A MORE

PERFECT
UNION

INQUIRY AND ANALYSIS

rm a more perfect Union, est

ecure the Blessings of Liber

ates, which shall consist of a

ly of the several

A MORE

PERFECT UNION

INQUIRY AND ANALYSIS

Brigid Harrison Montclair State University

Jean Wahl Harris University of Scranton

The McGraw·Hill Companies

Connect
Learn
Succeed™

Published by McGraw-Hill, an imprint of The McGraw-Hill Companies, Inc., 1221 Avenue of the Americas, New York, NY 10020. Copyright © 2011 by The McGraw-Hill Companies, Inc. All rights reserved. No part of this publication may be reproduced or distributed in any form or by any means, or stored in a database or retrieval system, without the prior written consent of The McGraw-Hill Companies, Inc., including, but not limited to, in any network or other electronic storage or transmission, or broadcast for distance learning.

1 2 3 4 5 6 7 8 9 0 DOC/DOC 0 9

ISBN: 978-0-07-352638-6
MHID: 0-07-352638-X

Vice President, Editorial: *Michael J. Ryan*
Director, Editorial: *Beth Mejia*
Director of Development: *Dawn Groundwater*
Senior Sponsoring Editor: *Mark Georgiev*
Senior Development Editor: *Carla Kay Samodulski*
Marketing Manager: *Caroline McGillen*
Editorial Coordinator: *Amy Flauaus*
Senior Production Editor: *Mel Valentín*
Manuscript Editor: *Thomas Briggs*
Design Manager and Cover Designer: *Cassandra Chu*

Interior Design: *Linda Beaupré*
Senior Photo Research Coordinator: *Alexandra Ambrose*
Photo Researcher: *David Tietz*
Art Editor: *Ayelet Arbel*
Media Project Manager: *Thomas Brierly*
Senior Production Supervisor: *Louis Swaim*
Composition: *10.5/12 Adobe Garamond Pro Regular by Aptara®, Inc.*
Printing: *45# New Era Matte, World Color*

Cover Images: iStock © Royce DeGrie

Credits: The credits section for this book begins on page C-1 and is considered an extension of the copyright page.

Library of Congress Cataloging-in-Publication Data

Harrison, Brigid C.
A more pefect union / Brigid Harrison, Jean Harris.—1st ed.
p. cm.
Includes bibliographical references and index.
ISBN-13: 978-0-07-352638-6 (alk. paper)
ISBN-10: 0-07-352638-X (alk. paper)
1. United States—Politics and government—Textbooks. 2. Political participation—United States—Textbooks. I. Harris, Jean (Jean Wahl), 1960– II. Title.
JK276.H37 2010
320.473—dc22

2009046161

The Internet addresses listed in the text were accurate at the time of publication. The inclusion of a Web site does not indicate an endorsement by the authors or McGraw-Hill, and McGraw-Hill does not guarantee the accuracy of the information presented at these sites.

www.mhhe.com

Brigid Callahan Harrison

Brigid Harrison specializes in the civic engagement and political participation of Americans, especially the Millennial Generation, the U.S. Congress, and the Presidency. Brigid has taught American government for over fifteen years. She takes particular pride in creating in the classroom a learning experience that shapes students' lifelong understanding of American politics, sharpens their critical thinking about American government, and encourages their participation in civic life. She enjoys supervising student internships in political campaigns and government and is a frequent commentator in print and electronic media on national and New Jersey politics. She received her B.A. from The Richard Stockton College, her M.A. from Rutgers, The State University of New Jersey, and her Ph.D. from Temple University. Harrison lives in Galloway, New Jersey, and has three children: Caroline (15), Alexandra (9), and John (6). Born and raised in New Jersey, Harrison is a fan of Bruce Springsteen and professor of political science and law at Montclair State University.

Jean Wahl Harris

Jean Harris's research interests include political socialization and engagement, federalism, and the evolution and institutionalization of the first ladyship and the vice presidency. She regularly teaches introductory courses in local, state, and national government and upper level courses in public administration and public policy. In the classroom, Jean seeks to cultivate students' participation in the political conversation so vital to American civic life and to convey the profound opportunities that the American political system affords an active, critical, and informed citizenry. She earned her B.A., M.A., and Ph.D. from the State University of New York at Binghamton. In 1994 the University of Scranton named her its CASE (Council for Advancement and Support of Education) professor of the year. She was an American Council on Education (ACE) Fellow during the 2007–08 academic year. Jean lives in Nicholson, Pennsylvania, with her husband Michael. She enjoys reading on her deck overlooking the Endless Mountains of Northeast Pennsylvania.

...their Services, to be ascertained...

...Peace, be privileged from Arr...

...any Speech or Debate in either...

...appointed to any civil Office...

...ing such time; and no Person...

...the Senate may propose or con...

...ll, before it become a Law, be pre...

BRIEF CONTENTS

CONTENTS

2 The Constitution 39

The Constitution of the United States of America 72

3 Federalism 97

PART II

Fundamental Principles 129

NATIONAL JOURNAL: NATIONAL SECURITY, TORTURE, AND CIVIL LIBERTIES 130

4 Civil Liberties 135

5 Civil Rights 173

marriage
equality

9 Elections, Campaigns, and Voting 321

10 The Media 361

PART IV

Institutions of Government 391

NATIONAL JOURNAL: HOW TOUGH SHOULD THE PRESIDENT BE? 392

11 Congress 397

12 The Presidency 435

13 The Bureaucracy 475

14 The Judiciary 507

PART V

Public Policy   543

NATIONAL JOURNAL: AFGHANISTAN: NEW LEASE ON A LONG WAR   544

15 Economic Policy   549

16 Domestic Policy 585

17 Foreign Policy and National Security 619

Appendixes

PREFACE

We the People of the United States, in Order to form a more perfect Union, establish Justice, insure domestic Tranquility, provide for the common defence, promote the general Welfare, and secure the Blessings of Liberty to ourselves and our Posterity, do ordain and establish this Constitution for the United States of America.

Why the title *A More Perfect Union*? Appearing in the preamble of the Constitution, this memorable phrase embodies in many ways what the citizens of a well-functioning democracy need to understand about their government. The founders considered the system of government they devised to be the best because it can always be made better. Establishing "a more perfect union" means that the American public will continually be asked to think critically about their government: they need to inquire, analyze, and act to make the United States a better republic. Each successive generation of Americans inherits a history of foundational principles and policies; as each generation faces new and urgent issues, its members must weigh their understanding of history in light of these contemporary pressures; and each generation must choose the next direction its members decide is best.

As instructors, we want our students to become critical consumers of political information, to ask questions and analyze information, and to apply what they learn in the classroom to American political life. When we ask ourselves, "What effect will our course have on our students five years later?" those are our humble expectations and the reason we wrote *A More Perfect Union*. The spirit of "a more perfect union"— that we as citizens are called upon to engage the past, present, and future of American political life—shapes the learning program and the framework for learning we have devised in this text. We aim to help students become critical thinkers about their government, to help them become the citizenry this country needs.

To give students the tools they will need to think critically about their government, *A More Perfect Union* teaches them a powerful formula for inquiry and analysis: How does what happened **Then,** and what is happening **Now,** shape what's coming **Next**? Students can use this three-part framework as a way to approach any political question: What historical context and foundational principles are relevant to the question? How should I take into account current political pressures in light of historical and conceptual precedents in considering this question? How can I use this understanding to decide what can or should happen next?

In *A More Perfect Union*, the *Then, Now, Next* formula frames each chapter. In this way, students are not expected simply to read, they are guided to inquire and analyze as they read—an *active* reading process that enables them to apply critical thinking to the information they are learning about American government.

Students need support as they learn how to ask intelligent questions and how to critically analyze the information presented to them. In *A More Perfect Union*, we wanted to create better pedagogy, not simply more of it. We set out to write a comprehensive text that does more with less. Therefore, our goal has been to focus the text, creating a framework for learning and a streamlined set of features that will support students as they learn to inquire about, analyze, and apply information.

Inquiry

Images, graphs, and charts in a book should engage students' curiosity and encourage them to ask questions. In *A More Perfect Union,* selected photos, figures, cartoons,

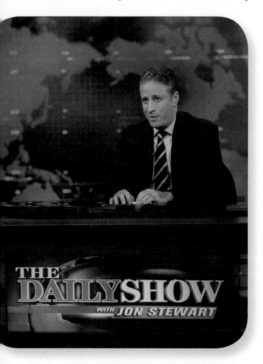

and tables are framed by a **Political Inquiry** assessment feature. Political Inquiry questions focus students' attention, making them realize that the photo contains political information, the graph requires interpretation, or the chart reveals more than merely meets the eye. The Political Inquiry questions are designed to help students learn to pull conclusions from information and understand the importance of the data they are asked to read.

Analysis

Analyzing original sources is one of the most important skills students need to learn to be successful students and informed citizens. Whether the source is the *Daily Show,* the *Washington Post,* the *Drudge Report,* or their senator's twitter feed, students must learn to analyze all sources of information—not just take what they hear or read at face value. The **Analyzing the Sources** feature is designed to help students sharpen their ability to engage a source of information and to pose questions, analyze data, and formulate their own opinion based on their enhanced understanding of the material.

Application

The active learning experience supported by *A More Perfect Union* encourages students to apply the knowledge they are gaining. We offer students two opportunities to consider how the issues discussed in the text relate to the world they read about every day:

- Each chapter contains a feature that helps the students use the **Then, Now, Next** framework to situate an issue confronting the Obama administration in terms of past precedent and current political pressures. It is designed to help students gain an informed understanding of the issue and how the political process may resolve it in the near future.

- At the beginning of each part is **an article from the *National Journal*** directly related to content in that part. These articles give students the opportunity to apply their understanding from the classroom to a specific issue presented and analyzed by a political journalist from one of the country's premier sources of information about government and policy.

By focusing their reading on inquiry and analysis, *A More Perfect Union* helps students learn and apply the skills that are at the heart of the course—critical thinking skills that allow them to make better-informed choices and to know why they made them. As students learn to balance the precedents of the past with the needs of the present to understand the directions of the future, they become the citizens who will continue to make the United States "A More Perfect Union."

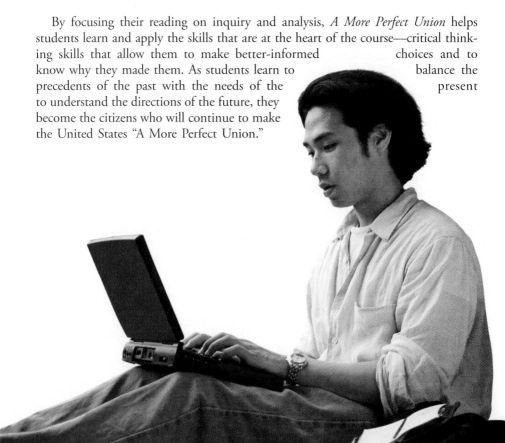

ACKNOWLEDGMENTS

We owe a debt of thanks to all of the people who have contributed their thoughts and suggestions during the stages of this book's development and whose many ideas have improved it immeasurably.

Manuscript Reviewers

Janet Adamski, *University of Mary Hardin-Baylor*

Ahrar Ahmad, *Black Hills State University*

Jeffrey Ashley, *Eastern Illinois University*

Lawrence Becker, *California State University–Northridge*

Nancy Bednar, *Antelope Valley College*

Steven S. Berizzi, *Norwalk Community College*

Jeffrey C. Berry, *South Texas College*

John Bolen, *San Jacinto College–South*

Shannon Bow, *University of Texas–Austin*

Robert C. Bradley, *Illinois State University*

Teresa Bush-Chavy, *American River College*

Richard D. Caldwell, *Eastern Illinois University*

Jamie Carson, *University of Georgia*

Anita Chadha, *University of Houston, Downtown*

Beatriz Chaslus-Cuartas, *El Paso Community College*

Grace Cheng, *Hawaii Pacific University*

Ann V. Clemmer, *University of Arkansas at Little Rock*

Paul W. Cooke, *Cy Fair College*

James W. Corey, *High Point University*

Denise DeGarmo, *Southern Illinois University–Edwardsville*

Louis DeSipio, *University of California–Irvine*

Robert E. Dewhirst, *Northwest Missouri State University*

Kevin Dockerty, *Kalamazoo Valley Community College*

Nelson Dometrius, *Texas Tech University*

John Forshee, *San Jacinto College–Central*

Jeffrey Fox, *Fort Lewis College*

David Garrison, *Collin County Community College*

Donald V. Gawronski, *Mesa Community College*

Dana K. Glencross, *Oklahoma City Community College*

Amy Glenn, *Tyler Junior College*

Anke L. Grussendorf, *Georgia State University*

Willie Hamilton, *Mount San Jacinto College*

Michelle Kukoleca Hammes, *St. Cloud State University*

Margaret Hankenson, *University of Wisconsin–Waukesha*

William T. Horner, *University of Missouri*

Terri Johnson, *University of Wisconsin–Green Bay*

Manoucher Khosrowshahi, *Tyler Junior College*

Richard Kiefer, *Waubonsee Community College*

Patricia Knol, *Triton College*

Lisa Langenbach, *Middle Tennessee State University*

John Linantud, *University of Houston, Downtown*

Shari L. MacLachlan, *Palm Beach Community College–Lake Worth*
Nathan Melton, *Utah Valley State College*
Leah Murray, *Weber State University*
Christopher Newman, *Elgin Community College*
Sunday P. Obazuaye, *Cerritos College*
William D. Pederson, *Louisiana State University–Shreveport*
Clarissa Peterson, *DePauw University*
Leonard Riley II, *Pikes Peak Community College*
Frauke Schnell, *West Chester University*
Ronnee Schreiber, *San Diego State University*
James Scott, *Oklahoma State University–Stillwater*
Margaret E. Scranton, *University of Arkansas at Little Rock*

Patrick L. Shade, *Edison Community College*
Henry Sirgo, *McNeese State University*
Michael W. Sonnleitner, *Portland Community College*
John Speer, *Houston Community College–Southwest*
Joseph L. Staats, *Valdosta State University*
Henry Steck, *SUNY Cortland*
Judy Tobler, *NorthWest Arkansas Community College*
Dennis Tombs, *San Jacinto College–North*
John Vanzo, *Bainbridge College*
Ronald W. Vardy, *University of Houston*
David G. Wigg, *St. Louis Community College*
Van Allen Wigginton, *San Jacinto College–Pasadena*
Zhiqun Zhu, *University of Bridgeport*

American Government Symposium

Since October 2006, McGraw-Hill has conducted a number of American Government Symposiums for instructors from across the country. These events offer forums for instructors to exchange ideas and experiences with colleagues they might not have met otherwise. They also provide an opportunity for editors from McGraw-Hill to gather information about the needs and challenges of instructors of American Government. The feedback we have received has been invaluable and has contributed—directly and indirectly—to the development of *A More Perfect Union* and its supplements. We would like to thank the participants for their insights.

Robert Ballinger, *South Texas College*
Jeffrey Birdsong, *Northeastern Oklahoma A&M College*
Amy Brandon, *San Jacinto College North*
Dan R. Brown, *Southwestern Oklahoma State University*
Monique Bruner, *Rose State College*
Anita Chadha, *University of Houston, Downtown*
Kathleen Collihan, *American River College*
Steven Collins, *Oklahoma State University, Oklahoma City*
Vida Davoudi, *Lonestar College, Kingwood*
Robert De Luna, *St. Philip's College*
Kevin Dockerty, *Kalamazoo Valley Community College*
Manar Elkhaldi, *University of Central Florida*
Karry Evans, *Austin Community College*
Pearl Ford, *University of Arkansas, Fayetteville*
John Forshee, *San Jacinto College–Central*
Jarvis T. Gamble, *Owens Community College*
William Gillespie, *Kennesaw State University*

Dana K. Glencross, *Oklahoma City Community College*
Larry Gonzalez, *Houston Community College–Southwest*
Nirmal Goswami, *Texas A&M University–Kingsville*
Daniel Gutierrez, *El Paso Community College*
Wanda Hill, *Tarrant County Community College*
Joseph Hinchliffe, *University of Illinois at Urbana-Champaign*
John Hitt, *North Lake College*
Lynn Jones, *Collin County Community College*
Brenda Jones, *Houston Community College–Central*
Franklin Jones, *Texas Southern University*
James Joseph, *Fresno City College*
Manoucher Khosrowshahi, *Tyler Junior College*
Michelle Kukoleca Hammes, *St. Cloud State University*
Chien-Pin Li, *Kennesaw State University*

Fred Lokken, *Truckee Meadows Community College*
Janna Merrick, *University of South Florida–Tampa*
Eric Miller, *Blinn College*
Kent Miller, *Weatherford College*
Eduardo Munoz, *El Camino College*
Kay Murnan, *Ozarks Technical Community College*
Blaine Nelson, *El Paso Community College*
James A. Norris, *Texas A&M International University*
Kent Park, *U.S. Military Academy at West Point*
Eric Rader, *Henry Ford Community College*
Ray Sandoval, *Richland College*
Craig Scarpelli, *California State University, Chico*
Louis Schubert, *City College of San Francisco*
Edward Senu-Oke, *Joliet Junior College*
Mark Shomaker, *Blinn College*
Thomas Simpson, *Missouri Southern University*
Henry Sirgo, *McNeese State University*
Amy Smith, *North Lake College*

John Speer, *Houston Community College–Southwest*
Sharon Sykora, *Slippery rock University*
Beatrice Talpos, *Wayne Community College*
Judy Tobler, *Northwest Arkansas Community College*
Beth Traxler, *Greenville Technical College*
Mathieu Turgeon, *University of North Texas*
William Turk, *University of Texas Pan American*
Ronald W. Vardy, *University of Houston*
Sarah Velasquez, *Fresno City College*
Ron VonBehren, *Valencia Community College–Osceola*
Van Allen Wigginton, *San Jacinto College–Central Campus*
Charlotte Williams, *Pasadena City College*
Robert Wood, *University of North Dakota*
Paul W. Wilson, *San Antonio College*
John Wood, *Rose State College*
Larry L. Wright, *Florida A&M University*
Ann Wyman, *Missouri Southern State University*
Kathryn Yates, *Richland College*

Supplements Team

A More Perfect Union is supported by a highly collaborative and integrated program of supplements for instructors teaching and students studying American Government. The critical-thinking approach within the text is continued within the supplements, resulting in a set of tools that will help students to learn the material and become more informed, engaged citizens.

The **Tools for Success** accompanying *A More Perfect Union* is an integrated program offering support to instructors teaching and students learning American Government. Available online at **www.mhhe.com/harrisonample**, the tool kit includes an Instructor's Manual that goes beyond lecture topics and outlines by tying all text features to individual and group projects in and out of class, a full test item bank tied to Bloom's taxonomy, and extensive resources for students.

- The **Instructor's Manual** by **Dana K. Glencross,** *Oklahoma City Community College,* **Beatriz Chaslus-Cuartas,** *El Paso Community College,* **Michelle Kukoleca Hammes,** *St. Cloud State,* and **Ronald W. Vardy,** *University of Houston,* includes chapter summaries, chapter outlines, lecture outlines with integrated PowerPoints, and abundant class activities.

- The **Test Bank** by **Paul W. Cooke,** *Cy Fair College,* **Elizabeth McLane,** *Wharton County Junior College,* **Michelle Kukoleca Hammes,** *St. Cloud State,* and **Ronald W. Vardy,** *University of Houston,* includes over 1000 multiple-choice and short-answer questions to accompany the chapters in *A More Perfect Union,* along with questions to be used in class (with PowerPoints) and student self check questions.

- **Resources for students** include quizzes; test questions; chapter summaries, outlines, and objectives; and access to PoliCentral, a dynamic interactive site that provides simulations, debate tools, participation activities, and video, audio, and speech activities.

In addition, **Facebook for Instructors and Students** by **Terri Towner,** *Oakland University (Michigan),* harnesses the power of Facebook as a classroom tool and guides you in creating an innovative learning opportunity for your students.

Expert Reviewers

Brian J. Brox, *Tulane University*
Brett Curry, *Georgia Southern University*
Brian Fogarty, *University of Missouri–St. Louis*
Mark R. Joslyn, *University of Kansas*
Hans Noel, *Georgetown University*
Jason MacDonald, *Kent State University*
Franco Mattei, *University of Buffalo*
Lawrence Rothenberg, *University of Rochester*
Saundra K. Schneider, *Michigan State University*
Robert Whaples, *Wake Forest University*
Jeff Worsham, *West Virginia University*

Personal Acknowledgments

We must thank our team at McGraw-Hill: Steve Debow, president of the Humanities, Social Science, and Languages group; Judy Ice, national sales manager; Mike Ryan, vice president and editor-in-chief; and Lisa Pinto, executive director of development have supported this project with amazing talent and resources. Beth Mejia, Director, Editorial, went the distance for this project and became a dear friend in the process. With kind and thoughtful leadership and sharp intellect, Mark Georgiev, senior sponsoring editor, took us by the hand and gently led us to where we needed to be. We benefited from steady guidance and wisdom from Rhona Robbin, director of development, and Lisa Moore, publisher for special projects. Senior development editor Carla Samodulski's enormous patience, sweet disposition, and impeccable insight made our book and our lives better. Marketing manager Caroline McGillen's energy, leadership, and skills have benefited the project, all while having fun. Mel Valentin, our production editor, and his team showed innovation and flexibility. We would particularly like to thank Cassandra Chu and Linda Beaupré, our designers; Ayelet Arbel, our art editor; Thomas Briggs, our manuscript editor; and Alex Ambrose and David Tietz, our photo researchers. Amy Flauaus provided invaluable support with good humor. We are extraordinarily grateful to all of you.

For their patience, understanding, and support, the authors also wish to thank: Ken, Caroline, Alexandra, and John Harrison, Rosemary Fitzgerald, Patricia Jillard, Kathleen Cain, John Callahan, Teresa Biebel, Thomas Callahan, Paula Straub, Sarah Griffith, Deborah Davies, Michael Harris, Jim and Audrey Wahl and the Wahl "girls"—Eileen Choynowski, Laura McAlpine, Audrey Messina, and Jaimee Conner; and Paul Meilak.

Brigid Callahan Harrison

Jean Wahl Harris

PART I

FOUNDATIONS
OF AMERICAN
DEMOCRACY

SURVEILLANCE AND THE CONSTITUTION

Has Obama held his position steady since the presidential campaign, made a course change from his 2008 promises, or pursued an issue new on his agenda?

It was February 12, 2008, and then-Sen. Barack Obama faced an easy vote. The Senate was about to take up the hotly debated question of whether telecommunications companies should be exempt from civil lawsuits alleging that they helped the Bush administration illegally spy on Americans. Opponents of the terrorist surveillance program, which bypassed federal law calling for court-approved search warrants for such eavesdropping, brought the suits, and Obama agreed with the litigants that if companies broke the law—regardless of the assurances they received from the government that their participation was lawful—they should be held to account. Obama's opposition to the so-called immunity provision during his quest for the Democratic presidential

nomination solidified his support among liberal activists, the technologically savvy Netroots of his party, and burnished his anti-Bush bona fides.

The Senate took up the controversy that morning, as an amendment to a pending bill that would modify the Foreign Intelligence Surveillance Act. (This was the law that the litigants accused the administration of violating.) The proposed revisions to FISA would dramatically expand the government's surveillance capabilities, giving it greater leeway to conduct surveillance of terrorism suspects and other foreign groups without obtaining individual search warrants from the FISA court. The communications of American citizens would undoubtedly be caught up in that electronic dragnet. Whether the immunity provision should be part of this new law was on the table. Obama voted to remove it, putting him at odds with the majority of his colleagues.

So, with the Senate in support of immunity, that left the question of whether Obama would oppose the overall changes to FISA, which the Senate took up later the same day. When the moment came to cast his vote, however, Obama didn't vote at all. He was one of three senators to take no position; the others were Hillary Rodham Clinton, then his chief rival for the Democratic nomination, and Republican Lindsey Graham of South Carolina. John McCain, the presumptive Republican presidential nominee, voted for the bill.

Obama had seemingly backed off his opposition to Bush-era surveillance policies. His position was challenged again a few weeks later when the candidate's top intelligence adviser said in an interview with *National Journal* that he personally favored immunity for the telecom companies. John Brennan's remarks ignited controversy, and some of Obama's supporters called upon the candidate to dismiss him. That would affirm, they seemed to think, Obama's loyal opposition to the legislation moving through Congress, which Brennan, in the interview, said had become "embroiled now in a partisan debate in some quarters."

Obama was still on record against immunity and through a spokesperson confirmed that he thought the companies' liability was "more appropriately a decision for the judiciary."

In July, almost five months after the immunity vote, Obama finally had to face the music. The Senate took up another FISA-changing bill, which the House had passed. It included immunity, and it would give the government broad authority to monitor communications outside the traditional search-warrant process. Sixty-nine senators voted in favor of the bill. Obama was one of them. President Bush signed the bill into law the next day.

No Turning Back

Candidate Obama's reversal on warrantless surveillance was the first major break with his most loyal supporters, and it remains a sore spot during the first months of his presidency. On his second full day in office, Obama earned some goodwill among the base by issuing two important executive orders. One would close the U.S. prison at

"The duty of the Justice Department is **to defend statutes that have been passed by Congress,** unless there is some very compelling reason not to." —Eric Holder

Guantánamo Bay within a year (although the fate of the nearly 250 prisoners there remains very much in question), and the other requires the CIA to follow the same interrogation rules as the military. That order effectively barred waterboarding, a harsh interrogation technique that intelligence officials say was rarely used but that many experts say is torture, and certainly was a potent symbol of past policies that Obama wanted to cleanly break from.

But on the hot-button issue of surveillance, Obama has shown no intention to turn back or break in a new direction. Indeed, most of what the Bush administration did under the cover of secrecy is now legal under the surveillance law that Obama voted

for last summer, seven weeks before he accepted the Democratic nomination for president. Obama has chosen Brennan, his onetime intelligence adviser and telecom immunity supporter, to be his chief homeland-security and counter-terrorism adviser in the White House. And in January, a federal Appeals Court strengthened Obama's hand when it published its opinion that the executive branch can claim an exemption to the Fourth Amendment's requirement for a court-ordered search warrant. If the government is monitoring the communications of foreigners overseas, it need not seek a warrant to do so, even if Americans are a party to those communications, the court ruled. When it comes to his surveillance authorities, then, Obama has clear sailing ahead of him and the wind at his back.

The opinion from the Foreign Intelligence Surveillance Court of Review—only the second in the history of this panel, which was set up to review FISA-related cases—doesn't settle the issue of whether President Bush violated the law when he authorized warrantless surveillance after the 9/11 attacks. Nor does it give Obama free rein to target Americans directly without search warrants. The law for which he voted forbids it.

"This was not a blank check by any means," legal scholar Orin Kerr wrote of the court opinion and its implications for future presidents.

Steven Schwinn, an associate professor of constitutional law at John Marshall Law School in Chicago, also stressed that the court opinion applies only to surveillance activities that Congress has specifically authorized in the various FISA acts. "It said nothing about the president's inherent Article II power to authorize the secret surveillance program," Schwinn wrote. (Bush had asserted an "extravagant" interpretation of his constitutional surveillance authorities, according to former Justice Department official Jack Goldsmith, who threatened to resign in 2004 over aspects of the surveillance program that he believed could not be supported by law.) "Bush administration supporters who praise this opinion as a vindication of Bush's sweeping claims of inherent Article II powers simply misread the opinion," Schwinn wrote.

But just because Obama's berth is wide doesn't mean it's free of conflict. The legal opinions justifying warrantless surveillance remain secret. And electronic privacy and civil-liberties groups are still pressing the president to circumvent the immunity provisions that he ultimately voted for, a potentially tricky legal maneuver that would also hold tremendous political consequences. Both McCain and Clinton questioned whether candidate Obama had the requisite experience and fortitude to fight a global war on terrorism; in that conflict, surveillance has been one of the United States' primary weapons.

The Legacy Question

Obama faces pressure from his base to make a demonstrable turn away from Bush-era policies. The Electronic Frontier Foundation, for one, wants the administration to put the civil lawsuits against the telecommunications companies back in play. Kevin Bankston, a senior staff attorney with the group, said that could happen in any one of a few ways, all of which involve the new attorney general, Eric Holder.

First, Obama could tell Holder to simply withdraw the government's current motion to dismiss the lawsuits based on the immunity provision, reversing course from the Bush Justice Department. Or, Obama could tell Holder to ask the courts to temporarily stay the proceedings while the administration comes up to speed on the cases and awaits the findings of several inspectors general, whose reports on the warrantless surveillance program are expected in July.

But there is a third route, Bankston said. Obama could instruct Holder not to appeal a case that Bankston's group brought last December before a federal District Court judge. It argues that the immunity provision violates constitutional separation of powers because the attorney general—not a judge—gets to determine unilaterally that any warrantless surveillance was both lawful and deemed necessary to protect national security. If the attorney general says that the surveillance met those criteria, then by law a judge must dismiss any lawsuit against a telecom company.

It's doubtful that the judge who is pondering the case will pick that fight with the new administration. Judge Vaughn Walker, the chief judge of the Northern District of California, heard oral arguments before Obama nominated Holder. "Why shouldn't the court wait to see what the new attorney general will do?" the judge asked.

During his confirmation hearing, Holder gave the response.

"President-elect Obama was against the [immunity provision]," he said, "but nevertheless voted for the statute that contained that immunity." The immunity question is now a matter of law, Holder said, and "the duty of the Justice Department is to defend statutes that have been passed by Congress, unless there is some very compelling reason not to.

"It would seem to me," he continued, "that unless there are compelling reasons, even given the opposition . . . I don't think that we would reverse course."

That could well be the new president's guiding mantra when it comes to his broad, and now legal, surveillance powers.

Cynicism, distrust, and apathy have characterized Americans' relationship with their government for the past generation.

New information technologies, new political leadership, and a diversifying population give many people cause for optimism as the nation responds to the changes of a new millennium.

NOW

6

1

People, Politics, and Participation

The United States was founded by individuals who believed in the power of democracy to respond to the will of citizens. Historically, citizen activists have come from all walks of life, but they have shared one common attribute: the belief that, in the ongoing conversation of democracy, their government listens to *people like them.* This idea is vital if individuals are to have an impact on their government; people who don't believe they can have any influence rarely try. From the Pilgrims' flight from religious persecution, to the War for Independence, to the Civil War, to the Great Depression, to World War II, and to the great movements for social justice—civil rights, women's liberation, and more—the story of the United States is the story of people who are involved with their government, who know what they want their government to do, and who have confidence in their ability to influence its policies.[1]

The history of democracy in the United States is rife with examples of ordinary people who have made and are making a difference.[2] Throughout this book, we describe the impact that individuals and groups have had, and continue to have, in creating and changing the country's institutions of government. We also explore how individuals have influenced the ways in which our governments—national, state, and local—create policy.[3] These stories are important not only in and of themselves but also as motivators for all of us who want to live in a democracy that responds to all of its citizens.

NEXT

Will the present generation break the cycle of cynicism that has pervaded the politics of the recent past?

Will new information technologies facilitate and energize political participation?

Will the face of American politics change as the nation's population grows and shifts?

A fundamental principle underlying this book is that your beliefs and your voice—and ultimately, how you use those beliefs and that voice—matter. Whatever your beliefs, it is important that you come to them thoughtfully, by employing introspection and critical thinking. Similarly, however you choose to participate, it is crucial that you take part in the civic life of your community. This book seeks both to inform and to inspire your participation. A sentiment voiced by American anthropologist Margaret Mead expresses a powerful truth: "Never doubt that a small group of thoughtful, committed citizens can change the world. Indeed, it's the only thing that ever has." This sentiment demonstrates our respect for the importance of your activism in the civic and political life of the United States and our desire to nurture that activism.

y shd u stdy am dem now? Or, Why Should You Study American Democracy Now?

Politics as practiced today is not your parents' brand of politics. **Politics**—the process of deciding who gets benefits in society and who is excluded from benefiting—is a much different process today than it was even a decade ago. Advances in technology have altered the political landscape in many ways, including how voters and candidates communicate with each other, how governments provide information to individuals, how people get their news about events, and how governments administer laws. The political landscape has also changed because of world events. In particular, the terrorist attacks of September 11, 2001, and the wars in Iraq and Afghanistan have markedly changed many aspects of American life. Americans have become immune to the latest reports of suicide bombings in Iraq, Afghanistan, and elsewhere; and they have become all too familiar with reports of local soldiers killed in war. These shifts in how Americans interact with government and in what issues concern them represent distinct changes that make the study of politics today interesting, exciting, and important.

How Technology Has Changed Politics

It would be difficult to overstate the impact of the technological revolution on politics as it is practiced today. In electoral politics, faster computers and the Internet have revolutionized a process that, until the advent of the personal computer and the Web, was not that different in 1990 from the way it was carried out in 1890. (See "Then, Now, Next.") Today, many voters get a good portion of their information from

How Will President Obama and Other Political Leaders Use the Latest Changes in Technology?

THEN: During the past half-century, television has been the most important medium candidates for public office and the presidency have used to get their messages across to the American public. Indeed, a president's ability to communicate to his constituents effectively on television often increased his political clout and heightened the chances of enacting his agenda. It could also insulate him from negative publicity.

NOW: As a presidential candidate, Barack Obama changed the way campaigns operate by using technology effectively to raise funds, inform supporters, mobilize volunteers, and organize grassroots activities. Upon his election, that structure has been replicated to try to generate support from the netroots for his policy agenda. Once again, his organization is using the Internet, social-networking sites, and Twitter to inform constituents and mobilize supporters to function as citizen lobbyists working for issues on his policy agenda.

WHAT'S NEXT?

- Will the Internet prove as effective a tool for governing as it has been for campaigning? Why or why not?
- What technologies will be most effective for informing constituents? Which constituents are most likely to rely on Web pages for their political news? On social-networking sites like Facebook and MySpace? On Twitter?
- How can Republicans make use of technology in opposing initiatives from either Obama or the Democratically controlled Congress?

Internet-based news sites and blogs. Campaigns rely on e-mail; instant and text messaging; Web sites; and social-networking pages on MySpace, Facebook, BlackPlanet, Cyloop, and similar sites to communicate with and organize supporters. State governments rely on computers to conduct elections.

But the impact of technology is not limited to elections. Would you like to help your grandfather apply for his Social Security benefits? You no longer need to go to the local Social Security office or even mail an application; instead, you can help him apply online, and his check can be deposited into his bank account electronically. Do you want to communicate your views to your representatives in Congress? You do not need to call or send a letter by snail mail—their e-mail addresses are available online. Do you want to find out which government agencies are hiring recent college graduates? Go to usajobs.gov. Do you need to ship a package using the U.S. Postal Service? The postal service Web site provides guidelines.

Because of these unprecedented shifts in the ways politics happens and government is administered, Americans today face both new opportunities and new challenges. How might we use technology to ensure that elections are conducted fairly? How might the abundance and reach of media technology be directed toward informing and enriching us rather than overwhelming us or perpetuating the citizen cynicism of recent years? What privacy rights can we be sure of in the present digital age? Whatever your age, as a student, you are a member of one of the most tech-savvy groups in the country, and your input, expertise, and participation are vital to sorting out the opportunities and obstacles of this next stage of American democracy.

The Political Context Now

The election of Barack Obama in 2008 was evidence of changes that have occurred in the U.S. political context in the past decade. Obama came to office to lead a nation facing the most serious recession since the Great Depression, and a populace divided over the nation's foreign policy. September 11, 2001, and the subsequent wars in Iraq and Afghanistan have had a marked effect on the U.S. political environment. These events have been a catalyst for changes in the attitudes of many Americans, including young Americans, about their government and their role in it.

Since the early 1970s—a decade blemished by the intense unpopularity of the Vietnam War and by scandals that ushered in the resignation of President Richard Nixon in 1974—Americans' attitudes toward government have been dismal.[4] Numerous surveys, including an ongoing Gallup poll that has tracked Americans' opinions, have demonstrated low levels of trust in government and of confidence in government's ability to solve problems.[5] Young people's views have mirrored those of the nation as a whole. In 2000, one study of undergraduate college students, for example, showed that nearly two-thirds (64 percent) did not trust the federal government to do the right thing most of the time, an attitude that reflected the views of the larger population.[6] Distrust; lack of **efficacy,** which is a person's belief that he or she has the ability to achieve something desirable and that the government genuinely listens to individuals; and apathy among young people were reflected in the voter turnout for the 2000 presidential election, when only 36 percent of eligible college-age voters went to the polls.

The events of 9/11 jolted American politics and the nation, and the altered political context provoked changes in popular views—notably, young people's opinions. "The attacks of 9/11 . . . changed the way the Millennial Generation thinks about politics. Overnight, their attitudes were more like [those of] the Greatest Generation [the generation of Americans who lived through the Great Depression and World War II]," observed John Della Volpe, a pollster who helped Harvard University students construct a national poll of young people's views.[7]

As patriotic spirits soared, suddenly 60 percent of college students trusted government to do the right thing. Ninety-two percent considered themselves patriotic. Some 77 percent thought that politics was relevant to their lives.[8] In the immediate aftermath of the 9/11 attacks, President George W. Bush and Congress enjoyed record-high approval ratings. Roughly 80 percent of young people and nearly that same percentage of all Americans supported U.S. military actions in Afghanistan. Beyond opinions, actions changed as well:

- More than 70 percent of college students gave blood, donated money, or volunteered in relief efforts.
- Nearly 70 percent volunteered in their communities (up from 60 percent in 2000).
- Some 86 percent believed their generation was ready to lead the Nation into the future.[9]

Then the political context changed again, over months and then years, as wars in Afghanistan and Iraq wore on, as casualties mounted, and as military spending skyrocketed. Trust in government, particularly of the president, plummeted. The changes after 9/11 continued to affect how Americans, particularly young Americans, participate in politics.

An important trend is visible in one of the most easily measured contexts: voter turnout. Figure 1.1 shows the jump in participation by young voters in the 2004 presidential election. (In contrast, for voters aged 66–74, participation actually *de*creased in 2004.) Among voters aged 18–21, the largest increases in turnout occurred among 19-year-olds, whose turnout rivaled that of voters in their 30s. Americans are debating the importance of this upswing in turnout over the long haul. In 2008, that trend continued, with estimates indicating that voters aged 18–20 increased by 2.2 million, surpassing the young voter turnout since 18-year-olds voted for the first time in 1972.

As these statistics demonstrate, lingering media characterizations of a cynical young electorate are off the mark. The evidence indicates that many young people are enthusiastic participants in civic and political life.[10] Witness the strong political support that the presidential campaign of Senator Barack Obama (D-Illinois) garnered from young people, some of whom packed their bags and traveled with the Obama team during the primary season that led to the Democratic convention in August 2008. Others are taking part in ways that have not traditionally been thought of, and measured as, participation. These include, for example, Internet activism and the use of one's power as a consumer to send political messages. For

Percent

- 30 and older
- 25 and older
- 18–29
- 18–24

U.S. ELECTIONS
2008

67
66
51
49

Year
1972 1976 1980 1984 1988 1992 1996 2000 2004 2008

POLITICAL INQUIRY

FIGURE 1.1 ■ VOTER TURNOUT BY AGE, 1972–2008
What trends led to increased voter turnout, especially among younger voters, in 2008?

Source: Emily Hoban Kirby and Kei Kawashima-Ginsberg, *The Youth Vote in 2008;* http://www.civicyouth.org/PopUps/FactSheets/FS_youth_Voting_2008.pdf; and Census CPS, Nov. 1972–2008.

many students, that foundation of political participation, volunteerism, or community action has already provided them with a rationale for increasing their knowledge of and participation in their communities.

Individuals who engage in politics and civic life experience many benefits. Engaged citizens are knowledgeable about public issues; actively communicate with policy makers and others; press government officials to carry out the people's will; advocate for their own self-interest and the interests of others; and hold public officials accountable for their decisions and actions. You will find that advocating for your own interests or working with others in similar situations will sometimes (perhaps to your surprise) lead to desired outcomes. This is efficacy in action. And you will discover that with experience you will become more effective at advocacy—the more you do, the better you get. Furthermore, you will derive social and psychological benefits from being civically engaged.

In addition, and importantly, local communities, states, and the nation benefit from an engaged populace. Governments are more effective when people voice their views. As we explore throughout this book, American democracy provides citizens and others with more opportunities to influence governmental action than at any other time in history. If you have the knowledge and tools, you should be able to make the most of these opportunities.

What Government Does

In this brief section, we look at the nature of government and the functions a government performs. Let's start with some important definitions. **Government** is an institution that creates and implements the policy and laws that guide the conduct of a nation and its citizens. **Citizens** are those members of a political community—town, city, state, or country—who, through birth or naturalization, enjoy the rights, privileges, and responsibilities attached to membership in a given nation. **Naturalization** means becoming a citizen by means other than birth, as in the case of immigrants. Although governments vary widely in how well they perform, most national governments share some common functions.

To get a clear sense of the business of government, consider the following key functions performed by government in the United States and many other nations:

- **To protect their sovereign territory and their citizenry and to provide national defense.** Governments protect their *sovereign territory* (that is, the territory over which they have the ultimate governing authority) and their citizens at home and abroad. Usually, they carry out this responsibility by maintaining one or more types of armed services. In the United States, the armed services include the Army, Navy, Marines, Air Force, and Coast Guard. Governments also preserve order domestically. In the United States, domestic order is preserved through the National Guard and federal, state, and local law enforcement agencies.

- **To preserve order and stability.** Governments also preserve order by providing emergency services and security in the wake of disasters. For example, after Hurricane Katrina struck the Gulf Coast and the city of New Orleans in August 2005, the National Guard was sent in to provide security in the midst of an increasingly dangerous situation (though in the eyes of many critics, including local and state elected officials, the action came too late to "preserve order"). Governments also maintain stability by providing a political structure that has **legitimacy:** a quality conferred on government by citizens who believe that its exercise of power is right and proper.[11]

- **To establish and maintain a legal system.** Governments create legal structures by enacting and enforcing laws that restrict or ban certain behaviors. In the United States, the foundation of this legal structure is the federal Constitution.[12] Governments also provide the means to implement laws through the actions of local police and other state and national law enforcement agencies. By means of the court system, governments administer justice and impose penalties.

- **To provide services.** Governments distribute a wide variety of services to their citizens. In the United States, government agencies provide services ranging from inspecting the meat we consume to ensuring the safety of the places where we work. Federal, state, and local governments provide roads, bridges, transportation, education, and health services. They facilitate communication, commerce, air travel, and entertainment.

  Many of the services governments provide are called **public goods** because their benefits, by their nature, cannot be limited to specific groups or individuals.

For example, everyone enjoys national defense, equal access to clean air and clean water, airport security, highways, and other similar services. Because the value and benefits of these goods are extended to everyone, government makes them available through revenue collected by taxes. Not all goods that government provides are public goods, however; some goods, like access to government-provided health care, are available only to the poor or to older Americans.

- **To raise and spend money.** All of the services that governments provide, from national protection and defense to health care, cost money.[13] Governments at all levels spend money collected through taxes. Depending on personal income, between 25 and 35 cents of every dollar earned by those working in the United States and earning above a certain level goes toward federal, state, and local income taxes. Governments also tax *commodities* (commercially exchanged goods and services) in various ways—through sales taxes, property taxes, sin taxes, and luxury taxes.

- **To socialize new generations.** Governments play a role in *socialization,* the process by which individuals develop their political values and opinions. Governments perform this function, for example, by providing funding for schools, by introducing young people to the various "faces" of government (perhaps through a police officer's visiting a school or a mayor's bestowing an honor on a student), and by facilitating participation in civic life through institutions such as libraries, museums, and public parks. In these ways, governments transmit cultural norms and values such as patriotism and build commitment to fundamental values such as those we explore later in this chapter. For a detailed discussion of political socialization, see Chapter 6.

Types of Government

When social scientists categorize the different systems of government operating in the world today, two factors influence their classifications. The first factor is *who participates in governing or in selecting those who govern.* These participants vary as follows, depending on whether the government is a monarchy, an oligarchy, or a democracy:

- In a **monarchy,** a member of a royal family, usually a king or queen, has absolute authority over a territory and its government. Monarchies typically are inherited—they pass down from generation to generation. Most modern monarchies, such as those in Great Britain and Spain, are *constitutional monarchies* in which the monarch plays a ceremonial role but has little actual say in governance, which is carried out by elected leaders. In contrast, in traditional monarchies, such as the Kingdom of Saudi Arabia, the monarch is both the ceremonial and the governmental head of state.

- In an **oligarchy,** an elite few hold power. Some oligarchies are *dictatorships,* in which a small group, such as a political party or military junta, supports a dictator. North Korea and Myanmar (formerly Burma) are present-day examples of oligarchies.

- In a **democracy,** the supreme power of governance lies in the hands of citizens. The United States and most other modern democracies are *republics,* sometimes called *representative democracies,* in which citizens elect leaders to represent their views. We discuss the idea of a republican form of government in detail in Chapter 2.

Social scientists also consider *how governments function* and *how they are structured* when classifying governments:

- Governments that rule according to the principles of **totalitarianism** essentially control every aspect of their citizens' lives. In these tyrannical governments, citizens enjoy neither rights nor freedoms, and the state is the tool of the dictator. Totalitarian regimes tend to center on a particular ideology, religion, or personality. North Korea is a contemporary example of a totalitarian regime, as was Afghanistan under the Islamic fundamentalist regime of the Taliban.
- When a government rules by the principles of **authoritarianism,** it holds strong powers, but they are checked by other forces within the society. China and Cuba are examples of authoritarian states because their leaders are restrained in their exercise of power by political parties, constitutions, and the military. Individuals living under an authoritarian regime may enjoy some rights, but often these rights are not protected by the government.
- **Constitutionalism,** a form of government structured by law, provides for **limited government**—a government that is restricted in what it can do so that the rights of the people are protected. Constitutional governments can be democracies or monarchies. In the United States, the federal Constitution created the governmental structure, and this system of government reflects both the historical experiences and the norms and values of the founders.

The Constitution's framers (authors) structured American government as a *constitutional democracy.* In this type of government, a constitution creates a representative democracy in which the rights of the people are protected. We can trace the roots of this modern constitutional democracy back to ancient times.

The Origins of Democracy

The ancient Greeks first developed the concept of a democracy. The Greeks used the term *demokratia* (literally, "people power") to describe some of the 1,500 *poleis* ("city-states"; also the root of *politics*) on the Black and Mediterranean seas. These city-states were not democracies in the modern sense of the term, but the way they were governed provided the philosophical origins of American democracy. For example, citizens decided public issues using majority rule in many of the city-states. However, in contrast to modern democracies, the Greek city-states did not count women and slaves as citizens. American democracy also traces some of its roots to the Judeo-Christian religion and the English common law, particularly the ideas that thrived during the Protestant Reformation.[14]

Democracy's Origins in Popular Protest: The Influence of the Reformation and the Enlightenment

We can trace the seeds of the idea of *modern* democracy almost as far back as the concept of monarchy—back to several centuries ago, when the kings and emperors who ruled in Europe claimed that they reigned by divine sanction, or God's will. The monarchs' claims reflected the political theory of the **divine right of kings,** articulated by Jacques-Benigne Bossuet (1627–1704), who argued that monarchies, as a manifestation of God's will, could rule absolutely without regard to the will or well-being of their subjects. Challenging the right of a monarch to govern or questioning one of his or her decisions thus represented a challenge to the will of God.

At odds with the theory of the divine right of kings was the idea that people could challenge the crown and the church—institutions that seemed all-powerful. This idea took hold during the Protestant Reformation, a movement to reform the Catholic Church. In October 1517, Martin Luther, a German monk who would later found the Lutheran Church, posted his *95 Theses,* criticizing the harmful practices of the Catholic Church, to the door of the church at Wittenberg Castle. The Reformation continued throughout the sixteenth century, during which time reform-minded Protestants (whose name is derived from *protest*) challenged basic tenets of Catholicism and sought to *purify* the church.

In England, some extreme Protestants, known as Puritans, thought that the Reformation had not gone far enough in reforming the church. Puritans asserted their right to communicate directly with God through prayer rather than through an intermediary such as a priest. This idea that an individual could speak directly with God lent support to the notion that the people could govern themselves. Faced with persecution in England, congregations of Puritans, known to us today as the Pilgrims, fled to America, where they established self-governing colonies, a radical notion at the time. Before the Pilgrims reached shore in 1620, they drew up the Mayflower Compact, an example of a **social contract**—an agreement between people and their leaders, whereby the people give up some liberties so that their other liberties will be protected. In the Mayflower Compact, the Pilgrims agreed to be governed by the structure of government they formed, thereby establishing consent of the governed.

In the late seventeenth century came the early beginnings of the Enlightenment, a philosophical movement that stressed the importance of individuality, reason, and scientific endeavor. Enlightenment scientists such as Sir Isaac Newton (1642–1727) drastically changed how people thought about the universe and the world around them, including government. Newton's work in physics, astronomy, math, and mechanics demonstrated the power of science and repudiated prevalent ideas based on magic and superstition. Newton's ideas about **natural law**—the assertion that the laws that govern human behavior are derived from the nature of humans themselves and can be universally applied—laid the foundation for the ideas of the political philosophers of the Enlightenment.

Technology and Political Participation

THEN (1970s)	NOW (2009)
47 percent of 18- to 20-year-olds voted in the 1976 presidential election.	About 53 percent of 18- to 20-year-olds voted in the 2008 presidential election.
People got their national news from one half-hour-long nightly news broadcast.	People get their news from an array of sources, including twenty-four-hour news networks and Internet news services available on demand on computers and cell phones.
Many people participated in civic life primarily through demonstrations, protests, and voting.	People still participate through demonstrations and protests but now also through volunteerism, Internet communities, and targeted purchasing; and a competitive Democratic primary in 2008 generated record-breaking voter participation and interest.

WHAT'S NEXT?

> How might advancing media technologies further transform the ways that people "consume" their news?

> Will the upswing of voter participation by 18- to 20-year-olds continue?

> What new forms of civic participation will emerge?

> Will the highly competitive 2008 presidential race motivate a new wave of voters to remain active participants in the electoral process?

The Modern Political Philosophy of Hobbes and Locke

The difficulty of individual survival under the rule of an absolute monarch is portrayed by the British philosopher Thomas Hobbes (1588–1679) in *Leviathan* (1651). Hobbes, who believed in the righteousness of absolute monarchies, argued that the strong naturally prey upon the weak and that, through a social contract, individuals who relinquish their rights can enjoy the protection offered by a sovereign. Without such a social contract and without an absolute monarch, Hobbes asserted, anarchy prevails, describing this state as one lived in "continuall feare, and danger of violent death; And the life of man, solitary, poore, nasty, brutish, and short."[15]

John Locke (1632–1704) took Hobbes's reasoning concerning a social contract one step further. In the first of his *Two Treatises on Civil Government* (1689), Locke systematically rejected the notion that the rationale for the divine right of kings is based on scripture. By providing a theoretical basis for discarding the idea of a monarch's divine right to rule, Locke paved the way for more radical notions about the rights of individuals and the role of government. In the second *Treatise,* Locke argued that individuals possess certain unalienable (or natural) rights, which he identified as the rights to life, liberty, and property. He stressed that these rights are inherent in people as individuals; that is, government can neither bestow them nor take them away. When people enter into a social contract, Locke said, they do so with the understanding that the government will protect their natural rights. At the same time, according to Locke, they agree to accept the government's authority; but if the government fails to protect the inherent rights of individuals, the people have the right to rebel.

The French philosopher Jean-Jacques Rousseau (1712–1778) took Locke's notion further, stating that governments formed by social contract rely on **popular sovereignty,** the theory that government is created by the people and depends on the people for the authority to rule. **Social contract theory,** which assumes that individuals possess free will and that every individual possesses the God-given right of self-determination and the ability to consent to be governed, would eventually form the theoretical framework of the Declaration of Independence.

The Creation of the United States as an Experiment in Representative Democracy

The people who settled the American colonies that eventually rebelled against Great Britain and became the first thirteen states were shaped by their experiences of living under European monarchies. Many rejected the ideas of absolute rule and the divine right of kings, which had been central to rationalizing the monarchs' authority. The logic behind the rejection of the divine right of kings—the idea that monarchs were not chosen by God—rested on the notion that people could govern themselves.

In New England, where many colonists settled after fleeing England to escape religious persecution, a form of **direct democracy**—a structure of government in which citizens discuss and decide policy through majority rule—emerged in *town meetings* (which still take place today). In every colony, the colonists themselves decided who was eligible to participate in government, and so in some localities, women and people of color who owned property participated in government well before they were granted formal voting rights under amendments to the federal Constitution.

Beyond the forms of direct democracy prevalent in the New England colonies, nearly all of the American colonies had councils structured according to the principle of representative democracy, sometimes called **indirect democracy,** in which citizens elect representatives who decide policies on their behalf. These representative democracies foreshadow important political values that founders like Thomas Jefferson and James Madison would incorporate into key founding documents, including the Declaration of Independence and the Constitution.

Political Culture and American Values

On September 11, 2002, the first anniversary of the terrorist attacks on the United States, the *New York Times* ran an editorial, "America Enduring." The author described how the United States and its residents had weathered the difficult year after 9/11: "America isn't bound together by emotion. It's bound together by things that transcend emotion, by principles and laws, by ideals of freedom and justice that need constant articulation."[16] These ideals are part of American **political culture**—the people's collective beliefs and attitudes about government and the political process. These ideals include liberty, equality, capitalism, consent of the governed, and the importance of the individual (as well as family and community).

> Thomas Jefferson's ideas about the role of government shaped the United States for generations to come. In 1999, descendants of Thomas Jefferson, including those he fathered with his slave, Sally Hemings, posed for a group photo at his plantation, Monticello, in Charlottesville, Virginia.

Liberty

The most essential quality of American democracy, **liberty** is both freedom from government interference in our lives and freedom to pursue happiness. Many of the colonies that eventually became the United States were founded by people who were interested in one notion of liberty: religious freedom. Those who fought in the War for Independence were intent on obtaining economic and political freedom. The framers of the Constitution added to the structure of the U.S. government many other liberties,[17] including freedom of speech, freedom of the press, and freedom of association.[18]

There is evidence all around us of ongoing tensions between people attempting to assert their individual liberty on the one hand and the government's efforts to exert control on the other. For example, issues of religious freedom are in play in school districts where some parents object to the teaching of the theory of evolution because the theory contradicts their religious beliefs. Issues of freedom of the press have arisen as the government has attempted to prevent the news media from photographing the flag-draped coffins of soldiers killed in Iraq. The struggle for privacy rights—and how these rights are defined—continues unabated as the government's counterterrorism efforts result in officials' seeking greater access to our communications.

Throughout history and to the present day, liberties have often conflicted with efforts by the government to ensure a secure and stable society by exerting restraints on liberties. When government officials infringe on personal liberties, they often do so in the name of security, arguing that such measures are necessary in order to protect the rights of other individuals, institutions (including the government itself), or society as a whole. As we consider in Chapter 4, these efforts include, for example, infringing on the right to free speech by regulating or outlawing hate speech or speech that incites others to violence. Governments may also impinge on privacy rights; think of the various security measures that you are subject to before boarding an airplane.

The meaning of liberty—how we define our freedoms—is constantly evolving. In light of the terrorist attacks of September 11, 2001, and the digital revolution, difficult questions have arisen about how much liberty Americans should have and how far the government should go in curtailing liberties to provide security. Should law enforcement officers be allowed to listen in on an individual's phone conversations if that person is suspected of a crime? Or should they be required to get a warrant first? What if that person is suspected of plotting a terrorist attack—should the officer be required to obtain a warrant first in that situation? What if one of the suspected plotters is not a U.S. citizen?

Equality

The Declaration of Independence states that "all men are created equal . . ." But the founders' notions of equality were vastly different from those that prevail today. Their ideas of equality evolved from the emphasis the ancient Greeks placed on equality of opportunity. The Greeks envisioned a merit-based system in which educated freemen could participate in democratic government rather than inheriting their positions as a birthright. The Judeo-Christian religions also emphasize the idea of equality. All three major world religions—Christianity, Judaism, and Islam—stress that all people are equal in the eyes of God. These notions of equality informed both Jefferson's assertion about equality in the Declaration of Independence and, later, the framers' structuring of the U.S. government in the Constitution.[19]

The idea of equality evolved during the nineteenth and twentieth centuries. In the early American republic, all women, as well as all men of color, were denied fundamental rights, including the right to vote. Through long, painful struggles—including the abolition movement to free the slaves; the suffrage movement to gain women the right to vote; various immigrants' rights movements; and later the civil rights, Native American rights, and women's rights movements of the 1960s and 1970s (see Chapter 5)—members of these disenfranchised groups won the rights previously denied to them.

Several groups are still engaged in the struggle for legal equality today, notably gay and lesbian rights organizations and groups that advocate for fathers', children's, and immigrants' rights. And historic questions about the nature of equality have very modern implications: Are certain forms of inequality, such as preventing gay couples from enjoying the rights of married heterosexual couples, acceptable in American society? Are the advantages of U.S. democracy reserved only for citizens, or should immigrants living legally in the United States also enjoy these advantages?

Beyond these questions of legal equality, today many arguments over equality focus on issues of economic equality, a concept about which there is substantial disagreement. Some in the United States believe that the government should do more to eliminate disparities in wealth—by taxing wealthy people more heavily than others, for example, or by providing more subsidies and services to the poor. Others disagree, however, and argue that although people should have equal opportunities for economic achievement, their attainment of that success should depend on factors such as education and hard work, and that success should be determined in the marketplace rather than through government intervention.

Capitalism

Although the founders valued the notion of equality, capitalism was equally important to them. **Capitalism** is an economic system in which the means of producing wealth are privately owned and operated to produce profits. In a pure capitalist economy, the marketplace determines the regulation of production, the distribution of goods and services, wages, and prices. In this type of economy, for example, businesses pay employees the wage that they are willing to work for, without the government's setting a minimum wage by law. Although capitalism is an important value in American democracy, the U.S. government imposes certain regulations on the economy: it mandates a minimum wage, regulates and inspects goods and services, and imposes tariffs on imports and taxes on domestically produced goods that have an impact on pricing.

One key component of capitalism is **property**—anything that can be owned. There are various kinds of property: businesses, homes, farms, the material items we use every day, and even ideas are considered property. Property holds such a prominent position in American culture that it is considered a natural right, and some aspects of property ownership are constitutionally protected.

Consent of the Governed

The idea that, in a democracy, the government's power derives from the consent of the people is called the **consent of the governed.** As we have seen, this concept, a focal point of the rebellious American colonists and eloquently expressed in Jefferson's Declaration of Independence, is based on John Locke's idea of a social contract. Implicit in Locke's social contract is the principle that the people agree to the government's authority, and if the government no longer has the consent of the governed, the people have the right to revolt.

The concept of consent of the governed also implies **majority rule**—the principle that, in a democracy, only policies with 50 percent plus one vote are enacted, and only candidates who attain 50 percent plus one vote are elected. Governments based on majority rule include the idea that the majority has the right of self-governance and typically also protect the rights of people who are in the minority. A particular question about this ideal of governing by the consent of the governed has important implications for the United States in the early twenty-first century: Can a democracy remain stable and legitimate if less than a majority of its citizens participate in elections?

Individual, Family, and Community

Emphasis on the individual is a preeminent feature of American democratic thought. In the Constitution, rights are bestowed on, and exercised by, the individual. The importance of the individual—an independent entity exercising self-determination— has powerfully shaped the development of the United States, both geographically and politically.

Family and community have also played central roles in the U.S. political culture, both historically and in the present day. A child first learns political behavior from his or her family, and in this way, the family serves to perpetuate the political culture. And from the earliest colonial settlements to today's blogosphere, communities have channeled individuals' political participation. Indeed, the intimate relationship between individualism and community life is reflected in the First Amendment of the Constitution, which ensures individuals' freedom of assembly—one component of which is their right to form or join any type of organization, political party, or club without penalty.

The Changing Face of American Democracy

In the spring of 2006, thousands of demonstrators took to the streets in cities across the United States, demanding reform of the nation's immigration laws. Immigration reform has become a hot-button issue in recent years. Advocates for the rights of undocumented immigrant workers have called on legislators to pass an amnesty law that would provide a structure for the legalization of these illegal immigrants. The immigrant-rights supporters have noted that the withdrawal of "undocumented workers" from the workforce would cripple the U.S. economy, in particular the agricultural and restaurant industries. On the other side of the controversy are countless concerned citizens who worry that low-income "illegal aliens" are draining the resources of already hard-pressed communities that suddenly must provide services to these individuals. Further, many of these citizens say that the undocumented immigrants are breaking the law and thus should not be rewarded with amnesty.

Though the debate has been passionate, it is not new, nor is the intense reaction to it by recent immigrants, both legal and undocumented. The questions and anxieties about demographic (population) change owing to immigration are as old as the nation itself. Figure 1.2 shows how the U.S. population has grown since the first census in 1790. At that point there were fewer than 4 million Americans. By 2000, the U.S. population had reached 281 million, and projections estimate that in 2010, it will top 310 million.

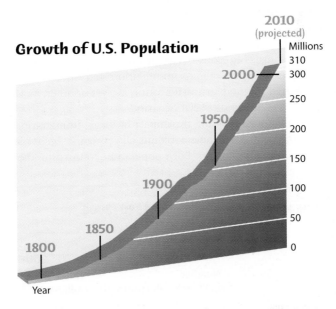

Growth of U.S. Population

FIGURE 1.2 ▧ From 1790 to 1900, the population of the United States increased gradually, and it did not reach 100 million until the second decade of the twentieth century. What factors caused the steep rise during the twentieth century? How will these forces continue to affect the size of the U.S. population during this century?

Source: U.S. Census, www.census.gov/population/www/documentation/twps0056.html.

Immigrants have always been part of the country's population growth, and over the centuries, they have made innumerable contributions to American life and culture.[20] Immigrants from lands all around the world have faced the kind of struggles that today's undocumented immigrants encounter. Chinese Americans, for example, were instrumental in pioneering the West and completing the construction of the transcontinental railroad in the mid-nineteenth century, but they were excluded by law from becoming U.S. citizens by the Chinese Exclusion Act of 1881. Faced with the kinds of persecution that today would be considered hate crimes, Chinese Americans used civil disobedience to fight against the so-called Dog Tag Laws that required them to carry registration cards. In one incident, in 1885, they fought back against unruly mobs that drove them out of the town of Eureka, California, by suing the city for reparations and compensation.[21]

A Population That Is Growing—and on the Move

Between 1960 and 2000, the population of the United States increased by more than 50 percent. As the population rises, measures of who the American people are and what percentage of each demographic group makes up the population have significant implications for the policies, priorities, values, and preferred forms of civic and political participation of the people. All of the factors contributing to U.S. population growth—including immigration, the birth rate, falling infant mortality rates, and longer life spans—have broad implications for both politics and policy as the ongoing debate about immigration reform shows. Generational differences in preferred methods of participation are yet another, as is the national conversation about the future of Social Security.

Although it is difficult to measure the impact of illegal immigration on the total U.S. population, the census attempts to count all residents, whatever their status. As Table 1.1 shows, the total foreign-born population counted by the U.S. census

TABLE 1.1

Nativity and Citizenship Status, 1990–2006

	1990 Number (millions)	1990 Percentage	2006 Number (millions)	2006 Percentage
Total population	249	100%	299	100%
Total native population	229	92	262	88
Total foreign-born population	20	8	37	12
Naturalized	8	3	16	5
Non-naturalized	12	5	21	7

Source: www.CensusScope.org, Social Science Data Analysis Network, University of Michigan, www.ssdan.net, and *Statistical Abstract of the United States, 2009,* Table 43, www.census.gov/compendia/statab/.

in 2000 increased slightly over 1990, with foreign-born residents accounting for 11 percent of the population (versus 8 percent in 1990).

Accompanying the increase in population over the years has been a shift in where people live. For example, between 1990 and 2000, 684 of the nation's 3,142 counties, most of them in the Midwest and Plains states, reported a loss in population. But 80 counties, primarily in the West and the South, had population growth of more than 50 percent. In five counties—two in Georgia and three in Colorado—the population jumped by more than 100 percent.

An Aging Population

As the U.S. population increases and favors new places of residence, it is also aging. Figure 1.3 shows the distribution of the population by age and by sex as a series of three pyramids for three different years. The 2000 pyramid shows the "muffin top" of the baby boomers, who were 36–55 years old in that year. A quarter-century later, the echo boom of the millennials, who will be between the ages of 30 and 55 in 2025, is clearly visible. The pyramid evens out and thickens by 2050, showing the effects of increased population growth and the impact of extended longevity, with a large number of people (women in particular) expected to live to age 85 and older.

Some areas of the United States are well-known meccas for older Americans. For example, Florida and the Southwest have the reputation as the premier retirement destinations in the United States. Older Americans are concentrated in these areas, as well as in the nation's midsection. Older people are concentrated in the Midwest and Plains states because of the high levels of emigration from these areas by younger Americans, who are leaving their parents behind to look for opportunity elsewhere.

A Changing Complexion: Race and Ethnicity in the United States Today

The population of the United States is becoming not only older but also more racially and ethnically diverse. Figure 1.4 shows the projected racial and ethnic composition of the U.S. population in 2010. Notice that Hispanics* now make up a greater proportion of the U.S. population than do blacks. As Figure 1.4 also shows, this trend has been continuous over the past several decades. Figure 1.4 also indicates that the percentage of Asian Americans and Pacific Islanders has doubled in recent decades, from just over 2 percent of the U.S. population in 1980 to over 4 percent today. The Native American population has increased marginally but still constitutes less than 1 percent of the whole population. Figure 1.4 also shows the

---

*A note about terminology: When discussing data for various races and ethnicities for the purpose of making comparisons, we use the terms *black* and *Hispanic,* because these labels are typically used in measuring demographics by the Bureau of the Census and other organizations that collect this type of data. In more descriptive writing that is not comparative, we use the terms *African American* and *Latino* and *Latina,* which are the preferred terms at this time. Although the terms *Latino* and *Latina* exclude Americans who came from Spain (or whose ancestors did), these people compose a very small proportion of this population in the United States.

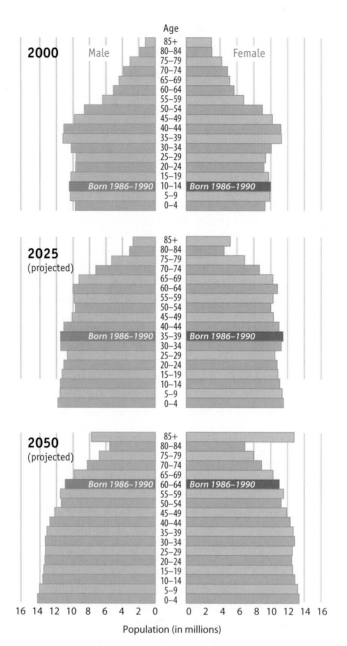

FIGURE 1.3

The Aging U.S. Population, 2000–2050

Source: U.S. Census Bureau, National Population Projections, www.census.gov/population/www/projections/natchart.html.

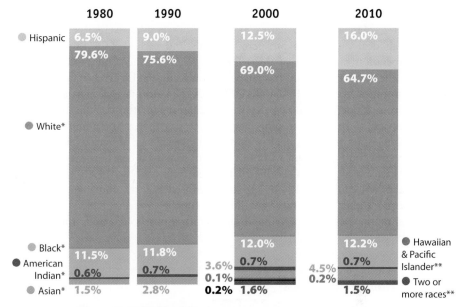

1980 **1990** **2000** **2010**

Hispanic 6.5% 9.0% 12.5% 16.0%

79.6% 75.6% 69.0% 64.7%

White*

Black* 11.5% 11.8% 12.0% 12.2% Hawaiian & Pacific Islander**
American Indian* 0.6% 0.7% 3.6% 0.7% 4.5% 0.7%
0.1% 0.2% Two or
Asian* 1.5% 2.8% 0.2% 1.6% 1.5% more races**

*Non-Hispanic only; in 1980 and 1990, "Asians" included Hawaiians and Pacific Islanders
** Option available for the first time in 2000 census

FIGURE 1.4

Population by Race Since 1980

Source: www.CensusScope.org, Social Science Data Analysis Network, University of Michigan, www.ssdan.net.

proportion of people reporting that they belonged to two or more racial groups, a category that was not an option on the census questionnaire until 2000.

Minority populations tend to be concentrated in different areas of the United States. At 12 percent of the population, African Americans are the largest racial minority in the United States (Hispanics are an ethnic minority). The African American population tends to be centered in urban areas and in the South, where, in some counties, African Americans constitute a majority of the population.

Hispanics, on the other hand, tend to cluster in Texas and California along the border between the United States and Mexico and in the urban centers of New Mexico. Concentrations of Hispanic populations are also found in Florida and the Northeast. Hispanics are the fastest-growing ethnic group in the United States, with a projected 16 percent of the 2010 U.S. population identifying themselves as Hispanic, nearly tripling in size since the 1980 census. Among people of Hispanic ethnicity, Mexicans make up the largest number (7 percent of the total U.S. population in 2000), followed by Puerto Ricans (1 percent in 2000) and Cubans (0.4 percent).

Changing Households: American Families Today

The types of families that are counted by the U.S. census are also becoming more diverse. The *nuclear family*, consisting of a stay-at-home mother, a breadwinning father, and their children, was at one time the stereotypical "ideal family" in the United States. Many—though hardly all—American families were able to achieve this cultural ideal during the prosperous 1950s and early 1960s. But since the women's liberation movement of the 1970s, in which women sought equal rights with men, the American family has changed drastically. As Figure 1.5 shows, these changes continued between 1990 and 2007, with the percentage of married couples declining from 55 percent to 52 percent. Explanations for this decline include the trend for people to marry at an older age and the fact that as the population ages, rising numbers of individuals are left widowed. The percentage of female householders without spouses (both with and without children) remained constant between 1990 and 2007 after experiencing a significant increase from 1970 to 1990. The proportion of male householders without spouses increased slightly, and men without a spouse are more likely to be raising children than they were in 1980. Finally, the proportion of the population living in nonfamily households, both those living alone and with others, rose slightly.

U.S. Household Trends

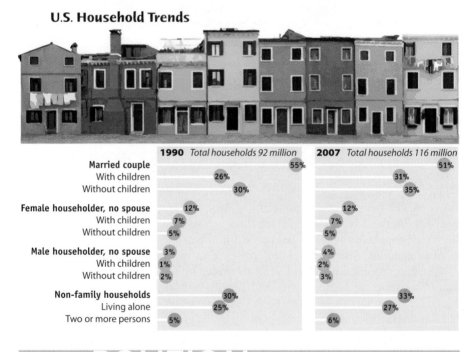

FIGURE 1.5 ■ What factors might explain the increase in male householders without spouses between 1990 and 2007? What factors might explain the increase in nonfamily households? What impact, if any, might these trends have on policy in the future?

Source: www.CensusScope.org/us/chart_house.html, Social Science Data Analysis Network, University of Michigan, www.ssdan.net, and *Statistical Abstract of the United States.*

Why the Changing Population Matters for Politics and Government

Each of the changes to the U.S. population described here has implications for American democracy. As the nature of the electorate shifts, different priorities may become important to a majority of the nation's people, and various policies may become more and less important (see "Analyzing the Sources" on page 30). For example, rapid U.S. population growth means that the demand for the kinds of services government provides—from schools, to highways, to health care—will continue to increase. The aging of the population will inevitably increase the burden on the nation's Social Security and Medicare health care systems, which will be forced to support the needs of that rising population.

Changes in the population's racial and ethnic composition also matter, as does the concentration of racial minorities in specific geographic areas. The racial and ethnic makeup of the population (along with other influences) can significantly affect the nation's political culture and people's political attitudes. It has implications, too, for who will govern, as more and more representatives of the country's various racial and ethnic groups become candidates for political office and as *all* political candidates must reach out to increasingly diverse groups of voters—or possibly pay the price at the ballot box for failing to do so.

Ideology: A Prism for Viewing American Democracy

Besides focusing on the demographic characteristics of the U.S. population, another way of analyzing political events and trends is by looking at them through the prism of ideology. **Political ideology** is an integrated system of ideas or beliefs about political values in general and the role of government in particular. Political ideology provides a framework for thinking about politics, about policy issues, and about the role of government in people's everyday lives. In the United States, one key component of various ideologies is the extent to which adherents believe that the government should have a role in people's everyday lives—in particular, the extent to which the government should promote economic equality in society.

In the twentieth century, the ideologies of liberalism and conservatism dominated U.S. politics. Although liberalism and conservatism have remained powerful ideologies in the early years of the twenty-first century, neoconservatism has also become increasingly important. Table 1.2 on page 32 summarizes the key ideologies we consider in this section.

Liberalism

Modern **liberalism** in the United States is associated with the ideas of liberty and political equality; its advocates favor change in the social, political, and economic realms to better protect the well-being of individuals and to produce equality within

What Current Events Do Young People Talk About?

The following data show responses to Harvard University's Institute of Politics (IOP) poll of young people aged 18–24. In 2007, the IOP conducted a national survey of college students and individuals who do not attend college. The IOP asked the respondents a variety of questions about the content of their conversations.* The topics of their conversations indicate what is important to young people in general. The results of the poll also suggest some real (and sometimes surprising) differences between the concerns of young people who attend college and those who do not.

In the last few weeks, have you and your friends talked about the following issues?

*Institute of Politics at Harvard University, "Attitudes Towards Politics and Public Service: A National Survey of College Undergraduates," April 11–20, 2000, www. iop.harvard.edu/pdfs/survey/2000.pdf.

Evaluating the Evidence

① Which topic was the most talked about among the young college students? Among young people who do not attend college?

② On which topics were there the greatest differences between college students and nonstudents? What do you think explains the differences?

③ Which topics were talked about by similar proportions of college students and nonstudents? Can you think of any reasons why the results for these two groups would be similar?

④ Ask yourself the questions in the survey. For each issue, which group does your response match? Why do you think this is the case? Are your responses similar to those of the college students who were polled? Why or why not?

---

society. They emphasize the importance of civil liberties, including freedom of speech, assembly, and the press, as outlined in the Bill of Rights. Modern liberals also advocate the separation of church and state, often opposing measures that bring religion into the public realm, such as prayer in the public schools. In addition, they support political equality, advocating contemporary movements that promote the political rights of gays and lesbians and voting rights for the disenfranchised.

The historical roots of modern liberalism can be found in classical liberalism, which emerged from the Enlightenment. The classical liberal ideals that emerged from the Enlightenment—freedom of thought and the free exchange of ideas, limited governmental authority, the consent of the governed, the rule of law in society, the importance of an unfettered market economy, individual initiative as a determinant of success, and access to free public education—were founding ideals that shaped American democracy as articulated in the Declaration of Independence and the Constitution.

Modern liberalism, which emerged in the early twentieth century, diverged from its classical roots in a number of ways. Most important, modern liberals expect

THE SITUATION IN IRAQ		
	NON-COLLEGE	COLLEGE
Yes	54%	64%
No	46	36

GENOCIDE IN DARFUR		
	NON-COLLEGE	COLLEGE
Yes	15	25
No	85	75

U.S. POLITICS		
	NON-COLLEGE	COLLEGE
Yes	51	66
No	49	34

CELEBRITY GOSSIP		
	NON-COLLEGE	COLLEGE
Yes	52	56
No	48	44

GLOBAL WARMING AND THE ENVIRONMENT		
	NON-COLLEGE	COLLEGE
Yes	49	59
No	51	41

THE JOB MARKET AND THE ECONOMY		
	NON-COLLEGE	COLLEGE
Yes	48%	51%
No	52	50

THE 2008 PRESIDENTIAL CAMPAIGN		
	NON-COLLEGE	COLLEGE
Yes	53	63
No	47	37

RELATIONS BETWEEN THE UNITED STATES AND IRAN		
	NON-COLLEGE	COLLEGE
Yes	24	30
No	76	70

LATEST SPORTS NEWS		
	NON-COLLEGE	COLLEGE
Yes	41	53
No	59	47

Source: "The 12th Biannual Youth Survey on Politics and Public Service," www.iop.harvard.edu/pdfs/survey_s2007_topline.pdf, accessed August 20, 2007.

government to play a more active role in ensuring political equality and economic opportunity. Whereas classical liberals emphasized the virtues of a free-market economy, modern liberals, particularly after the Great Depression that began in 1929, advocated government involvement in economic affairs. Today we see this expectation in action when liberals call for affirmative action; increases in social welfare programs such as Social Security, Medicare, and Medicaid; and government regulation of business and the workplace.

Conservatism

Advocates of **conservatism** recognize the importance of preserving tradition—of maintaining the status quo, or keeping things the way they are. Conservatives emphasize community and family as mechanisms of continuity in society. Ironically, some conservative ideals are consistent with the views of classical liberalism. In particular, the emphasis on individual initiative, the rule of law, limited governmental

The Traditional Ideological Spectrum

	Socialism	Liberalism	Middle of Road (Moderate)	Conservatism	Libertarianism
Goal of Government	Equality	Equality of opportunity, protection of fundamental liberties	Nondiscrimination in opportunity, protection of some economic freedoms, security, stability	Traditional values, order, stability, economic freedom	Absolute economic and social freedom
Role of Government	Strong government control of economy	Government action to promote opportunity	Government action to balance the wants of workers and businesses, and to foster stability	Government action to protect and bolster capitalist system, few limitations on fundamental rights	No governmental regulation of economy, no limitations on fundamental rights

TABLE 1.2

authority, and an unfettered market economy are key components of both classical liberalism and contemporary conservatism.

Traditionally, one of the key differences between modern liberals and conservatives has been their view of the role of government. In fact, one of the best ways of determining your own ideology is to ask yourself this question: To what extent should the government be involved in people's everyday lives? Modern liberals believe that government should play a role in ensuring the public's well-being, whether by regulating industry and the economy, by enacting antidiscrimination laws, or by providing an economic "safety net" for the neediest members of society. By contrast, conservatives believe that government should play a more limited role in people's everyday lives. They think that government should have a smaller role in regulating business and industry and that market forces, rather than the government, should largely determine economic policy. Conservatives believe that families, faith-based groups, and private charities should be more responsible for protecting the neediest, and the government less so. When governments must act, conservatives prefer decentralized action by state governments rather than a nationwide federal policy. Conservatives also believe in the importance of individual initiative as a key determinant of success. Conservative ideas are the fundamental basis of policies like the Welfare Reform Act of 1996, which placed the development and administration of welfare (Temporary Aid to Needy Families, or TANF) in the hands of the states rather than the federal government.

During the George W. Bush administration, **neoconservatives** gained prestige, as many Bush administration officials ascribed to this ideology, which often advocates military over diplomatic solutions to foreign policy challenges. Chiefly anti-Communist during the Cold War, today's neoconservatives are defined by their stance against predominantly Arab states that are alleged to support or harbor terrorists or pose a threat to the state of Israel. Neoconservatives are less concerned than traditional conservatives with restraining government in social policy. Since the end of the Bush administration, neoconservatives' influence has dwindled considerably both in government and within the Republican political party.

Other Ideologies on a Traditional Spectrum: Socialism and Libertarianism

Although liberals and conservatives dominate the U.S. political landscape, other ideologies reflect the views of some Americans. In general, those ideologies tend to be more extreme than liberalism or conservatism. Advocates of certain of these ideologies call for *more* governmental intervention than modern liberalism does, and supporters of other views favor even *less* governmental interference than conservatism does.

For example, **socialism**—an ideology that stresses economic equality, theoretically achieved by having the government or workers own the means of production (businesses and industry)—lies to the left of liberalism on the political spectrum.[22] Although socialists play a very limited role in modern American politics, this was not always the case.[23] In the early twentieth century, socialists had a good deal of electoral success. Two members of Congress (Representative Meyer London of New York and Representative Victor Berger of Wisconsin), more than seventy mayors of cities of various sizes, and numerous state legislators (including five in the New York General Assembly and many municipal council members throughout the country) were socialists. In 1912, Socialist Party presidential candidate Eugene Debs garnered 6 percent of the presidential vote—six times what Green Party candidate Ralph Nader netted in 2004.

According to **libertarianism,** government should take a "hands-off" approach in most matters. This ideology can be found to the right of conservatism on a traditional ideological spectrum. Libertarians believe that the less government intervention, the better. They chafe at attempts by the government to foster economic equality or to promote a social agenda, whether that agenda is the equality espoused by liberals or the traditional values espoused by conservatives. Libertarians strongly support the rights of property owners and a laissez-faire (French for "let it be") capitalist economy.

A Three-Dimensional Political Spectrum

The rise of neoconservatism demonstrates the limitations of a one-dimensional ideological continuum. For example, although an individual may believe that government should play a strong role in regulating the economy, he or she may also believe that the government should allow citizens a high degree of personal freedom of speech or religion. Even the traditional ideologies do not always fit easily into a single continuum that measures the extent to which the government should play a role in citizens' lives. Liberals supposedly advocate a larger role for the government. But although this may be the case in matters related to economic equality, liberals generally take a more laissez-faire approach when it comes to personal liberties, advocating strongly for privacy and free speech. And while conservatives support less governmental intervention in the economy, they sometimes advocate government action to promote traditional values, such as constitutional amendments to ban flag burning and abortion and laws that mandate prayer in public schools.

Because of these contradictions, scholars have developed various *multidimensional scales* that attempt to represent peoples' ideologies more accurately.[24] Many of these scales measure people's opinions on the proper role of government in the economy on one axis and their beliefs about personal freedom on a second axis. One Web site, *The Political Compass* (www.politicalcompass.org), allows visitors to plot their ideology on the site's multidimensional scale.

Civic Engagement: Acting on Your Views

One vitally important goal of this book is to encourage you to engage in respectful, continuing conversations about your views and to make the connection between having ideas and opinions and acting on them. Political scientist Michael Delli Carpini has defined **civic engagement** as

> individual and collective actions designed to identify and address issues of public concern. Civic engagement can take many forms, from individual voluntarism to organizational involvement to electoral participation. It can include efforts to directly address an issue, work with others in a community to solve a problem or interact with the institutions of representative democracy.[25]

The possibilities for citizen involvement are so broad and numerous that the idea of civic engagement encompasses a whole range of activities. Everything from tutoring an underprivileged child to volunteering at a conservative think tank exemplifies civic engagement. In this book, we focus in particular on civic engagement that takes the form of **political engagement**—that is, citizen actions that are intended to solve public problems through political means. As you will find as you read the book, a wide variety of political actions are possible, from boycotting and *buycotting* (buying goods produced by companies whose policies you agree with) to running for office.

CONTINUING THE CONVERSATION

- Now is an exciting time to study American democracy, and the fast-paced changes in American society today make participation in government and civic life more vitally important than ever. The effects of participating in the continuing conversation of American democracy through both words and actions are unequivocally positive—for you, for others, and for the government—and can have large ripple effects.

- The Millennial Generation is participating in the civic life of their communities and the nation through unprecedented—and efficacious—new forms of political participation and community activism. Technology will continue to play a significant role in how they and the population at large participate in politics and how government creates and administers policy.

- Demographic changes in American society—particularly the aging and growing diversity of the U.S. population—are giving rise to new public policy demands and creating new challenges. Challenges mean opportunities for those who are ready for them, and citizens who respond to those challenges will have an impact on the future of the nation.

STUDY NOW

Summary

1. y shd u stdy am dem now? Or, Why Should You Study American Democracy Now?

American democracy is at a crossroads with respect to the impact of technology, war, the continuing terrorist threat on politics, and the changing role young people are playing in politics.

2. What Government Does

Governments provide for the national defense, preserve order and stability, establish and maintain a legal system, distribute services, raise and spend money, and socialize new generations of citizens.

3. Types of Government

In categorizing governmental systems, political scientists evaluate two factors, including who participates in governing or in selecting those who govern, and how governments function and are structured.

4. The Origins of American Democracy

American democracy was shaped by individuals who believed in the right of citizens to have a voice in their government.

5. Political Culture and American Values

Political culture refers to the people's collective beliefs and attitudes about the government and the political process; important American values include liberty, equality, capitalism, and consent of the governed.

6. The Changing Face of American Democracy

The population of the United States is growing, aging, and becoming increasingly diverse.

7. Ideology: A Prism for Viewing American Democracy

Liberals emphasize civil liberties, separation of church and state, and political equality, while conservatives prefer small government, individual initiative, and an unfettered market economy.

For Critical Thinking and Discussion

1. In what ways do you use technology in your daily life? Do you use technology to get information about politics or to access government services? How? If not, what information and services may be obtained using technological tools?

2. Have the events of September 11, 2001, changed how you think about government? Explain. Have the wars in Iraq and Afghanistan changed how you view government? Describe.

3. Why do governments perform the functions they do? Can you think of any private entities that provide public goods?

4. Think of the advantages and disadvantages of direct versus indirect democracies. Do you participate in any form of direct decision making? If so, how well or poorly does it work?

Key Terms

authoritarianism 15

capitalism 21

citizens 13

civic engagement 34

consent of the
   governed 22

conservatism 31

constitutionalism 15

democracy 15

direct democracy 18
divine right of kings 16
efficacy 10
government 13
indirect democracy 19
legitimacy 13
liberalism 29
libertarianism 34
liberty 20

limited government 15
majority rule 22
monarchy 14
natural law 16
naturalization 13
neoconservatives 33
oligarchy 14
political culture 19
political engagement 35

political ideology 29
politics 8
popular sovereignty 18
property 21
public goods 13
social contract 16
social contract theory 18
socialism 33
totalitarianism 15

Internet Resources

A More Perfect Union **Web site**
www.mhhe.com/harrisonample Consult the book's Web site for study guides, interactive activities, simulations, and current hot-links that provide additional information on American politics and political and civic engagement in the United States.

Circle: the Center for Information & Research on Civic Learning & Engagement
www.civicyouth.org Circle is the premier clearinghouse for research and analysis on civic engagement.

Institute of Politics, Harvard University
www.iop.harvard.edu Harvard's IOP provides a host of information about civic participation, but particularly useful are its surveys of American youth (look under Research and Publications).

The Statistical Abstract of the United States
www.census.gov/compendia/statab This is "the authoritative and comprehensive summary of statistics on the social, political, and economic organization of the United States." It provides a plethora of data about the population of the United States.

Recommended Readings

Norris, Pippa. *Digital Divide: Civic Engagement, Information Poverty, and the Internet Worldwide.* Cambridge: Cambridge University Press, 2001. A comparative analysis probing how access to information and technology have an impact on civic and political engagement.

Putnam, Robert D. *Bowling Alone: The Collapse and Revival of American Community.* New York: Touchstone, 2000. A classic volume demonstrating the decline in traditional forms of civic participation.

Verba, Sidney, Kay Lehman Schlozman, and Henry E. Brady. *Voice and Equality: Civic Voluntarism in American Politics.* Cambridge, MA: Harvard University Press, 1995. An analysis of how people come to be activists in their communities, what issues they raise when they participate, and how activists from various demographic groups differ.

Zukin, Cliff, Scott Keeter, Molly Andolina, Krista Jenkins, and Michael X. Delli Carpini. *A New Engagement? Political Participation, Civic Life and the Changing American Citizen.* Oxford: Oxford University Press, 2006. A study of participation and political viewpoints across generations.

The Constitution's framers distributed government power and created checks and balances to ensure a representative democracy.

The courts continue to probe and interpret the Constitution's meaning, and members of Congress introduce proposed constitutional amendments annually.

2

The Constitution

The U.S. Constitution is the supreme law of the land, meaning that all laws and the procedures used to approve all laws must be in compliance with it. Yet, because the authors of the Constitution had to negotiate and compromise to win approval of the document, much of the language in the Constitution is vague and ambiguous. As a result, conflicts have erupted over its meaning—and hence over what the supreme law of the land is—since even before the Constitution was ratified, and they continue unabated today. The courts resolve many such conflicts when they are presented to them in lawsuits. Constitutional amendments are another means of resolving conflict over what the supreme law of the land is. Amendments clarify or even change that law. Ultimately, the majority of justices on the U.S. Supreme Court determine what is and what is not constitutional—what is the supreme law of the land.

Will the courts have to decide the constitutionality of presidential signing statements?

Will an amendment be ratified requiring presidential election by direct popular vote rather than by the Electoral College?

Will the Constitution's third century witness a greater volume of ratified constitutional amendments as the people's efforts to create "a more perfect union" continue?

What Is a Constitution?

A **constitution** is a document that describes three basic components of an organization: the organization's mission, its foundational structures, and its essential processes. Typically, constitutions begin with a description of the *mission,* the long-term goals of the organization as envisioned by its founders. Second, constitutions detail *foundational structures,* which are the bodies that will do what is necessary to accomplish the mission, and articulate the relationships among these bodies. For example, the U.S. Constitution describes three bodies, or branches, of government—legislative, executive, and judicial—and gives each responsibility for a different governmental function. The Constitution also describes how these bodies will monitor and check one another. Third, constitutions establish *essential processes,* which include the procedures for selecting the members of the organization, as well as the processes that the members will follow to fulfill their assigned functions. For example, the U.S. Constitution describes the basic procedures for electing and appointing officials to the three branches, making laws, resolving conflicts over the implementation and meaning of laws, and ratifying and amending the Constitution.

Approval (ratification) of any constitution gives birth to the organization described in the constitution, just as ratification of the U.S. Constitution gave birth to a new government. The legitimacy of a constitution and of the organization it creates depends on the means by which the organization came into existence, including what process was used to approve the constitution. Legitimacy of the organization also rests on its continued compliance with its constitution.

Today, the legitimacy of the national government created by the U.S. Constitution is clear. An overwhelming majority of U.S. citizens have complied with the

Mike Luckovich Editorial Cartoon © 2006 Mike Luckovich. Used with the permission of Mike Luckovich and Creators Syndicate.

laws made by the national government for more than 200 years (with the exception of the Civil War period) without governmental coercion or force, because they perceive the government to be legitimate. This compliance does not mean that the national government has served all citizens well, nor does it mean that all citizens have agreed with the government's interpretation or implementation of the Constitution all the time. In fact, citizens (as individuals and as members of a group) regularly question the constitutionality of government actions.

Moreover, government officials frequently lock horns over the proper interpretation of the Constitution. They are "trying to undermine the age-old checks and balances that the founding fathers placed at the center of the Constitution and the Republic," Senator Charles E. "Chuck" Schumer (D-New York) argued in 2005 when Republicans questioned the constitutionality of Democratic senators' use of the *filibuster* (a nonstop speech to prevent a vote in the Senate) to block Senate confirmation of the president's nominees.[1] Another battle over the proper interpretation of the Constitution broke out in 2006 over President George W. Bush's use of "signing statements," a device used by presidents to claim that a provision in the legislation being signed into law is unconstitutional and so need not be enforced. President Bush challenged more legislative provisions than all of his predecessors combined. In his first months in office, President Barack Obama issued several signing statements. Yet the question remains whether such signing statements are constitutional.[2]

Complicating the matter of constitutional interpretation is the fact that some of the language in the Constitution is vague and ambiguous, and hence subject to varying interpretations. The reason for this vagueness and ambiguity is that the Constitution is the product of vigorous deliberation, negotiation, and compromise, as we consider later in this chapter. Before we tune in to the conversations and compromises that produced this language, though, we first examine the governing principles that inspired the authors of the Constitution and the mission, structures, and essential governmental processes they established.

The Constitution of the United States

In March 1789, the United States began to function under the Constitution of the United States of America. This bold new blueprint for the federal government replaced the nation's first constitution, the Articles of Confederation, which had been in effect since 1781. The mission of the government that was created by the Constitution shared many characteristics with the national government's mission as described in the Articles of Confederation. But the organizational structures and essential processes that the authors of the Constitution—the *framers*—articulated were new, innovative, and unprecedented. Moreover, these structures and processes successfully established a system that has evolved into a government by and for the people, one that many Americans claim is the best government in the world.

Mission of the Constitution

If a foreign visitor asked you to tell her why the United States is a good country in which to live, what would you say? When U.S. citizens are asked what is good about their country, there are several common responses. They say that government in the United States

- is by and for the people
- is democratic
- protects individual liberties such as freedom of speech, freedom of religion, and freedom of the press
- protects people from unreasonable governmental searches and seizures of property
- guarantees the right of citizens to participate in government
- allows citizens to elect a large number of government officials, through regular, free elections, to represent and serve them
- ensures through its court systems that all people uphold the Constitution because no one is above the law

These typical responses dovetail with the principles of government developed by philosophers John Locke (1632–1704) and Jean-Jacques Rousseau (1712–1778) and articulated in the Declaration of Independence and the Constitution of the United States. Recall from Chapter 1 that a key tenet of Locke and Rousseau is that people agree to create a government as a way to protect their **natural rights** (also called *unalienable rights*). These are rights possessed by all humans as a gift from nature, or God, including the rights to life, liberty, and the pursuit of happiness. Viewed in this light, a government created by the people is a government *for* the people. In addition to expecting that their government will be *for the people,* U.S. citizens are guaranteed by their Constitution a government that will be *carried out by the people.* This kind of government, in which sovereign power is in the hands of the people, not a monarch or some other leader, is called a **republic.** In a republic, voters elect government officials to represent them in the processes by which laws are made. As we saw in Chapter 1, another common name for the U.S. system is *representative democracy.*

Built on the foundational principles of government for and by the people, the U.S. Constitution, in its *preamble* (introductory statement), lays out the mission of the newly created national government of the United States:

> We the People of the United States, in Order to form a more perfect Union, establish Justice, insure domestic tranquility, provide for the common defence, promote the general Welfare and secure the Blessings of Liberty to ourselves and our Posterity, do ordain and establish this Constitution for the United States of America.

As we shall see, the vision of a government by and for the people—a government that would provide justice, tranquility, defense, and liberty—would be at the heart of colonial Americans' dissatisfaction with the British crown. This vision would not only spark the War for Independence but also deeply motivate how the framers would shape the new national government.

A Key Foundational Structure: Separation of Powers with Integrated Checks and Balances

The Constitution's framers created a republic with governmental structures aimed at ensuring that a majority of the population could not pass laws that would take away the life, liberty, and pursuit of happiness of a minority of the population. Borrowing from French political thinker Baron de Montesquieu's (1689–1755) *The Spirit of the Laws* (1748), the framers separated the primary governing functions among three branches of government—referred to as the **separation of powers**—so that no one group of government officials controlled all the governing functions. Under the terms of the separation of powers, each branch of the government has specific powers and responsibilities that allow it to operate independently of the other branches: the legislative branch has authority to formulate policy; the executive branch has authority to implement policy; the judicial branch has authority to resolve conflicts over the law.

As suggested by Montesquieu's work, once the framers separated the primary functions, they established various mechanisms by which each branch can monitor and limit the functions of the other branches in order to ensure that no branch acts to the detriment of citizens' natural rights. These mechanisms collectively form a system of **checks and balances.** If one branch tries to move beyond its own sphere or to behave tyrannically, this arrangement ensures that the other branches can take action to stop it.

The following brief review of the first three of the seven articles that compose the Constitution should help to clarify the system of separation of powers, with its integrated checks and balances. For a complete compilation of the separation of powers and specific checks and balances, see Figure 2.1.

Article I: The Legislative Branch Article I of the Constitution delegates lawmaking authority to Congress, describes the structure of the legislative branch, and outlines the legislative process. Article I specifies that the legislature is **bicameral,** that is, composed of two chambers, which are the House of Representatives and the Senate. Each state is represented in the House based on its population. In contrast, state representation in the Senate is equal, with each state having two senators. Today, all citizens eligible to vote can participate in the election of one of their state's representatives in the U.S. House and both of their state's U.S. senators.

According to Article I, a proposed piece of legislation—a *bill*—requires simple majority votes (50 percent plus one vote) in both the House and the Senate in order to become law. This requirement means that the House and the Senate can check each other in the legislative process, because even if one chamber garners a majority vote, the other chamber can kill the bill if its majority does not support it. Because all pieces of legislation supported by the majority of the House and the majority of the Senate go to the president for approval or rejection, the president has a check on the legislative authority of Congress.

Article II: The Executive Branch Article II of the Constitution describes the authority of the president. This article gives the president authority to ensure

Separation of Powers with Checks and Balances

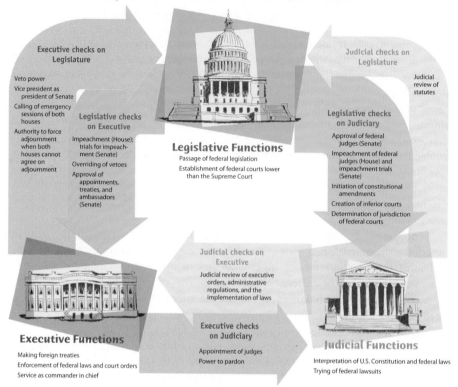

Executive checks on Legislature

Veto power

Vice president as president of Senate

Calling of emergency sessions of both houses

Authority to force adjournment when both houses cannot agree on adjournment

Legislative checks on Executive

Impeachment (House); trials for impeachment (Senate)

Overriding of vetoes

Approval of appointments, treaties, and ambassadors (Senate)

Legislative Functions

Passage of federal legislation

Establishment of federal courts lower than the Supreme Court

Judicial checks on Legislature

Judicial review of statutes

Legislative checks on Judiciary

Approval of federal judges (Senate)

Impeachment of federal judges (House) and impeachment trials (Senate)

Initiation of constitutional amendments

Creation of inferior courts

Determination of jurisdiction of federal courts

Judicial checks on Executive

Judicial review of executive orders, administrative regulations, and the implementation of laws

Executive Functions

Making foreign treaties

Enforcement of federal laws and court orders

Service as commander in chief

Executive checks on Judiciary

Appointment of judges

Power to pardon

Judicial Functions

Interpretation of U.S. Constitution and federal laws

Trying of federal lawsuits

POLITICAL INQUIRY

FIGURE 2.1 ■ Why did the Constitution's framers separate powers among the three branches of the federal government? What specific powers does each branch have? What is the purpose of the Constitution's checks and balances? For each branch of the government—legislative, executive, judicial—name a specific check that it can exert on each of the other two.

that the laws are faithfully executed, to appoint people to assist in administering the laws, to negotiate treaties, and to command the military. In addition to these executive functions, Article II allows the president several checks on the power of the other two branches of government.

As already noted, the president checks the legislative authority of Congress. All pieces of legislation approved by the House and the Senate are forwarded to the president's desk. The president has ten days to act on a bill, or it will automatically become law. Within those ten days, the president can either sign the bill into law or send it back to Congress—**veto** it—with his objections noted. Because Congress has primary responsibility for legislative functions, it can set aside the president's veto, that is, override the veto, by achieving positive supermajority votes of two-thirds of House members and two-thirds of the senators.

With respect to the legislature's checks on the executive, the Constitution gives the Senate a check on presidential authority to negotiate treaties by specifying that the Senate can approve or reject any negotiated treaties. The Senate also checks the executive power through its constitutional authority of **advice and consent,** which is the power to approve or reject the president's appointments. The Senate's advice and consent authority extends to the president's judicial nominees as well. Although the president nominates the individuals who will serve as judges in the federal judicial branch—ultimately, the people who will interpret the Constitution—the Senate must formally approve these candidates.

Article III: The Judicial Branch   Article III describes the judicial branch. More specifically, Article III establishes the U.S. Supreme Court, and it delegates to Congress the authority to establish other, inferior (lower) courts. The Supreme Court and the other federal courts established by Congress have the authority to resolve lawsuits arising under the Constitution, federal laws, and international treaties. In 1803, in the case of *Marbury v. Madison,* the Supreme Court interpreted Article III to mean that the Court has the authority to determine whether an action taken by any government official or governing body violates the Constitution; this is the power of **judicial review.**

In the *Marbury* case, the justices considered a portion of one of the first laws passed by Congress, the Judiciary Act of 1789. In its *Marbury* decision, the Court struck down the portion of the Judiciary Act that gave the Supreme Court new authority that was not specified in the Constitution. In so doing, the justices determined that it is in the Court's power to make rulings on what the Constitution means—that is, to interpret its often vague provisions. With its power of judicial review firmly established in *Marbury,* the Supreme Court has the authority to strike down laws, or portions of laws, approved by the other two branches (as well as by state and local governments) that it views as in violation of the Constitution. Some analysts consider the power of judicial review the ultimate check on the other two branches of government.

The framers intended that the national government created by the Constitution, with its separation of primary functions among the three branches, complemented by an integration of checks and balances, would work alongside the existing state governments. The Constitution did not describe the mission, foundational structures, or essential processes of the state governments because the states' own constitutions already did so. But the Constitution did spell out the distribution of authority between the national and state governments in this innovative governing system, as we now consider.

Another Key Structure: The Federal System

The framers created a federal system—a two-tiered government, comprising the national and state levels, each with ultimate authority over different matters. Article I of the Constitution lists the matters over which the national legislature (Congress) has ultimate lawmaking authority, such as regulating interstate and foreign commerce, coining money, raising and funding an army, and declaring war. Article I also prohibits state governments from engaging in certain specific activities, such as negotiating treaties. (Chapter 3 focuses on the constitutional distribution of power between the national and state governments.)

Yet the primary constitutional clause that acknowledges the establishment of a federal system of government is the Tenth Amendment, which in its entirety reads, "The powers not delegated to the United States by the Constitution, nor prohibited by it to the States, are reserved to the States respectively, or to the people." In this amendment, *United States* refers to the national government. Because there is no list of state responsibilities in the Constitution, the vagueness of the Tenth Amendment's "reserved to the states" clause has led to a perpetual battle between the national government and state governments over who is responsible for what.

Essential Processes of the National Government

In addition to the legislative process, the Constitution lays out the procedures governing the selection of national government officials. It also describes two procedures that have been vital for achieving representative democracy—the processes for formal amendment of the Constitution and for constitutional ratification. Consider that until the Constitution was amended, the national government had *no* authority to determine voting rights; *state law* determined who could vote in local, state, and national elections.

Selection of National Government Officials Members of the House and the Senate are elected by winning the majority of the people's direct vote (the popular vote) in their district and state, respectively. But when you cast your vote for a presidential candidate (which is an automatic vote for that candidate's vice-presidential running mate), you are not directly electing the president. Instead, in nearly every state, your presidential vote, combined with the votes of other citizens from your state, determines which political party's slate of representatives (*electors*) will participate on behalf of your state in the **Electoral College,** the body that actually selects the president and the vice president.

"I believe strongly that in a democracy, we should respect the will of the people, and to me, that means it's time to do away with the Electoral College and move to the popular election of our president," declared Senator Hillary Clinton (D-New York) in response to the outcome of the 2000 presidential election.[3] In that election, Democratic presidential candidate Al Gore won the popular vote, but Republican candidate George W. Bush ultimately won the electoral vote. In order to reform or eliminate the Electoral College, the Constitution would have to be formally amended by one of the methods we next consider.

Article V: The Amendment Process The Constitution's framers wanted to ensure that widespread deliberation among the American people would precede any and all changes in the written Constitution. Thus, they made it no easy matter to amend the U.S. Constitution formally—that is, to change its written language.

Amendment is a two-step process, entailing, first, the proposal of the amendment and, second, the ratification of the proposed amendment. Article V describes two different procedures for *proposing* an amendment (see Figure 2.2). The first method

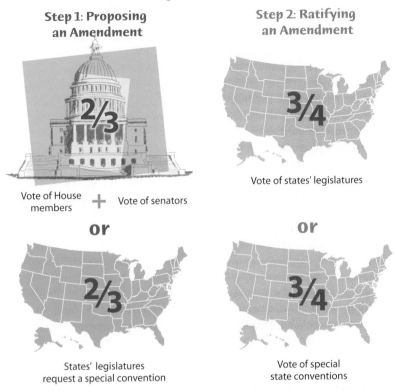

Amending the Constitution

Step 1: Proposing an Amendment

2/3

Vote of House members + Vote of senators

or

2/3

States' legislatures request a special convention

Step 2: Ratifying an Amendment

3/4

Vote of states' legislatures

or

3/4

Vote of special state conventions

POLITICAL INQUIRY

FIGURE 2.2 ■ **What steps are involved in proposing a constitutional amendment? In what two ways can an amendment be ratified? Who has the authority to ratify amendments to the Constitution? Why is the designation of this authority important to the balance of power between the national and state governments? Explain.**

requires a two-thirds majority vote in both the House and the Senate, after which the congressionally approved proposal is sent to the states for ratification. The second method (which has never been used) requires a special constitutional convention. If two-thirds of the state legislatures petition Congress to consider an amendment, such a convention, where state delegates vote on the possible amendment, takes place; an approved proposal then goes to the states for ratification.

Article V also outlines two avenues by which the second step, *ratifying* a proposed amendment, may occur. An amendment is ratified by a vote of approval in either three-quarters of the state legislatures or three-quarters of the special state conventions. Citizens have no vote in the process by which the U.S. Constitution is amended, nor did they have a vote in the original Constitution's ratification. In contrast, many countries and forty-nine of the fifty states in the United States do mandate citizen approval of constitutional amendments, as well as new constitutions.

Article VII: The Constitutional Ratification Process   According to Article VII of the Constitution, ratification of the Constitution required the affirmative vote of special conventions in nine of the thirteen original states. Notably, the ratification process did not authorize the state legislatures—whose elected officials might understandably have felt threatened by the new national government that the Constitution would create to work alongside them—to vote on the adoption of the Constitution. Instead, ratification would require special state conventions whose delegates would be selected by each state in a manner of its own determination.

The national-state competition underlying the ratification process exemplifies the many tensions and conflicts sparked by the plan to replace the Articles of Confederation (the nation's first constitution) with the Constitution of the United States. To appreciate the strength of this uneasiness requires a review of the history of the United States' founding.

The Creation of the United States

Understanding the American colonists' experiences in the period before the War for Independence (1775–1783) is central to comprehending the governments created by their first and second constitutions. Unlike their brothers and sisters in England, the colonists, most of whom viewed themselves as British subjects, were largely shut out of participating in the political processes taking place in England. As the eighteenth century unfolded, this exclusion increasingly rankled the American colonists, especially as an increasing number of the British government's policies put more and more restrictions on their freedoms and pursuit of economic well-being. Eventually, the colonists' public debates—in homes, taverns, town squares, and newspapers—coalesced around the principles of government by and for the people.

Colonization and Governance of America

In the 1600s, waves of Europeans undertook the dangerous sea voyage to America to start new lives. Some people with connections to the king of England were rewarded with large grants of land and the authority to govern. Many more voyagers came as *indentured servants,* who would work for a number of years for a master who paid for their passage. Others came to create communities with people of the same religion so that they could practice their faith without government interference. Countless others—Africans who were brought to the colonies as slaves—came against their will. In short, a diversity of people and a mix of economic classes migrated to the colonies, joining the Native American peoples who had lived there since ancient times.

By the early eighteenth century, a two-tier system of governing the American colonies had evolved, with governance split between the colonies and Britain. The colonists elected local officials to assemblies that had the authority to rule on day-to-day matters (including criminal law and civil law) and to set and collect taxes. Back in England, Parliament, with no representatives from the colonies, enacted laws with which the colonists had to comply. Governors appointed by the king oversaw the enforcement of British law in the colonies. Initially, these laws focused on international trade—the regulation of colonial imports and exports. But that focus would soon shift.

British Policy Incites a Rebellion

The towering costs of waging the Seven Years' War in Europe and its colonial extension, the French and Indian War (1756–1763), combined with costs of maintaining peace in America as westward-moving colonists encroached on Indian lands, convinced the British Parliament to turn to the colonies for increased revenues. The first new tariff imposed after the end of the war came by way of the Sugar Act (1764). In addition to increasing the taxes on such imported goods as molasses, coffee, and textiles, the Sugar Act directed that all the taxes thus collected be sent directly to Britain instead of to the colonial assemblies, as had been the practice until then.[4] Almost immediately, the colonists condemned the law, saying that because they had no representatives in Parliament, they had no obligation to pay taxes imposed by that body. Their anger intensified in 1765 when Parliament passed the Stamp Act, which taxed the paper used for all legal documents, bills of sale, deeds, advertisements, newspapers, and even playing cards.[5] The Stamp Act introduced a new level of British involvement (some thought interference) in the day-to-day matters of the colonies.

The colonists responded to the Sugar and Stamp acts by boycotting imported goods. Women, including groups of upper-class women known as Daughters of Liberty, substituted homegrown or homespun goods for the banned items. Although the boycotts were largely peaceful, other acts of resistance were not. The Sons of Liberty, founded by Boston brewer Samuel Adams in 1765, opposed the Stamp Act through intimidation of British stamp commissioners and sometimes violence.

Parliament followed the Sugar and Stamp acts with passage of the Quartering Act in 1765. The Quartering Act directed each colonial assembly to provide supplies to meet the basic needs of the British soldiers stationed within its colony. Parliament expanded this law in 1766 to require the assemblies to ensure housing for the soldiers.[6] Throughout the colonies, violent reactions to the quartering law erupted.[7] Since 1791, the Third Amendment to the Constitution has protected U.S. citizens from being required to quarter soldiers during times of peace.

Although Parliament repealed the hated Stamp Act in 1766, it paired this repeal with passage of the Declaratory Act. This new law gave Parliament the blanket power to assert control over colonies "in any way whatsoever."[8] This development was a clear indication that the two-tier system of colonial government, in which the colonies wielded some local governing authority, was dissolving. The next year, the colonists understood how momentous this law was, as Parliament used the Declaratory Act as the basis for a new series of laws that would culminate in war. Significant among these laws was the Townshend Duties Act of 1767, which not only expanded the list of imported goods that would be taxed but also stated that Parliament had unilateral power to impose taxes as a way of raising revenue and that the colonists had no right to object.[9] With this new law, the colonists dramatically stepped up their civic resistance.

A "Massacre" and a Tea Party By 1770, more than 4,000 British soldiers were quartered in the homes of the 16,000 civilians living in Boston. To make matters worse, the British soldiers quartered in the city sought additional work as rope makers and in other crafts, competing with the colonists for these jobs.[10] On March 5, 1770, an angry mob of nearly 1,800 struggling colonists clashed with the British soldiers, who shot into the crowd, leaving five dead and six wounded.

Almost immediately, Samuel Adams—an expert at "spinning" a news story—condemned the event as "the Boston Massacre." Partnering with Adams to shape public opinion were silversmith Paul Revere and wealthy shipping merchant John Hancock. The communications of the two men stressed that the colonists respected the rule of law but emphasized that the British king, George III, cared more about preserving his own power than about his subjects' well-being. Therefore, Revere and Hancock asserted, there could be no assurance that he would respect the colonists' rights and liberties. This problem, they argued, could be rectified only by the American colonists' ending their relationship with Britain.

In 1772, Adams created the Massachusetts Committee of Correspondence, a group dedicated to encouraging and maintaining the free flow of information and the spread of calls for rebellion among the Massachusetts colonists. Radicals in other colonies followed his lead.[11] Revere published pamphlets aimed at keeping the colonists together in their battle with the Crown, talking boldly about "our rights," "our liberties," and "our union."[12] These communication networks served as a kind of colonial-era Internet, facilitating the sharing of news among the colonists. But in this case, the swift transmission of information occurred by way of riders on horseback and printers at their presses rather than by the keystrokes of citizens typing on computers—today's vital communication network for rallying people behind a cause and mobilizing political activism.

Adding fuel to the fire, in 1773, Parliament passed the Tea Act, which gave Britain's East India Tea Company a monopoly on tea imported into the colonies. The questioning of the act's legitimacy by the Sons of Liberty successfully swayed public opinion and became the catalyst for an event that would become known as the Boston Tea Party. In November 1773, the first post–Tea Act shipment of tea arrived in Boston Harbor on three East India ships. Under cover of darkness on the night of December 16, 1773, fifty colonists, dressed as Mohawk Indians, boarded the three ships, broke open hundreds of crates, and dumped thousands of pounds of tea into the harbor.[13] The Boston Tea Party had a cataclysmic effect, not only on the relationship between Britain and the colonies but on the relationship among the colonists themselves.

Parliament responded with the Coercive Acts (Intolerable Acts), which closed the port of Boston until the colonists paid for the lost tea. In addition, the new laws imposed martial law, shut down the colonial assembly, and banned virtually all town meetings, thus curtailing legal opportunities for political engagement.[14] At the same time, the Crown stepped up enforcement of the Quartering Act.

The Continental Congress's Demands for Political Rights

Sympathy for Massachusetts's plight, along with rising concerns about how the Crown was generally abusing its powers, reinforced the colonists' growing sense of community and their shared consciousness of the need for collective action. The Massachusetts and Virginia colonial assemblies requested a meeting of delegates from all the colonies to develop a joint statement of concern that would be sent to the king. In September 1774, every colony but Georgia sent delegates to what became known as the First Continental Congress. The Congress (the assembled delegates) called for a boycott of all British goods and created Committees of Enforcement to impose the ban. Moreover, the Congress drafted and sent to the king a document demanding that the American colonists should have political rights to petition the government and to assemble, the right to select representatives to formulate tax policy, a guarantee of trial by peers, and freedom from a standing army.[15] The Congress also scheduled a second meeting—the Second Continental Congress—to discuss the king's response to these demands.

When the king refused to address the Congress's demands, civic discourse on the prospect of pursuing independence from Great Britain increased. On April 19, 1775, before the Second Continental Congress met, shots rang out at Lexington and Concord, Massachusetts, as British troops moved inland to seize the colonists' store of guns and ammunition. On May 10, 1775, the Second Continental Congress convened. The assembled delegates empowered the Congress to function as an independent government and to prepare for war with Britain, appointing George Washington to command the to-be-created Continental Army.

The Common Sense of Declaring Independence

In July 1775, the Second Continental Congress made one last effort to avert a full-blown war. The Congress petitioned King George III to end hostile actions against the colonists. The king refused and sent even more troops to the colonies to put down the rebellion. Yet even as the Congress made preparations for a likely war, many colonists remained unsure about whether the colonies should cut their ties with Britain. A brief pamphlet written by Thomas Paine, a recently arrived radical from Britain, and published in January 1776 transformed many such wavering colonists into patriots. Paine's *Common Sense* argued that war with Great Britain was not only necessary but unavoidable. Without war, the colonies and their people would continue to suffer "injuries" and disadvantages. Only through independence would Americans attain civil and religious liberty.[16]

In May 1776, Virginia delegate to the Congress Richard Henry Lee asserted "that these united Colonies are, and of right ought to be free and independent States, [and] that they are absolved from all allegiance from the British crown."[17] This "declaration of independence," which congressional delegates from other colonies subsequently echoed, led the Congress to approve a resolution empowering a committee of five to write down, in formal language, a collective declaration of independence. The committee selected Virginia delegate Thomas Jefferson, a wealthy plantation owner, to draft the declaration.

> Jefferson's Declaration of Independence, drawing on the work of philosophers John Locke and Jean-Jacques Rousseau, delivered the radical message that people have a right not only to choose their government but also to abolish it when it no longer serves them.

Unanimously endorsed by the Second Continental Congress on July 4, 1776, Jefferson's Declaration of Independence (Appendix A) drew upon the work of John Locke and Jean-Jacques Rousseau, as Table 2.1 highlights. The declaration was a radical statement. Its two central principles—that all men are equal and have rights that are unalienable (that is, fundamental) and that all government must be based on consent of the governed—may seem obvious from the vantage point of the twenty-first century. But in 1776, the idea that the people had a right not only to choose their government but to abolish it made the Declaration of Independence unlike anything before it.

After establishing these two central principles, the Declaration spelled out a list of grievances against King George in an attempt to convince the colonists and the European powers that the break with England was necessary and justified. The Declaration fulfilled this purpose of winning the hearts and minds of people both in the colonies and abroad. Until this point, the patriots had united in their hatred toward Britain but had little else around which to rally. The Declaration provided that rallying point by promising a new government that would be based on consent of the people, with liberty and equality as its central goals.

In 1777, as a brutal war over colonial independence raged between England and the colonies, the Second Continental Congress turned to the pressing task of establishing a new, *national* government by drafting a constitution, the Articles of Confederation. By that year, too, eleven colonies had written and ratified constitutions establishing new *state* governments, although two colonies continued to function under the structures and procedures established by their *royal charters* (constitutional

The Theories of Locke and Rousseau as Applied by Jefferson

What ideas did Jefferson take from Locke and Rousseau with respect to human rights and liberties? How would you summarize the views of the three men on the purposes of government and the source of government power?

TABLE 2.1

John Locke's Theories: *Two Treatises of Government* (1690)

All people are born free and equal.

All people are born into a "state of nature" and choose to enter into government for protection against being harmed.

Every person has the right to "life, liberty and property," and government may not interfere with this right.

Jean-Jacques Rousseau's Theories: *The Social Contract* (1762)

All power ultimately resides in the people.

People enter into a "social contract" with the government to ensure protection of their lives, liberties, and property.

If government abuses its powers and interferes with the people's exercise of their civil liberties, then the people have both the right and the duty to create a new government.

Thomas Jefferson's Application of Locke and Rousseau: Declaration of Independence (1776)

All men are created equal.

All men are endowed with certain unalienable rights, among which are life, liberty, and the pursuit of happiness.

To secure these rights, men create governments, which derive their powers from the consent of the governed.

King George III failed to respect the unalienable rights of the American colonists and instead created an "absolute tyranny" over them.

If government is destructive of people's rights, the people can alter or abolish it and create a new government.

documents initially approved by the British king).[18] In these ways, the colonies had become thirteen states with independent, functioning governments. It was to these governments that the Second Continental Congress sent the Articles of Confederation for ratification in 1777.

The State Constitutions

The states stood at the center of American politics when the nation was born. Every state constitution established a *mission* for the state government; *foundational structures* (including three branches of government, each with distinct primary governing functions and checks on the other branches), to organize the government and distribute power within it; and *essential processes* by which the government would operate. The state constitutions provided the governments they created with only limited powers, however. Most of these powers rested in the legislatures because of the prevailing view of people of the times that this was where the best prospects for representative government could be found.

Ensuring liberty was a crucial aspect of the mission of all the state governments. To this end, each state constitution included a *bill of rights*—a section enumerating the individual liberties with which the new state government could not interfere, including freedom of speech, press, and assembly; protection against unreasonable searches and seizures and taxation without representation; and the right to a jury trial. As you can see, the authors of the state constitutions wrote into them limits on the state governments to prevent these governments from infringing on individuals' life, liberty, and pursuit of happiness as the British Crown had done. Hence, the inclusion of a written list of citizens' liberties established a limited government by ensuring that both the people and the government knew what freedoms the government could not violate. In addition, most state constitutions explicitly asserted that power was held by the people, who created government and whom government served.

The states of the new American republic used their new constitutions to guide them in handling their day-to-day domestic matters. Meanwhile, members of the Second Continental Congress turned their attention to creating a national government that would allow the states to collectively address international affairs.

The Articles of Confederation (1781–1789)

Because of the colonists' bitter experience under the British Crown, the people and their delegates to the Second Continental Congress were leery of a strong, distant central government; they had a preference for government that was close to their homes. The delegates nevertheless recognized the need for a unified authority in the realms of international trade, foreign affairs, and defense.

The Articles of Confederation, which was submitted to the states for ratification in 1777 and ratified by the required thirteen states by 1781, established a **confederation:** a national government composed of a league of independent states and in which the central government has less power than the member states. Through the Articles of Confederation, the states created an alliance for mutual well-being in the international realm yet continued to pursue their own self-interest independently. Article II asserts that "each state retains its sovereignty, freedom, and independence" and that every power not specifically given to the central government is retained by the states. In addition, the national Congress that the Articles of Confederation established had the authority to negotiate treaties with other nations.

Structure and Authority of the Confederation   Structurally, the new national government had only one body, a Congress. Under the Articles, the Congress was **unicameral,** meaning that it had only one chamber, and every state had from two to seven delegates but only one vote in this body. Each state determined how its delegates would be selected. Approving policies and ratifying treaties required nine affirmative votes. The Articles did not create a judicial branch, an executive branch, or a chief executive officer. Conflicts of law were to be addressed by the state court systems, and national policies would be implemented and paid for by state governments. There was to be a president—one of the congressional members selected by his peers to preside over the meetings of Congress. Finally, and important to remember, amending the Articles of Confederation required unanimous agreement among all thirteen states.

What authority did the new national government have by way of this unicameral body? The answer is a very limited authority. Congress could approve policies relevant to foreign affairs, defense, and the coining of money. It was not authorized, however, to raise revenue through taxation; only state governments could levy and collect taxes. Therefore, in order to pay the national government's bills, Congress had to request money from each state. Moreover, the value of the money coined by the national government was not insured, because the national government did not control a source of revenue to back the value.

Weaknesses of the Confederation   Under the Articles of Confederation, the states retained ultimate authority in matters of commerce. As a result, other nations were not willing to negotiate trade policies with national officials. In addition, each state taxed all goods coming into the state from foreign nations and from other states. Moreover, the states issued their own money and required the use of this currency for all business within the state. The cumulative effect of these state policies hampered interstate and international commerce severely, putting the new nation's economic health in jeopardy.

In Massachusetts, economic pressures reached a head in 1786 when small farmers, many of whom had fought in the War for Independence, could not pay their legal debts and faced bankruptcy and the loss of their land. Farmer and war veteran Daniel Shays led an uprising of these debt-burdened farmers, today known as Shays's Rebellion. The rebels broke into county courthouses and burned all records of their debts. They then proceeded to the federal arsenal. Massachusetts asked Congress for assistance in putting down the rebellion. Congress appealed to each state for money to fulfill this request, but only Virginia complied. While eventually, through private donations, Massachusetts raised enough money to hire a militia to end the rebellion, the weaknesses of the national confederacy and a rationale for a stronger central government were becoming apparent.

In an attempt to deal with the weakness of the Articles, delegates from five states met in Annapolis, Maryland, in 1786. The delegates signed a resolution that called for a constitutional convention to be held in Philadelphia in 1787 and attended by all thirteen states. This resolution had a sweeping objective: delegates to the constitutional convention were to consider changes not only in commercial regulation but also in the overall structure of the new government that the Articles of Confederation had established.

Crafting the Constitution: Compromise, Ratification, and Quick Amendment

The delegates to the Constitutional Convention in 1787 were among the most elite Americans. Some 80 percent had served as members of the Continental Congress, and the vast majority were lawyers, businessmen, or plantation owners. Many were engaged in highly lucrative international trade, and all were wealthy. These elites contrasted sharply with the masses, who included the country's hard-pressed farmers and struggling local merchants and tradespeople. As a matter of fact, historian Charles Beard contended in 1913 that the Constitution's framers succeeded in forging a government that protected their elite status.[19]

Indeed, the delegates did write into the new constitution a much greater role for Congress in creating and maintaining a healthy economy, something that would be good for the delegates as well as the nation. For example, the new constitution gave Congress the authority to levy and collect taxes, regulate interstate and foreign commerce, coin money, and develop a system of weights and measures.

But although the delegates widely agreed about the need to create a stronger economic role for the national government, they differed significantly over other issues that loomed large in the new nation. There was considerable disagreement in particular about what powers to give the central government, how to ensure a representative democracy, and what to do about the entrenched institution of slavery. Delegates from southern states worried that the northern states would create barriers to their states' economic interests by either insisting on the abolition of slavery or diluting the voting strength of the South. In the North, a region on the cusp of the Industrial Revolution, people were concerned about how the new government's trade and tax policies would affect them. These regional concerns reflected continuing unease about the relative power of the national government and state governments and about the powers of the states relative to one another. These power concerns played out in the compromises written into the Constitution and in the ratification battle as well.

Many convention delegates, including James Madison of Virginia, believed that a closed environment would be necessary for hammering out the compromises that would be essential for creating an improved system of government. Therefore, the delegates met in secret. The framers ultimately succeeded in producing a new constitution by bargaining and by forging compromises on several thorny issues. Thereafter, proponents of the Constitution would win its ratification only after acknowledging the need to amend the ratified Constitution quickly by adding a bill of rights to limit the power of the national government.

Conflict and Compromise over Representative Democracy

Among the delegates' top points of contention was disagreement over representation in the national government.

The Changing Face of Popular Representation

	CONSTITUTIONAL CONVENTION (1787)	111TH CONGRESS (2009– 2010)	CURRENT U.S. POPULATION*
Women	0%	17%**	51%
African Americans	0%	8%†	12%
Asian Americans	0%	2%	4%
Hispanics	0%	6%	15%
Native Americans	0%	0%	1%

*U.S. Census Bureau, 2006 American Community Survey.
**www.cawp.rutgers.edu/Facts2.html.
†www.ethnicmajority.com/congress.htm.

WHAT'S NEXT?

> What is different about the composition of the delegates to the Constitutional Convention and the composition of the 111th Congress? What explains the differences?

> Why do you think the demographic representation among lawmakers in the 111th Congress does not mirror the composition of the U.S. population at large more closely?

> Do you think future Congresses will be more "representative" of the nation's population? Explain.

The Virginia and New Jersey Plans and the Connecticut Compromise Virginian James Madison arrived at the convention with a plan in hand for restructuring the national government. His proposal called for a radically revamped government, consisting of a bicameral legislature (Congress), a chief executive officer, and a separate national judiciary. Madison's proposal, which became known as the **Virginia Plan,** favored states with larger populations, because it called for the determination of state representation in the national legislature on the basis of population. The lower house would be chosen through popular election, but the members of the upper house would be elected by the lower house. Madison argued forcefully for a separation of powers, believing this arrangement to be the key to limiting the authority of the much expanded national government and to protecting individual rights and liberties.

The states with smaller populations quickly and aggressively responded to Madison's Virginia Plan with their own proposal, which became known as the **New Jersey Plan.** The small states' concerns about the Virginia Plan were obvious. Because Madison's plan based representation in Congress on state population, the small states stood to lose significant power (remember that under the Articles of Confederation, each state, no matter what its population and no matter how many representatives it had in the legislature, had one vote). Unlike the Virginia Plan, the New Jersey Plan was not a radical proposal—it essentially reworked the Articles of Confederation. Under the New Jersey proposal, a unicameral national legislature would remain the centerpiece of the government, and all states would have an equal voice (equal representation) in this government.

The conflict and negotiation over the Virginia and New Jersey plans resulted in several compromises, most notably the **Connecticut Compromise** (also known as the *Great Compromise*). This compromise created today's bicameral Congress, with state representation in the House of Representatives based on state population and equal state representation in the Senate (two senators per state).

The Constitution's Checks on Representative Democracy At the heart of representative democracy is the participation of citizens in electing their government officials. Yet the framers built a number of checks into the Constitution that significantly *limited* representative democracy, and in doing so they effectively took most of the institutions of governing out of the hands of the people. Although the Constitution allowed citizens to elect members of the House directly, it specified the election of senators by the state legislatures. This protocol remained in effect until 1913, when the ratification of the Seventeenth Amendment to the Constitution gave voters the power to elect the members of the Senate, too. And as we have seen, the Electoral College system that the framers devised for the election of the president and vice president prevented citizens from directly selecting the nation's chief executive and the second-in-command.

In addition to limiting the number of officials elected by citizens, the framers effectively limited voting rights to a minority of citizens. Existing state constitutions had established that only property-owning white men could vote. The one exception was New Jersey, where property-owning white women could also vote until 1807, when the state constitution was amended to deny women the right to the franchise.

The framers left to the states the authority to determine eligibility to vote. Hence, women and many men, including Native Americans and slaves, were denied the right to vote under the new Constitution.

The delegates spent most of the first two months of debate arguing about the national legislature and primarily focused on the question of state representation in Congress. They devoted less than a month to the rest of the issues before them, including the structure of the executive and judicial branches; the relationship between the federal and state governments; the process for amending the new plan of government, should the need arise to do so; the procedures for the Constitution's ratification; and a series of compromises over the slave trade.[20]

Conflict and Compromise over Slavery

Another major disagreement among the Constitutional Convention delegates centered on the "peculiar institution" (as Thomas Jefferson called it) of slavery. In 1790, slaves made up almost 20 percent of the U.S. population, and the overwhelming majority of slaves resided in the southern states.[21] The southern states' delegates worried that a strong central government would threaten the institution of slavery. During the constitutional debates, they therefore refused to budge on the slavery issue. Meanwhile, northern delegates, who were widely concerned that a weak national government would affect the United States' ability to engage in commerce and international trade, believed that the nation needed a more powerful central government than had existed under the Articles of Confederation. Ultimately, to get the southern states to agree to a stronger central government, the northern states compromised on the slavery issue.

A provision in Article I, Section 9, of the Constitution postponed debate on the legality of slavery—and consequently kept it legal—by prohibiting Congress from addressing the importation of new slaves into the United States until January 1, 1808. Moreover, Article IV, which deals with interstate relations, established the states' obligation to deliver all fugitive slaves back to their owners. This measure aimed to ensure that people in non-slaveholding states would continue to respect the property rights of slaveholders—including the right to own slaves, who were legally property, not people with natural rights.

Although the slaves were legally property, Article I, Section 2, established a formula for "counting" slaves for purposes of representation in the House of Representatives, apportionment of electors for the Electoral College, and the allocation of tax burdens among the states. This **Three-Fifths Compromise** counted each slave as three-fifths of a free man. The southern states benefited from this compromise: they gained greater representation in the House and the Electoral College than they would have if only nonslaves had been counted. The benefit to the northern states was that the South would pay more taxes than they would have if only nonslaves had been counted in taxation formulas.

James Madison, while deploring slavery, argued that the delegates' "compromise" over slavery was "in the spirit of accommodation which governed the Convention." He insisted that without the compromise, the Constitution would never have been signed.

> James Madison, Alexander Hamilton, and John Jay authored *The Federalist Papers,* a series of newspaper articles that justified and argued for the governing structures and procedures established in the U.S. Constitution. Because Madison and Hamilton had attended the Constitutional Convention, they had an insider's view of the arguments for and against the Constitution.

So in the delegates' debates and deliberations, they resolved some disagreements, such as the large state–small state conflict over congressional representation. They put on hold other differences, such as their divisions over slavery. In the end, the document that the framers sent to the states for ratification described a government structure that aimed to fulfill the principles of the Declaration of Independence, for a select group of people. Foremost among these principles was the idea that it is up to the people to found a government that protects their natural rights to life, liberty, and the pursuit of happiness. To ensure these rights, which were initially meant only for white, property-owning men, the framers devised two key arrangements: the separation of powers with an integrated system of checks and balances, and a federal system in which the national and state governments had distinct, ultimate authorities.

The Federalist–Anti-Federalist Debate

Signed by thirty-nine delegates on September 17, 1787,* the Constitution was published two days later in a special issue of a newspaper called the *Pennsylvania Packet.* Almost immediately, opponents of the proposed Constitution began to write letters, issue pamphlets, and make stirring speeches urging the state legislatures to reject the document. The debate developed as one between the Federalists and the Anti-Federalists. The **Federalists** supported the Constitution as presented by the convention delegates. The **Anti-Federalists** opposed the Constitution on the grounds that it gave the national government too much power—power that would erode states' authority and endanger individual freedoms.

It was in the Pennsylvania debate between the Federalists and the Anti-Federalists that the call first clearly emerged for the inclusion of a bill of rights that would limit the powers of the federal government. Geared toward addressing the main Anti-Federalist complaints about the Constitution, the proposal for a bill of rights became the dominant point of contention in the ratification campaign. In the end, the success or failure of the ratification process would hinge on it.

The Federalist Papers: In Support of a Strong National Government
The Federalists made their most famous arguments in a series of essays known as *The Federalist Papers,* which appeared in newspapers across the new nation. The authors—James Madison, Alexander Hamilton, and John Jay—knew that achieving ratification depended on convincing the public and state legislators that the Constitution would empower the new nation to succeed. They also understood that many of the Anti-Federalists' concerns centered on how much power the national government would have under the Constitution and how that authority would affect the states and individual freedoms. Consequently, they approached the ratification debate strategically, penning eloquently reasoned essays (in the form of letters) to speak to these specific issues.

Addressing fears of lost state power, Hamilton argues in *Federalist* No. 9 that "a FIRM Union will be of the utmost moment to the peace and liberty of the States, as a barrier against domestic faction and insurrection."[22] Similarly, in *Federalist* No. 51, Madison explains how the Constitution's provision of both a separation of powers and a system of checks and balances would prevent the national government from usurping the powers of the states and also ensure that no one branch of the federal government would dominate the other two.[23]

---

*In 2004, the national government approved a law establishing September 17 as Constitution Day. The law mandates that all educational institutions receiving federal funds, which includes almost every college in the country, must provide educational programs about the Constitution on that day.

> Mercy Otis Warren was one of the rare, respected, politically engaged women of the eighteenth century. Her significant influence extended to the citizenry and to the authors of the Constitution and the Bill of Rights, with many of whom she discussed and debated governance and politics. Her political writings include the *Anti-Federalist Papers* and her extraordinary *History of the Rise, Progress, and Termination of the American Revolution* (1805).

With regard to protecting individual rights, in *Federalist* No. 10, Madison reassuringly details how the republican government created by the Constitution would ensure that many views would be heard and that a majority of the population would not be permitted to trample the rights of the numerical minority.[24] And writing in *Federalist* No. 84, Hamilton argues that because "the people surrender nothing, and as they retain every thing" by way of the Constitution, there was no danger that the new government would usurp individual rights and liberties.[25]

The Anti-Federalist Response: In Opposition to a Strong Central Government   On the other side of the debate, Anti-Federalists penned countless letters, speeches, and essays warning of the dangers of the new government and urging Americans to reject it. Anti-Federalists agonized that the Constitution ceded much too much power to the national government, at the expense of both the states and the people. Without a bill of rights, they reasoned, there was no way of truly limiting the actions the new government might take to achieve its goals.

Articulating Anti-Federalist views, Thomas Jefferson insisted that the inclusion of a bill of rights in the Constitution was essential. Federalist Alexander Hamilton countered that listing these rights might in fact endanger the very kind of individual freedoms and rights they sought to safeguard. It was possible, Hamilton reasoned, that the list would be incomplete and that at some future time people might legitimately argue that because a given right was not specifically enumerated, it did not exist. (Was Hamilton correct? Consider the debate today about abortion.) Jefferson's response was that "half a loaf is better than no bread" and that "if we cannot secure all our rights, let us secure what we can."[26]

Along with Jefferson, Mercy Otis Warren was among the most influential Anti-Federalists. In addition to influencing public debate over declaring independence from Great Britain and ratifying the Articles of Confederation and the Constitution, Warren was a catalyst for the development of the Bill of Rights. She published her *Anti-Federalist Papers* under the pen name "A Columbian Patriot." The circulation of her pamphlet was larger than that of Hamilton, Madison, and Jay's *Federalist Papers.*

In the end, Jefferson's and Warren's views and the larger civic discourse about states' rights and individuals' liberties placed significant pressure on the Federalists to reconsider their opposition to a bill of rights. With the proviso that a bill of rights would be the first order of business for the new Congress, four holdout states—Massachusetts, Maryland, South Carolina, and New Hampshire—the last four states of the nine needed to ratify the Constitution, ratified it in 1788. Ultimately, all original thirteen states ratified the Constitution.

The Bill of Rights (1791): Establishing Civil Liberties

In the opening days of the first session of the newly constituted Congress in March 1789, Virginia congressman James Madison introduced a bill of rights. Comprising twelve amendments, this proposed addition to the Constitution powerfully reflected the public concerns voiced during the ratification debates by (1) enumerating limits on the government's right to infringe on the natural rights of life, liberty, and the pursuit of happiness, and (2) preserving the states' authority. Congress passed all twelve amendments and sent them to the states for approval. By 1791, the required number of states had ratified ten of the twelve amendments, which we refer to today as the **Bill of Rights.**

The Bill of Rights establishes the government's legal obligation to protect several specific liberties to which the Declaration of Independence referred when it stated that men were "endowed by their creator with certain unalienable rights." These natural rights became government-protected liberties, or *civil liberties,* through the ratification process. Chapter 4 focuses in depth on the civil liberties established in the Bill of Rights.

The Constitution as a Living, Evolving Document

The authors of the Constitution were pragmatic men who were willing to compromise to resolve the problems confronting the new nation.[27] To garner the votes needed to move the document from first draft through ratification, the framers had to negotiate and compromise over constitutional language. As a result of this give-and-take, the Constitution is replete with vague and ambiguous phrases, which the framers expected judges to interpret later. Alexander Hamilton wrote, "A constitution is in fact, and must be, regarded by judges as a fundamental law. It therefore belongs to them to ascertain its meaning as well as the meaning of any particular act proceeding from the legislative body. . . . The courts must declare the sense of the law. . . ."[28] As Supreme Court justice Charles Evans Hughes (1862–1948) more recently observed, "The Constitution is what the Judges say it is."[29]

Judges—and principally the justices sitting on the U.S. Supreme Court, which has the ultimate authority to rule on what the Constitution means—have reinterpreted the Constitution many times. The Constitution has been formally amended only twenty-seven times, however. The reason for the relatively low number of constitutional amendments is that the framers established a difficult amendment process, requiring supermajority votes in Congress and among the states. They did so to ensure that nationwide public discourse would take place before the Constitution, the supreme law of the land, could be formally changed.

The alteration of this document—through both the formal passage of amendments and the less formal, but no less important, judicial reinterpretation of key clauses—derives from a continuing conversation among citizens about the core beliefs and principles of the framers and the generations that have followed them, including Americans today. In 2007, political scientist Larry Sabato, in his book *A More Perfect Constitution: 23 Proposals to Revitalize Our Constitution and Make America a Fairer Country*, tried to energize public discourse on the need to amend the Constitution so as to make the country "a more perfect union."[30] In this concluding section, we consider the amendments that have been approved to date as the American people have undertaken efforts to perfect the union established by the Constitution, and we look at the process by which these amendments became a reality.

Formal Amendment of the Constitution

Every term, members of Congress introduce between 100 and 200 proposals for new constitutional amendments. Collectively, since 1789, this amounts to more than 10,000 proposals! Members of Congress who oppose a ruling by the U.S. Supreme Court or a law that engenders a great deal of public debate may propose an amendment to supersede the Court ruling or the law. Often members of Congress introduce these amendments knowing that they will never be ratified but wanting to appease their core constituencies by at least instigating public discourse about how our government should function and what rights and freedoms individuals should possess.

Only a tiny fraction of the 20,000-plus proposed amendments have cleared Congress—in fact, only thirty-three have achieved the two-thirds vote necessary in Congress—and, as noted, only twenty-seven have been ratified by the states. The amendments that the states have ratified fit into one of three categories: they have (1) extended civil liberties and civil rights (equal protection of laws for citizens), (2) altered the selection or operation of the branches of the national government, or (3) dealt with important policy issues. Table 2.2 summarizes the Eleventh through the Twenty-Seventh Amendments and organizes them by category.

TABLE 2.2

The Eleventh Through Twenty-Seventh Amendments to the U.S. Constitution

Amendments that Protect Civil Liberties and Civil Rights

Thirteenth	1865	Banned slavery
Fourteenth	1868	Established that all people have the right to equal protection and due process before the law, and that all citizens are guaranteed the same privileges and immunities
Fifteenth	1870	Guaranteed that the right to vote could not be abridged on the basis of race or color
Nineteenth	1920	Guaranteed that the right to vote could not be abridged on the basis of sex
Twenty-Third	1961	Defined how the District of Columbia would be represented in the Electoral College
Twenty-Fourth	1964	Outlawed the use of a poll tax, which prevented poor people from exercising their right to vote
Twenty-Sixth	1971	Lowered the voting age to 18 years

Amendments that Relate to the Selection of Government Officials or the Operation of the Branches of Government

Eleventh	1795	Limited federal court jurisdiction by barring citizens of one state from suing another state in federal court
Twelfth	1804	Required the electors in the Electoral College to vote twice: once for president and once for vice president
Seventeenth	1913	Mandated the direct election of senators by citizens
Twentieth	1933	Set a date for the convening of Congress and the inauguration of the president
Twenty-Second	1951	Limited to two the number of terms the president can serve
Twenty-Fifth	1967	Established the procedures for presidential succession in the event of the disability or death of the president; established the procedure for vice-presidential replacement when the position becomes vacant before the end of the term
Twenty-Seventh	1992	Required that there be an intervening election between the time when Congress votes itself a raise and when that raise can be implemented

Amendments that Address Specific Public Policies

Sixteenth	1913	Empowered Congress to establish an income tax
Eighteenth	1919	Banned the manufacture, sale, and transportation of liquor
Twenty-First	1933	Repealed the ban on the manufacture, sale, and transportation of liquor

Interpretation by the U.S. Supreme Court

Beyond the addition of formal amendments, the Constitution has changed over time through interpretation by the courts. This interpretation began with the U.S. Supreme Court's landmark *Marbury v. Madison* decision in 1803, in which the Court established the important power of judicial review—the authority of the courts to rule on whether acts of government officials and governing bodies violate the Constitution. Although the U.S. Supreme Court's interpretation is final, if the Supreme Court does not review constitutional interpretations made by lower federal courts, then the interpretations of these lower courts are the final word. For a taste of how the courts determine the meaning of the Constitution, see "Analyzing the Sources."

The power of judicial review has allowed the courts to continue to breathe life into the Constitution to keep up with societal norms and technological change. For example, in 1896, the Supreme Court decreed that the Fourteenth Amendment allowed laws requiring the segregation of white and black citizens.[31] Then in 1954, in the case of *Brown v. The Board of Education of Topeka, Kansas,*[32] the Supreme Court declared such segregation to be an unconstitutional violation of the Fourteenth Amendment.

Technology also drives constitutional reinterpretation. The framers naturally never conceived of the existence of computers and artificial intelligence. Yet by reviewing and freshly interpreting the Fourth Amendment, which prohibits unreasonable searches and seizures by government officials, the courts have uncovered the principles behind this amendment that apply to our technologically advanced society. Consequently, this provision, whose original intent was to limit governments' physical searches of one's property and person, can be used today to determine, for example, whether governmental surveillance of computer databases is permissible.

Sometimes the Supreme Court's opinions ignite a debate or intensify a debate already under way, such as the controversy over what to do with detainees at Guantánamo Bay (see "Then, Now, Next" on page 68). Court decisions that are viewed as a "win" for one side and a "loss" for the other often generate fierce responses in the other branches or levels of the government. For example, the executive branch might decide not to implement a Court decision. Or perhaps the legislative branch might write a new law that challenges a Court decision. Unless a lawsuit allows the Court to find the new law unconstitutional, the new law takes effect.

Although controversial Court decisions often capture significant media attention, in the vast majority of cases, the Court's rulings are in step with public opinion. Analysts note that the Court does not often lead public opinion—in fact, it more often follows it.[33] And even if the justices wanted to take some very controversial and unpopular action, the system of checks and balances forces them to consider how the other branches would react. Recall that the Court has the power to interpret the law; it does not have the power to implement or to enforce the law and must be concerned about how the other branches might retaliate against it for highly unpopular decisions. Therefore, for the most part, changes to the Constitution, both formal and informal, are incremental and further the will of the people because they are the product of widespread public discourse—an ongoing conversation of democracy.

Constitutional Principles in a Recent Second Amendment Case

Consider the following chronology related to the Second Amendment and its legal protections. Has the court made the meaning of the Second Amendment clear and unambiguous?

1791 **Second Amendment** passes, stating that "a well regulated Militia, being necessary to the security of a free State, the right of the people to keep and bear Arms, shall not be infringed."

1976 **Washington, D.C., law** is passed, banning all handguns in homes unless they were registered before 1976. The law's intent is to decrease gun violence.

2007 **Majority opinion of the U.S. Court of Appeals for D.C. Circuit,** *Parker v. District of Columbia,* finds the 1976 Washington, D.C., ban unconstitutional and explains, "We . . . take it as an expression of the drafters' view that the people possessed a natural right to keep and bear arms, and that the preservation of the militia was the right's most salient political benefit—and

thus the most appropriate to express in a political document."*

2008 **Majority opinion of the U.S. Supreme Court in** *Distrinct of Columbia and Adrian M. Felty v. Dick Anthony Heller* declares "There seems to us no doubt, on the basis of both text and history, that the Second Amendment conferred an individual right to keep and bear arms." The decision goes on to say, "Like most rights, the Second Amendment right is not unlimited. It is not a right to keep and carry any weapon whatsoever in any manner whatsoever and for whatever purpose."**

Evaluating the Evidence

① What do you think was the intent of the authors of the Second Amendment? Did they intend to protect a natural, individual right to bear arms? Did they mean to ensure that resources (that is, people with the right to bear arms) for protecting domestic tranquility and national defense would be readily available? Did they seek to ensure both?

② What do you imagine the majority of Americans think the Second Amendment means? Why? Where might you get data to support your prediction?

③ Do you agree with the majority opinion in the *Parker* case or the majority opinion in the *D.C. v. Heller* case? Explain.

④ What impact on public safety will the divergent interpretations of the Second Amendment have?

*Parker v. District of Columbia 478 F. 3d 370 (D.C. Circuit 2007).
**District of Columbia and Adrian M. Fenty v. Dick Anthony Heller 544 U.S.

What Should the Obama Administration Do with the Prisoners Held at Guantánamo Bay?

THEN: Shortly after the terrorist attacks of September 11, 2001, the Bush administration established a detention center for foreigners it classified as enemy combatants at the U.S. naval base in Guantánamo, Cuba. The enemy combatants were subject to trials by military tribunals, which provide very limited due process rights in comparison with trials in the

federal civilian court system. By 2008, the Supreme Court declared that the Guantánamo detainees had constitutionally guaranteed due process rights and the right to be heard in federal civilian courts.

NOW: Presidential candidate Barack Obama pledged to move the detainees' cases into the federal civilian courts and to close Guantánamo Bay. By June 2009, the federal government had cleared 50 of the over 200 remaining Guantánamo detainees for release. Bermuda, one of the handful of countries that agreed to take in released

detainees, is now home to several Chinese ethnic Uighurs released from Guantánamo.

WHAT'S NEXT?

- What constitutional obligations does the federal government have to released detainees if it fears they will be persecuted upon their return to their home countries?

- What arguments can you think of for using military tribunals to try detainees? What are the arguments for transferring the detainees to civilian courts?

- What effect, if any, do you think the renewed use of military tribunals might have on the treatment of U.S. military personnel captured in future international conflicts?

CONTINUING THE CONVERSATION

- Ratified in 1788 and in effect since 1789, the Constitution of the United States is remarkable for its long life—a longevity that owes much to the pragmatism of its framers.

- The structures and governing procedures the framers established, including the process by which the courts are able to interpret constitutional language in the context of contemporary societal values and technological advances, have ensured that the Constitution is a living, evolving document, not one that sits on a shelf accumulating dust.

STUDY NOW

Summary

1. What Is a Constitution?

A constitution is a document that describes the mission, foundational structures, and essential processes of an organization—including, as in the case of the U.S. Constitution, a government.

2. The Constitution of the United States of America

In 1788, the Constitution of the United States replaced the Articles of Confederation (1781–1788), creating innovative governmental structures in order to ensure government by and for the people, and protection of natural rights: (1) the separation of powers, (2) an integrated system of checks and balances, and (3) a federal system of government.

3. The Creation of the United States of America

By the mid-eighteenth century, the American colonists were persuaded by public discourse and eloquent revolutionaries that it was common sense to declare independence from Britain, yet the weak national government established by the Articles of Confederation did not serve the people well.

4. Crafting the Constitution: Compromise, Ratification, and Quick Amendment

In response to severe economic problems and tensions among the states, and to growing desires for a more perfect union of the states, the colonists debated and then ratified a second constitution in 1788, processes that were characterized by deliberation, compromise, and negotiation, resulting in vague constitutional language and quick constitutional amendment—the Bill of Rights (1791).

5. The Constitution as a Living, Evolving Document

Although the Constitution has been formally amended a mere twenty-seven times over its 220-plus year life, it is perpetually being revised through the process of judicial review and interpretation, with the U.S. Supreme Court having the final word on what is the supreme law of the land.

For Critical Thinking and Discussion

1. What was the relationship between the state constitutions, many of which were created right after the signing of the Declaration of Independence, and the U.S. Constitution, which was written more than a decade later?

2. Think about important debates in the American polity today. Describe one that you think is linked in some way to the compromises upon which the Constitution is based.

3. Pretend that you are a young adult living during the revolutionary era who is writing an article for a newspaper in England, and you are trying to explain why the colonists have destroyed thousands of pounds of British tea at the Boston Tea Party. How might you, as an English citizen living in Britain, characterize the colonists' motives? How might you, as an English citizen living in the colonies, characterize the colonists' motives?

4. The contest between the Federalists and Anti-Federalists over ratification of the Constitution was a very close one. What do you think would have happened had the Anti-Federalists prevailed? What kind of government would they have shaped? How would this government have dealt with the difficult issues facing the new republic—slavery, concerns about mob rule, and continuing hostility in the international community?

Key Terms

Internet Resources

A More Perfect Union Web site
www.mhhe.com/harrisonampule   Consult the book's Web site for study guides, interactive activities, simulations, and current hot-links that provide additional information on contemporary issues involving the Constitution.

FindLaw
www.findlaw.com   This site offers links to news regarding current cases before the U.S. Supreme Court, as well as access to decisions of all federal and state appellate courts.

Library of Congress Memory Project
www.loc.gov/rr/program/bib/ourdocs/PrimDocsHome.htm   This comprehensive Web site, created by the Library of Congress and part of its Memory Project, includes a wealth of information about the early American republic, including primary documents such as *The Federalist Papers.*

The U.S. Constitution Online
www.USConstitution.net   This interesting site helps to place the U.S. Constitution in a contemporary context. Its current events section discusses how the pending issues are affected by constitutional principles.

Recommended Readings

Breyer, Stephen. *Active Liberty: Interpreting Our Democratic Constitution.* New York: Random House, 2005. A short, readable book in which Supreme Court justice Stephen Breyer argues that constitutional interpretation must be guided by the foundational principle of government by the people and that the courts must ensure that they protect and facilitate citizens' participation in government.

Hamilton, Alexander, James Madison, and John Jay. *The Federalist Papers.* Cutchogue, NY: Buccaneer Books, 1992. A compilation of the eighty-five newspaper articles written by the authors to convince the voters of New York to ratify the proposed Constitution of the United States, featuring a comprehensive introduction that puts the articles in context and outlines their principal themes—and hence, the underlying principles of the Constitution.

Roberts, Cokie. *Founding Mothers: The Women Who Raised Our Nation.* New York: Perennial Press, 2004. An examination of the Revolution and its aftermath, focusing on how women contributed to the war effort and to wider discussions about how the new government should be structured and what goals it should advance.

THE CONSTITUTION OF THE UNITED STATES OF AMERICA

Preamble

We the People of the United States, in Order to form a more perfect Union, establish Justice, insure domestic Tranquility, provide for the common defence, promote the general Welfare, and secure the Blessings of Liberty to ourselves and our Posterity, do ordain and establish this Constitution for the United States of America.

▲ The Preamble states that "the People" are creating a new government, which is described in the Constitution.

ARTICLE I. (Legislative Branch)

Section 1. (Bicameral Legislative Branch)

All legislative Powers herein granted shall be vested in a Congress of the United States, which shall consist of a Senate and House of Representatives.

▲ Article I presents the organization, procedures, and authority of the lawmaking branch, the Congress, a bicameral (two-chamber) legislature comprising the House of Representatives and the Senate.

Section 2. (The House of Representatives)

Clause 1: The House of Representatives shall be composed of Members chosen every second Year by the People of the several States, and the Electors in each State shall have the Qualifications requisite for Electors of the most numerous Branch of the State Legislature.

▲ House members are elected to serve a two-year term.

Clause 2: No Person shall be a Representative who shall not have attained to the age of twenty five Years, and been seven Years a Citizen of the United States, and who shall not, when elected, be an Inhabitant of that State in which he shall be chosen.

▲ The Constitution specifies only three qualifications to be elected to the House: you must be at least 25 years old; you must be a U.S. citizen for at least seven years (so a foreign-born, naturalized citizen can be a House member) and you must be a resident of the state you will represent.

Clause 3: Representatives and direct Taxes shall be apportioned among the several States which may be included within this Union, according to their respective Numbers, which shall be determined by adding to the whole Number of free Persons, including those bound to Service for a Term of Years, and excluding Indians not taxed, three fifths of all other Persons. The actual Enumeration shall be made within three Years after the first Meeting of the Congress of the United States, and within every subsequent Term of ten Years, in such Manner as they shall by Law direct. The Number of Representatives shall not exceed one for every thirty Thousand, but each State shall have at Least one Representative; and until such enumeration shall be made, the

State of New Hampshire shall be entitled to chuse three, Massachusetts eight, Rhode-Island and Providence Plantations one, Connecticut five, New-York six, New Jersey four, Pennsylvania eight, Delaware one, Maryland six, Virginia ten, North Carolina five, South Carolina five, and Georgia three.

▲ Congress distributes House seats among the fifty states according to each state's share of the total population, as determined by a census (official count of the country's inhabitants) conducted every ten years. The "three-fifths" clause decreed that when conducting the census the government would not count Native Americans and would count each slave as three-fifths of a person while counting every other inhabitant as one person. The Fourteenth Amendment (1868) repealed the three-fifths clause.

Clause 4: When vacancies happen in the Representation from any State, the Executive Authority thereof shall issue Writs of Election to fill such Vacancies.

▲ Governors have the authority to call for a special election to fill any of their state's House seats that become vacant.

Clause 5: The House of Representatives shall chuse their Speaker and other Officers; and shall have the sole Power of Impeachment.

▲ House members select their presiding officer, the Speaker of the House. The Constitution gives the House a check on officials of the executive and judicial branches through its power of impeachment: the power to accuse such officials formally of offenses including treason, bribery, and abuse of power.

POLITICAL INQUIRY: *Because members of the House of Representatives run for reelection every two years, they are perpetually raising money for, and worrying about, their next election campaign. Recently, an amendment was introduced that would increase their term from two to four years. How would this change make members of the House more, or less, responsive to their constituents' concerns?*

Section 3. (The Senate)

Clause 1: The Senate of the United States shall be composed of two Senators from each State, chosen by the Legislature thereof, for six Years; and each Senator shall have one Vote.

▲ Initially, senators were selected by the members of their state's legislature. The Seventeenth Amendment (1913) changed this election process; today, senators are elected by the voters in their state. This amendment also authorized each state's governor to call for elections to fill vacancies.

Clause 2: Immediately after they shall be assembled in Consequence of the first Election, they shall be divided as equally as may be into three Classes. The Seats of the Senators of the first Class shall be vacated at the Expiration of the second Year, of the second Class at the Expiration of the fourth Year, and of the third Class at the Expiration of the sixth Year, so that one third may be chosen every second Year; and if Vacancies happen by Resignation, or otherwise, during the Recess of the Legislature of any State, the Executive thereof may make temporary Appointments until the next Meeting of the Legislature, which shall then fill such Vacancies.

▲ Every even-numbered year, congressional elections are held in which one-third of the Senate's 100 seats and all 435 House seats are up for election. Every state elects two senators, who serve six-year terms.

Clause 3: No Person shall be a Senator who shall not have attained to the Age of thirty Years, and been nine Years a Citizen of the United States, and who shall not, when elected, be an Inhabitant of that State for which he shall be chosen.

▲ Senators must be at least 30 years old, either natural-born citizens or immigrants who have been citizens for at least nine years, and residents of the state they are elected to represent.

Clause 4: The Vice President of the United States shall be President of the Senate but shall have no Vote, unless they be equally divided.

▲ The vice president serves as the president of the Senate, with the authority to preside over meetings of the Senate and to vote when there is a tie.

Clause 5: The Senate shall chuse their other Officers, and also a President pro tempore, in the Absence of the Vice President, or when he shall exercise the Office of President of the United States.

▲ While the president pro tempore, a senator elected by the other senators, has the authority to preside in the vice president's absence, the norm is to have the most junior senators preside on a rotating basis.

Clause 6: The Senate shall have the sole Power to try all Impeachments. When sitting for that Purpose, they shall be on Oath or Affirmation. When the President of the United States is tried the Chief Justice shall preside: And no Person shall be convicted without the Concurrence of two thirds of the Members present.

▲ The Senate exercises a check on officials of the executive and judicial branches of the federal government by trying them once they have been impeached by the House of Representatives.

Clause 7: Judgment in Cases of Impeachment shall not extend further than to removal from Office, and disqualification to hold and enjoy any Office of honor, Trust or Profit under the United States: but the Party convicted shall nevertheless be liable and subject to Indictment, Trial, Judgment and Punishment, according to Law.

▲ If the Senate convicts an impeached official, he or she is removed from office and may be subject to prosecution in the criminal courts.

POLITICAL INQUIRY: *The framers of the Constitution, who did not expect members of Congress to serve more than one or two terms, would be shocked to learn that Senator Robert C. Byrd (D-West Virginia), who was first elected to the Senate in 1959, is still serving in Congress. Some have proposed a constitutional amendment that would limit the number of times a House member or a senator could win reelection to the same seat. How would term limits benefit citizens? What problems might term limits cause?*

Section 4. (Congressional Elections)

Clause 1: The Times, Places and Manner of holding Elections for Senators and Representatives, shall be prescribed in each State by the Legislature thereof; but the Congress may at any time by Law make or alter such Regulations, except as to the Places of chusing Senators.

▲ Though states have the authority to organize and conduct elections, today they rely heavily on local governments to assist them. Congress has passed numerous laws to ensure constitutionally guaranteed voting rights and to make voter registration easier.

POLITICAL INQUIRY: *Voter turnout (the percentage of eligible voters that vote on election day) has increased in Oregon since that state changed its laws to allow voters to vote by mail. What are some arguments that could be made in support of a national law allowing citizens to vote by mail? What are some arguments that could be made against such a national law?*

Clause 2: The Congress shall assemble at least once in every Year, and such Meeting shall be on the first Monday in December, unless they shall by Law appoint a different Day.

▲ Congress must meet at least once each year. The Twentieth Amendment (1933) gives Congress the authority to determine the date on which its session begins.

Section 5. (Powers and Responsibilities of the House)

Clause 1: Each House shall be the Judge of the Elections, Returns and Qualifications of its own Members, and a Majority of each shall constitute a Quorum to do Business; but a smaller Number may adjourn from day to day, and may be authorized to compel the Attendance of absent Members, in such Manner, and under such Penalties as each House may provide.

▲ Each chamber decides whether the election of each of its members is legitimate. A majority of the members of each chamber must be present to conduct business: at least 218 members for the House and 51 senators for the Senate.

Clause 2: Each House may determine the Rules of its Proceedings, punish its Members for disorderly Behaviour, and, with the Concurrence of two thirds, expel a Member.

▲ After every congressional election, each chamber determines how it will conduct its business, selects from among its members a presiding officer and establishes codes of behavior.

Clause 3: Each House shall keep a Journal of its Proceedings, and from time to time publish the same, excepting such Parts as may in their Judgment require Secrecy; and the Yeas and Nays of the Members of either House on any question shall, at the Desire of one fifth of those Present, be entered on the Journal.

▲ The House and the Senate must keep and publish records of their proceedings, including a record of all votes for and against proposals, except those that they decide require secrecy.

Clause 4: Neither House, during the Session of Congress, shall, without the Consent of the other, adjourn for more than three days, nor to any other Place than that in which the two Houses shall be sitting.

▲ To close down business for more than three days during a session, or to conduct business at another location, each chamber needs to get approval from the other one. This ensures that one chamber cannot stop the legislative process by refusing to meet.

Section 6. (Rights of Congressional Members)

Clause 1: The Senators and Representatives shall receive a Compensation for their Services, to be ascertained by Law, and paid out of the Treasury of the United States. They shall in all Cases, except Treason, Felony and Breach of the Peace, be privileged from Arrest during their Attendance at the Session of their respective Houses, and in going to and returning from the same; and for any Speech or Debate in either House, they shall not be questioned in any other Place.

▲ Today, each member of Congress earns $150,000 per year, paid by taxes collected by the national government. Members of Congress are protected from civil lawsuits and criminal prosecution for the work they do as legislators. They are also protected from arrest while Congress is in session except for a charge of treason, of committing a felony, or of committing a breach of the peace.

Clause 2: No Senator or Representative shall, during the Time for which he was elected, be appointed to any civil Office under the Authority of the United States, which shall have been created, or the Emoluments whereof shall have been encreased during such time; and no Person holding any Office under the United States, shall be a Member of either House during his Continuance in Office.

▲ To ensure the separation of basic governing functions, no member of Congress can hold another federal position while serving in the House or Senate. Moreover, members of Congress cannot be appointed to a position in the executive or judicial branch that was created during their term of office.

Section 7. (The Legislative Process)

▲ This section details the legislative process.

Clause 1: All Bills for raising Revenue shall originate in the House of Representatives; but the Senate may propose or concur with amendments as on other Bills.

▲ While all revenue-raising bills, such as tax bills, must originate in the House, ultimately the House and the Senate must approve the identical bill for it to become law.

Clause 2: Every Bill which shall have passed the House of Representatives and the Senate, shall, before it become a law, be presented to the President of the United States: If he approve he shall sign it, but if not he shall return it, with his Objections to that House in which it shall have originated, who shall enter the Objections at large on their Journal, and proceed to reconsider it. If after such Reconsideration two thirds of that House shall agree to pass the Bill, it shall be sent, together with the Objections, to the other House, by which it shall likewise be reconsidered, and if approved by two thirds of that House, it shall become a Law. But in all such Cases the Votes of both Houses shall be determined by Yeas and Nays, and the Names of the Persons voting for and against the Bill shall be entered on the Journal of each House respectively. If any Bill shall not be returned by the President within ten Days (Sundays excepted) after it shall have been presented to him, the Same shall be a Law, in like Manner as if he had signed it, unless the Congress by their Adjournment prevent its Return, in which Case it shall not be a Law.

▲ After both the House and the Senate approve, by a simple majority vote in each chamber, the identical bill, it is sent to the president for approval or rejection. Congress can attempt to override a presidential rejection (veto) by garnering a supermajority vote of approval (two-thirds majority) in each chamber.

Clause 3: Every Order, Resolution, or Vote to which the Concurrence of the Senate and House of Representatives may be necessary (except on a question of Adjournment) shall be presented to the President of the United States; and before the Same shall take Effect, shall be approved by him, or being disapproved by him, shall be repassed by two thirds of the Senate and House of Representatives, according to the Rules and Limitations prescribed in the Case of a Bill.

▲ The president must approve or veto everything that Congress approves except its vote to adjourn or any resolutions that do not have the force of law.

Section 8. (The Lawmaking Authority of Congress)

▲ This section specifies the constitutionally established congressional powers. These powers are limited to those listed and any other powers that Congress believes are "necessary and proper" in order for Congress to fulfill its listed powers. Laws that appear to go beyond the listed powers can be challenged in the courts, with the Supreme Court ultimately deciding their constitutionality.

Clause 1: The Congress shall have Power To lay and collect Taxes, Duties, Imposts and Excises, to pay the Debts and provide for the common Defence and general Welfare of the United States; but all Duties, Imposts and Excises shall be uniform throughout the United States;

▲ The power to raise money and to authorize spending it for common defense and the general welfare is one of the most essential powers of Congress.

Clause 2: To borrow Money on the credit of the United States;

▲ Today, after years of borrowing money to pay current bills, the national government has a debt of over $11 trillion.

POLITICAL INQUIRY: *Some economists, politicians, and citizens fear that the national debt harms the United States by limiting the amount of money available to invest in growing the economy. Moreover, citizens worry that their children and grandchildren, saddled with the obligation of paying back this debt, may face limited government services. Therefore, there have been repeated calls for a balanced budget amendment, which would force Congress to spend no more than the money it raises in each budget year. What arguments might the members of Congress, elected officials who want to be reelected, put forth against ratification of a balanced budget amendment? What national situations might require spending more money than is raised in a budget year?*

Clause 3: To regulate Commerce with foreign Nations, and among the several States, and with the Indian Tribes;

▲ With the Supreme Court's support, Congress has interpreted Clause 3 in a way that has allowed it to expand its involvement in the economy and the daily lives of U.S. citizens.

Clause 4: To establish an uniform Rule of Naturalization, and uniform Laws on the subject of Bankruptcies throughout the United States;

▲ Congress has the authority to establish the process by which foreigners become citizens (Clause 4).

Clause 5: To coin Money, regulate the Value thereof, and of foreign Coin, and fix the Standard of Weights and Measures;

▲ The authority to make and regulate money and to standardize weights and measures is essential to the regulation of commerce (Clause 5).

Clause 6: To provide for the Punishment of counterfeiting the Securities and current Coin of the United States;

Clause 7: To establish Post Offices and post Roads;

Clause 8: To promote the Progress of Science and useful Arts, by securing for limited Times to Authors and Inventors the exclusive Right to their respective Writings and Discoveries;

Clause 9: To constitute Tribunals inferior to the supreme Court;

▲ Congress exercised its authority under Clause 9 to create the federal court system other than the Supreme Court, which was established under Article III of the Constitution.

Clause 10: To define and punish Piracies and Felonies committed on the high Seas, and Offences against the Law of Nations;

▲ Every nation in the world possesses the authority to establish its own laws regarding crimes outside its borders and violations of international law (Clause 10).

Clause 11: To declare War, grant Letters of Marque and Reprisal, and make Rules concerning Captures on Land and Water;

Clause 12: To raise and support Armies, but no Appropriation of Money to that Use shall be for a longer Term than two Years;

Clause 13: To provide and maintain a Navy;

Clause 14: To make Rules for the Government and Regulation of the land and naval Forces;

Clause 15: To provide for calling forth the Militia to execute the Laws of the Union, suppress Insurrections and repel Invasions;

▲ Clauses 11-15 collectively delegate to Congress the authority to raise and support military troops, to enact rules to regulate the troops, to call the troops to action, and to declare war. Clause 11 also provides Congress with the authority to hire an individual for the purpose of retaliating against another nation for some harm it has caused the United States—that is, to provide a *letter of Marque*, an outdated practice.

Clause 16: To provide for organizing, arming, and disciplining, the Militia, and for governing such Part of them as may be employed in the Service of the United States, reserving to the States respectively, the Appointment of the Officers, and the Authority of training the Militia according to the discipline prescribed by Congress;

▲ Clauses 15 and 16 guarantee the states the right to maintain and train a militia (today's National Guard), but state control of the militia is subordinate to national control when the national government needs the support of these militias to ensure that laws are executed, to suppress domestic uprisings, and to repel invasion.

Clause 17: To exercise exclusive Legislation in all Cases whatsoever, over such District (not exceeding ten Miles square) as may, by Cession of Particular States, and the Acceptance of Congress, become the Seat of the Government of the United States, and to exercise like Authority over all Places purchased by the Consent of the Legislature of the State in which the Same shall be, for the Erection of Forts, Magazines, Arsenals, dock-Yards and other needful Buildings;—And

▲ Congress has the authority to govern Washington, D.C., which is the seat of the national government. The national government also governs federal lands throughout the states that are used for federal purposes, such as military installations.

Clause 18: To make all Laws which shall be necessary and proper for carrying into Execution the foregoing Powers and all other Powers vested by this Constitution in the Government of the United States, or in any Department or Officer thereof.

▲ Clause 18 grants Congress authority to make all laws it deems necessary and proper to fulfill its responsibilities under the Constitution, including those listed in Section 8.

Section 9. (Prohibitions on Congress)

▲ Article I, Section 9, limits Congress's lawmaking authority and mandates that Congress be accountable to the people in how it spends the public's money.

Clause 1: The Migration or Importation of such Persons as any of the States now existing shall think proper to admit, shall not be prohibited by the Congress prior to the Year one thousand eight hundred and eight, but a Tax or duty may be imposed on such Importation, not exceeding ten dollars for each Person.

▲ Clause 1 barred Congress from passing laws to prohibit the slave trade until 1808 at the earliest. The Thirteenth Amendment (1865) made slavery illegal.

Clause 2: The Privilege of the Writ of Habeas Corpus shall not be suspended, unless when in Cases of Rebellion or Invasion the public Safety may require it.

Clause 3: No Bill of Attainder or ex post facto Law shall be passed.

▲ Clauses 2 and 3 guarantee protections to those accused of crimes.

▲ Congress cannot pass laws that declare a person or a group of people guilty of an offense (bills of attainder). Congress is also prohibited from passing a law that punishes a person tomorrow for an action he or she took that was legal today (ex post facto law).

Clause 4: No Capitation, or other direct, Tax shall be laid, unless in Proportion to the Census of Enumeration herein before directed to be taken.

▲ Clause 4 prohibits Congress from directly taxing individual people, such as imposing an income tax. The Sixteenth Amendment (1913) authorized congressional enactment of a direct income tax on individual people.

Clause 5: No Tax or Duty shall be laid on Articles exported from any State.

▲ Congress is prohibited from taxing goods that are exported from any state, those sent either to foreign lands or to other states (Clause 5).

Clause 6: No Preference shall be given by any Regulation of Commerce or Revenue to the Ports of one State over those of another: nor shall Vessels bound to, or from, one State, be obliged to enter, clear or pay Duties in another.

▲ Congress cannot favor any state over another in its regulation of trade (Clause 6).

Clause 7: No Money shall be drawn from the Treasury, but in Consequence of Appropriations made by Law; and a regular Statement and Account of the Receipts and Expenditures of all public Money shall be published from time to time.

▲ The national government can spend money only as authorized by Congress through enacted laws and must present a public accounting of revenues and expenditures.

Clause 8: No Title of. Nobility shall be granted by the United States: And no Person holding any Office of Profit or Trust under them, shall, without the Consent of the Congress, accept of any present, Emolument, Office, or Title, of any kind whatever, from any King, Prince or foreign State.

▲ Congress cannot grant individuals special rights, privileges, or a position in government based on their heredity (birth into a family designated as nobility). In addition, federal officials cannot accept gifts from foreign nations except those Congress allows (which today are gifts of minimal value).

Section 10. (Prohibitions on the States)

Clause 1: No State shall enter into any Treaty, Alliance, or Confederation; grant Letters of Marque and Reprisal; coin Money; emit Bills of Credit; make any Thing but gold and silver Coin a Tender in Payment of Debts; pass any Bill of Attainder, ex post facto Law, or Law impairing the Obligation of Contracts, or grant any Title of Nobility.

▲ Clause 1 specifically prohibits states from engaging in several activities that the Constitution delegates to the national government, including engaging in foreign affairs and creating currency. In addition, it extends several of the prohibitions on Congress to the states.

Clause 2: No State shall, without the Consent of the Congress, lay any Imposts or Duties on Imports or Exports, except what may be absolutely necessary for executing its inspection Laws: and the net Produce of all Duties and Imposts, laid by any State on Imports or Exports, shall be for the Use of the Treasury of the United States; and all such Laws shall be subject to the Revision and Control of the Congress.

▲ Clause 2 prevents states from interfering in foreign trade without congressional approval.

Clause 3: No State shall, without the Consent of Congress, lay any Duty of Tonnage, keep Troops, or Ships of War in time of Peace, enter into any Agreement or Compact with another State, or with a foreign Power, or engage in War, unless actually invaded, or in such imminent Danger as will not admit of delay.

▲ States cannot, without congressional approval, levy import taxes, sign agreements or treaties with foreign nations, or enter into compacts (agreements) with other states.

ARTICLE II. (Executive Branch)

▲ Article II outlines the authority of the president and the vice president and the process of their selection.

Section 1. (Executive Powers of the President)

Clause 1: The executive Power shall be vested in a President of the United States of America. He shall hold his Office during the Term of four Years, and, together with the Vice President, chosen for the same Term, be elected, as follows:

▲ The Constitution delegates to the president the authority to administer the executive branch of the national government. The term of office for the president and the vice president is four years. No term limit was specified.

Clause 2: Each State shall appoint, in such Manner as the Legislature thereof may direct, a Number of Electors, equal to the whole Number of Senators and Representatives to which the State may be entitled in the Congress: but no Senator or Representative, or Person holding an Office of Trust or Profit under the United States, shall be appointed an Elector.

▲ The Electoral College system provides each state government the authority to determine how its electors will be selected.

Clause 3: The Electors shall meet in their respective States, and vote by Ballot for two Persons, of whom one at least shall not be an Inhabitant of the same State with themselves. And they shall make a List of all the Persons voted for, and of the Number of Votes for each; which List they shall sign and certify, and transmit sealed to the Seat of the Government of the United States, directed to the President of the Senate. The President of the Senate shall, in the Presence of the Senate and House of Representatives, open all the Certificates, and the Votes shall then be counted. The Person having the greatest Number of Votes shall be the President, if such Number be a Majority of the whole Number of Electors appointed; and if there be more than one who have such Majority, and have an equal Number of Votes, then the House of Representatives shall immediately chuse by Ballot one of them for President; and if no Person have a Majority, then from the five highest on the List the said House shall in like Manner chuse the President. But in chusing the President, the Votes shall be taken by States, the Representatives from each State having one Vote; a quorum for this Purpose shall consist of a Member or Members from two thirds of the States, and a Majority of all the States shall be necessary to a Choice. In every Case, after the Choice of the President, the Person having the greatest Number of Votes of the Electors shall be the Vice President. But if there should remain two or more who have equal Votes, the Senate shall chuse from them by Ballot the Vice President.

▲ Electors have the authority to select the president and the vice president. Citizens' votes determine who their state's electors will be. Before passage of the Twelfth Amendment (1804), each elector had two votes. The candidate receiving the majority of votes won the presidency, and the candidate with the second highest number of votes won the vice presidency.

POLITICAL INQUIRY: *The Electoral College system is criticized for many reasons. Some argue that deciding the presidential election by any vote other than that of the citizens is undemocratic. Others complain that in 2000 the system allowed George W. Bush to become president, even though he had not won the popular vote. Many argue that the Electoral College system should be eliminated and replaced by direct popular election of the president and the vice president. What is(are) the benefit(s) of eliminating the Electoral College? What might be the potential harm to the nation of eliminating the Electoral College?*

Clause 4: The Congress may determine the Time of chusing the Electors, and the Day on which they shall give their Votes; which Day shall be the same throughout the United States.

▲ Today, by law, national elections are held on the Tuesday following the first Monday in November, in even-numbered years.

Clause 5: No Person except a natural born Citizen, or a Citizen of the United States, at the time of the Adoption of this Constitution, shall be eligible to the Office of President; neither shall any person be eligible to that Office who shall not have attained to the Age of thirty five Years, and been fourteen Years a Resident within the United States.

▲ The president (and the vice president) must be at least 35 years old and must have lived within the United States for at least fourteen years. Unlike the citizenship qualification for members of the House and Senate, the president and vice president must be natural-born citizens.

POLITICAL INQUIRY: *With the success of foreign-born politicians like Governor Arnold Schwarzenegger, Secretary of State Madeleine Albright, and Senator Mel Martinez, some have argued for a constitutional amendment to allow foreign-born citizens to be eligible for the presidency. Should the Constitution be amended so that foreign-born citizens would be eligible to become president of the United States? Why or why not? How would such an amendment change the nature of the presidential office?*

Clause 6: In Case of the Removal of the President from Office, or of his Death, Resignation, or Inability to discharge the Powers and Duties of the said Office, the Same shall devolve on the Vice President, and the Congress may by Law provide for the Case of Removal, Death, Resignation or Inability, both of the President and Vice President, declaring what Officer shall then act as President, and such Officer shall act accordingly, until the Disability be removed, or a President shall be elected.

▲ Clause 6 states that the powers and duties of the presidency are transferred to the vice president when the president is no longer able to fulfill them. It also states that Congress can pass legislation to indicate who shall act as president if both the president and the vice president are unable to fulfill the president's powers and duties. The Twenty-Fifth Amendment (1967) clarifies when the vice president acts as president temporarily and when the vice president actually becomes president.

Clause 7: The President shall, at stated Times, receive for his Services, a Compensation, which shall neither be encreased nor diminished during the Period for which he shall have been elected, and he shall not receive within that Period any other Emolument from the United States, or any of them.

▲ Currently, the president's salary is $400,000 per year plus numerous benefits including a nontaxable expense account.

Clause 8: Before he enter on the Execution of his Office, he shall take the following Oath or Affirmation:—"I do solemnly swear (or affirm) that I will faithfully execute the Office of President of the United States, and will to the best of my Ability, preserve, protect and defend the Constitution of the United States."

▲ Under the Constitution, the authority to ensure that laws are carried out is delegated to the president. The president and the vice president are elected to serve concurrent four-year terms.

Section 2. (Powers of the President)

Clause 1: The President shall be Commander in Chief of the Army and Navy of the United States, and of the Militia of the several States, when called into the actual Service of the United States; he may require the Opinion, in writing, of the principal Officer in each of the executive Departments, upon any Subject relating to the Duties of their respective Offices, and he shall have Power to Grant Reprieves and Pardons for Offences against the United States, except in Cases of Impeachment.

▲ The president is the commander of the military and of the National Guard (militia of the several states) when it is called to service by the president; is authorized to establish the cabinet, the presidential advisory body comprising the top officials (secretaries) of each department of the executive branch; and can exercise a check on the judicial branch by decreasing or eliminating sentences and even pardoning (eliminating guilty verdicts of) federal prisoners.

Clause 2: He shall have Power, by and with the Advice and Consent of the Senate, to make Treaties, provided two thirds of the Senators present concur; and he shall nominate, and by and with the Advice and Consent of the Senate, shall appoint Ambassadors, other public Ministers and Consuls, Judges of the supreme Court, and all other Officers of the United States, whose Appointments are not herein otherwise provided for, and which shall be established by Law: but the Congress may by Law vest the Appointment of such inferior Officers, as they think proper, in the President alone, in the Courts of Law, or in the Heads of Departments.

▲ The Constitution provides a check on the president's authority by requiring that treaties be ratified or appointments confirmed by the Senate. Congress can create additional executive branch positions and federal courts and can decree how these legislatively created positions will be filled.

Clause 3: The President shall have Power to fill up all Vacancies that may happen during the Recess of the Senate, by granting Commissions which shall expire at the End of their next Session.

▲ If vacancies occur when the Senate is not in session and is therefore not available to confirm presidential appointees, the president can fill the vacancies. The appointees serve through the end of the congressional session.

POLITICAL INQUIRY: *In recent years, Presidents Clinton and Bush both took advantage of the constitutional loophole that allows presidents to appoint people without Senate confirmation to make controversial appointments. Should the Constitution be amended to limit further the time an appointee who has not been confirmed can serve by requiring the Senate to consider the appointment when it next reconvenes? Why or why not?*

Section 3. (Responsibilities of the President)

He shall from time to time give to the Congress Information on the State of the Union, and recommend to their Consideration such Measures as he shall judge necessary and expedient; he may, on extraordinary Occasions, convene both Houses, or either of them, and in Case of Disagreement between them, with Respect to the Time of Adjournment, he may adjourn them to such Time as he shall think proper; he shall receive Ambassadors and other public Ministers; he shall take Care that the Laws be faithfully executed, and shall Commission all the Officers of the United States.

▲ As chief executive officer of the nation, the president is required to ensure that laws are properly implemented by overseeing the executive-branch agencies. The president is also required from time to time to give an assessment of the status of the nation to Congress and to make recommendations for the good of the country. This has evolved into the annual televised State of the Union Address. The president can also call special sessions of Congress.

Section 4. (Impeachment)

The President, Vice President and all Civil Officers of the United States, shall be removed from Office on Impeachment for and Conviction of, Treason, Bribery, or other high Crimes and Misdemeanors.

▲ Presidents, vice presidents, and other federal officials can be removed from office if the members of the House of Representatives formally accuse them of treason (giving assistance to the nation's enemies), bribery, or other vaguely defined abuses of power ("high Crimes and Misdemeanors") and two-thirds of the Senate find them guilty of these charges.

ARTICLE III. (Judicial Branch)

▲ Article III presents the organization and authority of the U.S. Supreme Court and delegates to Congress the authority to create other courts as its members deem necessary.

Section 1. (Federal Courts and Rights of Judges)

The judicial Power of the United States, shall be vested in one supreme Court, and in such inferior Courts as the Congress may from time to time ordain and establish. The Judges, both of the supreme and inferior Courts, shall hold their Offices during good Behaviour, and shall, at stated Times, receive for their Services, a Compensation, which shall not be diminished during their Continuance in Office.

▲ Federal judges serve until they retire, die, or are impeached by the House and convicted by the Senate. Congress cannot decrease a judge's pay.

Section 2. (Jurisdiction of Federal Courts)

Clause 1: The judicial Power shall extend to all Cases, in Law and Equity, arising under this Constitution, the Laws of the United States, and Treaties made, or which shall be made, under their Authority;—to all Cases affecting Ambassadors, other public ministers and Consuls;—to all Cases of admiralty and maritime Jurisdiction;—to Controversies to which the United States shall be a Party;—to Controversies between two or more States;—between a State and Citizens of another State;—between Citizens of different States;—between Citizens of the same State claiming Lands under Grants of different States, and between a State, or the Citizens thereof, and foreign States, Citizens or Subjects.

▲ Federal courts have the authority to hear all lawsuits pertaining to national laws, the Constitution of the United States, and treaties. They also have jurisdiction over cases involving citizens of different states and citizens of foreign nations. Note that the power of judicial review, that is, the power to declare acts of government officials or bodies unconstitutional, is not enumerated in the Constitution.

POLITICAL INQUIRY: *Today there are nine Supreme Court justices, yet the Constitution does not set a specific number for Supreme Court justices. With the increasing number of cases appealed to the Supreme Court, what would be the arguments for or against increasing the number of Supreme Court justices?*

Clause 2: In all Cases affecting Ambassadors, other public Ministers and Consuls, and those in which a State shall be Party, the supreme Court shall have original Jurisdiction. In all the other Cases before mentioned, the supreme Court shall have appellate Jurisdiction, both as to Law and Fact, with such Exceptions, and under such Regulations as the Congress shall make.

▲ Congress has the authority to regulate the Supreme Court's appellate jurisdiction.

Clause 3: The Trial of all Crimes, except in Cases of Impeachment, shall be by Jury; and such Trial shall be held in the State where the said Crimes shall have been committed; but when not committed within any State, the Trial shall be at such Place or Places as the Congress may by Law have directed.

▲ Defendants accused of federal crimes have the right to a jury trial in a federal court located in the state in which the crime was committed.

Section 3. (Treason)

Clause 1: Treason against the United States, shall consist only in levying War against them, or in adhering to their Enemies, giving them Aid and Comfort. No Person shall be convicted of Treason unless on the Testimony of two Witnesses to the same overt Act, or on Confession in open Court.

▲ This clause defines treason as making war against the United States or helping its enemies.

Clause 2: The Congress shall have Power to declare the Punishment of Treason, but no Attainder of Treason shall work Corruption of Blood, or Forfeiture except during the Life of the Person attainted.

▲ This clause prevents Congress from redefining treason. Those found guilty of treason can be punished, but their family members cannot be (no "Corruption of Blood").

ARTICLE IV. (State-to-State Relations)

▲ Article IV establishes the obligations states have to each other and to the citizens of other states.

Section 1. (Full Faith and Credit of legal proceedings and decisions)

Full Faith and Credit shall be given in each State to the public Acts, Records, and judicial Proceedings of every other State. And the Congress may by general Laws prescribe the Manner in which such Acts, Records and Proceedings shall be proved, and the Effect thereof.

States must respect one another's legal judgments and records, and a contract agreed to in one state is binding in the other states.

POLITICAL INQUIRY: *States have had the authority to legally define marriage since before the Constitution was ratified. Today, one of the many issues being debated is whether states with laws defining marriage as a contract between one man and one woman need to give full faith and credit to a same-sex marriage contract from a state where such marriages are legal, such as Massachusetts. Which level of government do you think has the right to define marriage? Explain your choice. Does the full-faith and credit clause require states that deny marriage contracts to same-sex couples to recognize legal same-sex marriage contracts from other states?*

Section 2. (Privileges and Immunities of Citizens)

Clause 1: The Citizens of each State shall be entitled to all Privileges and Immunities of Citizens in the several States.

▲ No matter what state they find themselves in, all U.S. citizens are entitled to the same privileges and rights as the citizens of that state.

Clause 2: A Person charged in any State with Treason, Felony, or other Crime, who shall flee from Justice, and be found in another State, shall on Demand of the executive Authority of the State from which he fled, be delivered up, to be removed to the State having Jurisdiction of the Crime.

▲ If requested by a governor of another state, a state is obligated to return an accused felon to the state from which he or she fled.

Clause 3: No Person held to Service or Labour in one State, under the Laws thereof, escaping into another, shall, in Consequence of any Law or Regulation therein, be discharged from such Service or Labour, but shall be delivered up on Claim of the Party to whom such Service or Labour may be due.

▲ Clause 3 created a state's obligation to return slaves fleeing from their enslavement in another state.

Section 3. (Admission of New States)

Clause 1: New States may be admitted by the Congress into this Union; but no new State shall be formed or erected within the Jurisdiction of any other State; nor any State be formed by the Junction of two or more States, or Parts of States, without the Consent of the Legislatures of the States concerned as well as of the Congress.

▲ Congress can admit new states to the union, but it cannot alter established state borders without the approval of the states that would be affected by the change.

Clause 2: The Congress shall have Power to dispose of and make all needful Rules and Regulations respecting the Territory or other Property belonging to the United States; and nothing in this Constitution shall be so construed as to Prejudice any Claims of the United States, or of any particular State.

▲ The federal government has authority to administer all federal lands, wherever they are located, including national parks and historic sites as well as military installations.

Section 4. (National Government Obligations to the States)

The United States shall guarantee to every State in this Union a Republican Form of Government, and shall protect each of them against Invasion; and on Application of the Legislature, or of the Executive (when the Legislature cannot be convened) against domestic Violence.

▲ The national government must ensure that every state has a representative democracy, protect each state from foreign invasion, and assist states in addressing mass breaches of domestic tranquility.

ARTICLE V. (Formal Constitutional Amendment Process)

▲ Article V details the process by which the Constitution can be amended.

The Congress, whenever two thirds of both Houses shall deem it necessary, shall propose Amendments to this Constitution, or, on the Application of the Legislatures of two thirds of the several States, shall call a Convention for proposing Amendments, which, in either Case, shall be valid to all Intents and Purposes, as Part of this Constitution, when ratified by the Legislatures of three fourths of the several States, or by Conventions in three fourths thereof, as the one or the other Mode of Ratification may be proposed by the Congress; Provided that no Amendment which may be made prior to the Year One thousand eight hundred and eight shall in any Manner affect the first and fourth Clauses in the Ninth Section of the first Article; and that no State, without its Consent, shall be deprived of its equal Suffrage in the Senate.

▲ Amendments can be proposed either by Congress or by a special convention called at the request of the states. Amendments to the Constitution must be ratified by the states.

ARTICLE VI. (Supremacy of the Constitution)

▲ Article VI decrees that the Constitution is the supreme law of the land.

Clause 1: All Debts contracted and Engagements entered into, before the Adoption of this Constitution, shall be as valid against the United States under this Constitution, as under the Confederation.

▲ This provision states that the new federal government created by the Constitution was responsible for the financial obligations of the national government created by the Articles of Confederation.

Clause 2: This Constitution, and the Laws of the United States which shall be made in Pursuance thereof; and all Treaties made, or which shall be made, under the Authority of the United States, shall be the supreme Law of the Land; and the Judges in every State shall be bound thereby, any Thing in the Constitution or Laws of any state to the Contrary notwithstanding.

▲ The Constitution, and all laws made to fulfill its mission that are in compliance with it, is the supreme law of the land; no one is above the supreme law of the land.

Clause 3: The Senators and Representatives before mentioned, and the Members of the several State Legislatures, and all executive and judicial Officers, both of the United States and of the several States, shall be bound by Oath or Affirmation, to support this Constitution; but no religious Test shall ever be required as a Qualification to any Office or public Trust under the United States.

▲ All national and state officials must take an oath promising to uphold the Constitution. This article also prohibits the government from requiring officeholders to submit to a religious test or swear a religious oath.

ARTICLE VII. (Constitutional Ratification Process)

▲ Article VII outlines the process by which the Constitution will be ratified.

Clause 1: The Ratification of the Conventions of nine States, shall be sufficient for the Establishment of this Constitution between the States so ratifying the same.

▲ The proposed second constitution decreed that it would replace the Articles of Confederation when nine states had ratified it. The first Congress met under the Constitution of the United States in 1789.

Clause 2: Done in Convention by the Unanimous Consent of the States present the Seventeenth Day of September in the Year of our Lord one thousand seven hundred and Eighty seven and of the Independence of the United States of America the Twelfth. In witness whereof We have hereunto subscribed our Names,

G. Washington—Presid't.
and deputy from Virginia

| | | New Hampshire | John Langdon |
| | | | Nicholas Gilman |

Delaware	George Read	Massachusetts	Nathaniel Gorham
	Gunning Bedford, Jr.		Rufus King
	John Dickinson	Connecticut	William Samuel Johnson
	Richard Bassett		Roger Sherman
	Jacob Broom		
Maryland	James McHenry	New York	Alexander Hamilton
	Daniel of St. Thomas Jenifer	New Jersey	William Livingston
	Daniel Carroll		David Brearley
Virginia	John Blair		William Patterson
	James Madison, Jr.		Jonathan Dayton
North Carolina	William Blount	Pennsylvania	Benjamin Franklin
	Richard Dobbs Spaight		Thomas Mifflin
	Hugh Williamson		Robert Morris
			George Clymer
South Carolina	John Rutledge		Thomas FitzSimons
	Charles Cotesworth Pinckney		Jared Ingersoll
	Charles Pinckney		James Wilson
	Pierce Butler		Gouverneur Morris
Georgia	William Few		
	Abraham Baldwin		

Amendments to the Constitution of the United States of America

THE BILL OF RIGHTS: AMENDMENTS I–X (RATIFIED IN 1791)

Amendment I (1791)

Congress shall make no law respecting an establishment of religion, or prohibiting the free exercise thereof; or abridging the freedom of speech, or of the press; or the right of the people peaceably to assemble, and to petition the Government for a redress of grievances.

▲ Government cannot make laws that limit freedom of expression, which includes freedom of religion, speech, and the press, as well as the freedom to assemble and to petition the government to address grievances.

POLITICAL INQUIRY: *Currently, freedom of speech protects symbolic speech such as the burning of the U.S. flag to make a statement of protest. What reasons are there to amend the Constitution to make burning the flag unconstitutional and hence a form of speech that is not protected by the Constitution? What reasons are there not to do so?*

Amendment II (1791)

A well regulated Militia, being necessary to the security of a free State, the right of the people to keep and bear Arms, shall not be infringed.

▲ Today, states and the federal government balance the right of the people to own guns with the need to protect the public.

POLITICAL INQUIRY: *Does the phrase "a well regulated Militia" limit the right to bear arms to those engaged in protecting public peace and safety? Why or why not?*

Amendment III (1791)

No Soldier shall, in time of peace be quartered in any house, without the consent of the Owner, nor in time of war, but in a manner to be prescribed by law.

▲ Military troops cannot take control of private homes during peacetime.

Amendment IV (1791)

The right of the people to be secure in their persons, houses, papers, and effects, against unreasonable searches and seizures, shall not be violated, and no Warrants shall issue, but upon probable cause, supported by Oath or affirmation, and particularly describing the place to be searched, and the persons or things to be seized.

▲ Government officials must obtain approval before they search or seize a person's property. The approval must come either from the person whose private property they are searching or seizing or from a judge who determines that the government is justified in taking this action.

Amendment V (1791)

No person shall be held to answer for a capital, or otherwise infamous crime, unless on a presentment or indictment of a Grand Jury, except in cases arising in the land or naval forces, or in the Militia, when in actual service in time of War or public danger; nor shall any person be subject for the same offence to be twice put in jeopardy of life or limb; nor shall be compelled in any criminal case to be a witness against himself, nor be deprived of life, liberty, or property, without due process of law; nor shall private property be taken for public use, without just compensation.

▲ The Fifth Amendment guarantees that before the government can take away a person's life, liberty, or pursuit of happiness it must follow certain procedures; it must follow due process of law. Due process guarantees include a grand jury hearing for those accused of a federal crime, protection from double jeopardy for those accused of any crime, and a fair price for private land the government takes for public use.

Amendment VI (1791)

In all criminal prosecutions, the accused shall enjoy the right to a speedy and public trial, by an impartial jury of the State and district wherein the crime shall have been committed, which district shall have been previously ascertained by law, and to be informed of the nature and cause of the accusation; to be confronted with the witnesses against him; to have compulsory process for obtaining witnesses in his favor, and to have the Assistance of Counsel for his defence.

▲ The Sixth Amendment lists additional components of due process, including the right of those accused of a crime to know the charges against them, hear from the witnesses, and defend themselves in a public trial held within a reasonable time after the government makes the charges. The government also must provide a lawyer to very poor people charged with a serious crime.

POLITICAL INQUIRY: *The resources needed to provide an adequate defense in a criminal case can be quite steep. For example, to ensure a fair trial, a lawyer may use government money to pay for expert witnesses. Argue for or against the need to limit such expenditures for indigent defendants accused of serious crimes.*

Amendment VII (1791)

In Suits at common law, where the value in controversy shall exceed twenty dollars, the right of trial by jury shall be preserved, and no fact tried by a jury, shall be otherwise re-examined in any Court of the United States, than according to the rules of the common law.

▲ Either party (the complainant or the person accused of causing harm or violating a contract) in a federal civil lawsuit involving more than $20 can demand a jury trial.

Amendment VIII (1791)

Excessive bail shall not be required, nor excessive fines imposed, nor cruel and unusual punishments inflicted.

▲ The Eighth Amendment protects those accused of crimes as well as those found guilty from overly punitive decisions. When judges set bail, a payment to the government that can be required to avoid incarceration before and during trial, it cannot be an excessively high amount.

POLITICAL INQUIRY: *When the Constitution was written, imprisonment was viewed as cruel and unusual punishment of the convicted. Today there is debate over whether the death penalty (capital punishment) is cruel and unusual. Whatever your opinion is of the death penalty itself, consider some of the techniques used by the government to put people to death. Are they cruel and unusual? Make a case for or against the use of lethal injection, for example.*

Amendment IX (1791)

The enumeration in the Constitution, of certain rights, shall not be construed to deny or disparage others retained by the people.

▲ The Ninth Amendment acknowledges that there are additional rights, not listed in the preceding eight amendments, that the government cannot deny to citizens.

Amendment X (1791)

The powers not delegated to the United States by the Constitution, nor prohibited by it to the States, are reserved to the States respectively, or to the people.

▲ The Tenth Amendment acknowledges that state governments retain all authority they had before ratification of the Constitution that has not been delegated to the national government by the Constitution.

Amendment XI (1795)

The Judicial power of the United States shall not be construed to extend to any suit in law or equity, commenced or prosecuted against one of the United States by Citizens of another State, or by Citizens or Subjects of any Foreign State.

▲ This amendment limits federal courts' jurisdiction; they do not have the authority to hear lawsuits brought by citizens against their own state or against another state, or brought by foreigners against a state.

Amendment XII (1804)

The Electors shall meet in their respective states and vote by ballot for President and Vice-President, one of whom, at least, shall not be an inhabitant of the same state with themselves; they shall name in their ballots the person voted for as President, and in distinct ballots the person voted for as Vice-President, and they shall make distinct lists of all persons voted for as President, and of all persons voted for as Vice-President, and of the number of votes for each, which lists they shall sign and certify, and transmit sealed to the seat of the government of the United States, directed to the President of the Senate;—The President of the Senate shall, in the presence of the Senate and House of Representatives, open all the certificates and the votes shall then be counted;—The person having the greatest Number of votes for President, shall be the President, if such number be a majority of the whole number of Electors appointed; and if no person have such majority, then from the persons having the highest numbers not exceeding three on the list of those voted for as President, the House of Representatives shall choose immediately, by ballot, the President. But in choosing the President, the votes shall be taken by states, the representation from each state having one vote; a quorum for this purpose shall consist of a member or members from two-thirds of the states, and a majority of all the states shall be necessary to a choice. And if the House of Representatives shall not choose a President whenever the right of choice shall devolve upon them, before the fourth day of March next following, then the Vice-President shall act as President, as in the case of the death or other constitutional disability of the President—The person having the greatest number of votes as Vice-President, shall be the Vice-President, if such number be a majority of the whole number of Electors appointed, and if no person have a majority, then from the two highest numbers on the list, the Senate shall choose the Vice-President; a quorum for the purpose shall consist of two-thirds of the whole number of Senators, and a majority of the whole number shall be necessary to a choice. But no person constitutionally ineligible to the office of President shall be eligible to that of Vice-President of the United States.

▲ Today, each elector has two votes; one for a presidential candidate and one for a vice-presidential candidate. The presidential candidate who wins the majority of electoral votes wins the presidency, and the same is true for the vice-presidential candidate. If no presidential candidate wins a majority of the votes, the House selects the president. If no vice-presidential candidate wins a majority of the votes, the Senate selects the vice president.

Amendment XIII (1865)

▲ This amendment abolished slavery.

Section 1. Neither slavery nor involuntary servitude, except as a punishment for crime whereof the party shall have been duly convicted, shall exist within the United States, or any place subject to their jurisdiction.

Section 2. Congress shall have power to enforce this article by appropriate legislation.

Amendment XIV (1868)

Section 1. All persons born or naturalized in the United States and subject to the jurisdiction thereof, are citizens of the United States and of the State wherein they reside. No State shall make or enforce any law which shall abridge the privileges or immunities of citizens of the United States; nor shall any State deprive any person of life, liberty, or property, without due process of law; nor deny to any person within its jurisdiction the equal protection of the laws.

▲ This amendment extends the rights of citizenship to all those born in the United States and those who have become citizens through naturalization. States are prohibited from denying U.S. citizens their rights and privileges and must provide all people with due process and equal legal rights.

POLITICAL INQUIRY: *Recently, some citizens and politicians have claimed that illegal immigrants and their children, who are citizens if they were born in the United States, cost the nation's taxpayers a great deal of money in public services guaranteed to all citizens, including public education. Argue for or against amending the Constitution to deny citizenship to those born in the United States to parents who are in the country illegally.*

Section 2. Representatives shall be apportioned among the several States according to their respective numbers, counting the whole number of persons in each State, excluding Indians not taxed. But when the right to vote at any election for the choice of electors for President and Vice President of the United States, Representatives in Congress, the Executive and Judicial officers of a State, or the members of the Legislature thereof, is denied to any of the male inhabitants of such State, being twenty-one years of age, and citizens of the United States, or in any way abridged, except for participation in rebellion, or other crime, the basis of representation therein shall be reduced in the proportion which the number of such male citizens shall bear to the whole number of male citizens twenty-one years of age in such State.

▲ This section of the Fourteenth Amendment requires that if a state denies men over the age of 21 the right to vote, its representation in the House will be diminished accordingly. The Fifteenth Amendment makes this section unnecessary.

Section 3. No person shall be a Senator or Representative in Congress, or elector of President and Vice President, or hold any office, civil or military, under the United States, or under any State, who, having previously taken an oath, as a member of

Congress, or as an officer of the United States, or as a member of any State legislature, or as an executive or judicial officer of any State, to support the Constitution of the United States, shall have engaged in insurrection or rebellion against the same, or given aid or comfort to the enemies thereof. But Congress may by a vote of two-thirds of each House, remove such disability.

▲ The intent of this section was to prevent government officials who supported the Confederacy during the Civil War from serving in government. In 1898, Congress voted to eliminate this prohibition.

Section 4. The validity of the public debt of the United States, authorized by law, including debts incurred for payment of pensions and bounties for services in suppressing insurrection or rebellion, shall not be questioned. But neither the United States nor any State shall assume or pay any debt or obligation incurred in aid of insurrection or rebellion against the United States, or any claim for the loss or emancipation of any slave; but all such debts, obligations and claims shall be held illegal and void.

Section 5. The Congress shall have power to enforce, by appropriate legislation, the provisions of this article.

POLITICAL INQUIRY: *According to the courts' interpretation, the Fourteenth Amendment prohibits discrimination under the law based on a person's race, religion, color, and national origin unless such discrimination is necessary for the government to accomplish a compelling public interest. However, the courts have allowed discrimination based on sex when a government successfully argues that the discrimination is substantially related to the achievement of an important public interest. Argue for or against amending the Constitution so that sex-based discrimination is treated the same as other forms of discrimination.*

Amendment XV (1870)

Section 1. The right of citizens of the United States to vote shall not be denied or abridged by the United States or by any State on account of race, color, or previous condition of servitude.

▲ All male citizens meeting their state's minimum age requirement are guaranteed the right to vote.

Section 2. The Congress shall have power to enforce this article by appropriate legislation.

Amendment XVI (1913)

The Congress shall have power to lay and collect taxes on incomes, from whatever source derived, without apportionment among the several States, and without regard to any census or enumeration.

▲ This amendment authorizes the national government to establish taxes on personal and corporate income.

Amendment XVII (1913)

The Senate of the United States shall be composed of two Senators from each State, elected by the people thereof, for six years; and each Senator shall have one vote. The electors in each State shall have the qualifications requisite for electors of the most numerous branch of the State legislatures.

When vacancies happen in the representation of any State in the Senate, the executive authority of such State shall issue writs of election to fill such vacancies: Provided, That the legislature of any State may empower the executive thereof to make temporary appointments until the people fill the vacancies by election as the legislature may direct.

This amendment shall not be so construed as to affect the election or term of any Senator chosen before it becomes valid as part of the Constitution.

▲ Since the ratification of the Seventeenth Amendment in 1913, senators have been elected by the citizens in each state rather than by state legislatures. The amendment also allows each state legislature to establish the process by which vacancies in the Senate will be filled, either through special election or by gubernatorial appointment.

Amendment XVIII (1919)

Section 1. After one year from the ratification of this article the manufacture, sale, or transportation of intoxicating liquors within, the importation thereof into, or the exportation thereof from the United States and all territory subject to the jurisdiction thereof for beverage purposes is hereby prohibited.

▲ The "Prohibition" amendment made it illegal to manufacture, sell, or transport alcoholic beverages in the United States.

Section 2. The Congress and the several States shall have concurrent power to enforce this article by appropriate legislation.

Section 3. This article shall be inoperative unless it shall have been ratified as an amendment to the Constitution by the legislatures of the several States, as provided in the Constitution, within seven years from the date of the submission hereof to the States by the Congress.

Amendment XIX (1920)

The right of citizens of the United States to vote shall not be denied or abridged by the United States or by any State on account of sex. Congress shall have power to enforce this article by appropriate legislation.

▲ All female citizens meeting their state's minimum age requirement are guaranteed the right to vote.

Amendment XX (1933)

Section 1. The terms of the President and Vice President shall end at noon on the 20th day of January, and the terms of Senators and Representatives at noon on the 3d day of January, of the years in which such terms would have ended if this article had not been ratified; and the terms of their successors shall then begin.

▲ The first two sections of the Twentieth Amendment establish new starting dates for the president's and vice president's terms of office (January 20). Section 2 also decrees that the annual meeting of Congress will begin on January 3 unless Congress specifies a different date.

Section 2. The Congress shall assemble at least once in every year, and such meeting shall begin at noon on the 3d day of January, unless they shall by law appoint a different day.

Section 3. If, at the time fixed for the beginning of the term of the President, the President elect shall have died, the Vice President elect shall become President. If a President shall not have been chosen before the time fixed for the beginning of his term, or if the President elect shall have failed to qualify, then the Vice President elect shall act as President until a President shall have qualified; and the Congress may by law provide for the case wherein neither a President elect nor a Vice President elect shall have qualified, declaring who shall then act as President, or the manner in which one who is to act shall be selected, and such person shall act accordingly until a President or Vice President shall have qualified.

▲ Sections 3 and 4 of this amendment establish that if the president elect dies before his or her term of office begins, the vice president elect becomes president. If the president elect has not been selected or is unable to begin the term, the vice president elect serves as acting president until the president is selected or is able to serve.

Section 4. The Congress may by law provide for the case of the death of any of the persons from whom the House of Representatives may choose a President whenever the right of choice shall have devolved upon them, and for the case of the death of any of the persons from whom the Senate may choose a Vice President whenever the right of choice shall have devolved upon them.

Section 5. Sections 1 and 2 shall take effect on the 15th day of October following the ratification of this article.

Section 6. This article shall be inoperative unless it shall have been ratified as an amendment to the Constitution by the legislatures of three-fourths of the several States within seven years from the date of its submission.

Amendment XXI (1933)

Section 1. The eighteenth article of amendment to the Constitution of the United States is hereby repealed.

▲ With this amendment, the Eighteenth Amendment's prohibition of the manufacture, sale, and transportation of alcoholic beverages was repealed.

Section 2. The transportation or importation into any State, Territory, or possession of the United States for delivery or use therein of intoxicating liquors, in violation of the laws thereof, is hereby prohibited.

Section 3. This article shall be inoperative unless it shall have been ratified as an amendment to the Constitution by conventions in the several States, as provided in the Constitution, within seven years from the date of the submission hereof to the States by the Congress.

Amendment XXII (1951)

Section 1. No person shall be elected to the office of the President more than twice, and no person who has held the office of President, or acted as President, for more than two years of a term to which some other person was elected President shall be elected to the office of the President more than once. But this Article shall not apply to any person holding the office of President, when this Article was proposed by the Congress, and shall not prevent any person who may be holding the office of President, or acting as President, during the term within which this Article becomes operative from holding the office of President or acting as President during the remainder of such term.

▲ This amendment established a two-term limit for the presidency, or in the case of a vice president succeeding to the presidency and then running for reelection, a maximum limit of ten years in office.

Section 2. This article shall be inoperative unless it shall have been ratified as an amendment to the Constitution by the legislatures of three-fourths of the several States within seven years from the date of its submission to the States by the Congress.

Amendment XXIII (1961)

Section 1. The District constituting the seat of Government of the United States shall appoint in such manner as the Congress may direct: A number of electors of President and Vice President equal to the whole number of Senators and Representatives in Congress to which the District would be entitled if it were a State, but in no event more than the least populous State; they shall be in addition to those appointed by the States, but they shall be considered, for the purposes of the election of President and Vice President, to be electors appointed by a State; and they shall meet in the District and perform such duties as provided by the twelfth article of amendment.

▲ Citizens living in Washington, D.C. are given the right to elect three voting members to the Electoral College. Before this amendment, these citizens were not represented in the Electoral College.

Section 2. The Congress shall have power to enforce this article by appropriate legislation.

Amendment XXIV (1964)

Section 1. The right of citizens of the United States to vote in any primary or other election for President or Vice President, for electors for President or Vice President, or for Senator or Representative in Congress, shall not be denied or abridged by the United States or any State by reason of failure to pay any poll tax or other tax.

▲ Governments are prohibited from requiring a person to pay a tax in order to vote.

Section 2. The Congress shall have power to enforce this article by appropriate legislation.

Amendment XXV (1967)

Section 1. In case of the removal of the President from office or of his death or resignation, the Vice President shall become President.

▲ The vice president becomes president if the president resigns or dies.

Section 2. Whenever there is a vacancy in the office of the Vice President, the President shall nominate a Vice President who shall take office upon confirmation by a majority vote of both Houses of Congress.

▲ The president can nominate a person to fill a vice-presidential vacancy. Congress must approve the nominee.

Section 3. Whenever the President transmits to the President pro tempore of the Senate and the Speaker of the House of Representatives his written declaration that he is unable to discharge the powers and duties of his office, and until he transmits to them a written declaration to the contrary, such powers and duties shall be discharged by the Vice President as Acting President.

▲ If the president indicates in writing to Congress that he or she cannot carry out the duties of office, the vice president becomes acting president until the president informs Congress that he or she is again fit to resume the responsibilities of the presidency.

Section 4. Whenever the Vice President and a majority of either the principal officers of the executive departments or of such other body as Congress may by law provide, transmit to the President pro tempore of the Senate and the Speaker of the House of Representatives their written declaration that the President is unable to discharge the powers and duties of his office, the Vice President shall immediately assume the powers and duties of the office as Acting President.

Thereafter, when the President transmits to the President pro tempore of the Senate and the Speaker of the House of Representatives his written declaration that no inability exists, he shall resume the powers and duties of his office unless the Vice President and a majority of either the principal officers of the executive department or of such other body as Congress may by law provide, transmit within four days to the President pro tempore of the Senate and the Speaker of the House of Representatives their written declaration that the President is unable to discharge the powers and duties of his office. Thereupon Congress shall decide the issue, assembling within forty-eight hours for that purpose if not in session. If the Congress, within twenty-one days after receipt of the latter written declaration, or, if Congress is not in session, within twenty-one days after Congress is required to assemble, determines by two-thirds vote of both Houses that the President is unable to discharge the powers and duties of his office, the Vice President shall continue to discharge the same as Acting President; otherwise, the President shall resume the powers and duties of his office.

▲ If the vice president, in concert with a majority of cabinet officials (or some other body designated by Congress), declares to Congress in writing that the president is unable to fulfill the duties of office, the vice president becomes acting president until the president claims he or she is again fit for duty. However, if the vice president and a majority of cabinet officials challenge the president's claim, then Congress must decide within three weeks if the president can resume office.

Amendment XXVI (1971)

Section 1. The right of citizens of the United States, who are eighteen years of age or older, to vote shall not be denied or abridged by the United States or by any State on account of age.

▲ The Twenty-Sixth Amendment guarantees citizens 18 years of age and older the right to vote.

Section 2. The Congress shall have power to enforce this article by appropriate legislation.

Amendment XXVII (1992)

No law varying the compensation for the services of the Senators and Representatives shall take effect, until an election of Representatives shall have intervened.

▲ Proposed in 1789, this amendment prevents members of Congress from raising their own salaries. Approved salary increases cannot take effect until after the next congressional election.

The newly created national government and the preexisting state governments acted independently as they implemented the innovative federal system of government established in 1789.

National, state, and local governments challenge one another regularly over the proper interpretation of the Constitution's distribution of power in the federal system.

NOW

3

Federalism

With more than 89,000 distinct governments in the United States today—one national, 50 state, and over 89,476 local governments—and given vague constitutional language regarding the proper authority of national and state governments, the courts frequently must interpret the framers' intent with respect to the distribution of authority. Among the conflicts over jurisdiction that have reached the courts are disagreements over which level of government has the authority to set the legal drinking age, to establish gun-free school zones, to legalize the medical use of marijuana, and to determine which votes count in a presidential election.

Wherever you live in the United States, at least four governments collect taxes from you, provide services to you, and establish your rights and responsibilities. With so many governments in action, citizens who are interested in influencing public policies have many access points. Yet which government has the authority to address your concerns may not be clear to you. It may not even be clear to government officials. Ultimately, the Constitution, as interpreted by the U.S. Supreme Court justices, determines which government is responsible for which matters.

Even as the wrangling continues over the proper interpretation of the constitutional distribution of authority between governments, the U.S. national, state, and local governments engage every day in *collaborative* efforts to fulfill the complex, costly needs

NEXT

Will Supreme Court justices continue to issue conflicting interpretations of federalism?

Will state and local governments maintain their efforts to be laboratories for the creation of effective policies?

Will intergovernmental relations evolve so that government can provide more efficient, effective public service?

of the people whom they serve. Such intergovernmental efforts are essential in today's world. But they complicate attempts to clarify which level of government is ultimately responsible for which services and policies.

An Overview of the U.S. Federal System

The U.S. Constitution established an unprecedented government structure characterized by a federal system of governance. A **federal system** has two constitutionally recognized levels of government, each with **sovereignty**—that is, ultimate governing authority, with no legal superior—over different policy matters and geographic areas. According to the Constitution, the national government has ultimate authority over some matters, and the state governments hold ultimate authority over different matters. The existence of two governments, each with ultimate authority over different matters—an arrangement called **dual sovereignty**—is what distinguishes the federal system of government from the two other most common systems of government, known as unitary and confederal. The American colonists' experience with a unitary system, and subsequently the early U.S. citizens' life under a confederal system (1781–1788), led to the creation of the innovative federal system.

Unitary System

Colonial Americans lived under Great Britain's unitary system of government. In fact, the majority of the world's nations today have unitary governments. In a **unitary system,** the central government is sovereign—it is the ultimate governing authority, with no legal superior. It can create other governments (regional governments) and delegate powers and responsibilities to them. The central government in a unitary system can also unilaterally take away any responsibilities it has delegated to any regional governments it creates and can even *eliminate* the regional governments.

Indeed, under Britain's unitary system of government during the American colonial period, the British Crown (the sovereign government) created colonial governments and gave them authority to handle day-to-day matters such as regulating marriages, resolving business conflicts, providing for public safety, and maintaining roads. As the central government in Britain approved tax and trade policies that harmed the colonists' quality of life, growing public discourse and dissension spurred the colonists to protest. It was their failed attempts to influence the central government's policies—by lobbying the king's selected colonial governors, sending petitions to the king, and boycotting certain goods—that eventually sparked more radical acts such as the Boston Tea Party and the colonists' declaration of independence from Great Britain.

Confederal System

When the colonies declared their independence from Great Britain in 1776, each became an independent sovereign state and adopted its own constitution. As a result, no state had a legal superior. In 1777, delegates from every state except Rhode Island met in a convention and agreed to a proposed alliance of the thirteen sovereign state governments. In 1781, the thirteen independent state governments ratified the Articles of Confederation, the first U.S. constitution, which created a confederal system of government.

In a **confederal system,** several independent sovereign governments (such as the thirteen state governments in the American case) agree to cooperate on specified matters while each retains ultimate authority over all other governmental matters within its borders. The cooperating sovereign governments delegate some responsibilities to a central governing body. Each sovereign government selects its own representatives to the central governing body. The sovereign governments retain ultimate authority in a confederal system for the simple reason that they can recall their delegates from the central government at any time and can either carry out or ignore the central government's policies.

As detailed in Chapter 2, the effectiveness of the confederation created by the Articles of Confederation increasingly came into question. In February 1787, the national Congress passed a resolution calling for a constitutional convention "for the sole and express purpose of revising the Articles of Confederation" in order to preserve the Union. Clear-eyed about the failures of the unitary and confederal systems, the colonists decided to experiment with a unique government system—a federal system. The federal system created by the Constitution of the United States has succeeded in preserving the union for over 220 years.

Federal System

The state delegates who met in Philadelphia in 1787 drafted a new constitution that created an innovative federal system of government with dual sovereignty. The Constitution's framers established dual sovereignty by detailing a new, sovereign national government for the United States and modifying the sovereignty of the existing state governments. The national government thus created has no legal superior on matters over which the Constitution gives it authority, and the state governments have no legal superior on the matters over which they are granted authority by the Constitution.

Such dual sovereignty does not exist in unitary and confederal systems, where sovereignty is held by one level of government (the central government in a unitary system and the regional governments in a confederal system). The federal system gives both the central (national) government and the regional (state) governments ultimate authority over different matters (see Figure 3.1).

Unitary System

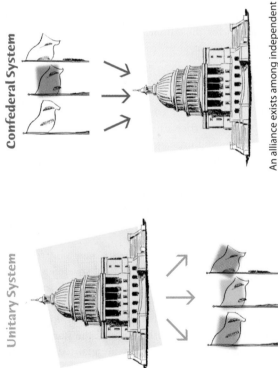

The central government is sovereign, with no legal superior. It may create state governments and delegate legal authority to them. It can also eliminate such governments.

Confederal System

An alliance exists among independent sovereign governments, which delegate limited authority to a central government of their making. The independent sovereign governments retain sovereignty, with no legal superior, over all matters they do not delegate to the central government.

Federal System

State governments are sovereign in specified matters, and a national government is sovereign in other specified matters. The matters over which each government is sovereign are set forth in a constitution, which is the supreme law of the land. Dual sovereignty is the distinguishing characteristic of a federal system.

POLITICAL INQUIRY

FIGURE 3.1 ■ Who is sovereign in a unitary system of government? In a confederal system of government? In a federal system of government? Which of the systems of government does the United States have, and why?

The federal system, as it works in the United States today, can be confusing—not only to citizens but also to elected officials and even Supreme Court justices. The confusion begins with the fact that in addition to the one national and 50 distinct state governments that are operating in the country today, more than 89,000 local governments are functioning, even though the Constitution does not mention local governments.

It is *state constitutions* that authorize states to create local governments. State governments delegate some of their responsibilities to these local governments through legislation and/or the approval of a *charter*, which is a local government's version of a constitution. At the same time, state governments have the authority to take back delegated responsibilities and even to eliminate local governments. Because the state government retains ultimate authority over all the matters it delegates to its local governments and can eliminate its local governments, the relationship between a state government and its local governments is *unitary* (following a unitary system of governmental structure).

Intergovernmental Relations (IGR)   In order to govern, a government must have the authority to formulate and approve a plan of action, to raise and spend money to finance the plan, and to hire workers to put the plan into action. In the U.S. federal system today, the responsibility for these three elements of any given public policy—the policy *statement,* the policy *financing,* and the policy *implementation*—may rest entirely with one level of government (national, state, or local), or it may be shared in a collaborative effort by two or more of these levels. Political scientists label the collaborative efforts of two or more levels of government working to serve the public **intergovernmental relations (IGR).**

The provision of elementary and secondary public education serves as an example of IGR. Although education is a policy matter that the U.S. Constitution distributes to the states, in all but four states, the state governments have created school districts—which are local-level governments—to implement elementary and secondary school policies. Funding for public elementary and secondary education comes from the property tax collected by the school district and grants of money collected by the federal and state governments through their taxes. In the majority of public school districts, only teachers certified by the state government can teach. These state-certified teachers, hired by local school districts, implement national policy mandating equal educational opportunity for all students (required by Titles VI and IX of the Civil Rights Act, and the Individuals with Disabilities Education Act) and proficiency tests (mandated by the No Child Left Behind Act). They also implement state policy with respect to curricula and the school calendar, as well as school district policy regarding school uniforms and discipline. The United States thus delivers the public service of elementary and secondary education through intricate intergovernmental relations, where three levels of government share policy making and policy financing and where school district employees implement national, state, and school district policies. (For more on how IGR can affect education policy, see "Then, Now, Next.")

We can measure the scope of IGR today by looking at the distribution of the workers whom national, state, and local governments hire to deliver specific

What Impact Will Federalism Have on Education during the Obama Years?

THEN: The No Child Left Behind Act, signed by President George W. Bush in 2002, imposes educational standards on state governments and their school districts. The act leaves it to the state to determine the curriculum needed to meet these standards and to create the tests that will assess whether students have achieved them. Critics of the act note that it does not provide states with the funds needed to meet its requirements.

NOW: Worried about the impact of the economic downturn on funding for education, President Barack Obama and Congress included $100 billion for education grants to states in the stimulus package enacted in February 2009.

WHAT'S NEXT?

■ What sources of funding might state and local governments turn to when the stimulus money runs out?

■ How might they be able to continue funding education at higher levels if the economy does not recover?

■ Will the federal grant money encourage greater intergovernmental cooperation?

Who Employs the Public Servants?

National defense — 100%

Postal service — 100%

Space research & technology — 100%

Elementary & secondary education — 1% — 99%

Hospitals — 14% — 37% — 50%

Higher education — 81% — 19%

Police protection — 14% — 9% — 77%

Fire protection — 100%

Streets & highways — 1% — 42% — 57%

% = National   % = State   % = Local

POLITICAL INQUIRY

FIGURE 3.2 ■ **What proportion of employees working on space research and technology is national? What proportion of employees working in elementary and secondary education is national? What explains the difference in these two cases?**

Source: U.S. Census Bureau, "Federal, State and Local Governments, Public Employment Data for 2005," www. census.gov/compendia/stat.ab/tables/08s0448.xls.

public services. The graphs in Figure 3.2 show some services that are purely national, one that is purely local, and several that are truly intergovernmental. Another gauge of the extent of IGR is the percentage of national grant money that state and local governments spend on the delivery of specific services. For example, in the policy area of public elementary and secondary education, the national government supplies approximately 9 percent of the funds needed; state governments provide 48 percent on average; and local governments contribute 42 percent on average.[1]

What a Federal System Means for Citizens For citizens, living in a federal system of government means that their legal rights and liberties and their civic responsibilities vary depending on where they live. The majority of U.S. citizens live under the jurisdiction of at least five governments: national, state, county (called *borough* in Alaska and *parish* in Louisiana), municipal or township, and school district. Each of these governments can impose responsibilities on the people living in its jurisdiction. The most obvious responsibility is to pay taxes. These taxes can include the national personal income tax; state sales and personal income taxes; and county, municipal, township, and school district property taxes. Each government can also guarantee personal liberties and rights. The Constitution lists individual liberties in the Bill of Rights. In addition, every state constitution has its own bill of rights, and some local governments offer further protections to their citizens. For example, some cities and counties prohibit discrimination based on an individual's sexual orientation, yet most states do not, nor does the national government.

Which government is responsible for what services, policies, and rights? Because the Constitution of the United States is the supreme law of the land, it is to the Constitution that we must turn to answer this question. Yet constitutional language is not always clear. As we saw in Chapter 2, the framers hammered out the Constitution through intensive bargaining and compromise that produced a text that is often vague and ambiguous. Also, as discussed in Chapter 2, the U.S. Supreme Court has the authority to determine what the constitution means and hence what is constitutional. This authority came from the Court's decision in the *Marbury v. Madison* case (1803), in which the justices found that the Constitution gives them, sitting as the Supreme Court, the ultimate authority to determine the Constitution's meaning and intent.[2] Significantly, and specifically, the *Marbury* case established the principle of judicial review: the Court's authority to determine whether an action of any government operating within the United States violates the Constitution.

Although the Supreme Court is the final interpreter of the Constitution, the Court's *constructions* (interpretations) have changed over time. For example, it is true that dual sovereignty—and therefore a federal system—still exists in the United States today, but the courts have interpreted the Constitution in such a way that the authority of the national government has expanded significantly over the last 220-plus years. In addition, the determination of which government has ultimate authority over specific matters has become even less clear due to the evolution of a complex arrangement of various levels of government working together to meet the various responsibilities that the Constitution delegates, implies, or reserves to them.

Later in this chapter, we consider this evolution of the U.S. federal system. Before we do, it is useful for us to examine the constitutional distribution of authority to the national and state governments.

Constitutional Distribution of Authority

By distributing some authority to the national government and different authority to the state governments, the Constitution creates the dual sovereignty that defines the U.S. federal system. The Constitution specifically lists the several matters over which the national government has ultimate authority, and it implies additional national authority. The Constitution spells out just a few matters over which the state governments have authority. The lack of constitutional detail on state authority is partially explained by the fact that at the time of the Constitution's drafting, the states expected to retain their authority, except for matters that, by way of the Constitution, they agreed to turn over to the newly created national government.

To fulfill their responsibilities to their citizens, both the national and the state governments have the authority to engage in the functions inherent to all sovereign governments. This authority extends to the concurrent powers, our first topic in this section.

Concurrent Sovereign Authority

In order to function, sovereign governments need the authority to make policy, raise money, establish courts to interpret policy when a conflict arises about its meaning, and implement policy. These authorities are recognized as *inherent* to all governments—they are defining characteristics of governments. In the U.S. federal system, we designate these inherent governing functions as the **concurrent powers** because the national and the state governments hold these powers jointly, and each can use them at the same time. For example, national and state governments make their own public policies, raise their own revenues, and spend those revenues to implement their policies. (State governments delegate these authorities, in limited ways, to the local governments they create so that they can function as governments.)

Just as the Supreme Court has had to step in to resolve conflicts over areas of concurrent authority, it must also resolve conflicts between the national and state governments over the constitutional powers that establish national and state sovereignty, as we now consider.

National Sovereignty

The Constitution distributes powers that are (1) enumerated, or specifically listed, and (2) implied for the national government's three branches—legislative, executive, and judicial. For example, Article I of the Constitution enumerates (lists) the matters over which Congress holds the authority to make laws, including interstate and foreign commerce, the monetary system, general welfare, and national defense. These are **enumerated powers** of the national government. The Constitution also gives Congress **implied powers**—that is, powers that are not explicitly described but may be interpreted to be necessary to fulfill the enumerated powers. Congress specifically receives implied powers through the Constitution's **necessary and proper clause,** sometimes called the **elastic clause** because the national government uses this passage to stretch its enumerated authority. The necessary and proper clause states that Congress has the power to "make all laws which shall be necessary and proper" for carrying out its enumerated powers.

Articles II and III of the Constitution also enumerate certain powers of the national government. Article II delegates to the president the authority to ensure the proper implementation of national laws and, with the advice and consent of the U.S. Senate, the authority to make treaties with foreign nations and to appoint foreign ambassadors. With respect to the U.S. Supreme Court and the lower federal courts, Article III enumerates jurisdiction over legal cases involving constitutional issues, national legislation, and/or treaties. The jurisdiction of the Supreme Court also extends to disagreements between two or more state governments, as well as to conflicts between citizens from different states. Figure 3.3 lists the national powers enumerated in Articles I, II, and III of the Constitution.

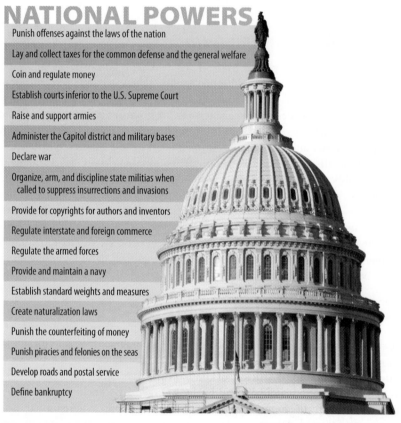

NATIONAL POWERS

Punish offenses against the laws of the nation

Lay and collect taxes for the common defense and the general welfare

Coin and regulate money

Establish courts inferior to the U.S. Supreme Court

Raise and support armies

Administer the Capitol district and military bases

Declare war

Organize, arm, and discipline state militias when called to suppress insurrections and invasions

Provide for copyrights for authors and inventors

Regulate interstate and foreign commerce

Regulate the armed forces

Provide and maintain a navy

Establish standard weights and measures

Create naturalization laws

Punish the counterfeiting of money

Punish piracies and felonies on the seas

Develop roads and postal service

Define bankruptcy

FIGURE 3.3

Enumerated Powers of National Government

The Supremacy Clause The country's founders obviously anticipated disagreements over the interpretation of constitutional language and prepared for them by creating the Supreme Court. The Court has mostly supported the national government when states, citizens, or interest groups have challenged Congress's use of the necessary and proper clause to take on new responsibilities beyond its enumerated powers. Unless the Supreme Court finds a national law to be outside of the enumerated or implied powers, that law is constitutional and hence the **supreme law of the land,** as defined by the **supremacy clause** in Article VI of the Constitution: "This Constitution, and the laws of the United States which shall be made in pursuance thereof; and all treaties made, or which shall be made, under the authority of the United States, shall be the supreme law of the land." State and local governments are thereby obligated to comply with national laws that implement national enumerated and implied powers, as well as with treaties—including treaties with Native American nations.

National Treaties with Indian Nations Throughout U.S. history, the national government has signed treaties with Native American nations, which are legally viewed as sovereign foreign nations. As with all treaties, treaties with Native American nations are supreme law with which the national government and state and local governments must comply. The core issue in the majority of these treaties is the provision of land (reservations) on which the native peoples could resettle after non-Indians took their lands during the eighteenth and nineteenth centuries. Today, the federal government recognizes more than 550 Indian tribes. Although the majority of Native Americans no longer live on reservations—most native peoples have moved to cities—approximately 300 reservations remain, in thirty-four states.[3]

Even though Indian reservations lie within state borders, national treaties and national laws, not state or local laws, apply to the reservation populations and lands. State and local laws, including laws having to do with taxes, crime, and the environment, are unenforceable on reservations. Moreover, Native American treaty rights to hunt, fish, and gather on reservations and on public lands supersede national, state, and local environmental regulations.[4]

Treaties entered into by the national government (including those negotiated with Indian nations residing within the states) and constitutional national laws are the supreme law of the land. Tensions frequently flare between the national government and state governments over the constitutionality of national laws. We now look at constitutional powers delegated and reserved to the states.

State Sovereignty

The Constitution specifies only a few state powers. It provides the states with a role in national politics and gives them the final say on formally amending the Constitution. The fact that the state governments were already functioning when the states ratified the Constitution partly explains the lack of constitutional specificity regarding state authority. Other than those responsibilities that the states agreed to delegate (and to imply) to the newly created federal government through their ratification of the Constitution, the states expected to retain their sovereignty over all the day-to-day matters internal to their borders that they were already handling. Yet the original Constitution did not speak of this sovereignty explicitly.

Powers Delegated to the States In addition to establishing the various electoral procedures that give voice to state interests in the national policy-making process, the Constitution creates a formal means by which the states can ensure that their constitutional authority is not changed or eliminated without their approval. Specifically, the Constitution stipulates that three-fourths of the states (through votes in either their legislatures or special conventions, as discussed in Chapter 2) must ratify amendments to the Constitution. By having the final say in whether the supreme law of the land will be changed through the passage of amendments, the states can protect their constitutional powers. Indeed, they did just that when they ratified the Tenth Amendment (1791).

Powers Reserved to the States The Constitution's extremely limited attention to state authority caused concern among citizens of the early American republic. Many people feared that the new national government would meddle in matters for which states had been responsible, thereby compromising state sovereignty. Citizens were also deeply concerned about their freedoms, corresponding to the protections listed in each state constitution's bill of rights. Anti-Federalists argued that without a bill of rights in the Constitution the national government would trample the people's natural rights to life, liberties, and the pursuit of happiness. As described in Chapter 2, the states ratified the Bill of Rights, the first ten amendments to the Constitution, in response to Anti-Federalist concerns.

The Tenth Amendment asserts that the "powers not delegated to the United States by the Constitution, nor prohibited by it to the states, are *reserved to the states* [emphasis added] respectively, or to the people." This **reserved powers** clause of the Tenth Amendment acknowledged the domestic matters over which the states had exercised authority since the ratification of their own constitutions. These matters included the ordinary, daily affairs of the people—birth, death, marriage, intrastate business, commerce, crime, health, morals, and safety. The states' reserved powers to protect the health, safety, lives, and property of their citizens are referred to as their **police powers.** It was over these domestic matters, internal to each state, that the states retained sovereignty according to the Tenth Amendment. In addition, state courts retained sovereignty over legal cases that involve their state's constitution and legislation (and that do not also raise issues involving the U.S. Constitution). Figure 3.4 summarizes the constitutionally reserved and enumerated powers of the states at the time of the Tenth Amendment's ratification.

The Tenth Amendment's affirmation of state sovereignty is brief and vague, and the Supreme Court continues to this day to resolve conflicts over its interpretation. New cases, leading to fresh interpretations, come before the Court when state governments challenge national laws that the states deem to infringe on their reserved powers but that the national government claims to fulfill its enumerated or implied powers. New interpretations by the Court also arise when the national government or citizens challenge the constitutionality of a state or local government action. Citizens, local governments, state governments, and the national government persistently ask the courts to resolve constitutional conflicts in order to protect their liberties, their rights, and, in the case of governments, their sovereignty.

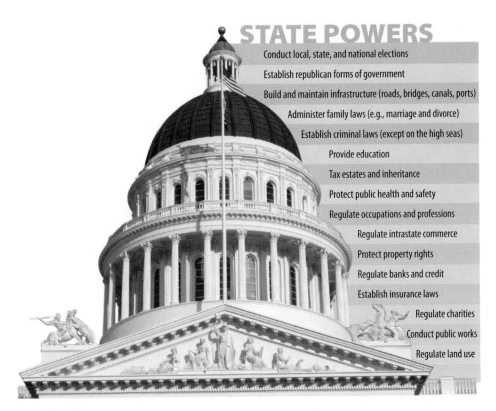

STATE POWERS

Conduct local, state, and national elections

Establish republican forms of government

Build and maintain infrastructure (roads, bridges, canals, ports)

Administer family laws (e.g., marriage and divorce)

Establish criminal laws (except on the high seas)

Provide education

Tax estates and inheritance

Protect public health and safety

Regulate occupations and professions

Regulate intrastate commerce

Protect property rights

Regulate banks and credit

Establish insurance laws

Regulate charities

Conduct public works

Regulate land use

FIGURE 3.4

Constitutionally Delegated and Reserved State Powers

The Supreme Court's Interpretation of Enumerated, Implied, and Reserved Powers

The landmark case of *McCulloch v. Maryland* (1819) exemplifies a Supreme Court ruling that established the use of the implied powers to expand the national government's delegated authority.[5] The case stemmed from Congress's establishment of a national bank, and in particular a branch of that bank located in the state of Maryland, which the Maryland state authorities tried to tax. Attorneys for the state of Maryland argued that if the federal government had the authority to establish a national bank and to locate a branch in Maryland, then Maryland had the power to tax the bank. On a more basic level, Maryland's legal counsel asserted that Congress did not have the constitutional authority to establish a national bank, noting that doing so was not an enumerated power. Lawyers for the national government in turn argued that federal authority to establish a national bank was implied and that Maryland's levying a tax on the bank was unconstitutional, for it impinged on the national government's ability to fulfill its constitutional responsibilities.

The Supreme Court decided in favor of the national government. The justices based their ruling on their interpretation of the Constitution's necessary and proper clause and the enumerated powers of Congress to "lay and collect taxes, to borrow money . . . and to regulate commerce among the several states." The Court said that, combined, these powers implied that the national government had the authority to charter a bank and to locate a branch in Maryland. In addition, the Court found that Maryland did not have the right to tax that bank, because taxation by the state would interfere with the exercise of federal authority. In addition to establishing that the necessary and proper clause justifies broad understandings of the enumerated powers, the Court affirmed once and for all that in the event of a conflict between national legislation (the law chartering the national bank) and state legislation (Maryland's tax law), the national law is supreme *as long as* it is in compliance with the Constitution's enumerated and implied powers.

The Power to Regulate Commerce   A few years later, in the case of *Gibbons v. Ogden* (1824), the Supreme Court again justified a particular national action on the basis of the implications of an enumerated power.[6] The *Gibbons* case was the first suit brought to the Supreme Court seeking clarification on the constitutional meaning of *commerce* in the Constitution's clause on the regulation of interstate commerce. The Court established a broad definition of commerce: "all commercial intercourse—meaning all business dealings." The conflict in this case concerned which government, New York State or the national government, had authority to regulate the operation of boats on the waterways between New York and New Jersey. The Court ruled that regulation of commerce implied regulation of navigation and that therefore the national government had authority to regulate it, not New York State.

Following the *Gibbons* decision, the national government frequently justified many of its actions by arguing that they were necessary to fulfill its enumerated powers to regulate interstate commerce, and the Court typically agreed. The case of *United States v. Lopez* (1995) is an example, however, of the Court's recent trend of being more critical of Congress's attempts to use the commerce clause to justify a national law.[7] The context for the case is the national Gun-Free School Zones Act of 1990, which mandated gun-free zones within a specified area surrounding schools. The lawyers for Alfonso Lopez, a twelfth-grader charged with violating this national law by bringing a .38-caliber handgun to school, successfully argued that the law was unconstitutional. The Court rejected the national government attorney's argument that the 1990 law was a necessary and proper means to regulate interstate commerce. Instead, the Court found that the law was a criminal statute, for which the state governments, not the national government, have authority.[8]

The Power to Provide for the General Welfare   Another enumerated power that has expanded through Court interpretation of what the Constitution implies is the power of the national government to provide for the general welfare. The national government's landmark Social Security Act of 1935 was a response to the Great Depression's devastating impact on the financial security of millions of Americans. The congressional vote to establish Social Security was overwhelmingly favorable. Yet the constitutionality of this very expansive program, which has become the most expensive national program, was tested in the courts shortly after its passage. In 1937, the Supreme Court had to decide: Was Social Security indeed a matter of general welfare for which Congress is delegated the authority to raise and spend money? Or was Social Security a matter for the state governments to address?[9] The Court found the national policy to be constitutional—a reasonable congressional interpretation, the justices wrote, of the enumerated and implied powers of the national government.

The Supreme Court's decisions in the *McCulloch, Gibbons,* and Social Security cases set precedents for the expansion of national power in domestic policy matters by combining the necessary and proper clause with such enumerated powers as regulating commerce and providing for the general welfare. The Court continues today to support Congress's use of the elasticity provided by the implied powers clause to expand its delegated powers. The Court also continues to protect national enumerated powers. Yet Congress does not always get its way, as the justices' decision in the *Lopez* case indicates.

In addition to establishing dual sovereignty and creating two independently operating levels of government, the Constitution enumerates some obligations that the national government has to the states—the topic to which we now turn.

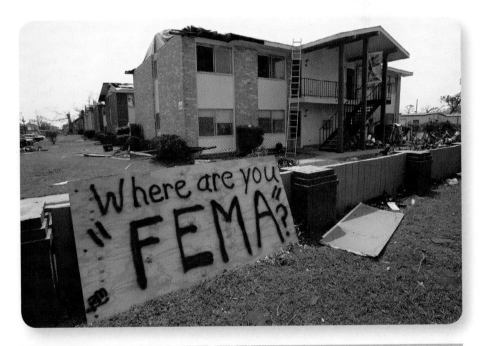

POLITICAL INQUIRY

> This sign raised by desperate apartment dwellers in Biloxi, Mississippi, five days after Hurricane Katrina battered the Gulf coastline sought to publicize the fact that FEMA's limited initial efforts were focusing on New Orleans, Louisiana, and leaving Mississippians to fend for themselves. What does this photo show? What is FEMA, and why have people posted a sign asking "Where are you, 'FEMA'?"

National Obligations to the States

On August 27, 2005, the day before Katrina (a powerful category 3 hurricane) hit the Gulf Coast states, National Hurricane Center director Max Mayfield personally called the governors of Mississippi and Louisiana and the mayor of New Orleans. Mayfield wanted to be sure that these state and local officials understood the severity of the approaching storm.[10] That same day, President George W. Bush declared a national state of emergency for the area, and Mississippi governor Haley Barbour did the same for his state. Louisiana governor Kathleen Blanco had declared a state of emergency for her state the day before. New Orleans mayor Ray Nagin ordered a mandatory evacuation of the city's 485,000 residents.[11] Federal Emergency Management Administration (FEMA) director Michael Brown told state and local officials in the Gulf states that FEMA was ready with all available assistance and was "going to move quick . . . and going to do whatever it takes to help disaster victims."[12]

Even with this apparent readiness at all levels of government, the impact of Katrina's subsequent flooding in New Orleans due to a levee break was devastating: over 1,200 people dead, more than 1 million evacuees, and an estimated $200 billion-plus of damage.[13]

The devastation prompted questions about the national government's obligations to local and state governments and citizens in times of disaster. The Constitution describes several obligations that the national government has to the states, including assistance during times of domestic upheaval (see Table 3.1). Yet does the national government have to wait for state or local officials to ask for help before it takes action? The Constitution is not clear about this question, and to date the courts have not rendered an interpretation on the matter.

Just as the Constitution establishes national obligations to the states, it also defines state-to-state obligations, our next subject.

TABLE 3.1

National Obligations to the States

The federal government:

- must treat states equally in matters of the regulation of commerce and the imposition of taxes
- cannot approve the creation of a new state from the property of an existing state without the consent of the legislatures of the states concerned
- cannot change state boundaries without the consent of the states concerned
- must guarantee a republican form of government
- must protect states from foreign invasion
- at their request, must protect states against domestic violence

State-to-State Obligations: Horizontal Federalism

In Article IV, the Constitution sets forth obligations that the states have to each other. Collectively, these state-to-state obligations and the relationships they mandate are forms of what scholars call **horizontal federalism.** For example, state governments have the right to forge agreements with other states, known as **interstate compacts.** Congress must review and approve interstate compacts to ensure that they do not harm the states that are not party to them and the nation as a whole. States enter into cooperative agreements to provide services and benefits for each other, such as monitoring paroled inmates from other states; sharing and conserving natural resources that spill over state borders, such as water; and decreasing pollution that crosses state borders. For example, in 2005, to improve air quality, the states of Connecticut, Delaware, Massachusetts, New Jersey, New York, Rhode Island, and Vermont agreed to an interstate compact establishing emissions caps on power plants in their states—caps that were higher than national standards.

States also cooperate through a procedure called **extradition,** the legal process of sending individuals back to a state that accuses them of having committed a crime and from which they have fled. The Constitution establishes a state governor's right to request the extradition of an accused criminal. Yet the courts have also supported governors' refusals to extradite individuals.

The Constitution asserts, too, that each state must guarantee the same **privileges and immunities** to all U.S. citizens—that is, citizens from other states who visit or move into the state—that it provides its own citizens. This guarantee does not prohibit states from imposing reasonable requirements before extending rights to visiting or new state residents. For example, states can and do charge higher tuition costs to out-of-state college students. In addition, in many states, new state residents must wait thirty days before they can register to vote. Yet no state can deny new state residents who are U.S. citizens the right to register to vote once they meet a reasonable state residency requirement.

Today, one very controversial state-to-state obligation stems from the full faith and credit clause of Article IV, Section 1, of the Constitution. The **full faith and credit clause** asserts that each state must recognize as legally binding (that is, valid and enforceable) the public acts, records, and judicial proceedings of every other state. For example, states must recognize the validity of out-of-state driver's licenses. Currently, public debate is ongoing about the impact of the full faith and credit clause on same-sex marriage contracts, and hence the constitutionality of the national Defense of Marriage Act (DOMA) of 1996, which allows states to determine whether they will recognize same-sex marriage contracts or same-sex civil union contracts legalized in other states.

The debates over same-sex marriage and civil unions raise several challenging constitutional questions. Because the Constitution is supreme, answers to these questions will eventually come from the Supreme Court's interpretation of the Constitution. Recently, the Supreme Court ruled that while the Constitution *is* the supreme law, state and local governments can guarantee their citizens more liberties and rights than are found in the Constitution, which guarantees only the required minimum.

The New Judicial Federalism

Political scientists use the phrase **new judicial federalism** to describe the practice whereby state judges base decisions regarding citizens' legal rights and liberties on their state constitutions when these laws guarantee more than the minimum rights or liberties enumerated in the U.S. Constitution. In fact, many state and local governments grant more liberties and rights than the Constitution guarantees, and can do so, according to the Supreme Court.

In *Pruneyard Shopping Center and Fred Sahadi v. Michael Robins et al.* (1980), the Court considered the case of a group of politically active high school students who had set up tables in a mall to hand out informational pamphlets and obtain signatures on a petition.[14] The pamphlets and petition dealt with opposition to the United Nations' stand on Zionism—that is, the existence of the Jewish state of Israel. After the owner of the shopping center asked the students to leave his private property, the students sued him on the basis of their belief that the California state constitution specifically protected their freedom of speech and expression, even in a privately owned shopping center. The Supreme Court agreed with the students that California's constitution gave its citizens more freedom of expression than the U.S. Constitution guaranteed, and judged that greater freedom to be constitutional.

New judicial federalism expands the authority of state governments in an era when the Supreme Court is ever more frequently being asked to clarify the constitutional distribution of authority. As we have seen, the delineation among national powers (enumerated and implied) and the states' reserved powers has never been clear. To complicate matters, over the course of U.S. history, national, state, and local governments' interactions have evolved into collaborative efforts whereby the creation, financing, and implementation of a given public policy are shared by two or more levels of government. We next explore the evolution of intergovernmental relations in the U.S. federal system.

Evolution of the Federal System

Evolution means changing slowly and continuously, often from the simple to the complex. The federal system established by the Constitution has evolved from a simple system of *dual federalism* to a complex system of *conflicted federalism*. The figure in "Analyzing the Sources" models both the original, simple federal system established in the Constitution and the current system, with its complex arrangement of intergovernmental relations. Specifically, evolution has occurred in the power relationship between the national government and the states. The United States is still a federal system of government with dual sovereignty. However, the power relationship between the national and state governments has changed over the years, as we now consider. We first survey four types of federalism, characterized by four different power relationships that have evolved in the U.S. federal system, all of which continue to this day. We then explore various means by which the national government has altered the power relationship between it and the state governments.

Three Models of Intergovernmental Relations in a Federal System

The diagram below presents Deil Wright's models of intergovernmental relations in the United States. The "coordinate" model indicates that the relationship between the national government and state governments is one of independence. Each government has autonomy over its functions. The "overlapping" model shows the interdependent relationships among all three levels of government in the United States. Wright argues that the authority pattern in the overlapping model is based on bargaining between the national and state governments. Finally, the "inclusive" model shows dependent relationships with a hierarchical pattern of authority.

Evaluating the Evidence

(1) Which of Wright's models do you think the Constitution's framers—the creators of the U.S. federal system—had in mind? Justify your selection.

(2) Which of Wright's models do you think best presents the relationships among the national, state, and local governments today? Explain.

(3) Which model displays the relationships and pattern of authority that you believe will best serve you and your family? Justify your selection.

	Coordinate model	Overlapping model	Inclusive model
Relationship	Independent	Interdependent	Dependent
Authority pattern	Autonomy	Bargaining	Hierarchy

From Wright. *Understanding Intergovernmental Relations, 3E.* © 1988 Wadsworth, a part of Cengage Learning, Inc. Reproduced by permission. www.cengage.com/permissions

Dual Federalism

Initially, the dual sovereignty of the U.S. federal system was implemented in such a way that the national and state governments acted independently of one another, as in Deil Wright's coordinate model (see "Analyzing the Sources"). Political scientists give the name **dual federalism** to this pattern of implementation of the federal system, whereby the national government takes care of its enumerated powers and the states independently take care of their reserved powers. From 1789 through 1932, dual federalism was the dominant pattern of national-state relations. Congresses and presidents did enact some laws that states argued infringed on their powers, and the Courts typically found in favor of the states in these cases. Yet as the 1819 *McCulloch* case shows, sometimes the Court ruled in favor of the national government.

Cooperative Federalism

A crippling economic depression that reached global proportions, known as the Great Depression, began in 1929. To help state governments deal with the domestic problems spawned by the economic collapse, Congress and President Franklin D. Roosevelt (1933–1945) approved numerous policies, collectively called the New Deal, that infringed on states' traditional reserved powers. Through these policies, the independent actions of national and state governments to fulfill their respective responsibilities evolved into cooperative efforts. **Grants-in-aid**—transfers of money from one level of government to another (also known as **intergovernmental transfers**)—became a main mechanism of President Roosevelt's New Deal programs.

The national grants of money offered to the state governments, and eventually also to local governments, during the Great Depression had few specific terms and conditions. State and local governments welcomed the national grants, which assisted them in addressing the domestic matters that fell within their sovereignty while allowing them to make most of the specific program decisions to implement the policy. The era of federalism that began during the Depression, with its growing number of collaborative, intergovernmental efforts to address domestic matters reserved to the states, is the period of **cooperative federalism** (1932–1963), described by Wright's overlapping model.

Centralized Federalism

By the time of Lyndon Johnson's presidency (1963–1969), a new kind of federalism was replacing cooperative federalism. In this new form of federalism, the national government imposed its own policy preferences on state and local governments. Specifically, in **centralized federalism,** directives in national legislation, including grant-in-aid programs with ever-increasing conditions or strings attached to the money, force state and local governments to implement a particular national policy. Wright's inclusive model comes closest to diagramming centralized federalism.

Presidents since Richard Nixon (1969–1974) have fought against this centralizing tendency by proposing to return policy responsibilities (policy making, policy financing, and policy implementation) to state and local governments. Presidents Nixon and Ronald Reagan (1981–1989) gave the name *new federalism* to their efforts to revert such obligations to state and local governments; today, we use the term **devolution** to refer to the return of policy responsibilities to state and local governments.

Republicans and Democrats (including presidents, members of Congress, and state and local lawmakers) broadly support devolution, but they debate *which elements of the policy-making process* should be devolved: policy creation, financing, and/or implementation. They also butt heads over *which policies* to devolve. The legislation and court decisions that result from these debates make for a complicated coexistence of dual federalism, cooperative federalism, and centralized federalism. In the evolution of

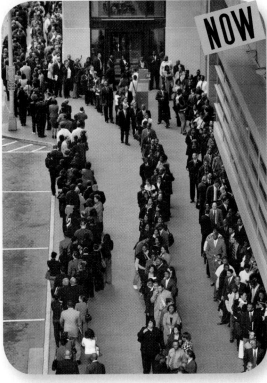

> With the unemployment rate climbing as high as 25 percent, thousands of Americans relied on soup kitchens and other charities to survive the Great Depression. In addition, through new grant-in-aid programs, the federal government worked with state and local governments to provide urgently needed financial support and services. As unemployment in the United States grew to over 9 percent in 2009, thousands of people lined up at a Federal Center Career Fair in Atlanta, Georgia, for information about federal jobs. As in the 1930s, the deep and prolonged recession forced the federal government to increase grants-in-aid to state and local governments for needed financial support and services for the unemployed.

federalism, we are now experiencing what David B. Walker, a preeminent scholar of federalism and intergovernmental relations, calls **conflicted federalism.**[15]

Conflicted Federalism

Because present-day national-state relations frequently feature conflicting tendencies, the label *conflicted federalism* has been used to describe intergovernmental relations today. Efforts to centralize policy making at the national level are evident, as are efforts to decentralize the implementation of national policies to the state and local levels. For some policy matters, the national and state governments operate independently of each other, and hence dual federalism is at work. For the majority of policies, however, intergovernmental efforts are the norm. These efforts may be voluntary and a means to advance state policy priorities (cooperative federalism), or they may be compelled by national legislation (centralized federalism).

The era of conflicted federalism has seen a jump in the number of legal challenges to national legislation that mandates state and local action. In the various cases that the Supreme Court has heard, the justices have ruled inconsistently, sometimes upholding or even expanding state sovereignty and other times protecting or expanding national sovereignty. For example, in 1976, the Supreme Court ruled in *National League of Cities v. Usery* that state and local governments were not legally required to comply with the national minimum wage law—hence protecting state authority.[16] Then, nine years later, in *Garcia v. San Antonio Transportation Authority* (1985), the Court ruled that national minimum wage laws did apply to state and local government employees—thus expanding national authority.[17]

Another policy matter that has been subject to conflicting Court decisions is the medical use of marijuana. California has fought an up-and-down battle with the national government over medical uses of marijuana. In 1996, California voters approved the Compassionate Use Act, allowing people to grow, obtain, or smoke marijuana for medical needs, with a doctor's recommendation. Then in 2001, the U.S. Supreme Court ruled that the national government could charge people who distributed marijuana for medical use with a crime, even in California, where the state law allowed such activity.[18] The Court found that national narcotics laws took precedence over California's law, which California had argued was grounded in the reserved police powers of the states. But in 2003, the Court refused to review a case challenging a California law allowing doctors to recommend marijuana use to their patients.[19] As a consequence of the Court's refusal to take on the case, the decision from the lower court prevailed. The lower court's ruling had been that doctors could *not* be charged with a crime for recommending marijuana to patients. To add to the confused legal status of medicinal marijuana in California, the U.S. Supreme Court in 2005 upheld the right of the national government to prosecute people who smoke the drug on the recommendation of their doctors, as well as those who grow it for medical purposes.[20]

In the case of medicinal marijuana, national and state actions and intents have been in clear conflict. Further, U.S. Supreme Court decisions have not yet clarified the confusion over constitutional authority to regulate medicinal marijuana. How did the federal system evolve from dual federalism to the conflicted federalism that is sharply in evidence today?

Landmarks in the Evolution of Federalism: Key Constitutional Amendments

Understanding the U.S. federal system's evolution from dual federalism to conflicted federalism requires a brief review of the tools the national government uses to expand its authority to direct state and local governments' domestic policies. Although the formal language of the Constitution with regard to the distribution of national and state sovereignty remains essentially as it was in 1791 (when the Tenth Amendment was ratified), three amendments—the Fourteenth, Sixteenth, and Seventeenth—have had a tremendous impact on the power relationship between national and state government. The Civil War, which was a catalyst for the ratification of the Fourteenth Amendment, also influenced the national-state power relationship.

The Civil War and the Postwar Amendments   The military success of the northern states in the Civil War (1861–1865) meant the preservation of the union—the United States of America. The ratification of the Thirteenth Amendment (1865) brought the legal end of slavery in every state. In addition, the Fourteenth Amendment (1868), which extended the rights of citizenship to individuals who were previously enslaved, also placed certain limits and obligations on state governments.

The Fourteenth Amendment authorizes the national government to ensure that the state governments follow fair procedures (due process) before taking away a person's life, liberty, or pursuit of happiness and that the states guarantee all people the same rights (equal protection of the laws) to life, liberty, and the pursuit of happiness, without discrimination. In addition, the amendment guarantees the privileges and immunities of U.S. citizenship to all citizens in all states. Accordingly, since the Fourteenth Amendment's ratification, Congresses and presidents have approved national laws that direct the states to ensure due process and equal protection. This legislation includes, for example, laws mandating that all government buildings, including state and local edifices, provide access to all persons, including individuals with physical disabilities. In addition, the Supreme Court has used the Fourteenth Amendment to justify extending the Bill of Rights' limits on national government to state and local governments (under incorporation theory, which Chapter 4 considers). And in *Bush v. Gore* (2000), the Supreme Court used the amendment's equal protection clause to end a controversial Florida ballot recount in the 2000 presidential election.[21]

In that electoral controversy, Democratic presidential candidate Al Gore first won a lawsuit in Florida State Supreme Court that challenged the official Florida vote count. As a result, ballots not initially counted were to be counted. In turn, Republican presidential candidate George W. Bush challenged the Florida Supreme Court's finding and asked the U.S. Supreme Court to determine the constitutionality of Florida's election law as interpreted by the state's supreme court. In its decision, the U.S. Supreme Court ruled that the Florida recount violated the Constitution's equal protection clause by not ensuring that each vote would be treated equally. The Court's ruling put an end to the recount, and candidate Bush became President Bush. (For more on the 2000 election, see Chapter 9.)

The Sixteenth Amendment   Passage of the Sixteenth Amendment (1913) powerfully enhanced the ability of the national government to raise money. It granted Congress the authority to collect income taxes from workers and corporations without apportioning these taxes among the states on the basis of population (which had been mandated by the Constitution before this amendment).

The national income tax provides the national government with access to tremendous financial resources. The national government uses these resources as leverage over state and local governments, encouraging or coercing them to pursue and implement policies that the national government thinks best. Specifically, by offering state and local governments grants-in-aid, national officials have gained the power to determine many of the policies these governments approve, finance, and implement. For example, by offering grants to the states for highways, the federal government encouraged each state to establish a legal drinking age of 21 years.

The Seventeenth Amendment   Prior to ratification of the Seventeenth Amendment in 1913, the Constitution called for *state legislators* to select U.S. senators. By this arrangement, the framers strove to ensure that Congress and the president would take the concerns of state governments into account in national policy making. Essentially, the original arrangement provided the state legislatures with lobbyists in the national policy-making process who would be accountable to the states. Once ratified, the Seventeenth Amendment shifted the election of U.S. senators to a system of popular vote by the citizens in a state.

With this change, senators were no longer directly accountable to the state legislatures because the latter no longer selected the senators. Consequently, state governments lost their direct access to national policy makers. Some scholars of federalism and intergovernmental relations argue that this loss has decreased the influence of state governments in national policy making.[22]

Further Evolutionary Landmarks: Grants-in-Aid

In 1837, the national government shared its revenue surplus with the states in the form of a monetary grant. But the government did not make a habit of such financial grants-in-aid until the Great Depression of the 1930s. Today, there is growing controversy over the strings attached to the various kinds of grants issued by the federal government.

Categorical Grants   Historically, the most common type of grant-in-aid has been the **categorical formula grant**—a grant of money for a narrow purpose, as defined by the national government. The legislation that creates such a grant includes a formula determining how much money is available to each grant recipient. The formula is typically based on factors related to the purpose of the grant, as well as political considerations (which assist in gaining the majority vote required to approve the legislation). Categorical grants come with strings—that is, rules and regulations with which the recipient government must comply.

One typical condition is a matching funds requirement, which obligates the grant recipient to spend some of its own money to match a specified percentage of the grant money provided. Matching funds requirements allow the national government to influence the budget decisions of state and local governments by forcing them to spend some of their own money on a national priority, which may also be a state priority, in order to receive national funding.

Since the 1960s, the national government has also offered categorical project grants. Like the categorical formula grant, a **categorical project grant** covers a narrow purpose (program area), but unlike the formula grant, a project grant does

Federal Homeland Security Grants to State and Local Governments

	THEN 2001 (MILLIONS)	THEN 2004 (MILLIONS)	NOW 2009 (MILLIONS)
Total home- land security grant outlays	$3,010*	$5,490**	$3,009**

*U.S. Census Bureau, *Statistical Abstract of the United States 2004–2005*, Table 424.
**http://www.dhs.gov/xnews/releases/pr_1225900531284.shtm.

WHAT'S NEXT?

> Why is 2001 an important year with regard to homeland security grants? Why have these grants increased since that year?

> Do you think that President Obama and Congress will increase the level of homeland security grant money provided to state and local governments? Why or why not?

not include a formula specifying how much money a recipient will receive. Instead, those interested in receiving such a grant must compete for it by writing a proposal detailing what program they wish to implement and what level of funding they need. A categorical project grant has strings attached to it and typically offers much less funding than a categorical formula grant.

Block Grants   Another type of formula-based intergovernmental transfer of money, the **block grant,** differs from categorical formula and categorical project grants in that the use of the grant money is less narrowly defined by the national government. While a categorical grant might specify that the money is to be used for a child care program, a block grant gives the recipient government more discretion to determine what program it will be used for within a broad policy area such as assistance to economically needy families with children. When first introduced by the Nixon administration in the 1970s, the block grant also had fewer strings attached to it than the categorical grants. Today, however, the number and specificity of conditions included in block grants are increasing.

State and local governments have grown dependent on national financial assistance, and so grants are an essential tool of national power to direct state and local government activity. Although the states welcome federal grant money, they do not welcome the strings attached to the funds.

State Attempts to Influence Grant-in-Aid Conditions   State government opposition to the strings attached to national grants came to a head in 1923 in the case of *Massachusetts v. Mellon*.[23] In this case, the Supreme Court found the conditions of national grants-in-aid to be constitutional, arguing that grants-in-aid are voluntary cooperative arrangements. By voluntarily accepting the national grant, the justices ruled, the state government agrees to the grant conditions. This 1923 Court decision was essential to the proliferation of national grants in subsequent years and to the evolution of federalism and intergovernmental relations as well. But the Court's decision did not end states' challenges to grant conditions.

In 1987, South Dakota challenged a 1984 national transportation law that penalized states whose legal drinking age was lower than 21 years. The intent of the national law was to decrease "drinking while intoxicated" (DWI) car accidents. States with legal drinking ages lower than 21 years would lose 5 percent of their national grant money for transportation. South Dakota argued that Congress was using grant conditions to put a law into effect that Congress could not achieve through national legislation because the law dealt with a power reserved to the states—determining the legal age for drinking alcoholic beverages.

In its decision in *South Dakota v. Dole*, the Court found that the national government could not impose a national drinking age because setting a drinking age is indeed a reserved power of the states.[24] Yet, the Court ruled, the national government could *encourage* states to set a drinking age of 21 years by threatening to decrease their grants-in-aid for highway construction. In other words, conditions attached to voluntarily accepted grants-in-aid are constitutional. Ultimately, the national policy goal of a 21-year-old drinking age was indeed accomplished by 1988—not through a national law but through a condition attached to national highway funds offered to state governments, funds on which the states are dependent.

Over time, the number and specificity of the grant conditions have grown. State and local governments have increasingly lobbied national lawmakers during the policy-making processes that create and reauthorize grants. One goal of this **intergovernmental lobbying** is to limit the grant conditions—or at least to influence them to the states' advantage. In other words, lobbyists for an individual state work to ensure that the conditions, including the grants' formulas, benefit that state. Beyond the efforts of lobbyists hired by individual states, coordinated lobbying on behalf of *multiple* states, municipal governments, and county governments is common.

If a state does not want to comply with a grant condition, then it need not accept the grant. The problem for state and local governments is that they have come to rely on national grant funds. Not long ago, approximately 31 percent of state and local general revenue came from national grants;[25] however, the severe economic downturn that began in 2008 propelled the federal government to increase grants-in-aid to state and local governments (for at least two years) through its economic stimulus package, the 2009 American Recovery and Reinvestment Act (ARRA). Yet the national government has no constitutional obligation to offer grants-in-aid to state or local governments. Therefore, intergovernmental lobbies persistently lobby Congress to ensure not only favorable grant formulas but also the survival of grants-in-aid on which state and local governments depend. They also lobby to prevent the passage of national laws mandating specific state and local actions.

Federalism's Continuing Evolution: Mandates

In our earlier analysis of the constitutional distribution of sovereignty, we considered specific examples of the Court's expansion of national authority through its decisions in cases involving conflicts over constitutional interpretation. The constitutional clauses most often questioned are the following: the necessary and proper clause, the national supremacy clause, the general welfare clause, and the regulation of interstate commerce clause.

With these Court decisions in hand, the national government is able to *mandate* certain state and local government actions. In addition, through a process known as *preemption,* the federal government can take away states' and localities' policy authority and impose its policy choices on state and local governments.

National **mandates** are clauses in national laws that direct state and local governments to do something specified by the national government. Most mandates relate to ensuring citizens' civil rights and civil liberties, as in the case of the mandate in the Rehabilitation Act of 1973 requiring that all government buildings, including those of state and local authorities, must be accessible to persons with disabilities. When the national government assumes the entire cost of a mandate, it is a *funded mandate.* When the state or local government must cover all or some of the cost, it is an *unfunded mandate.*

Also common is the federal government's use of preemption. **Preemption** means that a national policy supersedes a state or local policy because it deals with an enumerated or implied national power. Therefore, people must obey, and states must enforce, the national law even if the state or local government has its own law on the matter.

The Supreme Court typically has supported the federal government's arguments that the national supremacy clause and the necessary and proper clause—coupled with the powers delegated to the national government to provide for the general welfare and to regulate interstate commerce—give the federal government the authority to force state and local governments to implement its mandates. The Court has also supported the national government's argument that it can attach conditions to the grants-in-aid it offers state and local governments, hence forcing those that voluntarily accept national grants to implement policies established by national lawmakers.

Today's Federalism: The Good, the Bad, and the Inevitable

With more than 89,000 individual governments operating in the United States today, citizens have numerous opportunities to engage with government to ensure that it serves them. There are millions of government jobs for citizens who want to be in the front line of making or implementing public policy. There are multiple channels for citizens' requests for assistance, lobbying efforts, and complaints. Moreover, if one level of government does not respond, there are numerous other governments to approach. Ultimately, the courts may be called in to determine which government has the authority and responsibility to respond to citizens' specific requests.

The federal system also encourages public policy experimentation. A state or local government can act as a policy laboratory, and then other governments—state, local, and/or national—can choose to adopt a successful policy, without the expense of conducting their own experiments. For example, the 1990s witnessed numerous states' experimentation with public assistance programs for low-income families with children. A national welfare reform law passed in 1996, the Personal Responsibility and Work Opportunity Reconciliation Act, adopted some of the most successful of these state-level experiments. Today state, county, and city governments across the nation continue to experiment with innovative policies targeting such objectives as protecting the environment, preventing illegal immigration, and making health insurance affordable and available to all.

The United States' multiple governments increasingly offer redundant and overlapping protection of civil rights and civil liberties. (Chapters 4 and 5 explore these rights and liberties, including past and current initiatives to expand civil rights to groups historically denied equal protections.) Moreover, the involvement of multiple levels of government can yield a widely varying quality and quantity of services for the people. Because state constitutions require balanced state budgets, in any policy area for which state governments are sovereign, there is the potential for a "race to the bottom," in which the winner is the state that regulates and taxes businesses the least (thus achieving a low unemployment rate) and provides fewer and less responsive services to the poor (thus discouraging poor outsiders from entering the state). Differing financial capacities and political ideologies from state to state lead to policy variation across the states.

Citizens may like overlap and redundancy when these characteristics protect their liberties and rights. But like quickly turns to dislike if the result is higher taxes and an inefficient use of tax dollars as more than one level of government spends money to address the same problems. Overlap and redundancy in the provision of homeland security may be a good thing if it means that numerous levels of public officials are ensuring domestic tranquility. Yet an overlap of responsibilities requires careful coordination and communication to ensure a sharing of information and resources so that the public is served effectively and efficiently. As the experience of Hurricane Katrina has shown, coordination and communication problems are endemic to dual sovereignty implemented through intergovernmental efforts during crises.

Today's vexing societal problems demand the expertise and resources of multiple governments. From addressing economic and environmental problems to preparing for and dealing with disasters of natural and human origin, intergovernmental relations are essential to the provision of government services in the United States today. Whether national and state governments agree to cooperate by sharing responsibility to approve, finance, and implement policy or the national government mandates or preempts state policy, intergovernmental relations are inevitable in today's federalism. Conflicts over which government ultimately has sovereignty—is in change of which matters—are also inevitable in the U.S. system of federalism. These conflicts pervade public policy making and fill the docket of the Supreme Court.

CONCLUSION

CONTINUING THE CONVERSATION

- The dual sovereignty established by the creators of the U.S. federal system remains in effect today, yet the relations between the national government and the states have evolved over the years.

- Conflicted federalism (with characteristics of dual federalism, cooperative federalism, and centralized federalism) best describes the relations between the national government and the states today.

- Another characteristic of U.S. federalism is intergovernmental relation (IGR) created by collaborative efforts of two or more levels of government working to serve the public.

- Intergovernmental relations are inevitable as the 89,000-plus governments in the United States attempt to fulfill the mission of the Constitution in the context of present-day realities.

STUDY NOW

Summary

1. An Overview of the U.S. Federal System

Dual sovereignty is the defining characteristic of the U.S. federal system of government, with the national government sovereign over specific matters, and state governments sovereign over different matters.

2. Constitutional Distribution of Authority

The vagueness of some U.S. Constitution language providing for enumerated and implied national powers, reserved state powers, concurrent powers, and national supremacy has provoked ongoing conflict between the federal government and the states over the proper distribution of sovereignty.

3. Evolution of the Federal System

Amendments to the Constitution, together with the Supreme Court's interpretations of the Constitution's distribution of national and state government authority, have fostered federalism's evolution from a simple arrangement of dual federalism to a system of conflicted federalism with complex intergovernmental relations.

4. Today's Federalism: The Good, the Bad, and the Inevitable

For citizens, federalism provides many benefits, creates some confusion and burdens, and requires intergovernmental cooperation to ensure efficient and effective government.

For Critical Thinking and Discussion

1. Is the federal system of government that provides citizens with the opportunity to elect a large number of officials each year a benefit or a burden for citizens? Explain your answer.

2. Note at least three societal problems you believe the national government can address best (more effectively and efficiently than state or local governments). Discuss why you believe the national government is best suited to address these problems. Do these problems fit in the category of delegated national powers? Explain your answer.

3. Note at least three societal problems you believe state or local governments can address best (more effectively and efficiently than the national government). Discuss why you believe state or local governments are best suited to address these problems. Do these problems fit in the category of powers reserved to the states? Explain your answer.

Key Terms

block grant 121
categorical formula
  grant 120
categorical project grant 120
centralized federalism 116
concurrent powers 105
confederal system 99
conflicted federalism 117
cooperative federalism 116
devolution 116
dual federalism 115
dual sovereignty 98
enumerated powers 105
extradition 113

federal system 98
full faith and credit
  clause 113
grants-in-aid
  (intergovernmental
  transfers) 116
horizontal federalism 113
implied powers 105
intergovernmental
  lobbying 122
intergovernmental relations
  (IGR) 101
interstate compacts 113
mandates 123

McCulloch v. Maryland 109
necessary and proper clause
  (elastic clause) 106
new judicial federalism 114
preemption 123
police powers 108
privileges and immunities
  clause 113
reserved powers 108
sovereignty 98
supremacy clause 107
supreme law of the
  land 107
unitary system 98

Internet Resources

A More Perfect Union Web site
www.mhhe.com/harrisonampule   Consult the book's Web site for study guides, interactive activities, simulations, and current hot-links that provide additional information on federalism in the United States.

Bureau of the Census
www.census.gov   This site provides access to the *Statistical Abstract of the United States,* as well as other sources of data about national and state governments at this site.

Council of State Governments
www.csg.org   This site is a place where state officials can share information on common problems and possible solutions.

National Conference of State Legislatures
www.ncsl.org/statefed/statefed.htm   This site is dedicated to state-federal issues and relationships.

Recommended Readings

O'Toole, Laurence J. *American Intergovernmental Relations: Foundations, Perspectives, and Issues,* 3rd ed. Washington, DC: CQ Press, 2000. A collection of readings giving a comprehensive overview of U.S. federalism and intergovernmental relations, covering historical, theoretical, and political perspectives as well as fiscal and administrative views.

Rehnquist, William H. *The Supreme Court: Revised and Updated.* New York: Vintage Books, 2001. A history of the Supreme Court by the late chief justice, probing the inner workings of the Court, key Court decisions in the evolution of federalism, and insights into the debates among the justices.

Walker, David B. *The Rebirth of Federalism: Slouching Toward Washington,* 2nd ed. Washington, DC: CQ Press, 2000. Both a history of U.S. federalism and an assessment of the status of U.S. federalism today.

PART II

FUNDAMENTAL PRINCIPLES

NATIONAL SECURITY, TORTURE, AND CIVIL LIBERTIES

A bu Zubaydah wasn't giving up the goods. In the four months since March 2002, when U.S. agents captured and detained the man they believed was Al Qaeda's logistics chief, Zubaydah had said nothing that would lead investigators to other possible terrorist networks inside the United States. He was chatty. Even cordial at times. But in the estimation of CIA officials interrogating him, he had handed over no "actionable intelligence," hard facts that could lead investigators to other Qaeda plotters. And that was a problem, because counter-terrorism officials were becoming more and more convinced that a follow-up to the 9/11 attacks was in the offing.

Zubaydah's captors strongly suspected that he possessed information that could help disrupt a new terrorist assault. "There was a lot of concern that there would be multiple attacks, almost in sequence," a former senior CIA official who was directly involved in the agency's interrogation program for terrorist suspects told *National Journal*. "Things were moving rapidly. . . . It was, 'We know this guy's got more information.'"

The CIA passed its assessment along to lawyers at the Justice Department. "Specifically, [Zubaydah] is withholding information regarding terrorist networks in the United States or in Saudi Arabia and information regarding plans to conduct attacks within the United States or against our interests overseas," lawyers from Justice's Office of Legal Counsel wrote in a memo to the CIA's top lawyer, affirming for the record what they said CIA officials had told them. The memo was signed by then-Assistant Attorney General Jay Bybee, who is now a federal Appeals Court judge.

"Moreover, your intelligence indicates that there is currently a level of 'chatter' equal to that which preceded the September 11 attacks."

The Justice Department's memo, titled "Interrogation of Al Qaeda operative" and dated August 1, 2002, describes a high-level and secretive dialogue about whether the CIA should try to get more information from Zubaydah through aggressive and violent means, including suffocation by water, face slapping, and sleep deprivation. The lawyers based their analysis on whether these methods constituted torture entirely upon "facts" about Zubaydah's previous interrogations that they said had come from the CIA.

The memo was one of four documents declassified by President Obama [early in his presidency]. Collectively, the memos helped form the now-discarded legal rationale for using what the Bush administration, the International Committee of the Red Cross, and a host of military and intelligence officers say is torture. And yet, if the Justice lawyers can be believed to have acted in good faith, the documents are also illustrative of the mood hanging over the CIA officials who were interrogating Zubaydah as the first anniversary of the September 11 attacks approached. Both CIA and Justice officials seemed to be gripped by competing impulses: the urgent need to disrupt any other possible attacks and the belief that Zubaydah might know about them versus their personal desire to avoid the threat of indictment for torturing an unarmed prisoner.

Throughout the intelligence community in the summer of 2002, information about Al Qaeda was coming in quickly, but the spy agencies weren't well positioned to make sense of it.

"It was hard to differentiate whether this was reactionary chatter," tough talk from terrorists with little to back it up, "or planning," the former official said. The intelligence agencies had intercepted terrorists' phone calls and e-mails, and scoured purloined laptop computers and journals; they were also getting leads passed back through human sources in the field. The Qaeda refrain amounted to, "We need to follow up on

> After the waterboard was applied, "he answered every question," Kiriakou said. **"The threat information he provided disrupted a number of attacks,** maybe dozens of attacks."

this," the former official said, referring to 9/11.

Zubaydah's interrogators "tried the psychological routine, befriending him," the former official said. They didn't think it worked. The Justice Department memo states at the outset that the CIA believed that "Zubaydah has become accustomed to a certain level of treatment and displays no signs of willingness to disclose further information." The agency wanted to move to what it called "the increased pressure phase."

The August 2002 memo describes the application of said pressure in precise detail. The lawyers gave interrogators specific instructions on how to rough Zubaydah up

without, in their view, legally torturing him. The interrogation techniques are largely based on those developed by the Pentagon as part of a training program for combat pilots and Special Forces troops on how to withstand harsh interrogation if they were ever captured in battle.

"The amount of restraint [the interrogators] used was phenomenal," the former CIA official said. Arguing that many Americans would have been filled with rage at the mere sight of the self-confessed Qaeda planner, who told his captors he would kill again if released, the former official said that CIA interrogators stayed within the lines. "They followed the rules."

The CIA's inspector general has found, however, that Zubaydah and another prisoner captured later were subjected to waterboarding a total of 266 times, and that the application of the waterboard exceeded the limits spelled out in the August 2002 memo. The former CIA official interviewed by *National Journal* questioned whether the number was accurate, but he acknowledged that he had no evidence to refute it.

John Kiriakou, a CIA officer who was with the team that captured Zubaydah in Pakistan, later told ABC News that his personal rage led him to support harsh treatment of the prisoner. "I was so angry," he said. "And I wanted so much to help disrupt future attacks on the United States that I felt it was the only thing we could do." Kiriakou characterized waterboarding as torture, but he argued that it was necessary to get information from Zubaydah. After the waterboard was applied, "he answered every question," Kiriakou said. "The threat information he provided disrupted a number of attacks, maybe dozens of attacks."

The former senior CIA official said that information extracted from Zubaydah "prevented multiple attacks." On that point, he said, he was "certain." He elaborated, "We got some extremely useful tactical and strategic information." The first category included "names of individuals actively planning attacks," and the latter consisted of countries where the United States should focus its counter-terrorism efforts as well as the names of "targets" within those countries, the former official said.

The New York Times reported that National Intelligence Director Dennis Blair has said that Zubaydah's interrogation got results. "High-value information came from interrogations in

"Just how useful Zubaydah's information was and **whether his brutal interrogation was necessary** have been intensely debated. . . ."

which those methods were used and provided a deeper understanding of the Al Qaeda organization that was attacking this country," Blair wrote in a memo to his staff, after the Justice Department memos were released.

Just how useful Zubaydah's information was and whether his brutal interrogation was necessary have been intensely debated since the first details of his interrogation were revealed.

Among others, FBI officials who were involved in his interrogation have played down Zubaydah's contribution. Agent Daniel Coleman, who helped the FBI analyze some of Zubaydah's diaries, told New Yorker writer Jane Mayer

that the prisoner was a "schizophrenic personality" and that Qaeda chief Osama bin Laden would not have entrusted Zubaydah with secrets like those the CIA thought he possessed.

But this much is certain. In August 2002, with the chatter level and nerves running high, the interrogators had no way of knowing precisely what Zubaydah knew or didn't know. They believed he knew more than he was telling. They wanted to press him. "Frankly, there were lives at stake," Kiriakou told ABC News. "He had information, and we wanted to get it."

Obama has vowed that CIA employees who carried out interrogations and the agency officials who oversaw them will not face prosecution. But in comments to a reporter this week, he left the door open to prosecutions of the Justice Department lawyers who wrote the interrogation memos.

An extensive investigation of interrogation policy and practice, written by the Senate Armed Services Committee, has put those lawyers in the crosshairs. The report concludes that the principal authors of the August 2002 memo, John Yoo and Bybee, sought to "redefine torture." Before drafting the memo,

Yoo met with Alberto Gonzales, who was then top counsel to President Bush, and David Addington, Vice President Cheney's counsel, "to discuss the subjects he intended to address" in the memo, the report found.

Obama has said that as far as he is concerned, the CIA interrogators acted in good faith. Now the question is whether the same can be said of the lawyers who gave them the legal cover to act and the senior Bush administration officials who knew in advance what the lawyers planned to say.

The Bill of Rights protected citizens' rights to speak and act without undue monitoring or interference from the national government.

As part of a global war on terrorism, the national government increasingly monitors the words and actions of citizens and others.

NOW

4

Civil Liberties

Civil liberties protect people from government intrusion and allow them to follow their own belief systems. Civil liberties also empower people to speak out against the government, as long as they do not harm others.

Since the nation's founding, political discourse among the people has often focused on the ideals of liberty and freedom. The colonists took up arms against Britain because the king and Parliament refused to recognize their liberties as English citizens—freedoms their counterparts in Great Britain took for granted: freedom of speech and assembly and the right to be free from unrestrained governmental power, especially in the investigation and prosecution of crimes. As scholar Stephen L. Carter noted, by declaring their independence, the colonists engaged in the ultimate act of dissent.[1] Withdrawing their consent to be governed by the king, they created a new government that would tolerate political discourse and disagreement and that could not legally disregard the collective or individual will of citizens.

Since the War for Independence, the ideas of liberty and freedom have been a defining feature of American democracy.[2] Today, we continue to see the American polity struggle to balance the individuals' civil liberties with the government's need to provide protection and security for the populace.

NEXT

Will the Supreme Court uphold new laws allowing the president to place terrorist suspects under surveillance without a court order?

Will airports and federal agencies routinely implement security systems based on methods such as thumb print and retinal scan technology?

Will the Court uphold new laws that require Internet providers to secretly share personal information about their clients with the FBI?

Civil Liberties in the American Legal System

Civil liberties are individual liberties established in the Constitution and safeguarded by state and federal courts. We also refer to civil liberties as *personal freedoms* and often use the concepts of "liberty" and "freedom" interchangeably.

Civil liberties are different from civil rights. **Civil liberties** are constitutionally established guarantees that protect citizens, opinions, and property *against* arbitrary government interference. In contrast, civil rights (the focus of Chapter 5) reflect positive acts of government (in the form of constitutional provisions or statutes) *for* the purpose of protecting individuals against arbitrary or discriminatory actions. For example, the freedom of speech, a liberty established in the First Amendment to the U.S. Constitution, protects citizens against the government's censorship of their words—in particular, when these words are politically charged. In contrast, the right to vote, which the Constitution protects in a number of places, requires the government to step in to ensure that all citizens be allowed to vote, without restriction by individuals, groups, or governmental officials.

The Freedoms Protected in the American System

The U.S. Constitution, through the Bill of Rights, and state constitutions explicitly recognize and protect civil liberties. As Table 4.1 summarizes, the first ten amendments to the Constitution strictly limited the power of the legislative, executive, and judicial branches of the national government.

The freedoms established by the Bill of Rights are essential to individuals' and groups' free and effective participation in the larger community. Consider how the absence of freedom to speak one's mind or the absence of protection against the arbitrary exercise of police powers might affect the nature and extent of people's engagement in political and civic discourse. Without these protections, citizens could not freely express their opinions through rallies, protests, letters, pamphlets, public meetings, blogs, e-mail, and other forms of civic engagement. The Constitution's framers, who had been denied these liberties under British rule, saw them as indispensable to forming a new democratic republic.

These precious freedoms have had shifting meanings over the course of U.S. history, as presidents, legislators, judges, and ordinary citizens have changed their minds about how much freedom the people should have. When Americans have not perceived themselves as being under some external threat, they generally have adopted an expansive interpretation of civil liberties. At these times, citizens tend to believe that the government should interfere as little as necessary in individuals' lives. Accordingly, they strongly support people's right to gather with others and to speak their minds, even when the content of this speech is controversial. When the nation has been under some perceived threat, citizens

TABLE 4.1

The Bill of Rights: Limiting Government Power

Clause	Limitation
Amendment I: Limits on Congress	Congress cannot make any law establishing a religion or abridging the freedom of religious exercise, speech, assembly, or petition.
Amendments II, III, IV: Limits on the Executive	The executive branch cannot infringe on the right of the people to bear arms (II), cannot house soldiers in citizens' houses (III), and cannot search for or seize evidence without a legal warrant from a court of law (IV).
Amendments V, VI, VII, VIII: Limits on the Judiciary	The courts cannot hold trials for serious offenses without providing for a grand jury (V), a trial jury (VII), a fair trial (VI), and legal counsel (VI). The accused also have the right to hear the charges against them (VI), to confront hostile witnesses (VI), and to refrain from giving testimony against themselves (V); and they cannot be tried more than once for the same crime (V). In addition, neither bail nor punishment can be excessive (VIII), and no property can be taken from private citizens without "just compensation" (V).
Amendments IX, X: Limits	Any rights not listed specifically in the Constitution as held by the national government are reserved to the states or to the people (X), and the enumeration of certain rights in the Constitution should not be interpreted to mean that those are the only rights the people have (IX).

POLITICAL INQUIRY

Broadly speaking, what do the Bill of Rights amendments aim to recognize and protect? What do they aim to limit? Which amendments limit the powers of the legislative branch? Of the executive branch? Of the judicial branch?

have sometimes allowed the government to limit freedom of speech and assembly.[3] Limits have also extended to many criminal **due process** protections—legal safeguards that prevent the government from arbitrarily depriving people of life, liberty, or property without adhering to strict legal procedures. In this chapter, we consider not only the historical context for our civil liberties but also recent changes in how Congress, the president, and the courts are interpreting these liberties.

The Historical Basis for American Civil Liberties: The Bill of Rights

The framers vividly remembered the censorship and suppression of speech that they had suffered under British rule. Criticism of the British government, through both speech and the publication of pamphlets, had been harshly punished, often by imprisonment and the confiscation of property but sometimes even by death. The framers understandably viewed liberty as a central principle guiding the creation of a new democratic republic. Federalists such as Alexander Hamilton saw the Constitution itself as a bill of rights because it delegated specific powers to the national government and contained specific provisions designed to protect citizens against an abusive government (see Table 4.2).

The protections listed in Table 4.2 were designed to protect people from being punished, imprisoned, or executed for expressing political beliefs or opposition. However, the Anti-Federalists still stressed the need for a written bill of rights. As we saw in Chapter 2, the ratification of the Constitution stalled because citizens were worried about how the government might use its expanded powers to interfere with individual freedoms, particularly those associated with political speech and engagement. The First Amendment, which ensures freedom of religion, the press, assembly, and speech, was essential to political speech and to discourse in the larger society.

The freedoms embodied in the Bill of Rights are broad principles rather than specific prohibitions. From the nation's beginnings, the vagueness of the Bill of Rights led to serious disagreement about how to interpret its amendments. For example, the First Amendment's establishment clause states simply that "Congress shall make no law respecting an establishment of religion." Some commentators, most notably Thomas Jefferson, argued that the clause mandated a "wall of separation between church and state" and barred any federal support of religion. Others

TABLE 4.2

Citizens' Protections in the Original Constitution

Clause	Protection
Article I, Sec. 9	Guarantee of *habeas corpus*—a court order requiring that an individual in custody be brought into court and told the cause for detention
Article I, Sec. 9	Prohibition of *bills of attainder*—laws that declare a person guilty of a crime without a trial
Article I, Sec. 9	Prohibition of *ex post facto laws*—retroactive laws that punish people for committing an act that was legal when the act was committed
Article III	Guarantee of a trial by jury in the state where the crime was committed

more narrowly interpreted the clause as barring only the establishment of a national religion or the requirement that all public officials swear an oath to some particular religion. This disagreement about the breadth of the establishment clause is ongoing today, as the courts continue to try to determine what the proper relationship should be between church and state.

Other freedoms, too, have been subject to differing interpretations, including the First Amendment guarantees of freedom of speech, assembly, and the press. These conflicting interpretations often arise in response to public crises or security concerns. Security concerns also affect the protections offered to those accused of threatening the safety of the nation. For example, the USA PATRIOT Act, passed by Congress almost immediately after the 9/11 attacks and amended in 2002, allows law enforcement a good deal of legal leeway. It permits agents to sidestep well-established rules that govern how searches and seizures may be conducted and to restrict criminal due process protections severely, particularly for persons suspected of involvement in organizations thought to have ties to suspected terrorists.

Incorporation of the Bill of Rights to Apply to the States

The framers intended the Bill of Rights to restrict the powers of only the *national* government. They did not see the Bill of Rights as applicable to the state governments. In general, there was little public worry that the states would curtail civil liberties, because most state constitutions included a bill of rights that protected the individual against abuses of state power. Further, it was common thinking that because the state governments were geographically closer to the people than the national government, they would be less likely to encroach upon individual rights and liberties.

The Bill of Rights was assumed to apply to the national government, not the states, through most of early U.S. history. This assumption is illustrated by the case of *Barron v. Baltimore* (1833), in which a wharf owner named Barron sued the city of Baltimore. Barron claimed that the city had violated the "takings clause" of the Fifth Amendment, which bars the taking of private property for public use without just compensation. *Barron* argued that by paving its streets, the city of Baltimore had changed the natural course of certain streams; the resulting buildup of silt and gravel in the harbor made his wharf unusable. The case centered on the idea that the Fifth Amendment protects individuals from actions taken by both the national and state or local governments. The Supreme Court disagreed, ruling that the Fifth Amendment was restricted to suits brought against the federal government.[4]

In 1868, three years after the Civil War ended, the Fourteenth Amendment was added to the U.S. Constitution. The Fourteenth Amendment reads as if it were meant to extend the protections of the Bill of Rights to citizens' interactions with *state* governments:

> No State shall make or enforce any law which shall abridge the privileges or immunities of citizens of the United States; nor shall any State deprive any person of life, liberty, or property, without due process of law; nor deny to any person within its jurisdiction the equal protection of the laws.

Although this language sounds like an effort to protect citizens' rights and liberties from arbitrary interference by state governments, the Supreme Court rejected the doctrine of **total incorporation**—that is, the application of *all* of the protections contained in the Bill of Rights to the states. Instead, beginning with a series of cases decided by the Court in the 1880s, the justices formulated a narrower approach, known as **selective incorporation.**[5] This approach considered each protection individually, one case at a time, for possible incorporation into the Fourteenth Amendment and application to the states. In each case, the justices rejected the plaintiff's specific claims of protection against the state. But they held that due process mandates the incorporation of those rights that serve the fundamental principles of liberty and justice, those that were at the core of the "very idea of free government" and that were unalienable rights of citizenship.

Despite these early cases, the Supreme Court continued to embrace the idea that although citizenship meant being a citizen of a state and of the nation as a whole, the Bill of Rights protected citizens only against the national government. As Table 4.3 shows, not until 1925 did the Court gradually begin the process of incorporation, starting with the First Amendment protections most central to democratic government and civic engagement. That year, in the case of *Gitlow v. New York,* the Court held that freedom of speech is "among the fundamental personal rights and 'liberties' protected by the due process clause of the Fourteenth Amendment from impairment by the states."[6] In 1931, in its decision in *Near v. Minnesota,* the Court added freedom of the press, and in 1937, it added freedom of assembly to the list of incorporated protections.[7]

Incorporation progressed further with the landmark case of *Palko v. Connecticut* (1937), in which the Court laid out a formula for defining fundamental rights that later courts have used time and time again in incorporation cases, as well as in due process cases more generally. The justices found that fundamental rights were rooted in the traditions and conscience of the American people. Moreover, if these rights were eliminated, the justices argued, neither liberty nor justice could exist.[8] Judges in subsequent cases have used this formula to determine which Bill of Rights protections should be applied to the states. In case after case, the justices have considered whether such a right is fundamental—that is, rooted in the American tradition and conscience and essential for liberty and justice. The objectives of civic engagement and political participation are central to this judicial calculation, as the justices have tried to determine whether the right at issue is necessary for participation in the larger civil society.

Over time, the Supreme Court has incorporated most Bill of Rights protections, as Table 4.3 summarizes. Even rights that once were not incorporated—such as the right to compensation for the government's taking of private property—have now been incorporated. Yet a few notable exceptions to the trend of incorporation remain. For example, the Third Amendment's prohibition against the quartering of soldiers in citizens' homes has not been an issue since colonial times. The Fifth Amendment's provision for a grand jury indictment runs counter to a trend in state criminal cases away from grand juries and is not required to guarantee that states adhere to Fifth and Sixth Amendment protections during the arrest, interrogation, and trial of criminal defendants. Similarly, the Seventh Amendment's provision of a jury in a civil trial is widely viewed as less important than the Sixth Amendment's guarantee of a jury trial in criminal cases in which life and liberty may be at stake.

What do we mean by *selective incorporation?* According to the table, the Supreme Court applied most Bill of Rights protections to the states over time. What are some exceptions?

TABLE 4.3

Selective Incorporation of the Bill of Rights

Amendment	Liberty	Date	Key Case
I	Freedom of speech	1925	*Gitlow v. New York*
	Freedom of the press	1931	*Near v. Minnesota*
	Freedom of assembly and petition	1937	*DeJonge v. Oregon*
	Freedom to practice religion	1940	*Cantwell v. Connecticut*
	Freedom from government-established religion	1947	*Everson v. Board of Education*
II	Right to bear arms		Not incorporated
III	No quartering of soldiers		Not incorporated
IV	No unreasonable searches and seizures	1949	*Wolf v. Colorado*
	Exclusionary rule	1961	*Mapp v. Ohio*
V	Right to just compensation (for property taken by government)	1897	*Chicago, B&Q RR Co. v. Chicago*
	No compulsory self-incrimination	1964	*Malloy v. Hogan*
	No double jeopardy	1969	*Benton v. Maryland*
	Right to grand jury indictment		Not incorporated
VI	Right to a public trial	1948	*In re Oliver*
	Right to counsel in criminal cases	1963	*Gideon v. Wainwright*
	Right to confront witnesses	1965	*Pointer v. Texas*
	Right to an impartial jury	1966	*Parker v. Gladden*
	Right to a speedy trial	1967	*Klopfer v. North Carolina*
	Right to a jury in criminal trials	1968	*Duncan v. Louisiana*
VII	Right to a jury in civil trials		Not incorporated
VIII	No cruel and unusual punishments	1962	*Robinson v. California*
	No excessive fines or bail		Not incorporated

First Amendment Freedoms: Speech, Assembly, and Press

Civic discourse and free participation in the political process have certain requirements. As we consider in this section, an individual must be able to express his or her political views through speech, assembly, and petition. The person must also live in a society with a press that is independent of government censorship. Freedom of speech, assembly, petition, and the press is essential to an open society and to democratic rule. These freedoms ensure that individuals can discuss the important issues facing the nation and try to reach agreement about how to address these matters. Scholars have referred to this sharing of contrasting opinions as the **marketplace of ideas.** It is through the competition of ideas—some of them radical, some even loathsome—that solutions emerge. Freedom of the press allows for the dissemination and discussion of these varying ideas and encourages consensus building.

The marketplace of ideas serves as a means by which people can voice concerns and views freely and where individuals can reconsider their ideas on important national and local issues. The centrality of the freedom of political expression to the First Amendment reflects the founders' belief that democracy would flourish only through robust discussion and candid debate.

The First Amendment and Political Instability

Over time, the Supreme Court has distinguished between political expression that the First Amendment protects and expression that the government may limit or even prohibit. The government has tried to limit speech, assembly, and the press during times of national emergency, when it has viewed this expression as more threatening than it would be in normal times.

The Tension between Freedom and Order   A fundamental tension exists between the Bill of Rights, with its goal of protecting individual freedoms, and the government's central goal of ensuring order. Not even a decade had gone by after the Constitution's ratification when Congress passed the Alien and Sedition Acts (1798). These laws placed the competing goals of freedom and order directly in conflict. The Sedition Act, for example, criminalized all speech and writings judged to be critical of the government, Congress, or the president. This was just the first of many times in U.S. history that lawmakers sacrificed free speech and freedom of the press in an effort to ensure national security and order. For example, President Abraham Lincoln attempted to silence political dissidents during the Civil War by mandating that they be tried in military courts, without the due process protections afforded in a civilian court. Lincoln also suspended the writ of **habeas corpus** (Latin, meaning "you have the body"), an ancient right that protects an individual in custody from being held without the right to be heard in a court of law.[9] Again, it was political dissidents who were targeted for indefinite detention without trial.

The struggle for a balance between freedom and order continues today as the United States fights a global war on terrorism. Part of the 1789 Alien and Sedition

Acts, known as the Alien Enemies Act, empowered the president to deport aliens suspected of threatening the nation's security or to imprison them indefinitely.[10] After the September 11, 2001, terrorist attacks on U.S. soil, President George W. Bush invoked these same powers for combatants, insurgents, and suspected terrorists captured in the United States or abroad. Like President Lincoln, President Bush also argued that military combatants and suspected terrorists should be tried in military tribunals and denied the protections of civilian courts, including the right to a speedy and public trial.[11]

The Historical Context for Free-Speech Laws   The Supreme Court's willingness to suppress or punish political speech has changed over time in response to perceived internal and external threats to the nation. During World War I, the Court upheld the conviction of socialist and war protester Charles Schenck for distributing a pamphlet to recently drafted men urging them to resist the draft.[12] For the first time, the Court created through its ruling a test to evaluate such government actions, called the **clear and present danger test.** Under this standard, the government may silence speech or expression only when there is a clear and present danger that this speech will bring about some harm that the government has the power to prevent. In the *Schenck* case, the Court noted that the circumstances of war permit greater restrictions on the freedom of speech than would be allowable during peacetime. The justices ruled that Schenck's actions could endanger the nation's ability to carry out the draft and prosecute the war.

Soon after the *Schenck* case, a majority of the justices moved toward a far more restrictive test that made it easier to punish citizens for the content of their speech. This test, known as the **bad tendency test,** was established in the case of Benjamin Gitlow, who was convicted of violating a New York State criminal anarchy law by publishing pamphlets calling for a revolutionary mass action to create a socialist government.[13] The political context of Gitlow's conviction is revealing: a so-called red scare—fears that the socialist revolution in the Soviet Union would spread to other nations with large populations of workers—was sweeping the nation. Gitlow's lawyer contended that there was no proof that Gitlow's pamphlet created a clear and present danger of a violent uprising. The Court disagreed, ruling that any speech that had the tendency to incite crime or disturb the public peace could be silenced.

This highly restrictive test required only that the government demonstrate that some speech may at some time help to bring about harm. The threat did not need to be immediate or even direct. The test sacrificed the freedoms of speech and the press to concerns about public safety and protection of the existing order. The bad tendency test lasted only a short while; by the late 1930s, the Court had reverted to the clear and present danger test, which the justices interpreted more broadly to protect speech and participation. The relative peace and stability of the period between the two world wars is apparent in the Court's handling of speech and press cases, as the justices required government officials to demonstrate that the speech clearly posed a danger to public safety.

Even after the Court reverted to the clear and present danger test, however, it still allowed concerns about national security to dominate its handling of First

Amendment cases. In the wake of World War II, a war of conflicting ideologies emerged between the United States and the Soviet Union. Termed the *Cold War* because it did not culminate in a direct military confrontation between the countries, this development nevertheless created a climate of fear and insecurity in both nations. Concerns about the spread of communism in the United States led to the prosecution of individuals deemed to be sympathetic to communism and socialism, under the Smith Act of 1940. This federal law barred individuals from advocating or teaching about "the duty, necessity, desirability, or propriety of overthrowing or destroying any government in the United States by force or violence."

In the most important case of this period, the Supreme Court upheld the conviction of several individuals who were using the writings of German philosophers Karl Marx and Friedrich Engels, along with those of Soviet leaders Vladimir Lenin and Josef Stalin, to teach about socialism and communism.[14] In upholding the convictions, the justices found that although the use of these writings did not pose a risk of imminent danger to the government, it created the *probability* that such harm might result. Because there was a probability that these readings might lead to the destruction of the government, the Court reasoned, the speech could be barred. The seriousness of the evil was key to the test that came out of this ruling, known as the **clear and probable danger test.** Because the government was suppressing speech to avoid the gravest danger, an armed takeover of the United States, the Supreme Court majority ruled that it was justified in its actions—even if the risk or probability of this result was relatively remote.

As the Cold War subsided and concerns diminished about a potential communist takeover of the United States, the Court shifted to a broader interpretation of the First Amendment speech and press protections. Beginning with *Brandenburg v. Ohio* (1969), the Court signaled that it would give more weight to First Amendment claims and less to government concerns about security and order. In this case, the Court considered the convictions of the leaders of an Ohio Ku Klux Klan group who were arrested after they made a speech at a televised rally, during which they uttered racist and anti-Semitic comments and brandished guns and rifles. Local officials charged them with violating a state law that banned speech that disturbed the public peace and threatened armed overthrow. In overturning the convictions, the Court reverted to a strict reading of the clear and present danger test. The justices held that government officials had to demonstrate that the speech they sought to silence went beyond mere advocacy, or words, and that it created the risk of imminent disorder or lawlessness.[15]

The Standard Today: The Imminent Lawless Action Test   The Brandenburg test, known as both the **imminent lawless action test** and the **incitement test,** altered the clear and present danger test by making it even more stringent. Specifically, after the *Brandenburg* decision, any government in the United States—national, state, or local—trying to silence speech had to show that the risk of harm from the speech was highly likely and that the harm was imminent or immediate. The imminent lawless action test is the standard the courts use today to determine whether speech is protected from government interference.

Even though the Brandenburg test is well established, the issue of whether speech is protected continues to be important. For example, since the 9/11 attacks, public

> Cleveland police officers stand guard as Ku Klux Klan demonstrators exercise their rights to free speech and assembly. Even unpopular and racially intolerant groups like the Klan are protected by the First Amendment.

attention has increasingly focused on Web sites operated by terrorists and terrorist sympathizers, especially members of militant Islamic groups. Some of these sites carry radical messages; for example, one site urges viewers to eliminate all "enemies of Allah" by any necessary means and gives instructions on loading weapons. Do First Amendment guarantees protect such sites? Courts examining this question must determine not only whether the speech intends to bring about a bad result—we would probably all agree that intent is there—but also whether the speech incites lawless action that is imminent.

Freedom of Speech

The freedom to speak publicly, even critically, about government and politics is central to the democratic process. Citizens cannot participate fully in a political system if they are unable to share information, opinions, advice, and calls to action. Citizens cannot hold government accountable if they cannot criticize government actions or demand change.

Pure Speech versus Symbolic Speech   The Supreme Court has made a distinction between pure speech that is "just words" and advocacy that couples words with actions. With respect to civic discourse, both are important. When speech moves beyond words into the realm of action, it is considered to be **symbolic speech:** nonverbal "speech" in the form of an action such as picketing or wearing an armband to signify a protest.

Unless words threaten imminent lawless action, the First Amendment will likely protect them. But in civic discourse, words are often combined with action. For example, in the 1960s, antiwar protesters were arrested for burning their draft cards to demonstrate their refusal to serve in Vietnam, and public high school students were suspended from school for wearing black armbands to protest the war. When the two groups brought their cases to the Supreme Court, the justices had to determine whether their conduct rose to the level of political expression and merited First Amendment protection. Together, these cases help to define the parameters for symbolic speech.

In the first of these cases, *U.S. v. O'Brien,* the justices considered whether the government could punish several Vietnam War protesters for burning their draft cards in violation of the Selective Service Act, which made it a crime to "destroy or mutilate" these cards. The Court balanced the free-expression guarantee against the government's need to prevent the destruction of the cards. Because the cards were critical to the nation's ability to raise an army, the Court ruled that the government had a compelling interest in preventing their destruction.[16]

In contrast, when the Court considered the other symbolic speech case of this era, *Tinker v. Des Moines,* it found that the First Amendment did protect the speech in question. In this case, the justices ruled that the political expression in the form of the students' wearing black armbands to school to protest the Vietnam War was protected.[17] Unlike burning draft cards, which could be disruptive to government activity, the Court ruled that the symbolic speech engaged in by student protestors did not disrupt normal school activities and thus warranted greater protection.[18]

The highly controversial case of *Texas v. Johnson* (1989) tested the Court's commitment to protecting symbolic speech of a highly unpopular nature. At issue was a man's conviction under state law for burning the American flag at the Republican National Convention in 1984 to emphasize his disagreement with the policies of the administration of President Ronald Reagan (1981–1989). The Supreme Court overturned the man's conviction, finding that the flag burning was political speech worthy of protection under the First Amendment.[19] After the *Johnson* decision, Congress quickly passed the Flag Protection Act in an attempt to reverse the Court's ruling. Subsequently, however, in the case of *U.S. v. Eichman* (1990), the Court struck down the new law by the same 5–4 majority as in the *Johnson* ruling.[20]

The decisions in these flag-burning cases were very controversial and have prompted Congress to pursue the only remaining legal avenue to enact flag protection statutes—a constitutional amendment. Indeed, each Congress since the *Johnson* decision has considered creating a flag desecration amendment. Since 1995, the proposed amendment has been approved biennially by the two-thirds majority necessary in the U.S. House of Representatives, but it has consistently failed to achieve the same constitutionally required super majority vote in the U.S. Senate. Senate opponents of the ban argue that ratification of the amendment would undermine the principles for which the flag stands.

Not All Speech Is Created Equal: Unprotected Speech The Supreme Court long ago rejected the extreme view that *all* speech should be free in the United States. Whereas political speech tends to be protected against government suppression, other forms of speech can be limited or prohibited.

The courts afford **commercial speech,** that is, advertising statements, limited protection under the First Amendment. According to the Supreme Court, commercial speech may be restricted as long as the restriction "seeks to implement a substantial government interest, directly advances that interest, and goes no further than necessary to accomplish its objective." Restrictions on tobacco advertising, for example, limit free speech in the interest of protecting the health of society.

Other forms of speech, including libel and slander, receive no protection under the First Amendment. **Libel** (written statements) and **slander** (verbal statements) are false statements that harm the reputation of another person. In order to qualify as libel or slander, the defamatory statement must be made publicly and with fault, meaning that reporters, for example, must undertake reasonable efforts to verify allegations. The statement must extend beyond mere name-calling or insults that cannot be proven true or false. Those who take a legal action on the grounds that they are victims of libel or slander, such as government officials, celebrities, and people involved with specific public controversies, are required to prove that the defendant acted with malice—with knowledge that the statement was false or recklessly disregarded the truth or falsity of the statement.

Obscenity—indecent or offensive speech or expression—is another form of speech that is not protected under the First Amendment. After many unsuccessful attempts to define obscenity, in 1973, the Supreme Court developed a three-part test in *Miller v. California.*[21] The Court ruled that a book, film, or other form of expression is legally obscene if

- the average person applying contemporary standards finds that the work taken as a whole appeals to the prurient interest—that is, tends to excite unwholesome sexual desire
- the work depicts or describes, in a patently offensive way, a form of sexual conduct specifically prohibited by an anti-obscenity law
- the work taken as a whole lacks serious literary, artistic, political, or scientific value

Of course, these standards do not guarantee that people will agree upon what materials are obscene. What is obscene to some may be acceptable to others. In 2009, the Supreme Court did uphold a Federal Communications Commission (FCC) policy that penalizes broadcasters with fines if curse words are uttered on the air. When Nicole Richie and Cher (who were both referred to as "foul mouthed glitteratae from Hollywood" by Justice Antonin Scalia) and Bono used what Scalia referred to as the "F- and S- words" during the 2003 Billboard Awards, Fox Television challenged the FCC policy in the Supreme Court. But the Court allowed the policy, saying that profanity referring to sex or excrement is always indecent. Nonetheless, in most realms, the Court has been reluctant to limit free speech, even in the most controversial cases.

The Court may also ban speech known as **fighting words**—speech that inflicts injury or results in public disorder. The Court first articulated the fighting-words doctrine in *Chaplinsky v. New Hampshire* (1942). Walter Chaplinsky was convicted of violating a New Hampshire statute that prohibited the use of offensive, insulting language toward persons in public places after he made several inflammatory comments to a city official. The Court, in upholding the statute as constitutional, explained the limits of free speech: "These include the lewd and obscene, the profane, the libelous, and the insulting or fighting words—those which by their very utterance inflict injury or tend to incite an immediate breach of the peace."[22] Thus the Court ruled that, like slander, libel, and obscenity, "fighting words" do not advance the democratic goals of free speech.

Freedom of Assembly

The First Amendment says that people have the freedom to assemble peaceably and to seek redress of (compensation for) grievances against the government, yet there are limits placed on assembly. As the Supreme Court has considered the parameters of free-assembly cases, it has been most concerned about ensuring that individuals and groups can get together to discuss their concerns and that they can take action in the public arena that advances their political goals.

The Court's stance in free-speech cases provides insight into its leanings in cases concerning freedom of assembly. The Court is keenly aware of the need for order in public forums and will clamp down on speech that is intended and likely to incite public unrest and anger. This is one reason the Court has reaffirmed the fighting-words doctrine. Although officials cannot censor speech before it occurs, they can take action to limit speech once it becomes apparent that public disorder is going to erupt. In its rulings, the Court has also allowed content-neutral **time, place, and manner restrictions**—regulations regarding when, where, or how expression may occur. Such restrictions do not target speech based on content, and in order to stand up in court, they must be applied in a content-neutral manner. For example, people have the right to march in protest, but not while chanting into bullhorns at four o'clock in the morning in a residential neighborhood.

The Court's rulings in these various cases illustrate how the government is balancing the freedom of public assembly against other concerns—notably, public safety and the privacy rights of certain individuals. The Court is carefully weighing the freedoms of one group of individuals against another and attempting to ensure the protection of free public expression.

Freedom of the Press

Throughout American history, the press has played a crucial role in the larger debate about political expression. Before the War of Independence, when the British monarchy sought to clamp down on political dissent in the colonies, the king and Parliament quickly recognized the urgency of silencing the press. A free press is essential to democratic ideals, and democracy cannot survive when a government controls the press. The First Amendment's guarantees of a free press ensure not only that American government remains accountable to its constituents but also that the people hear competing ideas about how to deal with matters of public concern.

Certain well-established principles govern freedom of the press in the United States. First and foremost, the courts almost never allow the government to engage in prior restraint. **Prior restraint** means censorship—the attempt to block the publication of material that is considered to be harmful. The Supreme Court established the rule against prior restraint in 1931 in the landmark case of *Near v. Minnesota*.[7] After editor Jay Near wrote a story in the *Saturday Press* alleging that Jews were responsible for corruption, bribery, and prostitution in Minneapolis, a state judge barred all future sales of the newspaper. The Court overturned the state judge's ruling, finding that the sole purpose of the order was to suppress speech. Because freedom of the press has strong historical foundations, the Court concluded, censorship is clearly prohibited.

In the *Near* ruling, the Court recognized, however, that there might be times when government officials could limit the publication of certain stories. Specifically, such censorship might be justified under extraordinary circumstances related to ensuring public safety or national security or in cases involving obscenity. In reality, though, the Court has disallowed prior restraint in the vast majority of cases. For example, in the most important case examining the national security exception, *New York Times v. U.S.* (1971), the Court rejected the government's attempt to prevent publication of documents that detailed the history of the United States' involvement in Vietnam. In this case, also known as the Pentagon Papers case, the government argued that censorship was necessary to prevent "irreparable injury" to national security. But the Court dismissed this argument, asserting that full disclosure was in the interest of all Americans and that publication of the documents could contribute to the ongoing debate about the U.S. role in the Vietnam War.[23] In their ruling, the justices recognized that some materials are clearly necessary for full and fair discussion of issues facing the nation, while others are far less important to political discourse. (The Court, for example, has allowed the government to censor publications that are far less central to public debate, such as obscene materials.)

The Court is far more willing to allow the government to impose constraints on broadcast media than print media. Why should a distinction be made between print and broadcast media? Probably the most important justification is that only a limited number of channels can be broadcast, and the government is responsible for parceling out these channels. Because the public owns the airwaves, the people may also impose reasonable regulations on those who are awarded licenses to operate these channels.

The Court views the Internet to be more like print media than broadcast media. Thus far, the Court has signaled its interpretation that the Internet is an enormous resource for democratic forums, one that allows users access to virtually unlimited sites at very low cost (*Reno v. ACLU,* 1997). The Court's fine distinctions are between media that allow more versus less access to individuals and groups to engage in political discourse. The Court's assumption is that print media and the Internet provide relatively cheap and virtually unlimited access and enable people to tap easily into discussions about issues facing the nation. In contrast, broadcast media, with much scarcer channels, represent a much more limited arena for dialogue and thus can reasonably be regulated.

Freedoms of Religion, Privacy, and Criminal Due Process

The Constitution's framers understood that the government they were creating could use its powers to single out certain groups for either favorable or unfavorable treatment and in this way could interfere with the creation of community—and with citizens' engagement within that community. The founders' commitment to community building and citizens' engagement lies at the heart of several constitutional amendments in the Bill of Rights. Specifically, these are the amendments establishing the freedom of religion, the right to privacy, and the right to due process for individuals in the criminal justice system.

The First Amendment and the Freedom of Religion

The religion clauses of the First Amendment—the establishment clause and the free-exercise clause—essentially do two things. First, they bar the government from establishing or supporting any one religious sect over another, and second, they ensure that individuals are not hindered in the exercise of their religion. While the establishment clause requires that the government be neutral toward religious institutions, favoring neither one specific religion over others nor all religious groups over nonreligious groups, the free-exercise clause prohibits the government from taking action that is hostile toward individuals' practice of their religion. As we now consider, there is a tension between these two clauses.

The Establishment Clause   Stating only that "Congress shall make no law respecting an establishment of religion," the **establishment clause** does little to clarify what the relationship between church and state should be. The Constitution's authors wanted to ensure that Congress could not create a national religion, as a number of European powers (notably France and Spain) had done; the framers sought to avoid this level of government entanglement in religious matters. Further, many colonists had immigrated to America to escape religious persecution in Europe, and although many were deeply religious, uncertainty prevailed about the role that government should play in the practice of religion. This uncertainty, too, is reflected in the brevity of the establishment clause. The question arises, does the clause prohibit the government from simply preferring one sect over another, or is it broader, encompassing any kind of support of religion?

This is a crucial question because religious institutions have always been important forums for community building and engagement in the United States. Americans continue to be a very religious people. In 2007, over 82 percent of Americans surveyed said religion was fairly or very important in their lives.[24] But even given their strong religious affiliations, most Americans believe in some degree of separation between religious organizations and the government. The real question has centered on what amount of separation the establishment clause requires.

Over time, scholars and lawyers have considered three possible interpretations of the establishment clause. One interpretation, called *separationism,* is that the establishment clause requires a *strict separation of church and state* and bars most or all government support for religious sects. Supporters of the strict separationist view invoke the writings of Thomas Jefferson, James Madison, and others that call for a "wall of separation" between church and state.[25]

A second, and more flexible, interpretation allows the government to offer support to religious sects as long as this support is neutral and not biased toward one sect. This interpretation, known as *neutrality* or the *preferential treatment standard,* would permit government support provided that this support extended to all religious groups. The third interpretation is the most flexible and reads the establishment clause as barring only establishment of a state religion. This interpretation, known as *accommodationism,* allows the government to offer support to any or all religious groups provided that this support does not rise to the level of recognizing an official religion.[26]

Which of these three vastly different interpretations of the establishment clause is correct? Over time, the Supreme Court has shifted back and forth in its opinions, usually depending on the kind of government support in question. Overall, the courts have rejected the strictest interpretation of the establishment clause, which would ban virtually any form of aid to religion. Instead, they have allowed government support for religious schools, programs, and institutions if the support advances a secular (nonreligious) goal and does not specifically endorse a particular religious belief.

For example, in 1974, the Court upheld a New Jersey program that provided funds to the parents of parochial school students to pay for bus transportation to and from school.[27] The Court reasoned that the program was necessary to help students get to school safely and concluded that if the state withdrew funding for any of these programs for parochial school students, it would be impossible to operate these schools. The impact would be the hindrance of the free exercise of religion for students and their parents.

In another landmark case, *Lemon v. Kurtzman* (1971), however, the Court struck down a state program that used cigarette taxes to reimburse parochial schools for the costs of teachers' salaries and textbooks. The Court found that subsidizing parochial schools furthered a process of religious teaching and that the "continuing state surveillance" that would be necessary to enforce the specific provisions of the laws would inevitably entangle the state in religious affairs.[28]

In the *Lemon* case, the Court refined the establishment clause standard to include three considerations. First, does the state program have a secular, as opposed to a religious, purpose? Second, does it have as its principal effect the advancement of religion? And third, does the program create an excessive entanglement between church and state? This three-part test is known as the **Lemon test.** The programs most likely to withstand scrutiny under the establishment clause are those that have a secular purpose, have only an incidental effect on the advancement of religion, and do not excessively entangle church and state.

More recently, the Court upheld an Ohio program that gave vouchers to parents to offset the cost of parochial schooling.[29] The justices ruled that the purpose of the program was secular, not religious, because it was intended to allow parents an alternative to the Cleveland public schools. Any aid to religious institutions—in this case, mostly Catholic schools—was indirect, because the primary beneficiaries were the students themselves. Finally, there was little entanglement between the church and state, because the parents received the vouchers based on financial need and then were free to use these vouchers as they pleased. There was no direct relationship between the religious schools and the state.

So where the government program offers financial support, the Court has tended to evaluate this program by using either the preferential treatment standard or the accommodationist standard. Where the program or policy involves prayer in the school or issues related to the curriculum, however, the Court has adopted a standard that looks more like strict separationism.

A series of cases beginning with *Engel v. Vitale* (1962) has barred formalized prayer in the school, finding that such prayer has a purely religious purpose and that prayer is intended to advance religious, as opposed to secular, ideals.[30] For this reason, the Court has barred organized prayer in public elementary and secondary schools on the grounds that it constitutes a state endorsement of religion.

Recently, courts have begun to grapple with the decision of some school boards to mandate the inclusion of intelligent design in the curriculum.[31] **Intelligent design** is the theory that the apparent design in the universe and in living things is the product of an intelligent cause rather than of an undirected process such as natural selection. Though not stated by some of its primary proponents, many supporters believe that the designer is God, and they seek to redefine science to accept supernatural explanations.

Advocates of intelligent design claim that unlike **creationism,** which defends a literal interpretation of the biblical story of Genesis, intelligent design is a scientific theory. For this reason, they say, school boards should be permitted to include it in the curriculum, alongside evolution. Opponents claim that intelligent design is just another form of creationism, as it is based upon a belief in a divine being, does not generate any predictions, and cannot be tested by experiment. Mandating that schools teach intelligent design, critics argue, constitutes an endorsement of religion by the state.

The Free-Exercise Clause　　A real tension exists between the establishment and free-exercise clauses. Whereas the establishment clause bars the state from helping religious institutions, the **free-exercise clause** makes it illegal for the government to enact laws prohibiting the free practice of religion by individuals. Establishment clause cases often raise free-exercise claims, and so courts must frequently consider whether by banning state aid, they are interfering with the free exercise of religion.

Although free-exercise and establishment cases raise many of the same concerns, they are very different kinds of cases whose resolution depends on distinct legal tests. Establishment clause cases typically involve well-established and well-known religious institutions. Because establishment clause cases often center on state aid to religious schools, many involve the Roman Catholic Church, which administers the largest number of private elementary and secondary schools in the country. In contrast, free-exercise clause cases tend to involve less mainstream religious groups, among them Mormons, Jehovah's Witnesses, Christian Scientists, and Amish. These groups' practices tend to be less well known—or more controversial. For example, free-exercise clause cases have involved the right to practice polygamy, to use hallucinogens, to refuse conventional medical care for a child, and to refuse to salute the flag.

The Supreme Court has refused to accept that the government is barred from *ever* interfering with religious exercise. Free-exercise claims are difficult to settle because they require that courts balance the individual's right to free practice of religion against the government's need to adopt some policy or program. First and foremost, the Court has always distinguished between religious *beliefs*, which government may not interfere with, and religious *actions*, which government is permitted to regulate. For example, although adults may refuse lifesaving medical care on the basis of their own religious beliefs, they may not refuse medical procedures required to save the lives of their children.[32]

In assessing those laws that interfere with religiously motivated action, the Court has distinguished between laws that are neutral and generally applicable to all religious sects and laws that single out one sect for unfavorable treatment. In *Employment Division, Department of Human Resources v. Smith* (1990), the Court allowed the state of Oregon to deny unemployment benefits to two substance abuse counselors who were fired from their jobs after using peyote as part of their religious practice. Oregon refused to provide benefits because the two men had been fired for engaging in an illegal activity. The Court concluded that there was no free-exercise challenge, because Oregon had good reason for denying benefits to lawbreakers who had been fired from their jobs. The justices concluded that the state was simply applying a neutral and generally applicable law to the men as opposed to singling them out for bad treatment.[33]

In summary, people are free to hold and profess their own beliefs, to build and actively participate in religious communities, and to allow their religious beliefs to inform their participation in politics and civil society. However, individual *actions* based on religious beliefs may be limited if these actions conflict with existing laws that are neutrally applied in a nondiscriminatory fashion.

The Right to Privacy

So far in this section, we have explored the relationship between civil liberties and some key themes of this book: civic participation, inclusiveness, community building, and community engagement. We now shift our focus somewhat to consider the **right to privacy,** the right of an individual to be left alone and to make decisions freely, without the interference of others. Privacy is a core principle for most Americans, and the right to make decisions, especially about intimate or personal matters, is at the heart of this right. Yet the right to privacy is also necessary for genuine inclusiveness and community engagement, because it ensures that each individual is able to act autonomously and to make decisions about how he or she will interact with others.

The right to privacy is highly controversial and the subject of much public debate. In large part, the reason is that this right is tied to some of the most divisive issues of our day, including abortion, aid in dying, and sexual orientation. The right to privacy is also controversial because, unlike the freedoms of speech, the press, assembly, and religion, it is not explicitly mentioned anywhere in the Constitution. A further reason for the debate surrounding the right to privacy is that the Supreme Court has only recently recognized it.

The Emergent Right to Privacy   For more than one hundred years, Supreme Court justices and lower court judges have concluded that the right to privacy is implied in all of the other liberties spelled out in the Bill of Rights. Not until the landmark Supreme Court case *Griswold v. Connecticut* (1965) did the courts firmly establish the right to privacy. The issue in this case may seem strange to us today: whether the state of Connecticut had the power to prohibit married couples from using birth control. In their decision, the justices concluded that the state law violated the privacy right of married couples seeking access to birth control, and they struck down the law. The Court argued that the right to privacy was inherent in many of the other constitutional guarantees, most importantly the First Amendment freedom of association, the Third Amendment right to be free from the quartering of soldiers, the Fourth Amendment right to be free from unreasonable searches and seizures, the Fifth Amendment protection against self-incrimination, and the Ninth Amendment assurance of rights not explicitly listed in the Bill of Rights. Justice William O. Douglas and his colleagues effectively argued that a zone of privacy surrounded every person in the United States and that government could not pass laws that encroached upon this zone.[34]

In its ruling, the Court asserted that the right to privacy existed quite apart from the law. It was *implicit* in the Bill of Rights and fundamental to the American system of law and justice. The right to privacy hinged in large part on the right of individuals to associate with one another—and specifically, the right of marital partners to engage in intimate association.

In a 1984 case, the Supreme Court ruled that the Constitution protects two kinds of freedom of association: (1) intimate associations and (2) expressive associations.[35] The protection of intimate associations allows Americans to maintain intimate human relationships as part of their personal liberty. The protection of expressive associations allows people to form associations with others and to practice their First Amendment freedoms of speech, assembly, petition, and religion.

The Right to Privacy Applied to other Activities   The challenge for the Court since *Griswold* has been to determine which activities fall within the scope of the privacy right, and this question has placed the justices at the center of some of the most controversial issues of the day. For example, the first attempt to extend the privacy right, which raised the question whether the right protected the right to abortion, remains at least as controversial today as it was in 1973 when the Court decided the first abortion rights case, *Roe v. Wade*.[36] In *Roe* and the many abortion cases the Court has heard since, the justices have tried to establish whether a woman's right to abortion takes precedence over any interests the state may have in either the woman's health or the fetus's life. Over time, the Court has adopted a compromise position by rejecting the view that the right to abortion is absolute and

Sharing Personal Information on the Internet

WEB SITE	THEN (2003)	NOW (2010)
MySpace	0 accounts	> 200 million accounts
Facebook	0 active users	> 200 million active users
YouTube	0 videos shared	> Hundreds of millions of videos shared daily

WHAT'S NEXT?

> Will social-networking Web sites be required to share personal information about their clients, and their clients' Internet behavior, with federal investigators?

> How will our conceptions of privacy (and privacy rights) change as people post increasing amounts of information about themselves on the Web?

> Will the courts continue to protect virtually unlimited speech on the Web?

by attempting to determine when states can regulate, or even prohibit, access to abortion. In 1992, the Court established the "undue burden" test, which asks whether a state abortion law places a "substantial obstacle in the path of a woman seeking an abortion before the fetus attains viability."[37] Using this standard, spousal notification requirements were struck down, but other requirements, including waiting periods, mandatory counseling, and parental consent, have been upheld by the Court.

In cases involving the right to engage in consensual sexual activities with a partner of one's choosing, the Supreme Court has also employed a less than absolute approach. For many years the Court allowed states to criminalize homosexual activity, finding that the right to engage in consensual sexual activity did not extend to same-sex partners.[38] In a 2002 case, *Lawrence v. Texas,* however, the Court changed course by ruling that the right to engage in intimate sexual activity was protected as a liberty right, especially when the activity occurred inside one's home, and that states could not criminalize this activity.[39] Yet beyond the *Lawrence* decision, states are still free to prohibit a range of sexual activities, including prostitution, child sexual abuse, and sex in public places.[40] In the Court's view, these activities can be prohibited primarily because they are not consensual or not taking place in the home, a place that accords special protection by the privacy right.

Public discourse about privacy is constantly evolving as people voluntarily share more and more information about themselves through online networking sites such as Facebook, MySpace, and YouTube (see "Then, Now, Next"). Users share stories, photos, and videos of themselves—as well as of others, who may be unaware that they are the subject of a blog or video. Civil libertarians worry about the misuse and theft of personal information in a high-tech society where people's financial, employment, consumer, legal, and personal histories are so easily accessible. Government and law enforcement agencies are still deciding how they may use such materials in criminal investigations. Legal implications remain unclear.

The Fourth, Fifth, Sixth, and Eighth Amendments: Ensuring Criminal Due Process

The last category of civil liberties that bear directly on civic engagement consists of the criminal due process protections established in the Fourth, Fifth, Sixth, and Eighth amendments. Does it surprise you that so many of the Bill of Rights amendments focus on the rights of individuals accused of crimes? The context for this emphasis is the founders' concern with how the British monarchy had abused its power and used criminal law to impose its will on the American colonists. The British government had used repeated trials, charges of treason, and imprisonment without bail to stifle political dissent. The founders therefore wanted to ensure that there were effective checks on the power of the federal government, especially in the creation and enforcement of criminal law. As we have seen, the Bill of Rights amendments were incorporated to apply to the states and to their criminal codes through the process of selective incorporation. Thus, criminal due process protections are the constitutional limits imposed on law enforcement personnel.

These four amendments together are known as the **criminal due process rights** because they establish the guidelines that the government must follow in investigating, bringing to trial, and punishing individuals who violate criminal law. Each amendment guides the government in administering some facet of law enforcement, and all are intended to ensure justice and fairness in the administration of the law. Criminal due process is essential to guarantee that individuals can participate in the larger society and that no one person is singled out for better or worse treatment under the law. Like the First Amendment, due process protects political speech and freedom. Without these liberties, government officials could selectively target those who disagree with the laws and policies they advocate.

Moreover, without these rights, there would be little to stop the government from using criminal law to punish those who want to take action that is protected by the other amendments we have examined in this chapter. For example, what good would it do to talk about the freedom of speech if the government could isolate or punish someone who spoke out critically against it without having to prove in a public venue that the speech threatened public safety or national security?

The criminal due process protections are essential to ensuring meaningful participation and engagement in the larger community and to safeguarding justice and fairness.

The Fourth Amendment and the Protection Against Unreasonable Searches and Seizures
The Fourth Amendment requires police to get a warrant before engaging in a search and guides law enforcement personnel in conducting criminal investigations and in searching an individual's body or property. It has its roots in colonial history—specifically, in the British government's abuse of its law enforcement powers to prosecute and punish American colonists suspected of being disloyal.

The Fourth Amendment imposes significant limits on law enforcement. In barring police from conducting any unreasonable searches and seizures, it requires that they show probable cause that a crime has been committed before they can obtain a search warrant. The warrant ensures that police officers can gather evidence only when they have probable cause. Further, a judicially created ruling known as the **exclusionary rule** compels law enforcers to carry out searches properly. Established for federal prosecutions in 1914, the exclusionary rule forbids the courts to admit illegally seized evidence during trial.[41] This rule was extended to state court proceedings in the Supreme Court decision *Mapp v. Ohio* (1961).[42] In this case, the Court overturned an Ohio court's conviction of Dollree Mapp for the possession of obscene materials. Police had found pornographic books in Mapp's apartment after searching it without a search warrant and despite the defendant's refusal to let them in. Critics of the exclusionary rule note that securing a warrant is not always necessary or feasible and that guilty people sometimes go free due to procedural technicalities. They argue that reasonable searches should not be defined solely by the presence of a court-ordered search warrant.[43]

What are "reasonable" and "unreasonable" searches under the Fourth Amendment? Over time, the U.S. Supreme Court has established criteria to guide both police officers and judges hearing cases. The strictest definition of reasonableness requires that there is a warrant: where there is no warrant, the search is considered to be unreasonable. However, the Supreme Court has ruled that even without a warrant, some searches would still be reasonable. In 1984, for example, the Court held that illegally obtained evidence could be admitted at trial if law enforcers could prove that they would have obtained the evidence legally anyway.[44] In another case the same year, the Court created a "good faith" exception to the exclusionary rule by upholding the use of evidence obtained with a technically incorrect warrant, because the police officer had acted in good faith.[45]

More broadly, a warrantless search is valid if the person subjected to it has no reasonable expectation of privacy in the place or thing being searched. From colonial times to the present, the assumption has been that individuals have a reasonable expectation of privacy in their homes. Where there is no reasonable expectation of privacy, however, there can be no unreasonable search, and so the police are not required to get a warrant before conducting the search or surveillance. Since the 1990s, the Court has expanded the situations in which there is no reasonable expectation of privacy and hence no need for a warrant. For example, there is no reasonable expectation of privacy in one's car, at least in those areas that are in plain view, such as the front and back seats. There is also no expectation of privacy in public places such as parks and stores, because it is reasonable to assume that a person knowingly exposes his or her activities to public view in these places. The same is true of one's trash: because there is no reasonable expectation of privacy in the things that one discards, police may search this material without a warrant.[46]

In instances where there is a reasonable expectation of privacy, individuals or their property may be searched if law enforcement personnel acquire a warrant from a judge. To obtain a warrant, the police must provide the judge with evidence that establishes probable cause that a crime has been committed. Further, the warrant must be specific about the place to be searched and the materials that the agents are seeking. These requirements limit the ability of police simply to go on a "fishing expedition" to find some bit of incriminating evidence.

As society changes, expectations of privacy change as well. For example, technological innovation has given us e-mail and the Web, and Fourth Amendment law has had to adapt to these inventions. Is there a reasonable expectation of privacy in our communications on the Web? This is an important question, especially in light of citizens' heightened concerns about terrorism and white-collar crime.

The Fifth and Sixth Amendments: The Right to a Fair Trial and the Right to Counsel   The Fifth and Sixth amendments establish the rules for conducting a trial. These two amendments ensure that criminal defendants are protected at the formal stages of legal proceedings. Although less than 10 percent of all charges result in trials, these protections have significant symbolic and practical importance, because they hold the state to a high standard whenever it attempts to use its significant power to prosecute a case against an individual.

The Fifth Amendment bars **double jeopardy** and compelled self-incrimination. These safeguards mean, respectively, that a person may not be tried twice for the same crime nor forced to testify against him- or herself when accused of a crime. These safeguards are meant to protect people from persecution, harassment, and forced confessions. A single criminal action, however, can lead to multiple trials if each trial is based on a separate offense.

The Sixth Amendment establishes the rights to a speedy and public trial, to a trial by a jury of one's peers, to information about the charges against oneself, to the confrontation of witnesses testifying against oneself, and to legal counsel. The protection of these liberties is promoted by the ***Miranda* rights,** based on the Supreme Court decision in *Miranda v. Arizona* (1966).[47] In the *Miranda* case, the Court outlined the requirement that "prior to questioning, the person must be warned that he has a right to remain silent, that any statement he does make may be used against him, and that he has a right to the presence of an attorney, either retained or appointed." Subsequent cases have created some exceptions to *Miranda*.

Together, the Fourth, Fifth, and Sixth amendments ensure the protection of individuals against abuses of power by the state, and in so doing, they promote a view of justice that the community widely embraces. Because these rights extend to individuals charged with violating the community's standards of right and wrong, they promote a broad sense of inclusiveness—a respect even for persons who allegedly have committed serious offenses, and a desire to ensure that the justice system treats all people fairly.

The Court has considered the community's views in reaching its decisions in cases brought before it. For example, through a series of Supreme Court cases culminating with *Gideon v. Wainwright* (1963), the justices interpreted the right to counsel to mean that the government must provide lawyers to individuals who are too poor to hire their own.[48] The justices adopted this standard because they came to believe that the community's views of fundamental fairness dictated this result.

The Eighth Amendment: Protection Against Cruel and Unusual Punishment   The meaning of *cruel* and *unusual* has changed radically since the Eighth Amendment was ratified, especially with regard to the imposition of capital punishment—the death penalty. Moreover, Americans have always disagreed among themselves about the death penalty itself. Throughout the country's history, citizens and lawmakers have debated the morality of capital punishment, as well as the circumstances under which the death penalty should be used. Central to the public debate have been the questions of which crimes should be punished by death and how capital punishment should be carried out.

Generally, the Court has supported the constitutionality of the death penalty. An exception was the landmark case *Furman v. Georgia* (1972), in which, in a 5–4 decision, the Court suspended the use of the death penalty.[49] Justices Brennan and Marshall believed the death penalty to be "incompatible with evolving standards of decency in contemporary society." The dissenting justices argued in turn that capital punishment had always been regarded as appropriate under the Anglo-American legal tradition for serious crimes and that the Constitution implicitly authorized death penalty laws because of the Fourteenth Amendment's reference to the taking of "life." The majority decision came about due to concurring opinions by Justices Stewart, White, and Douglas, who focused on the arbitrary nature with which death sentences had been imposed. The Court's decision forced the states and the national legislature to rethink their statutes for capital offenses to ensure that the death penalty would not be administered in a capricious or discriminatory manner.[50] Over time, the courts have also interpreted the Eighth Amendment as requiring that executions be carried out in the most humane and least painful manner. Public discourse and debate have strongly influenced thinking about which methods of execution are appropriate.

Recent studies, however, suggest that states' administration of the sedative sodium pentothal has left individuals conscious and in agony but paralyzed and thus unable to cry out while they are dying. But in 2008, the Supreme Court ruled in a 7–2 decision that lethal injection does not constitute cruel and unusual punishment,[51] paving the way for ten states, which had halted lethal injections pending the case's outcome, to resume executions. The 2008 decision marked the first time the Supreme Court had reviewed the constitutionality of a method of execution since 1878, when the Court upheld Utah's use of a firing squad.[52] In that ruling, the Court said the Constitution prohibits executions that involve torture, such as burning alive or drawing and quartering an individual, as well as other infliction of "unnecessary cruelty" that the justices did not define. In the recent case, lawyers for the Kentucky inmates argued that the state is violating that standard by using drugs that pose a risk of extreme pain if something goes wrong and by failing to provide adequate safeguards. But in its decision in April 2008, the Court ruled that there is no Eighth Amendment requirement that a government-sanctioned execution be pain free, only that it does not involve a "substantial" or "objectively intolerable" risk of serious harm—a risk greater than possible alternatives.

The Second Amendment and the Right to Bear Arms

The fierce debate today over gun control illustrates much about the nature of political discourse and citizen action in the United States. Americans disagree about how to interpret the Second Amendment of the Constitution, but they do agree to have their disputes settled through laws and court rulings rather than armed conflict. Private citizens and political interest groups voice their opinions about the place of guns in society by using their First Amendment freedoms of speech and assembly. They also work behind the scenes to influence elected officials through campaign contributions and lobbying (see Chapter 7). At the heart of this debate is the question of the role guns play in creating a safe and free society.

Competing Interpretations of the Second Amendment

Americans disagree about the purpose and contemporary significance of the Second Amendment, which reads

> A well regulated Militia, being necessary to the security of a free State, the right of the people to keep and bear Arms, shall not be infringed.

Some people argue that the amendment gives individual citizens the right to bear arms, free from government control.[53] On the opposing side, others stress that the Second Amendment's original purpose was to ensure that state militias could back the government in maintaining public order.[54] These people suggest that the right to bear arms is thus a group right subject to regulation by Congress and the states.[55] The unorganized militia has not been activated since before the Civil War, and the government now has adequate weapons to defend the nation, these critics say.

As Figure 4.1 illustrates, states differ widely in the degree to which citizens have access to guns. Some states allow residents to carry concealed weapons for personal protection, but others do not. In 1976, Washington, D.C., passed the nation's toughest gun control laws, including a ban on handguns, rifles, and automatic weapons, except for individuals with a special permit—mostly police and security

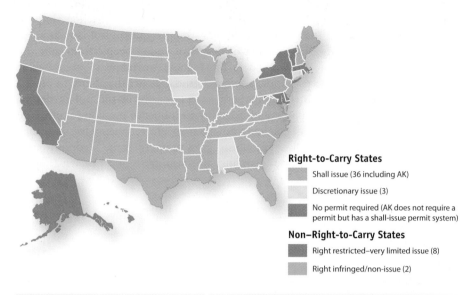

Right-to-Carry States

- Shall issue (36 including AK)
- Discretionary issue (3)
- No permit required (AK does not require a permit but has a shall-issue permit system)

Non–Right-to-Carry States

- Right restricted–very limited issue (8)
- Right infringed/non-issue (2)

POLITICAL INQUIRY

What do variations in states' laws regarding the right to carry arms indicate about interpretation of the Second Amendment? Geographically, where are most non–right-to-carry states located? What are some explanations for this trend?

FIGURE 4.1

State Conceal and Carry Gun Legislation There are forty right-to-carry (RTC) states. Of these, thirty-six have "shall issue" laws, which require that carry permits be issued to applicants who meet uniform standards established by the state legislature. Alabama, Connecticut, and Iowa have "discretionary-issue" carry permit systems. Vermont allows citizens to carry without a permit. (Alaska, which has a shall-issue provision for purposes of permit reciprocity with other states, adopted a no-permit-required law in 2003.) Of the ten non-RTC states, eight have discretionary-issue systems; two prohibit carrying altogether.

Source: http://www.nraila.org © 2009 NRA Institute for Legislative Action.

guards. In March 2007, a federal appeals court struck down the district's handgun ban, rejecting the city's argument that the Second Amendment right to bear arms applies only to militias (see "Analyzing the Sources" in Chapter 2). The city appealed the decision to the U.S. Supreme Court, which, in a 2008 ruling, affirmed the appeals court's ruling. In a 5–4 decision, the Supreme Court ruled that "the right of the people to keep and bear arms" is not limited to state militias but rather is a part of "the inherent right of self-defense."[56]

Citizens Engaged: Fighting for a Safer Nation

This disagreement over the Second Amendment's meaning is reflected in the actions of ordinary citizens and organized interest groups. For example, the Million Moms and the Second Amendment Sisters are two interest groups with clashing views on the issue of gun control. The Million Moms see stronger gun control laws as a way to prevent the alarmingly high number of deaths of young people from gun violence, an estimated ten deaths per day.[57] The Second Amendment Sisters believe that guns are a woman's best tool for self-defense and give her the ability to protect herself and her family.[58] Both groups have joined vocally in the public debate, exercising their freedom of speech and assembly to influence opinions about guns in the United States. They disagree over how best to protect themselves and their families in a dangerous world. Each group struggles to interpret the Second Amendment to fit its members' own understandings of social needs and problems today.

Civil Liberties in Post-9/11 America

Public discussion about the proper balance between individual freedom and public safety is not limited to gun control policies. Debate has intensified as the nation struggles with the aftermath of the 9/11 terrorist attacks and the continuing global war on terror. Citizens and government leaders are rethinking their beliefs about the proper scope of government power.

In the course of U.S. history, liberty and security have perennially coexisted in a state of tension. In the wake of 9/11, this tension has become more acute, as the federal, state, and local governments have taken certain actions that directly intrude upon individual freedoms. The government argues that these actions are necessary to protect life and property. But civil libertarians shudder at what they see as unprecedented violations of individual freedoms and rights.

Perceived Intrusions on Free Speech and Assembly

Following 9/11, a number of government agencies engaged in the surveillance of political groups in the United States. In late 2005, the media exposed a program by the Bush administration and the National Security Administration (NSA) to target U.S. civilians for electronic surveillance without judicial oversight. Members of the Bush administration claimed that they had monitored only communications where one party was suspected of links to terrorism and was currently overseas. Beginning in 2005, however, the American Civil Liberties Union (ACLU) issued a series of reports detailing how the FBI had spied not only on people suspected of taking part in terrorist plots but also on individuals involved in peaceful political activities.[59] In one instance, the FBI monitored the organizers of an antiwar protest who had gathered at a Denver bookstore, and agents compiled a list with the descriptions and license plates of cars in the store's vicinity. The ACLU has released similar reports describing the Pentagon's database of peaceful war protesters.[60]

What is the cartoonist's view of how civil liberties have changed since 9/11? Do you agree with this view? How might policies affecting civil liberties change in the Obama administration? Why?

Source: Ed Stein: © The Rocky Mountain News/Dist. By Newspaper Enterprise Association, Inc.

The ACLU and other critics of the domestic surveillance program have argued that the federal government is targeting political protest, not domestic terrorism plots. Opponents of the policy warn that the FBI and other agencies are infringing upon free speech, assembly, and expression. But former attorney general John Ashcroft and others in the Bush administration defended the government's expanded investigation and enforcement activities. They claimed that the threats to national security are grave and that the government must be given the power it needs to protect against these dangers.[61]

Perceived Intrusions on Criminal Due Process

Though about 10 years have passed since 2001, concern lingers about another terrorist attack on U.S. soil, and many Americans are willing to accept some infringement on their freedoms if it makes them safer. These citizens assume that real criminal activity may be afoot and that the surveillance is not being used to target groups that are politically unpopular or critical of the administration. Much of the debate about the surveillance activities of the FBI and other groups centers on this distinction.

To what extent must administration officials provide evidence of real criminal intent before placing a suspect under surveillance? In the aftermath of the 2001 terror attacks, the laws that govern domestic spying were modified in such a way

What Will Be the Legal Status of "Extraordinary Rendition" under President Obama?

The global "spider's web" of secret detentions and unlawful inter-state transfers
Rapporteur: Dick Marty, Switzerland, ALDE   Committee on Legal Affairs and Human Rights

AIRPORT KEY
Stopover points
Staging points
Pick-up points
Detainee transfer / drop-off points

Source: Council of Europe, The Venice Commission, http://assembly.coe.int/Doucument/WorkingDoes/doc06/edoc10957-1.jp

THEN: During George W. Bush's presidency, the CIA implemented a policy of "extraordinary rendition." Terrorist suspects were transferred to other nations where they faced the possibility of torture, thus circumventing U.S. law, which mandates due process rights for the accused and bars torture. This map shows where detainees were apprehended and where they were dropped off. When five individuals who charged that they had been apprehended and tortured under the extraordinary rendition program sued Jeppesen Dataplan, a subsidiary of Boeing that had arranged the rendition program, the Bush administration asserted the need to protect "state secrets" to obstruct judicial proceedings that would have challenged the legal basis of this program in the U.S. courts.

NOW: With the election of President Obama, many civil liberties interest groups believed that the courts would be able to investigate and rule on the extraordinary rendition policy. But when the Obama administration was forced to file a petition in the *Mohamed et al. v. Jeppesen Dataplan* lawsuit, Obama continued Bush's policy, again asserting that "state secrets" were at stake.

WHAT'S NEXT?

- Should the courts be allowed to rule on the legality of the policy of extraordinary rendition in the future? Why or why not?

- Why might the Obama administration continue to assert "state secrets" regarding extraordinary rendition throughout Obama's time in office? What might cause the administration to change its position?
- Why might the Obama administration continue the practice of extraordinary rendition? What reasons might the administration have for discontinuing it?

that the government has much more leeway in conducting searches and investigations, even where there is no real proof of criminal activity.

Terrorism led to important shifts in U.S. policy. One example is the USA PATRIOT Act, which Congress passed in 2001, just six weeks after the terror attacks with little debate in either the House or the Senate.[62] This law, reauthorized in 2005, allows the FBI and other intelligence agencies to access personal information and records without getting permission from, or even informing, targeted individuals. Much of the data come from private sources, which are often ordered to hand over their records. For example, the USA PATRIOT Act authorized the FBI to order Internet service providers to give information about their clients to the FBI. The act also empowered intelligence agencies to order public libraries to hand over records of materials that the targeted individuals had borrowed or viewed.

In addition, the Foreign Intelligence Surveillance Act (FISA) of 1978, which empowers the government to conduct secret searches where necessary to protect national security, has significantly broadened the powers of law enforcement agencies. Agencies must go before a specialized court, the Foreign Intelligence Surveillance Act Court, to justify the secret search. Civil libertarians are concerned about the FISA Court's secret location and sealed records, as well as its proceedings, in which the suspect is never told about the investigation and probable cause is not required to approve surveillance or searches of any person suspected of having some link to terrorism.

In July 2007, President Bush called on Congress to pass legislation to reform the FISA in order to ease restrictions on the surveillance of terrorist suspects in cases where one party or both parties to the communication are located overseas. The Protect America Act of 2007, signed into law on August 5, 2007, essentially legalized ongoing NSA practices.[63] Under the act, communications that begin or end in a foreign country may be wiretapped by the U.S. government without supervision by the FISA court. The act removes from the definition of "electronic surveillance" in FISA any surveillance directed at a person reasonably believed to be located outside the United States. As such, surveillance of these communications no longer requires an order from the FISA court. This means that the government may listen to conversations without a court order as long as the U.S. attorney general approves the surveillance. Supporters stress that flexibility is needed to monitor the communications of suspected terrorists and their networks. Critics, however, worry that the law is too vague and provides the government with the ability to monitor any group or individual it opposes, regardless of whether it has links to terrorism.

In addition to conversations about search and surveillance procedures, the nation is struggling with larger questions about the rights of detainees accused of conducting or supporting terrorist activities (see "Analyzing the Sources"). Some political

A Choice between Freedom and Security?

Source: www.anntelnaes.com Ann Telnaes Editorial Cartoon © 2002 Ann Telnaes. Reprinted with the permission of Ann Telnaes and the Cartoonist Group. All rights reserved.

Evaluating the Evidence

1. What message is the cartoonist trying to convey?
2. Do you think citizens must choose between freedom and security? Explain.
3. Do you support the central provisions of the USA PATRIOT Act and the NSA wiretapping program? Why or why not? Do such programs increase security or threaten liberty? Explain.

commentators argue that the torture of these individuals is appropriate in specific situations.[64] They point to a "ticking time bomb" scenario, in which the torture of a single suspect known to have information about the location of a nuclear bomb would be justified in order to save thousands or millions of innocent lives. Critics of this logic note that information obtained through torture is unreliable and not worth the price of violating our moral codes. Further, they argue that if the United States legalizes torture, Americans will lose their standing as a moral society and alienate potential allies in the war against terror.[65]

The debate over torture resulted in passage of the Detainee Treatment Act of 2005, which bans cruel, inhuman, or degrading treatment of detainees in U.S. custody.[66] Despite this legislation, questions remain. For example, the Hollywood film *Rendition* (2007) dramatized a controversial practice involving the transfer of custody of suspected terrorists to other nations for imprisonment and interrogation (see "Then, Now, Next" on page 164). Critics charge that the goal of such "extraordinary rendition" (which was based on an actual program the media uncovered in 2006) was to circumvent U.S. law, which requires due process and prevents torture. Former secretary of state Condoleezza Rice denied that U.S. officials transferred suspects to places where they knew these individuals would be tortured.[67] But according to a February 2007 European Parliament report, the CIA conducted 1,245 flights over European territory between 2001 and April 2006, many of them to destinations where suspects could have faced torture.[68] The 2007 confirmation hearings of Attorney General Michael Mukasey focused on the related issue of what constitutes torture. Critics of the nominee were upset by his refusal to define waterboarding—a controversial practice that simulates drowning—as illegal. While President Obama banned the practice of waterboarding as an interrogation tactic on terror suspects, unquestionably, the global war on terror has caused U.S. citizens and public officials to rethink the boundaries of acceptable behavior as they balance the need to protect the civil liberties of the accused with the desire to prevent terrorist attacks.

Perceived Discrimination Against Muslim Americans

Members of the Bush administration repeatedly said that the war on terror was not a war on immigrants or a war on Islam. Despite assurances, civil libertarians and leaders in the Muslim American community criticized administration policies targeting Muslims. Among these were policies allowing racial profiling of Arab and Muslim men; the use of secret evidence in national security cases; widespread FBI interviews of Muslims; raids of Muslim homes, schools, and mosques; the special registration and fingerprinting of Muslims from specific Arab nations; and the detention and deportation of many Arab and Muslim nationals without the right to legal representation.[69] Members of the Bush administration explained this aggressive policing in Muslim communities as a way to catch would-be terrorists and to cause them to delay or abandon their plans. Critics argued that the policies violate the civil liberties of Muslims by denying them due process.

In addition, the administration used the USA PATRIOT Act's provision barring "material support" for terrorist organizations to crack down on Muslim charitable organizations. Several Muslim charities were shut down for allegedly providing financial or other material assistance to groups the government designated as "terrorist." Critics of this policy stressed that officials used it to lock down three of the largest Muslim American charities without investigation and without proving that these organizations had links to terrorist organizations.[70] Muslims who had been donating to these nonprofit organizations as part of their *Zakat,* an Islamic charitable obligation, later found themselves questioned by the FBI.

Critics contend that administration policies have violated Muslims' freedoms of speech, religion, and association as law enforcers monitor their words, religious ceremonies, and organizational ties and as Muslims have become targets of government interrogation and even detention. In a government profiling program designed to catch would-be terrorists, race, age, and national origin, too, can lead to interrogation. Those in the Bush administration argued that it was required to do whatever it could to protect U.S. citizens from another terrorist strike. Critics worried that racial and religious profiling would alienate the 7 million Muslim citizens and would in fact jeopardize officials' ability to gather valuable intelligence. The nation's struggles to balance the demands of freedom and order are clearly illustrated in the ongoing conversation about how to protect personal liberty while ensuring national security.

CONTINUING THE CONVERSATION

CONCLUSION

- The Bill of Rights, the first ten amendments to the Constitution, reflects the U.S. political and legal systems' emphasis on individual liberties and rights. These freedoms ensure that individuals can freely participate in the political and social life of their communities, but such rights are also malleable; at times, the government has starkly limited them, as when officials perceive a threat to national security.

- The inevitable tension between freedom and order is heightened in a post-9/11 world, as Americans struggle to protect essential liberties while guarding against future terrorist attacks. This tension is reflected in contemporary debates over free speech, political protest, and due process.

- Do antiwar protests threaten the nation's success in Iraq? Should the government be able to track citizens' phone calls and e-mails? Is torture ever justifiable? These are some of the questions we confront as we struggle to maintain the commitment to liberty that defines our nation while preserving the nation itself.

STUDY NOW

Summary

1. Civil Liberties in the American Legal System

The U.S. Constitution—and more specifically, the Bill of Rights, the first ten amendments—protects individuals against the unrestrained exercise of power by the federal government, and over time, the Supreme Court has interpreted most of its protections as applying to the state governments as well.

2. First Amendment Freedoms: Speech, Assembly, and Press

Some of the civil liberties guaranteed in the Bill of Rights including the freedoms of speech, assembly, petition, and the press, exist in a state of tension with the goal of national security, and in times of crisis or instability, the judicial system has interpreted them narrowly.

3. Freedoms of Religion, Privacy, and Due Process

The freedom of religion, right to privacy, and criminal due process protections ensure that no one individual or group may be singled out for either favorable or unfavorable treatment.

4. The Second Amendment and the Right to Bear Arms

Americans actively disagree about the proper interpretation of the Second Amendment and about the role of guns in maintaining a free and safe society.

5. Civil Liberties in Post-9/11 America

In the wake of the terrorist attacks of September 11, 2001, federal and state law enforcement officials have limited the speech, assembly, and petition rights of some American citizens and nationals, and have curtailed the due process protections of those suspected of engaging in or supporting domestic and international terrorism.

For Critical Thinking and Discussion

1. Under what circumstances should the government be allowed to regulate or punish speech?

2. Under what circumstances should government be able to punish people for practicing their religious beliefs?

3. Do you believe that the USA PATRIOT Act and the NSA domestic surveillance program make the nation safer? Why or why not?

4. Will giving up liberty to enhance security protect the nation against terrorists, or will it destroy the fundamental values upon which the nation was founded? Defend your position.

Key Terms

Internet Resources

A More Perfect Union Web site
www.mhhe.com/harrisonampule   Consult the book's Web site for study guides, interactive activities, simulations, and current hot-links that provide additional information on civil liberties in the United States.

National Archives
www.archives.gov/national_archives_experience/charters/bill_of_rights.html   This organization is based in Washington, D.C.; go to this site to read an original copy of the Bill of Rights and information about its adoption.

Center for Democracy and Technology
www.cdt.org   The effect of new computer and communications technologies on American civil liberties is the subject of this site.

Electronic Privacy Information Center
www.epic.org/privacy   Find out more about privacy issues related to the Internet here.

Public Broadcasting Service
www.npr.org/news/specials/patriotact/patriotactprovisions.html   PBS provides a summary of controversial provisions of the USA PATRIOT Act, including major arguments for and against each provision.

Recommended Readings

Ackerman, Bruce. *Before the Next Attack: Preserving Civil Liberties in an Age of Terrorism.* New Haven, CT: Yale University Press, 2006. A recent work advocating the creation of an "emergency constitution" with specific time limits that would give the government enhanced national security powers in times of crisis while protecting civil liberties during normal circumstances.

Bollinger, Lee C., and Geoffrey R. Stone, eds. *Eternally Vigilant: Free Speech in the Modern Era.* Chicago: University of Chicago Press, 2002. Drawing on the work of legal scholars, an examination of the philosophical underpinnings of free speech, with a highlighting of the history of contentious free-speech disputes.

Carroll, Jamuna, ed. *Privacy.* Detroit, MI: Greenhaven Press, 2006. An edited volume of point-counterpoint articles exploring a wide variety of issues, including counterterrorism measures, Internet privacy, video surveillance, and employee monitoring.

Spitzer, Robert J. *The Politics of Gun Control,* 4th ed. Washington, DC: CQ Press, 2007. An analysis of the gun control debate in the United States, including its history, the constitutional right to bear arms, the criminological consequences of guns, citizen political action, and the role and impact of American governing institutions.

African Americans, women, Native Americans, Latinos, and other groups struggled to achieve equality in the United States.

Groups of citizens continue to struggle for their civil rights, including Asian Americans, lesbians and gay men, and citizens with disabilities.

NOW

5

Civil Rights

Although the Declaration of Independence promises equality, throughout U.S. history, this promise has seemed just beyond the grasp of many individuals and groups. The fact that people disagree strongly about what "equal treatment" requires is at the heart of many struggles for equality. Does equal treatment bar all differential treatment of any group or individual when it is based on innate characteristics, specifically race, national origin, sex, or religion? Should this list include sexual orientation and persons with disabilities?

In this chapter, we examine the concept of equality under the law, focusing on how, through various types of civic activism, groups that were originally deprived of equal protection in American society have been able to obtain their civil rights. For nearly the first century of our nation's history, much of the debate about equality focused on the plight of Africans and African Americans under slavery. After passage of the Thirteenth Amendment in 1865, which outlawed slavery, African Americans, Native Americans, and other disenfranchised groups shifted their attention to the challenge of obtaining the right to vote (suffrage).

Civil rights advocates have also pressed for equal access not only to voting but to all realms of public and private life, including the educational system, employment, housing, and public accommodations. Modern civil rights activists contend that the right to equal

NEXT

What groups of immigrants, racial or ethnic minorities, or other disadvantaged citizens will fight for their civil rights?

What criteria will the U.S. Supreme Court use in deciding cases concerning sex-based discrimination?

How will technology shape the issues and demands at the forefront of future civil rights battles?

protection under the law guarantees this access, though community resistance and continuing discrimination may thwart equal protection and render even the most ambitious court decisions ineffective.

The Quest for Equality Under the Law

When asked what principles or ideals they hold most dear, many Americans will mention freedom and equality, often in the same breath. As we discussed in Chapter 4, the ideal of freedom is very much at the heart of our commitment to civil liberties. Freedom of expression, the press, religion, and assembly are at the core of American political culture, as is the commitment to due process for criminal defendants. As we noted in Chapter 2, the Constitution was ratified only after the framers agreed to introduce the Bill of Rights in the first session of Congress. This Bill of Rights, comprising the first ten amendments to the Constitution, essentially bars the federal government from interfering with certain basic freedoms.

While the issue of protecting civil liberties was in the forefront at the nation's founding, the issue of guaranteeing civil rights reached the national agenda much later.[1] When we talk about **civil rights** in the United States, we mean the rights and privileges guaranteed to all citizens under the equal protection and due process clauses of the Fifth and Fourteenth amendments.[2] Included in these rights is the idea that individuals are protected from discrimination based on inherent characteristics such as race, national origin, religion, and sex. When a person or an organization interferes with a person's civil rights, the government has an obligation to intervene to remove these obstacles.

Inherent characteristics such as race, national origin, religion, and sex merit a greater level of protection than other qualities. When people are treated differently solely because of their membership in a particular racial or religious group, or because of their ancestry or sex, this discrimination is based on assumptions about the characteristics of the group, rather than on the unique qualities of the individual members of that group. Because no real consideration is given to the individual's unique characteristics, this kind of discrimination is arbitrary and unfair.

What is the government's role in ensuring equality? Most of us agree that no government should treat people differently based on race, ethnicity, national origin, or sex. But people disagree about whether this list should also include characteristics such as disability and sexual orientation. Americans also disagree about what should happen when a private person or an organization, and not a governmental

Fighting for Their Rights: How Groups and Issues Change

THEN (1960s AND 1970s)	NOW (2010)
African Americans, women, Native Americans, and Latinos fought for equal treatment under the law.	Asian citizens, citizens with disabilities, and lesbian, gay, bisexual, and transgendered citizens fight for equal treatment under the law.
Key strategies included nonviolent civil disobedience, protests, and the seeking of remedy through the justice system.	Protest and lawsuits remain important strategies, but today's activists also focus on petitioning Congress and state legislatures in attempts to pass legislation.
Important issues included equal access to schools, public accommodations, voting rights, and equal pay.	Important issues include spousal rights for gays and lesbians, voting rights, immigration policy, and discrimination against Muslim Americans.

WHAT'S NEXT?

> What groups will begin to seek ways of achieving their civil rights?

> How will new technologies change the strategies and tactics that civil rights activists use?

> What important issues will be at the forefront of the civil rights agenda in the future?

agency or official, engages in discriminatory behavior. Some believe that the government should vigorously pursue equality, even when its actions intrude upon individual freedoms or group privileges. Others accept a much more limited role for the government in these matters.

Let's use a familiar example of classifications. It may make sense for the government to require that people be at least 18 years old before they can vote because 18-year-olds have reached the level of maturity needed to make an informed decision.

It makes no sense, however, to impose a blanket ban on voting by racial, ethnic, or religious groups or by women. Race, religion, national origin, and sex are **suspect classifications** because the government considers distinctions based on these characteristics to be illegitimate. To establish whether a classification is "suspect," courts consider whether it is immutable (incapable of being changed), whether the group in question has experienced a history of discrimination, and whether the group is unable to effect change through the political process. Many argue that the list of suspect classifications should be expanded to include sexual orientation, ability or disability, and native language. While some states have barred discrimination against people who fit within these categories, there is less than full agreement among the states as to whether they merit the highest level of protection under the law.

For most of our nation's history, the law not only allowed unequal treatment for different racial, ethnic, and religious groups, as well as for men and women, but it also *required* this unequal treatment for a majority of the population. Women were not granted the right to vote until 1920, and they faced a variety of discriminatory practices. Ethnic and religious groups also faced widespread discrimination, some as a matter of law. For example, more than 120,000 people of Japanese ancestry

▷ In some places, segregation extended well beyond schools and housing, affecting every aspect of daily life. Irish American citizens were barred from applying for jobs. African Americans attending theaters were forced to use separate entrances, here with the ironic promise of "good shows in comfort."

were forcibly interned in camps during World War II. More recently, following the terrorist attacks of September 11, 2001, the federal government detained thousands of Arabs and Arab Americans in prisons without providing any criminal due process protections. But probably the most blatant example of discrimination in U.S. history is slavery. This practice was protected under the law, and slaves were considered to be the property of their owners. They had no protection under the law and could be treated in any way their owners saw fit.

Slavery and Its Aftermath

When it was first written, the Constitution implicitly endorsed the unequal and discriminatory treatment of African Americans.[3] Some of the most important provisions of the new constitution treated people of African descent as property, allowing states to continue to permit them to be enslaved. Although the movement to abolish slavery was in its early stages in 1787, the year the Constitution was completed, by the early to mid-1800s, it had gained significant momentum in the North, largely because of the activism of various religious and humanitarian groups.[4]

Slavery in the United States

In 1619, twenty Africans arrived in Jamestown as *indentured servants,* workers with a fixed term of service. But by the mid-1600s, slavery had begun to replace indentured servitude. Today most African Americans are the descendents of Africans who were forcibly brought to the New World.

Opposition to Slavery   Many chafed at the hypocrisy of those who sought freedom and equality but kept slaves. Among the first to challenge slavery were former slaves, who staged both peaceful protests and armed insurrections in the late 1700s and early 1800s. These activists successfully rallied support in the North for the abolition of slavery by 1804. They argued forcefully against the injustice of the slave system, moving the opponents of slavery to action by their horrifying firsthand accounts of the treatment of slaves.

Despite these arguments, the U.S. Congress, wary of the divisiveness caused by the slavery issue, sought to balance the antislavery position of the abolitionist states with the proslavery sentiments of the slaveholding states. One such attempt was the Missouri Compromise, passed by Congress in 1820. The compromise regulated slavery in the newly acquired western territories: slavery was prohibited north of the 36°30′ north parallel, except within the state of Missouri.

The abolitionists, including organizations like the American Anti-Slavery Society, objected to the efforts of Congress to accommodate the slaveholding states and called for the emancipation of all slaves. Members of the American Anti-Slavery Society were actively engaged in **civil disobedience**—nonviolent refusal to comply with laws and government policies that are morally objectionable—by supporting the Underground Railroad, a series of safe houses that allowed slaves to escape to the northern states and Canada. Between 1810 and 1850, an estimated 100,000 people escaped

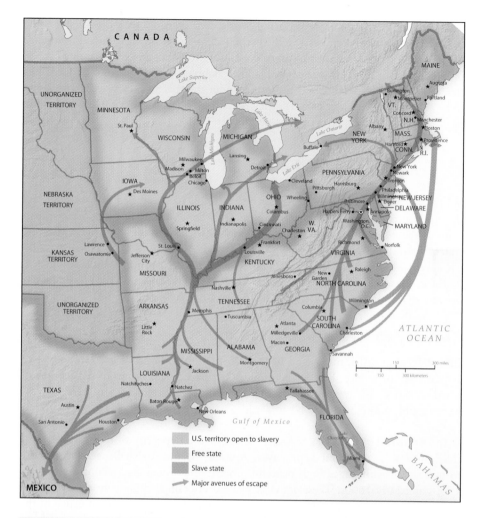

FIGURE 5.1 ■ ROUTES TO FREEDOM ON THE UNDERGROUND RAILROAD
Why did many escaping slaves use routes that followed the Mississippi River or the Atlantic coast? Which northern cities were important "stations" on the Underground Railroad? Why was legislation such as the Fugitive Slave Act ultimately powerless to stop this movement?

slavery through the Underground Railroad (see Figure 5.1). But in 1850, the U.S. Congress—in an attempt to stall or prevent the secession, or separation, of southern states from the Union—passed the Fugitive Slave Act. The law required federal marshals to return runaway slaves or risk a $1,000 fine (over $20,000 in today's dollars), while private citizens who harbored or abetted runaway slaves could be imprisoned for six months and fined $1,000. Passage of this statute meant that "conductors" on the Underground Railroad operated in clear violation of the law, risking their own livelihoods and property.

The Civil War Era   Abolitionists were bolstered in their efforts when Harriet Beecher Stowe's popular book *Uncle Tom's Cabin* was published in 1852. Vividly depicting the harsh reality of slavery in the United States, this work inspired many to actively challenge slavery. By the late 1850s, the widespread distribution of *Uncle Tom's Cabin,* as well as the trial and execution of John Brown, a white abolitionist who tried to ignite a slave insurrection in Harpers Ferry, in what was then Virginia and is now West Virginia, had convinced many northerners that slavery was immoral.

Yet the U.S. Supreme Court ruled otherwise. In 1857, Dred Scott, an African American slave held by a surgeon in the U.S. Army, sued for his freedom, arguing that because he had lived in both a free state (Illinois) and a free territory (the Wisconsin Territory, now Minnesota), he had become a free man, and as such could not be re-enslaved when he moved to Missouri. (Figure 5.1 shows states that did and did not allow slavery at this time.) The Supreme Court rejected Scott's claim and, in *Dred Scott v. Sandford,* ruled that the Missouri Compromise of 1820 was unconstitutional because the U.S. Congress lacked the authority to ban slavery in the territories.[5] It also ruled that Scott was not a U.S. citizen, asserting that slaves were property rather than citizens with **standing to sue,** or the legal right to bring lawsuits in court. While the *Dred Scott* decision appeared to be a victory for slaveholding states, it was also pivotal in mobilizing the abolitionist movement and swaying public opinion in favor of a war to prevent secession and to bring about emancipation.

Certain that their way of life was under siege and alarmed by the election of Abraham Lincoln as president in 1860, the southern states decided that they should secede from the union. By May 1861, eleven southern states had declared their independence and created the Confederate States of America. A long and bloody civil war followed as the North fought to bring the southern states back into the union.

One of the most important turning points of the Civil War was the Emancipation Proclamation, issued by President Lincoln in April 1862. This order abolished slavery in the states that had seceded from the Union. The Union army and navy were charged with implementing the order. The proclamation decreed that the abolition of slavery was a goal of the war, and in doing so, it effectively prevented Britain and France from intervening in the war on the southern side because these countries had both renounced the institution of slavery. When the South finally surrendered in April 1865, it did so knowing that its economic way of life, which depended on slave-based plantation farming, was over. At the end of the war, nearly 4 million slaves in the United States were freed, and three Constitutional amendments were ratified to codify the victories won on the battlefield:

- the Thirteenth Amendment (1865), which ended slavery throughout the United States and prohibited it in the future
- the Fourteenth Amendment (1868), which defined *citizens* as "all persons born or naturalized in the United States" and mandated the same privileges and immunities for all citizens and due process and equal protection for all people
- the Fifteenth Amendment (1870), which decreed that every man has the right to vote, regardless of color

Reconstruction and the First Civil Rights Acts

After the North won the war and Lincoln was assassinated in April 1865, members of Congress and others in government disagreed about the best way to proceed in the South. Many Republicans thought that the South should be stabilized and quickly brought back into the political fold. Like Lincoln, these moderates endorsed a plan that would enable the southern states to be quickly represented in Congress. Others, however, took a more radical view and argued that anyone who had ever supported the confederacy should be barred from national and state politics. As the 1860s drew to a close, many of these more radical Republicans had come to power and had strictly limited the people in southern states who could participate in politics. As a result of their activities, during the **Reconstruction era** between 1866 and 1877—when the institutions and the infrastructure of the South were rebuilt—freed slaves, who could easily say they had never supported the confederacy, made up a sizable portion of both the electorate and the candidate pool in the southern states. Federal troops provided protection that facilitated their participation. During this decade, African American voters made the most of their position in the South and elected a substantial number of other African Americans to legislative offices in the local, state, and federal governments. In some places, such as South Carolina, African American legislators outnumbered whites, giving them a majority during the Reconstruction years.

Between 1865 and 1875, Congress passed a series of laws designed to solidify the rights and protections outlined in the Thirteenth, Fourteenth, and Fifteenth amendments. Congress needed to spell out the rights of African Americans because of the pervasiveness of **Black Codes,** laws passed immediately after the Civil War by the confederate states that limited the rights of "freemen," or former slaves. These codes prevented freemen from voting, owning property, or bringing suit. To remedy this situation, Congress passed laws that sought to negate the Black Codes. One law, the Civil Rights Act of 1866, extended the definition of *citizen* to anyone born in the United States (including freemen) and granted all citizens the right to sue, own property, bear witness in a court of law, and enter into legal contracts. The Enforcement Act of 1870 bolstered the Fifteenth Amendment by establishing penalties for interfering with the right to vote. The Civil Rights Act of 1872, also known as the Anti–Ku Klux Klan Act, made it a federal crime to deprive individuals of their rights, privileges, or immunities. Although the Reconstruction-era Congress sought to remedy the new forms of inequality that emerged after the Civil War, its efforts would be short-lived.

Backlash: Jim Crow Laws

In 1877, the inauguration of President Rutherford B. Hayes (1877–1881) brought the Reconstruction era to a decisive end, almost immediately rolling back the gains African Americans had achieved in education and political participation. Under Hayes, the federal troops that had protected African Americans from physical reprisals were withdrawn. State and local governments throughout the South mandated racial segregation by enacting what came to be known as **Jim Crow laws.** These laws required the strict separation of racial groups, with whites and "nonwhites" going to separate schools, working in different jobs, and using segregated public accommodations, such as transportation and restaurants.

State and local governments in the South also found creative ways to prevent African Americans from exercising their right to vote. They relied on several tactics:

- The **white primary** was a primary election in which only white people were allowed to vote. Because Democrats dominated politics so heavily in the post–Civil War South, the only elections that really mattered were the primaries that determined the Democratic nominees. But Southern states restricted voting in these primaries to whites only.

- The **literacy test** determined eligibility to vote. Literacy tests were designed so that few voters would stand a chance of passing the exam administered to African American voters, while the test for white voters was easy to pass. Typically, white voters were exempt from literacy tests because of a grandfather clause (see below).

- A **poll tax,** a fee levied for voting, often presented an insurmountable obstacle to poor African Americans. White voters were often exempt from poll taxes because of a grandfather clause.

- The **grandfather clause** exempted individuals from conditions on voting (such as poll taxes or literacy tests) if they themselves or their ancestor had been eligible to vote before 1870. Because African Americans did not have the right to vote in southern states before the Civil War, the grandfather clause was a mechanism to protect the voting rights of whites.

These laws were enforced not only by government agents, particularly police, but by nongovernmental groups as well. Among the most powerful of these groups was the Ku Klux Klan (KKK). Throughout the late 1800s and into the 1900s, the Klan used its powers to threaten and intimidate those African Americans and whites who dared to question its core principle: that whites are in every way superior to African Americans. The Klan's particular brand of intimidation, the burning cross and the lynching noose, was reviled throughout the southern and border states, but few could dispute the power the Klan wielded in these areas.

Governmental Acceptance of Discrimination

The federal government too had seemingly abandoned African Americans and the quest for equality under the law. In the *Civil Rights Cases of 1883,* the Supreme Court ruled that Congress lacked the authority to prevent discrimination by private individuals and organizations. Rather, Congress's jurisdiction, the Court claimed, was limited to banning discrimination in official acts of state or local governments. The Court also declared that the Civil Rights Act of 1875, which had sought to mandate "full and equal enjoyment" of a wide variety of facilities and accommodations, was unconstitutional.

In 1896, the Court struck what seemed to be the final blow against racial equality. In 1890, Louisiana had passed a law that required separate accommodations for blacks and whites on railroad trains. Several citizens of New Orleans sought to test the constitutionality of the law and enlisted Homer Plessy, who was one-eighth African American (but still considered "black" by Louisiana state law) to serve as plaintiff. (The choice of Plessy, who could "pass" for white, was intended to show the arbitrary nature of the statute.) On June 7, 1892, Plessy boarded a railroad car designated for whites only. When asked to leave the whites-only car, Plessy refused. He was then arrested and jailed, charged with violating the state law. In 1896, the U.S. Supreme Court heard **Plessy v. Ferguson,** in which Plessy's attorneys argued that the Louisiana state law violated the **equal protection clause** of the Fourteenth Amendment, which states that no state shall "deny to any person within its jurisdiction the equal protection of the laws."

In a 7–1 decision, the Court rejected Plessy's arguments, claiming that segregation based on race was not a violation of the equal protection clause. Rather, the court made this argument:

> We consider the underlying fallacy of the plaintiff's argument to consist in the assumption that the enforced separation of the two races stamps the colored race with a badge of inferiority. If this be so, it is not by reason of anything found in the act, but solely because the colored race chooses to put that construction upon it.[6]

In its decision, the Court created the **separate but equal doctrine,** declaring that separate but equal facilities do not violate the Fourteenth Amendment's equal protection clause. Under this doctrine, the Court upheld state laws mandating that the races be separated in schools and all public accommodations such as businesses, public transportation, restaurants, hotels, swimming pools, and recreational facilities. The only condition the Court placed on these segregated facilities was that the state had to provide public facilities for both whites and nonwhites. The Court paid little attention to whether the school systems or public accommodations were comparable in quality. As long as the state had some kind of facilities in place for both whites and nonwhites, the segregation was permitted. This doctrine would become the legal backbone of segregationist policies for more than five decades to come.

The Civil Rights Movement

In the early decades of the twentieth century, African Americans continued their struggle for equality. Though the movement for civil rights enjoyed some early successes, the century was nearly half over before momentous victories by civil rights activists finally began to change the status of African Americans in revolutionary ways. These victories were the result of strong leadership at the helm of the movement, the effective strategies used by activists, and a national government that was finally ready to fulfill the promise of equality embodied in the Declaration of Independence.

Fighting Back: Early Civil Rights Organizations

In the early years of the twentieth century, the political climate was open to reform, with activists in the Progressive movement calling for an end to government corruption, reforms to labor laws, the protection of children from abusive labor practices, and an expansion of rights, including the right of women to vote and the civil rights of African Americans (see Chapter 8 for more on the Progressive movement). In 1909, influential African American social scientist W. E. B. Du Bois joined with Oswald Garrison Villard (publisher of the *New York Evening Post,* an influential newspaper, and grandson of the abolitionist leader William Lloyd Garrison) to form the National Association for the Advancement of Colored People (NAACP). One of the targets the NAACP would focus on over the next several decades was the separate but equal doctrine, which remained in place through the first half of the twentieth century.

Citing the lack of graduate schools, law schools, and medical schools for African Americans, the NAACP argued that the states had violated the equal protection clause by failing to make such schools available to African Americans. During the 1930s, lawsuits brought by the NAACP in several states ended discriminatory admissions practices in professional schools.[7] Momentum in the movement for equality continued to grow, fueled in part by the growing political activism of African American soldiers returning home after fighting against fascism abroad during World War II. Many of these soldiers began to question why they were denied freedom and equality in their own country, and they mobilized for civil rights in their communities. Though the Supreme Court had not yet overturned the separate but equal doctrine, by 1950, it had ruled that segregating classrooms, dining rooms, or library facilities in colleges, universities, and professional schools was unconstitutional.

Taking cues from these court decisions, by the 1950s, the NAACP and other groups had changed their tactics. Instead of arguing that states had to provide equivalent schools and programs for African Americans and whites, these groups began to argue that segregation itself was a violation of the equal protection clause. But it was not until 1954 that the U.S. Supreme Court struck down the separate but equal doctrine, finding it inherently unequal and therefore unconstitutional.

The End of Separate but Equal

In the fall of 1951, Oliver Brown, a welder at the Santa Fe Railroad yard in Topeka, Kansas, sought to have his daughter Linda enrolled in the third grade in an all-white public school seven blocks from their home. The act was not accidental; it was the calculated first step in a legal strategy that would result in sweeping changes to the nation's public school system, effectively shattering the segregated school system dominant in the South.[8] The Browns lived in an integrated neighborhood in Topeka, and Topeka schools were segregated, as allowed (but not required) under Kansas state law. Linda was denied admission, and instead was required to walk six blocks to a bus stop and then travel a mile by bus to attend her segregated school. Oliver Brown had spoken with a Topeka attorney and with the Topeka NAACP, which convinced him to join a lawsuit against the Topeka Board of Education and directed him to attempt to register his daughter at the all-white public school.

The stand taken by Oliver Brown and the other plaintiffs was not in vain. Thurgood Marshall, who would go on to become the first African American to sit on the U.S. Supreme Court, argued the case, and in a unanimous decision in 1954, the Supreme Court ruled in **Brown v. Board of Education of Topeka** that segregated schools violate the equal protection clause of the Fourteenth Amendment. In one stroke, the Court concluded that "separate but equal" schools were inherently unequal since they stamped African American children with a "badge of racial inferiority" that stayed with them throughout their lives.

In a second case the following year (sometimes called the second *Brown* decision or *Brown II*), the court grappled with the issue of how the first *Brown* decision should be implemented—recognizing that many southern states would be reluctant to enforce the decision unless they were made to do so. In its decision, the justices called on the states to dismantle the segregated school system "with all deliberate speed" but left it to local officials to determine how to achieve a desegregated system. Many have criticized the Court's unwillingness or inability to provide more concrete guidelines to local and state officials, contending that the Court's failure to act ultimately undermined the impact of the *Brown* opinion. Nevertheless, the Court's decision in this case signaled both a new era in civil rights law and a governmental climate favorable to changing centuries-long inequalities in American society.[9]

Rosa Parks's Civil Disobedience on a Montgomery Bus

In December 1955, a now-legendary woman named Rosa Parks was on a bus returning home from work as a seamstress at a Montgomery, Alabama, department store. In Montgomery and throughout the South, buses were segregated, with white riders boarding in the front and sitting front to back and African American riders sitting back to front.[10] The bus driver asked the 43-year-old African American woman to give up her seat for a white man; Parks refused and was arrested for violating a local segregation law. (See "Analyzing the Sources.")

The Montgomery chapter of the NAACP, of which Parks and her husband were active members, had sought a test case to challenge the constitutionality of the state's Jim Crow laws. Parks agreed to participate in the case, and her arrest came at a pivotal time in the civil rights movement. Activists were buoyed by the *Brown* decision. Momentum favored the civil rights activists in the South, and their cause was bolstered when civil rights and religious leaders in Montgomery chose a 27-year-old preacher relatively new to the city to lead a bus boycott to protest the segregated public facilities. His name was Martin Luther King Jr.[11]

Dr. Martin Luther King Jr. and the Strategy of Civil Disobedience

Over the course of the year-long bus boycott, King became a national symbol for the civil rights movement, as the boycott garnered national media attention. King's leadership skills were put to the test during the year-long battle: he was arrested; his home was bombed; death threats were made against him. But for 381 days, the buses of Montgomery remained virtually empty, resulting in a serious loss in revenue to the city and causing the NAACP to be banned in the state of Alabama. African Americans walked to and from work, day in and day out, for over a year. White employers drove some domestic servants to and from work. Finally, in

A Famous Image from the Civil Rights Era

Chances are you have seen this famous photograph before. It is a powerful image. Rosa Parks is the African American woman who refused to obey the law requiring her to give up her seat and move to the back of the bus for a white man. Her refusal and subsequent arrest were the catalyst for a 381-day bus boycott in Montgomery, Alabama, a boycott that ended when the Supreme Court ruled that Montgomery's segregated bus law was unconstitutional. This photo of Parks sitting on a bus in front of a white man was taken a month later.

Evaluating the Evidence

① The man sitting behind Rosa Parks is Nicholas Chriss, a reporter who was working for United Press International at the time the photograph was taken. Who do you think most people looking at this photograph assume that he is? Who did you think he was when you first saw the image?

② Journalists and civil rights advocates, who wanted to create a dramatic, lasting image of the landmark Court decision, had to talk Rosa Parks into having the picture taken. Do you think the photo's impact would be diminished if more people knew about its origin?

③ What is your opinion of the ethics of using a staged photograph such as this one? Can a staged photograph accurately depict a historic event? Why or why not?

December 1956, the U.S. Supreme Court ruled that segregated buses were unconstitutional.[12] The bus boycott was a success on many fronts: its righteousness was confirmed by the Supreme Court; the protests garnered national media attention and evoked public sympathy; and the civil rights movement gained an articulate leader who was capable of unifying and motivating masses and who had an effective strategy for challenging the racism of American society.

Nonviolent Civil Disobedience   King advocated protesting government-sanctioned discrimination through civil disobedience. Indeed, African American students, as well as white students and other civil rights activists from throughout the country, used the tactics of civil disobedience, including boycotts, sit-ins, and marches, to challenge the policies of segregation. One such demonstration was held in August 1963, in which hundreds of thousands of black and white Americans heard King deliver his famous "I Have a Dream" speech in the shadow of the Lincoln Memorial. (You can view the speech on YouTube at www.youtube.com/watch?v=PbUtL_0vAJk.)

The Reaction to Civil Disobedience   One famous series of marches occurred in early March 1965 from Selma to Montgomery, Alabama. On Sunday, March 7, about 600 civil rights activists began a march out of Selma, protesting the policies of intimidation and violence that prevented African Americans from registering to vote. The demonstrators, led by John Lewis (now a Democratic member of Congress from Georgia), walked only six blocks to Edmund Pettus Bridge, where law enforcement officials, including Alabama state troopers and members of the sheriff's office of Dallas County, Alabama, were waiting.[13] When the peaceful protesters attempted to cross the bridge, law enforcement officers brutally attacked them, using tear gas, bullwhips, and nightsticks. Dubbed Bloody Sunday, the march and the beatings were televised nationally and were instrumental in swaying public opinion in favor of civil rights. The marches sparked a renewed focus on the lack of voting rights for African Americans and ultimately helped to pressure Congress to pass the Voting Rights Act in 1965.[14]

King, who was not present at the Bloody Sunday march, returned to Selma to lead another march on the following Tuesday. When law enforcement officers again confronted the marchers at the bridge, King asked his followers to kneel in prayer and then turn around and return to their starting point. Critics charged that King was giving in to law enforcement and questioned his nonviolent tactics.[15] Differences over the use of nonviolent civil disobedience generated divisions within the civil rights movement,[16] with more militant leaders such as Stokely Carmichael and Malcolm X advocating more aggressive tactics.[17]

While the violence used against protesters generated positive opinions of the civil rights movement, another form of violence, urban riots, eroded feelings of goodwill toward the movement. For five days in 1965, rioting in the Watts neighborhood of Los Angeles resulted in thirty-four deaths, more than 1,000 injuries, and over 4,000 arrests. Though the immediate cause of the violence was an altercation between white police officers and an African American man who had been arrested for drunk driving, the frustration and anger that spilled over had long been brewing in this poor, predominantly African American neighborhood.

> On Sunday, March 7, 1965, Alabama state troopers move in on civil rights marchers with swinging clubs and tear gas. The ferocity of their attack, televised nationally, helped sway public opinion in favor of the marchers' cause.

On April 4, 1968, Martin Luther King was in Memphis, Tennessee, in support of African American sanitation workers who were striking for equal treatment and pay with white workers. Standing on a balcony at the Lorraine Motel, King was killed by an assassin's bullet. Heartbreak, hopelessness, and despair followed King's assassination—feelings manifested in part by further rioting in over a hundred cities. Many Americans, both black and white, objected to the looting depicted in nightly news broadcasts. But those who sympathized with the rioters noted that because of the accumulated injustices against African Americans, the government and the rule of law had lost legitimacy in the eyes of those who were rioting.

The Government's Response to the Civil Rights Movement

The civil rights movement is credited not only with ending segregation in public schools but also with desegregating public accommodations such as buses, restaurants, and hotels and with promoting universal suffrage. As a result of the movement, Congress passed the Voting Rights Act, which aggressively sought to counter nearly one hundred years of disenfranchisement, as well as the 1964 Civil Rights Act, which bars racial discrimination in accommodations and private employment, and the 1968 Civil Rights Act, which prohibits racial discrimination in housing.

The Civil Rights Act of 1964

Simultaneously expanding the rights of many Americans and providing them with important protections from discrimination, the Civil Rights Act of 1964 includes provisions that mandate equality on numerous fronts:

- It outlaws arbitrary discrimination in voter registration practices within the states.
- It bans discrimination in public accommodations, including in hotels, restaurants, and theaters.
- It prohibits state and local governments from banning access to public facilities on the basis of race, religion, or ethnicity.
- It empowers the U.S. attorney general to sue to desegregate public schools.
- It bars government agencies from discrimination and imposes the threat of the loss of federal funding if an agency violates the ban.
- It establishes a standard of equality in employment opportunity.

The last part of the act, Title VII, which established the equality standard in employment opportunity, provided the legal foundation for a body of law that regulates fair employment practices. Specifically, Title VII bans discrimination in employment based on inherent characteristics—race, national origin, religion, and sex. Title VII also established the Equal Employment Opportunity Commission (EEOC), a government body that still administers Title VII today.

Other Civil Rights Legislation in the 1960s

While the Civil Rights Act of 1964 sought to address discrimination in access to public accommodations, employment, and education, many civil rights leaders believed that further legislation was necessary to protect the voting rights of African Americans in the South because they had been so systematically intimidated and prevented from participating.[18] In some southern counties, less than a third of all eligible African Americans were registered to vote, while nearly two-thirds of eligible white voters were registered in the same counties.

The Voting Rights Act of 1965 (VRA) sought to rectify this disparity in two ways. First, the VRA banned voter registration practices, like literacy tests, that discriminated based on race. Second, the VRA mandated federal intervention in any county in which less than 50 percent of eligible voters were registered. Under this tough enforcement mechanism, dozens of federal voter registration agents were sent to many southern counties. During the summer of 1965, thousands of civil rights activists, including many college students, worked to register voters. Within months, a quarter-million new voters had been added to the voting rolls.

One component of the VRA provided for periodic review of some of its tenets. After a specified period of time, Congress must pass and the president must sign an extension of the law to have these requirements remain in effect. In 2008, the government again extended the VRA. Although the VRA permanently eliminated discriminatory practices such as literacy tests, the Department of Justice is responsible for monitoring other practices. The law includes a requirement that in some states (where less than 50 percent of eligible voters were registered)* "any voting qualification or prerequisite to voting, or standard, practice, or procedure with respect to voting" must first be cleared with the Department of Justice.

In 1968, in the aftermath of Martin Luther King's murder on April 4, Congress passed and President Lyndon Johnson signed an additional piece of civil rights legislation. The Civil Rights Act of 1968 sought to end discriminatory practices in housing, including mortgage lending. The act banned the practice of **steering,** in which realtors would steer African American families to certain neighborhoods and white families to others. One part of the act also made it a federal crime for individuals to tamper with the civil rights of others, thus offering protection for civil rights workers.

Impact of the Civil Rights Movement

The culmination of many acts of resistance by individuals and groups, the civil rights movement has had a momentous impact on society by working for the laws and rulings that bar discrimination in employment, public accommodations, education, and housing. The movement has also had a profound impact on voting rights by establishing the principle that the laws governing voter registration and participation should ensure that individuals are permitted to vote regardless of their race. As shown in Figure 5.2, as a result of the Voting Rights Act, in Mississippi, for example, the percentage of African Americans registered to vote jumped from 7 percent in 1965 to 72 percent in 2006. In some states, including Georgia, Mississippi, and North Carolina, a greater percentage of African Americans are registered than whites. In addition, all states, especially those in the South, have seen an enormous increase in the number of African Americans elected to serve in offices at the state, county, and municipal levels and in school districts. Indeed, more African Americans serve in elected office in Mississippi than in any other state, and all southern states boast among the highest numbers of African American elected officials.[19]

In addition to having a profound impact on race relations and civil rights law, the civil rights movement soon came to be regarded by other groups as a model of political engagement. Ethnic minorities, women, the disabled, and gays and lesbians have adopted many tactics of the movement in their own quest to secure their civil rights.

---

*These states include Alaska, Alabama, Arizona, Georgia, Louisiana, Mississippi, South Carolina, and Texas, plus some counties in California, Florida, New York, North Carolina, South Dakota, and Virginia.

The Voting Rights Act and Voter Registration Rates, 1965 and 2006

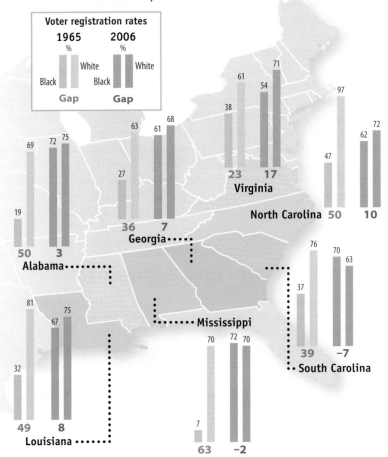

POLITICAL INQUIRY

FIGURE 5.2 ■ In view of the profound impact of the Voting Rights Act, as indicated by the data presented here, has the act outlived its usefulness? What might be some reasons for continuing the act? For discontinuing it?

Source: www.usdoj.gov/crt/voting/intro/intro_c.htm and authors' calculations based on www.census.gov/population/socdemo/voting/cps2006/tab04b.xls.

The Movement for Women's Civil Rights

As already noted, the pronouncement in the Declaration of Independence that "all men are created equal" initially applied only to white men, and usually only to those who owned property. Not only did the concept of equal protection of the laws not apply to nonwhite male citizens, until the Civil War amendments to the Constitution and subsequent pieces of national legislation such as the Voting Rights and Civil Rights acts, it did not apply to female citizens—white or nonwhite. Like African Americans, women had to wait until the Constitution was amended and civil rights legislation was adopted in response to the women's rights movement.

Advocates for women's civil rights began their efforts in the mid-1800s, initially focusing on gaining the right to vote for women citizens. This endeavor, the first wave of the women's rights movement, won suffrage for women in 1920. The cause of women's civil rights was rejuvenated in the 1960s, when the second wave of the movement began. This second wave continues today.

The First Wave of the Women's Rights Movement

The segregation of the women delegates at the 1840 World Anti-Slavery Conference in London was a defining moment for the first wave of the U.S. women's rights movement. Forced to sit in the balcony behind a drawn curtain, Lucretia Mott and Elizabeth Cady Stanton recognized that without improving their own legal and political status, women were not going to be successful in fighting for the legal rights of other groups of people.

In 1848, Mott and Stanton organized a meeting at Seneca Falls, New York, to discuss the lack of legal rights of U.S. citizens who happened to be born female. At the end of the convention, the participants signed the Declaration of Sentiments (see Appendix D). This declaration, modeled after the Declaration of Independence, listed many rights and opportunities that the law did not guarantee women, including the right to vote, educational and employment opportunities equal to those of white men, and married women's rights to own property and to sue.

Clearly, John Adams and the other architects of the Constitution had ignored Abigail Adams's request to her husband and his colleagues to "remember the ladies" when they created the new system of government. Adams warned her husband that not only would women not feel bound to obey laws in which they had no say but that the ladies would "foment a rebellion" if they were not provided a voice in government.

The signatories of the Declaration of Sentiments began Adams's forecasted rebellion. The document they signed insisted "that [women] have immediate admission to all rights and privileges which belong to them as citizens of these United States." For those women and men who joined this new movement for women's rights, the right to vote became the focal point. They recognized that this right was the foundational right that would enable women to win the other rights and privileges of citizenship.

Because the Constitution initially reserved for the states the authority to determine who had the right to vote, as well as to be employed and obtain the best possible education, many of the initial battles for women's rights took place at the state level of government. Eventually, as the national government's responsibilities expanded through court interpretations of the Constitution, especially the Fourteenth Amendment, its role in guaranteeing civil rights expanded as well.

State-Level Rights Even after ratification of the Fourteenth Amendment (1868) guaranteeing equal protection of the laws for all people and the same privileges and immunities to all citizens, women's educational and work opportunities were limited by social norms and by state laws. Education for girls prepared them to be good wives and mothers, not to be economically independent. By the late 1800s, a few colleges had begun to admit women, and several women's colleges were established. Yet most colleges did not offer women the same educational opportunities as men, and women who graduated and aspired to a career were limited in two ways. First, by choosing a career, these educated women gave up the possibility of marriage. They were not legally banned from marriage, but societal norms prevented them from having both a career and a husband. Second, their career choices were limited: teaching, the developing professions of nursing and social work, or missionary work.

In 1873, Myra Bradwell challenged women's limited career choices when she sued the state of Illinois over its refusal to let her practice law.[20] She argued that the Fourteenth Amendment's privileges and immunities clause protected her right to earn a living in a career of her choice. In this case, the Supreme Court found that women's God-given destiny was to "fulfill the noble and benign offices of wife and mother" and that allowing women to practice law would impinge on this destiny. The *Bradwell* case established the precedent for the Court to allow women to be treated differently from men (sex-based discrimination) if the different treatment was deemed a *rational* means by which the government could fulfill a *legitimate* public interest. This guideline for determining in a specific case whether sex-based discrimination is legal became known as the **ordinary scrutiny test** (also labeled the **rational basis test**). In the *Bradwell* case, the Court deemed it legitimate for the government to protect the role of women as wives and mothers, and in order to accomplish this protection, it was rational to deny them equal employment opportunities.

In 1875, another women's rights case came before the Supreme Court. In this case, Virginia Minor of Missouri (actually her husband, because she, like all married women, did not have legal standing to sue) challenged the constitutionality of Missouri's law that guaranteed the right to vote only to male U.S. citizens. In this case, *Minor v. Happersett,* the Court acknowledged that women were citizens, yet it also decreed that state governments established voting rights, not the U.S. Constitution.[21] Therefore, the justices argued, the Fourteenth Amendment's privileges and immunities clause did not give women rights not established in the Constitution, and so it did not extend to women the right to vote. While by 1875 some local governments (school districts specifically) had extended voting rights to women, no state other than New Jersey had granted women the right to vote. Women who owned property in New Jersey had the right to vote for a brief period between the end of the War for Independence and 1807, when it was taken away in response to the lobbying of politicians and professional men.

In 1890, when the Wyoming Territory became a state, Wyoming women, who had been voting in the territory since 1869, retained their voting rights. In this same year, two women's suffrage organizations, both of which had been established in 1869, merged to begin a new phase in their battle for women's suffrage.

The Nineteenth Amendment to the Constitution   The American Women's Suffrage Association (AWSA), directed by Lucy Stone, had been leading the battle to extend the right to vote to women in the states. At the same time, the National Women's Suffrage Association (NWSA), directed by Susan B. Anthony and Elizabeth Cady Stanton, was fighting to extend to women all rights of citizenship, including but not limited to the right to vote. Unlike the AWSA, the NWSA focused its suffrage battle on the federal level—specifically, on amending the U.S. Constitution. In 1890, frustrated by their lack of success in the battle to extend suffrage to women, the AWSA and the NWSA joined forces, creating the National American Women's Suffrage Association (NAWSA). The NAWSA focused its efforts on amending the U.S. Constitution.

In 1916, Alice Paul founded the National Women's Party, which adopted more radical tactics than the NAWSA had been willing to use in its fight for suffrage. Noting the lack of support on the part of national officials for suffrage, Paul's organization called on voters in the 1916 election not to vote for candidates who did not support women's suffrage, including President Woodrow Wilson, who was running for reelection. In 1917, after President Wilson was reelected, Paul and other suffragists chained themselves to the White House fence and called on Wilson to support the suffrage amendment. Arrested, jailed, and force-fed when they engaged in a hunger strike, the women gained media attention, which in turn brought national attention to their struggle for suffrage and the president's opposition. After several months and persistent media pressure, President Wilson called on the House and the Senate to approve the women's suffrage amendment.

By June 1919, the House and the Senate had approved what was to become the Nineteenth Amendment. In 1920, Tennessee became the thirty-sixth state to ratify the amendment, and it was added to the Constitution.

The Second Wave of the Women's Rights Movement

After the Nineteenth Amendment was added to the Constitution, the push for women's rights ceased to be a mass movement. Women were still organized in groups and lobbied the government for women's civil rights, but the many women's organizations were no longer working collectively toward one agreed-upon goal, such as the right to vote. Another mass women's movement did not arise until the 1960s. Several factors account for the mobilization of the second wave of the women's movement in the 1960s, which focused this time on the plethora of rights related to the social, economic, and political status of women, many of the same rights originally demanded in the Declaration of Sentiments.

By the 1960s, large numbers of women were working outside the home in the paid labor force. Working women talked with each other about their work and family lives and came to recognize common concerns and problems, including discrimination in educational opportunities, employment opportunities, and pay; lack of child care; domestic violence; the problem of rape, for which *they* were often blamed; and their inability to obtain credit (borrow money) without having a male cosign on the loan. Women recognized that as a class of citizens they did not have equal protection of the laws.

> Members of the Business and Professional Women (an advocacy and educational organization that has promoted women's equity since 1919) and Representative Catherine May (R-Washington), one of the thirteen women serving in Congress at the time, surround President John Kennedy as he signs the Equal Pay Act in 1963. President Barack Obama is surrounded by six of the ninety women serving in Congress in 2009, including Nancy Pelosi, the Speaker of the House of Representatives, as he signs the Lilly Ledbetter Fair Pay Act, which remedies loopholes in the Equal Pay Act. Ledbetter, standing to the left of the president, sued her employer after learning that—over a period of nineteen years—her pay was lower than that of her male coworkers who were doing the same job. Her failed discrimination lawsuit fueled the bill's passage.

In 1961, at the prodding of Esther Peterson, director of the Women's Bureau in the Department of Labor, President John F. Kennedy (1961–1963) established a Commission on the Status of Women, chaired by Eleanor Roosevelt. In 1963, the commission reported that women in the United States were discriminated against in many areas of life, including education and employment. In its report, the commission argued that women needed to pursue lawsuits that would allow the Supreme Court to interpret properly the Fourteenth Amendment's equal protection clause, hence prohibiting discrimination against women.

By the mid-1960s, the women's rights movement had been rejuvenated by a second wave of mass activity. The goal of this second wave was equal legal rights for women. The means to achieve this goal were legislation, litigation, and an as yet unsuccessful attempt to enact the Equal Rights Amendment (ERA), which had been written by Alice Paul and first introduced in Congress in 1923.

Federal Legislation and Women's Rights In 1955, Edith Green (D-Oregon) introduced into Congress the first piece of national legislation written specifically to protect women—the Equal Pay Act. Enacted into law in 1963, the act prohibited employers from paying women less than men were paid for the same job, which was the standard employment practice at the time. Indeed, beginning with school boards in the mid-1800s and the federal Mint during the Civil War, governments had hired women specifically because they could pay them less than men.

The 1964 Civil Rights Act as initially drafted prohibited discrimination in education, employment, and public accommodations based on race, ethnicity, and religion. Yet because of congressional women's efforts, Title VII of the proposed act was rewritten to prohibit discrimination in all personnel decisions based on *sex* as well as the other categories. Initially, the EEOC, the federal agency responsible for monitoring Title VII implementation, did not take sex-based discrimination complaints seriously. Women serving on state committees on the status of women responded by establishing the National Organization for Women (NOW) in 1966. NOW's initial statement of purpose is modeled on the requests of the 1848 Seneca Falls Declaration of Sentiments, demonstrating the continued lack of progress toward the goal of women's equality under the law.[22]

In order to take advantage of Title VII's promise of equal employment opportunities, women needed to pursue educational opportunities on an equal basis with men. Yet Title VI of the 1964 Civil Rights Act does not prohibit sex-based discrimination in institutions that receive federal funds, including educational institutions. By 1972, women's rights advocates had won an amendment to the 1964 Civil Rights Act, Title IX, which prohibits such sex-based discrimination in education.

The Equal Pay Act, Title VII, and Title IX are landmark pieces of national legislation that provide equal protection of the law for women. At the same time that Congress was enacting laws prohibiting sex-based discrimination, the courts were reinterpreting the equal protection clause of the Fourteenth Amendment.

Women's Rights and the Equal Protection Clause   In 1971, in the case of *Reed v. Reed,* the Supreme Court for the first time in history used the equal protection clause of the Fourteenth Amendment to find a law that discriminated against women unconstitutional.[23] In the *Reed* case, the Supreme Court found that an Idaho state law giving automatic preference to men to administer the estate of a deceased person who had not named an administrator was not a reasonable means to fulfill a legitimate government interest. Hence, using the ordinary scrutiny test established in the 1873 *Bradwell* case, the court ruled that this discriminatory treatment of women was unconstitutional.

Then, in 1976, the Supreme Court developed a new test for the legality of sex-based discrimination. Oklahoma law allowed women 18 years of age to buy beer with 3.2 percent alcohol content. Yet men in Oklahoma had to be 21 years of age to purchase 3.2 percent beer. Men challenged the law, asking the Court to decide if this sex-based discrimination was constitutional. In this case, *Craig v. Boren,* the Court established a **heightened scrutiny test** (also labeled the **intermediate scrutiny test**) for sex-based discrimination cases: different treatment is legal if it is *substantially* related to an *important* government interest.[24] The Court used this intermediate scrutiny test in the *Craig* case to find the Oklahoma law unconstitutional.

Today, courts sometimes use the ordinary scrutiny test and other times the intermediate scrutiny test when deciding sex-based discrimination cases, as well as other non–race-based discrimination cases. In comparison, the courts use the strict scrutiny test in race-based discrimination cases, as well as cases regarding certain liberties: freedom of religion, press, and assembly and privacy rights. The **strict scrutiny test** allows discrimination only if the different treatment is *necessary* to fulfill a *compelling* government interest. This test is much harder to pass than the ordinary scrutiny test.

Proponents of an ERA argue that the strict scrutiny test should be used in sex-based discrimination cases and that this will not happen until the Constitution is amended to explicitly guarantee equality of rights under the law whether a person is a man or a woman.

The Proposed Equal Rights Amendment During the 1970s, as the Supreme Court was reinterpreting the implications of the Fourteenth Amendment for sex-based discrimination, lobbying for the Equal Rights Amendment increased. In 1972, Congress approved the ERA, which states that "Equality of rights under the law shall not be denied or abridged by the United States or by any State on account of sex." Finally, forty-nine years after it was first introduced in Congress, the ERA was sent to the states for ratification.

Opponents of the ERA argued that it was a duplication of the Fourteenth Amendment and therefore was not needed. Opponents also claimed that passage of the amendment would make women subject to the military draft; would lead to the integration of all single-sex institutions, including schools and public bathrooms; and would result in the legalization of and public funding for all abortions. Moreover, they argued that the ERA was not needed because Congress was passing laws that guaranteed women equal protection in employment and education. Whether or not the claims of its opponents were accurate, they were successful in defeating the ERA, which had not been ratified by enough states by the deadline of 1982. The effort to ratify an ERA continues.

The first wave of the women's rights movement won the vote through constitutional amendment. The second wave successfully expanded women's civil rights through litigation and legislation. Yet many women's rights advocates argue that women still battle inequities, including unequal pay, sexual harassment, and the glass ceiling (aspiring to higher-level jobs but being unable to win them). Although the situation for women has greatly improved, some argue, not all women have benefited equally from gains in women's rights. Nonwhite women have two characteristics that can lead to discriminatory treatment, gender and color, necessitating a struggle for equal protection on two fronts: the women's rights movement and the civil rights movement of their racial group. We now explore the struggles of several other groups of citizens for equal civil rights.

Other Civil Rights Movements

Today, discriminatory treatment is still a reality for many groups of citizens. The Civil Rights Act notwithstanding, discrimination in employment, education, housing, and due process still occurs. Some employers make personnel decisions, from hiring to setting salaries, based on sex, race, ethnicity, English fluency, and disability. Because of the Supreme Court's ruling in the *Brown* case, no government in the

United States can write laws that segregate people based on their race or the color of their skin (unless such segregation passes the strict scrutiny test). **De jure segregation,** or segregation by law, is unconstitutional. Yet because people tend to live in neighborhoods with others of their race, religion, or ethnic group, schools are still segregated by race and color, producing **de facto segregation.** Poorer-quality schools are more common in communities dominated by African American and Latino residents. Housing discrimination can come in many forms: landlords illegally refuse to rent to and realtors selectively show homes for sale to people based on the color of their skin or their lack of fluency in English. Law enforcement officers may also select people for stopping, questioning, and even searching based on the color of their skin (racial profiling) instead of for reasonable cause based on their actions.

Unfortunately, we cannot discuss all of the civil rights movements that have occurred in the United States. Therefore, we will explore the civil rights battles of just a few groups of citizens: Native Americans, Hispanic Americans, Asian Americans, citizens with disabilities, and lesbian, gay, bisexual, and transgendered people. The hard-fought victories and aspirations of these groups offer an overview of both the history and the breadth of contemporary civil rights movements.

Native Americans' Rights

At first, the fledgling nation recognized the native residents of the land that became the United States as members of sovereign and independent nations with inherent rights. The federal government entered into more than 370 treaties with Native American tribes between 1778 and 1870.[25] Most of these treaties promised land to tribes that agreed to move, and almost all of these promises were empty, with the government reneging on most of these agreements. In addition, in 1830, Congress passed the Indian Removal Act, which called for the forced relocation of all native peoples to lands west of the Mississippi. In the end, most Native Americans were dispossessed of their lands and wound up living on reservations. The federal government treated Indians as subhumans, relegating them to second-class status, as they had African Americans.

Until Congress passed the Indian Citizenship Act in 1924, Native Americans had no rights to U.S. citizenship, and even the laws that allowed immigrants to become citizens did not apply to Native Americans. The Indian Rights Association, founded in 1882 and active in lobbying Congress and the state legislatures until the 1930s, was one of the most important of the early groups that actively campaigned for full suffrage for native peoples, in the belief that enfranchisement would help to "civilize" them. The early 1900s also saw the founding of the Society of American Indians and the American Indian Defense Association, both of which fought for citizenship for Native Americans and then for their civil rights. However, for more than forty years after passage of the Indian Citizenship Act, the basic rights enumerated in the Bill of Rights were not granted to Native Americans.

In the 1960s, Indian activists became more radical, occupying government buildings, picketing, and conducting protests. In 1968, the American Indian Movement

(AIM) was founded. In the same year, Congress passed the Indian Civil Rights Act, which ensured that Native Americans would have the full protection of the Bill of Rights. While this law had significant symbolic impact, it lacked an enforcement mechanism, and so native peoples continued to be deprived of basic due process protections and equal education and employment opportunites.

During the 1970s, Native American organizations began a new effort to force the federal government to honor treaties granting Indians fishing and hunting rights, as well as rights to the natural resources buried in their lands. Indians in New York, Maine, and elsewhere sued for land taken from them decades or even a century ago in violation of treaties. Starting with the 1975 Indian Self-Determination and Education Assistance Act, the national government has enacted laws that support greater autonomy for Indian tribes and give them more control of their assets.

The 1988 Indian Gaming Regulatory Act is the best known of the federal laws enacted to support Indian self-determination. This law authorizes Indian tribes to establish gaming operations on their property and requires them to negotiate compacts with the states in which their lands are located. The compacts typically include a profit-sharing understanding. The act mandates that the money made through gaming operations must be used for education, economic development, infrastructure (for example, roads and utilities), law enforcement, and courts. By 2003, there were 310 Indian gaming operations, operating under 198 tribe and state gaming compacts in twenty-eight states and accounting for about 10 percent of the U.S. gaming industry.[26] Clearly, one goal of the Gaming Act was to generate resources that would increase the educational and employment opportunities on Indian reservations.

Even with gaming profits, however, the prospects for many Native Americans today remain bleak. According to race and ethnic relations scholars Joe R. Feagin and Clairece Booher Feagin, "Native Americans have endured the longest Depression-like economic situation of any U.S. racial or ethnic group."[27] They are among the poorest, least-educated U.S citizens. Like many other groups of U.S. citizens with characteristics that identify them as non–white European descendants, Native Americans continue to fight in the halls of government, in the courtrooms, and in the public arena for their constitutionally guaranteed rights and privileges.

Citizens of Latin American Descent

U.S. citizens of Latin American descent (Latinos) include those whose families hail from Central America, South America, or the Caribbean. Latinos are the largest minority group in the United States, making up 15 percent of the total U.S. population in 2007 (45.5 million people). Sixty percent of this Latino population is composed of natural-born U.S. citizens.[28] Latinos make up a large percentage of the population of several states, including New Mexico, California, Texas, Arizona, and Florida.

Twenty-two percent of Latinos are eligible voters—U.S. citizens at least 18 years of age. In 2008, 50 percent of these eligible voters voted.[29] So far, the elections that have occurred in the twenty-first century have been followed by numerous lawsuits claiming that individual citizens, organized groups, and local governments have prevented eligible Latino voters from voting. For example, in 2006, the national government sued Philadelphia's city government for failing to assist voters effectively—specifically, Spanish-speaking voters who had limited English proficiency. Limited English proficiency continues to cause problems with access to voting and equal educational and employment opportunities for many U.S. citizens, including Latino citizens. We focus here on U.S. citizens of Mexican origin—the largest Latino population in the United States today.

Early Struggles of Mexican Americans   In 1846, because of land disputes sparked by white immigrants from the United States encroaching on Mexican territory, the United States declared war on Mexico. By the terms of the 1848 Treaty of Guadalupe Hidalgo, which ended the war, Mexico ceded territory to the United States for $15 million. The Mexican landowners living within this ceded territory had the choice of staying on their land and remaining in what was now the United States or relocating to Mexico. According to the treaty, those Mexicans who stayed on their land would become U.S. citizens, and their civil rights would be protected. While nearly 77,000 Mexicans chose to do so and became U.S. citizens, their civil rights were *not* protected.[30] Thus began a long and continuing history of discrimination against U.S. citizens of Mexican descent.

At the turn of the twentieth century, Mexican Americans organized to protest the various forms of discrimination they were experiencing, which included segregated schools, inequities in employment opportunities and wages, discrimination by law enforcement officers, and barriers to their voting rights such as poll taxes and English-only literacy tests. In 1929, several Mexican American organizations combined to create the League of United Latin American Citizens (LULAC).[31]

In 1945, LULAC successfully challenged the segregated school systems in California, which provided separate schools for Mexican children that were of poorer quality than the schools for white children. In this case, *Mendez v. Westminister,* the federal court set an important precedent by using the Fourteenth Amendment to guarantee equal educational opportunities.[32] In 1954, the U.S. Supreme Court followed this lower court's precedent when it ended legal race-based segregation in public schools throughout the nation in the *Brown v. Board of Education of Topeka* case.

The Chicano Movement   In addition to the women's rights movement and the civil rights movement for African American rights, the 1960s witnessed the birth of the Chicano movement, the mass movement for Mexican American civil rights. The Chicano movement was composed of numerous Latino organizations focusing on a variety of issues, including rights to equal employment and educational opportunities. One of the most widely recognized leaders in the Chicano movement was Cesar Chavez.

Cesar Chavez began his civil rights work as a community organizer in 1952, encouraging Mexican Americans to vote and educating them about their civil rights. In the early 1960s, Chavez, along with Jessie Lopez and Dolores Huerta, founded the Agricultural Workers Organizing Committee (AWOC) and the National Farm Worker Association (NFWA). Under Chavez's leadership, the AWOC and the NFWA merged

> Cesar Chavez began his civil rights work as a community organizer in 1952 by encouraging Mexican Americans to vote and use their civil rights. Together with Dolores Huerta, he founded the United Farm Workers. From the early 1960s until his death in 1993, Chavez was the leading voice for and organizer of migrant farmworkers in the United States. Today, Huerta is the most prominent Chicana labor leader in the country, developing leaders and advocating for the rights of immigrant workers, women, and children.

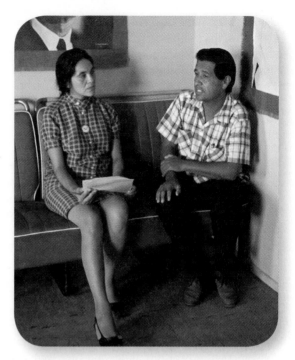

to form the United Farm Workers (UFW) in 1966. The UFW organized successful protests and boycotts to improve working conditions and pay for farmworkers.[33]

Until 1971, Latinos were not legally considered a racial minority group, and so antidiscrimination laws, such as the 1964 Civil Rights Act, did not apply to them. In the landmark case *Corpus Christi Independent School District v. Cisneros*[34] (1971), the Supreme Court upheld a lower court's ruling that Latinos are a racial minority group; therefore, they are covered by laws protecting the rights of minority groups.[35]

Employment Discrimination and Other Civil Rights Issues Since the 1986 Immigration Reform and Control Act went into effect, organizations that work to protect the rights of Latinos and other minority citizens have been receiving increasing numbers of complaints about employment discrimination. Under this act, employers who hire undocumented immigrant workers are subject to sanctions. In order to comply with this law, some employers refuse to hire—and thus discriminate against—any applicants for whom English is a second language and any who look Latino under the assumption that all such people could be undocumented immigrants. This means that employers are violating the equal employment rights of Latino citizens in many cases, for they are mistakenly assuming they are undocumented immigrants.

Today, U.S. citizens of Mexican descent continue to experience violations of their civil rights. LULAC, along with the Mexican American Legal Defense and Education Fund (MALDEF, founded in 1968) and other organizations, continues to fight for laws that will provide due process and equal protection, equal access to education, and other civil rights for Latino citizens and immigrants. They also work to educate Latinos about their rights and empower them to engage in the political process. Through the efforts of these and other groups, Hispanic voter registration and turnout has significantly increased in recent elections; however, Hispanic turnout is still lower than that of all other ethnic groups except Asian Americans.[36] We now turn to the history and ongoing efforts to obtain and protect the civil rights of Asian citizens.

Citizens of Asian Descent

Asian American citizens come from, or have ancestors from, a number of different countries with diverse cultures, religions, histories, and languages. Today, the largest percentage of Asian Americans have Chinese origins, followed by those of Filipino, Asian Indian, Vietnamese, Korean, and Japanese ancestry. Large numbers of immigrants from Japan came to the United States around the turn of the twentieth century, but it was not until the 1940s that the flow of immigrants from other Asian countries began to increase, beginning with the Philippines. In the 1960s, the number of immigrants from Korea and India began to increase significantly, and in the 1970s—as the Vietnam War ended—immigrants from Vietnam began to arrive in large numbers. Today, 4 percent of the U.S. population is of Asian descent.

Like other U.S. citizens with non–white European ancestry, Asian Americans have had to fight continually for their civil rights—specifically, for equal protection under the law and, particularly, for equal access to educational and employment opportunities, as well as citizenship. Asian immigrants and Asian Americans created organizations to fight for citizenship and equal protection of the law, such as the Japanese American Citizens League (JACL, founded in the 1930s). One successful result of these efforts was the 1952 Immigration and Nationality Act, which allowed Asian immigrants to become citizens for the first time. Before passage of this law, only U.S.-born children of Asian immigrants could be citizens.

Internment of Japanese Americans During World War II As noted previously, one of the most egregious violations of the civil rights of tens of thousands of Asian American citizens occurred during World War II when Americans of Japanese ancestry were forced to move to government-established camps. Under President Franklin Roosevelt's Executive Order 9066, over 120,000 Japanese Americans, two-thirds of whom were native-born U.S. citizens, were relocated from the West Coast of the United States after Japan's attack on Pearl Harbor. During this same period, the federal government also restricted the travel of Americans of German and Italian ancestry who were living on the West Coast (the United States was also fighting against Germany and Italy), but these citizens were not relocated. Many relocated Japanese Americans lost their homes and businesses.

The JACL fought for decades to obtain reparations for the citizens who were interned and for the repeal of a section of the 1950 Internal Security Act that allowed the government to imprison citizens deemed enemy collaborators during a crisis. Congress repealed the section of the 1950 law targeted by the JACL, and in

1987, President Ronald Reagan (1981–1989) signed a bill providing $1.2 billion in reparations.

Contemporary Issues for Asian Americans   During the 1960s and 1980s, the number of organizations and coalitions pressing for the civil rights of Asian Americans grew as large numbers of new immigrants from Asian countries arrived in the United States in response to changes in U.S. immigration laws. During the 1960s, Asian Americans on college campuses organized and fostered a group consciousness about the need to protect their civil rights. During the 1980s, Asian American organizations began to pay more attention to voting rights, as well as to hate crimes and employment discrimination. Then in 1996, numerous organizations, each representing Asian Americans with ancestry from one country, joined to form the National Council of Asian Pacific Americans (NCAPA), which presses for equal protection of the law for all Asians.

With the exception of Korean Americans and Vietnamese Americans, Asian Americans have the highest median income compared to the population as a whole.[37] Asian Americans are also twice as likely as the population as a whole to earn a bachelor's degree or higher.[38] Moreover, Asian Americans are better represented in professional and managerial positions than any other racial or ethnic group, including white Americans. Yet like women, Asian American citizens are not represented in the positions at the very top in the numbers their high levels of educational achievement suggest. Therefore, those advocating for Asian American civil rights are increasingly concentrating their efforts on discrimination in employment.

Citizens with Disabilities

The civil rights movements of the 1960s and 1970s made society more aware of the lack of equal protection of the laws for diverse groups of citizens, including people with disabilities. The first law to mandate equal protection for people with physical and mental disabilities was the 1973 Rehabilitation Act, which prohibited discrimination against people with disabilities in federally funded programs. In 1990, people with disabilities achieved a significant enhancement of this earlier victory in their fight to obtain protection of their civil rights. The Americans with Disabilities Act (ADA), enacted in that year, extends the ban on discrimination against people with disabilities in education, employment, health care, housing, and transportation to all programs and organizations, not just those receiving federal funds. The ADA defines a disability as any "physical or mental impairment that substantially limits one or more of the major life activities of the individual." The ADA does not enumerate every disability that it covers, resulting in much confusion over which conditions it covers and which it excludes.

Disability advocates disagree with recent Court decisions that specify a definition of "disability" that they believe is too narrow. The Court has determined that if an individual can take an action to mitigate an impairment (such as wearing eyeglasses for severe near-sightedness or taking medication for high blood pressure), then the impairment is not a disability requiring reasonable accommodation.[39] In response to these Court rulings, disability advocates, such as the National Coalition of Disability Rights and the ADA Watch, support the ADA Restoration Act that was proposed in 2007. Among other things, this act would broaden the category of impairments that are covered by the ADA by eliminating the need for an impairment to "substantially limit one or more major life activities."

Despite disagreement about the breadth of the law's coverage, there is no question that the ADA has enhanced the civil rights of citizens with disabilities. Before the ADA was enacted, people with disabilities who were fired from their jobs or denied access to schools, office buildings, or other public places had no recourse. Cities were under no obligation to provide even the most reasonable accommodations to people with disabilities who sought employment or the use of public transportation systems. And employers were under no obligation to make even the most minor modifications to their workplaces for employees with disabilities. For example, if a qualified job applicant was wheelchair bound, an employer did not have to consider installing ramps or raising desks to accommodate the wheelchair but could simply refuse to hire the individual. The ADA changed this situation by requiring employers and governmental organizations to make it possible for people with disabilities to participate meaningfully in their communities through reasonable accommodations.

Lesbian, Gay, Bisexual, and Transgendered Citizens

Lesbian, gay, bisexual, and transgendered people (people whose gender identity cannot be categorized as male or female)—a group often referred to with the abbreviation LGBT—also actively seek equal civil rights. Some of the specific rights that LGBT persons have organized to fight for include employment rights, housing rights, and marriage rights. Though the 1970s and 1980s saw some successes in these civil rights battles, there was some backlash in the 1990s and early in the twenty-first century. In this section, we focus mainly on the rights of lesbians and gay men.

The Gay Pride Movement   Several LGBT civil rights organizations were founded after the Stonewall Rebellion. In June 1969, groups of gay men and lesbians clashed violently with police in New York City, in a protest over the routine harassment by law enforcement of members of the lesbian and gay community. This influential conflict, which started at the Stonewall bar, marked the first time that members of this community acted collectively and in large numbers to assert their rights. Shortly after this event, in 1970, Lambda Legal, a national organization fighting for full recognition of the civil rights of LGBT citizens, was founded. Within a few years, gays and lesbians began to hold gay pride marches throughout the country, and many new groups, such as the Human Rights Campaign and the National Gay and Lesbian Task Force, began advocating for LGBT rights.

As a result of organized educational and lobbying efforts by the gay community, during the 1980s, a number of state and local governments adopted laws

THEN NOW NE**X**T

Will President Obama Allow Gays and Lesbians to Serve Openly in the Armed Forces?

THEN: Presidential candidate Bill Clinton promised to end the Defense Department's ban on allowing gays and lesbians to serve in the armed forces, but in 1993, he issued an executive order that (1) instructed the military no longer to ask recruits if they are homosexual and (2) instructed recruits and military personnel to keep silent about their sexual preferences. Moreover, Congress approved and President Clinton signed legislation that bans openly gay and lesbian people from serving in the military.

NOW: Presidential candidate Barak Obama's pledge to reverse the ban on gays and lesbians in military service has been relegated to the back burner as President Obama concentrates on getting the nation's economy back on a healthy track and succeeding in the U.S. military interventions in Iraq and Afghanistan.

WHAT'S NE**X**T?

■ In what ways might the increasing need for military personnel persuade military leaders and congressional members to support the repeal of the ban on gays and lesbians in the military?

■ According to public opinion polls, the overwhelming majority of Americans feel that the government should allow homosexuals to serve in the military. How might activists use these poll numbers to persuade military personnel and congressional members to support the repeal of the ban on gays and lesbians in the military?

■ How might those who oppose repeal of the ban overcome this public support?

prohibiting discrimination in employment, housing, public accommodations, and employee benefits—that is, guaranteeing equal protection of some laws—for LGBT persons. In 1982, Wisconsin was the first state to prohibit such discrimination. Yet during the same decade, numerous states had laws on the books prohibiting sex between mutually consenting adults of the same sex, typically in the form of antisodomy laws. In the 1986 case of *Bowers v. Hardwick,* the U.S. Supreme Court upheld Georgia's antisodomy law.[40] In 2003, another lawsuit challenging the constitutionality of a state antisodomy law came before the Supreme Court in the case of *Lawrence v. Texas.*[41] This time the Court overturned the 1986 *Bowers* decision, finding that the Fourteenth Amendment provides due process and equal protection for sexual privacy and therefore that the Texas law was unconstitutional.

Advocates for the rights of LGBT persons hoped this 2003 ruling would lead to federal protections of LGBT citizens' civil rights. But there is still no federal law prohibiting LGBT-based discrimination in employment, housing, or public accommodations. (One area of contention is the military's controversial "don't ask, don't tell" policy; see "Then, Now, Next" for more on this issue.) In contrast to the lack of federal legislation, today twenty states and the District of Columbia have antidiscrimination laws guaranteeing equal access to employment, housing, and public accommodations regardless of sexual orientation.[42]

Backlash Against the Movement for LGBT Civil Rights On the other side of the issue, in 1992, opponents of civil rights for LGBT persons succeeded in placing on the ballot in Colorado a proposed law that would prohibit all branches of the state government from adopting any law or policy making it illegal to discriminate against gay men, lesbians, bisexuals, or transgendered people. Immediately after Colorado voters approved the law, the state court placed an injunction on its implementation, preventing its enforcement, in order to allow a lawsuit challenging the law's constitutionality to work its way through the courts. In 1996, the U.S. Supreme Court, in *Romer v. Evans,* found the state law to be unconstitutional.[43] The parties who filed the suit challenging the law included the Boulder school district; the cities of Denver, Boulder, and Aspen; and the county of Denver.

Another civil rights battle for lesbians and gays is over the issue of marriage rights. The Hawaii state Supreme Court ruled in 1993 that it was a violation of the Hawaii state constitution to deny same-sex couples the right to marry. Opponents of same-sex marriage succeeded in their subsequent efforts to get a state constitutional amendment banning same-sex marriage on the ballot, and in 1996 the majority of Hawaiian voters approved it. The conflict over same-sex marriage that began in Hawaii quickly spread to other states. Since 1998, almost three-quarters of the states have banned same-sex marriage through constitutional amendment or legislation. What this means for gay and lesbian couples is that they are not able to obtain the same rights and benefits that are available to opposite-sex couples through marriage, including tax benefits, the right to receive joint mortgages, the right to make medical decisions for a partner who is unable to make such decisions, spousal Social Security benefits, and rights of inheritance when a deceased partner has no will.

In contrast, as of 2009, the states of Connecticut, Iowa, Maine, Massachusetts, New Hamsphire, and Vermont allow same-sex marriage, while California and New Jersey allow same-sex civil unions. Civil unions provide same-sex couples with many of the protections that married couples enjoy. However, the 1996 national Defense of Marriage Act states that the federal government does not recognize same-sex marriages, or civil unions, legalized by any state and that states do not need to recognize same-sex marriages that were legalized in other states.

Though the LGBT community is winning some of its civil rights battles in a growing number of states, in many areas, the battle has just begun. For example, in the area of family law, issues involving adoption rights and child custody, as well as divorce and property rights, are now battlegrounds. In addition, hate crimes continue to be a problem for members of the LGBT community, as well as for citizens (and noncitizens) with non–white European ancestry. Federal law defines a **hate crime** as a crime where the offender is motivated in part or entirely by her or his bias against the victim because of the victim's race, color, religion, or national origin. In October 2009, the federal law was amended to include crimes motivated by the victim's sexual orientation.

Affirmative Action: Is It Constitutional?

Laws reinforcing constitutional guarantees by prohibiting discriminatory treatment are the most common objectives of civil rights battles. Nevertheless, in the 1960s, the federal government also began implementing policies aimed at reinforcing equal access to employment by mandating recruitment procedures that actively sought to identify qualified minority men for government positions. This policy of **affirmative action** was extended to women in employment and then to educational institutions. However, affirmative action policies have been and continue to be very controversial.

How Affirmative Action Works

In 1961, President John F. Kennedy used the term *affirmative action* in an executive order regarding the recruitment of personnel by federal agencies and private businesses with contracts to do work for the federal government. The executive order required that these agencies and businesses do more than merely refrain from discriminating against minority men; it required that they engage in affirmative actions—intentional efforts to recruit qualified minority men for employment. The use of this term indicated that the government was attempting to take *proactive* measures to ensure equal employment opportunity.

In 1965, President Lyndon B. Johnson (1963–1968) extended the affirmative action requirement to include the recruitment of qualified women. Today, affirmative action policies cover personnel processes including hiring, training, and promoting. Private companies, nonprofit organizations, and government agencies that receive federal government contracts worth at least $50,000 are required by law to have an affirmative action plan for their personnel processes.

Affirmative action does not require organizations to hire unqualified candidates, nor does it require the hiring of a qualified minority candidate over a qualified nonminority candidate. Affirmative action does require that an organization make intentional efforts to diversify its workforce by providing equal opportunity to classes of people that have been historically, and in many cases are still today, subject to discrimination. It focuses attention on an employer's history of personnel decisions. If over the years an employer with an affirmative action plan does not hire qualified underutilized workers (women and minority men), it will appear to many that the employer is discriminating and is violating Title VII of the Civil Rights Act. However, critics of affirmative action argue that it discriminates against Caucasians, and they have questioned whether the way it is applied to personnel policies, as well as to college admissions policies, is constitutional.

In the 1970s, institutions of higher education began to make intentional efforts to expand educational opportunities for both men and women from various minority groups. In addition, colleges and universities use affirmative action to ensure a student body that is diverse in race, color, economic status, and other characteristics. These institutions believe that having students on campus from a wide variety of backgrounds enhances all students' educational experience and best prepares them to function successfully in a nation that is increasingly diverse. Yet like affirmative action in personnel policies, affirmative action in college admission policies has been controversial.

Opposition to Affirmative Action

In the important *Bakke* decision in 1978, the U.S. Supreme Court found unconstitutional the University of California at Davis's affirmative action plan for admission to its medical school.[44] The UC Davis plan set aside sixteen of the one hundred seats in its first-year medical school class for minorities (specifically, African Americans, Latinos, Asian Americans, and Native Americans). Justice Lewis Powell noted in his opinion that schools can take race into consideration as one of several factors for admission but cannot use it as the sole consideration, as Alan Bakke argued UC Davis had done.

Ward Connerly, chairman of the American Civil Rights Institute (ACRI), argues, "There can be no middle ground about the use of race. This is not an area where one can fudge or cheat just a little bit. Either we permit the use of 'race' in American life or we don't. I say, 'We don't!'"[45] Connerly is leading the battle against affirmative action in admissions and employment procedures. Connerly founded the ACRI in 1997, one year after his successful effort to have California voters repeal their state's affirmative action policies in college admissions and employment. After anti–affirmative action victories in Washington (1998) and Michigan (2006), the ACRI has also targeted Arizona, Colorado, Missouri, Nebraska, and Oklahoma for similar efforts.[46]

Opponents have challenged affirmative action in the courts and through legislative processes and statewide referenda. In two cases involving the University of Michigan in 2003, the U.S. Supreme Court upheld the *Bakke* decision that universities can use race as a factor in admissions decisions, but not as the overriding factor. Using the strict scrutiny test, the Court said in the *Grutter v. Bollinger* case that the school's goal of creating a diverse student body serves a *compelling public interest:* a diverse student body enhances "cross-racial understanding . . . breaks down racial stereotypes . . . and helps students better understand persons of different races."[47]

In 2007, however, the Supreme Court found unconstitutional two school districts' policies of assigning students to elementary schools based on race to ensure a diverse student body.[48] The majority of justices argued that these policies violated the equal protection clause of the Fourteenth Amendment. Chief Justice John Roberts,

POLITICAL INQUIRY

This cartoon suggests a number of the factors that colleges consider when making admissions decisions. Why is membership in a minority group controversial, whereas other factors—such as being able to play a certain sport or being the son or daughter of a graduate—are not? In the future, how can colleges achieve the goals of a diverse campus and a fair admissions process?

Signe Wilkinson Editorial Cartoon © 2003 Signe Wilkinson. Used with the permission of Signe Wilkinson and the Washington Post Writers Group in conjunction with the Cartoonist Group.

writing for the majority, argued that governments should not use laws to remedy racial imbalances caused by economic inequalities, individual choices, and historical biases (de facto imbalances). He stated that such laws put in place discrimination that the Court found unconstitutional in the *Brown* case back in 1954. The justices who dissented from the majority opinion noted that today's policies are trying to ensure inclusion of minorities, not create segregation of, and hence cause harm to, minorities. The dissenters view policies that take race into account to ensure inclusion and balance as necessary means to achieving the compelling public good gained by a diverse student body.

Are affirmative action policies aimed at ensuring equal educational and employment opportunities for women and minority men constitutional, or do they violate the equal protection clause of the Fourteenth Amendment? The answer to this question depends on how the majority of the members of the Supreme Court interpret the Fourteenth Amendment. Today, in order for an affirmative action policy for minority men to be constitutional, the government must pass the strict scrutiny test by showing that affirmative action is necessary to achieve a compelling public interest. In the case of affirmative action for women, the government must pass the heightened scrutiny test by showing that the policy is substantially related to the government's achievement of an important public interest. Much depends on how the courts define these interests.

CONTINUING THE CONVERSATION

CONCLUSION

- For most of U.S. history, the law has allowed, and in some cases even required, discrimination against people based on inherent characteristics such as race, ethnicity, and sex.

- This discriminatory treatment means that the U.S. government does not guarantee all citizens equal protection of their civil rights.

- African Americans, Native Americans, and women have endured long and continuing battles for equal civil rights.

- Latinos, Asian Americans, citizens with disabilities, and LGBT citizens are currently engaged in political, legal, and civic activities aimed at guaranteeing equal protection of their civil rights.

- Numerous other groups are working to gain equal civil rights, including older Americans, poor Americans, and children born in the United States to parents who are in the country illegally (the Fourteenth Amendment extends citizenship, and hence civil rights, to these children).

STUDY NOW

Summary

1. The Quest for Equality Under the Law
The law assumes that discrimination based on inherent characteristics such as race, national origin, religion, and sex is illegitimate.

2. Slavery and Its Aftermath
One legacy of slavery in the United States was state and federal governments providing unequal civil rights through legal racial discrimination and segregation of African Americans.

3. The Civil Rights Movement
Early and modern civil rights activists and organizations engaged in acts of civil disobedience, protests, lobbying, and lawsuits to ensure that the Fourteenth Amendment's guarantees of due process and equal protection of the law were a reality for African Americans.

4. The Government's Response to the Civil Rights Movement
The government responded to the demands for equal rights for African Americans with a series of laws that attempted to secure fundamental rights, including voting rights and equal rights to employment, education, public accommodations, and housing.

5. The Movement for Women's Civil Rights
The first wave of the women's rights movement, which succeeded in winning for women the right to vote in 1920, was followed by the second wave of the movement, which since the 1960s has been fighting for laws guaranteeing women equality of rights in all aspects of their lives.

6. Other Civil Rights Movements
Native Americans, Latino and Asian American citizens, citizens with disabilities, and lesbian, gay, bisexual, and transgendered citizens are just some of the other groups engaged in efforts to win equal civil rights, including employment and educational opportunities, housing, and marriage rights, among others.

7. Affirmative Action: Is It Constitutional?
In 1961, President Kennedy introduced the nation to a controversial policy he labeled affirmative action, a policy whose constitutionality is in question today.

For Critical Thinking and Discussion

1. Given the history of the attainment of civil rights for women and African Americans, what is your opinion of the result of the battle for the Democratic Party's presidential nomination in 2008?

2. Is it constitutional to deny any citizen the equal protection of marriage laws; is denying gay men and lesbians the right to marry a necessary means to a compelling public interest? Explain.

3. Today, more women than men are in college pursuing their bachelor's degrees. Should schools give preference to male applicants by accepting men with lower SAT scores and high school grade-point averages than women, in order to maintain sex balance in the student body? Explain.

4. Many organizations fighting for civil rights protections include in their name the phrase "legal defense and education fund." What do you think explains the common two-pronged focus of these organizations?

Key Terms

affirmative action 206
Black Codes 180
Brown v. Board of Education of Topeka 183
civil disobedience 177
civil rights 174
de facto segregation 197
de jure segregation 197
equal protection clause 182

grandfather clause 181
hate crime 206
heightened scrutiny test (intermediate scrutiny test) 195
inherent characteristics 174
Jim Crow laws 180
literacy test 181
ordinary scrutiny test (rational basis test) 192

Plessy v. Ferguson 182
poll tax 181
Reconstruction era 180
separate but equal doctrine 182
standing to sue 179
steering 189
strict scrutiny test 195
suspect classifications 176
white primary 181

Internet Resources

A More Perfect Union Web site
www.mhhe.com/harrisonampule   Consult the book's Web site for study guides, interactive activities, simulations, and current hot-links that provide additional information on civil rights.

Center for American Women and Politics
www.cawp.rutgers.edu   This premier Web site has historical as well as up-to-date information on women in elected and appointed positions in national, state, and local governments.

Equal Employment Opportunity Commission
www.eeoc.gov/facts/qanda.html   This federal government site offers a list of federal laws relevant to equal employment opportunities and includes answers to the most frequently asked questions regarding equal employment laws.

Leadership Conference on Civil Rights/Leadership Conference on Civil Rights Education Fund
www.civilrights.org   Founded by the LCCR and the LCCREF, this site seeks to serve as the "online nerve center" for the fight against discrimination in all its forms.

Recommended Readings

Branch, Taylor. *Parting the Waters: America in the King Years.* New York: Simon and Schuster, 1989. A Pulitzer Prize–winning book focusing on the civil rights movement from 1954 to 1963. It includes detailed descriptions of the leadership of Martin Luther King Jr. and describes the inner workings of the movement as it organized boycotts, sit-ins, and freedom rides.

Feagin, Joe R., and Clairece Booher Feagin. *Racial and Ethnic Relations.* Upper Saddle River, NJ: Prentice-Hall, 2003. A comprehensive look at the immigration of Africans, Asians, Europeans, Latin Americans, and Middle Easterners to the United States and the history of relations between Native Americans and the U.S. government. The initial chapters provide frameworks for analyzing the discrimination experienced by these groups of eventual citizens.

Herr, Stanley S., Lawrence O. Gostin, and Harold Hongju Koh. *The Human Rights of Persons with Disabilities: Different but Equal.* Oxford: Oxford University Press, 2003. A collection of essays explaining how Article I of the Universal Declaration of Human Rights, which states that all humans have equal and unalienable claims to dignity and freedom, defines the standard for rights for people with disabilities, including those with intellectual disabilities.

Rosenberg, Gerald. *The Hollow Hope: Can Courts Bring About Social Change?* 2nd ed. Chicago: University of Chicago Press, 2008. An argument that Congress, the White House, and civil rights activists—not the courts—bring about social change. The book reviews the evolution of federal policy in the areas of desegregation, abortion, and the struggle for LGBT rights.

PART III

PEOPLE AND THE GOVERNMENT

National
Journal

THE DEMOCRATIC WALL OF BLUE

State by state, election by election, Democrats since 1992 have methodically constructed the party's largest and most durable Electoral College base in more than half a century. Call it the blue wall.

After Barack Obama's sweeping victory in November, 18 states and the District of Columbia have now voted for the Democratic nominee in at least the past five presidential elections. The last time Democrats won that many states so consistently was from 1932 to 1948, when Franklin Roosevelt and Harry Truman won 22 states in five consecutive presidential races.

Together, D.C. and these 18 contemporary Democratic strong-holds—running up the East Coast from Maryland through Maine, through the Upper Midwest, and down along the Pacific Coast—are worth a combined 248 Electoral College votes.

That's more than 90 percent of the 270 votes required to win the presidency. The Democratic hold on all of them solidified in 2008.

Indeed, from the White House to the statehouse, Democrats now dominate these states up and down the ballot. Republicans hold just three of the 36 U.S. Senate seats in these 18 states. In the House, Democrats hold more than 70 percent of the seats from these 18 states, a net advantage of 89. In each chamber, the Democrats' advantage in these states provides their overall margin of majority.

How Blue States Are Alike

Almost all of the states in the blue wall fit a common demographic profile: affluent; well-educated; ethnically and racially diverse; culturally moderate to liberal; with below-average rates of church attendance and fewer evangelical Protestants than the

national mean. In an era in which each party's electoral coalition revolves more around cultural attitudes than economic interests, the Democratic advantage in these regions represents the flip side of the Republican edge in the culturally conservative South, Plains, and Mountain West that keyed Bush's victories in 2000 and 2004.

Those two triumphs demonstrated that the Democrats' hold on these states doesn't guarantee them the White House. Yet, because of Bush's inability to dent the blue wall, he won with two of the narrowest Electoral College majorities ever. And although Obama and other Democrats made substantial inroads in culturally conservative states in 2006 and 2008, the Republicans have been steadily losing ground in the culturally cosmopolitan blue states, especially since Bush first appeared on the national ballot in 2000.

That daunting trend is likely to sharpen the conflict between those in the GOP who believe that Republicans can recover only by adopting a more aggressive conservative message and those who fear that the party's current approach writes off too many voters and regions. Steve Schmidt, McCain's chief strategist, sides with the latter camp. "The party on its current trajectory is a shrinking party," Schmidt warns. "It needs to be an expanding party ... [and] to be a national party, it needs to compete in states like New Jersey, New York, and New Hampshire, Pennsylvania and California.... For the party to come back and grow, it must appeal to a broader majority of people. That is now the challenge."

"It's not quite a lock, but maybe it's a vise that really narrows the room for maneuver for Republicans," says Democratic pollster Mark Mellman. Ralph Reed, a Georgia-based veteran GOP strategist and activist, takes a similar view. "The next Republican nominee can't plan on carrying . . . the Rocky Mountain States and a solid South and then spend $60 million trying to flip Ohio," said Reed, the former executive director of the Christian Coalition. "You have to expand the map."

The Democrats' blue wall connects

three distinct groups of states.

Foundations of the Wall

It includes 10 from the Mid-Atlantic and Northeast—every state from Maryland to Maine except New Hampshire. In the Pacific West are California, Hawaii, Oregon, and Washington. Four more come from the Midwest: Illinois, Michigan, Minnesota, and Wisconsin. And finally, D.C.

After that geographic and ideological re-sorting, the Democrats' blue wall is now composed almost entirely of states that combine large numbers of well-educated, affluent, and less-religious whites with substantial numbers of racial and ethnic minorities, including sizable immigrant populations. Thirteen of the 18 blue states (plus the District of Columbia) rank among the 20 states with the highest proportion of college graduates, according to 2007 Census Bureau figures. Likewise, 13 of the states (plus D.C.) rank among the 20 states with the highest median income. Counting D.C., 12 of them rank among the 20 states with the highest percentage of foreign-born residents.

By contrast, these states are home to relatively few of the religiously devout, often evangelical, voters who are the core of the modern GOP coalition. The massive 2007 U.S. Religious Landscape survey conducted by the Pew Forum on Religion and Public Life found that the percentage of residents who described religion as very important in their life was lower than the national average in each of these 18 states, except for the survey's combined sample of Maryland and Washington, D.C.—and even that result probably represented the influence of heavily Democratic African-American voters.

At a time when social issues such as abortion divide the parties so starkly, many analysts see those cultural and religious trends as key to the Democratic grip on these states. "Basically, what they lack are the large numbers of white Protestants, especially the evangelicals, which have been the electoral base [for the GOP] in the South and the Mountain Plains," Black said. "Outside of those regions, the groups you have to compete for are much more diverse, and since the Republicans haven't been able to expand, they are really up against it when you have increased voting by minorities."

What changed? Two factors seem most important.

One is increasing racial diversity. Since 1988, according to network exit polls, the share of the vote cast by whites has declined in almost all of these states. In California, from 1988 through 2008, the white share of the vote fell from 79 percent to 63 percent; in New Jersey, from 87 percent to 73 percent; in Connecticut, from 94 percent to 78 percent; and in Illinois, from 90 percent to 73 percent. The offsetting increase has come among African-Americans, Asians, and Hispanics, all groups that are now voting overwhelmingly Democratic.

The other big change has been the growing Democratic strength among white voters with college or postgraduate degrees. In 1988, large, affluent, white-collar suburban counties such as Montgomery and Delaware in Pennsylvania, Bergen in New Jersey, Oakland in Michigan, and Fairfield in Connecticut, provided huge margins for George H. W. Bush. As these states move toward a postindustrial economy, college-educated voters constitute a larger share of the vote than they did 20 years ago in most of them, and a substantially larger share in some.

The Democratic gains in these upscale communities have paralleled the GOP's tightening identification since the early 1990s with a staunch Southern-flavored conservatism, particularly on cultural issues. Almost universally, Democrats believe they are advancing in these leafy suburbs largely because voters there have recoiled from that definition of the GOP.

Closely related, but distinct, other analysts say, is the perception in many of these places that the GOP elevates religion over science (on issues such as stem-cell research or the teaching of evolution) and prizes homespun "common sense" over advanced education—an inclination symbolized by the party's frequent portrayal of small towns like Sarah Palin's Wasilla, Alaska, as the "real America."

"The anti-intellectual side of the Republican Party is offensive to people who think what makes them different is they went to school and that they are smart," said Kieran Mahoney, a veteran Republican consultant in New York. "If we are going to glory in the notion that we are not thinking this through, don't be surprised if we offend those who are thinking it through."

But to seize that opportunity, Mahoney argued, Republicans will need to move away from a "moralist" definition of conservatism toward a more "libertarian" argument that links personal freedom and small government.

Schmidt, although he ran a campaign for McCain that ultimately saw vice presidential nominee Palin stress culturally polarizing themes, takes a similar view. Although the party will remain overwhelmingly "pro-life," he says, the GOP will not restore its competitiveness in these states without "tolerance for a type of conservatism and Republicanism that is closer to the British Conservative Party: pro-environment, competent in government, socially tolerant."

Learning from Obama?

Ralph Reed, reflecting a common view among religious conservatives, says that Republicans can regain ground in these blue states without moderating their views on social issues. The key, he says, is embedding those views in a compelling, larger agenda attractive to voters who may not agree with the party's cultural priorities. As proof that it can be done, Reed cites an unusual example: Obama's success at capturing states such as Virginia, Colorado, and North Carolina that were previously considered inhospitable to cultural liberals.

"I reject the idea that you have to trim your sails in terms of the core principles of your party in order to appeal everywhere," Reed said. "And I think Exhibit A of that is Obama. He ran advertising [advocating] the largest tax increase of any Democratic nominee in my lifetime, and a withdrawal from Iraq, and a very liberal position on the moral and social issues. But he competed everywhere, and he found ways to signal empathy [to conservatives]. A lot of this is a candidate who can build bridges to people who don't think you are sympathetic."

But Obama's success in Colorado and Virginia probably owes less to converting conservatives than to the influence on those states of the same electoral trends that flipped many of the blue-wall states away from the GOP in the 1990s. Key among those changes are an increasing number of minorities and a movement toward the Democrats among culturally moderate-to-liberal college-educated whites.

If anything, this explanation for Obama's breakthroughs underscores the magnitude of the choices facing the GOP, because it presents Republicans with the risk that the same cultural and demographic dynamics that have solidified the Democratic hold on the 18 blue-wall states could increasingly shift these battleground states into the Democrats' orbit. Measured on such yardsticks as income, education, and residents born abroad, Colorado and Virginia (and, to a lesser extent, North Carolina) now resemble the blue states more than they do the typical Republican bastions in the South or the Great Plains. If Republicans cannot crack the code with minority and well-educated, socially moderate white voters, states such as Colorado or Virginia that are now teetering between the parties eventually could become new bricks atop the Democrats' blue wall.

THEN

Families and schools were the most important influences on children as they developed their political views.

Families and schools remain influential, but the media are enormously important in developing the political views of the Millennial Generation.

NOW

6 Political Socialization and Public Opinion

The process of developing informed opinions about issues begins with the process of political socialization. Through socialization, we acquire our basic political beliefs and values. Through political socialization, we come to value the attributes of our own political culture. We also develop our ideological outlook and perhaps even begin to identify with a particular political party. While the process of political socialization begins in early childhood, throughout our lives, institutions, peers, and the media continue to influence our views.

Political socialization is a key component in the process of creating an engaged citizenry. Psychologist Steven Pinker once noted that "no matter how important learning and culture and socialization are, they don't happen by magic."[1] Joe Zavaletta, director of the Center for Civic Engagement at the University of Texas at Brownsville, would agree with Pinker's assertion: "Democracy is not magic. Why we expect our kids to magically become engaged citizens when they turn 18 when they haven't practiced . . . doesn't make any sense."[2]

Through the process of political socialization, individuals acquire the ideology and perspective that shape their political opinions. Though seemingly simple, public opinion is a fundamental building block on which American democracy rests. When we discuss public opinion, we often do so in the context of various public opinion polls that ask respondents everything from whether they approve of the president's job performance to how many sugars they take in their skim milk lattes. Political scientist V. O. Key Jr. wrote, "To speak

NEXT

How will technology affect the socialization of new generations of Americans?

How will polling organizations harness the power of the Internet to predict political behavior accurately?

How can pollsters find ways to measure the opinions of "celly-onlys"— potential respondents who own only cell phones?

with precision of public opinion is a task not unlike coming to grips with the Holy Ghost."[3] Key was referring to the nebulous nature of public opinion, which changes from day to day, is sometimes difficult to pinpoint, and is open to subjective interpretation. The glut in the number of "latest polls" has perhaps made us forget that the act of voting is itself simply the act of expressing one's opinion. Indeed, the word *poll* means to gauge public opinion, as well as the location where one casts a ballot.

Public opinion is one of the ways citizens interact with their government. Through public opinion surveys, people express their policy priorities ("What do you think is the country's most important problem?") and their approval or disapproval of both government officials ("Do you approve or disapprove of the way the president is handling his job?") and the policies they create ("Do you agree or disagree with President Obama's handling of the economy?). Much of the literature bemoaning the decline of civic involvement is based on public opinion research. But studies of civic involvement reveal that public opinion is the starting point for many forms of informed participation—participation that begins when individuals learn about an issue and choose to express their views on it using a variety of media.

Political Socialization and Civic Participation

How do we acquire our political views? Though an infant would be hard pressed to evaluate the president's job performance, of course, children begin to acquire political opinions at an early age, and this process continues throughout adulthood. As noted above, the process by which we develop our political values and opinions is called **political socialization.** As we develop our political values, we form the bedrock of what will become our political ideology. As this ideology emerges, it then shapes how we view most political subjects: our positions on public issues, how we evaluate candidates for office, and what our opinions on policies will be.

While many tend to think that political socialization occurs as people approach voting age, in reality, this process begins at home in very early childhood. Core tenets of our belief system—including our political ideology, our beliefs about people of different races and sexes, even our party identification—are often firmly embedded before we have completed elementary school.

A key aspect of political socialization is whether children are socialized to participate in politics. Simply put, civically engaged parents often have civically engaged children. Parents who engage in active forms of participation like volunteering on a campaign and passive forms like watching the nightly news or reading a newspaper demonstrate to children what matters to them. Parents who change the channel to a *Law and Order* rerun during an important presidential news conference are also socializing their children to their values. Children absorb the political views of their parents as well: a parent's subtle (or sometimes not so subtle!) comments about the president, a political news story, or a policy debate contribute to a child's political socialization by shaping that child's views.

The Process of Political Socialization

The beliefs and values we learn early in life also help shape how we view new information. While events may change our views, we often choose to perceive events in a way that is consistent with our earlier beliefs. For example, people's evaluation of which candidate "won" a debate often strongly coincides with their party identification. Thus, the process of political socialization tends to be cumulative.

Historically, most social scientists have agreed that family and school have the strongest influence on political socialization. Our families teach us that it is—or is not—valuable to be an informed citizen and coach us in the ways in which we should participate in the civic life of our communities. For example, if your mother is active in Republican Party politics in your town, you are more likely to be active in the

> Children are socialized to the views of their parents at a very early age. Where one family may socialize a child to participate in the environmental movement, another may teach a child about guns and Second Amendment issues. Here children are being socialized to varying political views. What opinions were you socialized to as a young child?

party than someone whose parents are not involved in a local party. Schools also influence our political socialization by teaching us shared cultural values. And in recent times, the omnipresent role that the media play in everyday life warrants their inclusion as one of the prime agents of political socialization.

Participating in Civic Life

Does the process of socialization matter in determining whether individuals are active in civic life? Studies indicate that socialization does matter in a number of ways. First, children whose parents are active in politics or in their community are more likely to be active themselves. Schools also play an important role in socializing young people to become active in civic life—high school and college students are more likely to participate than young people of the same age who are not attending school. Research also indicates that socialization actually *generates* participation. People who have been socialized to participate in civic life are more likely to volunteer for a charitable or a political organization in their communities when they are invited to do so.

From our families and schools, we also learn the value of becoming informed. Parents and schools, along with the media and the other agents of socialization that are discussed in the next section, provide us with important information that we can use to make decisions about our political actions. People who lack political knowledge, by contrast, tend not to be actively involved in their communities.[4] In fact, research indicates that when young people use any source of information regularly, including newspapers, radio, television, magazines, or the Internet, they are more likely to engage in all forms of civic participation. There is also a strong link between being informed and voting behavior. According to the results of one survey that measured civic engagement among young people, "youth who are registered to vote are more informed than their nonregistered peers. Eighty-six percent of young registered voters answered at least one of the knowledge questions (measuring political knowledge) correctly as opposed to 78 percent of youth who are not registered to vote."[5]

Agents of Socialization

Learning, culture, and socialization occur through **agents of socialization,** the individuals, organizations, and institutions that facilitate the acquisition of political views. Among the most important agents of socialization are the family, the media, schools, churches, peers, and political and community leaders. Our political views are also shaped by who we are: our race, ethnicity, sex, and age all influence how we become socialized to political and community life.

Family Influences on Activism and Attitudes

Family takes one of the most active roles in socializing us to politics and influencing our political views and behaviors. First of all, we learn whether our family members value civic activism by observing their actions and listening to their views. By example, parents show children whether community matters. Parents may teach different forms of political engagement—some young children might attend protests or demonstrations with their parents, while others might learn to boycott a particular product. When political activists discuss their own involvement, they often observe that "politics is in my blood." In reality, political activism is passed from one generation to the next *through example.*

In other homes, however, parents are not involved in politics or their communities. They may lack the time to participate in political activities, or they may fail to see the value of doing so. They may have a negative opinion of people who participate in politics, constantly making comments like "all politicians are corrupt," "they're just in it for themselves," or "it's all about ego." Such opinions convey to children that politics is not valued and may in fact be frowned upon. A parent's political apathy need not necessarily sour a son or daughter on politics or civic engagement permanently, however. Instead, first-generation activists often point to external influences such as school, the media, friends, and public policies, any of which can cause someone to become involved in civic life, regardless of family attitudes.

Our families influence not only whether we are civically active participants in the political process but also what we believe. While parents or older siblings may discuss specific issues or policies, their attitudes and outlooks also shape children's general political attitudes and ideology. Children absorb their parents' beliefs— whether their parents think the government should have a larger or smaller role in people's lives, whether they value equality between the sexes and races, whether they consider people in government to be trustworthy, and even what opinions they have about political leaders. In fact, we can see evidence of how strongly parents' views are transmitted to their children in one of the best predictors of the results of presidential elections: each election year, the *Weekly Reader,* a current events magazine that many school districts subscribe to, conducts a nonrandomized poll of its readers. Since 1956, the first- through twelfth-grade student poll has correctly predicted the outcome of every presidential election. Children know for whom their parents will vote and mimic that behavior in their responses to the poll.

The Media's Ever-Increasing Role in Socialization

An almost ever-present fixture in the lives of young Americans today, the media contribute to the political socialization of Americans in a wide variety of ways. Television, radio, the Internet, and various forms of electronic entertainment and print media help shape Americans' political perspectives. First of all, the media, especially television, help shape societal norms. The media impart norms and values on children's shows such as *Sesame Street, Barney,* and *Dora the Explorer,* which teach about racial diversity and tolerance. For example, Barney's friends include children with and without disabilities. These shows and others reflect changing societal standards and values. The media also reinforce core democratic values. Television programs such as *American Idol* and *The Biggest Loser,* and XM Radio's *20on20,* incorporate the principle of voting: viewers decide which contestant stays or goes, or listeners pick which songs are played. And organizations are using Internet tools like Web sites and Facebook and MySpace pages to socialize individuals to the value of political participation.

Second, the media help determine the national agenda. Whether they are covering health care reform, the war in Afghanistan, global climate change, or congressional policy debates, the media focus the attention of the American public. This attention may then have spillover effects as people demand action on a policy issue. We will see in Chapter 7, for example, how media coverage of the introduction of a bill concerning immigration spawned a nationwide protest movement in favor of immigration rights.

Third, the media educate the public about policy issues. Local and national news programs, newsmagazine shows, and even comedies like *The Daily Show with Jon Stewart* (yes, it really is a comedy, *not* a news, program) inform viewers about current events, the actions of policy makers, and public policy challenges in communities, states, and the nation.

Finally, the media, particularly television, can skew people's perception of public policy priorities and challenges. The oft-quoted saying "If it bleeds, it leads" demonstrates the attention that most local news stations focus on violence. While crime rates have dropped since the 1970s, the reporting of crime, particularly violent crime, on nightly news broadcasts has increased. Even national news broadcasts and talk shows fall prey to the tendency to emphasize "visual" news—fires, floods, auto accidents, and plane crashes. Although these stories are important to those involved, they have very little long-term impact on society as a whole. But because they pique viewer interest more effectively than, say, a policy debate in Washington or in a state capital, news programs devote more time to them. Internet news sources also cover these dramatic events, but the sheer number of Internet news sites and blogs makes it more likely that at least some of them will also cover more important news, and people interested in political events and debates can find Internet news sources that cover such events and issues.

Schools, Patriotism, and Civic Participation

As early as kindergarten, children in the United States are socialized to believe in democracy and express patriotism. Schools socialize children to the concept of democracy by making the idea tangible for them. On election day, children might vote for their favorite snack and wait for the results at the end of the day. Or they might compare different kinds of apples or grapes, or different books, and then vote for a favorite. Lessons such as these introduce children to processes associated with democracy at its most basic level: they learn about comparing attributes, choosing a favorite, voting, and winning and losing.

Children also are taught patriotism as they recite the Pledge of Allegiance every day, sing patriotic songs, and learn to venerate the "founding fathers," especially George Washington, and other American heroes, including Abraham Lincoln, Dr. Martin Luther King Jr., and John F. Kennedy. Traditionally, elementary and high schools in the United States have emphasized the "great men in great moments" form of history, a history that traditionally concentrated solely on the contributions of elites—usually white men in formal governmental or military settings. Increasingly, however, the curriculum includes contributions by women, African Americans, and other minorities.

Education also plays a pivotal role in determining *who* will participate in the political affairs of the community. Research indicates that higher levels of education are associated with higher levels of political activism. In a book on civic voluntarism, authors Sidney Verba, Kay Schlozman, and Henry Brady write, "Well-educated parents are more likely to also be politically active and to discuss politics at home and to produce children who are active in high school. Growing up in a politicized household and being active in high school are associated with political engagement."[6]

Churches: The Role of Religion

The impact of church and religion in general on one's political socialization varies a great deal from individual to individual. For some people, religion plays a key, defining role in the development of their political beliefs. For others, it is irrelevant.

For many years, political scientists have examined the impact religious affiliation—whether one is Catholic or Jewish, Protestant or Muslim—has on political preferences. For example, religion is related to how people view various issues, especially the issue of abortion. But more recent analysis shows that a better predictor of the impact of religion on voting is not so much the religion an individual practices, but rather how regularly he or she practices it. A Gallup poll estimated that in the 2008 presidential election, white voters who attended church weekly favored John McCain over Barack Obama 65 to 28 percent, while Obama outpolled McCain among those whites who never or seldom attended church 56 to 49 percent. McCain enjoyed an edge (53 to 41 percent) among those whites who attended services nearly weekly to monthly. Similar parallels cannot be seen among highly religious black voters, who overwhelmingly favored Obama (89 percent to McCain's 5 percent).[7] But the 2008 data are reflective of a historical trend in the United States, in which the Republican Party can count on the support of highly religious white voters in presidential elections.

In general, however, it seems that those who are faithful in their church attendance are more likely to share conservative values—and support Republican candidates in general elections—though this is less the case among Catholics, who are generally more Democratic. African American voters are even more likely than Catholics to vote for a Democratic candidate. But African Americans are also likely to have high levels of religiosity, as measured by frequency of church attendance. Table 6.1 shows the breakdown in party identification by frequency of church attendance. As the table shows, while African American churchgoers are slightly more likely to identify themselves as Republican than their non-churchgoing counterparts, nearly two-thirds still identify themselves as Democrats. This presence of two conditions or traits that pull a voter toward different parties is called **cross pressuring.**

Interestingly, Table 6.1 also shows that those who never attend church, particularly whites, are most likely to identify themselves as independents, with no party preference. Similarly, blacks who never attend church are more likely to identify themselves as independents than are those who attend at least occasionally.

Peers and Group Norms

Friends, neighbors, coworkers, and other peers influence political socialization. Through peers, we learn about community and the political climate and values of the area in which we live. For example, your neighbors might inform you that a

TABLE 6.1

Party Identification by Frequency of Church Attendance and Race

Race	Church Attendance	Republican	Independent	Democrat
White	Once a week	51%	25%	24%
	Almost every week	46	28	26
	Once a month	37	31	31
	Seldom	32	34	33
	Never	24	43	33
Black	Once a week	9	25	65
	Almost every week	6	22	71
	Once a month	5	23	72
	Seldom	4	26	70
	Never	4	38	58

particular member of the city council is a strong advocate for your neighborhood on the council, securing funds for recreational facilities or increased police protection. Or a coworker might let you know what your member of Congress is doing to help save jobs in the industry in which you work. Much research indicates that the primary impact of peers is to reinforce our already-held beliefs and values, however. Typically, the people with whom you are acquainted are quite similar to you. While diversity exists in many settings, the norms and values of the people you know tend to be remarkably similar to your own.

Political and Community Leaders: Opinion Shapers

Political and community leaders also help socialize people and influence public opinion. Positions advocated by highly regarded government leaders hold particular sway, and the president plays an especially important role in shaping Americans' views. For example, many commentators believe that when President Barack Obama made passage of a health care reform package a priority and instituted a self-imposed December 2009 deadline for this goal, his actions helped shape public opinion in favor of this agenda item. In July 2009, fully 41 percent of Americans said they would advise their congressional representatives to vote for a reform bill within the year, and another 30 percent said they would advise voting for the reforms, though not necessarily within the year.[8] At least part of the 71 percent who voiced a desire for reform were likely influenced by an Obama full-court press on the issue, including a news conference in which Obama said that he set the deadline in order to capitalize on momentum building around the issue, rather that allowing a protracted debate to sideline health care reform, as had occurred in previous administrations.

But the role of political leaders in influencing public opinion is not limited to the national stage. In your city, chances are that the views of community leaders—elected and not—influence the way the public perceives local policies. Perhaps the fire or police chief endorses a candidate for city council, or the popular coach for the Police Athletic League makes the funding of a new football field a policy priority in your town. Often we rely on the recommendations and priorities of well-respected leaders who have earned our trust.

Demographic Characteristics: Our Politics Are a Reflection of Ourselves

Who we are often influences our life experiences, which shape our political socialization and therefore what we think. The racial and ethnic groups we belong to, our gender, our age and the events that have shaped our lives, and where we live all play a role in how we are socialized to political and community life, our values and priorities, and even whom we vote for. Demographic characteristics also shape our levels of civic involvement and may even help determine the ways in which we contribute to the civic life of our communities and our nation.

Race and Ethnicity Whites, African Americans, Latinos, and Asian Americans prefer different candidates, hold different political views, and have different levels of civic involvement. Among the most salient of these differences are the candidate preferences of African Americans, who strongly support Democratic candidates over Republicans. But Figure 6.1 shows that in 2008, President Obama won majorities

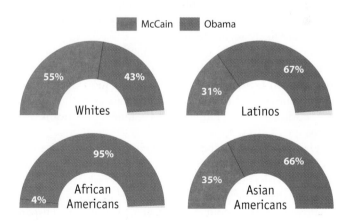

FIGURE 6.1

Support of the 2008 Presidential Candidates by Racial Group

Source: The Gallup Poll, "Candidate Support by Race," http://www.gallup.com/poll/108040/Candidate-Support-Race.aspx, and Jane Junn, Taeku Lee, S. Karthick Ramakrishnan, and Janelle Wong, the National Asian American Survey, *Asian Americans and the 2008 Election*, http://www.naasurvey.com/assets/NAAS-National-report.pdf; www.cnn.com/ELECTION/2008/results/polls/USP00p1.

TABLE 6.2

Latino Party Identification by National Origin, 2008

	Republican	Democratic	Independent	Other
Mexican	18%	50%	22%	6
Puerto Rican	11	61	24	7
Cuban	20	53	26	2
Other	12	52	24	12

Source: Changing Faiths: Latinosand the Transformation of American Religion. © 2006 Pew Hispanic Center, a Pew Research Center project, http://pewhispanic.org

from Latinos, Asian Americans, and particularly African Americans, 95 percent of whom voted for President Obama. This proportion exceeds the share of the African American vote that Democratic presidential candidates have garnered in recent years, which has averaged 84 to 90 percent. The 43 percent of the white vote that President Obama won exceeds the 41 percent that John Kerry received in 2004, and the average of 39 percent of white votes that Democratic candidates have received since 1964.

This breakdown of 2008 voter preferences is not unique, but rather reflects well-established differences in party affiliation and ideology between racial and ethnic minorities and whites. But there are also significant differences even within racial and ethnic groups.[9] Table 6.2 shows how the various categories of Latinos differ in terms of party identification. As the table shows, most Latinos of all national origins identify themselves as Democrats. But slightly higher percentages of Mexican and Cuban Americans are likely to be Republicans.

Party affiliation among ethnic groups within the Asian American community also varies somewhat, as Figure 6.2 shows. In general, about 60 percent of all Asian Americans are registered Democrats. South Asians are most likely to be Democrats, and majorities of Chinese and Koreans are Democrats as well. A quarter to a third of all Korean, Southeast Asian, Filipino, and Chinese Americans are unaffiliated with either party.

Beyond party affiliation and candidate preferences, racial and ethnic minorities and white voters differ on other issues as well. One example is their level of satisfaction with the state of the nation. Gallup frequently asks the question "Are you generally satisfied or dissatisfied with the way things are going in the United States at this time?" In June 2007, about 30 percent of whites and Hispanics reported being satisfied with the state of the nation, while 68 percent of whites and Hispanics were dissatisfied. But only 11 percent of blacks were satisfied, while 87 percent reported being dissatisfied.[10]

White, African American, Latino, and Asian American youths also differ significantly in their levels of civic engagement and in how they connect with their

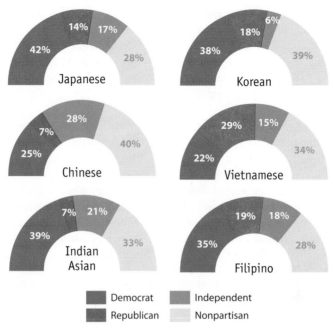

FIGURE 6.2

Asian Americans' Party Affiliation by Ethnic Group

Source: Jane Junn, Taeku Lee, S. Karthick Ramakrishnan, and Janelle Wong, the National Asian American Survey, *Asian Americans and the 2008 Election,* http://www.naasurvey.com/assets/NAAS-National-report.pdf

communities. Trends reported in *The 2006 Civic and Political Health of the Nation: A Detailed Look at How Youth Participate in Politics and Communities* include the following:

- African American youths are the most politically engaged racial or ethnic group. They are the most likely to vote, belong to political groups, make political contributions, display buttons or signs, canvass voters, and contact the media about political issues.
- Young Asian Americans are more likely to have been active in their communities. They are more apt to work to solve community problems, volunteer, engage in boycotts, sign petitions, and raise charitable contributions.
- Young Latinos are the least likely to be active in politics or their communities, but they are most likely to have engaged in political protests. One-quarter of Latinos (more than twice the proportion of any other group) have protested, primarily in immigration rights demonstrations. The lack of civic involvement may be a function of barriers to participation—including the fact that many Latino youths in the United States are not citizens, which would bar them from voting. The slogan of many immigration reform marches, "Hoy marchamos! Mañana votamos!" (Today we march! Tomorrow we vote!), may be a promise of increased political participation among young Latinos in the future.

- Young white people are moderately likely to engage in many community and political activities. They are more likely than other groups to run, walk, or bike for charity, and they are also more likely to be members of a community or political group. Of the groups of young people considered here, they are the least likely to protest, the least likely to contribute money to a political cause, and the least likely to persuade others to vote.[11]

Gender   Public opinion polls and voting behavior indicate that men and women hold very different views on issues, have different priorities when it comes to public issues, and often favor different candidates, particularly in national elections. This difference in men's and women's views and voting preferences is called the **gender gap,** the measurable difference in the way women and men vote for candidates and view political issues. The gender gap was first noticed by Eleanor Smeal, who at the time was president of the National Organization for Women. In the 1980 presidential election, Democratic incumbent Jimmy Carter lost to Republican challenger Ronald Reagan, but Smeal noticed that in poll after poll, women favored Carter.

Since that watershed 1980 election, the gender gap has been a factor in every subsequent presidential election: women voters are more likely than men to favor Democratic candidates. President Bill Clinton, first elected in 1992, had the smallest gender gap that year, with women voters favoring him by only 4 percent. Four years later, when he ran for reelection, he had the largest gender gap to that point, with women voters favoring him by 11 percent. In the 2008 presidential election, the gender gap continued to favor the Democratic nominee, with women voters favoring Barack Obama, over John McCain by 7 percent. The presence of Alaska governor Sarah Palin as the Republican vice presidential nominee appeared not to have swayed vast numbers of women voters.

Voting turnout patterns increase the effect of the gender gap. Women in most age groups—except those under age 25—are more likely to vote than their male counterparts. In addition, on average, women live longer than men, so older women constitute an important voting bloc. The difference in women's candidate preferences and their higher likelihood of voting means that the gender gap is a political reality that any candidate seeking election cannot ignore.

Young men and women also differ in their level of civic engagement, in the ways in which they are involved with their communities, and in their perspectives on the government. While majorities of young men and women believe it is their *responsibility* (rather than their choice) to get involved to make things better for society, how they choose to get involved varies by gender. As Figure 6.3 shows, women in particular are more likely to participate in certain forms of community activism such as volunteering and running, walking, biking, or engaging in other fund-raising activities for charity. Men and women are about equally likely to work on solving a community problem, such as volunteering for a nonprofit mediation service that helps negotiate disputes between neighbors. Men are more likely than women to choose formal political forms of activism, such as voting, persuading others to vote, and contributing money to political campaigns.

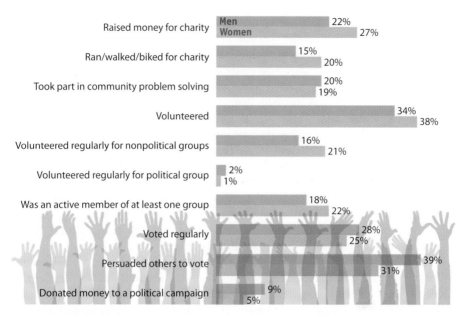

FIGURE 6.3

Participation in Civic Activities Among Young Men and Women

Source: Karlo Barrios Marcelo, Mark Hugo Lopez, and Emily Hoban Kirby, *Civic Engagement Among Young Men and Women* (College Park, MD: Circle: The Center for Information and Research on Civic Learning and Engagement, 2007).

Women's and men's opinions also differ on public policy issues, though often in unexpected ways. On the one hand, there is very little difference of opinion between men and women on the issue of abortion. On the other hand, men's and women's view on the optimal role of government vary greatly, with 66 percent of young women believe that government should do more to solve problems (versus 60 percent of young men), while only 27 percent of women believe that government does too many things better left to businesses and individuals, as opposed to 35 percent of men.[12] Women are also more likely to believe that the United States is at risk of another terrorist attack, and they are less likely to feel safe from terrorism. Women, too, are more likely to believe that going to war in Iraq was a mistake, and they were more likely to have reached this conclusion earlier than men were. When it comes to domestic priorities, men and women are equally likely to cite jobs and the economy as high priorities, but women are more likely to consider health care a priority. Men are about 10 percent more likely to favor the death penalty than are women.[13] Do the different life experiences of women and men help to explain some of their policy preferences, and hence their candidate preferences?

Age and Events   Differences in the candidates voters prefer—party, gender, the age of the candidates themselves—are one reflection of age and political opinions. People's opinions are also influenced by the events they have lived through and by their political socialization; an epic event may lead to a widespread change in political views.

Called the **generational effect** (or the *age-cohort effect*), this is the impact of a significant external event in shaping the views of a generation. Typically, generational effects
are felt most strongly by young people. As a result of the attacks that occurred on
September 11, 2001, people who were under age 30 on that day might place a heightened priority on keeping the United States safe in the face of a new kind of threat,
for instance. Other key events that have shaped the socialization of a generation include
the Great Depression and World War II for the oldest Americans and the war in
Vietnam and the changes in society that occurred during the 1960s for the Baby Boom
Generation born between 1946 and 1964. The major events that occur while we grow
up affect our socialization by shaping our viewpoints and our policy priorities.

One of the strongest examples of the generational effect is the Great Depression.
The oldest Americans, who came of age during the era of Democratic president
Franklin Roosevelt's New Deal social programs, remain most likely to vote Democratic. But often the impact of events is not immediately apparent. Political scientists continue to measure the effects of the September 11, 2001, terrorist attacks
and the subsequent war on terror on the views of the generation socialized to
politics during the first decade of the twenty-first century. In the 2008 presidential
election, young voters strongly preferred Senator Barack Obama over Republican
candidate Senator John McCain. But was this difference in candidate preference a
result of the generational effect? Will the Americans who grew up in the wake of
those attacks be more patriotic than their parents? Will they resist a militaristic
foreign policy throughout their lifetimes? These types of questions will interest
public opinion researchers in the decades to come.

Geographic Region Since the nation's founding, Americans have varied in
their political attitudes and beliefs and how they are socialized to politics, depending
on the region from which they come. These differences stem in part from historical
patterns of immigration: Irish and Italian immigrants generally settled in the northeastern seaboard, influencing the political culture of Boston, New York, Philadelphia,
and Baltimore. Chinese immigrants, instrumental in building the transcontinental
railroad in the nineteenth century, settled in California and areas of the Pacific
Northwest and have had a major impact on the political life of those areas.

Among the most important regional differences in the United States is the difference in political outlook between those who live in the Northeast and those in
the South. The differences between these two regions predate even our nation's
founding. During the Constitutional Convention in 1787, northern and southern
states disagreed as to the method that should be used to count slaves for the purposes of taxation and representation. The differences between these two regions were
intensified in the aftermath of the Civil War—the quintessential manifestation of
regional differences in the United States. Since the Republican Party was the party
of Lincoln and the North, the South became essentially a one-party region, with
all political competition occurring *within* the Democratic Party. The Democratic
Party dominated the South until the later part of the twentieth century, when
many Democrats embraced the civil rights movement (as described in Chapter 5).
Differences in regional culture and political viewpoints between North and South
remain. Today, in national elections, Republicans tend to carry the South, the West,

and most of the Midwest, except for large cities in these regions. Democrats are favored in the Northeast, the West Coast, and most major cities.

One factor that contributes to these differences in regional political climate is religious affiliation. Although differences in religious affiliation are often a function of people's heritage, church membership can alter the political culture of a region through the perpetuation of values and priorities. The South is much more Protestant than other regions of the United States. Not surprisingly, Republicans dominate in this area, particularly among religious Protestants, born-again Christians, and Evangelicals (see the discussion of the influence of churches on political socialization on page 225). Catholics and Jews tend to dominate in the Northeast along the East Coast; both groups are more frequently supporters of the Democratic Party. People without a religious affiliation, who tend to value independence and to have negative views of governmental activism, tend to live in the West and vote Republican.

Measuring Public Opinion

Public opinion consists of the public's expressed views about an issue at a specific point in time. Public opinion and ideology are inextricably linked because ideology is the prism through which people view all political issues; hence their ideology informs their opinions on the full range of political issues. Indeed, the growing importance of public opinion has even led some political scientists, such as Elizabeth Noelle-Neumann, to argue that public opinion itself is a socializing agent in that it provides an independent context that affects political behavior.[14] Though we are inundated every day with the latest public opinion polls on television, on the Internet, in magazines, and even on podcasts, the importance of public opinion is not a new phenomenon in American politics.

As early as the War of Independence, leaders of the Continental Congress were concerned with what the people thought. Popular opinion mattered because support was critical to the success of the volunteer revolutionary army. As discussed in Chapter 2, after the thirteen colonies won their independence, public opinion was an important concern of political and economic leaders during the early years of the new nation. The dissatisfaction of ordinary people troubled by debt caused Shays's Rebellion in Massachusetts in 1786–1787, which led to a shift in the thinking of the elites who came together in Philadelphia the following May to draft the new Constitution. And once the Constitution was drafted, *The Federalist Papers* were used as a tool to influence public opinion and generate support for the new form of government.

Public opinion is manifested in a variety of ways: demonstrators protesting on the steps of the state capitol; readers of the local newspaper writing letters to the editor on behalf of (or against) a proposal before the city council; citizens communicating directly with government officials, perhaps by telling their local city council member what they think of the town's plan to develop a recreational center or by calling their member of Congress to indicate their opinion of a current piece of legislation. One of the most important ways public opinion is measured is through the act of voting, which we discuss in Chapter 9. But another important tool that policy makers, researchers, and the public rely on as an indicator of public opinion is the **public opinion poll,** a survey of a given population's opinion on an issue at a particular point in time. Policy makers, particularly elected officials, care about public opinion because they want to develop and implement policies that reflect the public's views.[15] Such policies are more likely to attract support from other government leaders, who are also relying on public opinion as a gauge. Further, they help ensure that elected leaders will be reelected because they are representing their constituents' views.[16]

The Origins of Public Opinion Polls

In his book *Public Opinion,* published in 1922, political writer Walter Lippmann stressed both the importance of public opinion for policy makers and the value of measuring it accurately. Lippman's thought informed a generation of public opinion researchers, who in turn shaped two divergent areas of opinion research: (1) marketing research, used by businesses to increase sales, and (2) public opinion research, used to measure people's opinions on political issues.

Among the first efforts to gauge public opinion were attempts to predict the outcomes of presidential elections. In 1916, the *Literary Digest,* a popular magazine similar in format to today's *Reader's Digest,* conducted its first successful **straw poll,** a poll conducted in an unscientific manner to predict the outcome of an election. (The term comes from the use of a piece of straw to determine which way the wind is blowing; so too does a straw poll indicate how the winds of public opinion are blowing.) Between 1920 and 1932, *Literary Digest* correctly predicted the winner of every presidential race by relying on its subscribers to mail in postcards indicating their choice. The 1936 presidential election between Democrat Franklin Roosevelt and Republican governor Alfred M. "Alf" Landon of Kansas centered on one issue, however: the government's role in responding to the Great Depression. In effect, the election was a mandate on Roosevelt's New Deal policies. The *Literary Digest* poll predicted that Landon would defeat Roosevelt by 57 to 43 percent, but Roosevelt won that election by a landslide, receiving nearly 63 percent of the popular vote.

Where did the *Literary Digest* go wrong? The most fatal error the magazine committed was to use an unrepresentative sample to draw conclusions about the wider voting public. The straw poll respondents were derived from a list of subscribers to the magazine, automobile owners, and people listed in telephone directories. At the height of the Depression, this sample excluded most members of the working and middle classes. And class mattered in the 1936 election, with Roosevelt deriving his support primarily from poor, working-class, and middle-class voters. *Literary Digest* had committed what Lippmann termed an error of the casual mind: "to pick out or stumble upon a sample which supports or defies its prejudices, and then to make it the representative of a whole class."[17] Notice the similarity between *Literary Digest*'s faulty straw poll and many of today's voluntary Internet polls—self-selected respondents often differ dramatically in their views from those of the broader public.

Although the 1936 election destroyed the credibility of the *Literary Digest* poll, it was also the watershed year for a young, Princeton-based public opinion researcher named George Gallup. Gallup's entry in political public opinion research was driven in part by a desire to help his mother-in-law, Ola Babcock Miller, win election as Iowa's secretary of state, the first woman elected to that position. In 1935, Gallup founded the American Institute of Public Opinion, which would later become the Gallup Organization. Gallup gained national recognition when he correctly predicted the outcome of the 1936 election, and scientific opinion polls, which rely on the random selection of participants rather than their own self-selection, gained enormous credibility during this era.

Gallup's credibility suffered a substantial setback, however, after the presidential election of 1948 between Democrat Harry S Truman and Republican Thomas E. Dewey. That year, the "big three" polling organizations—Gallup, Roper, and Crossley—all concluded their polls in October, and all predicted a Dewey victory. By ending their efforts early, the polls missed the swing of third-party voters back to Harry S Truman's camp in the final days of the campaign. The organizations didn't anticipate that many voters would switch back to the Democratic nominee, who wound up winning the presidency. During his administration, Truman would sometimes offer a good-natured barb at the pollsters who had prematurely predicted his demise, and George Gallup responded in kind: "I have the greatest admiration for President Truman, because he fights for what he believes. I propose to do the same thing. As long as public opinion is important in this country, and until someone finds a better way of appraising it, I intend to go right ahead with the task of reporting the opinions of the people on issues vital to their welfare."[18]

How Public Opinion Polls Are Conducted

In politics, public opinion polls are used for a variety of reasons.[19] As political scientist Herbert Asher noted, "Polling plays an integral role in political events at the national, state, and local levels. In any major event or decision, poll results are sure to be a part of the news media's coverage and the decision makers' deliberations."[20] In addition, public opinion polls help determine who those decision makers will be: candidates for public office use polls to determine their initial name recognition, the effectiveness of their campaign strategy, their opponents' weaknesses, and the way potential voters are responding to their message. Once elected to office, policy makers often rely on public opinion polls to gauge their constituents' opinions and to measure how well they are performing on the job.

The process of conducting a public opinion poll consists of several steps. Those conducting the poll first need to determine the **population** they are targeting for the survey—the group of people whose opinions are of interest and about whom information is desired. For example, if your neighbor were considering running for the U.S. House of Representatives, she would want to know how many people recognize her name. But she would be interested only in those people who live in your congressional district. Further, she would probably narrow this population by looking only at those people in the district who are registered to vote. She might even want to narrow her target population further by limiting her survey to likely voters, perhaps those who have voted in past congressional elections.

The sponsor of any poll, whether a candidate, a political party, an interest group, or a news organization, needs to determine what information is desired from survey respondents. Sometimes this information is relatively clear—news media organizations track presidential approval ratings each month, for example. But other times

ANALYZING THE SOURCES

Examining Americans' Ideology

This graph shows a distribution of how Americans identify themselves by ideology, ranging from very liberal to very conservative (note that "neoconservative" was not offered as a possible response).

Evaluating the Evidence

1. What does the figure indicate about how most people identify themselves? Why do you think this is true?

2. If you were a candidate for the presidency, how might these data affect the policy stances you would take on specific issues?

3. The data are from a national sample of U.S. citizens. How do you think the data would vary in your state? In your community? If the sample included all U.S. residents, rather than just U.S. citizens?

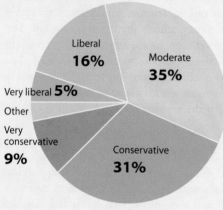

Liberal 16%
Moderate 35%
Very liberal 5%
Other
Very conservative 9%
Conservative 31%

Source: Lydia Saad, "'Conservatives' Are Single-Largest Ideological Group," Gallup News Service, June 15, 2009.

this process might be more complex. Polling organizations construct polls carefully to ensure that the questions actually measure what the client wants to know. Pollsters also recognize that many factors, including question design and question order, have an impact on the responses. For example, this chapter's "Analyzing the Sources" provides data on how Americans identify themselves ideologically: 5 percent of Americans identify themselves as very liberal, 16 percent as liberal, 35 percent as moderate, 31 percent as conservative, and 9 percent as very conservative. But past surveys have indicated that when the Gallup Organization has changed the term "liberal" to "progressive" in half of the surveys sent to respondents, those who have received the questionnaire with the "progressive" alternative have responded quite differently. In fact, fully 10 percent more (43 percent) identified themselves as moderates when the term "progressive" was used.[21] This simple change in terminology indicates that Americans may be more likely to identify themselves as "conservative" when the opposing term "liberal" rather than "progressive" is used.

Sampling Once the target population is determined and the survey measurement instrument, or poll, is designed, pollsters then must select a sample that will represent the views of this population. Because it is nearly impossible to measure all of the opinions of any given population, pollsters frequently rely on **random sampling,** a scientific method of selection in which each member of the population has an equal chance at being included in the sample. Relying on random sampling helps to ensure that the sample is not skewed so that one component of the population is overrepresented. To demonstrate this point, suppose the dean of students asks you as a class to conduct a public opinion survey that will measure whether students believe that parking facilities are adequate at your school. In this case, the population you need to measure is the entire student body. But clearly, how you conduct the sampling will have a bearing on the responses. If you ask only students in your 8:00 a.m. American government class, you might find that they have little trouble parking because the campus is not crowded at that hour. If you ask students who attend classes only during peak hours, you might get different, yet not necessarily representative, views as well, as these students may have more difficulty parking than average. How then would you obtain a random sample? The best way would be to ask the registrar for a list of all students, determine your sample size, randomly select every nth student from the list, contact each nth student, and ask for his or her views.

Researchers have noted, however, that one problem with polls is that even those conducted using random samples may not provide the accurate data needed to illuminate political opinions and behaviors. Part of the problem is that randomization can go only so far. One standard method for conducting telephone surveys is by using random-digit dialing of landline telephones.[22] Nearly every polling organization omits cellular lines from its population,[23] however, for a variety of reasons including the potential cost to the cell phone subscriber, the high rate of nonresponse because of the nearly universal use of caller ID, and the transportable nature of cell phones that makes their owners' willingness to participate in surveys unlikely.[24] Consider as well the population of individuals who rely exclusively on cell phones and do not use landlines. How might these people be different from those who use only landlines? People who rely exclusively on landlines are likely to be older than "celly-onlys." Indeed, one study found that 25 percent of young adults aged 18–29 years lived in celly-only households.[25] And some individuals who eliminate landlines from their homes do so in order to save money. In fact, in 2006, 17 percent of adults with household incomes below 200 percent of the federal poverty thresholds and 32 percent of low-income young adults lived in homes with only a cell phone.[26] So, by eliminating cell phone users from a potential sample, pollsters eliminate individuals who may be poorer or more concerned with the economy than those who pay to keep a landline.

One way pollsters attempt to address these types of concerns is through the use of a **quota sample,** a more scientifically sophisticated method of sampling than random sampling. A pollster using this method structures the sample so that it is representative of the characteristics of the target population. Let's say that your mother is running for mayor of your town, and you would like to conduct a poll that measures opinions of her among various constituencies. From census data, you learn that your town is 40 percent white, 35 percent African American, 20 percent Latino, and 5 percent Asian. Therefore, at a citywide event, you structure your sample so that it reflects the proportions of the population. With a sample of 200 voters, you would seek to include 80 white respondents, 70 African Americans, 40 Latinos, and 10 Asians. Pollsters routinely rely on quota sampling, though often they may not ask participants about their demographic characteristics until the end of the poll.

Another method used to address problems in sampling is **stratified sampling,** in which the national population is divided into fourths and certain areas within these regions are selected as representative of the national population. While some organizations still rely on quota sampling, larger organizations and media polls now use stratified sampling, the most reliable form of random sample. Today, nearly every major polling organization relies on U.S. census data as the basis of their four sampling regions. Stratified sampling is the basis for much of the public opinion data used by political scientists and other social scientists—in particular, the General Social Survey (GSS) and the National Election Study.

Sampling Error   As we have seen, to accurately gauge public opinion, pollsters must obtain an accurate sample from the population they are polling. A sample need not be large to reflect the population's views. In fact, most national polling organizations rarely sample more than 1,500 respondents; most national samples range from 1,000 to 1,500. To poll smaller populations (states or congressional districts, for example), polling organizations routinely use samples of between 300 and 500 respondents.

The key is having a sample that accurately reflects the population. Let's say that your political science instructor offers extra credit if you attend a weekly study group. The group initially convenes immediately after your regular class session. At the conclusion of the study group, the leader asks if this is a convenient time for everyone to meet. Since everyone present has attended the study group, chances are that the time is more convenient for them than it is for those students who did not attend—perhaps because they have another class immediately after your political science class, or they work during that time period, or they have child care responsibilities. In other words, the composition of the sample—in this case, the students in the study group—will skew the responses to this question. Similarly, if a poll is administered to a nonrepresentative sample of a population, the responses will not accurately reflect the population's views.

In selecting a representative sample, pollsters need to pay particular attention to the time of day a poll is administered: afternoons yield a disproportionate number of mothers with small children and retirees, while evenings may yield more affluent individuals who do not do shift work. And today's telephone technology presents pollsters with even more obstacles. As we have seen, many potential respondents, particularly young people, have opted out of telephone landlines in favor of cell phones, making them a subset of the population that is more difficult for pollsters to reach. People with caller ID or both cell phones and landlines frequently screen out unknown numbers or those of survey research companies.

Internet polls present their own set of obstacles, including the ability of some individuals to complete surveys (or vote for their favorite reality show contestant) repeatedly.[27] Nonetheless, market research firms, public opinion polling organizations, and even political candidates are increasingly relying on the Internet as a survey research tool.[28] Some organizations, such as the Harris Poll Online, offer "memberships": poll respondents can earn rewards for completing surveys that help the organization create a representative sample of their target population.

To adjust for problems with sampling, every poll that relies on a sample has a **sampling error** (sometimes called a **margin of error**), which is a statistical calculation

Public Opinion Polling

THEN (1970s)

NOW (2010)

THEN (1970s)	NOW (2010)
Telephone polls replaced mail-in and door-to-door polling because most American households had landlines.	Internet polls are at the cutting edge of public opinion research, but anonymity and multiple responses from the same person can damage a poll's accuracy.
Early telephone polls overrepresented the views of homemakers and retirees, who were more likely to answer the phone during the day.	The accuracy of telephone polls is affected by the difficulty of reaching people who use only cell phones or who screen calls using caller ID.
Pollsters remedied nonrepresentative sampling through quota sampling.	Pollsters rely on stratified sampling to ensure the most representative sample of the population they are targeting.

WHAT'S NEXT?

> How will new media technologies such as Twitter shape polling in the future?

> How might pollsters overcome the obstacles associated with Internet polls—in particular, anonymous respondents giving false answers or responding to the same poll multiple times?

> How will cell phones and text messaging change the process of measuring public opinion in the future?

of the difference in results between a poll of a randomly drawn sample and a poll of the entire population. Most polls have a sampling error of ±3 percentage points (plus or minus three percentage points). This means 3 percentage points should be added and subtracted from the poll results to find the range for the population. Consider the following story reported by Reuters News Service in 1996:

> WASHINGTON (Reuters)—President Clinton, hit by bad publicity recently over FBI files and a derogatory book, has slipped against Bob Dole in a new poll released Monday but still maintains a 15 percentage point lead. The CNN/USA Today/Gallup poll taken June 27–30 of 818 registered voters showed Clinton would beat his Republican challenger

if the election were held now, 54 to 39 percent, with seven percent undecided. The poll had a margin of error of plus or minus four percentage points.

A similar poll June 18–19 had Clinton 57 to 38 percent over Dole.[29]

The reporter who wrote this story did not understand the sampling error. In fact, with a margin of error of 4 percentage points, Clinton's standing remained virtually the same, because 54 percent (really 50–58 percent, as $54 - 4 = 50$ and $54 + 4 = 58$) encompassed the 57 percent he had garnered the previous week.

Types of Political Polls

Today, the process of measuring political opinions has evolved drastically from the days of the *Literary Digest*'s straw poll or even George Gallup's first successful predictions of the results of presidential elections.[30] Political candidates and parties and news organizations rely on several different types of polls, depending on their goals and objectives. These include tracking polls, push polls, and exit polls.

- **Tracking polls** measure changes in public opinion over the course of days, weeks, or months by repeatedly asking respondents the same questions. Since the 1992 presidential election, tracking polls have been an important tool, particularly for presidential candidates seeking to glean information about how campaign strategy has affected public opinion. Tracking polls are useful in indicating the effectiveness of the media strategy, the success of a day's worth of campaigning, or whether the campaign has gotten its message across in the most recent news cycle.

- **Push polls** are a special type of poll that both provides information to campaigns about candidate strengths and weaknesses and attempts to skew public opinion about a candidate. At their best, push polls help gauge voter priorities so that a campaign can better target its message. For example, a push poll might ask a respondent, "If you were aware that Senator John McCain was held prisoner while serving his country during the Vietnam War, would that make you more or less likely to vote for him?" Such questions enable the campaign to measure the importance to voters of a quality or stance of the candidate—in this case, service in Vietnam and McCain's POW status. The campaign can then determine whether to accentuate that message. But push polls have an unsavory reputation because some campaigns have used them to smear an opponent. Doing so in the hypothetical structure of push polls enables one campaign to make often baseless accusations against an opponent without having to substantiate the charges. For example, a pollster might ask, "If you knew that Jane Jones had been arrested for driving while intoxicated, would that make you more or less likely to vote for her?" Of course, the pollster is not saying that Jones had been arrested, but the hypothetical would lead some respondents to conclude that she had.

- **Exit polls** are conducted at polling places on election day to determine the winner of an election before the polls close. News organizations frequently sponsor exit polls, which help them predict the outcome of gubernatorial, congressional, and presidential elections. Because of exit polls, news organizations can frequently predict the outcome of a given election shortly after the polls have closed. Exit polls also provide the media, candidates, and political parties with information about why voters voted the way they did.

What Americans Think About Politics

Public opinion research is the means by which individuals can convey their opinions and priorities to policy makers. Consequently, polls connect Americans to their government.[31] Through public opinion polls, whether conducted by campaigns or media organizations, government officials come to know and understand the opinions of the masses.[32] Through polls, leaders learn what issues are important to people, which policy solutions they prefer, and whether they approve of the way government officials are doing their jobs.[33] The role of opinion polls in shaping citizens' involvement with their government is also circular: polls play a pivotal role in shaping public opinion, and the results of polls, frequently reported by the media, provide an important source of information for the American public.

The Most Important Problem

Several polling organizations routinely ask respondents to identify (either from a list or in their own words) what they view as "the most important problem" facing the country. As the graph in "Then, Now, Next" on page 242 shows, since April 2008, "the economy" has been most frequently cited as the most important problem (by 43 percent of those surveyed), having risen steadily in the rankings over the previous six-month period.[34] By March 2009, fully 80 percent of those surveyed identified the economy as the most important problem, though that figure tapered off, ebbing to 69 percent by May of that year. Not surprisingly, until November 2007, the war in Iraq was the top issue, with about a third of Americans—34 percent—citing it as the most important problem. By April 2008, only 23 percent named the war in Iraq as the most important problem. Until that time, Iraq had consistently been named the top problem for the four previous years. Interestingly, however, the percentage of Americans who were concerned about the situation in Iraq was not as high as it was for other wars, as reflected in the results of previous surveys conducted during earlier armed conflicts. For example, 56 percent of respondents identified the Korean War as the most important problem in September 1951, and 62 percent named the Vietnam War as the top problem in January 1967.[35] In general, other problems Americans identify as important include the state of the economy, gas prices, health care, immigration, and terrorism.

The Mood of the Nation

In October 2009, Americans' satisfaction with the state of the nation was low, with 26 percent of Americans saying they were satisfied and 71 percent saying they were dissatisfied. But these numbers mark an actual improvement in satisfaction: when President Obama was sworn into office in January 2009, only 14 percent of Americans were satisfied and 80 percent were dissatisfied.[36] Gallup reports that since it began asking the "mood of the nation" question in 1979, typically 43 percent of the

What Do Americans Consider to Be the Most Important Problem for the Obama Administration?

THEN: After the September 11, 2001, attacks, terrorism was the most important problem for many Americans, giving way to the war in Iraq in 2003. The situation in Iraq would remain the most important problem until 2008.

NOW: Since 2008, Americans have considered the economy to be the most important problem. During the 2008 presidential election campaign, nearly 80 percent mentioned it as their most pressing concern. The issue's dominance contributed to President Obama's election, with some voters blaming Republicans for the economic downturn during the Bush administration.

WHAT'S NEXT?

■ Will Americans continue to view the economy as the most important problem? Why or why not?

■ What might cause the situation in Iraq and Afghanistan to reemerge as an important problem, to most Americans?

■ What other issues do you see on the horizon as potential "most important problems"?

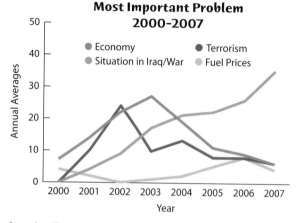

Most Important Problem 2000–2007

● Economy ● Terrorism
● Situation in Iraq/War ● Fuel Prices

Source: http://www.gallup.com/poll/27949/Americans-Views-Most-Important-Problem-Continues-Iraq.aspx.

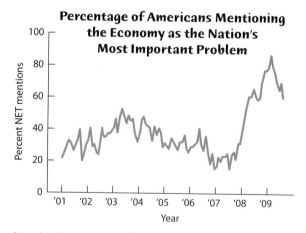

Percentage of Americans Mentioning the Economy as the Nation's Most Important Problem

Source: http://www.gallup.com/poll/1675/Most-Important-Problem.aspx.

American people report being satisfied.[37] When George W. Bush took office in 2001, 56 percent of Americans reported being satisfied; that percentage jumped to an unsustainable 70 percent in the aftermath of the 9/11 attacks and has since declined steadily, most precipitously in 2008. As noted, during that year, the economy emerged as one cause of high levels of dissatisfaction, replacing dissatisfaction with the war in Iraq.

Public Opinion About Government

Analysts of public opinion, government officials, and scholars of civic engagement are all concerned with public opinion about the government at all levels—in particular, about the institutions of the federal government. For decades, public opinion researchers have measured the public's trust in government by asking survey respondents to rate their level of trust in the federal government's ability to handle domestic and international policy matters and to gauge their amount of trust and confidence in the executive, legislative, and judicial branches of government.

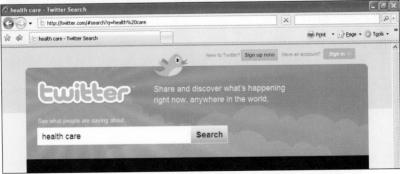

> Bumper stickers, traditionally a means of voicing opinions on the issues of the day, provide a (very unscientific) way of observing public opinion. Today, however, many individuals are likely to voice their views through tweets and by following the causes they care about on Twitter. Do Internet-based services like Twitter provide a more accurate gauge of public opinion than older media like bumper stickers? Does the absence of bumper stickers or tweets about an issue necessarily mean that members of the public lack opinions on it?

The responses to these questions are important for several reasons. First, although these measures indicate public opinion about institutions rather than individuals, individual office holders nonetheless can use the data as a measure of how well they are performing their jobs. Lower levels of confidence in the institution of the presidency, for example, tend to parallel lower approval ratings of specific presidents.[38] Second, trust in government is one measure of the public's sense of efficacy, their belief that the government works for people like them, as discussed in Chapter 1. If people trust their government, they are more likely to believe that it is responsive to the needs of citizens—that it is working for people like themselves.

The public's trust in the ability of the federal government to handle both international affairs and domestic problems declined during President Bush's second term in office but has rebounded somewhat since President Obama took the oath of office in January 2009. Many analysts attribute the decline during the Bush administration to widespread dissatisfaction with both foreign policy as it relates to the war in Iraq and the economic downturn. But as shown in Figure 6.4, in 2009,

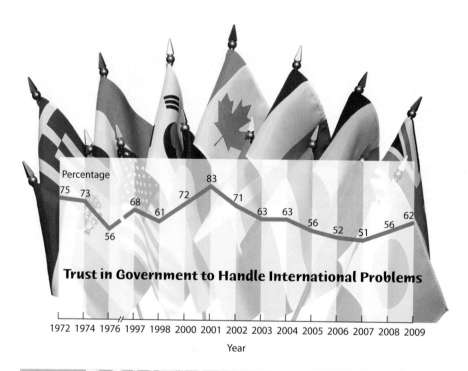

Trust in Government to Handle International Problems

FIGURE 6.4 ▮ As you can see, public trust in the government's ability to deal with international problems increased significantly in 2009. What explains this increase in trust? Has the international context changed a great deal, or can you think of other events or situations that may have affected the public's judgment?

Source: The Gallup Organization, http://www.gallup.com/poll5392/Trust-Government.aspx.

Trust in Government to Handle Domestic Problems

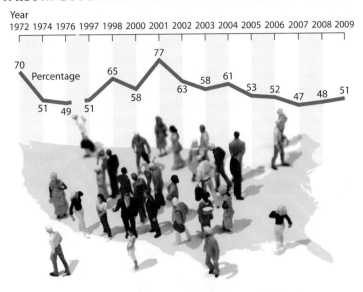

Year
1972 1974 1976 1997 1998 2000 2001 2002 2003 2004 2005 2006 2007 2008 2009

70
Percentage 65
77
63 58 61
58
53 52
51 49 51 58 47 48 51

POLITICAL INQUIRY

FIGURE 6.5 ■ **What impact does the state of the economy have on the public's trust in the government's ability to handle domestic problems? What can you infer about the state of the economy in May 1972? In September 2004? In September 2009?**

Source: The Gallup Organization, http://www.gallup.com/poll5392/Trust-Government.aspx.

62 percent of Americans said they trusted the government to handle international problems, an increase from 56 percent during the last year of the George W. Bush presidency. During the Bush administration we can see the impact of both the September 11, 2001, terrorist attacks (resulting in a record high 83 percent trust rating) and the American people's weariness of the war in Iraq, which showed in the low levels of trust during Bush's second term (2005–2009). The rating reached a nadir of 51 percent in 2007 before rebounding a bit in 2008.

The public's trust in the government's ability to handle domestic matters has also declined, as shown in Figure 6.5, which indicates a decrease in the number of people who trust the government to handle domestic problems a great deal or a fair amount since President Bush's record highs after September 11, 2001. From Figure 6.5, it is clear, that the government—here primarily reflecting President Obama and the Democratic majority in Congress—has fared less well in garnering trust to handle domestic problems than international challenges. Perhaps this is partially due to the unease associated with President Obama's health care reform proposals in 2009. That year, only 51 percent of Americans trusted the government to handle domestic problems, barely up form 48 percent the year before and from President Bush's 2007 low of 47 percent. During the Bush administration, a significant dip in the assessment of the government's ability to handle domestic matters occurred in 2005, immediately after Hurricane Katrina devastated parts of Louisiana, Mississippi, and other southern states. The widely perceived inability of the government to manage this crisis was reflected in this drop in confidence, and confidence continued to decline as the nation's worries about the economy persisted into 2008. The low levels of confidence seen in 2007 rival the record low confidence levels of 51–49 percent seen in the period between 1974 and 1976, following the Watergate scandal.

When examining the public's trust in specific branches of government, the impact of external events is apparent. For example, trust in all branches of government hit record highs in the aftermath of the September 11, 2001, terrorist attacks. An examination of the trust in the executive branch also demonstrates that peoples' trust in that branch is reflective of the popularity of an individual president. Witness, for example, in Figure 6.6 the increase in trust in the executive branch after Barack

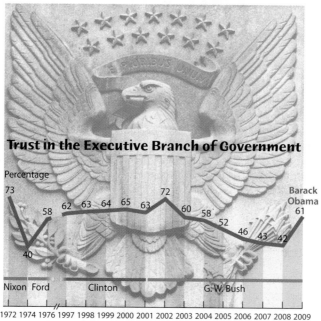

POLITICAL INQUIRY

FIGURE 6.6 ■ As the graph shows, the public's trust in the executive branch declined steeply (from 73 percent to 40 percent in two years) during the Nixon presidency as a result of the Watergate scandal. The decline during George W. Bush's presidency was more gradual, from 72 percent to 42 percent in six years. Is this decline partly to be expected for any second-term president?

Source: The Gallup Organization, http://www.gallup.com/poll5392/Trust-Government.aspx.

Obama became president: trust increased from 42 percent in 2008 during the Bush administration to 61 percent in 2009, marking the first increase in trust in the executive branch since 2001. The Bush administration was characterized by declining levels of trust in the executive branch. For example, in 2007, public trust in the executive branch dropped to 43 percent, marking a 9-percentage-point decline from 2005. The only time the level of public trust in the executive branch was lower (at 40 percent) since Gallup began measuring trust in institutions was in 1974, at the height of the Watergate scandal and just months before Richard Nixon resigned the presidency.[39] As previously noted, the decline in trust in the institution of the presidency is closely related to public approval of individual presidents: in the 2007 survey, only 36 percent of those surveyed approved of the way President Bush was handling his job.

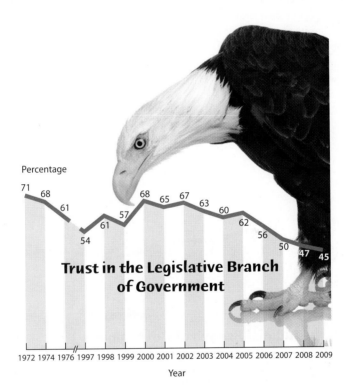

Percentage

Trust in the Legislative Branch of Government

71 68 61 54 61 57 68 65 67 63 60 62 56 50 47 45

1972 1974 1976 1997 1998 1999 2000 2001 2002 2003 2004 2005 2006 2007 2008 2009

Year

POLITICAL INQUIRY

FIGURE 6.7 ■ Trust in the legislative branch plummeted from 62 percent in 2005 to 45 percent in 2009. What factors can explain this trend? Why do you believe that trust in both the executive and the legislative branches was low from 2006 to 2008, despite the fact that those branches were controlled by different political parties?

Source: The Gallup Organization, http://www.gallup.com/poll5392/Trust-Government.aspx.

Often there is an inverse relation in levels of trust between the executive and the legislative branches (when one enjoys high levels of trust, the other suffers low). For example, in 2009, the executive branch enjoyed a 61 percent trust rating, while the legislative branch's was a mere 45 percent. But this was not the case in 2007, however. As Figure 6.7 shows, trust in the legislative branch also declined to 50 percent from 62 percent in 2005. Before 2006, part of this decline of trust could be attributed to the public's dissatisfaction with the Republican Congress's consent to Bush administration policies concerning Iraq. But since 2006, the continuing decline indicates widespread dissatisfaction with the Democratic majority in Congress. Public dissatisfaction could be attributed to the Democrats' inability to make good on their campaign promise to end the war in Iraq, as well as dissatisfaction with the U.S. economy.

The judicial branch of government consistently scores higher in levels of public trust than the other two branches reaching 76 percent in 2009. Figure 6.8 shows that confidence in the judiciary typically hovers between 65 and 75 percent, sometimes climbing into the high 70s (or even 80 percent in 1999). The judiciary's lowest rating came in 1976, when there was widespread dissatisfaction with government as a whole in the aftermath of the Watergate scandal.

Percentage

66   71   63   71   78   80   75   74   75   67   65   68   69   69   69   76

Trust in the Judicial Branch of Government

1972 1974 1976 1997 1998 1999 2000 2001 2002 2003 2004 2005 2006 2007 2008 2009

Year

POLITICAL INQUIRY

FIGURE 6.8 ▮ While trust in the judicial branch rebounded to 76 percent in 2009, it was lower than usual from 2003 to 2008, with ratings consistently below 70 percent—especially in 2004, when the percentage almost reached the Watergate level. What could have caused these ratings to dip?

Source: The Gallup Organization, http://www.gallup.com/poll5392/Trust-Government.aspx.

CONTINUING THE CONVERSATION

- The process of political socialization is quite different from even a generation ago. While some agents of socialization such as families, peers, and churches remain important, other agents, particularly the media, are more pervasive and influential than ever before.

- Technology has drastically changed the way public opinion is measured. The advent of the computer alone—from powerful mainframes to personal computers—has revolutionized the data collection process; today computers facilitate near-instant access to polling data. They also provide the means to generate and survey increasingly representative samples in order to gauge the public's views with a high degree of accuracy.

- The catch-22 has been the pervasiveness of public opinion polls. People's opinions are solicited by every kind of survey, from cheesy Internet polls to reputable polling organizations. As a result, the public has become poll weary, dubious of the value of the pollster's next set of questions.

- Technology has provided—and will continue to provide—ways to solve the problems that technology itself has generated in accurately measuring public opinion. Stratified samples and other increasingly sophisticated microsampling techniques have improved the ability of reputable pollsters to gauge public opinion. And pollsters are incorporating new technologies, including text messaging and cell phone surveys, as they work to develop new ways to accurately measure and convey the public's views to candidates, to policy makers, and, through the media, to the public itself.

STUDY NOW

Summary

1. Political Socialization and Civic Participation

Political socialization begins at home in very early childhood, when our political ideology, our beliefs about people of different races and sexes, and even our party identification can be firmly embedded, and the beliefs and values we learn early help shape how we view new information as we age.

2. Agents of Socialization

Among the agents of socialization—including family, the media, schools, churches, peers, community and political leaders, and demographic characteristics—the most important are the family and the media.

3. Measuring Public Opinion

The measurement of public opinion has evolved and become increasingly complex and reliable when done scientifically; in measuring public opinion, reputable pollsters identify the target population, design an accurate measure, select a sample, and administer the poll.

4. What Americans Think About Politics

Americans identify the state of the economy as the "most important problem," and their trust in both the presidency and Congress is at near-record lows, while trust in the judiciary remains relatively stable.

For Critical Thinking and Discussion

1. Were you brought up in a family in which joining groups was important? Do your parents belong to any interest groups? Do you? If not, why do you think that is the case?

2. How have your demographic characteristics—your age, the area of the country in which you were raised, and so on—contributed to the formation of your political views? How relevant are the generalities described in the chapter to your own experience and beliefs?

3. What do you think is the "most important problem" facing the United States? Is it a problem discussed in this book? Is it one shared by your classmates?

4. What factors influence how satisfied you feel about the direction of the country?

5. Which branch of government do you trust the most? Why?

Key Terms

agents of socialization 222
cross pressuring 225
exit polls 240
gender gap 230
generational effect 232
political socialization 220

population 235
public opinion 233
public opinion poll 233
push polls 240
quota sample 237
random sampling 236

sampling error (margin of error) 238
stratified sampling 238
straw poll 234
tracking polls 240

Internet Resources

A More Perfect Union Web Site
www.mhhe.com/harrisonampule   Consult the book's Web site for study guides, interactive activities, simulations, and current hot-links that provide additional information on socialization and public opinion in the United States.

Annenberg National Election Studies
www.electionstudies.org   The ANES Web site contains a plethora of information on American public opinion, as well as a valuable user guide that can help acquaint you with using the data. It also provides a link to other election studies, including some cross-national studies at www.electionstudies.org/other_election_studies.

The Gallup Organization
www.galluppoll.com   You will find both national and international polls and analysis on this site.

The Roper Center
www.ropercenter.uconn.edu   This Web site features the University of Connecticut's Roper Center polls, the General Social Survey, presidential approval ratings, and poll analysis.

Zogby International
www.zogby.com   For a wide variety of political, commercial, and sociological data, go to this site.

Recommended Readings

Fiorina, Morris P. *Culture War: The Myth of a Polarized America.* New York: Pearson Longman, 2006. A critical view of the notion that the United States is divided along ideological lines. Fiorina asserts that Americans are generally moderate and tolerant of a wide variety of viewpoints.

Jamieson, Kathleen Hall. *Electing the President, 2004.* Philadelphia: University of Pennsylvania, 2006. A fascinating "insider's view" of how public opinion shaped the 2004 presidential campaigns by the director of the Annenberg National Election Studies.

Page, Benjamin I., and Robert Y. Shapiro. *The Rational Public: Fifty Years of Trends in Americans' Policy Preferences.* Chicago: University of Chicago, 1992. An analysis of the policy preferences of the American public from the 1930s until 1990. The authors describe opinion on both domestic and foreign policy.

Traugott, Michael W., and Paul J. Lavrakas. *The Voter's Guide to Election Polls.* New York: Chatham House, 2000. A user-friendly approach, written in question-and-answer format, that helps beginners understand the polling process and how to interpret public opinion data.

Welch, Susan, Lee Sigelman, Timothy Bledsoe, and Michael Combs. *Race and Place: Race Relations in an American City* (Cambridge Studies in Public Opinion and Political Psychology). Cambridge: Cambridge University Press, 2001. An analysis of the impact of residential changes on the attitudes and behavior of African Americans and whites.

THEN

Individuals joined voluntary organizations to achieve goals of value to their members and to influence the direction of society and government.

Organization and money are crucial predictors of how successfully an interest group will influence policy.

NOW

7

Interest Groups

Organizations that seek to achieve their goals by influencing government decision making are called **interest groups**. Also called *special interests,* interest groups differ from political parties in that interest groups do not seek to control the government, as parties do. Interest groups simply want to influence policy making on issues. Interest groups are more important in the political process of the United States than anywhere else in the world.[1] Their strong role is partly due to the number of interest groups that attempt to influence U.S. policy.

Take just one issue—the environment, say—and chances are that you or someone in your class is a member of one of the almost 200 organizations concerned with the environment, conservation, or ecology in the United States.[2] The multitude of interest groups focused on any given issue is an important component of how government policy is formulated. Interest groups shape the policy process by helping determine which issues policy makers will act on and which options they will consider in addressing a problem.

When we think of interest groups, the typical images that come to mind are of wealthy lobbyists "schmoozing" with easily corrupted politicians. While this may sometimes be the case, interest groups do not require the leadership of the rich and well connected to be effective. Even the least powerful members of society, through collective action, can influence policy making. Although moneyed interests may dominate politics, interest groups play a crucial role in leveling the political playing field by providing access for organized "average" people.

Will digital fund-raising, organizing, and communicating strengthen the clout and efficacy of interest groups?

Will expanding Web-based activism change the face of *who* participates in interest groups?

Will digital group activism have unintended negative consequences?

The Value of Interest Groups

The nineteenth-century French historian and writer Alexis de Tocqueville, author of the influential work *Democracy in America,* dubbed Americans "a nation of joiners" in 1835, and his analysis still rings true today.[3] Indeed, estimates indicate that about 80 percent of all Americans belong to some kind of voluntary group or association, although not every group is an interest group.[4] The key role interest groups would play in politics was foreseen by the founders—James Madison acknowledged the idea that people with similar interests would form and join groups to prompt government action. He believed that the only way to cure "the mischiefs of faction" was by enabling groups to proliferate and compete with one another.[5]

Yet despite this heritage, some contemporary scholars argue that Americans today are increasingly staying at home. Political scientist Robert Putnam, author of *Bowling Alone: The Collapse and Revival of American Community,* found a marked decrease in the number of people who belong to interest groups and other types of clubs and organizations. These organizations, Putnam argues, are essential sources of **social capital,** the relationships that improve our lives by giving us social connections with which to solve common problems. Putnam demonstrates that social capital improves individual lives in very concrete ways: those with a greater number of social ties live longer, happier, and healthier lives. But social capital also improves communities, and

> Can a conversation over skim milk latte create social capital? People may not be joining gardening clubs, and women may not be gathering for afternoon Tupperware home parties, at quite the same rate as they used to, but are they less connected than in the past? Or are their connections just different?

even larger polities, because it stimulates individuals to communicate and interact with their government. Efficacy increases, because when people are engaged and communicate with government officials, government responds by meeting their needs more effectively. This response in turn creates the feeling among individuals that government listens to people like them. And when government responds, it becomes more likely that those affected will try to influence government decisions again.[6]

Critics of Putnam's work have noted that although the number of people belonging to the kinds of groups Putnam analyzed may be declining, people are engaged in other types of groups and clubs and enjoy various forms of group recreation.[7] For example, it is unlikely that you are a member of a gardening club such as those that Putnam researched (but if you are, good for you!). Yet it is likely that you belong to an online community such as MySpace or Facebook. Such communities facilitate social relationships and may even provide the opportunity for participants to solve community problems. And although people may be less likely to entertain friends and relatives in their homes today (another activity Putnam measured), they are *more likely* to socialize with friends and relatives over meals in restaurants. So even if Putnam may be correct in his analysis that we are no longer socially engaged the way Americans used to be, we may still be engaged—but through different channels and in different settings. Research supports this interpretation: in 2005, more than one-quarter of college freshmen surveyed said they believed that it was important to participate in community action programs, and over two-thirds said they believed it was important to help others in need, *the highest proportion to say so in twenty-five years.*[8]

Political scientist E. E. Schattschneider has written, "Democracy is a competitive political system in which competing leaders and organizations define the alternatives of public policy in such a way that the public can participate in the decision-making process."[9] One of the key types of competitive organizations Schattschneider was describing is interest groups. Schattschneider and other political scientists study and assess the value that interest groups provide in American democracy. This value centrally includes interest groups' usefulness in channeling civic participation—serving as a point of access and a mechanism by which people can connect with their government. Political scientists also explore interest groups, on the one hand, as valuable avenues by which people can influence the policy process and, on the other hand, as resources for policy makers. In this section, we consider various perspectives on the role of interest groups in a democracy, the diverse value that interest groups confer, and the drawbacks of interest groups.

Interest Groups and Civic Participation

Scholars who study civic engagement acknowledge the significant ways in which interest groups channel civic participation. Interest groups afford a way for people to band together to influence government as a *collective force.* Interest groups also seek to involve *individuals* more actively in the political process by encouraging them to vote and to communicate their views one-on-one to their elected officials. In addition, interest groups assist in the engagement of *communities* by providing a forum through which people can come together and form an association. Importantly, too, interest groups offer an alternative means of participation to individuals who are disenchanted with the two-party system.

How Group Participation Has Changed in the United States

THEN (1960s)	NOW (2010)
Individuals joined bowling leagues, civic associations, and community service organizations.	People join Internet-based organizations and use social-networking sites to keep in touch with others who share their personal and public interests.
Many people entertained and socialized a great deal at home.	People are more likely to visit with friends and relatives in restaurants, cafés, and other public settings, as well as online through "virtual visits."
Groups used traditional activities to communicate their interests to policy makers, including letter writing and lobbying.	Groups rely on traditional activities but also increasingly use new technologies to communicate with members, to fund-raise, and to lobby policy makers.

WHAT'S NEXT?

> What new media technologies and strategies might shape how interest groups organize and mobilize members in the future?

> Are there *negative* consequences to relying on the Internet as an organizing tool? What obstacles will some Internet-based organizations face in mobilizing their supporters around a given issue?

> In what ways will technology change how policy makers are influenced in the future?

Pluralist Theory vs. Elite Theory

An interest group can represent a wide variety of interests, as in the case of a community Chamber of Commerce that serves as an umbrella organization for local businesses. Alternatively, an interest group can restrict itself to a narrower focus, as does the Society for the Preservation and Encouragement of Barbershop Quartet Singing. Scholars who support **pluralist theory** emphasize how important it is for a democracy to have large numbers of diverse interest groups representing a wide variety of views.[10] Indeed, pluralists view the policy-making process as a crucial competition among diverse groups whose members attempt to influence policy in numerous settings, including agencies in the executive branch of government, Congress, and the courts.[11] Pluralists believe that interest groups are essential players in democracy because they ensure that individual interests are represented in the political arena *even if some individuals opt not to participate.* Like some of the founders, pluralists argue that individuals' liberties can be protected only through a proliferation of groups representing diverse competing interests, so that no one group dominates.

Pluralists believe, moreover, that interest groups provide a structure for political participation and help ensure that individuals follow the rules in participating in civic society. Following the rules means using positive channels for government action rather than extreme tactics such as assassinations, coups, and other forms of violence. Pluralists also stress that groups' varying assets tend to counterbalance one another. Pluralists contend that this is frequently the case with many policy debates. And so, although an industry association such as the American Petroleum Institute, an interest group for the oil and natural gas industry, might have a lot of money at its disposal, an environmental group opposing the industry, such as Greenpeace, might have a large membership base from which to launch grassroots activism.

Proponents of elite theory dispute some claims of pluralist theory. In particular, elite theorists point to the overwhelming presence of elites as political decision makers. According to **elite theory,** a ruling class composed of wealthy, educated individuals wields most of the power in government and also within the top universities, corporations, the military, and media outlets. Elite theorists claim that despite appearances that the political system is accessible to all, elites hold disproportionate power in the United States. They also emphasize that elites commonly use that power to protect their own economic interests, frequently by ensuring the continuation of the status quo. And so while non-elites represented by interest groups may occasionally win political victories, elites control the direction of major policies. But elite theorists posit that there is mobility into the elite structure. They emphasize that (in contrast to the situation in aristocracies) talented and industrious individuals from non-elite backgrounds can attain elite status in a democracy, often through education. This mobility, they say, gives the political system an even greater façade of accessibility.

Although these theories offer competing explanations for the role and motivation of interest groups in the United States, many political scientists agree that aspects of both theories are true: elites do have disproportionate influence in policy making, but that power is checked by interest groups. Undisputed is that interest groups are an essential feature of American democracy and provide an important medium through which individuals can exercise some control over their government.

Key Functions of Interest Groups

Many Americans join interest groups, and yet interest groups have a generally negative reputation. For example, it has been said of many a politician that he or she is "in the pockets of the special interests." This statement suggests that the politician is not making decisions based on conscience or the public interest but rather that the individual can be "bought." This notion is closely linked to the ideas held by elite theorists, who argue that elites' disproportionate share of influence negatively impacts the ability of the "average Jill or Joe" to get the government to do what she or he wants it to. Yet despite the criticisms frequently leveled by politicians, pundits, and the populace about interest groups' efforts to influence government, they serve several vital functions in the policy-making process in the United States:

- **Interest groups educate the public about policy issues.** Messages from interest groups abound. For example, thanks to organizations such as Mothers Against Drunk Drivers (MADD), most pee are aware of the dangers of drinking and driving. In educating the public, interest groups often provide a vehicle for civic discourse, so that genuine dialogue about policy problems and potential solutions is part of the national agenda.
- **Interest groups provide average citizens with an avenue of access to activism.** Anyone can join or form an interest group. Although wealthy and well-educated people are most likely to do so, interest groups can speak for all kinds of people on all kinds of issues. Historically in the United States, groups have been significant forces for advocates of civil rights for African Americans[12] and for supporters of equal rights for women,[13] gays and lesbians, and ethnic minorities.
- **Interest groups mobilize citizens and stimulate them to participate in civic and political affairs.** Some people are "turned off" by politics because they feel that neither the Democratic Party nor the Republican Party represents their views. In these cases, interest groups, with their typically narrower area of focus, can sometimes fill the void. Moreover, interest groups nurture community involvement by encouraging the formation of local chapters of larger interest groups. They support public education activities by private citizens. And interest groups not only can facilitate the ongoing conversation of democracy between people and their government officials but also encourage voting.
- **Interest groups perform electoral functions.** By endorsing and rating candidates and advertising their positions, interest groups provide voters with cues as to which candidates best represent their views. Interest groups also mobilize campaign volunteers and voters. These activities facilitate informed civic participation.
- **Interest groups provide information and expertise to policy makers.** The private sector often has greater resources than the public sector and can be a source of meaningful data and information for policy makers on pressing social issues.
- **Interest groups can protect the common good.** The federal government is structured so that only one individual (the president) is elected from a national constituency. Interest groups can work to protect the nation's interest as a whole, rather than just the needs of a specific constituency.
- **Interest groups are an integral part of the government's system of checks and balances.** Interest groups often "check" each other's influence with competing interests, and they can similarly check the actions of policy makers.

The Downside of Interest Groups

Despite the valuable functions of interest groups, certain criticisms of these organizations are valid. Interest groups do contribute to the appearance of (and sometimes the reality of) corruption in the political system. Indeed, there are various criticisms of the "interest group state." Former president Jimmy Carter bemoaned the influence of special interests, saying that they are "the single greatest threat to the proper functioning of our democratic system," while former president Ronald Reagan charged that interest groups are "placing out of focus our constitutional balance."[14]

Another criticism is that interest groups and their political action committee (PAC) fund-raising arms (which we consider briefly later in this chapter and in more detail in Chapter 9) make money a vital force in American politics. By contributing large sums of money to political campaigns, interest groups' PACs make campaigns expensive and often lopsided; candidates without well-stuffed campaign war chests have a difficult, if not impossible, task in challenging those who receive large PAC contributions. Money also changes the nature of campaigns, making them less engaging for citizens on a grassroots level and more reliant on the mass media.

Moreover, interest groups are faulted with strengthening the advantages enjoyed by incumbents. Most interest groups want access to policy makers, regardless of these elected officials' party identification. Realizing that the people already in office are likely to be reelected, interest groups use their resources disproportionately to support incumbent candidates. Doing so increases incumbency advantage even further by improving the odds against a challenger.

Finally, although the option to form an interest group is open to any and all activists and would-be activists, elites are more likely to establish and to dominate interest groups than are non-elites. This fact skews the policy process in favor of elites. Interest group activism is much more prominent among the wealthy, the white, the upper-middle class, and the educated than among the poor, the non-white, the working class, and the less educated. Although Internet-based interest groups have been particularly effective in attracting young people and others not traditionally drawn to such organizations, many of the most effective national interest groups remain dominated by traditional interest-group populations.

Who Joins Interest Groups, and Why?

People are not all equally likely to join or form interest groups, and this reality has serious consequences for the ability of interest groups to represent everyone's views. Political scientists agree that income and education tend to be the best predictors of interest group membership. This said, enormous diversity exists in the types of people who choose to join or form interest groups.

Patterns of Membership

Interest group participation is related to three demographic characteristics: income, social class, and education. People with higher incomes are more likely to participate in interest groups than those with lower incomes. Also, many surveys show that those who identify themselves as upper-middle or middle class are more likely to join interest groups than those who self-identify as lower-middle or working class.

Similarly, higher education levels are a strong predictor of interest group participation. But interest group participation also frequently reflects one's occupation: people tend to belong to associations related to their work.

Interest Group Participation Based on Occupation   There are several reasons for interest group membership patterns, some of which, as we shall see, are interconnected. For example, people with higher incomes have more disposable income to spend on membership dues for organizations. They are also likely to have occupations in which interest group activity is useful (or even required, as in some professional fields such as the law).

Doctors and lawyers, for example, are likely to be members of professional associations such as the American Medical Association (AMA) and the American Bar Association. These organizations give incentives for membership, such as accreditation of qualified professionals. They also confer benefits by providing various services to members and by attempting to influence government policy on members' behalf. The AMA accredits qualified physicians, promotes opportunities for continuing education to members, and lobbies the government on policy issues related to health care. During the 2008 presidential campaign, the AMA began a three-year media campaign designed to get the presidential candidates and the new president to tackle the issue of insurance coverage for the estimated 47 million Americans who do not have health insurance. Ads placed in the *New York Times* and *USA Today* feature a person holding a stethoscope as if it were a microphone, and part of the message says that the uninsured have "a voice and a vote."

Workers such as teachers and tradespeople are likely to belong to labor unions.[15] Many labor unions are influential in local politics, generating grassroots support for candidates through their membership base. A few of the national labor unions, especially the National Education Association (NEA), the largest teachers' union in the country, and the American Federation of Labor–Congress of Industrial Organizations (AFL-CIO), an organization of many different labor unions, are strongly influential in national politics.

Executives in business and industry are likely to be members of industry-specific and general business organizations that advocate on behalf of their members. All of these professional associations, labor unions, and business organizations are types of interest groups.

Interest Group Participation and Social Class   Differentiating the influence of income from that of class can be difficult when examining the impact of social class on the likelihood of joining an interest group. But in general, people who identify themselves as working class are less likely to have been socialized to participate in interest groups, with the important exception of labor unions, which historically have been most likely to organize working-class occupations. As we considered in Chapter 6, an important predictor of political participation (and interest group participation specifically) is whether a person learns to take part and join from a young age. If your mother participated in your town's historical preservation society, and your father attended meetings of the local Amnesty International chapter, you are likely to view those behaviors as "what people do" and do them yourself. If you come from a working-class family, you are generally less likely to see your parents engage in these participatory behaviors, rendering you similarly less likely to participate. Although scholars trace much of the lack of participation of working-class people to how they are socialized, the overlapping occurrence of working-class status and lower income is also a factor.[16] That is, working-class people are likely to have lower incomes and less job security than their middle-class counterparts. Thus they might not be able to afford membership dues and contributions to interest groups or might not have access to child care that would allow them to attend meetings. Their lower likelihood of owning a computer limits their chances of taking an active role in Internet-based groups. Or they might simply lack the leisure time to participate.

Interest Group Participation and Education   Educational attainment also has a strong impact on whether a person will join an interest group. One recent study surveyed 19- to 23-year-olds and found that those who were college students were more than twice as likely to join a politically motivated interest group as their age-group peers who did not attend college.[17] Individuals with higher education levels are more likely to be informed about issues and more willing to invest the time and energy in joining an interest group that represents their views. They might also be more likely to understand how important interest groups are in shaping public policy.

College students are among the most avid participants in Internet-based activist groups. But "belonging" to these groups varies a great deal (not unlike the situation in "real world" interest groups). A member of an Internet-based interest group may play a highly active role—communicating with other members regularly, attending rallies and other campus events, and taking concrete actions such as signing an Internet petition and participating in a protest. Or members may be more passive: they may limit their activity to reading the regular e-mails from the group that inform them of issues and events, and may only occasionally participate. Or they may be members of a group in name only. But this phenomenon is not unique to Internet-based groups. Many interest groups are dominated by a cadre of committed activists supported by "sometimes-activists." And nearly every group has a contingent of "members" who signed up mainly for the free T-shirt, tote bag, or umbrella.

Motivations for Joining Interest Groups

Some people may join an interest group for the benefits they can gain. Others might gravitate to a group sponsoring a particular cause. Still others might become members of a group for the simple reason that they want to meet new people. Recognizing that individuals have various motivations for joining, interest groups typically provide a menu of incentives for membership. For example, the National Association for the Advancement of Colored People (NAACP) offers a wide range of motivations for people to join the group (see "Analyzing the Sources"). In doing so, the NAACP, like many other interest groups, attempts to attract as many members as possible.

Solidary Incentives   Some people join interest groups because they offer **solidary incentives**—the feeling of belonging, companionship, friendship, and the satisfaction derived from socializing with others. Solidary incentives are closely linked to Robert Putnam's idea of social capital: both solidary incentives and social capital

Incentives for Participating in Interest Groups

The NAACP's Web site lists reasons why an individual should join the NAACP. Often, interest groups offer a wide variety of incentives for membership in order to attract members with different motivations.

Evaluating the Evidence

① In your view, what are the most important incentives the NAACP offers?

② What incentives are purposive? Does the NAACP offer solidary incentives? Monetary incentives? Which incentives fit in which categories?

③ Why might all of these types of incentives motivate someone to join the NAACP?

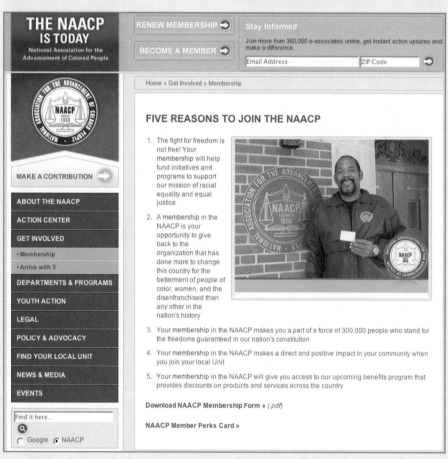

THE NAACP IS TODAY
National Association for the Advancement of Colored People

RENEW MEMBERSHIP ➡

BECOME A MEMBER ➡

Stay Informed
Join more than 360,000 e-associates online, get instant action updates and make a difference.

Email Address   ZIP Code   ➡

MAKE A CONTRIBUTION ➡

ABOUT THE NAACP
ACTION CENTER
GET INVOLVED
• Membership
• Arrive with 5
DEPARTMENTS & PROGRAMS
YOUTH ACTION
LEGAL
POLICY & ADVOCACY
FIND YOUR LOCAL UNIT
NEWS & MEDIA
EVENTS

Find it here...   🔍
◯ Google ⦿ NAACP

Home » Get Involved » Membership

FIVE REASONS TO JOIN THE NAACP

1. The fight for freedom is not free! Your membership will help fund initiatives and programs to support our mission of racial equality and equal justice

2. A membership in the NAACP is your opportunity to give back to the organization that has done more to change this country for the betterment of people of color, women, and the disenfranchised than any other in the nation's history

3. Your membership in the NAACP makes you a part of a force of 300,000 people who stand for the freedoms guaranteed in our nation's constitution

4. Your membership in the NAACP makes a direct and positive impact in your community when you join your local Unit

5. Your membership in the NAACP will give you access to our upcoming benefits program that provides discounts on products and services across the country

Download NAACP Membership Form » (.pdf)

NAACP Member Perks Card »

Source: http://www.naacp.org/get-involved/membership/fivereasons/index.htm

are related to the psychological satisfaction derived from civic participation. For example, a person might join the Sierra Club because she wants to participate in activities with other people who enjoy hiking or care deeply about wilderness protection. Your uncle might join the National Rifle Association because he likes to compete in shooting contests and wants to get to know others who do the same.

Purposive Incentives   People also join interest groups because of **purposive incentives,** that is, because they believe in the group's cause from an ideological or a moral standpoint. Interest groups pave the way for people to take action with like-minded people. And so you might join People for the Ethical Treatment of Animals (PETA) because you strongly object to animal abuse and want to work with others to prevent cruelty to animals. A friend who is passionately pro-life might join the National Right to Life Committee (NRLC), whereas your pro-choice cousin might join NARAL Pro-Choice America (formerly the National Abortion Reproductive Rights Action League).

The Internet is a particularly effective forum for attracting membership through purposive incentives. Accessible anyplace and anytime, the Internet provides resources for you to join an interest group even during a bout of insomnia at 3:00 a.m. Suppose a conversation earlier in the day got you thinking anew about the brutal genocidal conflict in Darfur. In those dark predawn hours, you can google "save Darfur" and within seconds have a variety of access points for becoming civically engaged by participating in an interest group. Some interest groups might ask you to contribute money; others might urge you to sign an online petition or to call the White House to make your opinions known. You can also learn about demonstrations sponsored by other groups right on your college campus and in your community. You might even find out about state and national demonstrations. The media contacts provided by online interest groups make it easy for you to write a letter to an editor, attempting to convince others of your views. Just learning about the wide variety of activities available can make you feel that you are "doing something" about a cause you believe in.

Economic Incentives   Many people join interest groups because of material or **economic incentives;** that is, they want to support groups that work for policies that will provide them with economic benefits. For example, the National Association of Police Organizations lobbies Congress concerning many appropriations measures that could affect its membership, including bills that would provide or increase funding for Community Oriented Policing Services (COPS) programs, bulletproof vests, and overtime pay for first responders to disasters.

Nearly all corporate and labor interest groups offer economic incentives to their members. They sometimes do so by advocating for policies that support business or labor in general, such as policies focused on the minimum wage, regulations concerning workplace conditions, and laws governing family leave or health coverage.

Other interest groups offer smaller-scale economic benefits to members. Many Americans over age 50 join the American Association of Retired Persons (AARP) because of the discounts members receive on hotels, airfares, and car rentals. Other organizations provide discounts on health insurance, special deals from merchants, or low-interest credit cards.

Most people join and remain in interest groups for a combination of reasons. A person might initially join an interest group for purposive incentives and then realize some solidary benefits and remain in the group because of the friendships formed. Or someone might join a professional association for the economic benefits but then develop rewarding social networks. Many individuals who join and stay in interest groups do so because of overlapping incentives.

How Interest Groups Succeed

In a single week in early 2006, the defense corporation Lockheed Martin won more than $2.5 billion worth of defense contracts from the federal government. First, the Defense Department contracted with the company for a $2.1-billion project that would create a network system to connect the department's earth-based global information grid to Defense Department users around the world. Then the company won a $491-million contract to build a third spacecraft for the Advanced Extremely High Frequency satellite system.

As it happens, Lockheed Martin, with annual revenues of over $37 billion, wins more federal contracts than any other company that contracts with the federal government. Similarly to many other big businesses, Lockheed Martin acts like an interest group. That is, it attempts to influence government policy by using the kinds of strategies on which interest groups rely to sway policy makers. In Lockheed Martin's case, such strategies include joining with competitors to form the National Defense Industrial Organization for the purpose of achieving policies benefiting all member corporations.

Contrast this powerful corporate interest with the "nuclear freeze" groups that coalesced in opposition to President Ronald Reagan's proposal in the 1980s to build a space-based shield to protect the United States from nuclear attack. Dubbed "Star Wars," the proposal attracted vocal and widespread opposition from nuclear freeze activists in the nation's capital and in cities throughout the United States. Although the groups continued their "no nukes" campaign more modestly during the George H. W. Bush administration, their efforts largely fizzled during the Clinton presidency. Despite the fact that Lockheed Martin is researching what has been called the "Son of Star Wars" weapon system advocated by President George W. Bush, the effectiveness of the no-nukes activists has dissipated.

Given that interest groups attempt to influence all kinds of policies, why are some interest groups better at getting what they want than others? Political scientists agree on various factors that influence whether an interest group will succeed. These factors include the interest group's *organizational resources*—the tools it has at its disposal to help achieve its goals—and its *organizational environment*—the setting in which it attempts to achieve those goals.

Organizational Resources

The effectiveness of interest groups in influencing government policy often depends on the resources they use to sway policy makers.[18] Interest groups rely on two key types of resources: (1) membership, the people who belong to a given group, and (2) financial resources, the money the group can spend to exert influence.

How Membership Affects Success A large membership enhances an interest group's influence because policy makers are more likely to take note of the group's position. The age-old concept of "strength in numbers" applies when it comes to interest groups. The sheer number of a group's membership is often an important factor in forcing policy makers, the media, and the public to pay attention to an issue. Among the largest U.S. interest groups is the American Association of Retired Persons (AARP), which boasts a membership of more than 35 million people. This vast size gives the organization incredible clout and historically has made policy makers unwilling to take on any issue that would unleash the wrath of AARP's formidable membership. For example, for years many economic analysts have suggested increasing the age at which people become eligible to receive Social Security. They reason that the average life span has risen significantly since the eligibility age was set and that people are working longer because they remain healthier longer. But this potential policy solution has long simmered on the back burner. The reason? Politicians in Congress and the White House have not wanted to incur the disapproval of the AARP's members, who would widely oppose increasing the eligibility age and might respond by voting unsympathetic officials out of office. While he was Speaker of the House of Representatives, Dennis Hastert (R-Illinois) remarked that he took "the AARP very seriously"—as had Newt Gingrich when he was Speaker before—and that "Republicans had been courting AARP for some time, listening to them, engaging in a give-and-take dialogue that none of the capital's pundits even suspected was going on."[19]

But size is not the only important aspect of an interest group's membership. The *cohesion* of a group, or how strongly unified it is, also matters to participants and to policy makers.[20] For example, the Human Rights Campaign (HRC) lobbies for federal legislation to end discrimination on the basis of sexual orientation and provides research to elected officials and policy makers on issues of importance to people who are gay, lesbian, bisexual, or transgender. The HRC has a membership of about 600,000, but because the organization limits its advocacy to issues impacting gay, lesbian, bisexual, and transgendered people, it is an extremely cohesive association.

Another significant aspect of an interest group's membership is its *intensity*. Intensity is a measure of how strongly members feel about the issues they are targeting. For example, pro-life interest groups such as the National Right to Life Committee, environmental groups such as the Sierra Club and Greenpeace, and animal rights groups such as People for the Ethical Treatment of Animals (PETA) are known for sustaining high levels of intensity. These organizations are more adept at attracting new members and younger members than are older, more entrenched kinds of groups. These newer, youthful members are a significant force behind the persistence and intensity of these groups.

The *demographics* of a group's membership also may increase its success. Members who know policy makers personally and have access to them mean greater influence for the group.[21] In the case of Lockheed Martin, the defense contractor discussed above, the company enjoyed the benefit of having had connections with some well-placed members of the George W. Bush administration. These included Vice President Dick Cheney, whose wife, Lynne, served on Lockheed's board of directors until 2001; former transportation secretary Norman Mineta, who served as a vice president with the company; and Deputy Secretary of Homeland Security Michael Jackson, a former chief operating officer (COO) at Lockheed.

In addition to an interest group's members' connections, other demographic attributes also matter. Members who are well educated, geographically dispersed (because they can influence a broader network of policy makers than a geographically consolidated membership), or affluent tend to have more influence. Policy makers perceive these attributes as important because the groups' membership is more likely to lobby and to contribute financial resources on behalf of the organization's cause.

How Financial Resources Affect Success   For an interest group, money can buy power.[22] Money fuels the hiring of experienced and effective staff and lobbyists, who communicate directly with policy makers, as well as the undertaking of initiatives that will increase the group's membership. Money also funds the raising of more money.[23] For example, the Business Roundtable represents the interests of 150 chief executive officers of the largest U.S. companies, including American Express, General Electric, IBM, and Verizon. In 2007, it spent over $10 million lobbying the president, Congress, and several cabinet departments for policies that would benefit its member corporations, their shareholders, and their 10 million employees. Issues of concern to the Business Roundtable include policies such as Securities and Exchange Commission rules, laws concerning corporate ethics, and reform to the nation's class action lawsuit regulations.

Sometimes interest groups form a separate entity, called a **political action committee (PAC),** whose specific goal is to raise and spend money to influence the outcome of elections (see Chapter 9 for a detailed discussion of PACs). Interest groups use PACs to shape the composition of government; that is, they contribute money to the campaigns of favored candidates, particularly incumbents who are likely to be reelected.[24] While this is but one specific example of the influence that interest groups' money has on politics, interest groups representing the economic concerns of members—business, industry, and union groups—generally tend to have the greatest financial resources for all of these activities.[25]

Organizational Environment

The setting in which an interest group attempts to achieve its goals is the *organizational environment.* Key factors in the organizational environment include its leadership and the presence or absence of opposition from other groups.[26]

Leadership   Strong, charismatic leaders contribute to the influence of an interest group by raising public awareness of the group and its activities, by enhancing its reputation, and by making the organization attractive to new members and contributors. An example of a dynamic leader who has increased his interest group's effectiveness is James P. Hoffa, the son of powerful Teamsters Union president Jimmy Hoffa, who disappeared without a trace in 1975. Since 1999, he has served as the president of the Teamsters Union, which primarily represents unionized truck drivers.

Opposition   The presence of opposing interest groups can also have an impact on an interest group's success. When an interest group is "the only game in town" on a particular issue, policy makers are more likely to rely on that group's views. But if groups with opposing views are also attempting to influence policy, getting policy makers to act strongly in any one group's favor is more difficult. Consider this example: Hotel Employees and the Restaurant Employees International Union supported increasing the minimum wage, but the National Restaurant Association, which advocates for restaurant owners, opposed a minimum wage hike, arguing that the higher wage would cut into restaurant owners' profits or limit its members' ability to hire as many employees as before. In the face of such opposing interests, policy makers are often more likely to compromise than to give any one group exactly what it wants.

Although each of these factors—organizational resources and the organizational environment—influences how powerful an interest group will be, no single formula determines an interest group's clout. Sometimes an interest group has powerful advocates in Congress who support its cause. Other times a single factor can prove essential to an interest group's success.

Types of Interest Groups

A wide variety of political interest groups exercise their muscle in the case of virtually every type of policy question, from those concerning birth (such as what the minimum hospital stay an insurance company must cover after a woman gives birth should be) to matters related to death (such as what practices by funeral directors should be banned by the government). Despite the broad range of issues around which interest groups coalesce, political scientists generally categorize interest groups by what kinds of issues concern them and who benefits from the groups' activities. For example, some interest groups focus primarily on economic decisions that affect their members. Other interest groups pursue ideological, issue-based, or religion-based goals. Yet others lobby for benefits for society at large, while still others advocate on behalf of foreign interests.

Economic Interest Groups

When economic interest groups lobby government, the benefits for their members can be direct or indirect. In some cases, the economic benefits flow directly from the government to the interest group members, as when an agricultural interest group successfully presses for *subsidies,* monies given by the government to the producers of a particular crop or product, often to influence the volume of production of that commodity. For example, as a result of the lobbying efforts of several large dairy cooperatives, including the Dairy Farmers of America, the 2007 Farm Bill Extension Act earmarked over $800 million in subsidies to large and small dairy farmers.[27]

In other instances, economic interest groups lobby for or against policies that, while not directly benefiting their members, have an indirect impact on the interest group's membership. This was the case when many unions, including the AFL-CIO, lobbied against the creation of private Social Security accounts, fearing that this privatization would result in a decrease in Social Security retirement benefits for their members.

Corporate and Business Interests
Large corporate and smaller business interest groups are among the most successful U.S. pressure groups with respect to their influence on government. These groups typically seek policies that benefit a

particular company or industry. For example, the Motion Picture Association of America (MPAA) represents the seven major U.S. manufacturers and distributors of movies and television programs. The MPAA lobbies policy makers (often by hosting prerelease screenings of films and lavish dinner receptions) with the goal of securing the passage of antipiracy laws, which aim to prevent the illegal copying of movies and to penalize individuals who sell them. This advocacy benefits the group's members and their employees, because antipiracy laws help to ensure that any copies of movies sold are legal and thus profitable for MPAA members.

Certain industries' associations are stand-alone organizations, such as the National Association of Realtors and the National Beer Wholesalers Association. But industry and business groups also commonly advocate for policies using **umbrella organizations,** which are interest groups representing groups of industries or corporations. Examples of umbrella business organizations include the Business Roundtable and the U.S. Chamber of Commerce, a federation of local chambers of commerce that represents about 3 million large and small businesses.

Often corporate and business groups compete against labor groups. This rivalry is a natural result of having different constituencies. Typically, corporate interests advocate on behalf of the company owners, stockholders, and officers, whereas labor unions champion employees' interests.

Labor Interests   Like corporate interest groups, labor interest groups include both national labor unions and umbrella organizations of unions. The AFL-CIO, an umbrella organization made up of more than 50 labor unions, is among the nation's most powerful interest groups, although its influence has waned over the past several decades as union membership has declined generally. During the 1950s and 1960s, nearly 35 percent of all U.S. workers were union members. By 1983, membership had decreased to about 20 percent, and today about 13 percent of all U.S. workers belong to unions. In part, this decline stems from changes in the U.S. economy, with many highly unionized manufacturing jobs being replaced by less unionized service sector jobs. Given the drop in union membership, labor interest groups' influence has also waned, although the unions' reduced clout is in part due to a lack of cohesion among labor union members.

Like corporate and business interest groups, labor unions pursue policies that benefit their members, although these are frequently at odds with corporate and business interest groups' positions. And like corporate and business interest groups, labor unions sometimes press for policies that primarily benefit their own members, while at other times they promote policies that benefit all union workers and sometimes even non-union workers. For example, in 2007, the AFL-CIO successfully lobbied Congress for an increase in the federal minimum wage, which benefited the members of many unions whose contracts are based on federally mandated minimum wages but also many non-union workers who are paid the minimum wage.

Agricultural Interests   Of all types of U.S. interest groups, agricultural interest groups probably have the most disproportionate amount of influence given the relatively small number of farmers and farmworkers in the country relative to the general population. And because agricultural producers in the United States are also very

Top Agricultural Subsidies in the United States, 2007

TABLE 7.1

Rank	Program	Number of Recipients	Subsidy Total
1	Corn	755,358	$2,048,116,614
2	Wheat	637,403	1,092,800,323
3	Cotton	118,843	586,187,836
4	Soybeans	572,147	574,640,511
5	Rice	32,816	414,411,200
6	Sorghum	255,425	189,455,101
7	Barley	135,314	76,598,425
8	Peanuts	16,816	67,670,907
9	Sunflower	30,042	12,838,968
10	Canola	10,249	4,811,215

Source: The Environmental Working Group, http://farm.ewg.org/farm/region.php?fips=00000.

diverse, ranging from small farmers to huge multinational agribusinesses, it is not surprising to see divergent opinions among people employed in the agricultural sector.

The largest agricultural interest group today is the American Farm Bureau Federation (AFBF), which grew out of the network of county farm bureaus formed in the 1920s. With more than 5 million farming members, the AFBF is one of the most influential interest groups in the United States, primarily because of its close relations with key agricultural policy makers. It takes stands on a wide variety of issues that have an impact on farmers, including subsidies, budget and tax policies, immigration policies that affect farmworkers, energy policies, trade policies, and environmental policies.

In addition to large-scale, general agricultural interest groups such at the AFBF, there is an industry-specific interest group representing producers for nearly every crop or commodity in the agricultural sector. Table 7.1 shows that corn producers are among the most effective groups in securing subsidies for their growers. Between 1995 and 2006, more than 1.5 million corn farmers across the United States received in excess of $56 billion in government subsidies. Table 7.1 reveals that in 2007 alone, corn growers netted over $2 billion in government subsidies. Wheat producers received over $1 billion in 2007, while cotton and soybean growers received more than a half billion.

Trade and Professional Interests   Nearly every professional occupation—doctor, lawyer, engineer, chiropractor, dentist, accountant, and even video game developer—has a trade or professional group that focuses on its interests. These interest groups take stands on a variety of policy matters, many of which indirectly affect their membership. For example, in the aftermath of the September 11, 2001, terrorist attacks, members of the American Hotel and Lodging Association (AH&LA), a trade group representing state and city partner lodging associations, lobbied for passage of a law that would aid insurance companies in the event of a future terrorist strike. Congress subsequently passed the Terrorism Risk Protection Act, which provides up to $100 billion in subsidies to insurers in the event of a catastrophic terrorist attack. The AH&LA argued for the bill because its members would benefit from greatly reduced costs of terrorism insurance under the bill. When President George W. Bush signed the bill into law in 2002, representatives of the AH&LA attended the signing ceremony.

Public and Ideological Interest Groups

Public interest groups typically are concerned with a broad range of issues that affect the populace at large. These include social and economic issues, such as Social Security reform and revision of the federal tax structure, and environmental causes, such as clean air and clean water. Examples of public interest groups include the National Taxpayers Union, Common Cause, and the Sierra Club. Usually, the results of the efforts of a particular public interest group's advocacy cannot be limited to the group's members; rather, these results are **collective goods** (sometimes called *public goods*)—outcomes that are shared by the general public. Collective goods are "collective" and "public" because they cannot be denied to people who are not group members. For example, if the Sierra Club succeeds in winning passage of an environmental bill that improves water and air quality, *everyone* shares in the benefits. Specifically, it is impossible to make pure drinking water and clean air a privilege restricted to Sierra Club members.

The nature of collective goods—the fact that they cannot be limited to those who worked to achieve them—creates a **free rider problem,** the situation whereby someone derives a benefit from the actions of others. You are probably familiar with the free rider problem. Suppose, for example, that you form a study group to prepare for an exam, and four of the five members of the group come to a study session having prepared responses to potential essay questions. The fifth member shows up but is unprepared. The unprepared group member then copies the others' responses, memorizes them, and does just as well on the exam. The same thing happens to interest groups that advocate for a collective good. The group may work hard to improve the quality of life, but the benefits of its work are enjoyed by many who do not contribute to the effort.

Economist Mancur Olson asserted in his **rational choice theory** that from an economic perspective it is not rational for people to participate in a collective action designed to achieve a collective good when they can secure that good without participating. So, in the study group example, from Olson's perspective, it is not economically rational to spend your time preparing for an exam when you can get the benefits of preparation without the work. Of course, taking this idea to the extreme, one might conclude that if no one advocated for collective goods, they would not exist, and thus free riders could not derive their benefit.

Current scholarship on civic engagement has focused on the free rider problem. Researchers have investigated the increased benefits of widespread citizen participation in interest groups, citing evidence that groups with higher levels of public participation may be more effective, and may provide greater collective benefits, than groups with lower rates of participation. Studies also indicate that through the act of participating in civic life, individuals derive some benefit themselves in addition to the benefits created by their work. So, if the fifth person in the study group prepares for the exam, too, *all* members of the group may perform better on the exam. And if more people are civically involved in groups, then their potential to have an impact on their government increases. In addition, civic engagement scholars cite the psychic benefit to an individual of knowing that a collective good was achieved in part because of *her* participation, and these researchers also mention the other benefits derived from collective action, including solidary and purposive benefits.

Consumer Interests   Well before attorney and activist Ralph Nader gained nationwide attention as a Green Party candidate for the presidency in 2000, he founded numerous organizations to promote the rights of consumers. In the 1970s and 1980s, these organizations lobbied primarily—and successfully—for changes in automotive design that would make cars safer. One result was the mandatory installation of harness safety belts in rear seats, which then typically had only lap belts. In 1971, Nader founded the interest group Public Citizen, which lobbies Congress, the executive branch, and the courts for openness in government and consumer issues, including auto safety, the safety of prescription drugs, and energy policy. Each December, the group issues a list of unsafe toys to guide gift-buyers' holiday purchases.

Environmental Interests   Many groups that advocate for the protection of the environment and wildlife and for the conservation of natural resources came about as a result of a broader environmental movement in the 1970s, although the Sierra Club was founded more than a century ago, in 1892. Some environmental groups, particularly Greenpeace, have been criticized in the media and by their opponents for their use of confrontational tactics. But many environmental activists say that the power of corporate interests (with which they are frequently at odds) is so pervasive that they can succeed only by taking strong, direct action to protect the natural environment, thus rationalizing their sometimes extreme tactics. And so, while some environmentalists follow the conventional route of lobbying legislators or advertising to raise public awareness of their causes, others camp out in trees to attempt to prevent their removal or sit on oil-drilling platforms to halt drilling into a coral reef. In addition to stalling the undesired action, the confrontational protest tactic also has the advantage of attracting media attention, which serves to increase public awareness.[28] Such environmental groups hope that they can prevent environmental destruction by embarrassing the corporation or government involved.

Religious Interests   For a long time, organized religions in the United States were essentially uninvolved in politics, partly because they were afraid of losing their tax-exempt status by becoming political entities. But formal religions increasingly have sought to make their voices heard, usually by forming political organizations separate from the actual religious organizations. Today, religious interests are among the most influential interest groups in U.S. politics.

In the early stages of their activism, Christian organizations typically were most politically effective in the Republican presidential nomination process, when the mobilization of their members could alter the outcome in low-turnout primaries. During the 1970s, several conservative Christian organizations, most notably the Moral Majority, founded by the late Reverend Jerry Falwell, were a force in national politics. The Moral

Majority helped to elect Ronald Reagan, a Republican, to the presidency in 1980 and was instrumental in shaping the national agenda of the Reagan years, particularly regarding domestic policy. In 1989, another conservative Christian organization, the Christian Coalition, took shape, marking a new era in the politicization of religious groups. The Christian Coalition advocates that "people of faith have a right and a responsibility to be involved in the world around them" and emphasizes "pro-family" values.[29] During its first decade, the Christian Coalition's influence grew gradually. During the 2000 election, the organization was an important supporter of George W. Bush's candidacy for the presidency, and with his election, the group's influence grew considerably. In the 2004 presidential election, conservative Christian organizations proved enormously important in activities such as voter registration and get-out-the-vote campaigns, thus aiding President Bush's reelection efforts.

The Christian Coalition and other religious groups—including Pax Christi USA (the national Catholic peace movement), B'nai Brith (an interest group dedicated to Jewish interests), and the Council on American-Islamic Relations (CAIR, a Muslim interest group)—also advocate for the faith-based priorities of their members. Many of these organizations have become increasingly active in state and local politics in recent years. For example, since 2000, members of the Christian Coalition, recognizing the influence that local school boards have in determining how religion is integrated into the classroom, have made national headlines by running organized slates of candidates for election to local school boards, many of whom have won. By 2008, lawmakers in more than twenty states had considered various pieces of legislation that would include instruction in creationism in school curricula. Many such proposals came at the behest of Christian school board members.

Foreign Interest Groups

In the United States, advocacy by interest groups is not limited to U.S.-based groups. Foreign governments, as well as international corporations based abroad, vigorously press for U.S. policies beneficial to them. Foreign governments might lobby for U.S. aid packages; multinational corporations might work for beneficial changes to tax regulations. Often a foreign government will rely on an interest group made up of U.S. citizens of the foreign nation's heritage to promote its advocacy efforts. Indeed, one of the more influential interest groups lobbying for foreign concerns is the U.S.-based American Israel Public Affairs Committee (AIPAC), which has 65,000 members. AIPAC lobbies the U.S. government for pro-Israel foreign policies such as the grant of nearly $2.5 billion in economic and military aid for Israel in 2007. Despite its relatively small membership, AIPAC is considered highly influential because of its financial resources and well-connected membership base, which enjoys access to many policy makers.

Sometimes it is readily apparent when foreign interests are lobbying for their own causes—as, for example, when a trading partner wants better terms. But in other cases, particularly when international corporations are lobbying, it is difficult to discern where their "American" interest ends and their "foreign" interest begins. So while only U.S. citizens and legal immigrants can contribute to federal PACs, American employees of foreign companies do form and contribute to PACs. Many people would be surprised at the large amounts of money that international corporations' PACs contribute to both of the major U.S. political parties. But because many subsidiaries of these corporations are important American businesses, their lobbying activities are not necessarily a foreign encroachment on U.S. politics.

Interest Group Strategies

Interest groups use two kinds of strategies to advance their causes. *Direct strategies* involve actual contact between representatives of the interest group and policy makers. *Indirect strategies* involve using intermediaries to advocate for a cause or generally to attempt to persuade the public, including policy makers, to embrace the group's position. Most interest groups use a combination of direct and indirect strategies to accomplish their goals.

Direct Strategies to Advance Interests

Groups often opt for direct strategies when they seek to secure passage or defeat of a specific piece of legislation. These strategies include lobbying, entering into litigation to change a law, and providing information or expert testimony to decision makers.

Lobbying, Issue Networks, and Iron Triangles   Interest groups hire professionals to **lobby,** or communicate directly with, policy makers on the interest groups' behalf. President Ulysses S. Grant coined the term *lobbyist* when he walked through the lobby of the Willard Hotel in Washington, D.C., and commented on the presence of "lobbyists" waiting to speak to members of Congress.

Today lobbying is among the most common strategies that interest groups use, and the practice may include scheduled face-to-face meetings, the "buttonholing" of members of Congress as they walk through the Capitol, telephone calls, and receptions and special events hosted by the interest groups. The professional lobbyists whom interest groups hire are almost always lawyers, and their job is to cultivate ongoing relationships with members of Congress (and their staff) who have influence in a specific policy area. In many situations, lobbyists help navigate access to these policy makers for industry and interest group members.

Interest groups have learned that one of the most effective ways of influencing government is to hire former government officials, including cabinet officials, members of Congress, and congressional staffers, as lobbyists. Because these ex-officials often enjoy good relationships with their former colleagues and have an intimate knowledge of the policy-making process, they are particularly effective in influencing government. Frequently, this practice creates an **issue network,** the fluid web of connections among those concerned about a policy and those who create and administer the policy.

Similarly, an interest group's efficacy often depends on its having close relationships with the policy makers involved in decisions related to the group's causes, as discussed in "Then, Now, Next." During the rough-and-tumble policy-making process, the interaction of mutual interests among a "trio" comprising (1) members of Congress, (2) executive departments and agencies (such as the Department of Agriculture or the Federal Emergency Management Agency), and (3) organized interest groups is sometimes referred to as an **iron triangle,** with each of the three players

Will K Street and the Obama Administration Call a Truce?

THEN: During the administration of George W. Bush, critics frequently criticized the cozy relationship between the Bush administration and corporate campaign donors, who wielded influence through lobbyists with easy access to Bush. The problem, critics said, was that the Bush administration would reward businesses that

contributed to Republican campaigns with weakened environmental regulations, key administration appointments, and lucrative government contracts.

NOW: Several interest groups are decrying new Obama administration policies that restrict contacts between lobbyists and government officials in connection with the American Recovery and Reinvestment Act of 2009 (the stimulus package). Stringent guidelines have been instituted for lobbyists: no lobbyist is eligible for employment in the administration, and there is a ban on phone calls and meetings about specific stimulus projects or proposals. Instead, communications (in writing) about specific projects will be posted on Recovery.gov, the government Web site designed to bring transparency to stimulus spending. Critics of these new rules have said they will challenge them in court on First Amendment grounds.

WHAT'S NEXT?

- How might interest groups find a way to influence government spending, despite the restrictions imposed by the Obama administration?

- With new lobbying guidelines in place, how can resources like Recovery.gov help citizens in the future remain informed about interest group activity concerning stimulus spending?

- What other new technologies, besides Web sites, might shape how interest groups and government interact?

being one side of the triangle (see Figure 7.1). Although each side in an iron triangle is expected to fight on behalf of its own interests, constituents, or governmental department, the triangle often seeks a policy outcome that benefits all three sides. Often this outcome occurs because of close personal and professional relationships that develop as a result of the interactions among the sides in an issue-based triangle. And sometimes the individual players in a triangle that is focused on a particular issue—say, military policy or subsidies for tobacco growers—share a personal history, have attended the same schools, come from the same region of the country, and have even worked together at one time. Such long-term relationships can make it difficult for opposing interests to penetrate the triangle. (See Chapter 13 for further discussion of the role of iron triangles in policy making.)

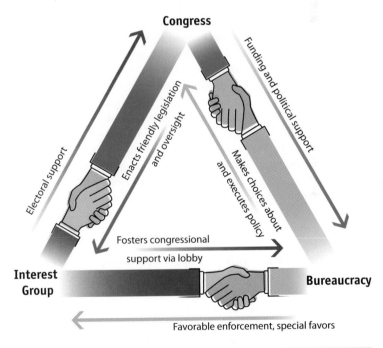

POLITICAL INQUIRY

FIGURE 7.1 ■ AN IRON TRIANGLE
Who are the players in an iron triangle? How do interest groups benefit from their iron triangle relationships? Why do you think the triangular relationship has been described as "iron"?

Litigation by Interest Groups   Sometimes, interest groups challenge a policy in the courts. For example, in 2004, the Recording Industry Association of America (RIAA), a trade association representing manufacturers of music compact discs, filed five separate lawsuits against 531 defendants in Philadelphia, Orlando, and Trenton, claiming that the defendants had illegally swapped copyrighted songs by sharing computer files with other Internet users. The RIAA, which has continued to target college students in its lawsuits, said that the litigation was designed to protect the interests of its members, who had seen a slump in CD sales since song swapping had become more popular. By prosecuting offenders, the RIAA aimed to deter others from sharing files and hoped that law enforcement would view the issue more seriously than it had. Although few prosecutions and convictions have resulted from the RIAA lawsuits, media coverage of these legal actions is thought to have deterred some individuals from sharing copyrighted songs via the Internet.

In other instances, interest groups sue to prevent a particular public policy from being enacted or to prompt a court ruling on the constitutionality of an issue. The latter was the case when in 1992, Planned Parenthood of Pennsylvania, an abortion rights advocacy group, sued the state's governor, claiming that the state's Abortion Control Act violated the constitutional protections on abortion outlined in the Supreme Court's decision in *Roe v. Wade* (1973). In particular, Planned Parenthood argued that the clauses in the state legislation that required a pregnant woman to notify her husband, a pregnant teen to get parental consent, and any abortion seeker to satisfy a twenty-four-hour waiting period after receiving counseling presented an undue burden and violated the spirit of *Roe*. In *Roe v. Wade*, the Supreme Court had ruled that a woman's right to abortion was essentially guaranteed in the first trimester, could be regulated by the states in the second, and could be banned by the states in the third. The Supreme Court agreed to hear the Planned Parenthood case and struck down some components of the Pennsylvania legislation, including the requirement for spousal notification, while allowing other components not specified in *Roe*, including the parental consent requirement and the twenty-four-hour waiting period, to stand.

By litigating, interest groups can ensure that laws passed by legislatures and signed by executives are in keeping with current constitutional interpretation. By bringing their causes before the courts, they also can shape policy and encourage enforcement by executive agencies.

Providing Information and Expert Testimony   Interest groups are one of the chief sources of information for policy makers. Interest groups have the resources to investigate the impact of policies. They have access to data, technological know-how, and a bevy of experts with extensive knowledge of the issues. Most interest groups provide information to policy makers, and policy makers understand that the information received is slanted toward the group's interest. But if competing interest groups supply information to policy makers, then policy makers can counterbalance the various sets of information.

Sometimes interest groups use celebrities as "experts" to testify, knowing that they will attract greater attention than most policy experts. Elmo, the furry red *Sesame Street* Muppet, testified in 2002 on behalf of a bill that would provide $2 million in federal funding to public schools for music education. The House Appropriations

Subcommittee on Labor, Health and Human Services, and Education heard testimony from Elmo, who apparently is an authority on music education. Elmo told the subcommittee, "Elmo loves to sing and to dance and to make music with all his friends on *Sesame Street*. It helps Elmo learn ABCs and makes it easier for Elmo to remember things. Sometimes it makes Elmo excited, and sometimes it calms Elmo down. Elmo's teacher really likes that! My friend [American Music Conference Executive Director] Joe Lamond says some kids don't have music in school. That makes Elmo sad."[30]

Indirect Strategies to Advance Interests

Reaching out to persuade the public that the interest group's position is right, deploying citizens as grassroots lobbyists, and electioneering are some of the indirect strategies interest groups use to pursue their public policy agendas. Indirect tactics are likely to be ongoing rather than targeted at a specific piece of legislation, although that is not always the case.

Public Outreach   Interest groups work hard—and use a variety of strategies—to make the public, government officials, their own members, and potential members aware of issues of concern and to educate people about their positions on the issues. Some interest groups focus solely on educating the public and hope that through their efforts people will be concerned enough to take steps to have a particular policy established or changed. In doing so, the groups promote civic engagement by informing individuals about important policy concerns, even if the information they provide is skewed toward the group's views. The groups also encourage civic discourse by bringing issues into the public arena. Often they do so by mounting advertising campaigns to alert the public about an issue.

Sometimes interest groups and corporations engage in **climate control,** the practice of using public outreach to build favorable public opinion of the organization or company. The logic behind climate control is simple: if a corporation or an organization has the goodwill of the public on its side, enacting its legislative agenda or getting its policy priorities passed will be easier because government will know of, and may even share, the public's positive opinion of the organization. For example, when Wal-Mart started to see opposition to the construction of its superstores in communities across the country, it relied on public relations techniques, particularly advertising, to convince people that Wal-Mart is a good corporate citizen. As critics complained about Wal-Mart's harmful effects on smaller, local merchants, the firm's ads touted Wal-Mart's positive contributions to its host communities. When opponents publicized the company's low-wage jobs, Wal-Mart countered with ads featuring employees who had started in entry-level positions and risen through the ranks to managerial posts. These ads would be viewed both by policy makers (municipal planning board members, for example) and by citizens, whose opinions matter to those policy makers. This type of climate control is designed to soften opposition and increase community goodwill.

Other groups, especially those without a great deal of access to policy makers, may engage in protests and civil disobedience to be heard. Sometimes leaders calculate that media attention to their actions will increase public awareness and spark widespread support for their cause.

TABLE 7.2

Contributions by Business, Labor, and Ideological Political Action Committees

	Total	Democrat (%)	Republican (%)
Corporate	$158,311,196	$76,009,131 (48%)	$82,302,065 (52%)
Labor	62,635,944	57,967,217 (93)	4,668,727 (7)
Nonconnected	66,591,015	35,401,045 (53)	31,189,970 (47)
Trade/Membership/ Health	112,880,369	58,038,677 (51)	54,841,692 (49)
Cooperative	6,859,823	3,554,604 (52)	3,305,219 (48)
Corporations Without Stock	5,459,525	2,898,323 (53)	2,561,202 (47)
Total	$412,737,872	$233,868,997 (57%)	$178,868,875 (43%)

Source: http://www.fec.gov/press/press2009/20090415PAC/20090424PAC.shtml.

Electioneering   Interest groups often engage in the indirect strategy of **election-eering**—working to influence the election of candidates who support their issues. All of the tactics of electioneering are active methods of civic participation. These techniques include endorsing particular candidates or positions and conducting voter registration and get-out-the-vote drives. Grassroots campaign efforts often put interest groups with large memberships, including labor unions, at an advantage.

Campaign contributions are considered a key element of electioneering. The importance of contributions puts wealthier interest groups, including corporate and business groups, at an advantage. Table 7.2 shows the breakdown of contributions by business, labor, and ideologically driven PACs. Business PACs and individuals with business interests compose the largest sources of revenue for political candidates and tend to favor Republicans over Democrats. Labor groups and individuals associated with them give overwhelmingly to Democratic candidates but contribute a great deal less money than do business PACs. Ideologically driven PACs and individuals are nearly evenly divided between Democrats and Republicans.

Interest groups also commonly use the tactics of endorsements and ratings to attract support for the candidates whom they favor and to reduce the electoral chances of those whom they do not. Through endorsements, an interest group formally supports specific candidates and typically notifies its members and the media of that support. An endorsement may also involve financial support from the interest group's PAC. And by the technique of rating candidates, the interest group examines candidates' responses to a questionnaire issued by the group. Sometimes a group rates members of Congress on the basis of how they voted on measures important to the group. The ratings of a liberal interest group such as the Americans for Democratic Action (ADA) or a conservative interest group such as the American Conservative Union (ACU) can serve as an ideological benchmark. So, for example, as senators in 2007, both Hillary Clinton and Barack Obama had ADA ratings of

75, while Republican John McCain had an ADA rating of 10. McCain had an ACU rating of 82, and Clinton and Obama each had about an 8. Interest group ratings are used by voters and the media to evaluate candidates and also by candidates themselves, who may advertise their rating to targeted group constituencies.

The Influence of Political Action Committees

The influence of money on politics is not a recent phenomenon. Louise Overacker, one of the first political scientists to do research on campaign finance, wrote in 1932, "Any effective program of control must make it possible to bring into the light the sources and amounts of all funds used in political campaigns, and the way in which those funds are expended. . . . Negatively, it must not attempt to place legal limitations upon the size of contributions or expenditures."[31] Years later, Congress would see the wisdom of Overacker's analysis: federal regulations now stipulate that a group that contributes to any candidate's campaign must register as a political action committee (PAC). For this reason, most interest groups form PACs as one arm of their organization.

POLITICAL INQUIRY

The cartoon refers to a scandal involving contaminated pet food imported from China. What point does this cartoon make about the nature of 2008 political campaign contributions? Exactly what are these contributions buying, according to the cartoonist?

© Joe Heller, 2008. www.cagle.com

Whereas the interest group pursues the group's broad goals by engaging in a variety of activities, its PAC raises and spends money in order to influence the outcome of an election. Typically, it will do so by contributing to candidates' campaigns. Funding campaigns helps an interest group in various ways. For one thing, it establishes the interest group as a formal supporter of one or more candidates. And importantly, campaign contributions are a door opener for an interest group's lobbyists. For a lobbyist, access to policy makers is crucial, and campaign contributions provide a means of contact and help ensure that a phone call will be returned or an invitation responded to, even if the policy maker does not support the group's position on every issue.

Table 7.3 lists the PACs that contribute the most money to U.S. campaigns and highlights the party their contributions favor. As the table (along with Table 7.2)

TABLE 7.3

Top Twenty PAC Contributors to Candidates, 2009–2010

PAC	Total	Democrats	Republicans
Operating Engineers Union	$1,947,500	89%	11%
Intl. Brotherhood of Electrical Workers	970,650	98	3
National Community Pharmacists Assn.	970,500	65	35
AT&T Inc.	776,775	48	51
American Crystal Sugar	694,000	73	27
Machinists/Aerospace Workers Union	693,500	99	1
National Beer Wholesalers Assn.	646,000	60	40
American Assn. for Justice	586,000	97	3
American Bankers Assn.	559,000	47	53
Carpenters & Joiners Union	535,000	81	19
Honeywell International	532,000	68	32
Boeing Co.	445,500	63	37
Raytheon Co.	425,500	64	36
National Air Traffic Controllers Assn.	395,250	81	19
United Food & Commercial Workers Union	395,048	100	0
AFLAC Inc.	378,500	65	35
Blue Dog	370,000	100	0
United Parcel Service	348,268	47	53
Lockheed Martin	344,500	63	37
Teamsters Union	341,500	99	1

Source: Center for Responsive Politics, http//www.opensecrets.org/pacs/toppacs.php.

illustrates, Democrats have dominated the 2008–2010 election cycle, garnering disproportionate support from labor unions, while Republicans fared better with business and corporate PACs that often split their contributions evenly between members of the two parties. More consistently, PACs, particularly those formed by economic interest groups, overwhelmingly favor incumbents. PACs' powers-that-be know that incumbent candidates are most likely to be reelected, and thus the PACs support their reelection bids. As we will examine further in Chapter 9, interest groups rely on political action committees to channel their support to candidates that espouse their views.

CONTINUING THE CONVERSATION

CONCLUSION

- Although there are competing opinions about the role and value of interest groups in U.S. politics, their influence in policy making is unquestioned. Thus interest groups offer enormous potential for people who wish to become civically engaged. The abundance of groups for virtually every cause (and the ability of anyone to form his or her own group) means that like-minded individuals can work together to ensure that government policy represents their views.

- Today, through the Internet and other digital technology, interest groups can provide individuals with instantly accessed information and organizational tools. Advances in computing, telephone communications, and television have opened the doors to participation in politics and government in ways that were undreamed of a few decades ago, and the potential exists for interest groups to reach new and ever-widening audiences. As we have seen, however, the potential audience currently excludes many members of the working class, who may lack the time and means to join groups or access computer technology. This lack of access poses a challenge to interest groups as they rely ever more heavily on digital recruiting, communicating, organizing, and fund-raising.

- In becoming increasingly dependent on relatively low-cost technological tools, interest groups also have to deal with the challenges of paying for the expertise needed to design, build, and maintain their Web sites and blogs. Once such issues are resolved, and once access is opened to those not currently wired, digital strategies will further strengthen the clout and efficacy of interest groups, and these groups will speak for a broader swath of Americans.

STUDY NOW

Summary

1. The Value of Interest Groups

Interest groups offer individuals a vehicle for engaging in civic actions and improving their communities and nation, and the positive impacts of improved social capital are reciprocal: as participation benefits individuals, it also benefits communities and larger governments, which in turn provide benefits to individuals.

2. Who Joins Interest Groups, and Why?

In general, people with high incomes, individuals who are upper-middle and middle class, and those with high levels of education are more likely to join interest groups than are people with low incomes, those who are lower-middle and working class, and those who have less education.

3. How Interest Groups Succeed

Organizational resources consist of groups' membership and financial resources; the organizational environment comprises the group's leadership and the presence of opposing or competitive interest groups in the policy-making environment.

4. Types of Interest Groups

Interest groups typically fall into one of three categories: economic interest groups, public and ideological interest groups, and foreign governments and corporations.

5. Interest Group Strategies

Direct strategies typically involve lobbying a policy maker, while indirect strategies might include using public outreach to build favorable public opinion of the organization (climate control), using campaign contributions and electioneering to influence who will be making policy, and educating the public so that they share a group's position and can convey that view to policy makers.

6. The Influence of Political Action Committees

PACs, the tool by which interest groups contribute to electoral campaigns, are sometimes partisan, but in general they tend to support incumbent candidates, making it difficult for nonincumbents effectively to challenge those already in office.

For Critical Thinking and Discussion

1. Were you brought up in a family in which joining groups was important? Do your parents belong to any interest groups? Do you? If not, why do you think that is the case?

2. What kinds of interest groups are you and your friends most likely to be involved in (even if you are not)? Why are the issues these groups advocate important to you?

3. How has the Internet changed how interest groups operate? What kinds of groups has it made more effective? Has it made any groups less effective?

4. Select a controversial issue such as abortion or gun control, and use the Internet to search for and learn about the interest groups that represent opposing views. What tactics does each group use? Is one strategy more effective than the other?

5. The Supreme Court has ruled that political expenditures constitute a form of free speech. Do you agree? Can you think of any other ways in which "money talks"?

Key Terms

climate control 277
collective goods 270
economic incentives 263
electioneering 278
elite theory 257
free rider problem 270
interest groups 253

iron triangle 273
issue network 273
lobby 273
pluralist theory 256
political action committee
  (PAC) 266
purposive incentives 263

rational choice theory 270
social capital 254
solidary incentives 261
umbrella organizations 268

Internet Resources

A More Perfect Union Web site
www.mhhe.com/harrisonampule   Consult the book's Web site for study guides, interactive activities, simulations, and current hot-links that provide additional information on interest groups in the United States.

Center for Responsive Politics
www.opensecrets.org   This nonpartisan Web site provides information on the campaign financing of candidates for federal office.

Common Cause
www.commoncause.org   This Web site features a special section on money and politics and provides links to sites related to its endorsed reform measures.

Federal Election Commission
www.fec.org   You'll find a plethora of information about campaign financing, including regulations, contributions and expenditures, specific candidates, individual donors, political action committees, and political parties.

Recommended Readings

Berry, Jeffrey M., and Clyde Wilcox. *The Interest Group Society,* 4th ed. New York: Longman, 2006. Analyzes the proliferation of various types of interest groups in the United States, as well as the strategies interest groups use to sway policy makers.

Cigler, Alan J., and Burnett A. Loomis. *Interest Group Politics,* 7th ed. Washington, DC: CQ Press, 2007. A classic analysis, first published in 1983, detailing the impact of interest groups in modern American politics.

Herrnson, Paul S., Ronald G. Shaiko, and Clyde J. Wilcox. *The Interest Group Connection: Electioneering, Lobbying, and Policymaking in Washington*, 2nd ed. Washington, DC: CQ Press, 2004. A collection of essays describing the role of interest groups on the federal level. The essays focus on elections, Congress, the president, and the judiciary.

Wright, John. *Interest Groups and Congress* (Longman Classics Edition). New York: Longman, 2002. A study of the influence of both historical and modern interest groups, asserting that interest groups' practice of providing specialized information to members of Congress increases their influence there, has an impact on the resultant policy, and shapes opinion.

TYLER OVERMAN
MEMPHIS, TN

THEN

Political parties relied on patronage and voter loyalty to become powerful entities in American politics.

NOW

Voter loyalty has declined, but parties remain an important force for mobilizing citizens.

Political Parties

Political parties are essential channels for the realization of American democracy. Political parties serve the American system in many crucial capacities, from recruiting candidates, to conducting elections, to distributing information to voters, to participating in governance. One of their essential functions is to provide an open arena for participation by civic-minded individuals, while reaching out to involve those who do not participate.

Because Americans place high value on independent thought and action, some citizens view political parties with suspicion. For such observers, the collective activity of parties brings worries about corruption and control by elite decision makers. But even though party insiders sometimes do exert considerable power, parties remain one of the most accessible forums for citizens' participation in democracy. Indeed, political scientist E. E. Schattschneider, who believed that parties represented the foremost means for citizens to communicate with political decision makers and in this way to retain control over their government—wrote that "modern democracy is unthinkable save in terms of political parties."[1]

Will the dominance of the Democratic and Republican parties continue?

Will political parties decline in their ability to perform key functions?

How will digital technologies further shape parties' strategies and expand their reach—and change the membership of parties?

NEXT

Parties Today and Their Functions

In the United States today, two major political parties—the Democratic and the Republican parties—dominate the political landscape. Generally, a **political party** is an organization of ideologically similar people that nominates and elects its members to office in order to run the government and shape public policy. Parties identify potential candidates, nominate them to run for office, campaign for them, organize elections, and govern. But given some overlapping roles, political scientists agree that parties can be distinguished from other political organizations, such as interest groups and political action committees, through four defining characteristics.

Defining a Political Party

First, *political parties run candidates under their own label, or affiliation.* Most candidates who run for office are identified by their party affiliation. Running a candidate under the party label involves a host of party functions, including recruiting candidates, organizing elections, and campaigning.[2] And political parties typically are the only organizations that regularly run candidates under their party label.

Second, unlike interest groups, which hope to have individuals sympathetic to their cause elected but which typically do not want to govern, *political parties seek to govern.* Political parties run candidates hoping that they will win a majority of the seats in a legislature or control the executive branch. Such victories enable the party to enact a broad partisan agenda.

A third defining characteristic is that *political parties have broad concerns, focused on many issues.* The major parties in the United States are made up of coalitions of different groups and constituencies who rely on political parties to enact their agendas. That is, if we were to look at a party's **platform**—the formal statement of its principles and policy objectives—we would find its stance on all sorts of issues: war, abortion rights, environmental protection, the minimum wage, and so on. These positions are one articulation of the interests of that party's coalition constituencies. Typically, interest groups have narrower issue concerns than parties do, and some focus on only a single issue. For example, we know that the National Rifle Association opposes governmental controls on gun ownership, but what is this interest group's position on the minimum wage? On the environment? Chances are high that the NRA does not have positions on these matters because its concern is with the single issue of gun ownership.

Finally, *political parties are quasi-public organizations that have a special relationship with the government.* Some functions of political parties overlap with governmental functions, and some party functions facilitate the creation and perpetuation of government (running elections, for example). The resulting special status subjects political parties to greater scrutiny than private clubs and organizations.

What Political Parties Do

As we have seen, by promoting political activity, political parties encourage civic engagement and citizen participation and in this way foster democracy. Parties provide a structure for people at the grassroots level to volunteer on party-run campaigns, make campaign contributions, work in the day-to-day operations of the party, and run for office. On the local level, a political party's ability to promote citizen participation varies with its relative influence within the community. Viable political parties—those that effectively contest and win some elections—are more effective at promoting citizen participation than weak political parties. A party that typically is in the minority in a local government—on town council, in the county legislature—will find it more difficult to attract volunteers, to bring people out to fund-raisers, and to recruit candidates. And it naturally follows that parties that are better at attracting public participation are more likely to win elections.

Political parties also foster cooperation between divided interests and factions, building coalitions even in the most divisive of times. In 2004, Democrats helped to bring together a coalition of groups—including medical researchers, physicians, support and research groups that provide services to people with diseases such as Alzheimer's and Parkinson's, and individuals with those diseases—to oppose the Bush administration's limitations on embryonic stem cell research. This coalition succeeded in lobbying Congress to pass a bill, the Stem Cell Research Enhancement Act of 2006. Although President Bush vetoed the legislation, the coalition continues to attempt to influence stem cell research policy, now concentrating on the states. Civic engagement researchers point out that political parties' work in building coalitions and promoting cooperation among diverse groups often occurs away from the bright lights of the media-saturated public arena, where the parties' differences, rather than their common causes, often are in the spotlight.

Political parties also grease the wheels of government and ensure its smooth running. Nearly all legislatures, from town councils to Congress, consist of a *majority party*, the party to which more than 50 percent of the elected legislators belong, and the *minority party*, to which less than 50 percent of the elected legislators belong. Thus, if five of the nine members of your town council are Republicans and four are Democrats, the Republicans are the majority party and the Democrats are the minority party. The majority party elects the legislature's leaders, makes committee assignments, and holds a majority on those committees.

By serving as a training ground for members, political parties also foster effective government. This role of parties is particularly important for groups that traditionally have not been among the power brokers in the government. Historically, African Americans, Latinos, and women have gained valuable knowledge and leadership experience in party organizations—by volunteering on party-run campaigns, assisting with candidate recruitment, or helping with fundraising endeavors—before running for office.[3] Party credentials established by serving the party in these ways can act as a leveling device that can help make a newcomer's candidacy more viable.

Perhaps most important, political parties promote civic responsibility among elected officials and give voters an important "check" on those elected officials. Midterm congressional elections, like those held in 2010 in the middle of President Obama's term, can be viewed as an opportunity for voters to check the power of the president and the majority party in Congress. When an elected leader, particularly a chief executive, is the crucial player in enacting an important policy, the existence of political parties enables voters to hold party members responsible *even if that particular elected official is not running for reelection.* The system thus provides a check on the power of elected officials, because it makes them aware that the policy or position they are taking may be unpopular.

Historically, according to one theory, political parties have also made government more effective and have provided important cues for voters. The **responsible party model,** developed by E. E. Schattschneider, posits that a party tries to give voters a clear choice by establishing priorities or policy stances different from those of the other rival party or parties. Because a party's elected officials tend to be loyal to their party's stances, voters can readily anticipate how a candidate will vote on a given set of issues if elected, and can thus cast their vote according to their preferences on those issues.

The Three Faces of Parties

American political parties perform their various functions through three "faces," or spheres of operation.[4] The three components of the party include the party in the electorate, the party organization, and the party in government (see Figure 8.1).

The Party in the Electorate

All of the individuals who identify with or tend to support a particular party make up the **party in the electorate.** Several factors influence which party an individual will identify with, including personal circumstances, race, and religion, as well as the party's history, ideology, position on issues of importance to the voter, and candidates.[5]

Measuring the Party in the Electorate The term **party identifier** refers to an individual who identifies him- or herself as a member of one party or the other; party identifiers typically are measured by party registration. In most states, party registration is a legal process in which a voter formally selects affiliation with one political party. This declaration of affiliation often occurs when a person

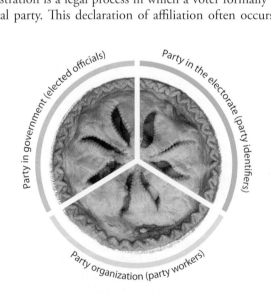

FIGURE 8.1

The Three Faces of Parties

Will African Americans Remain Loyal to President Obama's Democratic Party?

THEN: Since the civil rights movement of the 1960s, about three quarters of African voters identify themselves as Democrats. When then-Republican National Committee (RNC) chairman Ken Mehlman addressed the National Association for the Advancement of Colored People (NAACP) in 2005, he noted that "some Republicans gave up on winning the African-American vote, looking the other way or trying to benefit politically from racial polarization." He added, "I am here as Republican chairman to tell you we were wrong."* However, the Republican Party made few inroads among African Americans during Mehlman's tenure and that of his successor, Robert Duncan.

NOW: With the historic election of Barack Obama as the nation's first African American president, the Republican Party also made history: in 2009, the RNC elected Maryland governor Michael Steele as its first African American chair. Addressing the NAACP, Steele outlined a different strategy for bringing African Americans to the Republican Party. "Certainly my visit here today does not represent some miraculous breakthrough in GOP–NAACP relations. This is the first baby step in many more baby steps to come. After all, we all know that old loyalties and attitudes die hard. But the question is, if the GOP is willing to take those steps, will the NAACP be willing to do the same? . . . Think about it this way: if a black man can become chairman of the Republican National Committee, then anything is possible."**

WHAT'S NEXT?

- As more African Americans become affluent and move into the middle class, will the Republican Party be able to attract increasing numbers of this key Democratic constituency to the GOP? Why or why not?

(Continued)

- How will Barack Obama's historic election affect the loyalty to the Democratic Party that many African American voters have traditionally shown?

- How can both political parties make use of new technologies to attract diverse constituencies to their parties?

*John Rondy, "GOP Ignored Black Vote, Chairman Says," Reuters/July 15, 2005, http/www.boston.com/news/nation/articles/2005/07/15/gop_ignored_black_vote_chairman/says/. **http://www.youtube.com/watch?v=+Act4mapWSo.

registers to vote; the prospective voter selects his or her party identification by filling out a voter registration form or party declaration form. Depending on the state, a voter may select the Democratic or Republican Party, a variety of third parties, or no party. When a voter does not select a party, he or she is technically an unaffiliated voter, but often analysts refer to such a voter as an **independent.**

Determining Who Belongs to Each Political Party   Although we commonly speak in terms of which groups affiliate with and "belong to" each of the political parties, these are just generalizations, with many exceptions. In general, each political party counts specific demographic groups as part of its base of support. A party will often draw party activists and leaders from the ranks of this bloc of individuals whose support can be counted on.

Figure 8.2 shows the breakdown of party membership among various groups in the United States. Although whites, men, and people with some college education are naturally found in both parties, they are more likely to be Republicans. For the Democrats, key voting blocs include African Americans, ethnic minorities, women, and people with no college education. (For more on the strong preference of African American voters for the Democratic party, see "Then, Now, Next.") Individuals with a college degree or more are evenly divided between the two parties. Social class also plays a role in party preference. The working class is largely Democratic, and the upper-middle class, largely Republican; the middle class, by far the largest class in the United States, is divided between the two parties. But the best predictor of a person's party identification is his or her ideology. People who identify themselves as conservative are much more likely to be Republicans; people who identify themselves as liberal are much more likely to be Democrats (see the discussion of ideology in Chapter 1).

Differences Between Democrats and Republicans   We can trace some of the differences—in both ideologies and core constituencies—between today's Democrats and Republicans to the 1930s. This was the era of the **Great Depression,** a time of devastating economic collapse and personal misery for people around the world. President Franklin D. Roosevelt's drive to expand the role of government by providing a safety net for the most vulnerable in society has remained part of the Democratic agenda to this day. In the past several decades, this agenda has centered on pressing for civil rights for African Americans and for the expansion of social welfare programs. Today, key components of the Democratic agenda include gay rights, health care reform, environmental protection, and freedom of choice with respect to abortion.

Traditionally, Republicans have countered this position by advocating a smaller government that performs fewer social welfare functions. But a major priority for the Republican Party today is advocacy of a stronger governmental role in regulating traditional moral values. Because of this stance, a solid voting bloc within the

	Republican	Democrat	Independent
Gender			
Men	37%	32%	31%
Women	34	43	23
Education			
Less than high school diploma	28	51	21
High school	33	43	24
Some college	36	36	27
College degree or more	37	34	29
Age			
18–29 years old	31	43	26
30–44 years old	37	37	26
45–64 years old	35	37	28
65 and over	37	36	27
Household income			
Below $35,000	25	42	24
$35,000 to below $75,000	33	33	26
$75,000 and over	38	29	26
Race			
Whites	41	31	28
African Americans	7	75	18
Hispanics/Latinos	23	44	23
Asian Americans	25	37	28
Native Americans	22	36	28
Geographic region			
Northeast	26	44	30
Midwest	38	37	25
South	41	35	24
West	34	37	30

POLITICAL INQUIRY

FIGURE 8.2 ■ DEMOGRAPHIC CHARACTERISTICS OF PARTY IDENTIFIERS
Which two racial groups are likeliest to identify with the Demographic Party? Which party do people with incomes below $35,000 per year favor? What might explain these data?

Source: The National Annenberg Election Study polls conducted between October 7 and November 16, 2004, www.annenbergpublicpolicycenter.org/ NewsFilter.aspx?mySubType=ALL&. Used by permission of Annenberg Public Policy Center.

Republican Party comprises conservative Christians, sometimes called the Christian Right or Religious Right, who agree with the Republicans' pro-life position on abortion (which includes support for increased regulation of abortion) and appeals for a constitutional amendment banning gay marriage. Republicans also emphasize the protection of business and business owners and in general support a decreased role for the federal government, particularly with respect to the economy and social welfare issues, and a corresponding larger role for state governments. ("Analyzing the Sources" on page 296 looks at the popularity of both parties during the past decade.)

It is not surprising that the base constituencies of the parties are drawn from the groups that each party's platform emphasizes. The base of the Democratic Party prominently includes women, the majority of whom, since 1980, have voted for the Democratic presidential nominee. Since Franklin Roosevelt's New Deal social welfare policy during the 1930s, African Americans have been an important voting bloc within the Democratic Party, although they have faced struggles and strife in asserting and securing their rights, particularly during the civil rights movement of the 1960s. Other ethnic minorities, including Latinos and Asian Americans, also tend to support the Democratic Party (as described in Chapter 6), as do many working-class voters. The base of the Republican Party prominently includes many small-business owners, citizens who identify themselves as being very religious, and upper-middle-class voters.[6]

The Party Organization

Thomas P. "Tip" O'Neill (D-Massachusetts), Speaker of the House of Representatives from 1977 until 1987, is often quoted as saying, "All politics is local." In no case is this statement truer than it is for American political parties.

Party organization refers to the formal party apparatus, including committees, headquarters, conventions, party leaders, staff, and volunteer workers. In the United States, the party organization is most visible at the local level. Yet county and local parties tend to be *loosely* organized—centered predominantly around elections—and may be dormant when election season passes.[7] Except during presidential elections, state and local political parties typically function quite separately from the national party. Although the number of individuals who actually participate in the party organization is quite small when compared with the party in the electorate, on the local level, political parties offer one of the most accessible means for individuals to participate in politics.

But with respect to political *power*, county and local parties are the most important components of a party organization. Theoretically, political parties' organization resembles a pyramid (see Figure 8.3), with a broad base of support at the bottom and power flowing up to a smaller group at the state level and then to an even smaller, more exclusive group at the national level.[8] In reality, the national committees of both major U.S. political parties exist separately from the committees of the state and local parties (see Figure 8.4), and real political power can usually be found at the local or county party level, as we will see in the following discussion.

The National Parties Every four years, political party activists meet at a national convention to determine their party's nominee for the presidency. Here the delegates also adopt rules and develop a party platform that describes the party's policy priorities and positions on issues.

FIGURE 8.3

Theoretical Structure of Political Parties: A Hierarchical Model of Party Organizations

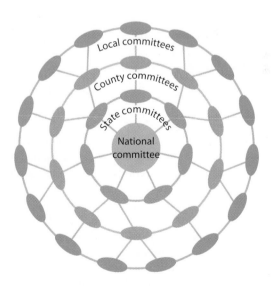

FIGURE 8.4

Modern Structure of Political Parties: Power Diffused Through Many Party Organizations

The People's Opinion of the Parties

The figure below shows the percentage of survey respondents who have a favorable view of the Republican and Democratic parties at selected dates between September 2001 and August 2009.

Evaluating the Evidence

(1) What is the general trend with regard to party favorability ratings? Is one political party consistently viewed more favorably than the other? What is the trend over time regarding the favorability of Democrats versus Republicans?

(2) Look at particular high and low points for each political party. What events may have caused people's opinions of the parties to be more or less favorable?

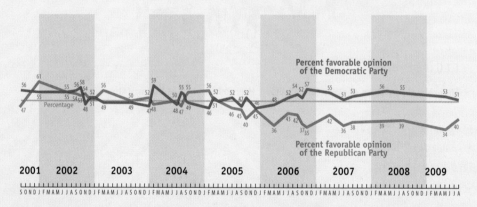

Source: The Gallup Poll, "Party Images," www.gallup.com/poll/24655/Party-Images.aspx.

The national party committees (the Democratic National Committee, or DNC, and the Republican National Committee, or RNC) are the national party organizations charged with conducting the conventions and overseeing the operation of the national party during the interim between conventions. The national committee elects a national chair, who is often informally selected by the party's presidential nominee. The national chair, along with the paid staff of the national committee, oversees the day-to-day operations of the political party.

But the role of the national chair depends to a large extent on whether the party's nominee wins the presidency. If the party's nominee is victorious, the national chair has a less prominent role because the president serves as the most public representative of the party. If the party's nominee loses, however, the national chair may take on a more public persona, serving as the spokesperson for the **loyal opposition**—the out-of-power party's objections the policies and priorities of the government in power. In recent years, regardless of whether the party's nominee has won or lost, one of the most important roles of the national chair has been to fund-raise. Money donated to the national parties is often redirected to the state and local parties, which use it to help contest elections and mobilize voters.

State Parties   Both national parties have committees in each state (the Illinois State Democratic Committee, for example) that effectively *are* the party in that state. State committees act as intermediaries between the national committees and county committees. Typically, state committees are made up of a few members from each county or other geographical subdivision of a given state.

Historically, state parties were important because of their role in the election of U.S. senators, who until 1913 were elected by their states' legislatures. Since the ratification of the Seventeenth Amendment in that year, the voters of each state have directly elected their senators by popular election.

Later in the twentieth century, state political parties began to regain power, partly due to the U.S. Supreme Court's decision in *Buckley v. Valeo* (1976). In this case, the Court ruled that political parties are entities with special status because their functions of educating and mobilizing voters and contesting elections help to ensure democracy.[9] This ruling created the so-called **soft money loophole,** through which the political parties could raise unlimited funds for party-building activities such as voter registration drives and get-out-the-vote (GOTV) efforts, although contributions to specific candidates were limited. The Court's decision strengthened the influence of the state parties, which the national parties often relied upon to coordinate these efforts. The Bipartisan Campaign Reform Act of 2002 eliminated the soft money loophole, but until that time, state parties were strengthened by their ability to channel those contributions to political parties. (See Chapter 9 for further discussion of soft money.)

County and Local Parties   County committees consist of members of municipal, ward, and precinct party committees. The foot soldiers of the political parties, county committees help recruit candidates for office, raise campaign funds, and mobilize voters. The importance of a given county committee's role largely depends on whether its candidates are elected and whether its party controls the government. Party success tends to promote competition for candidates' slots and for seats on the county committee.

In most major cities, ward committees and precinct committees dominate party politics. Because city council members are often elected to represent a ward, ward committees are a powerful force in city politics, providing the grassroots organization that turns voters out in city elections. Precinct committees (a precinct is usually a subdivision of a ward) also help elect city council members.

Besides fund-raising, county and local political parties still play key roles in shaping both community engagement and individual participation in the political process, as they have done historically. During election season (in most places, from the end of August through the first week in November), county and local parties recruit and rely on volunteers to perform a host of functions, including answering phones in party headquarters, registering voters, coordinating mailings, doing advance work for candidates, compiling lists for get-out-the-vote efforts, supervising door-knocking campaigns, and phone-banking to remind voters to vote on Election Day.

The Party in Government

When candidates run for local, state, or national office, their party affiliation usually appears next to their name on the ballot. After an elected official takes the oath of office, many people do not think about the official's party affiliation. But in fact, the **party in government**—the partisan identification of elected leaders in local, county, state, and national government—significantly influences the organization and running of the government at these various levels.

In most towns, the party identification of the majority of the members of the legislative branch (often called *city council* or *town council*) determines who will serve as the head of the legislature (sometimes called the *president of city council*). And in most towns, the president of the city council hails from the majority party. In addition, paid professional positions such as city solicitor (the town's lawyer), town planner, and city engineer are often awarded on the basis of the support of the majority of the council. Even though the entire council votes on appointments, the minority party members often defer to the majority, as appointments typically are viewed as a privilege of winning a majority. Other appointments might include positions on voluntary boards such as a town planning or zoning board.

On the state level, the party in government plays a similarly prominent role in organizing government work. Typically, state legislatures are organized around political party. Seating assignments and committee assignments are made by the majority party leadership and are based on a legislator's party affiliation. Figure 8.5 illustrates the partisan breakdown of state legislatures. In each state, the party with a majority (shown in the figure) in the legislature also has a majority on the legislature's committees, which decide the outcome of proposed legislation. Parties moreover are important in the executive branch of state government, as state governors typically appoint party loyalists to key positions in their administrations. Depending on the appointment powers of the governor, which vary from state to state, a governor may also appoint party members to plum assignments on state regulatory boards. In states where the governor appoints the judiciary, the governor also frequently selects judicial nominees from his or her own political party.

Parties perform a similar role in the federal government. Presidents draw from party loyalists to fill cabinet and subcabinet appointments and typically appoint federal judges from their own political party. Congress is organized based on the party affiliation of its members. When representatives or senators refer to a colleague "on the other side of the aisle," they are referring to a member of the other political party, as congressional Democrats and Republicans sit across the aisle from one another. As in state legislatures, the party with the majority in Congress essentially runs the legislative branch. From its ranks comes the congressional leadership, including the Senate Majority Leader, the Speaker of the House of Representatives, and the House Majority Leader (see Chapter 11).

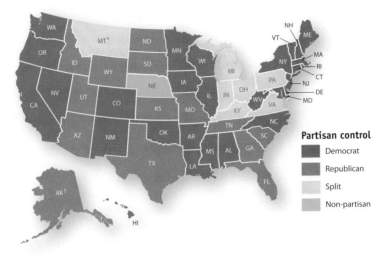

FIGURE 8.5

Partisan Control of State Legislature Before the Election of 2009

*Republicans control Montana's State Senate; it's lower house is split 50–50.

†Upper house is split 50–50; lower house is Republican controlled.

Source: The National Conference of State Legislatures, www.ncsl.org/statevote/partycomptable2008.htm.

Divided Government   There are limits to a party's power. Probably the most important check comes from the opposition party, which can openly criticize the party in power and aggressively investigate alleged misconduct on the part of its officials. During parts of the Bill Clinton and George W. Bush administrations, for example, the president and the members of Congress functioned with a **divided government,** the situation in which one party controls Congress and the other party, the presidency.[10]

Divided government prevailed after 1994 when Democrat Bill Clinton was president and Republicans won control of the House of Representatives. The Republicans not only opposed Clinton's policy priorities but also condemned his sexual improprieties with White House intern Monica Lewinsky, as well as his and Hillary Clinton's ties to a controversial land deal dubbed Whitewater. In 2000, when Republican president George W. Bush was elected, the Senate was evenly divided between Democrats and Republicans. Divided government emerged again after the 2006 midterm elections, when the Democrats won control of both houses of Congress. Democrats in Congress alleged administration misconduct when it appeared that Bush's attorney general, Alberto Gonzales, had dismissed federal prosecutors for reasons of politics rather than competence. In these instances of a divided government, both administrations' attention was diverted from pursuing policy initiatives to dealing with the scandals, and both presidents suffered a loss of prestige that negatively affected their ability to achieve their legislative priorities.

Political Parties in U.S. History

Modern Americans' divided opinions of political parties would not be surprising to the founders, who viewed political parties with suspicion.[11] Thomas Jefferson said, "If I could not go to heaven but with a party, I would not go there at all." This sentiment was shared by George Washington, who warned of "the baneful effects of the spirit of party."[12] Despite these reservations, political parties began to emerge in the United States during the debate over ratification of the Constitution (with both Washington and Jefferson instrumental in their creation). Those who advocated ratification and a strong central government were called Federalists, and those who opposed ratification and favored states' rights were called Anti-Federalists. Thus began the first party system in the United States. **Party system** refers to the number and competitiveness of political parties in a polity[13]—for example, a government may have a two-party system in which one party is ascending in power. As we will see, the demarcation of party systems typically occurs in hindsight, when social scientists recognize points where there has been a **realignment,** a shift in party allegiances or electoral support.[14]

While these shifting allegiances have played a pivotal role in shaping the context of politics since the country's early days, the founders generally believed that parties threatened the stability of the fledgling democracy.[15] Most thought that political parties enabled individuals and groups to pursue self-serving interests that were often contrary to the common good. Some of the founders argued that parties discouraged independence in thought and action. Some thought that parties exacerbated conflicts and disagreements among the people rather than building consensus. Yet their formation and continued evolution testifies to their important role in achieving political and policy goals for their members.[16]

The First Party System:
The Development of Parties, 1789–1828

In 1788, George Washington was elected president, but the consensus surrounding his election proved short-lived. Washington deeply opposed the idea of political parties and ruled during an era without formal parties. But he recognized that despite his popularity, he needed legislators who would push his initiatives through Congress. Washington's secretary of the treasury and close ally, Alexander Hamilton, gathered legislators into a loosely knit party, the Federalists, that favored a strong national government.

Thomas Jefferson, secretary of state during Washington's first term (1789–1793), feared a strong central government, and he and his backers opposed Hamilton's Federalists. But Jefferson's primary concern was that the new government should succeed, and so despite his opposition, he remained in Washington's cabinet during the president's first term. When Jefferson later resigned his secretarial post, in 1793, many of those who shared his apprehensions about a strong central government remained in Congress.

Although Jefferson lost to Federalist John Adams in the 1796 presidential election, he paved the way for his future electoral success by building a base of support—including partisan groups in the states and newly established political newspapers—that allowed him to get his message out.[17] This direct communication with voters marked a significant step in the civic development of the U.S. electorate. The strategy was effective: Jefferson won election to the presidency in 1800 over Adams, and Adams's defeat marked the end of the Federalist Party. Jefferson was reelected in 1804, and both of his elections demonstrated the important function that political parties would play in elections.[18] His supporters became known as Jeffersonian Republicans; later, Democratic-Republicans. The modern descendants of the Democratic-Republicans today are called Democrats.

The Jeffersonian Republicans' effective campaign tactics of communicating with voters, along with the absence of well-organized opposition, resulted in their continued dominance from 1815 to 1828. Historians call these years the Era of Good Feelings, largely because of the widespread popular support for Democratic-Republican presidents James Madison (1809–1817), James Monroe (1817–1825), and John Quincy Adams (1825–1829).

The Second Party System: The Democrats' Rise to Power, 1828–1860

By 1828, some dissension among the Jeffersonian Republicans was becoming apparent. Members of the party, including the charismatic general and politician Andrew Jackson of Tennessee, chafed at the elitism of the party and the era. The Jacksonian Democrats—the name for the new coalition that Jackson formed—emphasized leadership through merit rather than birth.[19] They espoused **populism,** a philosophy supporting the rights and empowerment of the masses, particularly in the area of political participation, and the **spoils system,** in which political supporters were rewarded with jobs (from the phrase "to the victor go the spoils"). The Jacksonian Democrats succeeded in mobilizing the masses, sweeping Jackson to victory in the presidential election of 1828.[20] Political parties had become the medium through which many Americans were politicized, and in 1828, for the first time, more than one million Americans cast their ballots in the presidential contest.

Jackson's populism marked a critical step in opening up the civic life of the polity to a much wider swath of citizens.[21] It redefined not only who was eligible to succeed as political leaders but also who should be eligible to participate in the selection of those leaders. Historian Richard P. McCormick noted that the Jacksonian Democrats extended voting rights to all white adult males, changed the mechanism for selecting presidential electors to popular elections by voters instead of by the state legislatures, and increased the importance of the party convention, in effect giving party members more say in candidates' selection. And although women would not gain the right to vote until 1920, the Jacksonian era saw the formal beginnings of the women's suffrage movement with the formation of the two major women's suffrage organizations and the advent of the Seneca Falls Convention (1848) in support of expanded rights for women.[22]

During the 1830s, southern plantation owners and northern industrialists became concerned about the impact the Democrats' populism would have on economic elites.[23] Their mutual interests crystallized in the formation of the Whig Party in 1836, which succeeded in electing two presidents, William Henry Harrison (succeeded by John Tyler upon his death) and Zachary Taylor.[24] But the era of the Second Party System ultimately was defined by the long-standing effects that Jacksonian principles would have on U.S. politics, namely through the politicization of a previously excluded mass of citizens—many of whom had been initiated into the rites of full citizenship, and others of whom had begun the struggle to win their own status as full citizens.[25]

The Third Party System: The Republicans' Rise to Power, 1860–1896

In the 1850s, slavery became the primary concern for both the Whigs and the Democrats.[26] This highly charged issue divided the Whig Party into proslavery and abolitionist factions, and the party consequently faded away.[27] In its place, a new antislavery party, the Republicans (also called the Grand Old Party, or GOP), took shape in 1854 and gained the support of abolitionist Whigs and northern Democrats.[28] The victory of the Republican presidential nominee, Abraham Lincoln, in the election of 1860 marked the beginning of a period of dominance of the antislavery Republicans, which continued even after the Civil War.[29] During this time, the Republican Party enjoyed strong support from newly franchised African American

THE CURIOUS EFFECT OF CLEAN LINEN UPON
THE DEMOCRATIC PARTY

POLITICAL INQUIRY

In this cartoon by the famous nineteenth-century caricaturist and cartoonist Thomas Nast, what does the tiger represent? What point is the cartoonist making about the "clean linen" the tiger is wearing?

Party Politics in Flux

THEN (1889)	NOW (2010)
Powerful political parties were in their heyday, and party bosses ruled the cities with an iron fist.	The era of party politics in the United States is over, according to some scholars.
The patronage system was in high gear, and political parties derived enormous power and loyalty from the recipients of jobs and lucrative contracts.	A merit-based civil service system has largely replaced patronage, and parties are weakened because of a decline in the number of loyal members.
Elected officials toed the party line, because they depended on the party for their office.	Elected officials pride themselves on their "independence," and "bipartisanship," and sometimes owe very little to their political party.

WHAT'S NEXT?

> How are advancing technologies likely to change political parties and their operations in the future? Will these weaken or strengthen the parties? Explain.

> Do you think that the next elections will mirror the partisan loyalties among voters in the 2008 presidential campaign?

> How do parties today help voters evaluate candidates? Will they still perform this function in the future? Will the nature of this process change? Explain.

voters. Although many African Americans in the South were prevented from exercising their right to vote through threats, intimidation, and tactics such as the white primary (see Chapter 5), African Americans in the North widely voted Republican. They would remain strong supporters of the "party of Lincoln" for decades.

During this time, political parties grew very strong, and political machines came to dominate the political landscape. A **political machine** was both a corrupt and a useful organization that dominated politics around the turn of the twentieth century, particularly in cities. Each political machine was headed by a "boss," whose power rested on a system of patronage. A party leader used **patronage** as a device to reward political supporters—rather than individuals who might demonstrate greater merit or particular competence—with jobs or government contracts. In exchange, those receiving patronage would vote for the party and might be expected to volunteer on a campaign or kick back some of their wages to the party.

Although political machines were known for corruption, they did accomplish some good. Richard Croker was political boss of Tammany Hall, New York City's Democratic Party political machine from 1886 until 1902. He explained: "Think of what New York is and what the people of New York are. One half are of foreign birth. . . . They do not speak our language, they do not know our laws. . . . There is no denying the service which Tammany has rendered to the Republic, there is no such organization for taking hold of the untrained, friendless man and converting him into a citizen. Who else would do it if we did not?"[30]

On that score, Croker was right. At the time, political machines provided the vital service of socializing a generation of immigrants to democracy and to the American way of political life. Some machines, including Tammany Hall, generated widespread political participation, and some allowed the participation of women.[31] Political machines helped integrate immigrants into the social, economic, and political fabric of the United States, usually by awarding jobs for loyalty to the party. And in an era when the federal government had not yet become a large-scale provider of social services, urban political machines also provided a safety net for the injured, the elderly, and widows.

The Fourth Party System: Republican Dominance, 1896–1932

The 1896 presidential election between populist Democrat William Jennings Bryan and Republican William McKinley marked the beginning of a new era in party politics. Bryan appealed widely to Protestants, southerners, midwesterners, and rural dwellers who were suspicious of Catholic, ethnic, working-class immigrants in the urban Northeast. McKinley emphasized economic growth and development and garnered support from industrialists, bankers, and even working-class factory workers, who saw his backing of business as being good for the economy. McKinley won the election handily, his victory ushering in an era of Republican dominance in presidential politics that would last until the election of 1912.

That year, Theodore Roosevelt (who had succeeded McKinley as president in 1901 after the latter's assassination, and who had been elected president as a Republican in 1904) ran in the presidential election as a Progressive. The Progressive Party advocated widespread governmental reform and sought to limit the power of political bosses. The Republicans' split between William Howard Taft's regular Republicans and Roosevelt's Progressives powered Democrat Woodrow Wilson to the presidency with only 42 percent of the popular vote.

As Wilson's Democratic administration ended up enacting many of the Progressive Party's proposals, the power of the urban political machines declined. For example, recorded voter registration and secret ballot laws were passed, the direct party primary was established, and civil service reform was expanded. The national leaders who spearheaded these measures designed them to take political power out of the bosses' hands and give it to the electorate.

After Wilson's two terms, the Republicans continued to enjoy the support of business elites and the industrial working class. They also benefited from the backing of the many African Americans in the northern cities who continued to support the party of Lincoln, and of women voters, many of whom had been activists in the Progressive movement. With this widespread and diverse support, the Republicans retained control of the presidency throughout the 1920s.

The Fifth Party System: Democratic Dominance, 1932–1968

When the stock market crashed in 1929, the economy entered the deep downturn that history remembers as the Great Depression. In the election of 1932, a broad constituency responded to the calls of the Democratic candidate, Franklin D. Roosevelt, for an increased governmental role in promoting the public welfare. Roosevelt pressed tirelessly for a **New Deal** for all Americans, a broad program in which the government would bear the responsibility of providing a "safety net" to protect the weakest members of society.

A new alignment among American voters swept "FDR" into presidential office. In fact, the **New Deal coalition**—the name for the voting bloc comprising traditional southern Democrats, northern city dwellers (especially immigrants and the

> African American voters were a key constituency in electing both Franklin Roosevelt and Barack Obama to the presidency. Here, voters in Harlem wait to cast their ballots for President Roosevelt in 1936 and President Obama in 2008.

poor), Catholics, unionized and blue-collar workers, African Americans, and women—would give Roosevelt the presidency an unprecedented four times.[32]

The era of the Fifth Party System significantly opened up party politics and civic activity to a widening spectrum of Americans. Notably for African Americans and women, Franklin Roosevelt's elections marked the first time that they had been actively courted by political parties, and their new political activism—particularly in the form of voting and party activities—left them feeling they had a voice in their government.

Vice President Harry Truman assumed the presidency on Roosevelt's death in 1945 and was elected in his own right in 1948, but subsequent Democrats were unable to keep Roosevelt's coalition together. Republican Dwight Eisenhower won the White House in 1952 and again in 1956. And although Democrats John F. Kennedy and Lyndon Johnson held the presidency through most of the 1960s, the events of that decade wreaked havoc on the Democratic Party, with deep divisions opening up over the Vietnam War and civil rights for African Americans.[33]

A New Party System?

Between 1968 and 2008, Republicans held the presidency for all but the Jimmy Carter (1977–1981) and Bill Clinton (1993–2001) administrations. With the passage of time and the gaining of perspective on the significance of these relatively recent events, some political scientists contend that the years since 1968 can be characterized as a period separate from the Fifth Party System—an era that has given rise to a new party system.

Other political scientists have noted certain changes within the electorate that help to explain the prevalence of Republican victories at the national level. One such change is the tendency of southern whites to vote Republican, a trend that began with Ronald Reagan's election to the presidency in 1980. The migration of southern whites—historically, a core constituency of the Democratic Party—to the Republicans has provided a crucial boost for Republican candidates. In his book *Whistling Past Dixie,* political scientist Thomas F. Schaller asserts that the deep conservatism of southern whites has rendered the region no longer a competitive ground for Democrats. Schaller argues that the Democrats would be better off focusing on strengthening their constituencies in the Southwest and Midwest, where their ideological positions would have greater voter appeal.[34]

Additional characteristics of this new party system, according to scholars, include *intense party competition,* in which the two major U.S. political parties have been nearly evenly matched and neither one has dominated, and *divided government,* where a president of one party has to deal with a Congress of the other. This fierce partisan competitiveness is clearly apparent in the outcomes of recent national elections. In particular, the 2000 presidential campaign demonstrated the ferocious rivalry of the two parties, with a presidential election so close that the outcome was in question for weeks after the voting had ended. That year, voters also evenly divided the Senate, electing fifty Democrats and fifty Republicans.

Moreover, some scholars see **dealignment,** the phenomenon in which fewer voters support the two major political parties and instead self-identify as independent, as a notable characteristic of this new party system.[35] Others view the increasing trend toward supporting candidates from both parties—(**ticket splitting**)—or from third parties as evidence of a new party system's emergence.

The period since 1968 has also been characterized by the growing importance of candidate-centered politics. The rise of **candidate committees,** organizations that candidates form to support their individual election as opposed to the party's slate of candidates, is one reflection of how politics has increasingly become candidate-centered. Candidate committees compete with political parties in many arenas. They raise and spend money, organize campaigns, and attempt to mobilize voters. One impact of their enhanced influence has been that elected officials, particularly members of Congress, are less indebted to their parties than in previous eras and thus sometimes demonstrate less loyalty when voting on bills in the legislature.

Some political scientists argue that these characteristics of the new party system demonstrate that the responsible party model (discussed earlier) is not as strong as it once was. The rise of candidate committees and the increase in ticket splitting mean that parties are less helpful to voters as they assess candidates, because the differences between Republican and Democratic candidates may dissipate in the face of constituent opinion. Yet most Americans disagree: a recent Gallup poll indicated that nearly two-thirds of those surveyed believe that there are important differences between the Democratic and Republican parties.[36] And the research of some scholars, including David Karol, Hans Noel, John Zaller, and Marty Cohen, indicates that party elites, including elected officials and former elected officials, have increased their control in selecting presidential nominees, suggesting a potential revival of the importance of parties as players in politics today.[37]

Two-Party Domination in U.S. Politics

Since the ratification of the Constitution in 1787, the United States has had a two-party system for all but about thirty years in total. This historical record stands in marked contrast to the experience of the many nations that have third parties.[38] A **third party** is a political party organized as opposition or an alternative to the existing parties in a two-party system. Many countries even have *multi*party systems.

The United States' two-party system has had two contradictory influences on people's civic engagement. On the one hand, the dominance of only two political parties through most of American history has made it easy for individuals to find avenues for becoming civically engaged. Further, at various historical points, political parties have worked for the outright extension of political rights to groups that were excluded, although often with the foremost aim of bolstering their core supporters. On the other hand, the dominance of just two political parties that tend to be ideologically moderate discourages the political participation of some people, particularly those who are strongly ideological.

Although the grip of the United States' two-party system is frustrating to people who support a greater diversity of parties, the reasons for the two-party system are numerous and difficult to change.

The Dualist Nature of Most Conflicts

Historically, many issues in the United States have been dualist, or "two-sided," in nature. For example, the debate over ratification of the U.S. Constitution found people with two basic opinions. On one side, the Federalists supported ratification of the Constitution, which created a federal government that separated powers among three branches and shared power with state governments. They were opposed by the Anti-Federalists, who campaigned against ratification of the Constitution, supported stronger states' rights, and wanted to see states and individuals enjoy greater protections. This split provided the initial structure for the two-party system, and a multitude of issues followed that format.

Political scientists Seymour Martin Lipset and Stein Rokkan asserted that the dualist nature of voter alignments or cleavages shapes how political parties form. In particular, these alignments or cleavages concern the character of the national fabric (for example, whether religious ideals or secular notions should prevail), and they are determined by function (business versus agrarian interests, for example).[39] These cleavages shaped party formation during the nineteenth century, when the dualist nature of conflict continued to be in evidence in public affairs. Some states wanted slavery; other states opposed "the peculiar institution" of human bondage. In some states, commercial and industrial interests dominated; in other states, agricultural interests held the reins of power. Immigrants, often Catholics, controlled the politics of some states, whereas native-born Protestants held sway in others.

By the twentieth century, the dualist conflict had become more ideological. Some Americans agreed with President Franklin D. Roosevelt's plan to help lift the country out of the Great Depression by significantly increasing the role of government in people's everyday lives. Others opposed this unprecedented expansion of the federal government's power. In later decades, debates over civil rights and women's rights demonstrated the continued dualist nature of conflict in American society and culture.

The Winner-Take-All Electoral System

In almost all U.S. elections, the person with the most votes wins. If a competitor gets just one vote less than the victor, he or she wins nothing. If a third party garners a significant proportion of the vote in congressional elections nationwide but does not win the most votes in any given district, the party will not win any seats in Congress.

Compare the winner-take-all system to the proportional representation system found in many nations. In a **proportional representation system,** political parties win the number of parliamentary seats equal to the percentage of the vote each party receives. So, for example, if the Green Party were to capture 9 percent of the vote in a country's election, it would get nine seats in a one-hundred-member parliament. In a proportional representation system, the 19 percent of the vote that Reform Party candidate Ross Perot won in the 1992 U.S. presidential election would have given the Reform Party about 85 seats in the House of Representatives!

In nations with proportional representation, third parties (which we consider in more detail later in the chapter) are encouraged because such parties can win a few seats in the legislature and use them to further their cause and broaden their support.[40] In addition, in proportional representation systems, third parties sometimes form a *coalition,* or working union, with a larger party so that the two together can control a majority of a legislature. And so, for example, the Green Party that won nine seats in Parliament in the example mentioned above might form a coalition with another party that had received 42 percent of the vote, together forming a majority government. In this way, a third party can get members appointed to key positions as a reward for forming the coalition. Consequently, societies with proportional representation systems can sometimes be more inclusive of differing points of view because even those winning a small proportion of the vote achieve representation, and that representation can be pivotal in the formation of coalitions.

Continued Socialization to the Two-Party System

Another reason that the two-party system dominates in the United States is that party identification—like ideology, values, and religious beliefs—is an attribute that often passes down from one generation to the next. Hence many an individual is likely to be a Democrat or Republican because his or her parents were one or the other. Many people first learn about government and politics at home. Around the dinner table, a child may have heard her parents rail against Barack Obama's health care proposal or criticize George W. Bush's Iraq policy. Having become socialized to their household's political culture, children are likely to mimic their parents' views.

Even children who do not share their parents' political outlook or who grow apart from it over time (as commonly occurs during the college years) have been socialized to the legitimacy of the two-party system—unless, of course, their parents routinely criticized both Democrats and Republicans or voiced dissatisfaction with the two-party system.

Election Laws That Favor the Two-Party System

At both the federal and the state level in the United States, election laws benefit the two major parties because they are usually written by members of one of those parties. Although some local governments mandate nonpartisan elections, in most cities and towns, getting on the ballot typically means simply winning the party's nomination and collecting a state-specified number of signatures of registered party members on a nominating petition. Usually, the party organization will circulate this petition for a candidate. Third parties have a much steeper climb to get their candidates in office. In the 2008 presidential election, candidate Ralph Nader, who ran as an independent, had difficulty just getting his name on the ballot in some states.

Scholars of civic engagement point to the structural impediments to the formation of third parties as key to the low level of civic engagement on the part of individuals who are dissatisfied with the two-party system. Facing seemingly insurmountable structural obstacles to the formation of successful third parties, some Americans shy away from political engagement.

The Two-Party System Today: In Decline or in Resurgence?

Given the various historical changes to the U.S. political party system that we examined above, many political scientists have inquired into what the impact of these changes will be. Do the changes signify an end to party control in American politics? Or can political parties adapt to the altered environment and find new sources of power?

The Party's Over

Some scholars argue that changes in the political environment have rendered today's political parties essentially impotent to fulfill the functions that parties performed during stronger party systems. In 1982, political scientist Gary Orren wrote, "In a world in which political scientists disagree on almost everything, there is remarkable agreement among the political science profession that the strength of American political parties has declined significantly over the past several decades."[41] Although some political scientists would subsequently challenge Orren's perspective, many agreed with him at the time.

These theorists note several key factors that have contributed to party decline. Some argue that the elimination of political patronage through the requirement of civil service qualifications for government employees has significantly hurt parties' ability to reward loyal followers with government jobs. Patronage jobs still exist, but most government positions are now awarded upon an applicant's successful performance on a civil service exam that is designed to measure qualifications based on objective criteria. Whereas the recipients of patronage jobs were among the most loyal party members in previous decades, party loyalty has decreased as political parties have lost a significant amount of control in the awarding of jobs.

Other political scientists emphasize the government's increased role over time in providing social welfare benefits as a contributor to the decline of political parties. Before President Franklin D. Roosevelt's New Deal, the government bore little if any responsibility for providing a safety net for those on the bottom economic rungs of society, a role often filled by political parties. With the coming of the New Deal and the subsequent passage of social welfare legislation, the government has come to be the largest provider of social services, and the parties typically no longer perform that function. Thus changing times have brought the elimination of another source of party loyalty.

Primary elections—elections in which voters choose the party's candidates who will run in the later general election—also have decreased parties' power by taking the control of nominations from party leaders and handing it to voters. In the past, when a party machine anointed nominees at nominating conventions, those nominees became indebted to the party and typically responded with loyalty if they got elected. But today's candidates are less likely to owe their nomination to the party: instead, in many cases, they have fought for and won the nomination by taking their campaign directly to primary voters.

Changes in the mass media have also meant a drastically decreased role for political parties. In their heyday, political parties were one of the most important providers of news. Parties published so-called penny papers that reported information to the public. Today, political parties may still provide some information to voters at election time, but most voters rely on other, independent media outlets—newspapers, television, radio, and Internet news sources—rather than exclusively partisan sources.

The rise in candidate-centered campaigns has also weakened political parties. **Candidate centered campaigns,** in which an individual seeking election, rather than an entire party slate, is the focus, have come about because of changes in the parties' functions, the advent of direct primaries, and trends in the mass media that have shifted the focus to individual office-seekers. Candidate-centered campaigns also must rely more heavily on paid professional campaign workers (instead of party volunteers), a reality necessitating campaign contributions to individual candidates rather than to the party.

These changes in the nature of political parties and in their ability to perform their traditional functions have led some political scientists to conclude that the era of party rule is ending. Other players, they say—including interest groups, candidate-based organizations, and the media—will come to assume the roles traditionally performed by political parties.

The Party's Just Begun

Pointing to the record-breaking turnout in the 2008 presidential primaries, other political scientists strongly disagree that U.S. parties' prime has passed.[42] While conceding that political parties' functions have changed, these theorists observe that parties have proved themselves remarkably adaptable. When the political environment has changed in the past, political parties have responded by assuming different functions or finding new avenues by which to seed party loyalty. According to this view, the parties' ability to rebound is alive and well.

These scholars also argue that the continued dominance in the United States of two political parties—through decades of threats to their survival—has demonstrated a strength and resilience that are likely to prevail. Today's Republicans, the party of Lincoln, have endured the assassinations of party leaders, the Great Depression, the four-term presidency of popular Democrat Franklin D. Roosevelt, and the Watergate scandal during the Nixon presidency. Today's Democrats are the same party that opposed suffrage for African Americans in the aftermath of the Civil War and that survived internal divisions over civil rights through the 1960s to become strong supporters of African American rights in recent decades. The Democrats too have endured assassinations, and scandals and have weathered Republican control of the White House for all but twelve years since 1968. Both political parties have remained remarkably competitive despite the challenges to their success.

Scholars who argue that the two main U.S. political parties are once again rebounding cite the lack of viable alternatives to the two-party system. Yes, third parties have made a mark in recent presidential elections. But the present-day party system has not seen the emergence of a strong, viable third party with a cohesive ideology that has attracted a significant portion of the vote in more than one election. And civic education scholars agree that third parties have served an important function by encouraging the political participation of people who are disenchanted with the current two-party system. They also acknowledge, however, the continued dominance of the two main parties in creating opportunities for civic engagement within communities.

Third Parties in the United States

As we have seen, the absence of viable U.S. political parties beyond the Democrats and Republicans is a source of frustration for some Americans. This frustration is borne out by the data in Figure 8.6, which illustrates that a majority of Americans favor a third party. Notably, the data show a significant increase in popular dissatisfaction with both political parties. Why should this be the case? Most pollsters would argue that the failure of both the Republicans and the Democrats to end the war in Iraq has contributed to the electorate's growing dissatisfaction with both political parties.

Despite the fact that a majority of Americans think a third party is needed, third parties have had little success in contesting elections. In recent times, Ralph Nader was an influential candidate in 2000, not because he netted a sizable proportion of votes but because the 3 percent that he did win was enough to change the outcome of that razor-close election. Other third-party candidacies have proved influential because of their role in focusing attention—particularly the attention of the victorious candidate—on an issue that might not otherwise have been addressed.[43] Such was the case in 1912 when Progressive Party candidate Theodore Roosevelt ran

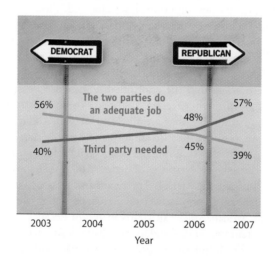

POLITICAL INQUIRY

FIGURE 8.6 ■ IS A THIRD PARTY NEEDED?
What trend do the polling data in this figure show? What factors in political and social environments might explain this trend?

Source: The Gallup Poll, "Party Images," www.galluppoll.com/content/default.aspx?ci=24655, accessed October 4, 2007.

against Woodrow Wilson. Although he lost the presidency, Roosevelt succeeded in shaping public opinion so that Wilson felt compelled to enact part of the Progressives' national agenda, including sweeping changes to the nation's child labor laws.

One of the most significant obstacles to the formation of a viable third party is that people who are dissatisfied with the two dominant parties fall across the ideological spectrum: some are very liberal; others, quite conservative; still others, moderate. Thus, although many Americans are dissatisfied with the current parties, a third party would have difficulty attracting enough support from among these diversely dissatisfied party members.

Nonetheless, third parties have played, and continue to play, an influential role in American electoral politics. Third parties are particularly effective at encouraging the civic engagement of people who feel that the two dominant parties do not represent their views or do not listen to them. Third parties give such citizens a voice. And even though third parties often do not succeed electorally, their mere presence in the political arena enlivens civic discourse and frequently encourages debate about urgent policy issues that the two major parties ignore or slight.

Types of Third Parties

Third parties have existed in the United States since the early nineteenth century. Over the nation's history, third parties typically have fallen into one of three general categories: issue advocacy parties, ideologically oriented parties, and splinter parties.

Issue Advocacy Parties   Formed to promote a stance on a particular issue, many issue advocacy parties are short-lived. Once the issue is dealt with or fades from popular concern, the mobilizing force behind the party disintegrates. An example is today's Green Party, which promotes environmental protection as a primary issue and also emphasizes human rights, childhood poverty, globalization, health care, and corporate corruption and greed in its party platform. In the 2000 presidential election, the Green Party sought to win 5 percent of the vote for its presidential candidate, Ralph Nader. If the Greens had succeeded, they would have automatically qualified their party for federal matching funds in the 2004 campaign. The Green Party fell short, however, as it captured only 3 percent of the vote. Its share of the vote then dropped drastically in the 2004 presidential election.

Ideologically Oriented Parties   The agenda of an ideologically oriented party is typically broader than that of an issue-oriented party. Ideologically oriented parties are structured around an *ideology*—a highly organized and coherent framework concerning the nature and role of government in society (see Chapter 6). Such parties have broad views about many different aspects of government. For example, the Libertarian Party, which holds the ideological position that government should not interfere with individuals' social, political, and economic rights, advocates a very limited role for government: no guarantees of minimum wages or other forms of governmental regulation of the economy, including environmental regulation; no governmental interference in individuals' privacy; the legalization of prostitution and drugs; and the elimination of major governmental bureaucracies, including the Central Intelligence Agency, the Internal Revenue Service, and the Federal Bureau of Investigation.

Another ideologically oriented party is the Socialist Party, which lies at the other end of the ideological spectrum from the Libertarian Party. The Socialist Party, formed in 1901, is one of the longest-standing ideologically oriented parties in the United States. Socialists believe that government should play a large role in ensuring economic equality for all people. Historically, the Socialist Party has advocated various policies that ultimately were addressed in legislation by the two major parties, including Social Security, workers' compensation, disability insurance, and unemployment insurance. Currently, the Socialist Party is calling for a 50 percent cut in the military budget and proposes to replace that expenditure with spending on education, child care, health care, and low-cost housing.[44]

Splinter Parties   A splinter party is a political party that breaks off, or "splinters," from one of the two dominant parties. Often a group splinters off because of intraparty (internal, or within the party) disagreement on a particular issue. For example, in 1948, a group of southern Democrats who opposed the Democratic Party's support of civil rights for African Americans splintered from the Democratic Party to form the States' Rights Party, which quickly became known as the Dixiecrat Party. The party called itself the States' Rights Party because it claimed that Congress had no power to interfere with the administration of laws made by the states. It used this claim to retain the policies that created a system of racial segregation in the South. Although the States' Rights Party was a separate, formal organization, many southern Democratic elected officials and party leaders who agreed with the States' Rights Party's platform supported its views from within the Democratic Party.

The Impact of Third Parties

Despite the difficulties associated with sustaining support in American electoral politics, third parties have important effects in the political arena. First, although U.S. third parties usually do not win elections, they can influence electoral outcomes. For example, given the closeness of the 2000 presidential race, many Democrats believe that Green Party candidate Ralph Nader caused Democrat Al Gore to lose the election. They reason that Nader voters would have been more likely to vote for the liberal Gore than for the conservative George W. Bush if Nader had not been a candidate. In a state such as Florida where the electorate was evenly divided, Nader's candidacy in fact could have changed the outcome of that state's balloting and thus the results of the national election as well. Of course, many third-party advocates claim that supporters of a third-party candidate may not have voted at all if their party had not been on the ballot.

Second, third parties provide a release valve for dissatisfied voters. People who are disgruntled with the two major parties can join or form another political party. And although a third party's chances of electoral success are not great, such parties provide a mechanism for like-minded people to come together to try to effect change. Sometimes, these efforts result in a victory, especially on the local level. A well-known third-party victor is Jesse Ventura, a former professional wrestler who

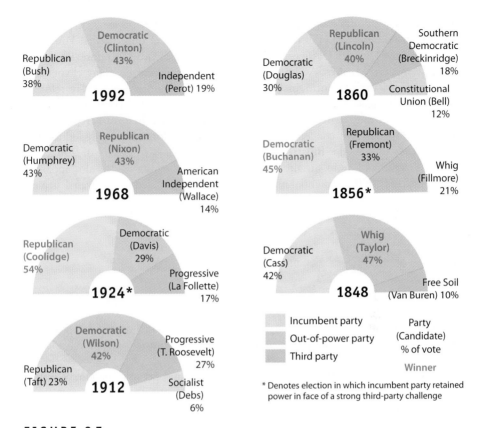

FIGURE 8.7

Third Parties Help the Out-of-Power Party

Note: Candidate appears in parentheses; percentage is percentage of vote won by candidate.

was elected governor of Minnesota in 1998 as a candidate of the Reform Party. With respect to the national level, the impact of third parties as a release valve for discontented voters may be seen in several elections, as shown in Figure 8.7. In U.S. history, third-party presidential candidates have won more than 10 percent of the vote seven times, the latest being in 1992, when Independent Party candidate H. Ross Perot captured 19 percent of the vote. As the figure illustrates, in five of those seven cases, the incumbent party's presidential nominee lost the presidency. Thus, third parties tend to help the major out-of-power party win election.

Finally, third parties put a variety of issues on the national political agenda. When a third party, especially an issue-oriented third party, draws attention to an issue of concern, sometimes government officials respond to that concern even if the third party fails in its election bid. In some such cases, the issue has not previously been given priority, and the attention the third party draws to it serves to create a groundswell of political pressure that forces action. In other cases, the policy makers might act to address the issue in order to woo the supporters of the third party who have expressed that particular issue concern.

Historically, the two major parties' co-option of issues that were first promoted by third parties has sometimes contributed to the demise of third parties. For example, as we have seen, the Progressives' presidential candidate, Theodore Roosevelt, lost to Democrat Woodrow Wilson in 1912, but Wilson enacted many elements of the Progressive Party's platform, including antitrust regulations, corporate law reforms, and banking regulations. Lacking a unique platform, and with comparatively little electoral success, the Progressives faded away. More recently, Reform Party candidate H. Ross Perot's activism concerning campaign finance reform eventually led the two major parties to pass the Bipartisan Campaign Finance Reform Act of 2002. The Reform Party's inability to sustain voter support over the long haul is also apparent: after the party's 2000 presidential nominee Pat Buchanan failed to net even 1 percent of the national vote, the party did not nominate a candidate in 2004, instead backing Green Party nominee Ralph Nader.

New Technologies: The Parties in the Twenty-First Century

American political parties have changed dramatically in recent years. Global realities such as the end of the Cold War, international and domestic terrorism, and the impact of the Internet have partly driven the changes.

The ways in which party members and voters give and get information, as well as the methods by which parties campaign, have changed drastically in recent years. More and more people in the electorate are finding information about issues through social networking sites, tweets, instant and text messages, and through the Internet. For example, those interested in receiving text updates from Barack Obama's organization Organizing for America can simply text "go" to "OBAMA" (62262), and they will receive updates from the organization, including appearance notifications. During the 2008 campaign, both the McCain and Obama campaigns used their Web sites to plug their supporters into assorted outlets for their interest and activism. Both offered downloadable widgets that allowed supporters to link their social-networking pages and to fund-raise by linking the campaign site to their own Web sites. Both also hosted a wide variety of ways for individuals to stay connected to the campaigns, including listing candidates' favorites on del.icio.us; links to campaign videos on YouTube and to Facebook and MySpace pages; a Twitter micro-blog through which the campaign sent short, updated communications to instant messaging and e-mail accounts and to the Twitter Web site; and campaign photos available at the flickr Web site.

The Internet has also democratized the party process. Partisan activism is no longer limited to individuals who can attend meetings. Whole new forms of Internet activism have emerged. People with access to the Internet can chat, organize, plan, lobby, fund-raise, contribute, and mobilize without leaving their desks.

Today, each party relies heavily on the Internet for communicating with supporters, as, for example, the Democratic Party's blog "Kicking Ass" and the Republican Party's "podcasts to go" reveal. Each party's Web site gives visitors information and plenty of opportunities to volunteer. Moreover, adopting a strategy first employed by individual candidates, parties are also using the Internet as a fund-raising tool: they solicit contributions via special e-mail accounts and on party Web sites and accept donations through online credit card payments. At the end of this chapter you will find URLs for the Web sites of the Democratic National Committee, the Republican National Committee, and a nonpartisan organization, where you can explore your own opportunities for Internet activism.

CONTINUING THE CONVERSATION

- Despite the cynicism with which people often view them, political parties are a vital institution for the civic engagement of Americans and are essential to democracy.
- For many citizens, political parties are the gateway to political participation.
- For others, they provide cues that guide decisions at the ballot box.
- The two major U.S. political parties have demonstrated enormous adaptability over time. The ability to change in response to constituent demands is a consistent trait of these two dominant parties.
- The cultural and structural forces that perpetuate the two-party system show little sign of relenting.
- Although third parties such as the Green Party provide rich fodder for political pundits who speculate about their importance, in electoral terms third parties have demonstrated very little ability to win elections.

STUDY NOW

Summary

1. Parties Today and Their Functions

Political parties run candidates in elections in an effort to control government. They advance the cause of civic engagement by facilitating citizens' participation, providing unity and cohesiveness, encouraging civic discourse, and communicating important cues to voters.

2. The Three Faces of Parties

Three aspects of parties are the party in the electorate (the individuals who tend to support a particular party), the party organization (the formal party apparatus), and the party in government (the partisan identification of elected leaders).

3. Political Parties in U.S. History

Political scientists have identified five U.S. party systems. Through these party systems, we see the ideological roots and political foundations of the two dominant political parties today.

4. Two-Party Domination in U.S. Politics

Explanations of why two political parties dominate include the ideas that parties reflect the dualist nature of conflict in the United States, that the winner-take-all election system creates a two-party structure, that people are socialized to the two-party system, and that election laws strengthen and perpetuate that structure.

5. The Two-Party System Today: In Decline or in Resurgence?

Some political scientists argue that recent times show a decline in the influence of the two major U.S. parties. Other scholars assert that parties are rebounding, and they note parties' adaptability, as well as the lack of viable alternatives to the two major parties.

6. Third Parties in the United States

Third parties, which include issue advocacy parties, ideologically oriented parties, and splinter parties, sometimes act as a spoiler for one of the two major parties. Although third-party candidates typically lose elections, they do succeed in getting various issues on the national agenda.

7. New Technologies: The Parties in the Twenty-First Century

Social networking sites are becoming an increasingly important tool used by both political parties in communicating with and mobilizing supporters. Supplementing other Web-based technologies, these new mediums have transformed the practice of party politics.

For Critical Thinking and Discussion

1. How were you socialized to the two-party system? Do your views reflect your parents' views? Were third parties even mentioned in your house when you were growing up?
2. What factors explain the demographic bases of the two major parties? How could each party expand its base of support?
3. What impact do you think the Internet and other technologies will have on parties over time? Why?
4. What evidence is there that a new party system is emerging? Do the 2008 election results support the claim that a new party system is taking shape?
5. In what ways beyond those discussed in the chapter might the Internet be used as a communication tool between voters and parties? In your view, what are the most important uses for the Internet in partisan politics?

Key Terms

candidate-centered campaign 311	candidate committees 307	divided government 299
	dealignment 306	Great Depression 292

Internet Resources

A More Perfect Union Web site
www.mhhe.com/harrisonampule   Consult the book's Web site for study guides, interactive activities, simulations, and current hot-links that provide additional information on political parties in the United States.

Democratic National Committee
www.democrats.org   The Democrats' Web site contains links for state and local party Web sites and opportunities for volunteering, internships, and employment, as well as party position papers and platforms and candidate information.

Pew Research Center for the People and the Press
http://people-press.org/reports/display.php3?ReportID=242   This the Web site for the report "Beyond Red vs. Blue: Republicans Divided About Role of Government, Democrats by Social and Personal Values," which provides a quiz so you can determine where your political beliefs fall on Pew's typology of voters.

Project Vote Smart
www.vote-smart.org   This nonpartisan site provides independent, factual information on candidates and elected officials of all political parties.

Republican National Committee
www.gop.org   The Republicans' site also has links for state and local party sites and opportunities for volunteering, internships, and employment, as well as party position papers and platforms and candidate information.

Recommended Readings

Flammang, Janet. *Women's Political Voice.* Philadelphia: Temple University Press, 1997. A well-researched account of women's political participation in general and women's participation in political parties in particular.

Hershey, Marjorie Random, and Paul Allen Beck. *Party Politics in America,* 10th ed. New York: Longman, 2003. A classic work on American political parties, analyzing the changing roles of parties in the twentieth century and the impact of the campaign finance system on political parties.

Lijphart, Arend. *Electoral Systems and Party Systems: A Study of Twenty-Seven Democracies 1945–1990.* New York: Oxford University Press, 1994. An exploration of the nature of party systems in many industrialized democracies both historically and in modern times.

Schattschneider, E. E. *Party Government.* New York: Rinehart, 1942. A classic work that explains the nature of political parties and their impact on party government.

Political party–dominated campaigns and grassroots activism were deciding factors in how people voted.

Candidate-centered campaigns rely on paid professionals to shape and spin candidates' messages—and on costly media buys to disseminate it.

NOW

9 Elections, Campaigns, and Voting

When Americans think about politics, their first thought is often about elections, campaigns, and voting. In the eyes of many of us, these activities are the essence of political participation, because it is through the electoral process that we feel we participate most directly and meaningfully in our democracy. Often viewed as the pinnacle of the democratic experience, the act of voting is the culmination of a wide range of forms of political engagement. In the discussion that follows, we see the interconnectedness of many aspects of political campaigns and elections, including fund-raising, grassroots organizing, candidate selection, and voter mobilization. These opportunities for civic participation in the democratic process are present in such a broad variety of forms that they are accessible to everyone who wants to be engaged.

How will continuously advancing technologies drive and change campaigns?

How will changes in the campaign finance structure affect how campaigns are conducted?

What new faces and voices will determine the campaign environment?

Civic Engagement and Political Participation

Elections, campaigns, and voting are fundamental aspects of the civic engagement of Americans and are important both for the polity as a whole and for the individuals who participate.[1] But intensive political engagement—working on a campaign or running for office, say—rarely represents an individual's first foray into a civically engaged life. Rather, people who are so engaged in the political process usually are initiated through smaller, less intensive steps. Perhaps a group of classmates who especially enjoy the political discussions in your American government class might continue their conversations of democracy over a cup of Starbucks after class. Those same classmates might begin regularly reading political blogs and daily newspapers to become better informed about candidates and issues. Some members of the informal group might decide to hear a candidate who is giving a speech on campus—and wind up volunteering on his or her campaign. Political engagement often begins with small steps such as these, but the cumulative results are large: they help to ensure that the government is representative of the people and responsive to their needs. Representative governments, which are the product of individuals' political engagement, tend to be more stable and to make decisions that best reflect the needs and will of the people who elect them.

Direct forms of political participation such as voting, volunteering on a campaign, and running for office are of keen interest to scholars of civic engagement. Many scholarly analysts have noticed an overall decrease in levels of political participation. As discussed in Chapter 7, political scientist Robert Putnam argues that the United States is seeing a decline in its social capital, the social networks and reciprocal relationships characteristic of a community or society. These networks are varied and include formal organizations such as clubs, fraternities, sororities, interest groups, and sports teams. But there are also informal networks such as babysitting co-ops, car pools, and study groups. Putnam details how solitary pursuits such as watching television and using a computer have pervasively replaced group activities related to civic participation.

Some scholars have challenged Putnam's assertion that social capital has declined. They point out that new forms of social capital have arisen in the form of Internet social networks, instant messaging, and Internet activism to replace the traditional social networks that Putnam studied. Despite these differing views, there is consensus that civic participation is essential and that among its most important forms is electoral political participation.

Indeed, elections offer a wealth of opportunities for citizen involvement:

- Members of political parties recruit candidates to run for election.
- Cadres of volunteers organize campaign events, including fund-raisers, rallies, and neighborhood leafleting.
- Phone bank volunteers try to persuade other people to participate in the electoral process—for instance, by giving a campaign contribution, putting a candidate's sign on their lawn, or simply voting for the candidate.

> Are more people really *"Bowling Alone"*? Political scientist Robert Putnam has argued that the United States is experiencing a decline is social capital because its citizens are participating less in civic life. But perhaps Americans are engaged in civic life in very different ways from those of previous generations. While perhaps they are not joining bowling leagues as in decades past (left), bowling enthusiasts may still be experiencing similar social rewards and companionship over a game of Wii bowling, as they are in this Illinois restaurant (right).

■ Other volunteers focus exclusively on **GOTV**—that is, they work to get out the vote. They register voters for both primary and general elections, and they provide absentee ballots to people who are ill or who will be out of town on election day. On election day itself, they remind people to vote by phoning them or knocking on their door and asking if they need a ride to the polls.[2]

■ Others (who may be paid) volunteer to work at the polls on election day.

While each volunteer effort plays a part in ensuring the success of a democracy, a key form of political participation is running for office. Electoral contests in which more than one candidate seeks to win office are a fundamental component of a democracy.

Elections in the United States

Every state holds at least two types of elections. A *primary election* comes first and determines the party's nominees—those who will run for office. For most political offices, there is little or no competition in the primary election. But in presidential and gubernatorial primary elections, vigorous contention is often the rule, particularly within the out-of-power party. House and Senate primary elections that lack an incumbent candidate (that is, one who has been elected to that office before) are also often highly competitive as many candidates attempt to win their party's nomination.

In a **general election,** the parties' respective nominees run against each other, and voters decide who should hold office, as the person with the most votes wins. (Presidential elections, discussed later in this chapter, are a notable exception.) The degree of competition in general elections depends on a number of factors, including the presence of and strength of incumbency, the degree of party competition, and the level of the office. In recent times, presidential elections have been brutally competitive, as have been certain gubernatorial races and many congressional contests where no incumbent was seeking reelection. Some communities, particularly big cities, may also experience intense competition for office in general elections.

Nominations and Primary Elections

In a primary election, voters decide which nominees the political parties should run in the general election. But *which* voters decide varies greatly from state to state. In some states, only registered party members are eligible to vote in primary elections, whereas in other states, any registered voter can vote in any party's primary, and in North Dakota, voters are not even required to register.

In U.S. presidential primaries, voters do not vote directly for the candidate whom they would like their party to nominate. Instead, the popular vote determines which candidate's delegates will attend the party's nominating convention and vote for that party's nominee. This system of selecting delegates through primary voting is different from the earlier system, when party leaders selected the presidential nominee with little or no input from the rank-and-file party members.

The two major U.S. parties made reforms to the earlier delegate selection process after the 1968 Democratic National Convention in Chicago. Anti–Vietnam War activists outside the convention protested the presumed nomination of Vice President Hubert Humphrey as the Democratic Party's presidential candidate. Humphrey had not won any primaries but was favored among the convention's delegates who had been hand-picked by party leaders. The activists instead supported the candidacy of Senator Eugene McCarthy (D-Minnesota), an outspoken war opponent. The demonstrations turned into riots when Chicago police beat the protesters. The Democratic National Committee, in an attempt to address the concerns of those complaining that they had been excluded from the nomination process, appointed the McGovern-Fraser Commission (named after its co-chairs), which recommended a series of reforms to the delegate selection process.

The reforms, many of which both the Democratic Party and the Republican Party adopted, significantly increased the influence of party voters. Voters could now select delegates to the national conventions, a power previously restricted to the party elite. Party voters today select the delegates at statewide conventions or through primary elections or **caucuses**—meetings of party members held to select delegates to the national convention. The reforms also included provisions that would ensure the selection of a more representative body of delegates, with certain delegate slots set aside for women, minorities, union members, and young party voters. These slots roughly correspond with the proportion of support the party receives from those groups.

When an individual is elected to be a delegate at the national convention, often that delegate has pledged to vote for a specific candidate. This pledge is nonbinding, however, as delegates of a losing candidate often switch their support to the apparent victor.

Types of Primary Elections   In an **open primary** election, any registered voter can vote in any party's primary, as can independent voters not registered with a party. In an open primary, parties' ballots are available in the voting booth, and the voter simply selects privately or publicly one on which to register his or her preferences.

In a **closed primary** election, voting in a party's primary is limited to members of that party. In some states, voters must declare their party affiliation well in advance of the primary election—sometimes as many as sixty days before. In other states, voters can declare their party preference at the polling place on the day of the election. Such restrictions on who can vote in a party's primary originated in the parties' maneuvering to have the strongest candidate nominated. For example, if a popular incumbent president were running unopposed in a primary election, members of the president's party might choose to vote in the other party's primary as a way of scheming to get a weak candidate nominated. A closed primary aims to thwart this strategy.

Presidential Primaries   The states determine the timing of primary elections. Historically, states that held their presidential primary earlier in the year had a greater say in determining the nominee than did states with later primaries. The reason is that candidates tended to drop out if they did not win primaries, did not meet media expectations, or ran out of funds. In general, past presidential primaries gave great sway to the agricultural states, as many of the more urban states' primaries fell later in the season.

All of this changed in 2007 when, in an attempt to increase their political clout, a number of diverse states banded together to hold their primaries on the same day, so that presidential candidates would be forced to address issues of the keenest interest to those states. These states modeled their objective on **Super Tuesday,** the day in early March on which the most presidential primary elections took place, many of them in southern states. Super Tuesday had been the fruit of a successful effort in 1988 by several southern and rural states to hold their primaries on the same day so as to increase their political importance and allow expression of southern voters' political will.[3] But in 2007, the Super Tuesday strategy was challenged by state legislators in some of the most populous states, including California, New York, Illinois, and New Jersey, who sought to have their presidential primaries on the earliest day that national political party rules allowed. In 2008, that day, February 5, was dubbed "Super-Duper Tuesday" by the media, with twenty-four states holding their primaries on the same day. Although under normal circumstances, such a change would have muted the impact of other primaries because the most populous states control an enormous number of delegates to the national conventions, in 2008 this was not the case. That year, the highly competitive Democratic primary between Senator Hillary Clinton (D-New York) and Senator Barack Obama (D-Illinois) meant that states such as New Mexico and Oregon (which had late primaries, in early June) were competitive and received national media coverage.

General Elections

In a general election, voters decide who should hold office from among the candidates determined in the primary election. Most general elections, including presidential elections, are held on the first Tuesday after the first Monday in November.

But because the states schedule and oversee elections, you might find that your gubernatorial election, state legislative election, or town council election occurs at different times of the year.

General elections for Congress and most state legislatures feature a winner-take-all system. That is, the candidate who receives the most votes wins that office (even if that total is not a majority, or even if an opponent receives only one vote less than the victor). Thus, a member of the U.S. House of Representatives or Senate can be elected with less than a majority of the votes in his or her district, particularly when three or more candidates are seeking that seat.

Because electoral law varies from state to state, and counties and municipalities within those states have their own structures of governance, less common kinds of elections are possible and are used in some locales. For example, some states require a runoff election when no candidate receives the majority of the votes cast. In a **runoff election,** if no candidate receives more than 50 percent of the vote, several of the top vote-getters (usually the top two) run in another, subsequent election. Typically, the field of candidates is winnowed down until one candidate receives the requisite 50 percent plus one vote. Runoff elections often occur in *nonpartisan* municipal elections where candidates do not run on a party label.

Owing to advances in technology, runoff elections can occur immediately in some states when needed. In an **instant runoff election,** a computerized voting machine simulates the elimination of last-place vote-getters. How does this system work? In an instant runoff, voters rank candidates in order of preference (first choice, second choice, and so on). If any candidate garners more than 50 percent of all of the first-choice votes, that candidate wins. But if no candidate gets a majority of first-choice votes, the candidate in last place is electronically eliminated. The voting machine computer then recalculates the ballots, using the second-choice vote for those voters who voted for the eliminated last-place finisher; in effect, every voter gets to choose among the candidates remaining on the ballot. This process is repeated until a candidate who receives more than 50 percent of the votes emerges. Today's voting machines allow this process to take place instantly.

Referendum, Initiative, and Recall

Whereas primary elections and general elections select an individual to run for and serve in office, various other kinds of elections are held for the purpose of deciding public policy questions. Although no national mechanism allows all Americans to vote for or against a given policy proposal, citizens can directly decide policy questions in their states by referendum or initiative.[4]

A **referendum** is an election in which voters in a state can vote for or against a measure proposed by the state legislature. Frequently, referenda concern matters such as state bond issues, state constitutional amendments, and controversial pieces of legislation. An **initiative,** sometimes called an initiative petition, is a citizen-sponsored proposal that can result in new or amended legislation or a state constitutional amendment. Initiatives differ from referenda in that they are typically propelled to public vote through the efforts of citizens and interest groups.[5] The initiative process usually requires that 10 percent of the number of the voters in the previous election in that state sign a petition agreeing that the **proposition,** or proposed measure, should be placed on the ballot.

A third type of special election, the recall, differs from referenda and initiatives in that it is not concerned with policy-related issues. Rather, the **recall** election allows voters to cut an officeholder's term of office short. Recall elections are typically citizen-sponsored efforts that demonstrate serious dissatisfaction with a particular officeholder. Concerned citizens circulate a petition, and after they gather the required number of signatures, an election is held to determine whether the official should be thrown out of office.

The Act of Voting

The process of voting begins when a voter registers to vote. Voting registration requirements vary greatly from state to state. Some states require registration months in advance of an election; others allow voters to register on the day of voting. In the United States, the voters use an **Australian ballot,** a secret ballot prepared by the government, distributed to all eligible voters, and, when balloting is completed, counted by government officials in an unbiased fashion, without corruption or regard to individual preferences. Because the U.S. Constitution guarantees the states the right to conduct elections, the mechanics and methods of voting vary widely from state to state. Some states use touch-screen technology; others employ computerized ballots or punch cards that are counted by computers. Still other states use traditional lever ballots, in which voters pull a lever to register their vote for a particular candidate. Despite these differences, all ballots are secret ballots.

The 2000 Election and Its Impact

In the 2000 presidential election between Democrat Al Gore and Republican George W. Bush, an enormous controversy erupted over the voting in Florida. Because of the closeness of the electoral vote, the outcome of the Florida vote turned out to be pivotal. But the tallies in that state's election were in question, not only because of the narrow difference between the number of votes won by each candidate but also because of the voting process itself. Florida citizens cast their vote on a punch card by poking through a **chad,** a ready-made perforation, next to the name of their candidate of choice. Officials then counted the punch card ballots using a computer program that calculated votes by counting the absence of chads. But in the case of the 2000 election, thousands of ballots could not be read by the computer and needed to be counted by hand. This unexpected development put election officials in the difficult, and ultimately deeply controversial, position of gauging "voter intent." If a chad was hanging by one perforation only, did the voter intend to vote for that candidate? What if the chad was "pregnant" (that is, sticking out but not removed; see the photo)? What if the chad was dimpled, and the voter had cast his or her entire ballot by only dimpling the chads?

In the end, the U.S. Supreme Court had the final say. On December 12, 2000, the Court halted the hand counting of ballots in Florida, with the Court's majority

> The problems with chads: A hanging chad . . . and a pregnant chad.

ruling that the differing standards of hand counting ballots from one county to the next and the absence of a single judicial officer charged with overseeing the hand counts violated the equal protection clause of the U.S. Constitution. The ruling meant that George W. Bush, who was leading in the count, was certified the winner of the Florida race, thus securing that state's twenty-five Electoral College votes and the presidency of the United States.

Indignation surrounding the 2000 election resulted in federal policy changes to the conduct of elections by the states. The key policy revision came through the passage of the Help America Vote Act of 2002 (HAVA). HAVA allocated $650 million to assist states in changing from punch card ballots to electronic voting systems and set a deadline of 2005 for states to comply, although some states have not yet done so.

Types of Ballots

There are two types of ballots most commonly used in general elections in the states today. The first, the **party-column ballot,** organizes the candidates by party, so that all of a given party's candidates for every office are arranged in one column. The opposing party's candidates appear in a different column.

The impact of a party-column ballot is twofold. First, party-column ballots increase voters' tendency to vote the "party line," that is, to vote for every candidate of a given party for every office. In fact, some states provide a party lever, which allows a voter to vote for all of a given party's candidates simply by one pull of a lever or one press of a "vote party" button. Second, because they increase the tendency to vote the party line, party-column ballots also increase the **coattail effect,** the phenomenon whereby *down-ballot candidates* (candidates who are running for lower-level offices, such as city council) benefit from the popularity of a top-of-ticket nominee. Often, the composition of city councils, county legislatures, and even state legislatures changes because of a coattail effect from a popular presidential or gubernatorial candidate. Because party-column ballots strengthen political parties, parties tend to favor this type of ballot, which is the most commonly used ballot in the United States.

Another type of general election ballot is the **office-block ballot,** which arranges all candidates for a particular office under the name of that office. Office-block ballots are more likely to encourage ticket splitting, where voters "split their ticket"—that is, divide their votes—between candidates from different parties.[6] Because office-block ballots deemphasize political parties by breaking up the party line, the parties do not tend to favor them.

Why Ballot Design Matters

The 2000 presidential election voting in Florida provides evidence that not only the voting process but also the design of ballots can make a difference in outcomes. Specifically, with respect to the vote in Florida's Palm Beach County, where voters push a button on their voting machine ballot to register their vote, critics charge that the ballot in use, the *butterfly ballot* (so called because candidates are listed on two "wings" with a common "spine"), was particularly confusing to voters.

On this particular ballot, the Democratic ticket of Al Gore and Joe Lieberman was listed second in the left column, or wing. But in order to vote for them, a voter had to select the *third* button down. Hitting the second button would have registered a vote for the Reform Party candidates. Because of the lack of ballot clarity and voters' widespread assumption that the two major party candidates would lead the ballot, many Democrats complained that this ballot layout put the Gore/Lieberman ticket at a disadvantage. Although supporters of Reform Party candidate Pat Buchanan in Palm Beach County projected that he should have received at best 1,000 votes there, Buchanan received over 3,400 votes. Many people, including Buchanan himself, believed that these votes were mistakenly cast for him and intended for Al Gore.[7]

In fact, an additional 19,000 votes were nullified in the Palm Beach County election because voters cast *two* votes for president, presumably with balloters

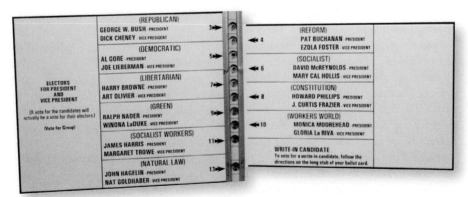

> The controversial butterfly ballot used by Palm Beach County, Florida, in the 2000 election.

Source: © AP Photo/Gary I. Rothstein.

realizing too late that they had pushed the wrong button. Buchanan himself addressed this issue, saying, "If the two candidates they pushed were Buchanan and Gore, almost certainly those are Al Gore's votes and not mine. I cannot believe someone would vote for Gore and say, 'I made a mistake, I should have voted for Buchanan.' Maybe a small minority of them would have done that. But I—I've got to think that the vast majority of those [votes] would naturally belong to Al Gore and not to me."[8]

Voting by Mail

One form of voting, **absentee voting,** is a long-standing tradition by which voters cast their ballots in advance by mail when disability, illness, school, work, service in the armed forces, or travel prevents them from casting a ballot in their voting precinct. To cast an absentee ballot, an individual must typically apply (before a specific state-designated deadline) to vote by absentee ballot in the county where he or she usually votes. The superintendent of elections then mails a ballot to the voter, who votes and then mails the ballot back. The absentee ballots are counted and added to the votes cast in the voting precincts. Requirements for absentee ballots vary from state to state. Some states require a legitimate excuse, but increasingly, many states accept ballot applications simply because absentee voting is more convenient for the voter.

A relatively recent development is the advent of statewide voting by mail, a practice that states have adopted in an attempt to increase voter participation by making voting more convenient (see "Analyzing the Sources"). The first experiment with statewide vote by mail occurred in Oregon in 1996. In a special election there, where officials had predicted a turnout of less than 50 percent, more than 66 percent of voters cast their ballots. This experiment brought another benefit: it saved taxpayers more than $1 million. Oregon decided to continue the practice in the 2000 presidential election, in which voter turnout hit 80 percent, and in the 2004 presidential race, where the turnout approached 85 percent. Oregon has now taken the drastic step of abandoning voting in polling places on election day.

There are obvious advantages to voting by mail. As Oregon's experience demonstrates, more people participate when voting becomes easier. Further, increased participation may bring to office candidates who are more representative of the will of the people because more people had a say in their election.

Some scholars, however, have criticized the vote-by-mail trend. One important criticism is that voting by mail means that people vote before the final days of the campaign, thus casting their ballot before some additional last-minute information might be revealed about a candidate. Indeed, some voters may cast their ballots before the political rivals' debates occur or before candidates fully articulate their message. Consider one case in Bainbridge Island, Washington, where it was revealed just days before the election that a candidate for mayor had padded his résumé. By the time the exaggerations came to light, some voters had already cast their ballots by mail.[9]

Early Voting

Voters are increasingly opting to cast their ballot prior to election day. These charts show how early voting during the 2008 presidential election (either by absentee or mail-in ballot) breaks down according to age and geography. The polls measure whether an individual had already voted an (before the October 17–22, 2008 polling period), intended to vote before the November 4 election, or planned to vote on election day.

Evaluating the Evidence

1. According to the charts, which voters are the most likely to say they will vote early?

2. In examining the age of early voters, you can see a distinct trend regarding who is most likely to vote early. Why do you think this is the case?

3. It is clear from the second graph that voters in some regions are much more likely to vote early than others. What might explain this difference?

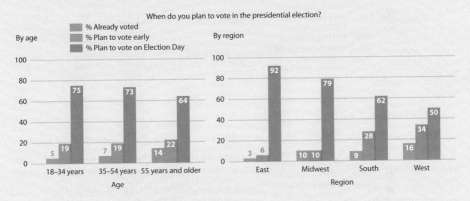

When do you plan to vote in the presidential election?

Source: http://www.gallup.com/poll/111430/Early-Voting-Now-11-Could-Reach-30.aspx

Voting by mail also increases the chances of vote fraud. Even though states take measures to ensure the principle of "one person, one vote," voting by mail presents opportunities for corruption. Voting at the polls requires a face-to-face encounter, but voting by mail does not, so ballots could be stolen from individuals' mailboxes or intercepted after having been mailed by a voter.

Voting by mail also may eliminate the privacy associated with voting in recent times. With mail balloting, the vote occurs in a less controlled setting, and the voter might feel pressured by others to select a particular candidate. In contrast, booth voting affords privacy and secrecy that go far toward ensuring that the votes cast behind the curtain reflect the individual voter's will.

Finally, voting by mail may undermine feelings of civic engagement by eliminating a source of psychological rewards for voters. Going to a polling place, signing the voting registry, entering the voting booth, and casting your vote can elicit feelings of patriotism, civic pride, and fulfillment of civic responsibility: the sense that you are doing your duty to help ensure the election of the best-qualified candidates. Although the results may be the same with voting by mail, some evidence suggests that voting by mail does not bring with it the same sense of civic satisfaction that voting at a polling place confers.

Running for Office: The Choice to Run

The reasons that individuals become political candidates vary almost as much as the individuals do. Yet four types of motivation are generally in play when a person decides to declare a candidacy:

- a sense of civic responsibility—the feeling on the candidate's part that he or she has an obligation to govern
- a sense of party loyalty—of filling the need for parties to run viable candidates
- personal goals, and in particular, interest in electoral politics and officeholding as a career
- interest in increasing the candidate's name recognition and stature in the community, often for business reasons

Some people believe they have an obligation to put their experience, knowledge, and skills to work for the greater good of the community or country. Often these civically motivated people become politically involved out of concerns about specific issues. They might object to a specific policy or want to see the government take action on a given issue. For example, Representative Carolyn McCarthy (D-New York) ran for and won a seat in the House of Representatives after her husband was killed and her son was injured in a mass shooting on the Long Island Railroad. While nursing her adult son's injuries after the senseless tragedy, McCarthy decided to run when her congressman voted to repeal a ban on assault weapons.

Sometimes an individual may choose to run for office out of a sense of party duty. The candidate may run as a "sacrificial lamb" for a seat he or she has little chance of winning, mainly with the intent of ensuring that the party offers an alternative to the favored candidate. Or an elected official may decide to run for another office because he or she has the best chance of winning an election and allowing the party to attain control of that office.

Other people are motivated to run for a particular office because of personal goals. Many of these individuals seek elected office as their career. Whereas presidents and governors typically serve no more than eight years, members of Congress, state legislators, county commissioners, and council members often serve for decades.

Holding office is what they do—and because of the advantages of incumbency, once elected, many remain in office for years. Other candidates run for office because of political ambitions: a town council member who aspires to serve in the state legislature might run for county commissioner even if she thinks she will not win because she realizes that mounting a viable campaign might help her in a later bid for the statehouse.

Finally, some people run for office because of the heightened stature that a candidacy brings to their "regular" careers. Lawyers may run for the state legislature, realtors for the city council, or insurance brokers for county commissioner because a candidacy makes them more successful in their daily occupations. Running for office enhances a person's name recognition so that, for example, the realtor sitting on the city council might get more business because people in the community know his name. Running for office also opens doors to networks of potential business contacts, as many candidates address civic groups and get to know people in the community. These networks can be useful in business as well as politics.

Many candidates, of course, run for office for a combination of reasons. They might believe, for example, that they have a responsibility to serve their country *and* that they have something valuable to contribute.

Formal Eligibility Requirements

Article I of the U.S. Constitution specifies some minimum criteria for those seeking election to federal office:

- **President:** A candidate for the presidency must be a natural-born citizen. Naturalized citizens, who are born citizens of another country and then choose to become American citizens, such as Ileana Ros-Lehtinen (R-Florida), a member of the House of Representatives and a native of Cuba, cannot run for president. Presidential candidates also must be at least 35 years old and must have been a resident of the United States for fourteen years by the time of inauguration.
- **Vice president:** A vice-presidential candidate, like a contender for the presidency, must be a natural-born citizen and must be at least 35 years old; he or she must not be a resident of the same state as the candidate for president with whom he or she will serve.
- **U.S. senator:** A candidate for the Senate must have citizen status of at least nine years, must be at least 30 years old when taking office, and must be a resident of the state from which he or she is elected.
- **U.S. representative:** A candidate for the House of Representatives must be a citizen for at least seven years, must be at least 25 years old when taking office, and must be a resident of the state from which he or she is elected.

Typically, a state's constitution determines the minimal qualifications for the governorship and state legislature, and these vary from state to state. In general, state requirements address the same issues as federal guidelines—citizenship, age, and residency.

Informal Eligibility Requirements

In addition to the legal eligibility requirements prescribed by the federal and state constitutions, informal eligibility criteria—that is, the characteristics that voters expect officeholders to have—help to determine who is qualified to run for a particular office. By and large, the eligibility pool for elected office depends on the office—and so, although your car mechanic might be considered a good candidate for your town council, he would not likely meet the informal eligibility criteria to be elected president of the United States.

Generally, the higher and more prestigious the political office, the greater the informal eligibility requirements are. On the local level, particularly in smaller communities, an individual would be considered eligible to run for town council if he or she were liked and respected in the community, had lived in the community long enough to know the voters, and were either gainfully employed, a homemaker, or retired.

Farther up the political office ladder, state legislative candidates in most states are expected to have some kind of professional career. Still, there is a great deal of variation from state to state, and certainly nonprofessionals occupy many state legislative seats. State legislatures tend to be dominated by lawyers and business professionals, occupations that offer the prestige to be considered part of the informal eligibility pool and that allow enough flexibility to facilitate campaigning and legislative work.

The informal eligibility requirements for federal office are even more stringent. Voters expect candidates for the House of Representatives, the U.S. Senate, and the presidency to have higher qualifications than candidates for state and local offices. Among most congressional constituencies, candidates for federal office would be viewed as "qualified" to hold office if they had a college degree, considerable

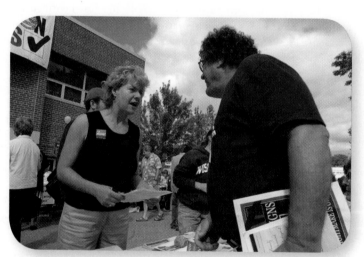

> Informal qualifications for Congress vary according to the political culture in the district. Openly gay members of Congress are a rarity. Representative Tammy Baldwin (D-Wisconsin), the only openly lesbian member of Congress, talks here with a constituent.

professional and leadership experience, and strong communication skills. But informal qualifications vary according to the political culture in a district, with some districts favoring a particular religious affiliation, ethnicity, or other characteristic. In races for the U.S. Senate and the presidency, the popular press examines the minutest details of candidates' professional and educational background. For example, sometimes it is not enough that candidates are college graduates; where they went to college, whose university is more prestigious, and who had the higher grade point average are all fodder for the media and political pundits.

Political Campaigns Today

Campaigns today are a different animal from the campaigns of the 1980s or even the early 1990s. The main reasons for the changes are the professionalization of campaign staffs, the dramatically expanded role of the media and the Internet, and candidates' ever-rising need for funding to keep pace with the unprecedented demands of contemporary campaigning.[10]

The Professionalization of Political Campaigns

One of the most significant changes in the conduct of campaigns is the rise in prominence of **campaign consultants,** paid professionals who specialize in the overall management of political campaigns or an aspect of campaigns, such as fund-raising or advertising. Previously, volunteers who believed in the party's ideals and in the candidate ran most campaigns. Although some volunteers may have been motivated by the expectation that they would personally benefit from the election of their candidate, their efforts focused largely on the election itself—of a single candidate or slate of candidates.

In contrast, professional consultants dominate modern campaigns for federal offices, many state offices, and some municipal offices. Typically, these advisers receive generous compensation for their services. Although professional consultants may not be as dedicated to a single candidate as earlier grassroots volunteers were, these strategists are typically committed to seeing their candidate elected and often are quite partisan, usually working only for candidates of one party throughout their careers.

One of the top jobs in a political campaign is that of **campaign manager,** a professional whose duties comprise a variety of strategic and managerial tasks. Among these responsibilities might be the development of the overall **campaign strategy,** the blueprint for the campaign, which includes a budget and fund-raising plan, an advertising strategy, and staffing objectives. Once the campaign strategy is set, the campaign manager often hires and manages the office staff; selects the campaign's theme, colors, and slogan; and shapes the candidate's image. Another crucial campaign professional is the pollster, who conducts focus groups and polls that help develop the campaign strategy by identifying the candidate's strengths and weaknesses and by revealing what voters care about.

Other professionals round out the candidate's team. A **fund-raising consultant** works with the candidate to identify likely contributors and arranges fund-raising events and meetings with donors. Policy directors and public relations consultants help to develop the candidate's stance on crucial issues and to get the candidate's positions out to the voters, and a **media consultant** brings the campaign message to voters by creating handouts and brochures, as well as newspaper, radio, and television promotions. Media consultants rely increasingly on the Internet to bring the campaign to voters through e-mail campaigns, Web-based advertising, blogs, and message boards.[11]

Media and New Technologies: Transforming Political Campaigns

Today, with the presence everywhere of the media in all its forms—television, Internet news sites, blogs, radio, podcasts, newspapers, magazines—citizens' access to information is unprecedented. Today twenty-four-hour news channels such as CNN and MSNBC compete with Internet news outlets, satellite radio programming, and news text messages to grab audience attention. But not all of this bombardment of information is accurate.

Given the abundance of information disseminated today, and in light of its diverse and sometimes questionable sources, engaged citizens have a greater responsibility to be discerning consumers of the news, including coverage of campaigns, voting, and elections. They cannot be passive listeners and spoon-fed watchers of news as it is dished out by daily newspapers, nightly newscasts, and the occasional weekly or monthly periodical. Vivé Griffith of the University of Texas at Austin's Think Democracy Project writes, "The challenge for the contemporary citizen is to be more than an audience member. . . . An informed polity is essential to a democracy, and it can be difficult to sort through whether our media-saturated world ultimately serves to make us more or less informed."[12] We consider media coverage of elections, campaigns, and voting in detail in Chapter 10.

Personality versus Policy   In sorting through the abundance of "news," citizens must also contend with changes in how information is presented by the media. When news was less available—that is, when TV networks aired a single fifteen-minute nightly news broadcast—the content tended to be policy-oriented and hard-hitting. Today, networks have much more time to fill: in addition to their nightly thirty-minute news broadcasts, most metropolitan areas have an hour and a half of local news in the evening, with two additional half-hour broadcasts in the morning and at noon. This all-day banquet of news programming does not include national morning talk shows such as *Good Morning America* and the *Today Show,* nor does it include evening news magazines such as *60 Minutes, 20/20,* and *48 Hours.* Because of the many hours that networks and twenty-four-hour cable news shows must fill, the focus has shifted more and more from the policy stances of candidates and government officials to the personalities of these individuals. Many Americans are well equipped to describe the personality traits and lifestyle preferences of elected leaders: President George W. Bush's penchant for exercise, former president Bill Clinton's reputation as a fast-food junkie, Barack Obama's pack-a-day smoking habit. The reason for this shift is twofold: (1) many viewers enjoy lighter content when watching so much television, and (2) personality-oriented coverage is less likely to offend viewers and advertisers.

How Political Campaigns Have Changed in the Past 30 Years

THEN (1980s)	NOW (2010)
Many campaigns were managed and staffed by volunteers.	Campaigns are increasingly professionally managed by "guns for hire" and often have an extensive staff dedicated to strategy setting, fund-raising, and media relations.
Grassroots activism was the norm in all but the largest campaigns.	*Netroots* activism uses the Internet as a complement to traditional grassroots campaign efforts.
Money was a crucial consideration in campaigns, but grassroots activism de-manded fewer financial resources.	Money rules the day in most campaigns.

WHAT'S NEXT?

> How can the Internet change the need for money in political campaigns?

> Given the extent of Web activism during the 2008 campaigns, is there still a role for grassroots activism in post-2008 campaigns? Explain.

> Will campaigns continue to be dominated by professional staffers? Why or why not?

Revolutionizing the Campaign: The Internet The Internet has dramatically changed the conduct of political campaigns. As its use has steadily grown, the ways in which the Internet is impacting political campaigns is continuously evolving. Among the new tools used by candidates for the presidency, the Internet is among the most valuable and powerful. The Internet serves as an efficient means by which office seekers can communicate with supporters and potential supporters, as well as a mechanism to mobilize citizens. Candidates' Web sites provide a unique and easily accessed forum where the electorate can find out about candidates' experience, views, and policy priorities—and potentially make more informed choices in the voting booth.

Internet communities provide a powerful mechanism for political engagement. Some Internet communities may be dedicated to advancing the electoral chances of a particular candidate. Other communities host forums for political discourse, including Facebook pages that facillitate policy discussions among group members.

Candidates for government office also increasingly use the Internet for fund-raising. In discussing the growth of campaign fund-raising on the Internet, Eli Pariser, founder of MoveOn.org's Peace Campaign, noted that "candidates are wasting their time with rubber-chicken donors,"[13] an allusion to the donors who contribute to candidates by paying to attend campaign dinners.

Regulating Campaign Finance

Money—lots of it—is essential in electoral races today. Money and the modern campaign are inextricably linked because of the importance of costly media advertising in modern campaigns.[14] Federal regulations require any group that contributes to candidates' campaigns to register as a political action committee (PAC), and many interest groups form PACs as one arm of their organization. Though they are a fixture in U.S. politics, PACs are a relatively recent phenomenon. But the influence of money in electoral politics goes back a long time, as do the efforts to regulate it.[15] Reformers have attempted to limit the impact of money on political campaigns for almost as long as campaigns have existed. One of the foremost obstacles to reforming the campaign finance system is that the people charged with fixing the problem—the members of Congress—have successfully used the system to get elected. Still, despite the significant obstacles, legislators have made efforts historically and in recent times to overhaul the country's campaign finance system.

An early attempt at regulating campaign finance took root after a scandal that erupted during the administration of President Warren Harding (1921–1923). In 1921, the president transferred oil reserves at Teapot Dome, Wyoming, from the Department of the Navy to the Department of the Interior. The following year, Harding's secretary of the interior leased the oil fields without competitive bidding. A Senate investigation into the deal revealed that the lessee of the fields had "loaned" the interior secretary more than $100,000 in order to win political influence. The interior secretary was convicted and sentenced to a year in prison and a $100,000 fine. Dubbed the Teapot Dome scandal, this sordid affair led Congress to try to limit influence of money on politics through legislation.

The Federal Corrupt Practices Act of 1925 sought to prevent future wrongdoing. This act aimed to regulate campaign finance by limiting campaign contributions and requiring public disclosure of campaign expenditures, and it was one of the first attempts at campaign finance regulation. But because the act did not include an enforcement mechanism, it was a weak attempt to fight corruption, and candidates found numerous loopholes.

The Political Activities Act of 1939, also known as the Hatch Act, marked another congressional attempt to eliminate political corruption. With the growth of the federal bureaucracy as a result of the New Deal programs of President Franklin D. Roosevelt, several scandals had emerged, demonstrating the problems that could arise when government employees took an active role in politics. The Hatch Act banned partisan political activities by all federal government employees except the president, vice president, and Senate-confirmed political appointees. The act also sought to regulate the campaign finance system by limiting the amount of money a group could spend on an election and placing a $5,000 cap on contributions from an individual to a campaign committee. Although the Hatch Act was more effective than the Federal Corrupt Practices Act of 1925, it also contained a significant loophole: groups that wanted to spend more than the legislated limit of $3 million simply formed additional groups.

Congress again attempted to curtail the influence of special interests in 1946 with the passage of the Federal Regulation of Lobbying Act. Title III of this law stated that any person who received money in order to influence congressional legislation was a lobbyist and must register his or her activities. The law's goal was to provide for public disclosure of lobbyists' activities, but it fell short because it too lacked an enforcement mechanism.

In 1971, Congress passed the Federal Election Campaign Act (FECA), the most significant attempt at overhauling the nation's campaign finance system. The law was sponsored by Democrats in Congress who were concerned about the enormous fund-raising advantage the Republicans had had during the 1968 presidential election. This law placed considerable limitations on both campaign expenditures and campaign contributions, and it provided for a voluntary tax-return check-off for qualified presidential candidates. This provision enables you, when filling out your federal income tax return, to contribute three dollars, which will go toward the matching funds that qualified presidential candidates receive.

In 1974, FECA was amended to place more stringent limitations on individual contributions and to limit expenditures by PACs, and it revamped the presidential election process by restricting spending and providing public financing for qualified candidates who abided by the limits. The act also required public disclosure of contributions and expenditures by all candidates for federal office. Most important, the act created an enforcement mechanism in the Federal Election Commission, the agency charged with enforcing federal campaign finance laws.

In the subsequent, highly significant Supreme Court case *Buckley v. Valeo* (1976), however, the plaintiffs contended that placing limitations on the amount an individual candidate could spend on his or her own campaign violated First Amendment protections of free speech. The Court agreed, ruling that "the candidate . . . has a First Amendment right to engage in the discussion of public issues and vigorously and tirelessly to advocate his own election."[16] This ruling paved the way for the subsequent explosion in the formation of PACs, as the Court recognized political expenditures as a protected form of speech and removed limits on overall campaign spending, on personal expenditures by an individual candidate, and on expenditures not coordinated with a candidate's campaign that are made by independent interest groups. In its *Buckley* ruling, the Court boldly overturned the limitations on expenditures that to that point had been written into law.

Regulatory Loopholes: Independent Expenditures

The determination that campaign expenditures constitute free speech uncovered an important loophole in the Federal Election Campaign Act of 1974. Because expenditures are protected from limitations, many PACs now use the independent expenditure loophole to spend unlimited sums for or against political candidates.[17] **Independent expenditures** are outlays, typically for advertising for or against a candidate, that are uncoordinated with a candidate's campaign. Although PAC contributions to a candidate are limited, a PAC can spend as much as it wants on mailings, television promotions, or other advertisements supporting (or working against) candidates for federal office. This tactic is legal if these expenditures are not coordinated with the candidates' campaigns and if they do not "expressly advocate" a candidate by saying "Vote for . . . ," "Elect . . . ," or using similar language.[18]

Regulatory Loopholes: Soft Money

Another loophole in the amended Federal Election Campaign Act of 1974 proved important in the 1990s. Soft money constitutes contributions to the political parties that are not subject to contribution limits and are designated for use on so-called party-building activities. The soft money loophole allowed donors who had contributed the maximum to federal candidates to give even more money by contributing to the national party committees. The party committees then gave the money to state parties, which subsequently spent the funds on party-building activities under more lenient state regulations. Frequently, such soft money contributions benefited federal candidates by paying for voter registration drives, polls, and general, party-based advertisements. Then, during the 1990s, the political parties began to use soft money for television advertisements that featured the presidential candidates but did not expressly advocate their election. The Bipartisan Campaign Finance Reform Act of 2002 (see pages 341–342) banned soft money contributions to political parties.

The Impact of Regulation: The Growth of PACs

Throughout the 1970s, Congress continuously sought to redress problems that arose out of the changes to the law and the *Buckley* decision through a series of amendments to the Federal Election Campaign Act. One of the most significant amendments lifted the ban on the formation of PACs by businesses and organizations that do business with the federal government. Because of this amendment and the assertion of free-speech protections in the *Buckley* case, the number of political action committees shot up dramatically, as Figure 9.1 demonstrates. The figure shows that the number of corporate PACs alone nearly doubled between 1977 and 1980. Many of these PACs were formed by corporations that do business with the federal government and by associations whose members' livelihoods are significantly affected by federal regulations, including defense contractors, agricultural producers, and government employee unions.

The ballooning of the number of PACs over time is indicative of the increased power that PACs have wielded in campaigns for federal office since 1980. And

PAC Count, 1974 to present

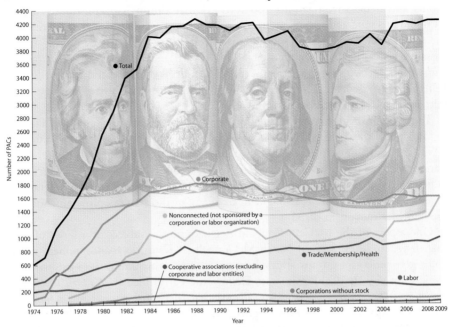

FIGURE 9.1 ▇ **What trends does the figure show with respect to the number of political action committees since 1977? For which groups has the growth in PACs risen most steeply?**

Source: Federal Election Commission, www.fec.gov/press/press2008/20080117paccount.shtml.

although the growth in the number of political action committees has leveled off since 1995, there is little evidence that their influence is waning.

The Bipartisan Campaign Finance Reform Act of 2002

Throughout the 1980s and 1990s, campaign finance reform was a perennial topic in presidential campaigns, and candidates roundly criticized the role of "special interests" in politics. But members of Congress had little to gain from reforming the system that had brought them to office. Although various campaign finance proposals were considered, only one passed both the Senate and the House, in 1992, and President George H. W. Bush vetoed it.

Then in 2002, the world's largest energy-trading company and one of the nation's biggest corporations, Enron, collapsed after an internal accounting scandal, leaving in its wake furious stockholders, employees, and retirees whose financial health depended upon the company. Investigations revealed massive corporate fraud, including accounting improprieties that had enabled corporate leaders to lie about profits and debt. Investigations also revealed that Enron had contributed nearly $4 million to state and federal political parties for "party-building activities" through the soft money loophole. Public indignation at the scandal flared, leading to the passage of the McCain-Feingold Act. This bipartisan campaign reform proposal, named after its two sponsors, Senator John McCain (R-Arizona) and Senator Russell Feingold (D-Wisconsin), had been making its way at a snail's pace through committees before the Enron scandal broke.

The McCain-Feingold Act, formally known as the Bipartisan Campaign Finance Reform Act (BCRA) of 2002, banned nearly all soft money contributions, although PACs can contribute up to $5,000 to state, county, or local parties for voter registration and get-out-the-vote drives. Table 9.1 shows that the law also increased individual contribution limitations and regulated some independent expenditure advertising. Although BCRA sought to fix many of the system's problems, some of the remedies remain in dispute.

One aspect of the McCain-Feingold Act became the subject of a series of legal challenges. In 2003, Senator Mitch McConnell (R-Kentucky), an opponent of the act, and a variety of groups affected by the new law (including the National Rifle Association and the California State Democratic Party) filed *McConnell v. the Federal Election Commission*.[19] The suit alleged that McCain-Feingold was a violation of the plaintiffs' First Amendment rights. One aspect of the law to which the groups objected was a ban on independent issue ads (thirty days before a primary election and sixty days before a general election), in which a group purchases advertising targeting a particular candidate for federal office. But the Supreme Court upheld the constitutionality of McCain-Feingold in a 5–4 decision.

Then in 2007, the Court (in another 5–4 decision) did an about-face and created an exception to the ban on issue-based ads. In *Federal Election Commission v. Wisconsin Right to Life, Inc.*,[20] the justices held that advertising within the thirty- and sixty-day window could not be prohibited, thus paving the way for its extensive use in the 2008 presidential race.

Regulatory Loophole: 527s

Another loophole in the campaign finance law became apparent with the emergence of a new form of political group, the so-called 527. Named after the section of the Internal Revenue Service tax code that regulates such organizations, a **527** is a tax-exempt group that raises money for political activities, much like those allowed under the soft money loophole. If a 527 engages only in activities such as voter registration, voter mobilization, and issue advocacy, it does not have to report its activities to the Federal Election Commission, only to the government of the state in which it is located or to the IRS. Disclosure to the FEC is required only if a 527 engages in activities expressly advocating the election or defeat of a federal candidate, or in electioneering communications. (For insight into the effect of 527s on the 2004 and 2008 presidential elections, see "Then, Now, Next" on page 344.)

Campaign finance reform advocates note that several 527s have been partially funded by large contributions from a few wealthy individuals, a claim bolstering the charge that 527s are a way to evade the soft money ban. In 2008, 527s spent

Campaign Finance Rules Under the Bipartisan Campaign Finance Reform Act, 2009–2010 Cycle

	To Each Candidate or Candidate Committee per Election	To National Party Committee per Calendar Year	To State, District, & Local Party Committee per Calendar Year	To Any Other Political Committee per Calendar Year[1]	Special Limits
Individual May Give	$2,400*	$30,400*	$10,000 (combined limit)	$5,000	$115,500* overall biennial limit: • $45,600* to all candidates • $69,900* to all PACs and parties[2]
National Party Committee May Give	$5,000	No limit	No limit	$5,000	$42,600* to Senate candidate per campaign[3]
State, District, & Local Party Committee May Give	$5,000 (combined limit)	No limit	No limit	$5,000	No limit
PAC (Multicandidate)[4] May Give	$5,000	$15,000	$5,000 (combined limit)	$5,000	No limit
PAC (Not Multicandidate) May Give	$2,400*	$30,400*	$10,000 (combined limit)	$5,000	No limit
Authorized Campaign Committee May Give	$2,000[5]	No limit	No limit	$5,000	No limit

*These contribution limits are indexed for inflation.

[1] A contribution earmarked for a candidate through a political committee counts against the original contributor's limit for that candidate. In certain circumstances, the contribution may also count against the contributor's limit to the PAC. 11 CFR 110.6. See also 11 CFR 110.1(h).

[2] No more than $45,600 of this amount may be contributed to state and local party committees and PACs.

[3] This limit is shared by the national committee and the national Senate campaign committee.

[4] A multicandidate committee is a political committee with more than 50 contributors which has been registered for at least 6 months and, with the exception of state party committees, has made contributions to 5 or more candidates for federal office. 11 CFR 100.5(e)(3).

[5] A federal candidate's authorized committee(s) may contribute no more than $2,000 per election to another federal candidate's authorized committee(s). 11 CFR 102.12(c)(2).

Source: Federal Election Commission, www.fec.gov/ans/answers_general.shtml#How_much_can_I_contribute.

TABLE 9.1

Will 527s Continue to Shape Our Perceptions of President Obama and Other Candidates?

KEN CORDIER
P.O.W. Dec. 1966 - Mar. 1973
www.swiftvets.com

THEN: In the 2004 presidential election campaign, 527s (named after the tax code that regulates such groups) became prominent when one such organization, Swift Boat Veterans and POWs for Truth, began campaigning against Senator John Kerry, the Democratic nominee. They claimed that he was unfit to serve as president, that he had exaggerated his war record, and that he had betrayed veterans and POWs by protesting the Vietnam War. Though many veterans who had served with Kerry stepped forward to refute the group's claims, the campaign conducted by the Swift Boat Veterans was effective in many swing states, and many analysts cite "swift boating" as an important factor in Kerry's loss to President George W. Bush.

NOW: In the 2008 presidential elections, 527s again emerged as important players, spending more than $255 million to shape voters' perceptions of the candidates. But unlike in 2004, when conservative 527s dominated, in 2008, four of the five largest 527s were liberal organizations engaging in "issue advocacy" that shaped the campaign context primarily in favor of Democratic candidates, as shown in the accompanying table.

COMMITTEE	EXPENDITURES
Service Employees International Union (Liberal)	$27,839,177
America Votes (Liberal)	$24,491,324
American Solutions Wining the Future (Conservative)	$22,966,088
EMILY's List (Liberal)	$12,910,515
The Fund for America (Liberal)	$12,142,044

■ In what ways could 527s continue to play an important role in federal politics?

■ Why might current members of Congress be reluctant to reform campaign finance laws to close the 527 loophole?

■ Will conservatives or liberals dominate the 527 landscape in the 2012 presidential election? Why?

about $200 million to influence the outcome of federal elections through voter registration and mobilization efforts and through ads that, while purportedly issue based, typically criticized a candidate's record.

Presidential Campaigns

To many Americans, presidential campaigns epitomize the democratic process. In presidential election years, nonstop campaigning affords ample opportunities for the public to learn about the candidates and their positions. Campaigns also provide avenues for participation by the people—for example, by volunteering in or contributing to candidates' campaigns or even just by debating candidates' views around the water cooler. Although these opportunities for citizen engagement are especially abundant during a presidential election, they arise well before, because potential candidates typically position themselves years in advance of a presidential election to secure their party's nomination and to win the general election.

Party Conventions and the General Election Campaign

As Figure 9.2 illustrates, political parties hold conventions to select their party's nominee for president of the United States. As discussed in Chapter 8 and as reviewed earlier in this chapter, the delegates to the national conventions are chosen by citizens in each state who vote in their party's primary election. After the conventions are over and the nominees have been decided (typically by late August or early September of the election year), the nominees and their vice-presidential running mates begin their general election campaign. Usually, the parties' choice of nominee is a foregone conclusion by the time of the convention. Eligible incumbent presidents (who have served only one term) are nearly always renominated, and the nominee of the opposing party is often determined by the primary results.

The Electoral College

The votes tallied on election day determine which presidential candidate's slate of electors will cast their ballots, in accordance with state law. There are 538 electors in the Electoral College because the number of electors is based on the number of

Fall preceding election year–January of election year—
Campaigning by candidates for party nomination in early primary
and caucus states, especially Iowa and New Hampshire

January of election year—Early caucuses and primaries held

February—Super Tuesday primaries and caucuses held

March–July—Primaries and caucuses continue

August–early September—Party conventions

September–early November—General election campaign

First Tuesday after the first Monday in November—
Election Day, including election of electors

Monday following the second Wednesday of
December—Electoral College voting in state capitals

December—Votes transported to the
House of Representatives

Early January
following the election—
Votes announced at a joint
session of Congress

January 20
Inauguration of president

FIGURE 9.2

Timeline of Presidential Elections U.S. presidential elections occur every four years; the next one will take place in November 2012.

> Every four years, electors determined by popular presidential elections in the states convene at state capitals in December to cast their votes for president. At the Ohio Statehouse, Eugene Miller, one of Ohio's twenty electors, signs his name on a certificate of votes on Monday, December 15, 2008.

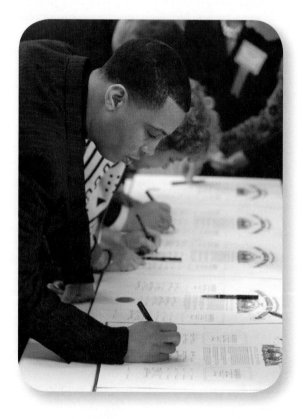

members of Congress—435 in the House of Representatives, 100 in the Senate—plus 3 electors who represent the District of Columbia. A presidential candidate needs a simple majority of votes (270) to win.

On the Monday following the second Wednesday of December, the slate of electors chosen in each state meets in the state capital and casts their electoral votes. The results are then announced in a joint session of Congress in early January. In most presidential elections, however, the winner is known on election night, because analysts tabulate the outcome in each state and predict the electoral vote. The winner takes the oath of office as president in inaugural ceremonies on January 20.

Who Votes? Factors in Voter Participation

Not all people are equally likely to participate in the process of voting for the president or other government officials. Yet of all the forms of political participation, the act of voting has been analyzed perhaps more than any other.[21] Scholars such as Angus Campbell, Philip E. Converse, Warren Miller, and Donald Stokes have examined what factors influence who votes and how voters decide.[22] They and others have analyzed how characteristics such as education level, income, age, race, and the degree of party competitiveness in a given election influence whether a person will vote.[23] Of course, in considering demographic characteristics such as voter age and income level, we must remember that these are merely generalizations.

Education Level—the Number One Predictor of Voting

An individual's level of education is the best predictor of whether that person will vote. Table 9.2 shows that in 2008, less than 40 percent of all U.S. citizens without a high school diploma voted. As education increases, so too does the likelihood of voting, with measurable differences even between those who have only attended

TABLE 9.2

U.S. Voting by Educational Attainment, 2008

Education	2008 Turnout Rate
Less than high school diploma	39%
High school diploma	55
Some college to bachelor's degree	72
Postgraduate education	83

Source: U.S. Census Bureau, Current Population Survey, Voting and Registration Supplement.

college and those who have graduated, particularly in the proportion registered to vote. Among those with a college or an advanced degree, nearly three-quarters are registered, and about one-half vote.

The Age Factor

During any presidential campaign, you will hear much about age as a factor in the likelihood of voting. Despite efforts by organizations such as MTV's Rock the Vote and despite campus-focused initiatives by presidential campaigns, young adults are less likely to vote than Americans who are middle-aged and older though that figure has increased in recent years.[24] But in the 2008 election, we saw that the turnout rate among young Americans—those aged 18–29—continued to climb, reaching about 53 percent, the highest turnout rate for voters of that age group since 18-year-olds were first granted the right to vote in 1972. While the turnout rate may not have broken records, the youth vote was key in President Obama's election: 66 percent of young voters favored Obama. Figure 9.3, which plots the percentage of people in various age groups who voted in the 2008 presidential election, shows a historic trend: as Americans age, they are more likely to vote. While 51 percent of individuals aged 18–29 years reported that they had voted, more than 70 percent of people aged 60 and over said that they had. There are numerous reasons why young people are less likely to vote. Among 18- to 29-years-olds, the reason most often cited is that they were too busy or had a schedule conflict, but

POLITICAL INQUIRY

FIGURE 9.3 ■ AGE AND VOTING IN THE 2008 PRESIDENTIAL ELECTION
For which age group was the percentage of people voting highest? For which age group was the voting percentage lowest? What overall pattern does the graph show? How do you explain it? Why did the youth vote matter in 2008?

Source: U.S. Census Bureau, Current Population Survey, Voting and Registration Supplement.

members of this age group are also more likely to report that they forgot to vote or were out of town. Age also is related to mobility—young people might move when they leave for college or to start a new job, and mobility depresses voter turnout.

Race and Voter Participation

As the 2008 presidential contest demonstrated, race plays a significant role in voter turnout. For decades after the Voting Rights Act of 1965 ensured that African Americans could freely exercise the right to vote, turnout rates among African Americans lagged substantially behind those of non-Hispanic white Americans. Today, however, voter participation among African Americans nearly equals that of whites, as Figure 9.4 indicates. The figure also shows that voting participation among Hispanics and Asian Americans lags behind that of whites and African Americans.

Figure 9.4 shows that the percentage of non-Hispanic whites who reported they voted in the 2008 presidential election was 66 percent, and for African Americans, the voting rate was 65 percent. Importantly, in addition to increased turnout by African Americans, Barack Obama's candidacy netted him 95 percent of all votes cast by African Americans.

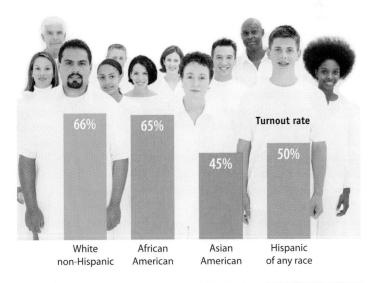

FIGURE 9.4 ■ **VOTER TURNOUT IN THE 2008 PRESIDENTIAL ELECTION, BY RACE**
Which demographic group had the highest turnout of the four groups shown? Which had the lowest? Which groups do you believe increased the most in the 2008 election? Why? Looking ahead to the next presidential election in 2012, what do you predict about the voting turnout rates for each of the groups shown?
Source: http://www.census.gov/population/www/socdemo/voting/cps2008.html.

Income—a Reliable Predictor of Voting

Besides education, income is one of the best predictors of whether an American will vote.[25] Typically in recent years, U.S. citizens with the lowest income level have had voter turnout levels of 50–60 percent; whereas, those with the highest income level have had turnout levels above 85 percent.[26] As income increases, so too does the likelihood of voting.

The reasons for the close correlation between income and likelihood of voting are complex.[27] One possibility is that people with lower incomes may have less belief than higher-income earners that the government listens to people like them. Another factor may be that individuals with lower incomes have less leisure time in which to learn about candidates and issues and even to vote. Further, in contrast to the situation in many European democracies, U.S. political parties and political organizations tend not to be highly class based. Whereas European voters are often mobilized—by class-based trade unions and by the parties themselves—to vote on the basis of their economic interests, in the United States, the lowest-income workers are less likely to be members of organized labor unions and thus are less likely to be mobilized to vote on the basis of their own economic interests.

Party Competitiveness and Voter Turnout

Finally, researchers have found that party competitiveness in elections also influences voter turnout.[28] In tight contests, in which either party has a viable chance of winning, voter turnout typically is high because the race generates more voter interest than an election in which the winner is a foregone conclusion. Sometimes turnout is high in competitive elections because voter efficacy is higher—a voter may believe that her vote "counts" more in a close election than in a less competitive race. Voter turnout also runs high in competitive elections because the parties and other campaign organizations work harder to get out the vote when they think they have a chance at winning but know that victory is not guaranteed.

Competitive races also draw ratcheted-up media attention. A tightly competitive local mayoral race might get greater than usual regional news attention, and a close race for the White House brings nearly nonstop media reports and candidate advertisements. The barrage of media coverage increases public awareness and may also boost voter efficacy by conveying the message that every vote counts.

The impact of this fierce party competitiveness was clearly evident in the 2004 presidential voting, when more than 120 million Americans cast their ballots. In absolute numbers, this is the largest number of voters of any race in history, although the **turnout rate,** the proportion of eligible voters who actually voted, was only 59 percent. The 2004 turnout rate was less than the 60.2 percent level seen in the 1992 election between George H. W. Bush and Bill Clinton, which was also extremely competitive. But in the 2004 election, voter turnout rose significantly in the sixteen key battleground states where both parties believed they had a chance of winning: Arizona, Colorado, Florida, Iowa, Maine, Michigan, Minnesota, Missouri, Nevada, New Hampshire, New Mexico, Ohio, Oregon, Pennsylvania,

West Virginia, and Wisconsin. In those states, the turnout rate was 65.3 percent, more than 6 percent higher than the national rate, highlighting the powerful role of party competitiveness in attracting voter interest and increasing turnout.[29]

How Voters Decide

When deciding for whom they will vote, some voters evaluate candidates on the basis of their positions on issues and then cast their ballots for those who best represent their views. Called **prospective voting,** this method of candidate evaluation focuses on what the candidates will do in the future. A more common form of candidate evaluation is **retrospective voting,** in which a voter evaluates an incumbent candidate on the basis of whether the incumbent's past decisions and actions are satisfactory to the voter.[30] If they are satisfactory, the voter will likely support the incumbent. If not, the voter will be disposed to support the incumbent's opponent. The prevalence of an incumbency advantage in election outcomes indicates that many voters have a favorable view of the decisions and actions of incumbent candidates for most offices.[31]

The most important factor that plays into how a voter decides on a candidate and perceives specific candidates, however, is the voter's party identification. Other influential determinants include those specific to a given election, such as candidates' attributes and the impact of the candidates' campaigns.

Major Factors in Voter Decision Making

The strongest bearing on voter preference is party identification, with about half of all voters basing their candidate choice on which party they identify with. Table 9.3 shows that in the 2008 presidential election, party identification was a potent influence on how voters decided among candidates. As shown in the table, among voters who identified themselves as either Democrats or Republicans, loyalty to their party's candidate was high, with at least 90 percent of both Democrats and Republicans voting for their party's nominee for president. President Obama's victory came in part because of his support among the nation's

TABLE 9.3

Party Loyalty in the 2008 Presidential Election

	Voting for McCain	Voting for Obama
Democrats	7%	93%
Independents	49	51
Republicans	93	7

Source: http://www.gallup.com/poll/112132/Election-Polls-Vote-Groups-2008.aspx.

independent or unaffiliated voters—those who do not identify themselves as either Democrats or Republicans.

Often a significant determinant in why people vote the way they do, policy priorities are to a certain extent aligned with party identification (or, even more generally, with ideology), because the political parties usually embrace differing viewpoints on issues. National issues that top the list of concerns among voters have remained consistent over many years and include several domestic policy matters, such as the economy, education, crime, health care, and Social Security. Since the terrorist attacks of 2001, homeland security and issues related to terrorism and then the wars in Iraq and Afghanistan have also ranked high in the list of issue concerns on which voters base their vote choices.

But how do voters decide which party and which candidate to support at the polls, based on the issues? First and foremost, an issue must be **salient** to voters— that is, it must resonate with them and reflect something that they care deeply about, an issue they are willing to base their vote on.[32] The ability of voters to cast an issue-based vote increases when candidates differ in their positions on an issue.

Incumbency, the situation of already holding an office or official position, as we've seen, is also a key factor influencing how people vote. Because an incumbent is a "known commodity" with demonstrated experience to serve in office, voters are much more likely to vote for incumbents than for their challengers. Thus, for most offices, incumbents are much more likely to be reelected than their challengers are to be elected. Indeed, in congressional elections, generally more than 90 percent of incumbent U.S. senators and 95 percent of incumbent members of the House of Representatives win reelection. But incumbency is also an influence in presidential elections, gubernatorial and state legislative elections, and probably even your local city council elections. Incumbents have notable advantages over challengers, namely, greater name recognition, a track record that voters can evaluate, and access to campaign contributions that help get their message out.

Campaign Influences on Voter Choice

As we have seen, parties and candidates conduct campaigns to influence voters' choices at the polls. Campaigns today vary a great deal in how they are waged. Whereas a candidate for a small town's board of selectmen might knock on the door of every voter in the community, a U.S. Senate or gubernatorial candidate might spend most of his or her time raising money to pay for expensive television and radio advertisements. Generally, the lower the level of office, the greater the likelihood that the candidate will rely on grassroots activism.

Trends in modern campaigns, including a far greater reliance on paid professional staffers and the prevalence of the media as a tool for communicating with voters, are catapulting the costs of campaigns sky-high. Voter choices are also affected by increasingly negative campaigns, one outcome of the modern political campaigns' reliance on paid professionals. Outside consultants typically have far fewer qualms about "going negative" than do activists in the all-community volunteer-run campaigns that were more typical of earlier times.

Consultants use negative campaign tactics for a simple reason: research shows that the approach sways voter opinion.[33] Although the candidates themselves often prefer to accentuate a positive message that highlights their background, experience, and qualifications, paid campaign consultants generally do not hesitate to sling the mud. Once a candidate establishes name recognition and credibility with voters, many consultants believe highlighting the opponent's negative qualities and actions is an effective campaign strategy.

But the impact of negative campaigning is not limited merely to swaying voters from one candidate to another. Research by political scientists shows that negative campaigning can suppress voter turnout in several ways. For example, Shanto Iyengar and Jennifer A. McGrady note that negative advertising may suppress voter turnout among the attacked candidate's supporters.[34] Other political scientists' research shows that negative campaigning undermines the democratic process by decreasing civic engagement among all voters. According to these findings, the electorate becomes disenchanted with the candidates (about whom voters get a barrage of negative information), with the campaigns (because campaigns serve as the primary messengers for delivering negative information about opponents), or with the entire electoral process that facilitates this negativity. Some voters view negative campaigning as being completely at odds with their idealized conception of the democratic process, and this may discourage them from voting.

Why Some People Do Not Vote

Negative campaigning is one reason some people do not vote, but political scientists have proposed several others. Lack of civic engagement on the part of voters underlies many of these ideas. Other reasons have to do with the nature of campaigns and the structure of elections.

Lack of Efficacy

Some voters do not vote because they do not participate in civic affairs, either locally or at the national level. Many of these nonvoters lack efficacy.[35] They do not believe that the government listens to people like themselves or that their vote actually matters in determining the outcome of elections and the business of government.[36]

Scholars have determined that individuals who lack efficacy exist across the social and economic spectrums but that poorer people are more likely than better-off individuals to feel that the government does not listen to people like them. Yet, although it is a common notion that people are alienated from politics or think that the government does not listen to their concerns, a recent study estimated that only about 9 percent of the U.S. population feels this way.[37] This same survey indicated that people lacking efficacy—a group that the study called the "disaffecteds"—typically had a low level of educational attainment and were less likely to follow current events than more engaged citizens.

Voter Fatigue and Negative Campaigns

Another explanation for why some Americans do not vote stems from the nature of political campaigns. In the United States, campaigns tend to be long, drawn-out affairs. For example, presidential campaigns typically last for more than a year, with some candidates positioning themselves three or four years in advance of an election. Contrast this with many parliamentary systems, including Germany's, in which an election must be held within sixty days of the dissolution of parliament because of a "no confidence" vote of the chancellor (similar to a prime minister). Some scholars say that the lengthiness of the campaigns leads to **voter fatigue,** the condition in which voters simply grow tired of all candidates by the time election day arrives, and may thus be less likely to vote.

American journalist and humorist Franklin Adams commented that "elections are won by men and women chiefly because most people vote against somebody rather than for somebody." The prevalence of negative campaigning compounds the impact of voter fatigue. Even the most enthusiastic supporters of a candidate may feel their advocacy withering under the unceasing mudslinging that occurs in many high-level campaigns. And so while evidence shows that negative advertising is effective in swaying voters' opinions, sometimes it also succeeds in suppressing voter turnout by making voters less enthusiastic about voting.

The Structure of Elections

Political scientists also cite the structure of U.S. elections as a reason why more Americans do not vote. For years, voting rights activists claimed that the registration requirements in many states were too complicated and discouraged people from voting by making it too difficult to register. In 1993, Congress sought to remedy this situation by passing the National Voter Registration Act, frequently called the "Motor Voter" Act, which allows eligible people to register to vote when they apply for a driver's license or enroll in a public assistance program or when they submit the necessary information by mail. Although there was enormous anticipation that the motor voter law would significantly boost voter registration and turnout, in fact its impact has been negligible.

Critics of the structure of elections also point to their frequency. In the United States, the number of elections varies from municipality to municipality, and local government charters may call for more than four elections for municipal offices alone. Although most federal offices require only two elections (a primary and a general), these elections are not always held in conjunction with state, county, and municipal elections.

The timing of elections also affects voter participation. Most general elections are held on a weekday—the first Tuesday after the first Monday in November. Moreover, although states decide when to hold primary elections, state legislative elections, and municipal and school board elections, these elections, too, typically occur on a weekday. Critics say that holding elections on weekends or over a two-day period instead, or establishing a national voting holiday, would increase voter turnout by ensuring that voters had ample opportunity to cast their ballots.

The Rational Abstention Thesis

A final explanation as to why some people do not vote is that they make a conscious choice that not voting is a rational, logical action. Called the **rational abstention thesis,** this theory states that some individuals decide that the "costs" of voting—in terms of the time, energy, and inconvenience required to register to vote, to become informed about candidates and elections, and actually to vote—are not worth the effort when compared to the expected "benefits," or what the voters could derive from voting.

In light of these cumulative "costs," it is perhaps surprising that so many people choose to vote.[38] One explanation for why they do is that most voters report that they derive psychological rewards from exercising this citizen's right—feelings of being civically engaged, satisfied, and patriotic. But when the costs associated with voting increase too much, turnout drops; more people choose not to vote when voting becomes too inconvenient. This drop-off occurs, for example, when municipalities shorten voting hours and during inclement weather.

The Impact of Nonvoting

From a civic engagement perspective, nonvoting is both a symptom and a result of a lack of civic involvement on the part of individuals.[39] Your roommate might not vote because she is not civically engaged—because she feels that she has little to contribute and that the government does not listen to "people like her" anyway. But by not voting, she perpetuates this lack of efficacy by remaining outside the process rather than staking a claim to what is rightfully hers: the idea that every individual has the right to a voice in the composition and priorities of the government. Only by becoming civically engaged—learning about the candidates, discussing issues, and voting—can she break the cycle of inefficacy. Voting will make her pay more attention to campaigns, candidates, and issues.

Beyond the effects of nonvoting on individuals, low voter turnout affects the polity. When relatively few people vote in a given election, the outcome is likely to represent the will of only that subset of the electorate who voted. This impact is important: consider that polls indicate that the outcomes of the 2000 and 2004 presidential elections would have been different if voter turnout had been higher. In each of these elections, the Democratic nominee (Al Gore and John Kerry, respectively) was the favored candidate among several groups whose turnout falls below average, including voters under age 24, African American voters, and voters with lower incomes. The process becomes cyclical: these nonvoters who disagree with the outcome conclude that the government does not represent them, feel less efficacious, and are less inclined to vote in the future.

Moreover, some scholars assert that democracies with low voter turnout are more likely to generate threats to their own well-being.[40] In democracies with low turnout, these scholars say, charismatic, popular political figures may rise to power and become authoritarian leaders. Corruption, too, can be a problem in low-turnout democracies where government officials might feel relatively unconcerned about the disapproval of disgruntled constituents.

Other researchers, however, contend that nonvoting is not a big problem, especially in cases where large numbers in the electorate are relatively uninformed about candidates and issues.[41] A number of scholars in this camp argue that participation by the uninformed is undesirable, as it may lead to drastic changes in government. Opponents of this view counter that because of political parties' role in selecting candidates, the menu for voter choice is actually quite limited in most elections. Those who argue that nonvoting does not matter also ignore the fact that voting tends to produce more engaged citizens who, because they vote, feel a duty to be informed and involved.

Other scholars who claim that low voter turnout is not a problem argue that low voting rates are simply a function of people's satisfaction with the status quo: their nonvoting simply means that they do not seek change in government. This argument, however, does not explain why lower turnout is most likely to occur in populations that are least likely to be satisfied with their situation. For example, people with lower incomes are much less likely to vote than those with higher incomes. Whatever the reason—a lack of efficacy as argued by some, satisfaction as argued by others—nonvoters' best chances of having their views reflected in the policy process is to articulate them through voting.

CONCLUSION

CONTINUING THE CONVERSATION

- The nature of political campaigns in the United States has continuously evolved, but the changes in recent decades have been especially dramatic.

- An era in which political parties and grassroots activism dominated campaigns has given way to the present-day realities where money, media, and mavens of strategy are key forces in shaping campaigns, which have grown increasingly candidate-centered.

- Prominently driving the changes are the simultaneous *decrease* in political party clout and *increase* in the need for money—money to pay for the small army of professional staffers that run the campaigns, and money to cover the expensive media buys that candidates, especially those running for national and state office, heavily depend on for communicating with the electorate.

- Technology offers the potential to bring the politics of electoral campaigns back to the grassroots—now perhaps more appropriately called the netroots. Although campaigns' use of technology certainly is not free, digital communication is cost-effective and rapid.

- Through the new mediums of communication, there is great potential, too, for the inclusion of a variety of new voices in the political campaigning process. Groups that want to influence campaigns and voters have at their disposal a vast arsenal of new technology that makes such influence possible.

Summary

1. Civic Engagement and Political Participation

Active political engagement benefits both the individual and the polity. Although some civic activities, such as working full-time on a campaign, might represent enormous commitments, others, including casting a ballot and engaging in political discourse, are less time-consuming and are manageable for even the busiest people.

2. Elections in the United States

U.S. elections include the primary election, in which a party's nominee to run in the general election is selected; the general election, in which the winning candidate attains the office being sought; and special-purpose elections such as the initiative, referendum, and recall, which are citizen-sponsored efforts to have a greater say in the political process.

3. The Act of Voting

Although all of the states rely on the Australian (secret) ballot, the types of ballots used in states vary significantly. The type of ballot can have an impact on election outcomes, as in the 2000 presidential election.

4. Running for Office: The Choice to Run

Most offices have formal eligibility requirements, but there are also more subjective requirements by which voters view candidates as qualified to hold a given office. Often these characteristics have to do with occupation, education, and experience.

5. Political Campaigns Today

Today's political campaigns hire a wide variety of professionals who perform the tasks that were once accomplished by volunteer staffs. Office seekers' increasing reliance on electronic media, first television and now the Internet, has drastically changed both the ways in which campaigns are conducted and the costs of those campaigns.

6. Regulating Campaign Finance

Government efforts over the years to regulate campaign contributions have led to laws with numerous loopholes. The latest attempt to curtail the influence of money on politics is the Bipartisan Campaign Finance Reform Act of 2002.

7. Presidential Campaigns

Presidential campaigns are of increasing duration. They begin with the primary process, continue through the national party conventions, proceed to the general election campaign and voting, and end with the Electoral College vote.

8. Who Votes? Factors in Voter Participation

Influences on voter participation include education, age, race, income, and party competitiveness.

9. How Voters Decide

Party identification, policy priorities, incumbency, and campaigns are factors influencing how voters decide for whom to vote.

10. Why Some People Do Not Vote

The many reasons why people don't vote include a lack of efficacy, the impact of voter fatigue and negative campaigns, the structure of elections, and the rational abstention thesis. Whatever the reason, nonvoting has a harmful impact on individuals and the government.

For Critical Thinking and Discussion

1. Why do formal and informal eligibility requirements for office differ? What are the informal eligibility requirements to run for the state legislature where you live? What are the requirements for the city or town council in your hometown or the community where your school is located? How do these differences reflect the nature of the constituency for the office being sought?

2. How has the increasing cost of political campaigns changed the nature of American politics? Why have costs escalated?

3. What has been the impact of the increasing negativity in American political campaigns?

4. Using the text discussion of factors influencing whether a person votes, assess a classmate's likelihood of voting based solely on those factors. Then ask the person if he or she votes. Was your assessment accurate?

5. In your view, what is the impact of nonvoting?

Key Terms

absentee voting 330
Australian ballot 327
campaign consultant 335
campaign manager 335
campaign strategy 335
caucuses 324
chad 327
closed primary 325
coattail effect 328
527 342
fund-raising consultant 335
general election 323

GOTV 323
incumbency 352
independent
   expenditures 340
initiative 326
instant runoff election 326
media consultant 336
office-block ballot 329
open primary 324
party-column ballot 328
proposition 327
prospective voting 351

rational abstention
   thesis 355
recall 327
referendum 326
retrospective voting 351
runoff election 326
salient 352
Super Tuesday 325
turnout rate 350
voter fatigue 354

Internet Resources

A More Perfect Union **Web site**
www.mhhe.com/harrisonampule   Consult the book's Web site for study guides, interactive activities, simulations, and current hot-links that provide additional information on voting, campaigns, and elections in the United States.

The Living Room Candidate
www.livingroomcandidate.org This site, maintained by the Museum of the Moving Image, provides videos of television commercials run by presidential campaigns from 1956 to 2008.

Project Vote Smart
www.vote-smart.org This nonpartisan Web site provides independent, factual information on election procedures in each state.

Rock the Vote
www.rockthevote.org This nonprofit, nonpartisan organization encourages political participation by young people and provides resources on policies of interest, as well as voting information.

Vote, Run, Lead
www.voterunlead.org This is the Web site for an organization that encourages the civic engagement of young women as voters, activists, and candidates for political office.

Recommended Readings

Faucheux, Ron. *Campaigns and Elections: Winning Elections.* New York: M. Evans, 2003. A collection of the "best of the best" articles from *Campaigns and Elections* magazine; a practical guide to conducting campaigns.

Herrnson, Paul S., Richard G. Niemi, Michael J. Hanmer, Benjamin B. Bederson, and Frederick C. Conrad. *Voting Technology: The Not-So-Simple Act of Casting a Ballot.* Washington, DC: Brookings Institution Press, 2008. An explanation of the intricacies of voting technology, including the electoral implications of how votes are cast.

Patterson, Thomas E. *The Vanishing Voter.* New York: Knopf, 2002. An analysis of the decline in voter turnout, with recommendations for reversing the trend.

Wattenberg, Martin P. *Is Voting for Young People?* New York: Longman, 2007. An explanation of why young people have not voted historically and analysis of the importance of voter participation from the viewpoint of young Americans.

Zukin, Cliff, Scott Keeter, Molly Andolina, Krista Jenkins, and Michael X. Delli Carpini. *A New Engagement? Political Participation, Civic Life, and the Changing American Citizen.* New York: Oxford University Press, 2006. A description of the changing ways in which Americans are participating in the political life of their country and communities.

CAN FACEBOOK
REPLACE
FACE TO FACE?

NATIONAL CONFERENCE
ON
CITIZENSHIP

THEN

The relationship between the media and consumers was one-way.

Technology has created a two-way relationship between the media and consumers, involving the exchange of a seemingly limitless amount of information.

NOW

10

The Media

If you are like most Americans—and indeed like multitudes of people across the globe—the media are a fixture in your daily life. You may wake up to a radio show each morning or read a newspaper over breakfast or while commuting on a bus or train. You may watch televised news stories or receive real-time news updates on your cell phone, Internet news sites, and blogs or tune in to the twenty-four-hour news channels available virtually everywhere. There is no escaping that as a citizen of the twenty-first century, you are bathed in a sea of news and information. Some of what the media offer you is meant to entertain, and some is meant to inform, but increasingly the lines between the two have blurred.

The sheer amount of information and entertainment available courtesy of the media has increased immeasurably over the past few decades. Within a generation, the modern media have transformed American life. Where once people had to seek out news and information, today they are inundated with it, and they must develop the skill to filter the good from the bad.

Although this abundance of information at times may rise to the level of a blitz, information is empowering. It serves as the basis on which people shape well-founded opinions. These opinions are the building blocks for meaningful civic engagement and political participation. In the discussion that follows, we see how the media continuously shape the ways we receive information and exercise the rights and privileges of our American democracy.

Will the abundance and reach of the media overload people with information?

Will people select media sources that serve only to confirm their views?

Will the ever-increasing speed and volume of information affect its quality?

NEXT

The Political Functions
of the Media

In the United States today, the media in all their forms—including print, television, radio, and the Internet—fulfill several key functions. Much of what the media do revolves around entertaining us, whether that means watching *CSI* or reading the Sunday funnies. But the media are a vital element of our democracy because of the political role they perform in our society. Specifically, the media perform the following functions:

- provide political information
- help us to interpret events and policies and help set the national policy agenda
- provide a forum for political conversations
- socialize children to the political culture

Providing Information

One long-standing function of the mass media is to serve up a steady diet of news and information to readers, viewers, and listeners. Indeed, the media, particularly the electronic media, are the primary source of information for most individuals. Coverage includes everything from weather watches, to sports scores, to the latest legislative developments on Capitol Hill, to serious analysis of top domestic policy issues and international problems. From this steady diet arises the problem of information overload—the constant availability of news information to the point of excess, which may cause media consumers to ignore, dismiss, or fail to see the significance of particular events. Media critics fault the television networks in particular for injecting entertainment into news shows. They dub this combination **infotainment** (a hybrid of the words *information* and *entertainment*). More recent is the trend of uniting comedy with political content, as in Jon Stewart's *The Daily Show* and Stephen Colbert's *The Colbert Report,* both of which interpret news events with a comedic slant.

Sound Bites and Soft News   Journalists blame the public for a lack of interest in real issues and an addiction to negative news and **sound bites**—short audio or video clips taken from a larger speech. In turn, reporters must please the public in order to maintain ratings. Media representatives argue that today's media consumers prefer infotainment to a probing discussion of the issues. Those who are interested can find in-depth, balanced information online if they know where to look but are often hard pressed to locate it in the average newspaper or commercial radio or television broadcast.

Why do some news organizations dedicate so much coverage to events or topics that are not serious or broadly important—in other words, to **soft news?** Some scholars point to the profit-seeking motivations of media moguls. Indeed, it is no secret that most media outlets are in a race to boost their profits, and their typical strategy is to attract higher numbers of consumers. So television networks and cable television stations strive to increase their viewers; newspapers and magazines, their subscribers; radio stations, their listeners; and Internet sites, the number of hits they receive—often by disseminating material molded to mass tastes.

The Profit Motive Media consumers generally do not directly create media profit. Instead, rising use by consumers means that media channels can charge advertisers more because their ads are reaching more people. Only public television and public radio (which are nonprofit institutions that depend on private and government grants and donations from viewers and listeners), as well as satellite radio provider Sirius/XM (which does not accept advertising but charges listeners subscription fees), do not rely on advertising dollars.

What influence does profit seeking have on the quality of political reporting and people's attitudes about government? Some analysts, including James Hamilton, say that profit seeking creates a kind of media bias.[1] They point out that media outlets may avoid political controversy in an effort not to offend their audiences. Other scholars, among them Matthew Robert Kerbel, argue that the media's emphasis on negativity—particularly the misdeeds and character flaws of government officials, which have a powerful attraction for the general public—contributes to the public's declining trust in governmental institutions.[2] Other commentators argue that the abundance of profit-making media outlets has negatively affected the quality and accuracy of the information they provide (see "Analyzing the Sources"). For example, William V. Kennedy argues that reporters covering wars are often ill equipped to "ask the right questions," with the result that news consumers get misinformation about military actions and outcomes.[3]

Interpreting Matters of Public Interest and Setting the Public Agenda

Besides reporting information, the media help people to comprehend and interpret matters of public interest and to make informed decisions about public policies. Political scientist Shanto Iyengar asserts that the process of interpretation often begins with media **framing**—setting a context that helps consumers understand important events and matters of shared interest.

Political scientist Pippa Norris has analyzed the process of framing as it relates to gender. She asserts that gender has become a common frame through which journalists provide context for different kinds of political stories.[4] Norris explains that voters, candidates, public opinion, and issues all may be viewed from a gender-based perspective. For example, in the 2008 presidential campaign, the media initially covered the race for the Democratic nomination by accentuating the gender of Senator Hillary Clinton (D-New York) and played up Clinton's potential to be the first woman president of the United States. Media reporting defined her opponent, Senator Barack Obama, as potentially the first African American president. Similarly, when Senator John McCain announced that Alaska governor Sarah Palin would be his running mate in the 2008 general election campaign, the media emphasized the gendered aspects of her nomination, particularly her role as a mother.

Confidence in the Media

The Gallup Organization has asked the following question in surveys since 1972:

"In general, how much trust and confidence do you have in the mass media—such as newspapers, T.V., and radio—when it comes to reporting the news fully, accurately, and fairly: a great deal, a fair amount, not very much, or none at all?"

The line graph illustrates survey respondents' views on these questions, showing survey data at various times between May 1972 and September 2009. You can see that people's assessment of news organizations has varied considerably during this period.

Evaluating the Evidence

① Describe trends in the 1970s in people's confidence in the media, citing specific data from the graph.

② Describe trends since 2001 in people's confidence in the media, citing specific data.

③ What do the latest surveys indicate about respondents' opinions on the issue of confidence in the media?

④ What do the data say about the *overall* trends with regard to people's confidence in the media?

⑤ What factors could have contributed to the changes in people's assessment of the media over time? Explain.

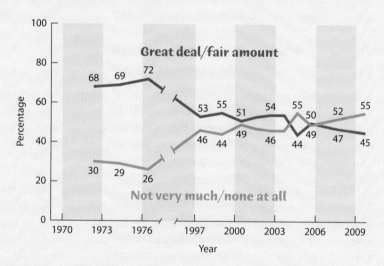

Source: The Gallup Poll, *Media Use and Evaluation*, www.galluppoll.com/poll/1663/Media-Use-Evaluation.aspx.

The media also help to shape the **public agenda**—public issues that most demand the attention of government officials. The media commonly influence the setting of the public agenda by **priming**—using their coverage to bring particular policies on issues to the public agenda.

Providing a Forum for Conversations About Politics

Throughout their existence, the media have provided an often lively forum for conversations about politics. The prominence of this role has reached new heights in the Internet era. Historically, information flowed from the media—which through the years have included everything from the political broadsides and leaflets of colonial times to modern newspapers, radio news, and television programming—to the people. The people then formed opinions based on what they read, heard, and saw. Traditionally, this communication was one-way and typically featured little give-and-take between media sources and their consumers. A notable exception has been the **letter to the editor,** in which a reader responds to a newspaper story, knowing that the letter might be published in that paper.

The advent of talk radio gave listeners one of their first regular opportunities to express their views publicly. Television took note, and call-in shows such as *Larry King Live* now are common fare on cable television stations.

But no other medium has expanded the ability of people to communicate their views to the degree that the Internet has. David Weinberger, who served as marketing consultant and Internet adviser to Democratic 2004 presidential hopeful Howard Dean, describes the phenomenon: "Don't think of the Internet as a broadcast medium . . . think of it as a conversational space. Conversation is the opposite of marketing. It's talking in our own voices about things we want to hear about."[5] Blogs facilitate this conversation by inviting an ongoing dialogue between the blog hosts and posters. Discussion boards (even those that are "nonpolitical") are filled with political discussion and opinions. Chat rooms permit people of a given political persuasion to discuss and organize with like-minded thinkers. Social-networking sites such as MySpace, Facebook, BlackPlanet, MyBatanga, AsiaAve, and Faithbase allow individuals to share their stories, interests, and political viewpoints.

Socializing Children to Political Culture

The media also socialize new generations to the political culture. For young children, television remains the dominant medium for both entertainment and socialization. TV-viewing toddlers receive regular messages about important cultural values. Shows such as *Sesame Street* and *Barney* send powerful messages about the value of diversity in society. TV programming for older children similarly takes on political issues. In *Arthur,* the main character comes face-to-face with censorship when adults in his town have the "Scare Your Pants Off" book series removed from the public library, thus providing a concise fifteen-minute lesson on civil liberties issues.

Even television and radio programs not specifically aimed at youths often reinforce democratic principles and practices. What is *American Idol* if not a televised election? And when the tribe speaks on *Survivor*, they do so through the process of voting. Talk radio and television call-in programs rest on the assumption that individuals' opinions matter and that they have the right to voice them. These various kinds of programming may not directly spur a particular political behavior on the part of viewers. Nonetheless, television and other forms of media that we often think of as pure entertainment frequently reinforce and legitimize dominant American political values.

The Press and Politics: A Historical View

The sheer volume of information available today through the media makes the influence of the media in our times beyond dispute. Historically, too, the media have played an essential role in setting the political agenda and shaping public policy. The power of the media was evident, for example, as early as pre-Revolutionary times, such as when newspaper owners and readers rallied against the Stamp Act's (1765) imposition of taxes on newspapers and other kinds of legal documents. Newspaper publishers sympathetic to the colonists' cause of ejecting Great Britain from American shores used their "power of the pen" to arouse public opinion, and they strongly supported the patriot cause throughout the Revolution. Taking sides in an internal conflict was a new role for the press, one that would sow the seeds of future media influence on the country's domestic and foreign policy. The early history of media development also raised issues that continue to create conflict about the media's role in society.

The Early Role of the Press

Great leaders learned early how intimately their careers were linked to favorable press coverage and influence. From the 1790s to the 1830s, the press served primarily as a vehicle for the leaders of political parties, who expressed their opinions through newspapers known to reflect their particular viewpoints in reporting the news. Were these newspapers forerunners of today's liberal and conservative media outlets? Their circulation was small, but so was their audience; most people could not read and write and did not vote.

By the 1830s the environment had changed. For openers, the average American was now able to read. New technology made possible the **penny press**—newspapers that sold for a penny. Circulation increased, and the working class became interested in what the newspapers had to offer. Another reason newspapers reduced their price was the advent of advertising; newspaper owners figured out that if they sold advertising, they could increase both their profits and their papers' circulation. The 1830s was the first time advertising became part and parcel of the newspaper business, and although pressures from advertisers sometimes affected coverage and editorial opinion, few readers noticed this practice, and even fewer challenged it.

> Yellow journalism can influence the national policy agenda. When the battleship *Maine* exploded in Havana harbor in February 1898, newspaper coverage significantly molded public opinion, and in turn, Congress declared war on Spain. What recent media coverage has influenced public opinion about an event or issue?

Yellow Journalism and Muckraking

Throughout the last part of the nineteenth century, newspapers competed vigorously with each other for ever-greater shares of readership. Publishers found that stories about sex, gore, violence, and government corruption sold papers faster than reports about garbage collection and school budgets. Well-known publishers William Randolph Hearst and Joseph Pulitzer established their reputations and their fortunes at this time, Hearst with the *New York Journal American* and Pulitzer with the *New York World.* Along with Hearst and Pulitzer at the beginning of the twentieth century came the practice of yellow journalism, so named after the yellow ink used in the "Yellow Kid" cartoons in the *New York World.* The term **yellow journalism** has come to signify an irresponsible, sensationalist approach to news reporting and is used to this day to criticize certain elements of the press.

By contrast, shortly after the turn of the century came the era of **muckraking,** an about-face that placed journalists in the heroic role of exposing the dark underbelly of government and industry. The most famous of the muckrakers included Ida Tarbell, who exposed the oil industry in a series of articles running from 1902 to 1904 in *McClure's* magazine called "The History of the Standard Oil Company"; Lincoln Steffens, who published *The Shame of the Cities* in 1904; and Upton Sinclair, whose novel *The Jungle* (1906) revealed the horrors of the meat-processing industry, leading to passage of the Pure Food and Drug Act and later to the establishment of the Food and Drug Administration.[6]

A Widening War for Readership

Yellow journalism died down after World War I, and newspapers entered a period during which they valued objectivity, at least on the surface. Newspapers increasingly found themselves competing with the new media that were just coming into being: radio stations from 1920 to 1950; television from the 1940s to 1980; and from then on, the explosion of the **new media**—cable television, the Internet, blogs, and satellite technology.

This increased competition has had several impacts on the newspaper industry. First, newspaper readership has steadily declined, particularly the audience for local newspapers. For example, Figure 10.1 shows that between 1998 and 2008, the proportion of people who read a local newspaper every day or several times a week decreased from 68 percent to 53 percent. Further, although readership of national newspapers increased slightly after the terrorist strikes of September 11, 2001, since that time readership has ebbed to the same level as before the attacks. Partly as a result of a long-term decline in local newspaper relationship, the number of daily newspapers has decreased dramatically, with many cities that used to support three

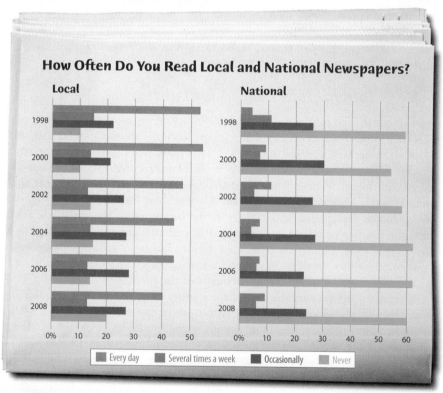

FIGURE 10.1

Declining Readership of Newspapers

Source: The Gallup Poll, *Media Use and Evaluation*, www.galluppoll.com/poll/1663/Media-Use-Evaluation.aspx.

FIGURE 10.2 ■ NEWSROOM EMPLOYMENT BY GENDER, 2009
In the past, "newsmen" were in fact news*men*. What does the graph indicate about women's employment in today's newsrooms?

Source: The American Society of Newspaper Editors, "Newsroom Employment Census," Table M, www.asne.org/index.cfm?id=5660.

or four "dailies" now typically having only one newspaper. Second, competition has resulted in consolidation of the newspaper industry so that today a single large parent company typically owns local newspapers as well. For example, the Gannett Corporation, which publishes *USA Today*, also publishes numerous daily and weekly newspapers in cities and towns throughout the country. Third, competition has forced nearly every newspaper to offer free online editions. Thus you can receive nearly any newspaper at no cost in your e-mail inbox each morning.

As the industry has changed, so, too, has the human face of the newsrooms. Figure 10.2 shows that in 2009, more than one-third of all newsroom supervisors were women, as were some two-fifths of all layout and copy editors and reporters. These figures reflect the societal changes from the times in which "newsmen" were in fact news*men*. Among all positions measured in the annual newsroom census, women were least likely to hold jobs in the visual arts, such as photographer and artist.

Table 10.1 shows another measure of how modern newsrooms have changed along with American society. The table illustrates the proportion of minority journalists working at newspapers in eight different circulation categories. From Table 10.1, we can see that minority journalists are much more likely to be employed at larger-circulation newspapers, with minorities constituting one-fifth of the journalists at papers having a circulation of 250,000 to 500,000. That proportion is nearly identical at the largest-circulation newspapers and steadily tapers off among newspapers with circulation of less than 250,000.

TABLE 10.1

Minority Journalists as a Percentage of the Professional Workforce of Newspapers in Eight Circulation Categories

NEWSPAPER CIRCULATION	YEAR				
	1980	1992	1997	2002	2009
Over 500,000	7.2	15.6	17.3	18.5	19.9
250,001 to 500,000	6.4	13.3	16.2	18.8	21.1
100,001 to 250,000	6.3	10.4	13.1	14.5	17.1
50,001 to 100,000	5.6	9.3	11.3	10.5	13.3
25,001 to 50,000	4.2	5.7	7.1	7.9	8.7
10,001 to 25,000	3.1	5.7	7.0	7.1	6.4
5,001 to 10,000	2.4	4.5	5.1	4.8	5.6
5,000 and Under	2.8	5.4	4.6	4.8	5.7

Source: The American Society of Newspaper Editors, "Newsroom Employment Census," Table F, www.asne.org/index.cfm?id=5653. Copyright © 2008 The American Society of Newspaper Editors.

The Media Go Electronic: The Radio and Television Revolutions

It is impossible to overemphasize the transformative impact of the early electronic media. From the time of the first U.S. radio broadcasts in the early 1920s, radio allowed listeners to hear news in real time. This immediacy marked a drastic change from the standard, delayed method of receiving news, which was by reading the morning and evening editions of newspapers, plus the occasional "extra edition" published when important breaking news warranted it. Radio also altered the relationship between politicians—particularly presidents—and their constituents, as it enabled listeners to hear the voices of their elected leaders. Television further revolutionized this relationship by making it possible for people to see their leaders (though initially only in black and white).

How Radio Has Opened Up Political Communication

Radio was the first electronic medium that brought people into direct contact with their leaders. Beginning in the 1920s, radios became a fixture in American living rooms, and families who could not afford a radio of their own would often spend evenings at the homes of friends or neighbors who could.

How Will President Obama Attempt to Get His Message Across in the Digital Age?

THEN: President Franklin Roosevelt was recognized as a master political communicator. Roosevelt relied on a folksy, conversational tone and the relatively new medium of radio to bring his message to the people.

NOW: Some seventy-five years later, another president, Barack Obama, is widely recognized as a skilled political speaker. Obama's charismatic delivery combined with his effective use of technology contributed to his successful candidacy, and he is continuing to use these assets to further his agenda as president.

WHAT'S NEXT?

- What new technologies will be instrumental for presidential candidates in the 2012 election?
- What impact will President Obama's use of technology have on his ability to communicate with constituents? To convince legislators to support his proposals?
- How will politicians' use of technology effect how the media covers them in the future?

FDR'S Fireside Chats   Franklin D. Roosevelt was the first politician to realize the value of radio as a device for political communication—and to exploit that value (see "Then, Now, Next" on page 371). As governor of New York (1928–1932), Roosevelt faced a Republican state legislature hostile to many of his liberal social welfare programs. To overcome the opposition, Roosevelt used radio addresses to appeal directly to his constituents, who would then lobby the legislators for his policies. Indeed, after some of Roosevelt's radio addresses, legislative offices were flooded with letters from constituents asking lawmakers to support a particular policy.

By the time Roosevelt became president in 1933, he had grasped the importance of radio as a tool for communicating directly with the people. FDR often began his radio addresses to the country—his **fireside chats**—with the greeting, "Good evening, friends," highlighting the personal relationship he wished to cultivate between himself and his listeners. (You can download many of Roosevelt's fireside chats in MP3 format from the Vincent Voice Library at Michigan State University.) Through the folksy fireside chats, Americans learned about presidential initiatives on the banking crisis, New Deal social welfare programs, the declaration of war on Japan after that nation's attack on Pearl Harbor, and the progress of U.S. forces during World War II. In all, Roosevelt had thirty fireside chats with Americans over his twelve years as president. Although political and news radio programming remained popular during the 1950s and 1960s, radio generally took a backseat to television during this era.

Talk Radio: Talking the Political Talk   Radio began to emerge from the shadows of television in the 1970s and 1980s. These decades brought a renaissance of sorts for radio, as the medium saw tremendous growth in **talk radio**—a format featuring conversations and interviews about topics of interest, along with call-ins from listeners. As many AM station owners switched to an all-talk format in these years, music programming migrated to the FM band.

In 1987, the Federal Communications Commission (FCC) repealed the **fairness doctrine,** which had required stations to provide equal time to all sides regarding important public issues and equal access to airtime to all candidates for public office. Since the law's repeal, partisan radio programming has grown dramatically. Today, listeners tend to tune in to radio hosts who share—many say, reinforce—their opinions, and they interact with them through call-in opportunities. Figure 10.3 shows the rise in listenership for talk radio programs since 1995. Daily listenership of such programs has nearly doubled, increasing from 11 percent in 1995 to 18 percent in 2008. The percentage of people who listen to talk radio several times a week has doubled in that time.

The appeal of talk radio, particularly as broadcast via the Internet, mirrors the allure of Internet blogs. The messages of both mediums have become highly personal and emotional, targeted to a narrow segment of the public. Conservative radio commentators tend to draw an audience dominated by middle-aged conservative males, while the much smaller liberal market segment tends to draw the coveted younger audience.

2006
2008
2004
2002
1999
1998
1995

44%
43%
27%
28%
42%
9%
10%
25%
12%
20%
18%
39%
21%
29%
10%
22%
12%
8%
47%
33%
12%
9%
12%
21%
12%
58%
5%
35%
48%

Never
Occasionally
Several times per week
Every day

**Radio
Talk Show
Listenership,
1995-2008**

POLITICAL INQUIRY

FIGURE 10.3 ▮ What has been the trend in talk radio listenership since 1995? What factors might explain this trend?

Source: http://www.gallup.com/poll/1663/Media-Use-Evaluation.aspx.

Television and the Transformation of Campaigns and Elections

Although radio predates television, TV nonetheless has been the centerpiece of U. S. home entertainment for a long time. Television began to make a mark on the American scene in the 1940s, when small TV sets—their screens flecked with static snowflakes—hit the market. Today, the images we view are crystal clear, as high-definition, big-screen TVs increasingly dominate households. Hundreds of channels compete for audience share, ending the previous dominance of the three major networks—ABC, NBC, and CBS.

Figure 10.4 illustrates these changes. Viewership of nightly network news broadcasts on ABC, CBS, and NBC plummeted between 1995 and 2008. In 1995, well over a

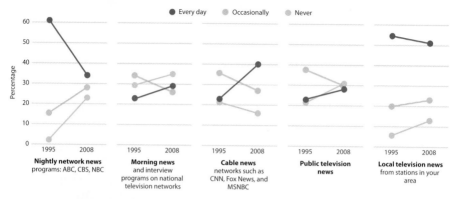

FIGURE 10.4

Where Do Americans Get Their News?

Source: The Gallup Poll, *Media Use and Evaluation,* poll administered August 11–14, 1995, and December 4–7, 2008, www.gallup.com/poll/1663/Media-Use-Evaluation.aspx.

majority of Americans watched a nighttime network news broadcast; by 2008, only 35 percent did, and the number who never watched grew to 22 percent. Compare these figures with the data for the networks' cable news counterparts, where daily viewership has increased by more than 10 percent. Among the other categories of TV news (morning shows such as *Good Morning America* and the *Today* show, public television news broadcasts, and local news shows), viewership has essentially stagnated.

As cable news channels such as CNN and Fox News have increased their viewing audience, it is no wonder the word *broadcasting* has spawned the term **narrowcasting:** the practice of aiming political media content at specific segments of the public, divided according to political ideology, party affiliation, or economic interests. This winnowing of audiences has led to **media segmentation,** the breaking down of the media in general according to the specific audiences they target. Examples of segmented media include Black Entertainment Television (BET), the U.S.-based Spanish-language television network Telemundo, and the Lifestyle Network, which includes the Food Network and HGTV. Through media segmentation, advertisers can tailor their advertising to the tastes of their targeted market.

The Media Revolution Continues: The Internet

The modern media revolution continued with the birth of the Internet. As a medium of communication, a source of news and information, and a tool for political engagement and grassroots organizing, the Internet has had an incalculable—and a global—impact on the way people interact.

But access to the Internet is not equal, because affluent individuals are more likely than the less affluent to have computers and Internet connections. The

How the Media Have Shaped Entertainment and the Information Highways

THEN (1960s)	NOW (2010)
Television programming matured and revolutionized how the media entertain and provide information.	The Internet matures and revolutionizes how we are entertained and how we get information.
Television accentuated a new set of candidate qualities—including being telegenic—that had not mattered much in earlier political campaigns.	The Internet accentuates a new set of candidate qualities—including being tech savvy and Net organized—that were unheard of a generation ago.
Communication between the media and voters was one-way: people got information but could not "talk back."	Information flow is two-way, thanks to talk radio and the Internet—including blogs, YouTube, social networking sites, Twitter, and instant messaging.

WHAT'S NEXT?

> What new media technologies will shape campaigns and political participation in the future?

> For individuals seeking information about policy issues and political campaigns, what might be the negative consequences of the abundance of information flowing through the electronic media?

> How will technology change political participation in the future?

term for this unequal access to computer technology is the **digital divide.** Sociologist Mark Wheeler has examined the digital divide, particularly when it comes to high-speed Internet connectivity. He has noted that income and wealth affect individuals' access to high-speed Internet service, even in the world's most affluent democracies.[7]

Yet even for those without computers of their own, the Internet has broadly transformed life in the United States. How the average U.S. citizen is educated, communicates, gets news, shops, receives information about politics, and participates in the political process all have changed because of the Internet. As political scientist Michael Cornfield noted, "I can't think of anything except kissing babies that you can't do online."[8] The influence of the Internet has been both positive and negative, and it continues to evolve.

The Internet and Civic Engagement

Over time, the Internet has transformed the media's function as a conveyor of information and a resource for civic engagement. Communications scholar Howard Rheingold argues that the digital media in particular serve as a key avenue by which young people can use their "public voice" to consume and share information.[9]

The Evolution of the Internet   In its early years, the Internet functioned in much the same way that traditional media formats such as newspapers and periodicals functioned: it provided a convenient but "one-way" means for people to get information at times determined by the publishers. As **bandwidth**—the amount of data that can travel through a network in a given time period—has increased, so, too, has the sophistication of Web content, as well as the venues and formats that serve as information sources. Today's news Web sites—including those of all the network and cable news stations, plus sites maintained by Internet service providers such as AOL—give Internet users news stories when they want them instead of at predetermined times. Users can selectively search for specific information about public issues that matter to them, potentially building their knowledge base with a mouse click. Moreover, many contemporary news outlets, including magazines and radio programs, are now making available downloadable podcasts of content that users can view or listen to at their convenience. These podcasts are giving individuals even greater access to information, including reports on social issues, policy initiatives, and politics. Civic participation has been facilitated by the rise of these news Web sites and other sites, which host blogs and forums that allow readers to engage in virtual civic discourse and even to form virtual communities.

The Internet as a Source of Information and Community   YouTube provides a compelling example of how the evolving Internet has worked to the benefit of civic engagement. This Web site, which debuted in February 2005 and is now owned by Google, allows individuals to post and watch original videos. The success of the YouTube experiment is inconceivable in the world of the dial-up Internet connection that was the norm just a few years ago. YouTube's YouChoose '08 was an online network of YouTube members who uploaded political videos related to the 2008 presidential campaign so that others could view them. And so if you want to watch a political advertisement, see an interview with the French president, or participate in Citizen Tube (YouTube's video blog, or **vblog**), today's technology makes it possible for you to do so in seconds. In 2007, YouTube partnered with CNN to host both Democratic and Republican presidential primary debates, promoting civic engagement by making it possible for Web site users not only to watch the debates but also to submit questions to the candidates. The interactivity embodied in viewing, commenting, posting, and vblogging has revolutionized civic discourse.

Today's Internet technology also facilitates the formation of virtual communities. These networks of interested participants, while different from their IRL (in real life) counterparts, share features with those real-world groups. Many blogs, for example, have community leaders, regular contributors, expert commentators, and participants with established roles. Blogs promote civic engagement by disseminating information, exposing readers to the viewpoints of others, providing a forum allowing bloggers to share their own views, serving as a venue for the formation of online communities that can foster feelings of efficacy among participants, and channeling activism, both virtual and real.* In short, the Internet has led to the phenomenon of the **prosumer**—the individual who simultaneously consumes information and news and produces information in forms such as videos, blogs, and Web sites.

The Internet as a Source of News

Internet users in the United States spend an average of three hours per day online, according to research conducted by the Stanford Institute for the Quantitative Study of Society (SIQSS)—far more than they spend watching TV or reading newspapers.[10] Perhaps more important, the number of individuals using the Internet as a source of news continues to increase dramatically. Figure 10.5 shows that in the eleven-year span from 1996 to 2008, the proportion of Americans who get news from the Internet grew exponentially. In fact, by 2008, a majority of Americans got news from the Internet at least sometimes, and one-fourth used the Internet as a news source daily. It is no wonder Nielsen TV ratings and newspaper subscriptions have declined.

The old adage that a "week is an eternity in politics" has become an understatement in the age of the Internet and the twenty-four-hour news cycle. Things happen in the click of a mouse button, and increasingly, politicians are making snap statements in front of ever-present cell phone video cameras and regretting them later. Vermont governor Howard Dean, candidate for the 2004 Democratic nomination for president, certainly regretted his wild scream to a crowd during a campaign stop, the video of which was later played and replayed on the Internet and on TV screens around the world.

Internet news sites could be doing some things better, though. For example, many news outlets present a news story as either an article or a video, but few major media outlets offer hot-links to original source data that would aid interested site users in delving more deeply into the story. Instead of a synthesized news article on a Supreme Court decision, for instance, media outlets could provide links to the original opinions on the case, as well as to audio recordings of the arguments

---

*A note about content: the authors recognize the enormous variation in the quality of information available on the Internet in general and in blogs in particular. So when using the Internet as a source of information, a healthy dose of skepticism can be quite useful.

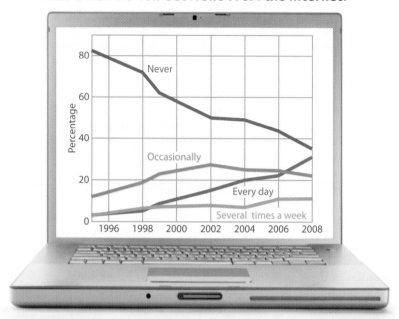

How Often Do You Get News From the Internet?

FIGURE 10.5

Percentages of Americans who Get News from the Internet

Source: The Gallup Poll, *Media Use and Evaluation*, poll administered December 4–7, 2008, www.gallup.com/poll/1663/Media-Use-Evaluation.aspx.

before the court, records of lower court decisions, and briefs filed with the court, supporting or opposing one side or the other, which are available elsewhere online *if* one is willing to search for them. Instead, most outlets offer only broad coverage with links to related stories—an approach that does not make it easy for an individual to research a matter of interest more deeply.

The Internet's Influence on Political Participation and Campaigns

Even more than talk radio, the Internet has made politics participative. People can express their preferences online on issues from health reform to term limits, from income tax credits to repealing the inheritance tax. But besides acting as a gauge for public opinion, the Internet can also be a useful tool for citizens' political activism. The traditional media have not had nearly the impact on political participation that the Internet has had. For example, the left-of-center wing of the Democratic Party has not achieved the same media dominance in radio as the conservative wing of the Republican Party. One radio station targeting liberal listeners, Air America, was formed in 2004, but it has never succeeded in attracting a competitive share of the radio audience. What *has* worked in attracting the liberal wing of the youth vote are blogs and Web sites such as www.moveon.org.

Using the Internet to Mobilize Voters   Jesse Ventura, a professional wrestler who served as the governor of Minnesota from 1999 to 2003, credits the Web for opening up the political process by enabling grassroots mobilization through **e-campaigning**—the practice of mobilizing voters using the Internet—which allowed an outsider like himself to be elected governor. Winning half of the under-thirty vote, Ventura conducted a campaign without any physical headquarters—at least at first. Armed with a large e-mail list, he enlisted pledges of support that short-circuited the traditional doorbell ringing and telephone calls that go with the terri-tory when running for office. His tactics gave him the final surge of voters that he needed to win. Ventura's victory testifies to the power of the Internet as a political campaign tool.

The potential of the Internet as a force in political campaigns came into sharp focus again in 2004, when liberal Democratic governor Howard Dean of Vermont used the Web extensively for recruiting volunteers and raising money. Dean's efforts proved so successful that other candidates quickly followed his strategy. By the 2008 campaign, every major presidential candidate had a staff of Web site designers, Internet campaign managers, and blog managers. The Internet has even changed how candidacies are announced and presidential campaigns unfold. A campaign video of former senator John Edwards announcing his candidacy in New Orleans ran on YouTube, and both Senator Barack Obama and Senator Hillary Rodham Clinton announced their candidacies via their Web sites, followed by the posting of the corresponding videos on YouTube.

How the Internet can Affect a Political Campaign   The Internet has also changed the nature of political organizing. On the day that Senator Obama announced his bid for the presidency, Farouk Olu Aregbe, a student government adviser at the University of Missouri, logged on to www.facebook.com and announced the formation of a group called "One Million Strong for Barack." Within a month, Aregbe's Facebook group had over a quarter of a million members, and other Face-book users had formed more than 500 groups supporting the candidate.

But the rapid expansion of Internet technology has also made it more difficult for presidential campaigns (and administrations) to manage the news.[11] As a case in point, in January 2007, just after Senator Clinton launched her White House bid, a video appeared on YouTube featuring her singing an off-key rendition of the national anthem (the moment had been captured by an MSNBC news video crew). After the blog site *The Drudge Report* featured a link to the video, it logged nearly 800,000 hits. What was the campaign to do? Ignore the video? Apologize for the senator's inadequate singing voice? Promise that she would not sing publicly again? The campaign decided to ride it out and do nothing, and this strategy seemed to work, as the story and fanfare soon fizzled. Wrote Patrick Healy of the *New York Times:* "The video clip may have been trivial, but the brief episode surrounding it illustrated how visual and audio technologies like video streaming have the potential to drive political news in unexpected directions, and how White House candidates are aggressively monitoring and trying to master them."[12]

Today's Blogosphere

Clearly, the widespread use of the Internet has also contributed to the spread of blogs. A new language has sprouted to incorporate this development, beginning with **blogosphere**—the community, or social network, of bloggers. The owner of the Dallas Mavericks basketball team, Mark Cuban, says that he runs his Internet blog as a means of correcting all the media accounts about him. As in every other corner of the Internet, there are no checks on what he posts: Cuban, who claims an audience of 300,000 readers, has called sports columnists "clueless," "morons," and purveyors of "slime reporting."[13]

Estimates indicate that the number of blogs has doubled every five months since 2003 to a current level of over 20 million individual blogs.[14] As the number has multiplied, their variety and credibility have increased. Bloggers received press credentials at both the Democratic and the Republican conventions in 2008. Traditional television and print media outlets now host blogs as well.

The blog's rise as a tool of grassroots organizing has given birth to the term **netroots** to describe Net-centered political efforts on behalf of candidates and causes. A blog makes information available to large numbers of users immediately, spreading news and energizing supporters more rapidly than any other medium. It also differs from traditional media in one important way: bloggers make no attempt to be impartial. A blog is an opinion journal, offering a specific perspective and appealing to a specific segment of the public. In that respect, it cannot replace traditional journalism, especially because there is no check on whether the facts it presents are correct. But blogs continue to change the face of political campaigning and grassroots organization—for better and for worse.

Media Convergence

The concept of convergence has taken hold among media observers today. **Convergence** refers to the merging of various forms of media—newspapers, television stations, radio networks, and blogs—under one corporate roof with one set of business and editorial leaders. The emergence of Politico, a multimedia start-up that debuted in Washington, DC, in January 2007, is an example of this concept come to life. What would have been regarded in the past as a violation of antitrust laws is now considered the wave of the future. Politico's mission is to report on the daily politics on Capitol Hill and in the White House. Politico is a publication of Capital News Corp., which is financed by Allbritton Communications, a company that used to own a now-defunct newspaper called the *Washington Star*.

The Negative Political Impact of the Internet

The explosion of the Internet in politics has also opened a Pandora's box of problems. One key problem is misinformation. Unlike newspapers, magazines, and television networks, where editors and fact-checkers are responsible for ensuring accuracy, the

Internet is almost entirely unmonitored. In political campaigns, misinformation can be devastating.

Another problem is that the Internet has contributed to the decline in civility in political discourse. Some bloggers and anonymous message board posters seek to destroy their opponents' reputations. The nature of the Internet means that lies and slanderous accusations can often be leveled with no consequence to the poster. This problem occurs not just in national politics but in community politics as well.

The Internet also poses a host of unknown potentialities. What will be the cross-over effects, for example, of such present-day crimes as identity theft and the stealing of social security numbers and state secrets, both of which have been "hacked into" via the Net? Consider the problems of a national election conducted through computer terminals. How would a recount be managed? Would the outcome be fair? Would the losers view it as fair? Would the average citizen trust the results?

And although new communications tools allow politicians substantially to reduce the amount of legwork and "flesh pressing" required in a typical campaign, the absence of such glad-handing could also destroy the flavor of local politics. Politicians would no longer have to stand in front of supermarkets and kiss babies, but neither would the voters be able to get to know the candidates or to probe into their views on the issues.

How the Media Influence Government Policy

Media reporting can have an effect on government policy making, particularly when policy makers' opinions are divided, as coverage of the wars in Afghanistan and Iraq shows. In the patriotic cultural climate following September 11, 2001, public confidence in the Bush White House's policy grew as favorable media reporting increased significantly. The media heavily covered the Bush administration's plan to invade Afghanistan, with its objective to overthrow the Islamic fundamentalist Taliban regime that was allowing the operation of al-Qaeda terrorist training there and to track down terrorist leader Osama bin Laden. There was also saturated media reporting on the intent to invade Iraq, as the Bush administration claimed that Iraqi president Saddam Hussein's regime was sponsoring terror and manufacturing weapons of mass destruction.

Initially, media and public support for Bush policy and the military invasions was strong. Figure 10.6 shows that in April 2003, 73 percent of Americans surveyed by the Gallup Organization believed it was "worth going to war." On May 1, 2003, the media approvingly covered President Bush's triumphant announcement on the USS *Abraham Lincoln* that "major combat operations had ended" and the "mission [was] accomplished," and Americans widely cheered. Clearly, media coverage had cultivated powerful public support for policy initiatives.

If positive media coverage of a policy can create favorable public opinion, can negative coverage create unfavorable opinion? For example, would the 73 percent of people who thought it was worth going to war in Iraq change their minds if media coverage turned negative, or would they hold fast to their views? Figure 10.6 shows the impact that negative media coverage can have on policy. Clearly, as the

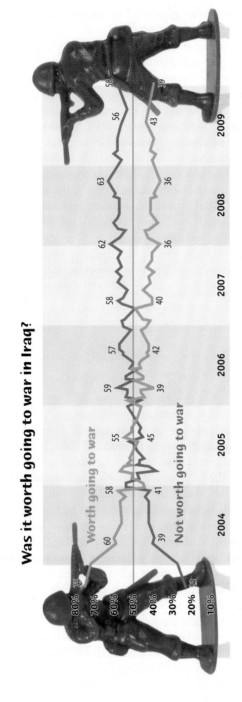

Was it worth going to war in Iraq?

FIGURE 10.6 ■ What did Americans think in 2004 about the worth of the United States' going to war in Iraq, according to Gallup polling? Did those attitudes remain consistent through 2009? What main reasons do you think explain the shifts in public opinion? Was media coverage a factor?

Source: The Gallup Poll, "Iraq," www.gallup.com/poll/1633/Iraq.aspx.

POLITICAL INQUIRY

war in Iraq dragged on, public support dwindled. Although support sagged for numerous reasons, including the escalating body count, the war's protracted nature, and the failure to find the weapons of mass destruction that motivated the war, the graph shows that media coverage of one event sparked a significant decline in public support for the war. That event was the spring 2004 attacks on four U.S. military contractors who were killed, mutilated, and burned in Fallujah by a band of Iraqi insurgents. Figure 10.6 shows the sea change that occurred after this particular insurgent attack and the media coverage it generated, with the percentage of those who thought it was worth going to war dropping nearly 20 percent.

A Biased Media?

A recent joke about how the media will cover the end of the world stereotyped the nation's major newspapers while also emphasizing their importance in reporting world events. As the story goes, the *New York Times* headline would be, "World Ends; Third World Hit Worst." The *Washington Post*'s front page would blare, "World Ends; Unnamed Source Says White House Had Prior Knowledge." In *USA Today*, a newspaper with a huge national and international circulation, the story would be titled, "We're Dead; State-by-State Analysis, page 4D; Sports, page 6C." And the *Wall Street Journal*? "World Ends; Stock Market Goes Down."

Media critics today are everywhere. All of them claim that both print and electronic media exhibit bias in their reporting, in their selection of what issues to cover, and in their favoring of one side of an issue (or one politician) over another. One of the most common complaints is that the media have an ideological bias.

The Question of Ideological Bias

A long-standing complaint is that the media—particularly big-city newspapers—evidence a liberal bias. For example, former House majority leader Tom DeLay (R-Texas) protested the liberal leanings of two of the country's major newspapers, the *New York Times* and the *Washington Post*, when they ran stories about his ethics problems. Those media, he claimed, ignored the same practices when Democrats such as Nancy Pelosi (D-California), then House minority leader, engaged in them. The day after the *New York Times* published an article revealing that DeLay's congressional campaign had paid his wife and daughter more than $500,000 for their services, DeLay lashed out, stating that the article was "just another seedy attempt by the liberal media to embarrass me."

The notion that the media have a liberal bias is an often-heard criticism. In 1964, former president Dwight D. Eisenhower, in his address to the Republican National Convention, condemned a liberal media bias:

My friends, we are Republicans. If there is any finer word in the field of partisan politics, I have not heard it. So let us particularly [scorn] the divisive efforts of those outside our family, including sensation-seeking columnists and commentators, who couldn't care less about the good of our party.[15]

Many conservatives point to studies indicating that a majority of newsroom reporters identify themselves as liberal or Democrat. Conservatives charge that the ideological bent of the journalists carries through to the topics covered and to the perspectives of the stories. But studies conducted by various political scientists, including C. Richard Hofstetter, Michael J. Robinson, and Margaret A. Sheehan, refute the idea that journalists' personal viewpoints tinge the content of the news in a liberal way.[16] Indeed, studies suggest that most news stories take the form of a debate, with the journalist presenting the various sides of an issue and leaving the conclusion to the reader's interpretation.

Changes in the nature of the mass media have led to increasingly vocal charges, especially by Democratic elected officials, that newer media outlets, particularly talk radio and the blogosphere, are dominated by conservatives. Among the most vocal critics of the alleged conservative media bias was former Democratic president Bill Clinton. Clinton blamed the media for his troubles over Whitewater—an investment scandal involving shady real estate dealings by Clinton and his wife, Hillary Rodham Clinton—and later for his woes over his affair with White House intern Monica Lewinsky. Hillary Clinton included the press in her controversial remarks about the existence of a "vast right-wing conspiracy" that sought to discredit her husband's presidency.

The Public's View on Media Bias

What does the public think about partisan bias? Figure 10.7 shows that when asked the question "In general, do you think the news media are—?" (the survey rotated the potential responses: "too liberal," "just about right," and "too conservative"), 47 percent responded that they thought the news media were too liberal. Thirty-six percent said they thought the media were "just about right" ideologically, while 13 percent said they believed the news media were too conservative.

Thus more than half (60 percent) of those surveyed believed that the media are biased (either liberally or conservatively). Yet research by William P. Eveland Jr. and Dhavan V. Shah into people's perception of media bias concluded that it is often linked to whether people have conversations with others whose views differ from theirs. When they do not have such dialogues, they are more likely to believe that the media are biased against their view.[17]

The Issue of Corporate Bias

Most professional journalists hold journalistic objectivity to be important, and that principle well serves the interests of the large corporations that dominate the U.S. media industry today. Within most of the giant media conglomerates, motivated as they are by the drive for profits, reporters are strongly discouraged from displaying bias. Newspapers and television stations rely on advertisers, and advertisers want not only to attract the largest number of readers or viewers but also to avoid offending the largest numbers. Thus, given the corporate nature of today's media, neutrality is generally a guiding principle.

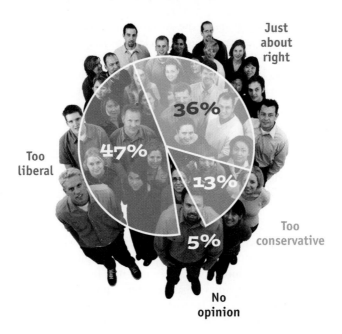

Just about right

36%

47%

Too liberal

13%

5%

Too conservative

No opinion

FIGURE 10.7

Public Opinion of Ideological Media Bias

Source: The Gallup Poll, *Media use and Evaluation*, poll administered September 8–11, 2008, www.gallup.com/poll/1663/Media-Use-Evalution.aspx.

Critics on the left, however, argue that these corporate structures create their own bias and that this bias has altered what is considered news and how that news is covered.[18] Corporate bias—and the desire to attract, keep, and please an audience—produces skewed programming. Will corporate conglomerates be willing to report on situations that may put themselves and their advertisers in a negative light? How does the drive for profits influence what is in the news? Are viewers being fed "news" that is not particularly newsworthy? There is no doubt that profits influence the media to cover the kinds of stories that viewers and readers want. In particular, violence dominates most local news programming, so much so that the principle of "if it bleeds, it leads" now extends into the first fifteen minutes of many local news broadcasts. Fires; political, sports, and sex scandals; and celebrity-heavy news are also powerful audience attractors.

Regulation of the Media: Is It Necessary?

The framers of the Constitution had to be concerned only with print media when they guaranteed freedom of the press—one of the fundamental liberties they ensured in the Bill of Rights. As the media evolved beyond print into electronic formats, so, too, did thinking about the government's role in regulating the media, especially media outlets such as radio and television stations. But technology has outpaced the ability of the government to regulate certain forms of electronic media, including the Internet and satellite radio services such as Sirius/XM. Nonetheless, television and regular radio transmissions are still subject to government regulation.

Control of the Business Side of the Media

Through the independent regulatory agency known as the Federal Communications Commission (FCC), founded in 1934, the government regulates and controls the ownership of radio and television stations. Most of the FCC's rules have concerned ownership, such as the number of outlets a network may own.

In 1996, Congress passed the Telecommunications Act, which opened the communications markets to telephone companies. This sweeping law allowed competition in the communications industry. It presented new (often confusing) options for consumers, as individual companies began to offer a suite of services, from local and long-distance telephone service, to Internet access, to cable and satellite television.

With the combination of all of these services under single companies, large conglomerates have increasingly gained control of the media. Firms such as Disney, Viacom, News Corporation, and Time Warner exert a powerful influence over what news the average American sees and reads on a given day. The advent of these media titans has given rise to concerns about whether this type of control will deter balanced reporting of the news and unbiased presentations of issues. In addition, public conversations about our democracy are probing into the question of whether the relative lack of competition (because there are so few competitors) means that a valuable check on what the media do and how they do it has been lost.

Congress is currently considering another question of control over the business of the media. The issue, a controversial one, centers on **Net neutrality:** the idea that Internet traffic—e-mail, Web sites, videos, and phone calls—should flow through the Internet pipeline without interference or discrimination by those who own or are running the pipeline. *Should* these broadband behemoths be able to use their market power to control information or to favor certain clients online? Critics charge that congressional passage of legislation supporting the service providers would destroy the neutrality and openness of the Internet. Tim Berners-Lee, the inventor of the World Wide Web, says, "The neutral communications medium is essential to our society. . . . It is the basis of democracy, by which a community should decide what to do."[19] Do you agree with Berners-Lee? In what ways would you say that neutral media are the basis of a democracy?

Control of Media Content

To avoid government regulation, the broadcasting industry has established its own code of conduct, although the National Association of Broadcasters' code remains purely voluntary. The Telecommunications Act of 1996, however, did provide for the inclusion of V-chip technology in television sets. The **V-chip,** an electronic chip installed in all TV units thirteen inches or larger in size and made for the U.S. market since January 1, 2000, lets parents block programming they consider unsuitable for children. A further provision of the act, aimed at limiting the transmission of pornographic materials on the Internet so that minors could not access them, was struck down by the courts as an unconstitutional limitation of freedom of speech. Consequently, the broadcast media, as well as Internet sites, have been free to provide whatever content they believe will draw an audience—often to the detriment of civil discourse.

CONTINUING THE CONVERSATION

CONCLUSION

- The surge in the number and variety of media outlets— along with the changes in the nature of the media and in people's interactions with them—has affected politics and government in many ways. Narrowcasting and the resulting segmentation of media markets, a central feature of media growth, might raise the comfort level of many people, but it also limits the exposure of many people to new ideas. Like gated communities, segmented media are also segregated media, detached environments that expose people only to viewpoints with which they agree, thus cordoning them off from society and from many of its problems.

- Technology has created a two-way relationship between the media and consumers, involving the exchange of seemingly limitless information in a vast conversation of democracy. The openness and easy accessibility of the new media have led to considerable criticism of them, but the good news is that almost all public—and to a lesser extent, private—institutions have become much more transparent in recent years. This two-way relationship has also meant that citizens are afforded greater opportunities to use their public voice to influence government and the policies it creates.

- The modern media have opened the door more widely to citizens' direct participation in the democratic process. In light of Americans' high levels of cynicism about their elected leaders, might this powerful new opportunity to be heard make our democracy more participatory than the Constitution's framers ever intended or imagined? Will the availability of the Internet as a forum for citizens and a tool for organizing lead to a meaningful expansion of participation in civic life and in the conversation of democracy? Will citizens use the new technology productively?

STUDY**NOW**

Summary

1. The Political Functions of the Media

The media perform several key political functions, including disseminating information, helping to interpret matters of public interest and to set the national policy agenda, providing a forum for political conversations, and socializing children to the political culture.

2. The Press and Politics: A Historical View

Since early in American history, the press has played a vital role in shaping the political context. As the format of the media has evolved over the centuries, so has media's impact on politics and policy making.

3. The Media Go Electronic: The Radio and Television Revolutions

The advent of the electronic media has revolutionized the impact of media on politics. Television and talk radio have altered the nature of politics and campaigning, the former affecting everything from how campaigns are conducted to how candidates dress, and the latter providing a forum for political discourse open to participation by virtually everyone.

4. The Media Revolution Continues: The Internet

The Internet has drastically altered the political landscape by making available, in a key-stroke, an abundance of information and by serving as a medium for the broad, rapid dissemination of information and opinion. The Internet has changed approaches to fund-raising, voter mobilization, candidacy announcements, and campaign strategy.

5. How the Media Influence Government Policy

The media exert an impact on government policy making by creating popular support or disapproval for government policies and by covering some public issues but not others.

6. A Biased Media?

In addressing the question of media bias, we must consider the issues of both content bias and ideological bias. But research stresses that most news stories take the form of a debate that presents the various sides of an issue and leaves the conclusion to the reader's interpretation.

7. Regulation of the Media: Is It Necessary?

The Telecommunications Act of 1996 allowed competition in the communications industry and presented new options for consumers, as individual companies began to offer a suite of services. With the combination of all of these services under single companies, large corporate conglomerates increasingly have gained control of the media, making the job of the Federal Communications Commission (FCC) more complex.

For Critical Thinking and Discussion

1. Has the Internet changed how you personally participate in politics? Does virtual activism make real-world activism less likely or more likely? Explain.

2. What do you think are the *most important* functions the media perform? Why? Does the diversity of media outlets hinder the media's ability to serve some of their more traditional functions? Explain.

3. Compare and contrast the penny papers of the nineteenth century with today's blogs. What are the similarities and differences between the two? How will blogs evolve given the evolution of other media forms?

4. Discuss the dangers of the unchecked Internet in the political world. Can these dangers be combated? If so, how?

5. What difficulties are associated with government regulation of the media in an era of cable television, the Internet, and satellite radio?

Key Terms

bandwidth 376
blogosphere 380
convergence 380
digital divide 375
e-campaigning 379
fairness doctrine 372
fireside chats 372
framing 363
infotainment 362

letter to the editor 365
media segmentation 374
muckraking 367
narrowcasting 374
Net neutrality 386
netroots 380
new media 368
penny press 366
priming 365

prosumer 377
public agenda 365
soft news 362
sound bites 362
talk radio 372
vblog 376
V-chip 387
yellow journalism 367

Internet Resources

A More Perfect Union **Web site**
www.mhhe.com/harrisonampule   Consult the book's Web site for study guides, interactive activities, simulations, and current hot-links that provide additional information on the media and politics in the United States.

State of the Media
www.stateofthemedia.org   Run by the Project for Excellence in Journalism, this site features an annual report on the media and tracks trends in media usage and confidence in the media.

The Pew Research Center for People and the Press
http://people-press.org   This site provides independent research, surveys, data sets, and commentary on the media and issues of media interest.

Media Watch
www.mediawatch.com   Visit this site to learn about the initiatives of an activist group that monitors media content and seeks to combat stereotypes and violence in the media.

Recommended Readings

Arnold, R. Douglas. *Congress, the Press, and Political Accountability*. Princeton, NJ: Princeton University Press, 2004. An analysis of how local newspapers cover members of Congress in their districts throughout a legislative session.

Bennett, W. Lance. *News: The Politics of Illusion,* 7th ed. New York: Longman, 2006. A behind-the-scenes tour of the media in politics while grappling with the question, How well does the news, as the core of the national political information system, serve the needs of democracy?

Crouse, Timothy. *The Boys on the Bus*. New York: Random House, 1973. A classic tale of the presidential campaign press corps.

Graber, Doris. *Media Power and Politics*. Washington, DC: CQ Press, 2006. An analysis of the influence of the media on opinions, elections, and policies, as well as efforts to shape the content and impact of media coverage.

Iyengar, Shanto, and Jennifer A. McGrady. *Media Politics: A Citizen's Guide*. New York: W.W. Norton, 2006. A survey of how politicians use the media to get elected, wield power in office, and achieve policy goals.

Plissner, Martin. *The Control Room: How Television Calls the Shots in Presidential Elections*. New York: Free Press, 1999. A description of the effect of television news and advertising on presidential elections.

PART IV

INSTITUTIONS OF GOVERNMENT

National Journal

How Tough Should the President Be?

A year ago, vice presidential candidate Joe Biden offered up one of his classic off-script observations that pained Barack Obama's political advisers. "Mark my words, it will not be six months before the world tests Barack Obama like they did John Kennedy," he predicted. "Watch, we're gonna have an international crisis, a generated crisis, to test the mettle of this guy."

A narrative is emerging among some columnists, pundits, and academics across the political spectrum that Obama's low-key, cool, cerebral style, while reassuring on many levels, lacks the punch that is sometimes needed to advance an agenda in Washington, and in a perilous world.

Neither foreign leaders nor U.S. lawmakers fear the president, according to this critique. They are comfortable defying Obama's wishes and pursuing their own agendas without concern for the consequences. Even when the president has made it clear—publicly and privately—that he strongly favors a certain course of action, others sometimes appear to find it easy to reject his appeals.

"Obama has created an atmosphere of no fear," says Douglas Brinkley, a history professor at Rice University and the author of several presidential biographies. "Nobody is really worried about the revenge of Barack Obama, because he is not a vengeful man. That's what we love about him—he is so high-minded, and a conciliatory guy, and he tries to govern with a sense of consensus—all noble goals, but they don't get you very far in this Washington knifing environment."

"He has been all carrots and no sticks so far," observed a veteran Senate Democratic aide, speaking on condition of anonymity. Obama's style "has to be more Lyndon Johnson. Half, 'I love you, but I'll stick this screwdriver right through your heart in a second if it is to my advantage.' On the fear question, I don't think he or his team is feared."

Brinkley agrees: "He needs to be more like LBJ or Theodore Roosevelt. He has to change his tactical framework, if his personality will allow it, to being a much more in-your-face, cutthroat, high-minded nationalist, pushing the country's agenda to the people."

Even Obama's friends on Capitol Hill privately grumble that he foolishly set a deadline to close Guantánamo by January 2010 without first developing a plan to pull it off. That failure invited Democratic lawmakers to jump ship on what has become a hot political issue as Republicans whip up fears among constituents that keeping detainees in prisons in their communities will invite terrorist attacks.

"He should not have put a timetable on it," said Simon Serfaty, who follows global affairs at the Center for Strategic and International Studies and has written many books on international relations. "He is now finding out it's harder than he thought."

Meanwhile, on his top domestic priority—the most sweeping health care legislation since LBJ's push for Medicare as part of his Great Society—Obama is faulted in some quarters for his mixed signals on the importance of the so-called government-run insurance program, or "public option," to compete with the private sector.

Is it important as a counterweight "to keep insurance companies honest," as he said in his September 9 speech to a joint session of Congress, or is it "just one sliver of [reform], one aspect of it," as he commented at a town hall meeting in August?

The president has also struggled in the international arena with recalcitrant friends as well as determined enemies. U.S. allies have provided only modest support for the Afghanistan war; entreaties to other countries to take custody of Guantánamo Bay detainees have had limited success; and Israel summarily rejected Obama's repeated public demands to freeze its settle-

> "There are moments **when fear is useful,** when people have to realize who's in charge. . . ."
> —Bruce Buchanan

ments in the West Bank as an inducement to Arab leaders to engage in the peace process.

"There are moments when fear is useful, when people have to realize who's in charge and there may be consequences for bucking the person in charge," said Bruce Buchanan, a professor of government at the University of Texas (Austin).

Style or Substance?

The most immediate challenge concerns Obama's very public reassessment of U.S. strategy in Afghanistan. Somewhat stunningly, Gen. Stanley McChrystal, the top U.S. commander in the region, publicly and bluntly dismissed a course of action under consideration by the White House (and reportedly favored by Biden) that would reduce the scale of the U.S. effort in Afghanistan.

That alternative, McChrystal opined, would

lead to "Chaos-istan." When asked if it could work in practice, the general said, "The short answer is no," and he called it "a shortsighted strategy."

Those comments sparked glee among conservatives and provoked push-back in the form of editorial commentary and headlines about the effrontery of the military commander.

McChrystal's frankness startled experts in international relations. "I find it amazing that McChrystal would be speaking out the way he is at the very moment when the White House is engaging in a review of his recommendations, and [McChrystal is] explaining that there is no alternative to what he is suggesting," Serfaty said.

Helpful or not, an inevitable question arises: Would such a high-ranking military officer have been so publicly dismissive of military options under consideration by previous presidents?

James Thurber, director of the Center for Congressional and Presidential Studies at American University, said he could not imagine such a scenario during the George W. Bush administration. Referring to Bush's vice president and Defense secretary, Thurber said, "Cheney and [Donald] Rumsfeld were feared, and [Bush] went along with them. Then, once they made a decision, they didn't [mess] around."

Despite all of the questions about whether Obama might be more successful if he had the element of fear to go along with the goodwill toward him, nobody can doubt the president's willingness to tackle some of the most difficult issues, from pressing for health care reform despite obvious political risks to intervening in the economy in ways unfathomable a few years ago.

"He is having problems for just one reason—he is trying to do big things," said David Rohde, a political scientist at Duke University. "He is trying to make big changes. If he were to propose a health bill that made just a little, incremental change, it would have flown through the House and Senate with no trouble at all. Very few presidents of recent vintage have tried to do big things. When they did try, except at the very beginning of their administrations, they often failed. Lyndon Johnson didn't face anything like this when he was doing his big things."

Buchanan of the University of Texas has his own list of high-risk stances where the president has shown strength. "Near as I can tell,

Obama is willing to make calls that aren't necessarily popular. He may be about to do so in connection with Afghanistan. He made some calls that were challenging, to say the least; remember the pirate hostage situation [in April 2009, when Obama authorized Navy snipers to shoot Somali pirates who were holding an American captive], which was a high-risk call because if it backfired, it would have been a messy, sticky situation."

Afghanistan Test

The debate over Afghanistan became personal when Sen. John McCain, R-Ariz., took to the Senate floor to push his proposal to require McChrystal and Gen. David Petraeus, the top U.S. commander for the wars in Iraq and Afghanistan, to testify before Congress. His move was obviously designed to increase pressure on Obama to grant McChrystal's request for as many as 40,000 more troops for Afghanistan.

McCain then unloaded on Obama's top advisers, charging that they were reluctant to send more troops out of political caution. The administration was "trying to find the exit sign" out of Afghanistan, he said. "It has been broadcast all over television that there are individuals—including the vice president; now, unfortunately, the national security

adviser [James Jones]; the chief political adviser to the president, Mr. Rahm Emanuel— who don't want to alienate the left base of the Democratic Party. That is what this is all about."

When a reporter asked McCain if this decision was a test for Obama as commander-in-chief, McCain was quick to respond. "Of course it is," he said.

No Marching Orders

When Obama spoke to a joint session of Congress on his priorities for health reform, he took a markedly different approach from that of Bill Clinton 15 years before. In 1994, Clinton issued a blunt warning in his State of the Union address.

"If you send me legislation that does not guarantee every American private health insurance that can never be taken away, you will force me to take this pen, veto the legislation, and we'll come right back here and start all over again," he said.

Clinton later reflected that his threat was a mistake. "I did it because a couple of my advisers had said that people wouldn't think I had the strength of my convictions unless I demonstrated that I wouldn't compromise," he wrote in his memoir, *My Life.* "It was an unnecessary red flag to my opponents in

Congress. Politics is about compromise, and people expect presidents to win, not posture for them."

In contrast to Clinton, Obama has not tried to dictate to Congress the details of the legislation; instead, he has provided general principles that he favors. That strategy has prompted plenty of second-guessing.

"It's hard to march if you don't have marching orders," said Charles Jones, a political science professor emeritus at the University of Wisconsin who has written several books on presidents' relations with Congress. "If it's 'We may go this way or we may go that way,' it is hard to go back to the office and say, 'We know what we are doing here.'"

But Sen. Sheldon Whitehouse, D-R.I., says that the more hands-off style does not show weakness but rather reflects a strategic decision by the White House about the best way to get major legislation passed.

"Once the White House made the decision to let Congress try to work out these issues, certain consequences followed," Whitehouse said. But I think that speaks more to the strategic decision to let us try to work this out through that period than it does to any lack of toughness on the part of the man himself."

Ultimately, the verdict on the efficacy of Obama's style will depend in significant part on whether health care legislation passes, said Larry Sabato, a professor of politics at the University of Virginia. "Health care could be his hammer—if he gets it, he will have proven that his style works, that you don't have to be an in-your-face LBJ type to get significant health care reform. But if it falls apart or he gets a tiny piece of it, then there will be criticism that he is ineffective and not tough enough."

The framers granted to Congress certain explicit powers, as well as key implied powers; through the evolution of both the national government strengthened and broadened its authority.

A much more demographically diverse Congress exercises wide powers, its decision making influenced by shifting constituencies in a fast-growing, fast-changing country.

NOW

Congress

First and foremost, Congress is an institution shaped by the people elected to serve there, men and women acting as the trusted representatives of the constituents who voted them into office. Congress and the policies it sets are molded by the times; laws passed in one generation may seem antiquated to the next. And Congress and the policies it creates are influenced by a wide variety of other factors, including the legislative body's institutional history, the lawmaking process, and the internal and external actors—congressional leaders, political parties, interest groups, the president, staff members, ordinary citizens, and the media—who seek to influence congressional actions.

The Constitution's framers structured the government so that Congress—more so than the two other institutions of the federal government—would be responsive to the needs and will of the people. In representing their constituents, members of Congress provide an easily accessed point of contact for people to connect with their government and to have their voices heard.

Citizens today have countless opportunities to participate in shaping Congress's agenda and influencing how the members of Congress vote. Constituents communicate by e-mail, the Internet, and telephone and meet face-to-face with members of Congress on issues that concern them. Constituents meet with congressional staff members for help in understanding how to deal with government bureaucracy. Through congressional campaigns and elections,

How will technology affect the ability of "average" citizens to influence Congress?

Will the composition and policy making of Congress more broadly reflect the changing face of the United States?

What pressing new issues will Congress be forced to consider?

NEXT

citizens learn about issues of national importance and can participate in a variety of ways, such as volunteering in support of a candidate's run for office, contributing to the individual's campaign, becoming informed about the candidates and issues, and casting a ballot on election day.

Throughout this chapter, we view Congress through the lens of civic engagement, seeing that Congress—the people's branch of the federal government—while imperfect, is structured to empower citizens to play a role in determining public policy priorities. And ultimately, it is the people, through their choices at the ballot box, who decide who the creators of those policies will be.

The Origins of Congress

For the United States' founders, creating the national Congress was a crucially important task. Fearful of a powerful executive, but having endured the problems stemming from the weak national government under the Articles of Confederation, the framers of the Constitution believed that the legislature should be the key branch of the newly formed national government. In their vision, Congress would be the institution responsible for making laws that would create effective public policy. In structuring Congress, the framers strove to create a legislative branch that was at once powerful enough to govern and to check the power of the president and yet not so powerful that the legislature itself would exercise tyrannical rule.

As they debated the shape of Congress, the Constitution's framers had to balance the desires of representation of two opposing groups. The Constitution created a bicameral, or two-house, legislature in which one house, the House of Representatives, would be based on population, and the other chamber, the Senate, would be based on state representation.[1] The constitutionally specified duties of each house of Congress reflect the framers' views of the essential nature of the two chambers and the people who would serve in them.

The House of Representatives, with the smallest constituencies of any federal office (currently about 647,000 people reside in each congressional district), is the chamber closer to the people. As such, the framers intended the House to closely represent the people's views. The Constitution thus requires, for example, that all revenue bills (bills that would create taxes) must originate in the House of Representatives. In the framers' eyes, unwarranted taxation was an egregious offense. By placing the power to tax in the hands of the members of the House of Representatives—the officials who face more frequent federal elections—the framers sought to avoid the types of unpopular, unfair taxes that had sparked the American Revolution. A short electoral cycle, they reasoned, would allow disfavored politicians to be voted out of office. Like all other bills, revenue bills must be passed in identical form by both the House and the Senate to become law, but requiring revenue bills to originate in the House reflected a victory by the large states at the Constitutional Convention (smaller states wanted taxation power to reside with the Senate).

Although the framers viewed the House as the "people's chamber," they conceived the Senate to be a more elite, more deliberative institution, one not subject to the whims of mass politics like its lower-house counterpart. Today the Senate remains a more deliberative body than the House. This quality is made possible by the Senate's smaller size and the less frenetic electoral schedule of its members, who face elections less frequently than House representatives. In addition, because of the specific constitutional duties mandated to the upper house, particularly the requirement that treaties must be ratified in the Senate, many U.S. senators have specialized in U.S. foreign policy issues. (See "The House and the Senate Compared" later in this chapter for further discussion of House-Senate differences.)

The framers' vision was to structure the Congress to embody republican principles, ensuring that in its central policy-making responsibilities, the national legislature would be responsive to the needs and will of the people. Both historically and continuing in the present day, civically engaged citizens have exerted a strong influence on the outcome of the policy-making process. One important avenue by which individuals influence Congress and its acts is through congressional elections, a topic we now consider.

Congressional Elections

The timetable for congressional elections reflects the framers' views of the differing nature of the House of Representatives and the Senate. House members, as public servants in the legislative body that the framers conceived as closer to the people, are elected every two years, in even-numbered years (2010, 2012, and so on). But the framers also sought to check the power of the people, who they believed could be irrational and unruly, and so members of the Senate originally were chosen by state legislatures. Ratification of the Seventeenth Amendment to the Constitution in 1913 shifted the election of senators to popular election within the states. Senators serve six-year terms, which are staggered so that one-third of the Senate is elected every two years. Thus in any given congressional election year, thirty-three or thirty-four seats in the Senate are up for election. Usually, the two senators from a given state will not be elected in the same cycle, unless the death or resignation of a sitting senator requires a special election. As we saw in Chapter 2, the Constitution requires that the number of seats in the House of Representatives awarded to each state be based on that state's population and that each state have two U.S. senators. On average, a successful campaign for a seat in the House of Representatives cost about $1.1 million in 2008. This is a veritable bargain compared to the price tag for a successful bid for the U.S. Senate, which averaged about $6.5 million that year. Compare this to the annual salary of $174,000 that rank-and-file members of the House and Senate collect.

Incumbency

The status of already holding office—known as **incumbency**—strongly influences a candidate's ability to raise money and is probably the most important single factor in determining success in a congressional campaign. Indeed, in any election year, about 95 percent of incumbent members of the House of Representatives running for reelection win, and about 88 percent of their Senate counterparts do. These outcomes may indicate what *individual* members of Congress are doing right: representing their own constituencies effectively, engaging with their constituents, and listening to and addressing their needs. But voters typically think about Congress in terms of *a whole,* rather than individuals, viewing it as a body that is overwhelmingly composed of "other people's" representatives, who do not reflect their views.[2] Thus the voting public frequently holds negative views about Congress as a collective entity.

Why do incumbents so often win reelection? Several factors make it more likely that someone already in office will be returned to that office in a reelection bid:

- **Stronger name recognition.** Having run for election before and served in government, incumbents tend to be better known than challengers.
- **Easier access to media coverage.** Media outlets routinely publicize the activities of elected congressional officials, rationalizing that they are covering the institution of Congress rather than the individuals. Nonincumbent challengers face an uphill battle in trying to get coverage of their campaigns.
- **Franking.** The privilege of sending mail free of charge is known as *franking.* Federal law allows members of Congress free mailings to every household in their state or congressional district. These mailings make it easy for members of Congress to stay in touch with their constituencies throughout their tenure in office.

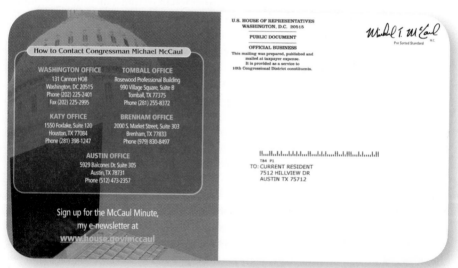

> A piece of franked mail from a congressional office. Note the signature of the sending member of Congress, which serves as a postage stamp.

- **Campaign contributions.** Political action committees and individuals are interested in supporting candidates who will be in a position to help them once the election is over. Because donors are aware of the high reelection rates of incumbent candidates, incumbents garner an enormous proportion of contributions, sometimes as much as 80 percent in any given congressional election year.
- **Casework.** Incumbents who personally help constituents solve problems with the federal bureaucracy can win their loyalty–and burnish their own reputation—which helps them to attract support for their candidacy during a run for reelection.

Thus, incumbency is a powerful obstacle for outsiders who seek to unseat an elected member of Congress. Despite the incumbency advantage, in each congressional election, many individuals challenge incumbent members of Congress, often doing so knowing that the odds are stacked against them but believing in giving voters a ballot choice. Others run because they seek to bring attention to a particular issue or to shape the policy agenda—or sometimes because they simply underestimate the power of incumbency.

Reapportionment and Redistricting

Sometimes the advantages of incumbency can be diminished, as in election years after reapportionment and redistricting. **Reapportionment** (sometimes called *apportionment*) is the reallocation of seats in the House of Representatives on the basis of changes in a state's population since the last census. Every ten years, in the year ending in zero (2000, 2010, and so on), the federal government counts the number of people in the country as a whole. If the census indicates that a state's population has changed significantly, that state may gain or lose seats in the House of Representatives. **Redistricting,** the redrawing of congressional district boundaries within a state, is based on the reapportionment from the census.

Because the composition of a given congressional district can change as a result of reapportionment and redistricting, this process can mitigate the impact of incumbency. Frequently, the greatest shifts in the composition of the House of Representatives occur in election years ending in 2 (2002, 2012, and so on), when the first elections take place that incorporate the changes from reapportionment and redistricting. As a result of reapportionment in 2002, for example, New York and Pennsylvania each lost two House seats. Five states in the Midwest lost one House seat each, while several states in the South and Southwest gained seats. When a state loses a seat, the result is that an incumbent member of Congress is likely to lose a seat. When a state gains a seat, a new member of Congress can be elected to the open seat.

In some states, the goal of congressional redistricting is to protect House incumbents. The redrawing of congressional boundaries for the purpose of political advantage is a form of **gerrymandering,** the practice of drawing legislative district boundaries to benefit an incumbent, a political party, or some other group. The term was coined in reference to Massachusetts governor Elbridge Gerry after a district shaped like a salamander was created to favor his party in 1811. The illustration on page 402 shows the first gerrymander.

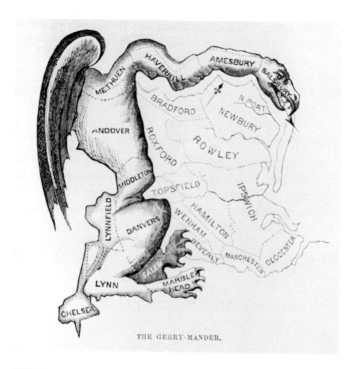

THE GERRY-MANDER.

What point does Gilbert Stuart's famous satirical cartoon of 1812, representing Massachusetts legislative districts, make about the nature of a gerrymander? What do people today mean when they talk about gerrymandering? What are your own views on the practice?

Most forms of gerrymandering are legal. The U.S. Supreme Court ruled in 1986 that a gerrymandering plan is unconstitutional only when it eliminates the minority party's influence statewide.[3] Because of the strict standards, only one partisan gerrymandering plan filed after the 1990 census was successfully challenged.

State legislatures have attempted to address the issue of racial imbalance in the House of Representatives by constructing a kind of gerrymander called a majority-minority district. A **majority-minority district** is composed of a majority of a given minority community—say, African Americans—and the creators' intent is to make it likely that a member of that minority will be elected to Congress. The Supreme Court has ruled that such racial gerrymandering is illegal unless the state legislature redrawing the district lines creates majority and minority districts at the expense of other redistricting concerns. Typically, these concerns include preserving the geographic continuity of districts, keeping communities within one legislative district, and reelecting incumbents.

Powers of Congress

The primary source of congressional authority is the U.S. Constitution. As shown in Table 11.1, the Constitution enumerates to Congress a number of different powers. The nature of these responsibilities reveals that the Constitution is both very specific in describing congressional powers (as in punishing illegal acts on the high seas) and at the same time quite vague (as in its language establishing the federal court system). Many of the specific duties of Congress reflect Americans' bitter experience in the colonial era, in that the framers granted powers to Congress that they did not want to place in the hands of a strong executive. For example, the

TABLE 11.1

Enumerated Powers of Congress

Judicial Powers
Establish the federal court system
Punish counterfeiters
Punish illegal acts on the high seas

Economic Powers
Impose taxes
Establish import tariffs
Borrow money
Regulate interstate commerce
Coin and print money, determine the value of currency

National Security Powers
Declare war
Raise and regulate national armed forces
Call up and regulate state national guard
Suppress insurrections
Repel invasions

Regulatory Powers
Establish standards of weights and measures
Regulate copyrights and patents

Administrative Powers
Establish procedures for naturalizing citizens
Establish post offices
Govern the District of Columbia

economic powers granted to Congress, including the ability to tax and spend, to establish tariffs, and to borrow money, all limit the power of the president.

Powers specifically granted to Congress still have a distinct impact on our everyday lives. For example, Congress regulates currency, establishes weights and measures, and administers post offices. As we have seen, the connection between Congress, particularly the House, and the people was crucial to the framers, and so the Constitution requires that all taxation and spending measures originate in the House because the framers believed this chamber would be nearest to the people— and that House members would therefore ensure that the people's will was done.

The Constitution imbues Congress with an additional source of power, one that has proved very important in the expansion of legislative authority over time. As discussed in Chapter 2, the necessary and proper—or elastic—clause states that Congress shall have the power to "make all Laws which shall be necessary and proper for carrying into Execution the foregoing powers, and all other Powers vested by this Constitution in the Government of the United States, or in a Department or Officer thereof." This clause has been responsible for Congress's ability to legislate in many matters not described in the enumerated powers. Deciding whether oil companies should be allowed to drill for oil in the Arctic National Wildlife Refuge, determining the powers of law enforcement in investigating terrorism, and regulating stem cell research are all examples of powers not enumerated in the Constitution but that Congress exercises because of the broad scope of authority provided by the necessary and proper clause.

In addition to the Constitution, Congress derives power from Supreme Court decisions, the media, and the people. Supreme Court decisions often uphold the constitutionality of a law, in a sense verifying Congress's ability to create policy on a given subject. The media grant Congress power by providing members with a forum in which to communicate with constituents, sway public opinion, and create a favorable climate for the passage of legislation. The people are a key source of congressional power through civic participation in the electoral and legislative processes. Citizens communicate their views and priorities to their representatives, who then can claim public support in their endeavors to enact policy.

Functions of Congress

The Constitution is far more explicit in defining the responsibilities of the national legislature than it is in describing the function of the other branches of the government.[4] In its shaping of congressional functions, the Constitution's concerns with limited government, checks and balances, the separation of powers, and the creation of a federal system are all readily apparent.

Representation Comes in Many Forms

In delineating the composition of the federal legislature and the procedures for electing its members, the Constitution shapes the congressional function of representation in several ways. Representation traditionally involves a House or Senate member's articulating and voting for the position that best represents the views of his or her constituents.[5] But sometimes a member of Congress may speak for other constituencies as well. For example, a feminist legislator might "represent" feminists nationwide,[6] just as a gay legislator might "represent" the collective interests of gays across the United States.

Often Congress's policy-making function is at odds with its representation function. A legislator may be pressured—by his or her political party or own conscience—to vote for a policy that clashes with constituents' interests or views. In representing constituents, legislators frequently follow one of two models of representative behavior.

Models of Representation   According to the **trustee model** of representation, a member of the House or the Senate is articulating and voting for the position that best reflects constituents' views. This model was espoused by British political theorist Edmund Burke (1729–1797), who served in Parliament as a representative of Bristol, England. Explaining his conception of representation, Burke emphasized to his constituents, however, that a member of Parliament "is not a member of Bristol, he is a member of Parliament."[7] Burke accordingly argued that a member of Parliament should follow his conscience when making decisions in the legislature: "Your representative owes you, not his industry only, but his judgement [sic]; and he betrays, instead of serving you, if he sacrifices it to your opinion."[8] In this trustee view, a legislator may act in opposition to the clear wishes of his or her constituents, such as in cases where an action is "for their own good" or the good of society.

> Rep. John Lewis (D-Georgia) has served in Congress since 1986. While Lewis formally represents Georgia's fifth congressional district, Lewis' leadership in the civil rights movement of 1960s has meant that many African Americans and others concerned with civil rights view Lewis as a representative of their views.

Another model of representation is the **instructed delegate model,** the idea that a legislator, as a representative of his or her constituents, should vote in keeping with the constituents' views, *even if those views contradict the legislator's personal views.* This model of representation conceives of legislators as the agents of their constituents. A legislator hewing to the instructed delegate model faces a dilemma when his or her constituency is evenly divided on an issue.

Given these two different models of representation, which one do legislators typically follow? Most analyses of representation indicate that legislators are likely to combine the approaches. Specifically, with regard to many important or high-profile issues, legislators act as instructed delegates, whereas for more mundane matters about which their constituents are less likely to be aware or to hold a strong position, they rely on the trustee model.

Pork Barrel and Earmarks Members of Congress also represent their constituencies through pork barrel politics. **Pork barrel** (also called simply *pork*) refers to legislators' appropriations of funds for special projects located within their congressional district. Because pork brings money and jobs to a particular district, reelection-seeking legislators work aggressively to earmark monies for their states or districts—to "bring home the bacon."[9] Members frequently use transportation bills as a means of creating pork barrel projects for their districts. One analysis estimates, for example, that every $1 billion spent on highway and mass transit projects creates about 47,500 jobs, and members of Congress are happy to take credit for the jobs and for highway and mass transit improvements when running for reelection.[10]

Members of Congress also use **earmarks** as a means of representing constituent interests: a designation within a spending bill that provides for a specific expenditure. A striking example of both pork barrel politics and an earmark is the infamous Bridge to Nowhere in Ketchikan, Alaska, a city with only 8,000 residents but a large tourist industry. City leaders wanted to make the land of nearby Gravina Island (currently accessible via a seven-minute ferry ride) available for development by constructing a huge bridge that would allow tourist-carrying cruise ships to pass under. Ketchikan officials had an ally in Representative Don Young (R-Alaska), chair of the House Committee on Transportation and Infrastructure, who earmarked $223 million as a federal contribution to the bridge in a federal highway and mass transit bill, the Transportation Equity Act. Steve Ellis, of the taxpayer watchdog group Taxpayers for Common Sense, called the project "an abomination."[11] A thunderous public uproar followed media coverage of the appropriation, and the earmark was removed from the budget. But Young succeeded in keeping the allocation, so the state of Alaska could still choose to spend the money on the bridge project. The issue became a lightning rod in the 2008 presidential race when critics alleged that as governor of Alaska, Republican vice presidential nominee Sarah Palin had supported the project before reversing her position.

Casework A special form of representation called **casework** involves providing representation in the form of personal aid to a constituent or group of constituents, typically by getting the government to do something the constituent wants done.

Members of Congress and their staffs commonly assist constituents in dealing with bureaucratic agencies. In doing so, they serve in the capacity of an **ombudsperson,** an elected or appointed representative who acts as a citizens' advocate by listening to their needs and investigating their complaints with respect to a particular government agency. For example, a member of Congress might intervene with the Immigration and Naturalization Service (INS) to request that a constituent's relative in a foreign country be granted a visa to travel to the United States.

According to political scientist Morris Fiorina, casework is a valuable tool for legislators. Fiorina points out that servicing constituents is relatively easy for members of Congress, because bureaucrats—who depend on Congress for their funding— typically respond quickly to the requests of legislators.[12] The loyalty derived from assisting constituents is one aspect of the incumbency advantage that makes incumbent members of Congress more likely to be elected than their challengers, who do not enjoy that source of constituent loyalty.[13]

Policy Making: A Central Responsibility

Each year Congress passes laws determining everything from incentives for the creation of alternative energy sources, to what restrictions should govern gun purchases, to what law enforcers can do when they suspect someone of being a terrorist. The Constitution invests Congress with other policy-making powers as well, including the authority to tax and spend, to declare war, to establish courts, and to regulate the armed forces. This policy-making function is the central responsibility that the Congress carries out, and nearly all of its other functions are related to its policy-making role. Congressional policy-making power also extends to the operations and priorities of governmental departments and agencies. For example, Congress has directed the State Department to select a secure domestic production facility to create ePassports, next-generation passports with an embedded microchip.

Oversight: A Check on the Executive Branch

In creating a system of checks and balances in the Constitution, the framers established the key congressional function of oversight.[14] **Oversight** is the process by which Congress "checks" the executive branch to ensure that the laws Congress passes are being administered in keeping with legislators' intentions. Congressional oversight is a check on the executive branch because the federal bureaucracy that implements laws is part of the executive branch.

In carrying out their oversight function, members of Congress use a variety of tools, some of which are listed here:

- congressional hearings, in which government officials, bureaucrats, and interest groups testify as to how a law or policy is being implemented and examine the impact of its implementation
- confirmation hearings on presidential appointees to oversee executive departments or governmental agencies

- investigations to determine whether a law or policy is being implemented the way Congress intended it to be, and inquiries into allegations of wrongdoing by government officials or bureaucrats
- budgetary appropriations that determine the level of funding of an executive department or a government agency.

These tools ensure that Congress has some say in how the executive branch administers the laws that Congress creates. Members of Congress increasingly have viewed their role of checking the executive branch as crucially important.

Agenda Setting

Congress engages continuously in **agenda setting:** determining which public policy issues the federal legislature should consider.[15] Indeed, political scientists such as Gary Cox and Matthew D. McCubbins assert that agenda setting relieves the pressure parties face in getting their members to vote with the party.[16] At the beginning of a congressional term, House and Senate leaders announce their goals for the coming session. These goals reflect the issues and positions that predominated during the electoral campaign and that congressional leaders perceive to represent the people's priorities.

Managing Societal Conflict

Congress also has a significant influence in managing the societal conflict inherent in a divided society such as the United States. Some citizens want policies benefiting rural areas, while others give higher priority to urban areas. Some want more money for programs for senior citizens; others seek funding for children's programs. With respect to abortion policy, some people are pro-life and others are pro-choice. In addition, there are divisions related to social class, race, geography, gender, sexual orientation, religion, and so on. Congress manages these conflicts by representing a wide range of views and interests.

The House and the Senate Compared

Although the House of Representatives and the Senate share numerous functions, the two chambers of Congress differ in significant ways. As President Woodrow Wilson remarked, the "House and Senate are naturally unalike."[17] Constitutionally, the two houses are conceived as unique organizations, and the framers designated their duties to match the strengths and expertise of the people who would come to hold office in each chamber. Table 11.2 highlights these major differences. For example, the Constitution empowers the House of Representatives, as the legislative body closer to the people, to initiate any bills that result in taxes; whereas it

TABLE 11.2

Differences Between the House and the Senate

House	Senate
Larger (435 members)	Smaller (100 members)
Shorter electoral cycle (two-year term)	Longer electoral cycle (six-year term)
Narrow constituency (congressional districts)	Broad constituency (states)
Less prestigious	More prestigious
Originates all revenue bills	Ratifies treaties; confirms presidential nominees
Less reliant on staff	More reliant on staff
Power vested in leaders and committee chairs	Power more evenly distributed

empowers the Senate, as the more deliberative house, to give the president advice and consent on appointments and the ratification of treaties. The differences between the House and Senate are not limited merely to their functions, however. The electoral and legislative structures also differ between the two houses.

The 435 current members of the House of Representatives each represent a legislative district determined by the reapportionment and redistricting process that occurs every ten years, as we considered earlier in this chapter. In more populated areas, these congressional districts are often homogeneous, cohesive units in which a House member's constituency is likely to have fairly unified positions on many issues.[18] Senators, however, are elected by the population of an entire state, and although the political culture in some states is somewhat cohesive (for example, Massachusetts voters are more liberal on most issues than are Kansas voters), in many states, there are notable differences in constituents' views, ideology, and policy priorities. For instance, Senators Barbara Boxer and Dianne Feinstein both represent the entire state of California, and both are Democrats. Although California is generally viewed as having a liberal political culture, Boxer and Feinstein must represent the interests of both liberal voters in the western coastal areas of the state and more conservative voters inland to the east. At times, moreover, the interests of a senator's constituents divide over a given issue: in California, for example, environmental activists and fishers have argued against programs that divert water from lakes and streams so that it can be used for irrigation on commercial farms, while affluent agribusinesses advocate water diversion. A U.S. senator must balance such conflicting positions when making policy decisions.

The differing length of representatives' and senators' terms of service affects how members of each chamber of Congress relate to their constituents. Given their short two-year terms, members of the House of Representatives naturally are reluctant to defy the will of the electorate on a given issue because of the likelihood that their opposition will be used against them during their reelection campaign. As the framers structured it, the House remains "the people's house," the chamber in which civically engaged individuals can effectively have their interests represented. And although U.S. senators naturally also want to please their constituents, they recognize that voting against their constituents' will on a particular issue might be less significant than such an action would be for a House member, especially if the issue arises early in their term and is not important enough for people to hold against them six years down the road.

The size of the chambers and length of terms also affect the relative prestige of each chamber. In general, the smaller Senate is considered more prestigious than the House of Representatives, although some individual House members may enjoy more prestige than some senators.

Although the House and Senate differ in their constitutionally determined duties, both must pass any piece of legislation before it can become law. But the way in which legislation is considered and voted upon differs in each house of Congress.

The larger size of the House of Representatives, with its 435 members, necessitates a more formal legislative structure in order to prevent unruliness. The House, for example, generally has more, and more formal, rules guiding debate than the Senate. Despite the differences between the two chambers, the legislative process is remarkably similar in both.

The Legislative Process

Article I, Section 1, of the Constitution states, "All Legislative Powers herein granted shall be vested in a Congress of the United States, which shall consist of a Senate and House of Representatives." A **bill** is a proposed piece of legislation. As shown in Figure 11.1, every bill must be approved by *both houses* (the House and the Senate) *in identical form.* In general, bills must pass through five steps in order to become law:

1. **Introduction.** A member of the House of Representatives or the Senate formally proposes the bill.

2. **Committee review.** Subgroups within the House and Senate, composed of legislators who have expertise in the bill's subject matter, review the bill.

3. **House and Senate approval.** If the bill makes it out of committee, a majority of members in both the House and Senate must approve it.

4. **Conference committee reconciliation.** The conference committee reconciles the bill when different versions have passed in the House and the Senate.

5. **Presidential approval.** If the president signs the bill, it becomes law. But even after this arduous process, a presidential veto will kill the bill unless the veto is overridden.

The Legislative Process

Concept for legislative consideration

- Bill introduced in House
- Bill introduced in Senate

Bill assigned to committee, then usually referred to subcommittee

House	Senate
Subcommittee	Subcommittee
Committee	Committee
Rules committee schedules debate	Senate leadership schedules debate
Floor action	Floor action
House bill	Senate bill

Differences?
- Yes → Conference committee → Conference bill → Floor action
- No →

Presidential approval?
- Yes → Bill becomes law
- No → Veto

Override veto?
- Yes → Bill becomes law
- No → Start legislative process again

POLITICAL INQUIRY

FIGURE 11.1 What do you notice about the initial stages of the legislative process whereby a bill becomes a law? How do the Senate and the House resolve differences in versions of a bill passed in each chamber? What outcomes are possible once a bill goes to the president for approval?

Introducing a Bill

Bills are introduced differently in each chamber of Congress. In the House of Representatives, a member of a legislator's staff drafts the proposed legislation, and the House member puts the bill into the **hopper,** a wooden box that sits on a desk at the front of the House chamber. Upon introduction, a bill is referred to as "H.R.," meaning House of Representatives, followed by a number that indicates the order in which it was introduced in a given legislative session—for example, "H.R. 207."

In the Senate, the process is less formal. Here, senators can announce proposed legislation to colleagues in a speech on the Senate floor (see "Analyzing the Sources"). Alternatively, a senator can submit a written draft of the proposed legislation to an official known as the Senate clerk, or sometimes a senator will propose legislation simply by offering it as an amendment to an already pending piece of legislation. Once a bill is introduced in the Senate, it is referred to as "S.," or "Senate," followed by its number reflecting the order in which it was introduced in a given legislative session—for example, "S. 711."

Before 1995, a bill introduced in the House of Representatives could be subject to **joint referral,** the practice of referring the bill simultaneously to two different House committees for consideration. But the 104th Congress abolished joint committee referrals. Today bills introduced in the House are referred to one committee, called the **lead committee.** Occasionally, when the substance of a bill warrants additional referrals to other committees that also have jurisdiction over the subject of the bill, the bill might be subsequently referred to a second committee.[19] In the Senate, bills typically are referred to only one committee.

The Bill in Committee

After introduction by a member of the House or Senate, a bill is read into the *Congressional Record,* a formal record of all actions taken by Congress. Because of the large number of bills introduced, both chambers rely on an extensive committee structure that facilitates the consideration of so high a volume of bills.[20] Most bills that are introduced "die" in committee. That is, a committee does not consider the bill (sometimes because the committee does not have the time in a legislative session to take up the measure) or declines to forward the bill to the full chamber.

Each congressional committee and subcommittee is composed of a majority of members of the majority party in that chamber. For example, if 218 or more members (a majority in the House) elected to the House of Representatives are Republicans, then every committee and subcommittee in the House has a majority of Republicans. The parties in each chamber decide members' committee and subcommittee assignments.

Though the selection of committee chairs varies between chambers and parties, committee chairs are often chosen using the **seniority system,** by which the member with the longest continuous tenure on a standing committee receives preference when the committee chooses its chair. The committee chairs run committee meetings and control the flow of work in each committee. Although the seniority system is an institution in Congress, it is an informal system, and seniority does not always determine who will be the committee chair.[21] Chairs are chosen by a secret ballot, and in recent years, junior members sometimes have won out over senior committee members.

Standing committees are permanent committees with a defined legislative jurisdiction. The House has twenty-four standing committees, and the Senate twenty. The House Committee on Homeland Security and the Senate Armed Services Committee are examples of standing committees.

Select committees are specially created to consider a specific policy issue or to address a particular concern. Select committees have focused on such issues as homeland security and terrorism, aging, and transportation.

Joint committees are bicameral committees composed of members of both chambers of Congress. Sometimes these committees offer administrative or managerial guidance of various kinds. For example, one joint committee oversees the presidential inauguration, and another supervises the administration of the Library of Congress.

In addition to the congressional committees, the House has more than ninety subcommittees, and the Senate sixty-eight. **Subcommittees** typically handle specific areas of the committees' jurisdiction. For example, the Committee on Homeland Security is a standing committee in the House. Within the committee, there are six subcommittees, each of which handles bills relevant to its specified jurisdiction.

When a committee or subcommittee favors a measure, it usually takes four actions:

1. **Agency review.** During **agency review,** the committee or subcommittee asks the executive agencies that would administer the law for written comments on the measure.

2. **Hearings.** Next the committee or subcommittee holds **hearings** to gather information and views from experts, including interest groups, concerned citizens, and sometimes celebrity spokespersons.

3. **Markup.** During **markup,** the committee "marks up" the bill with suggested language changes and amendments. The committee does not actually alter the bill; rather, members recommend changes to the full chamber. In a typical bill markup, the committee may eliminate a component of the proposal or amend the proposal in some way.

4. **Report.** After agreeing to the wording of the bill, the committee issues a **report** to the full chamber, explaining the bill and its intent. The bill may then be considered by the full chamber.

In the House of Representatives, a special measure known as a **discharge petition** is used to extract a bill from a committee in order to have it considered by the entire House. A discharge petition requires the signature of a majority (218) of the members of the House.

Navigating Congress

As shown in the accompanying map, a large part of Congress's work takes place in the office buildings surrounding the Capitol Rotunda that are considered part of "Capitol Hill." Members of the House of Representatives are typically assigned an office in one of three buildings on the south side of the Capitol Rotunda: the Cannon Office Building, the Longworth Office Building, and the Rayburn Office Building. Senators work out of an office in one of the three office buildings located on the north side of the rotunda: the Russell Office Building, the Dirksen Office Building, and the Hart Office Building.

Many of the buildings boast beautiful architecture and amenities such as gymnasiums, post offices, kitchens, and recording studios. In the Rayburn Office Building, members can travel to the Capitol via a subway tunnel with two cars, and pedestrian tunnels join it to the Longworth Building. A double-track subway system connects Dirksen, Russell, and the Capitol, and tunnels beneath the Cannon and Russell buildings connect to the Capitol.

Although political scientists seldom analyze office space and layout, the proximity of members of Congress to their office neighbors, along with the common facilities they share, surely has an impact on the legislative process. In the Capitol Hill office buildings, senators and representatives of diverse backgrounds become familiar with colleagues whom they see regularly in the hallways, elevators, gyms, kitchens, and subway trains between buildings.

Evaluating the Evidence

1. You also have a network of relationships based on your daily activities. What people do you see regularly because of your work or school schedule? What unlikely relationships have you formed because of your daily activities?

2. In what ways might the time spent in their Capitol Hill offices and common facilities breed familiarity among federal legislators? What different kinds and backgrounds of people might this daily contact bring together?

3. How might legislators' interactions in their office buildings affect their political decision making?

Debate on the House and Senate Floor

Table 11.3 shows some key differences in the legislative process between the House and Senate. For example, if a House bill is "discharged," or makes it out of committee, it then goes to the **Rules Committee,** one of the most important committees in the House, which decides on the length of debate and the scope of amendments that will be allowed on a bill. The Rules Committee sets the structure for the debate that ensues in the full House. For important bills, the Rules Committee tends to

Legend

HOB: House Office Building
LOC: Library of Congress Building
SOB: Senate Office Building
USBG: United States Botanic Garden

Union Station Metro Station

Marshall Federal Judiciary Building

Russell SOB

Dirksen SOB

Hart SOB

Constitution Ave.

U.S. Supreme Court

U.S. Capitol

USBG Conservatory

Jefferson LOC

Adams LOC

Rayburn HOB

Independence Ave.

Cannon HOB

Madison LOC

Bartholdi Park

Ford HOB

Longworth HOB

Capitol South Metro Station

First St., SE

Federal Center SW Metro Station

0   0.25 mile

0   0.25 kilometer

Source: www.aol.gov/cc/cc-map.cfm

set strict limits on the types of amendments that can be attached to a bill. In general, the Rules Committee also establishes limits to floor debate in the House.

The Senate does not have a committee to do the work of the Rules Committee, but the Senate's small size allows members to agree to the terms of debate through **unanimous consent** agreements. Unanimous consent must be just that: every senator needs to agree to the terms of debate (including time limits on debate), and if even one senator objects, unanimous consent does not take effect. Senators do

TABLE 11.3

Differences in the Legislative Process in the House and Senate

House	Senate
Bill introduced by member placing bill in hopper	Bill introduced by member
Relies on Rules Committee to schedule debate on House floor and to establish rules for amendments	Relies on unanimous consent agreements to determine rules for debate and amendments
Has a rule barring nongermane amendments	No rule banning nongermane amendments
Does not allow filibusters	Allows filibusters
Discharge petition can be used to extract a bill from a committee	No discharge petitions allowed

not look favorably on objections to unanimous consent, and so such objections are rare. Objecting to unanimous consent agreements can potentially undermine a senator's ability to get legislation passed by provoking the ire of other senators.

If the Senate does not reach unanimous consent, the possibility of a **filibuster** arises—a procedural move that attempts to halt passage of the bill.[22] Sometimes the mere threat of a filibuster is enough to compel a bill's supporters to alter a bill's content. During a filibuster, a senator can speak for an unlimited time on the Senate floor. Filibustering senators do not need to restrict themselves to speaking only on the subject of the bill—they just need to keep talking. Some senators have read the Bible, cookbooks, and even the Nynex Yellow Pages into the *Congressional Record.* Former Republican South Carolina senator Strom Thurmond holds the Senate record for the longest filibuster. In an attempt to block passage of the Civil Rights Act of 1957, Thurmond filibustered for twenty-four hours and eighteen minutes. A filibuster can end by a vote of **cloture,** in which a supermajority of sixty senators agrees to invoke cloture and end debate. Cloture is initiated if sixteen senators sign a cloture petition.

After a bill is debated by the full chamber, the members vote on it. Before a bill can become law, identical versions of the bill must pass in both the House and the Senate. If only one chamber passes a bill during a congressional term, the bill dies. If both the House and Senate pass bills on the same topic, but with differences between the bills, the bills are then sent to a **conference committee,** a bicameral, bipartisan committee composed of legislators whose job is to reconcile the two versions of the bill. Typically, the legislators appointed to the conference committee will be members of the standing committees that considered the bill in their chambers. After the committee develops a compromise version of the bill, the bill then goes back to both chambers for another vote. If the bill does not pass in both chambers during a congressional term, the bill is dead, although it can be reintroduced in the next session. If both chambers approve the bill, it then goes to the president for signature or veto.

Presidential Action

When both the House and Senate manage to pass a bill in identical form, it proceeds to the president, who may take one of three actions. First, the president may sign it, in which case the bill becomes a law. Second, the president may choose to do nothing. If the president does nothing and Congress is in session, the bill becomes law after ten days without the president's signature. A president may take this route if he or she does not support the bill but knows that Congress would override a veto. If, however, Congress has adjourned (that is, the bill was passed at the end of a legislative session), the president may exercise a pocket veto. A **pocket veto** occurs when Congress has adjourned and the president waits ten days without signing the bill; the president effectively "puts the bill in his pocket," and the bill dies. Finally, a president may exercise the executive power of a *veto:* rejecting the bill and returning it to Congress with a message explaining why the bill should not become law. Congress can override the veto by a two-thirds vote in both houses, in which case the bill becomes law. But overriding a presidential veto is a difficult and rare achievement.

Congressional Leadership

The House and the Senate alike choose the majority and minority leaders for their adept negotiating skills, their finely honed ability to guide compromise, and their skills of persuasion. A majority leader nurtures compromise in the legislative process by knowing the members' positions on legislation well enough to recognize which issues are negotiable and which are deal-breakers; by engineering trade-offs between players; and by convincing committee chairs that a negotiated compromise is the best outcome they can expect.

In earlier eras, forceful leaders rose to the position of majority leader in both houses and strongly influenced congressional priorities and legislation.[23] But as political parties have come to play a less important role in the election of members of the House and Senate, allegiance to party leaders in these institutions has dwindled.[24] The era has long passed in which individuals could essentially control what Congress did through their assertive personalities.[25] Today's congressional power brokers face members whose loyalty to the party and the leadership is tempered by the need to please constituencies that themselves are less loyal to the parties than in bygone times.[26] Nonetheless, despite the evolution in the role of congressional leader, partisanship remains a strong aspect of congressional politics, particularly since 1994. Table 11.4 shows the leaders of the 111th Congress (2009–2011).

Leadership in the House of Representatives

Although Article I, Section 2, of the Constitution states, "The House of Representatives shall choose their Speaker and other Officers," and all members of the House vote for the Speaker, it is really the members of the majority party who select their **Speaker of the House.** Second in the line of presidential succession (after the vice president), the Speaker serves as the presiding officer and manager of the House. In this capacity, the Speaker chairs floor debates, makes majority party committee

TABLE 11.4

The Leaders of the 111th Congress (2009–2011)

House of Representatives

Speaker of the House	Nancy Pelosi (D-California)
House majority leader	Steny Hoyer (D-Maryland)
House majority whip	James E. Clyburn (D-South Carolina)
House minority leader	John Boehner (R-Ohio)
House minority whip	Eric Cantor (R-Virginia)

U.S. Senate

Senate majority leader	Harry Reid (D-Nevada)
Senate majority whip	Dick Durbin (D-Illinois)
Senate majority leader	Mitch McConnell (R-Kentucky)
Senate minority whip	Jon Kyl (R-Arizona)

assignments, assigns members to the powerful Rules Committee, negotiates with members of the minority party and the White House, and guides legislation through the House.[27] But the Speaker is also the leader of his or her party in the House, and a key duty associated with this role is helping party members get reelected. Finally, the Speaker is him- or herself an elected member of the House.

The House leadership—which, in addition to the Speaker, includes the majority leader, the minority leader, and the party whips—is chosen at the beginning of each session of Congress through a conference also known as a *caucus.* During a caucus, all of the members of the political party meet and elect their chamber leaders, approve committee assignments, and elect committee chairpersons. Party leaders also may call a party caucus during a legislative session to shore up support on an issue being voted upon or to formulate the party's position on an issue on the agenda.[28]

In 1999, the then-majority Republican Party caucus elected Representative Dennis Hastert (R-Illinois) Speaker of the House. Hastert was little known on the national scene, particularly when compared with his predecessor, Newt Gingrich (R-Georgia), whose abrasive leadership style was often highlighted in the national media. But the mild-mannered Hastert's tenure as Speaker came to an abrupt end in 2006, when Republicans failed to win a majority in the House elections. With this turn of events, many commentators faulted Hastert for being weak and ineffectual. As the Democrats swept into office that year, they also made history, electing Representative Nancy Pelosi (D-California) the first woman to serve as Speaker. Pelosi is an unabashed liberal who railed against the Bush administration, particularly its policies in Iraq, during the 2006 congressional elections. But Pelosi recognized early that the Speaker's role is one of leading not just her own political party but the entire House of Representatives, with its wide span of views and interests: "You have to govern from the center. We are in a completely different place now. We are setting our legislative agenda."[29]

During Pelosi's tenure in the House, she has earned a reputation for the ability to form a coalition within her party—nurturing the loyalty of junior members; unifying moderate, liberal, and conservative Democrats; and building coalitions composed of representatives from different districts, generations, ethnicities, and sexes. These skills are essential attributes for the Speaker of the House.

The Speaker relies on the **House majority leader** to help develop and implement the majority party's legislative strategy, work with the minority party leadership, and encourage unity among majority party legislators. In this last task, the Speaker and the House majority leader are assisted by the **majority whip,** who acts as a go-between with the leadership and the party members in the House. The term *whip* comes from the English hunting term *whipper-in,* a hunter whose job is to keep the foxhounds in the pack and to prevent them from straying during a fox hunt. Similarly, the job of the party whip is to keep party members together, encouraging them to vote with the party on issues and preventing them from straying off into their own positions. The minority party in the House also elects leaders, the **House minority leader** and the **minority whip,** whose jobs mirror those of their majority party colleagues but without the power that comes from holding a majority in the House.

Leadership in the Senate

In the Senate, the vice president of the United States serves as the president of that body, according to the Constitution. But in actual practice, vice presidents preside over the Senate only rarely. Vice presidents, however, have one power in the Senate that, although rarely exercised, is enormously important. If a vote in the upper house of Congress is tied, the vice president breaks the tie.

The majority party in the Senate elects a Senate leader called the **president pro tempore.** Meaning "president for the time," this position is often referred to as "president pro tem." The job of the president pro tem is to chair the Senate in the vice president's absence. Historically, this position has been honorary in nature, with the majority party senator who has the longest record of continuous Senate service being elected to the office. Despite the honorary nature of the position, the Senate's president pro tem is third in the line of presidential succession (following the vice president and the Speaker of the House). Robert Byrd (D-West Virginia), who has served in the Senate since 1959, is the current president pro tem.

The real power in the U.S. Senate is held and wielded by the **Senate majority leader,** whose job is to manage the legislative process so that favored bills are passed; to schedule debate on legislation in consultation with his or her counterpart in the minority party, the **Senate minority leader;** and to act as the spokesperson for the majority party in the Senate. The majority and the minority leaders both play crucial roles in ushering bills through the Senate, and the majority leader facilitates the numerous negotiations that arise when senators bargain over the content of a given piece of proposed legislation.[30]

Senate majority leader Harry Reid (D-Nevada) was elected after the Democrats won a majority of seats in the 2006 Senate elections. Reid is a soft-spoken politician who was elected partly because of his talent at building consensus, a necessary skill given his desire to tackle some highly partisan and controversial issues when he assumed his leadership role, including ethics reform, funding for stem cell research, and an increase in the federal minimum wage.

Decision Making in Congress: The Legislative Context

When deciding whether to "tow the party line" on a legislative vote, members of Congress do not operate independently and in isolation. Throughout the legislative process, they face a variety of external pressures that influence their views. Some of these influences are subtle; others are more pronounced. Moreover, the impact of the influence varies according to the timing and type of legislation being considered. For example, political scientist Barry C. Burden has noted that the personal experiences of legislators sometimes have a bearing on their policy stances on issues.[31] Among the most important influences on members of Congress with respect to the legislative process are political parties, members' colleagues and staff, interest groups, the president, and of course their constituents—the people who elected them to serve as their representatives in our system of republican government.

Political Parties and Partisanship in Decision Making

Figure 11.2 shows the party breakdown in Congress since 1985. The data show that 1994 was a pivotal year, ending Democratic control in the House and Senate. For nearly all of the next twelve years, Republicans retained control over both the House and the Senate. (Republicans lost their narrow majority in the Senate in 2001 when one Republican senator switched parties, but they regained control in the 2002 elections.) But in 2006, the balance of power shifted back to the Democrats, who won majorities in both houses. That year, Democratic candidates benefited from President George W. Bush's unpopularity and public weariness with the war in Iraq. As shown in Figure 11.3 on page 422, in 2008, Democrats increased their majorities in both houses, again benefitting from George W. Bush's unpopularity and—for some Democratic congressional candidates—riding in on Barack Obama's coattails. While significantly increasing their numbers in both houses, the Democrats formally fell short of the sixty members necessary for a filibuster-proof majority in the Senate, forcing them to rely on the votes of the two independents elected to the Senate to avoid filibusters.

The partisan breakdown of Congress is important because most major legislative votes cast are "party votes," meaning that most members of one political party vote one way, while most members of the other party vote the other way. In some cases, this divide is due to the differing ideologies the parties represent. In other instances, party voting is simply pure partisanship: Democrats vote against something because Republicans vote for it, and vice versa.

Partisan voting increased after the Watergate scandal in the 1970s and again after the 1994 congressional elections, in which Republicans took control of Congress.

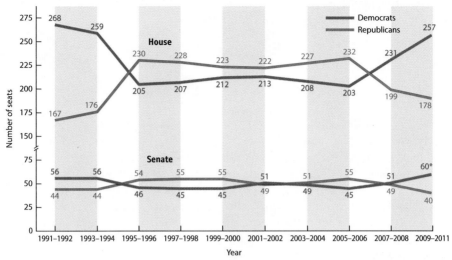

Party Breakdowns in the House and Senate, 1991–2011

* Two Independent members of the Senate typically vote Democratic.

POLITICAL INQUIRY

FIGURE 11.2 ■ **What trends does this graph show with respect to party representation in the House of Representatives since 1991? What trends does it indicate for the Senate? Generally, do the patterns for the House resemble those for the Senate?**

Partisanship tends to be particularly acrimonious immediately before congressional and presidential elections. It occurs more often when members are voting on domestic policy issues, such as environmental or economic regulatory policy and entitlement programs, that tend to crystallize ideological differences between the parties. But often partisan votes are politically motivated, plain and simple. One of the most partisan votes on record in Congress was the 1998 vote on whether President Bill Clinton should be impeached. In that vote, 98 percent of all members of Congress voted the party line—Republicans for impeachment, Democrats against.

Scholars believe that changes in how congressional district maps are drawn partly explains increased partisan voting in the House of Representatives. In earlier times, redistricting occurred through a simple redrawing of the lines of a congressional district to accommodate population changes. But today, with the widespread use of computer-driven mapmaking technology, congressional seats can be configured to ensure a "safe seat"—one in which the party identification of the majority of a district's voters makes it likely that a candidate from a given party will win election. Sometimes, for example, more than 60 percent of a district's population identifies with one political party. The advent of safe seats means that a House member generally can be partisan with immunity because his or her constituency so often agrees with the representative's partisan stance. In contrast, when congressional districts were more competitive, a

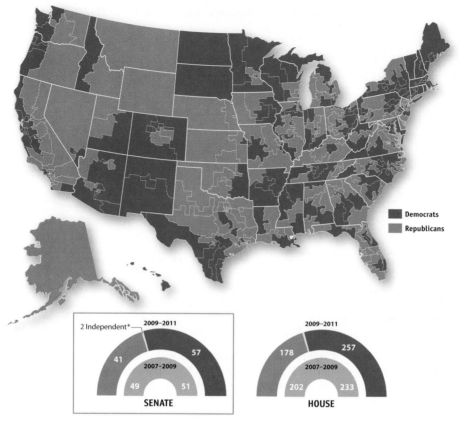

* Senators Joseph Lieberman (CT) and Bernie Sanders (VT) caucus with the Democrats

FIGURE 11.3 ■ Which party has a majority of seats in the U.S. House of Representatives? In the U.S. Senate? Which party gained seats in the 2008 election? Why do you think this was the case? In your view, how will the party breakdown in Congress likely change in the 2010 congressional elections?

House member typically would have to temper partisan impulses to placate the sizable proportion of his or her constituency that identified with the opposing party. Today that is no longer the case, and it appears that Republicans in the House of Representatives have become more conservative and their Democratic counterparts have become increasingly liberal. Consequently, House members are less likely to compromise or to be moderate in their positions in negotiating issues with the opposition.

Many scholars assert that a similar bifurcation of political ideology has not occurred in the Senate. They claim that because state populations as a whole tend to be more ideologically diverse and less homogeneous than House districts, U.S. senators often must temper their views to reflect the wider range of their constituents' perspectives. Thus senators tend to be more willing to compromise and to take a more moderate

Partisanship in Congress

THEN (1980s)	NOW (2010)
Congress was divided; Democrats controlled the House of Representatives, and Republicans controlled the Senate.	Democrats control both houses of Congress.
Although incumbents enjoyed a considerable advantage, many congressional districts were a mix of constituents of both major parties.	Fewer congressional districts are competitive. Many districts are more homogeneous because district boundaries can be drawn with sophisticated computer programs.
Partisan voting was evident, but legislators were often forced to base their positions on constituent preferences in addition to their own party loyalty.	With the advent of less competitive districts, legislators are more partisan than their predecessors.

WHAT'S NEXT?

> Has the outcome of the 2008 elections increased or decreased party tensions, in your view? Why?

> In recent years, partisanship has increased when there has been a president of one party and a Congress controlled by another. Does such a scenario exist today? What implications does that have for the future of partisanship in Congress for the next several years?

> Increases in technological sophistication could make redistricting an even more exact science. What impact would this have on partisanship in Congress?

stance in negotiating with the opposing party than their House counterparts. Nonetheless, on some issues, other scholars note that the Senate is increasingly dividing along strongly partisan lines.[32] In the 2006 Senate confirmation hearings for Supreme Court nominee Samuel Alito, Democrats opposed Alito's nomination, fearing that the conservative judge would provide the swing vote to overturn the landmark Supreme Court ruling *Roe v. Wade*, which legalized abortion in the United States. In the Senate's vote to confirm Alito, forty out of forty-four Democratic senators voted against Alito's confirmation, whereas all but one of the fifty-four Republicans (Rhode Island senator Lincoln Chafee) voted for Alito's confirmation. (For a view of an area where votes have tended to be bipartisan—war funding—see "Then, Now, Next" on page 425.)

Colleagues and Staff: Trading Votes and Information

Congressional colleagues provide cues for members of the House and Senate in their decision making over whether to vote for a pending piece of legislation. Members may seek the opinions of like-minded colleagues in determining how to vote on a proposed bill. In addition, legislators may consult with peers who are policy experts, such as Senators Chris Dodd (D-Connecticut) and Jon Kyl (R-Arizona), both of whom are experts on health care policy.

Members of Congress also engage in **logrolling,** the practice of trading votes between members. Logrolling is a reciprocal tactic by which a member agrees to vote on one piece of legislation in exchange for a colleague's vote on another.

In addition, House and Senate members rely on their staffs to inform their decision making on legislation.[33] Staff members frequently have policy expertise that can guide a legislator's decision on an upcoming vote. They also figure in the legislative voting process by communicating with legislators about the desires of constituents and interest groups with respect to a pending piece of legislation.

Interest Groups: Influence Through Organization

In various ways, interest groups also influence congressional elections. They can affect electoral outcomes, for example, through an endorsement process by which a group notifies its members that it backs a certain candidate in the hope that members get on the bandwagon and express their support at the polls. In addition, through their political action committees, interest groups make financial contributions to congressional campaigns. And interest groups whose memberships are mobilized to support or oppose a candidate often provide grassroots activists to political campaigns.[34]

As we considered in Chapter 7, interest groups also shape the legislative process. They make their mark by influencing congressional campaigns, by providing information to members of Congress as they try to decide whether to vote for a particular piece of legislation, and by lobbying members of Congress to support or oppose legislation.[35]

The President's Effect on Decision Making

As we have seen, the president determines whether to sign or to veto legislation. But often, before a bill reaches the signing stage, the president's position on it carries enough influence to sway members of Congress, particularly members of his political party, to vote for or against the proposed legislation.

The president can be a lightning rod with respect to some legislative matters. In 2006, President George W. Bush's support for proposed legislation awarding a contract to manage U.S. ports to Dubai (a nation on the Persian Gulf) generated enormous

Will Congress Continue to Fund War during Obama's Administration?

THEN: During the final two years of the Bush administration, the Democrat-controlled Congress allocated staggering sums to fund the wars in Iraq and Afghanistan, increasing military spending by more than 30 percent. Continuing the practice set by previous Republican congresses, they funded wars through emergency war-spending measures and didn't factor them into the federal budget. Even after public opinion had largely turned against the wars, Congress continued to allocate funds: in May 2007, it allocated $120 billion*; in September 2007, $9 billion**; and in June 2008, $162 billion.[†]

NOW: Since President Obama's election, the Democrat-controlled Congress has again allocated staggering sums to fund the wars in Iraq and Afghanistan, voting for $84.9 billion in June 2009[††] to fund the war through September 30, 2009, through emergency war-spending measures. While President Obama has said that this will be the last emergency request he will make to Congress, continued funding of the wars in Iraq and Afghanistan as part of the federal budget is likely.

WHAT'S NEXT?

■ What obstacles could impede an attempt by Congress to halt funding of the wars in Iraq and Afghanistan in the future?

■ Why might President Obama continue to advocate for similarly high levels of funding for these wars in Congress? Why might he begin to decrease funding levels?

(continued)

■ What impact might the decision to continue funding have on the public's perception of the Democratic Congress in the future?

*http://www.washingtonpost.com/wp-dyn/content/article/2008/06/18/AR2008061802556.html?nav=rss_politics/congress.
**http://www.reuters.com/article/politicsNews/idUSN1225097720070912.
†http://www.washingtonpost.com/wp-dyn/content/article/2008/06/18/AR2008061802556.html?nav=rss_politics/congress.
††http://appropriations.senate.gov/News/2009_06_12_Text_of_2009_Supplemental_Conference_Report.pdf?CFID=1596735&CFTOKEN=91884035.

congressional opposition. The bill's opponents included not only Democrats but also some members of Bush's own political party, who saw the bill as an opportunity to distance themselves from an unpopular president in a congressional election year.

Constituents: The Last Word

Of all the players with a voice in the legislative process, congressional constituents—the people whom the members of Congress represent—wield perhaps the strongest, if indirect, influence with respect to congressional decision making. Most members of Congress want to be reelected, and representing constituents' views (and being able to convince voters that their views are represented well) is a major avenue to reelection. Thus, constituents influence the legislative process by ensuring that their representatives in Congress work hard to represent their perspectives and policy interests, whether those concerns are over environmental pollution, crime, or the soaring cost of higher education.

In fact, some research shows that the public's "potential preferences" can motivate legislators to espouse a policy position likely to be embraced by constituents.[36] But other research shows that most voters are not especially vigilant when it comes to monitoring their elected officials in Congress. In fact, only a very small percentage of voters, sometimes called the **attentive public,** pay careful attention to the public policies being debated by Congress and to the votes cast by their representatives and senators. But the fact that the attentive public is a relatively small minority does not mean that votes taken in Congress are insignificant as far as constituents' opinions go. Indeed, if a member of Congress should disregard constituents' views in voting on a major issue, it is quite likely that an opposing candidate or political party will bring this misstep to the public's attention during the individual's next congressional campaign.

The People and Their Elected Representatives

Although members of Congress may make it a priority to represent the viewpoints and interests of their constituents, demographically speaking, they do not represent the American public at large. As Table 11.5 shows, Congress, especially the Senate, is older, whiter, more educated, wealthier, and more likely to be male than the population as a whole. That said, Congress is not designed to be a perfect sampling of American demographics.[37] It is logical that the leaders of government would

Demographic Characteristics of the 111th Congress Compared to the U.S. Population

	House	Senate	U.S. Population
Average Age	57 years	63 years	38 years
Party			
Democrat	59%	57%	32%
Republican	41	41	29
Independent/unaffiliated	0	2	37
Sex			
Male	83	83	49
Female	17	17	51
Race			
White	85	95	80
Black	9	1	13
Hispanic (any race)	6	3	15
Asian/Pacific Islander	2	2	4
Native American	0.22	0	1
Education			
Bachelor's degree	91	98	25
Master's degree	19	19	7
Law degree	41	58	1
PhD	5	0	1
MD	3	4	2
Religion*			
Protestant	58	57	44
Roman Catholic	29	24	25
Jewish	6	11	1.5
Muslim**	0.45	0	0.5
Buddhist**	0.45	0	0.5
Wealth*			
Net assets over $1 million (household)	16	33	7

*Data for 109th Congress.
**Muslim, Buddhist counts are for 111th Congress.
Sources: Mildred L. Amer, *Membership in the 111th Congress: A Profile* (Washington, DC: Congressional Research Service); U.S. Census Bureau, *The Statistical Abstract of the United States, 2004–05* (Washington, DC: 2004).

more closely resemble individuals who have achieved leadership positions in other realms, such as the corporate world and academia.

Yet importantly, Congress is more diverse today than at any other point in history. Figure 11.4 shows that no women have ever been elected to Congress from three states (Iowa, Mississippi, and Vermont), and fourteen other states have sent women to Washington in the past but currently have no women serving in Congress. Three states—California, Maine, and Washington—have two women U.S. senators. Yet the proportion of women in Congress is not nearly equal to their proportion of the national population: women constitute about 17 percent of the House and the Senate but about 51 percent of the U.S. population. Today, 17 women (13 Democrats and 4 Republicans) serve in the Senate, and 73 women (56 Democrats and 17 Republicans) serve in the House of Representatives. Despite this upward trend, the United States lags behind many industrialized democracies with respect to the proportion of women serving in the national legislature.

Similarly, African Americans have historically been underrepresented in Congress. To date, only six African Americans have served in the Senate, including two—Hiram Revels and Blanche Bruce—who served during the Reconstruction era that followed the Civil War. After Bruce left the Senate in 1881, no other African American would be elected to the Senate until 1967, when Senator Edward Brooke (R-Massachusetts) was elected for one term. More recently, Senator Carol Moseley Braun (D-Illinois) was elected in 1992 and served for one term, and Barack Obama was elected from the state of Illinois in 2004. With his election to the presidency, Obama's Senate seat was vacated, and Illinois Governor Rod Blagojevich appointed Roland Burris to serve the remainder of Obama's term. Today, Burris is the only African American U.S. senator.

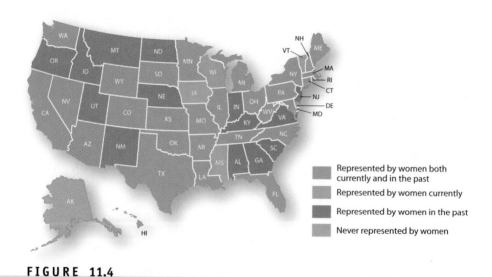

FIGURE 11.4

States Represented by Women in Congress.

Source: http://womenincongress.house.gov/data/wic-by-state.html

Figure 11.5 traces the increasing success of African Americans in getting elected to the House of Representatives. The figure shows that as in the Senate, African Americans' initial service in the House came about in the Reconstruction period. But the successes of that era were short-lived, and the numbers of African Americans in Congress would not match those of the immediate post-Reconstruction period until after the civil rights movement of the 1960s. Today, as in the case of women, more African Americans serve in Congress than at any other point in U.S. history.

Latinos' success at winning election to Congress still drastically lags behind their proportion of the population, with Latinos constituting nearly 14 percent of the population but just 5 percent (25 members) of the House of Representatives and 3 percent of the Senate. But in many states, including New Mexico, California, Texas, and Arizona, increasing numbers of Latinos are being elected to state legislatures, providing a pool of candidates who could move on to run for

FIGURE 11.5 ▓ **What explains the rise in African American representation in the house from 1871 through 1887? Why did blacks' representation fall after 1877? What pattern do you see since the late 1960s, and what political and social changes explain it?**

Congress. As women, African Americans, and ethnic minorities take up an increasing proportion of the eligibility pool—the group of people deemed qualified for office—diversity in Congress is sure to grow.

CONCLUSION

CONTINUING THE CONVERSATION

■ Congress is shaped by the framers' vision that created it; by the groups and individuals that seek to, and do, influence it; and by the broader electorate who vote for the representatives who serve in it.

■ The Constitution's framers ingeniously created a strong legislative system designed to dominate the national government. In doing so they simultaneously—and significantly—checked the power of the executive.

■ Today, Congress is more demographically diverse than ever before in history. It has also responded to modern challenges by exercising a wider scope of powers, concerning issues that were unimaginable even two decades ago.

■ For groups and individuals alike, Congress stands as a crucial resource for civic engagement, political participation, and efficacy. The digital technologies of today and tomorrow will continuously provide citizens with powerful tools for communicating with congressional policy makers and influencing policy.

STUDY NOW

Summary

1. The Origins of Congress

The Constitution's framers intended Congress to be the strongest and most important branch of the federal government, a body both representative and deliberative. The Constitution provided a flexible framework for the evolution of Congress to meet changing times.

2. Congressional Elections

One of the most important factors shaping congressional elections is incumbency, which confers numerous advantages to those already serving in elective office. Congressional elections are also shaped by the processes of reapportionment and redistricting, which occur every ten years.

3. Powers of Congress

The Constitution enumerates certain powers for Congress, including judicial, economic, national security, regulatory, and administrative powers. Other powers of the federal legislature have evolved through national legislators' interpretation of the Constitution's necessary and proper clause, which has been a mechanism for the expansion of congressional authority.

4. Functions of Congress

The primary functions of Congress are public policy making, popular representation, oversight of the executive branch to ensure the proper administration of laws, civic education, and management of societal conflict.

5. The House and the Senate Compared

Members of the House of Representatives and the Senate serve different constituencies for different terms of office. House members are elected for a two-year term from a congressional district, and senators serve for a six-year term and represent an entire state.

6. The Legislative Process

A bill, the precursor to a law, can be introduced by a member of the House or the Senate. Once proposed, the bill is then referred to a committee, where it is debated, reviewed, and amended. If it passes out of committee, it is debated by the full chamber; if it passes in both the House and Senate, the president may sign the bill, veto it, or take no action.

7. Congressional Leadership

House leadership consists of the Speaker of the House of Representatives and the House majority and minority leaders, plus the majority and minority whips. In practice the Senate majority leader wields the power in the upper chamber of the national legislature.

8. Decision Making in Congress: The Legislative Context

Political parties, congressional colleagues, interest groups, the president, and constituent viewpoints all play roles in influencing members of Congress.

9. The People and Their Elected Representatives

Although Congress is not demographically representative of the United States, it is more demographically diverse than the leadership structure of other institutions, and is becoming increasingly diverse, with higher proportions of women, African Americans, and Latinos serving today than ever before.

For Critical Thinking and Discussion

1. If you were serving in Congress, would you tend to follow the instructed delegate model of representation or the trustee model? Why? What might be the likely outcome of your choice?

2. How does the legislative process differ in the House and Senate? In which chamber is the process more streamlined? More deliberative? Why?

3. What do you and the people you know think about the work and contributions of Congress? Would you give Congress high or low approval ratings as an institution,

or something in between? Who is your own congressional representative, and what rating would you give her or him? Why?

4. Log on to the Library of Congress Web site (http://thomas.loc.gov/), and read about issues currently on the floor of the House of Representatives. Can you see the impact of any of the external influences mentioned in this chapter on the legislative process? Describe these influences and discuss how they are shaping the process.

5. Why do you think so few women and racial and ethnic minorities have been elected to Congress? Why is this situation changing? What do you imagine that Congress will look like, demographically speaking, in the year 2050?

Key Terms

agency review 413
agenda setting 408
attentive public 426
bill 410
casework 406
cloture 416
conference committee 416
discharge petition 413
earmark 406
filibuster 416
gerrymandering 401
hearings 413
hopper 412
House majority leader 419
House minority leader 419

incumbency 400
instructed delegate
   model 406
joint committee 413
joint referral 412
lead committee 412
logrolling 424
majority whip 419
majority-minority
   district 402
markup 413
minority whip 419
ombudsperson 407
oversight 407
pocket veto 417

pork barrel 406
president pro tempore 419
reapportionment 401
redistricting 401
report 413
Rules Committee 414
select committee 413
Senate majority leader 419
Senate minority leader 419
seniority system 412
Speaker of the House 417
standing committee 413
subcommittee 413
trustee model 405
unanimous consent 415

Internet Resources

A More Perfect Union **Web site**

www.mhhe.com/harrisonample Consult the book's Web site for study guides, interactive activities, simulations, and current hot-links to additional information on Congress.

C-Span

www.c-span.org The cable television network C-Span provides a plethora of information on Congress, including Internet video, audio, and podcast programs of congressional hearings and committee meetings; C-Span video series; and a wide variety of public affairs information.

Library of Congress

http://thomas.loc.gov (note the absence of www) Thomas (named for Thomas Jefferson) is the Web site for the Library of Congress, the most important clearinghouse for information about Congress, legislation, hearings, votes, and other federal matters.

Roll Call

www.rollcall.com This Web site for *Roll Call*, the "newspaper of Capitol Hill since 1955," offers an insider's look at the world of Capitol Hill, including issue analysis, politics, and opinions.

U.S. Senate and U.S. House of Representatives
www.senate.gov and **www.house.gov** These Web sites for the Senate and House provide information about members of Congress, votes, pending legislation, committees, and session schedules, plus information about the Capitol building and information for visitors.

Recommended Readings

Ahuja, Sunil and Robert Dewhirst (eds.). *The Roads to Congress.* Belmont, CA: Wadsworth, 2006. A reader examining several key congressional races, including safe seats, open seats, and contested seats in the House and Senate.

Dodd, Lawrence C., and Bruce J. Oppenheimer. *Congress Reconsidered,* 8th ed. Washington, DC: CQ Press, 2004. The most recent edition of a classic series providing comprehensive coverage of the evolution of the American Congress.

Fenno, Richard F., Jr. *Home Style: House Members in Their Districts.* New York: Longman, 2002. An examination of members of Congress at home in their districts and how constituent interaction affects congressional decision making.

Loomis, Burdett, and Wendy J. Schiller. *The Contemporary Congress.* Belmont, CA: Wadsworth, 2005. A concise yet comprehensive analysis of Congress, particularly the legislative context that influences the legislative process.

Thomas, Sue. *How Women Legislate.* New York: Oxford University Press, 1994. A groundbreaking analysis of the differences and similarities between how men and women approach the task of legislating.

Presidential power grew over the centuries to "imperial" proportions and then ebbed in the late twentieth century in the wake of scandals.

The imperial presidency has reemerged as a model for viewing presidents today.

NOW

12

The Presidency

E ach presidency is shaped not only by the person who holds the office but also by the support of constituencies within the public, the support of Congress for presidential policy priorities, and the societal context of the day. Each presidential term can be molded and manipulated in many ways, with the result that one president may appear strong, and the next, weak—or a president may be both effective and ineffectual during the course of just one term. In looking at the roles presidents play in conducting their office, as well as the sources of their power, we consider in this chapter why some presidents are more effective than others.

The presidency is constantly evolving. The institution of the presidency that George W. Bush left behind is not the one that George Washington left behind. In the discussion that follows, we examine the development of the presidency in order to gain historical perspective on how the individuals who have served as president have changed the nature of the institution over time and what the impacts of those changes are for presidents today.

The presidency has changed in part because of the way this institution—which for many Americans embodies their government—has evolved.[1] It is fitting, therefore, that this chapter often looks through the prism of civic engagement to probe into the complicated relationship between the people and the presidency. We consider that even within this most "imperial" of the American institutions of government, the people play a vital part in

Will future presidents continue down the path of an imperial presidency?

What checks will constrain future presidents' exercise of power?

How will the relationship between presidents and the people change in the future?

determining not only who serves as president but also how effective and successful the president is in exercising executive power.[2]

Presidential Elections

The relationship between Americans and their president begins well before a president takes the oath of office. In presidential election years, nonstop campaigning provides ample opportunities for the public to learn about presidential candidates and their positions on issues. Campaigns also present many avenues for participation by the people—for example, by volunteering in or contributing to candidates' campaigns or even just by debating candidates' views around the water cooler. Although these opportunities for citizen engagement are especially abundant during a presidential election year, similar chances to get involved arise well before, because potential candidates typically position themselves years in advance of Election Day to secure their party's nomination and to win the general election.

As discussed in Chapter 8, the delegates to the national conventions are chosen by citizens in each state who vote in their party's primary election. After the nominees have been decided, typically by late August, they and their vice-presidential running mates begin their general election campaign. Usually, the parties' choice of nominee is a foregone conclusion by the time of the convention. Eligible incumbent presidents (that is, those who have served only one term) are nearly always renominated, and the nominee of the opposing party is often determined by the primary results.

The votes tallied on Election Day determine which presidential candidate's slate of electors will cast their ballots, in accordance with state law. There are 538 electors in the Electoral College because the number of electors is based on the number of members of Congress—435 in the House of Representatives, 100 in the Senate—plus three electors who represent the people of the District of Columbia. A presidential candidate today needs a simple majority of votes (270) to win the presidency. On the Monday following the second Wednesday of December, the slate of electors chosen in each state meet in their respective state capitals and cast their electoral votes. The results are then announced in a joint session of Congress in early January. In most presidential elections, however, the winner is known on election night because analysts tabulate the outcome in each state and predict the electoral vote. The winner takes the oath of office as president in inaugural ceremonies on January 20.

Presidential Roles in the Domestic Sphere

A newly elected president quickly discovers that the presidential office requires the performance of a variety of functions each day. Many of these roles involve leadership in domestic policy issues,[3] whether it is Barack Obama's desire to overhaul health care,

George W. Bush's priority of reforming schools, or all presidents' need to keep the economy sound and growing. As leaders in the domestic sphere, presidents must interact with Congress, manage the economy, and serve as the leader of their party.[4]

Chief Legislator

Although the separation of powers precludes the president from actually creating laws, presidents nonetheless have significant legislative power.[5] Presidents can influence Congress by lobbying its members to support or oppose pending legislation and by defining the congressional agenda in the annual presidential State of the Union message. Presidents also "legislate" when they submit the budget for the entire federal government to Congress annually, although Congress ultimately passes the spending plan.

Today one of the most important legislative tools at a president's disposal is the authority either to sign legislation into law or to veto it,[6] as described in Chapter 2. Although a veto allows the president to check the power of Congress, it also provides Congress with the opportunity to check presidential power by overriding the veto with a two-thirds majority vote.[7] In giving the president the right to veto laws, the Constitution essentially integrates the executive into the legislative process.[8]

As discussed in Chapter 11, there are several variations on the veto. During a regular legislative session, if the president does not sign or veto a bill within ten days after receiving it from Congress, the bill becomes law even without the president's consent. But if the president receives a congressional bill for his signature and Congress is scheduled to adjourn within ten days, the president can exercise a pocket veto by taking no action at all. Further, during the presidency of Bill Clinton, Congress statutorily equipped the president with a new kind of veto power: the **line-item veto** allowed the president to strike out specific line items on an appropriations bill while allowing the rest of the bill to become law. In 1997, however, the Supreme Court declared the line-item veto unconstitutional, asserting that it violated the separation of powers because the Constitution grants Congress the inherent power to tax and to spend.

Figure 12.1 shows that the use of the veto varies widely from president to president. Modern presidents are generally much more likely to veto legislation than their earlier counterparts were. A primary determinant of whether a president will regularly exercise veto power is whether the president's party has a majority in Congress.

An exception to this trend was the presidency of Franklin D. Roosevelt. As Figure 12.1 shows, during Roosevelt's twelve-year term in the White House, he issued 372 vetoes, or 12 percent of all presidential vetoes. Roosevelt chalked up this exceptional record despite having strong Democratic majorities in Congress throughout his tenure. But Roosevelt used the veto much differently than most presidents do. Because he was such a strong president, he exercised his veto power to prevent the passage of even small pieces of legislation with which he disagreed. Most presidents save the veto for important legislative matters, as they are unwilling to offend members of Congress over smaller laws that they do not favor.

President George W. Bush vetoed relatively few (eleven) pieces of legislation during his two terms of office. His first veto came in 2006, when a congressionally passed measure that would have eased restrictions on federal funding for stem cell

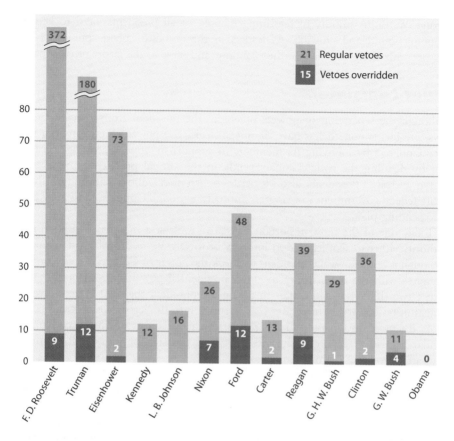

FIGURE 12.1 ■ **PRESIDENTIAL VETOES, 1933–2009.**
What trend is evident in presidents' use of the veto from the administration of Franklin Roosevelt to the present? Why do you think a president is more likely to veto legislation when one party controls Congress and the other controls the presidency?

research reached Bush's desk. One explanation for Bush's scant use of vetoes is that while the Republicans controlled Congress, Bush did not need to veto legislation often because he effectively convinced Congress to act on his legislative priorities and avoid passing legislation he disagreed with. For example, Bush threatened to veto the Lilly Ledbetter Fair Pay Act, but the Senate failed to pass the legislation in the wake of the threat, an issue discussed in "Analyzing the Sources." Indeed, ten of President Bush's eleven vetoes occurred after the Democrats took control of Congress in 2006.

Because President Obama has had Democratic majorities in Congress during his first two years in office, he has not yet used the veto, though he threatened to use it if Congress included a $1.75 billion appropriation to fund the purchase of F-22

Should Time Limits Be Placed on Lawsuits That Claim Discrimination?

While planning for her retirement, Lilly Ledbetter learned that during the nearly twenty years she had been employed as a salaried worker in Goodyear Tire Company's Gadsden, Alabama, plant, she had received less pay than had men employed in the same job. In 1998, Ledbetter filed a lawsuit claiming that Goodyear had for years engaged in wage discrimination based on gender. In 2007, the U.S. Supreme Court ruled in the case *Ledbetter v. Goodyear Tire Co.* that because Ledbetter had not filed her suit within 180 days of the first discriminatory paycheck, the statute of limitations on her claims had passed. In response to this decision, Congress in 2007 considered legislation that would have essentially reversed the Court's ruling by defining each paycheck as an act of discrimination. What follows are two presidential administrations' positions on this legislation (you can access the full text of Bush's statement at http://www.whitehouse.gov/omb/legislative/sap/110-1/hr2831sap-r.pdf; you can acccess the full text of Obama's speech at http://www.whitehouse.gov/blog_post/AWonderfulDay/).

President George W. Bush

STATEMENT OF ADMINISTRATION POLICY

H.R. 2831—Lilly Ledbetter Fair Pay Act of 2007

(Rep. Miller (D) CA and 31 cosponsors)

The Administration supports our Nation's anti-discrimination laws and is committed to the timely resolution of discrimination claims. For this and other reasons, the Administration strongly opposes the Ledbetter Fair Pay Act of 2007. H.R. 2831 would allow employees to bring a claim of pay or other employment-related discrimination years or even decades after the alleged discrimination occurred. H.R. 2831 constitutes a major change in, and expanded application of, employment discrimination law. The change would serve to impede justice and undermine the important goal of having allegations of discrimination expeditiously resolved. Furthermore, the effective elimination of any statute of limitations in this area would be contrary to the centuries-old notion of a limitations period for all lawsuits. If H. R. 2831 were presented to the President, his senior advisors would recommend that he veto the bill.

H.R. 2831 purports to undo the Supreme Court's decision of May 29,

(continued)

2007, in *Ledbetter v. Goodyear Tire & Rubber Co.* by permitting pay discrimination claims to be brought within 180 days not of a discriminatory pay decision, which is the rule under current law, but rather within 180 days of receiving any paycheck affected by such a decision, no matter how far in the past the underlying act of discrimination allegedly occurred. As a result, this legislation effectively eliminates any time requirement for filing a claim involving compensation discrimination. Allegations from thirty years ago or more could be resurrected and filed in federal courts. . . .

* * * * *

President Barack Obama

REMARKS BY THE PRESIDENT UPON SIGNING THE LILLY LEDBETTER BILL
East Room
January 29, 2009

It's . . . fitting that we're joined today by the woman after whom this bill is named—someone who Michelle and I have had the privilege to get to know ourselves. And it is fitting that we are joined this morning by the first woman Speaker of the House of Representatives, Nancy Pelosi. . . .

Lilly Ledbetter did not set out to be a trailblazer or a household name. She was just a good hard worker who did her job—and she did it well—for nearly two decades before discovering that for years, she was paid less than her male colleagues for doing the very same work. . . .

[S]he set out on a journey that would take more than ten years, take her all the way to the Supreme Court of the United States, and lead to this day and this bill which will help others get the justice that she was denied.

Because while this bill bears her name, Lilly knows that this story isn't just about her. It's the story of women across this country still earning just 78 cents for every dollar men earn—women of color even less—which means that today, in the year 2009, countless women are still losing thousands of dollars in salary, income and retirement savings over the course of a lifetime. . . .

[T]oday, I sign this bill not just in her honor, but in the honor of those who came before—women like my grandmother, who worked in a bank all her life, and even after she hit that glass ceiling, kept getting up and giving her best every day, without complaint, because she wanted something better for me and my sister.

And I sign this bill for my daughters, and all those who will come after us, because I want them to grow up in a nation that values their contributions, where there are no limits to their dreams and they have opportunities their mothers and grandmothers never could have imagined. . . .

So thank you, Lilly Ledbetter.

Evaluating the Evidence

① How does the Bush administration shape—and justify—its threatened rejection of the Ledbetter Fair Pay Act? What is your opinion of the argument for vetoing the bill?

② How does the Obama administration frame its advocacy for the Ledbetter Fair Pay Act? What is your opinion of the argument presented in Obama's speech?

③ In his remarks upon signing the bill, President Obama refers to his wife, his grandmother, his daughters, and House Speaker Nancy Pelosi. What is the desired impact of referring to these women in his life in this speech? How might the Bush administration answer this type of appeal?

jets in the 2009 defense authorization measure. But Congress backed down, and the president was not forced to veto the measure.

But President Bush used a different tactic—the signing statement—to put his mark on the way policies were to be administered during his tenure of office. A presidential **signing statement** is a written message that the president issues upon signing a bill into law. A presidential signing statement may, for example, direct executive departments in how they should implement a law, taking into account constitutional or political considerations. Controversy arose over the perception that the president used the tool of the signing statement to modify the intent of the laws. Critics, including the American Bar Association, complained that by using signing statements, President Bush was asserting unconstitutional legislative authority, and some critics compared the presidential directives to invoking the line-item veto in some pieces of legislation.[9] In all, President Bush issued more than 750 signing statements during his two terms of office.

Chief Economist

Although the Constitution makes no mention of presidential responsibilities with respect to the economy, the president's submitting a budget to Congress reflects what has become another key presidential role: the manager of the economy. Of course, the president does not exert a great deal of control over the enormous national economy, but presidents have numerous tools at their disposal that powerfully influence the country's economic performance. For example, in 2008, when Wall Street reacted unfavorably to ongoing financial crises in the banking, mortgage, insurance, and financial services sector, the Bush administration was at the forefront in urging Congress to shore up the corporations with a bailout plan. In addition, by submitting a budget to Congress, presidents set the economic priorities of the legislative agenda. Presidents also help to establish the regulatory and economic environment in which businesses must operate, and in this way they can influence economic growth and employment levels.

Central in presidents' oversight of economic performance is the appointment of the Federal Reserve Board ("the Fed") and its chair, who play a crucial role in managing the economy. The position of Fed chair tends to be less partisan than many other appointments, and a given chair often serves under presidents of both political parties. In 2005, President Bush named Ben Bernanke as Fed chair, replacing Alan Greenspan, who had served for eighteen years under both Democrats and Republicans. And in 2009, President Obama reappointed Bernanke.

The appointment of a Fed chair has a lot to do with consumer confidence, as well as with support from economically influential individuals on Wall Street, including investment bankers, stockbrokers, and mortgage lenders. The fact that a Fed action (such as increasing the interest rate) can send the stock market plummeting sheds light on why presidential appointments to the Fed are watched so closely.

Party Leader

One of the most important domestic roles for the president is political: the function of party leader. As chief of one of the two main parties, the president is a symbolic leader for the party members and asserts influence in the party's operations by selecting the national party chair and serving as the party's premier fund-raiser. The presidential function of party leader has become even more significant in recent White House administrations, with presidents working ever more aggressively to promote the reelection of candidates from their party by ensuring that enough money is available for their campaigns.

The president also acts as party head in the day-to-day operations of the executive branch, as many of the staff appointments to the White House Office, cabinet, subcabinet, ambassadorships, and judiciary typically come from party ranks. Finally, at the end of a term, presidents usually campaign for their party's presidential nominee.

Presidential Roles in the Foreign Policy Sphere

Presidential responsibilities also extend to setting and executing foreign policy. The president's foreign policy powers are for the most part constitutionally derived.[10] Specifically, the Constitution gives the president the authority with which to carry out the roles of chief diplomat and commander in chief of the U.S. armed forces.

Chief Diplomat

Serving in the capacity of chief diplomat, the president (along with advisers) shapes and administers the nation's foreign policy. Supported by a wide array of foreign policy resources, including the State Department, the National Security Council, the Central Intelligence Agency, and the various branches of the U.S. military, the president creates and administers foreign policy. In setting foreign policy, the president can act more unilaterally than with most domestic policies. Presidents are much less likely to be challenged in the foreign policy arena by members of Congress, who, in reflection of their constituents' main interests, tend to be primarily concerned with domestic policy issues.

As chief diplomat, the president, in conjunction with his or her staff, negotiates treaties and other international agreements with foreign nations and represents the United States at international summits. The president also has the authority to enter into an **executive agreement,** a kind of international accord. Executive agreements are based on the constitutional authority vested in the president, and unlike treaties, they may not be binding on future presidents, nor do they require Senate approval.

The Constitution also empowers the president to appoint ambassadors to other nations. As high-ranking diplomats, ambassadors are the official representatives of the United States in their host nation. Ambassadors' duties vary widely, depending upon the locale of their appointment. Some ambassadors play an influential, highly visible role in carrying out U.S. foreign policy, but others remain in the background.

The president, acting in the role of chief diplomat, is the leader of the diplomatic corps. In the capacity of chief diplomat, the president also hosts state dinners at the White House and formally receives the ambassadors of other nations.

Commander in Chief

As commander in chief, the president is the supreme military commander of the U.S. Army, Navy, Air Force, Marines, and Coast Guard. Counseled by advisers, the president decides when to send troops into battle (although only Congress can formally declare war) and sets military strategy in times of both peace and war.[11] For example, in 2009 President Obama had to decide whether to increase the number of troops in Afghanistan after U.S. military leaders there requested additional forces. The president also confers with world leaders and visits foreign nations. These kinds of gestures aim to demonstrate that as commander in chief, the president commands the respect both of the U.S. military and of the foreign nations dependent upon U.S. military power.

Overlap in the Domestic and Foreign Policy Roles: Chief Executive and Chief of State

Some presidential functions overlap the domestic and foreign policy spheres. This spillover notably exists in the president's role as chief executive—in which the president, as head of the executive branch, appoints his advisers and staff—and the role of chief of state, the ceremonial function of the president.

Chief Executive

As the nation's leader in domestic and foreign policy initiatives, the president serves as chief executive. In this capacity, the president appoints the *secretaries* (top administrators) of the cabinet—the fifteen departments of the federal government—as well as the heads of other federal government agencies charged with developing and implementing the administration's policy. As chief executive, the president also appoints other staff members and numerous advisers, including staff in the Executive Office of the President. In the capacity of chief executive, the president determines how the bureaucracy will implement the laws Congress has passed and which policies—those concerning education, crime, social welfare, and so on—will be emphasized.[12]

Chief of State

The president's role as chief of state reflects the chief executive's embodiment of the values and ideals of the nation, both within the United States and abroad. The function of chief of state is similar to the ceremonial role played by the constitutional monarch in parliamentary systems such as Great Britain's. In the United States, the role of symbolic leader of the nation enhances the president's image and authority and promotes national unity. We may experience this sense that we are one indivisible nation, for example, when the president, as chief of state, makes a formal state visit to another nation, hosts Olympic medalists at the White House, or visits the sites of national tragedies, as when President Obama offered comfort and paid tribute to those who lost their lives or were injured in the Fort Hood, Texas, shooting rampage in 2009.

The President and the Executive Branch

Because daily news reports so often showcase the president acting as head of state and chief diplomat, one of the president's primary responsibilities—administering the federal government—is easily overlooked. As chief executive, the president is constitutionally charged with ensuring that the "laws be faithfully executed." Today this responsibility means that the president oversees a bureaucracy of more than 4 million government employees, including the members of the military, while presiding over an astonishing $3 *trillion* annual federal budget. In addition, as we now consider, the president is the leader of the executive branch of government, which includes the vice president, the cabinet, the offices within the White House, and the entire federal bureaucracy.

The Vice President's Role

John Nance Garner, Franklin D. Roosevelt's vice president from 1933 to 1941, vulgarly commented that "the vice presidency isn't worth a pitcher of warm piss."[13] This insider's observation on the vice-presidential office matches the perceptions of many Americans fairly well. But although the media and the public tend to ignore the vice presidency and to marginalize the responsibilities of the second-in-command, vice presidents have an enormously important function. They are first in the line of succession to the presidency if the president should die or become incapacitated. Only eight presidents have died while in office, and although presidential succession may not be the foremost consideration in selecting a running mate for many presidential candidates, it can be an issue. Bill Clinton, in describing his selection of Tennessee senator Al Gore as his running mate, explained that his choice of Gore in part reflected Clinton's belief that Gore would make a good president "if something happened to me."[14]

The Vice President's Job   Many vice presidents serve a largely ceremonial function that revolves around activities such as attending state dinners, visiting foreign nations, and attending the funerals of foreign dignitaries. But vice presidents may have more substantive responsibilities, depending upon their skills and the needs of the administration. Sometimes, for example, a vice president acts as legislative

> Presidental candidates often choose a running mate who complements their attributes. Vice President Joe Biden, who served thirty-six years in the U.S. Senate, brought experience to President Barack Obama's ticket in 2008.

liaison with Congress, particularly if the vice president has more experience in dealing with the legislative branch than the president. Such was the case with Al Gore, who had served eight years in the House of Representatives and eight years in the Senate, whereas the president under whom he served, Bill Clinton, lacked Washington experience. In other instances, vice presidents' policy expertise is a crucial resource for the administration. In the case of George W. Bush' vice president, Dick Cheney, experience in foreign policy and national security determined the pivotal role he played in developing the Bush's administration's foreign policy.

Choosing a Vice President   In selecting a vice-presidential running mate, presidential candidates weigh several considerations. Would-be presidents strive for a **balanced ticket;** that is, to broaden their appeal to the electorate and increase their chances of getting elected, they select a running mate who brings diversity of ideology, geographic region, age, gender, race, or ethnicity to the slate. Or they may base their vice-presidential selection on their own shortcomings, whether in policy expertise or governing experience. For example, as a candidate vying for the presidency against Senator John McCain, an older and respected member of the U.S. Congress, Barack Obama chose Senator Joe Biden, who was thought to complement Obama in terms of age (Biden was 65 years old to Obama's 47), experience (Biden had served in the Senate since 1972, Obama since 2000), and expertise (Biden was chair of the Senate Foreign Relations Committee, while Obama had faced criticism in the media about his lack of foreign policy experience). In naming Alaska governor Sarah Palin as his running mate, McCain also sought to bring youth, vigor, and enthusiasm to complement his experience and expertise. McCain's selection was also designed to attract the votes of women and cultural conservatives.

The Cabinet

Since George Washington's presidency, every president has depended upon the advice of a **cabinet,** the group of experts chosen by the president to serve as advisers on running the country. These advisers serve as the heads of each of the executive departments. Figure 12.2 shows the fifteen departments of the cabinet. Each cabinet member except the head of the Department of Justice is called the *secretary* of that department. In the Obama administration, Hillary Rodham Clinton serves as head of the Department of State, and thus her title is secretary of state. The head of the Department of Justice is called the attorney general.

Figure 12.2 shows cabinet departments and their respective Web sites. The newest department, the Department of Homeland Security, was created by President George W. Bush in 2002. This department is charged with increasing the nation's preparedness, particularly with respect to catastrophic events such as terrorist attacks and natural disasters. George Washington's cabinet consisted of the heads of only four departments—justice, state, treasury, and war (the latter is now called the Department of Defense). Subsequent presidents added other departments.

Each president may also designate cabinet rank to other advisers whose agencies are not permanent cabinet departments. Typically, presidents have specified that their national security adviser, director of the Office of Management and Budget, and administrator of the Environmental Protection Agency be included in their administration's cabinet.

Today, presidents and the public scrutinize presidential cabinet appointments to determine whether, in the words of Bill Clinton, they "look like America." As the data in Table 12.1 confirm, this is a relatively new gauge, as only three women and two members of ethnic minority groups had served in presidential cabinets before the Carter administration. Increasingly, however, as the table shows, presidential cabinets have become more diverse, with significant strides made during the Clinton administration.[15] President Clinton became the first president to appoint a woman to any of the "big four" posts when he named Janet Reno attorney general and Madeleine Albright secretary of state. George W. Bush named Colin Powell the first black secretary of state, and when Powell resigned, Bush replaced him with Condoleezza Rice, an African American woman who had served previously as national security adviser. Female members of President Obama's cabinet include Hillary Rodham Clinton as secretary of state; Labor Secretary Hilda Solis, who is Latina; Secretary of Homeland Security Janet Napolitano; Secretary of Health and Human Services Kathleen Sebelius; Chairwoman of the Council of Economic Advisors Christina Romer; Environmental Protection Agency Administrator Lisa Jackson, who is African American; and United Nations Ambassador Susan Rice, who is African American. Other African Americans in Obama's cabinet include Attorney General Eric Holder and U.S. Trade Representative Ron Kirk. Latinos also include Interior Secretary Ken Salazar. And three Asian Americans—Secretary of Commerce Gary Locke, Secretary of Veterans' Affairs Eric Shinseki, and Energy Secretary Stephen Chu—serve in the Obama cabinet.

The Executive Office of the President

Whereas the cabinet usually functions as an advisory board for the president, the **Executive Office of the President (EOP)** typically is the launch pad for the implementation of policy. The offices, counsels, and boards that compose the EOP help the president to carry out the day-to-day responsibilities of the presidency and

Department of Agriculture
Secretary Thomas J. Vilsack
www.usda.gov

Department of Commerce
Secretary Gary F. Locke
www.commerce.gov

Department of Defense
Secretary Robert M. Gates
www.defenselink.mil

Department of Education
Secretary Arne Duncan
www.ed.gov

Department of the Interior
Secretary Kenneth L. Salazar
www.doi.gov

Department of Justice
Attorney General Eric H. Holder, Jr.
www.usdoj.gov

Department of Labor
Secretary Hilda L. Solis
www.dol.gov

Department of State
Secretary Hillary Rodham Clinton
www.state.gov

Department of Energy
Secretary Steven Chu
www.energy.gov

Department of Health & Human Services
Secretary Kathleen Sebelius
www.hhs.gov

Department of Homeland Security
Secretary Janet A. Napolitano
www.dhs.gov

Department of Housing & Urban Development
Secretary Shaun L.S. Donovan
www.hud.gov

Department of Transportation
Secretary Raymond L. LaHood
www.dot.gov

Department of the Treasury
Secretary Timothy F. Geithner
www.ustreas.gov

Department of Veterans Affairs
Secretary Eric K. Shinseki
www.va.gov

POLITICAL INQUIRY

FIGURE 12.2 ■ THE DEPARTMENTS OF THE PRESIDENT'S CABINET
The presidential cabinet consists of the heads of the fifteen departments shown in
the figure. Which department is concerned with finding alternatives to the use of
fossil fuels? Which one addresses the problems of the dedicated servicemen and
-women who serve in Iraq and Afghanistan? Which department arose as a result of
the 9/11 terrorist strikes?

Women and Minorities Appointed to Presidential Cabinets

President	Number of Women Cabinet Members*	Number of Minority** Cabinet Members	Tenure
Obama	7	9	2009–
G. W. Bush	7	10	2001–2009
Clinton	13	11	1993–2001
G. H. W. Bush	4	3	1989–1993
Reagan	4	2	1981–1989
Carter	4	1	1977–1981
Ford	1	1	1974–1977
Nixon	0	0	1969–1974
Johnson	0	1	1963–1969
Kennedy	0	0	1961–1963
Eisenhower	1	0	1953–1961
Truman	0	0	1945–1953
F. Roosevelt	1	0	1933–1945

*Includes Cabinet and Cabinet-level appointments.
**Includes African Americans, Latinos/as, and Asian Americans.

Sources: Brigid C. Harrison, *Women in American Politics: An Introduction* (Belmont, CA: Wadsworth, 2003); the Center for the American Woman and Politics, *National Information Bank on Women in Public Office*, Eagleton Institute of Politics, Rutgers University; www.whitehouse.gov, and various presidential library Web sites.

TABLE 12.1

similarly assist the First Lady and the vice president in their official activities. The EOP also coordinates policies among different agencies and departments.

Among the EOP offices, several are particularly important, including the White House Office, the National Security Council, the Office of Management and Budget, and the Counsel of Economic Advisers. These offices are crucial not only because of the prominent issues with which they deal but also because of their strong role in developing and implementing policy in these issue areas.[16]

The White House Office   Playing a pivotal role in most presidential administrations, the **White House Office (WHO)** staff members develop policies favored by the presidential administration and protect the president's legal and political interests. They research policy and keep the president informed about policy issues on the horizon. WHO staffers also regularly interact with members of Congress, their primary goal being to get presidential policy priorities enacted into law. They strive to ensure that these policies, once passed into law, are administered in keeping with the president's expectations.

Because of the enormous influence of staff members in the WHO, presidents take pains to ensure their loyalty and trustworthiness. Among the top staff members of the White House Office is the **chief of staff,** who serves as both an adviser to the president and the manager of the WHO. Other staff members with clout include the **press secretary,** the president's spokesperson to the media, and the **White House counsel,** the president's lawyer. The president's secretary and appointments secretary are also influential WHO employees; they act as gatekeepers by controlling access to the president by other staffers and by members of Congress and the cabinet.

National Security Council   The president consults members of the **National Security Council (NSC)** on domestic and foreign matters related to national security. Since its creation in 1947 during the Truman administration,[17] the NSC has advised presidents on key national security and foreign policy decisions and assisted in the implementation of these decisions by coordinating policy administration among different agencies. For example, once the president has decided on a specific policy, the NSC might coordinate its implementation among the Department of State, the Central Intelligence Agency, various branches of the military, and diplomatic officials.

The president officially chairs the National Security Council. Its other regular members include the vice president, secretary of defense, secretary of state, secretary of the treasury, and the assistant to the president for national security affairs, who is responsible for administering the day-to-day operations of the NSC and its staff. Other administration officials serve the NSC in advisory capacities or are invited to meetings when matters concerning their area of expertise are being decided.

Office of Management and Budget   Once part of the Department of the Treasury, the **Office of Management and Budget** (**OMB**—originally called the Bureau of the Budget) has been a separate office within the WHO since 1939. Its chief responsibility is to create the president's annual budget, which the president submits to Congress each January. The budget outlines all of the anticipated revenue that the government will receive in the next year, usually from taxes and fees paid by businesses and individuals. The budget also lists the anticipated expenditures for the coming year, detailing how much money the various departments and agencies in the federal government will have available to spend on salaries, administrative costs, and programs. The OMB is among the president's most important agencies for policy making and policy implementation.

The director of the Office of Management and Budget, a presidential appointee confirmed by the Senate, has a staff of about 600 career civil servants. In recent decades, the OMB director has figured prominently in presidential administrations and typically has been designated a member of the cabinet. The director's job is complex. He or she interacts intensively with Congress, trying to ensure that the budget that passes resembles the president's proposed budget as closely as possible. The director also lobbies members of Congress with the goal of ensuring that the key provisions of the budget that are important to the president remain intact in the congressionally approved version.

Once Congress approves the budget, the director of the OMB monitors its implementation, as it is the job of the OMB staff to manage the budget's execution by federal departments and agencies—to ensure that monies are spent on their designated purposes and that fraud and financial abuse do not occur. This managerial responsibility of the Office of Management and Budget was the reason for the change in the office's name (from the Bureau of the Budget) in 1970.

Presidential Succession

No examination of the executive branch would be complete without considering the question, What happens if the president dies? Presidential succession is determined by the Presidential Succession Law of 1947. But sometimes incapacitation other than death prevents presidents from fulfilling their duties. In such cases, the Twenty-Fifth Amendment, ratified in 1967, determines the course of action.

When the President Dies in Office

When the president dies, the course of action is clear in most cases: the vice president assumes the presidency. Such was the situation when Harry Truman became president upon Franklin D. Roosevelt's death from natural causes in 1945 and when Lyndon Johnson was sworn in as president after the assassination of John F. Kennedy in 1963. Vice presidents sometimes fill the unexpired term of their president for reasons other than the president's death, as when Gerald Ford acceded to the presidency upon the resignation of Richard Nixon after the Watergate scandal.

The Presidential Succession Law of 1947 determines presidential succession if the vice president also dies or is unable to govern. Table 12.2 shows that after the vice president, the next in line for the presidency is the Speaker of the House of Representatives, then the president pro tem of the Senate, followed by a specified order of the members of the cabinet. Notice that as new cabinet departments have been established, their secretaries have been added to the bottom of the line of succession.

> When a president dies in office, the line of presidential succession is clear. Crowds watched the funeral procession for President Franklin D. Roosevelt, who died in office in 1945 and was succeeded by his vice president, Harry S. Truman.

TABLE 12.2

The Line of Presidential Succession

1. Vice president
2. Speaker of the House of Representatives
3. President pro tem of the Senate
4. Secretary of state
5. Secretary of the treasury
6. Secretary of defense
7. Attorney general
8. Secretary of the interior
9. Secretary of agriculture
10. Secretary of commerce
11. Secretary of labor
12. Secretary of health and human services
13. Secretary of housing and urban development
14. Secretary of transportation
15. Secretary of energy
16. Secretary of education
17. Secretary of veterans affairs
18. Secretary of homeland security

When the President Cannot Serve: The Twenty-Fifth Amendment

What happens when a president is alive but unable to carry out the responsibilities of the office? Until the ratification of the Twenty-Fifth Amendment in 1967, the course of action was not clear. Such was the case in 1881, when an assassin shot President James Garfield, and Garfield lived two and a half months before succumbing to his injuries. In another such instance, President Woodrow Wilson was so ill during his last months in office that he was incapacitated. First Lady Edith Wilson assumed some of his responsibilities and decision making. Questions about presidential health also arose toward the end of Franklin D. Roosevelt's tenure; and during the Eisenhower administration, the president authorized Vice President Richard Nixon to determine whether Eisenhower was competent to govern after battling a series of illnesses. President Kennedy, who suffered from a host of physical ailments including severe, chronic back pain and Addison's disease, similarly empowered Vice President Lyndon Johnson: in an informal agreement, the men arranged that if Kennedy was physically unable to communicate with Johnson, Johnson was authorized to assume the presidency.

After Kennedy's assassination, the ratification of the Twenty-Fifth Amendment (1967) finally put codified procedures in place for dealing with an incapacitated president. According to the Twenty-Fifth Amendment, if a president believes he or she is unable to carry out the duties of the office, the president must notify Congress, and the vice president becomes the acting president until the president can resume authority. The amendment would apply in the case when a president is anesthetized for surgery, for example, or perhaps recuperating from a debilitating illness.

In other situations, a president might be incapable of carrying out the duties of office and incapable of notifying Congress. In such a case, the Twenty-Fifth Amendment requires that the vice president and a majority of the cabinet notify Congress, and the vice president becomes the acting president. If a question arises as to whether the president is fit to reassume the duties of office, a two-thirds vote of Congress is required for the acting president to remain.

Sources of Presidential Power

The presidency that Barack Obama assumed on January 20, 2009, scarcely resembled the one executed by the first president, George Washington, in the 1790s. In the interim, the powers of the president have evolved, reflecting the expansion of the

> In describing the powers that would guide presidents for centuries to come, the framers of the Constitution created a unique office. The Oval Office is symbolic of the powers of president—those bestowed by the founders, those granted through legislation, those resulting from Supreme Court decisions, and those that have evolved with the office of the presidency itself.

federal government since that time, changes in public attitudes about the proper role of government, and the personalities and will of those who have served as president.

In describing the powers that would guide presidents for centuries to come, the framers of the Constitution created a unique office. These visionary authors had lived through a repressive era in which an authoritarian monarch had exercised absolute power. They subsequently had witnessed the new American nation's struggles under the ineffectual Articles of Confederation, in which the federal government had too little power and the states too much. Thus the framers sought to establish an office that would balance the exercise of authority with the preservation of the rights and will of the people.

Given their colonial experience, it was no surprise that the framers granted the president both expressed powers and inherent powers in the Constitution. Congress grants president additional powers, called statutory powers, through congressional action. We consider these various powers in this section.

Additional presidential powers have emerged over time. These newer authorities reflect both changes in the institution of the presidency and shifts in popular views on the appropriate role of government and the president. These powers include emergency powers granted in Supreme Court decisions and powers that, while not formalized, are given to the president by the public through election mandates, presidential popularity, or unified public opinion on a particular issue or course of action.

The Constitution: Expressed Powers

The primary source of presidential power comes from the Constitution in the form of the **expressed powers.** These powers, which are enumerated in Article II, Sections 2 and 3, include the following:

- serve as commander in chief of the armed forces
- appoint heads of the executive departments, ambassadors, Supreme Court justices, people to fill vacancies that occur during the recess of the Senate, and other positions
- pardon crimes, except in cases of impeachment
- enter into treaties, with two-thirds consent of the Senate
- give the State of the Union address to Congress
- convene the Congress
- receive ambassadors of other nations
- commission all officers of the United States

The expressed powers outlined in the Constitution provide a framework for presidential responsibilities and an outline of presidential power. They also shape how presidents themselves develop their authority.

The Constitution: Inherent Powers

One of the principal ways by which the Constitution provides for presidents themselves to assert additional powers, beyond those expressed in the Constitution, is the **take care clause,** which states that "the executive Power shall be vested in a

President of the United States of America" and that "he shall take Care that the Laws be faithfully executed." On the basis of this clause, presidents throughout U.S. history have asserted various **inherent powers,** which are powers that are not expressly granted by the Constitution but are inferred.

President Thomas Jefferson exercised inherent powers in his far-reaching Louisiana Purchase in 1803. Jefferson authorized this $15-million purchase of 800,000 square miles of land, even though the Constitution did not authorize any such action on the part of a president. Interestingly, in the civic discourse over the Constitution, Jefferson, an Anti-Federalist, had argued for states' rights and against a strong central government and a powerful presidency. Jefferson had believed that the powers enumerated in the Constitution defined the powers of the government. But he thought that the purchase of the Louisiana Territory was of crucial strategic and economic importance. He believed that the deal was key to the United States' averting war with France and securing the port of New Orleans, which was essential to the new American republic's fortunes in trade. Jefferson could not wait for a constitutional amendment to authorize the transaction, and so he forged ahead with the purchase. Congress and many Americans of the day agreed with his actions, and so there were no negative consequences to them.

More recently, in the 1930s, President Franklin D. Roosevelt drew on the inherent powers when he expanded the size of the federal government in order to administer his New Deal programs, designed to relieve the economic and human distress of the Great Depression. Beginning in 2002, President George W. Bush used the inherent powers when he suspended the civil liberties of foreign nationals being held in a military prison at the U.S. naval base at Guantánamo Bay, Cuba, as part of the administration's war on terror. The individuals at Guantánamo Bay have been detained indefinitely for questioning about their possible terrorist activities. These instances of presidents' exercise of inherent powers generated varying degrees of controversy among Americans of the times.

Statutory Powers

The Constitution's expressed and inherent powers provided a foundation for presidential power that has evolved over time. These powers have been supplemented by additional powers—**statutory powers**—explicitly granted to presidents by congressional action.

An example of such a grant of statutory powers is the 1996 Line Item Veto Act, discussed earlier, which gave the president the power to strike down specific line items on an appropriations bill while allowing the rest of the bill to become law. As noted, in 1997, the Supreme Court declared the line-item veto unconstitutional on the grounds that the congressional action violated the separation of powers.

Special Presidential Powers

Presidents also have special powers that have evolved from various sources, including the Constitution, Supreme Court decisions, and congressional statutes. These powers, which numerous presidents have exercised, have come to be regarded as accepted powers and privileges of the presidency. They include executive orders, emergency powers, and executive privilege.

Executive Orders   The president has the power to issue **executive orders** that have the force of law. Executive orders carry the same weight as congressional statutes and have been used in a variety of circumstances to guide the executive branch's administrative functions.[18] In general, executive orders do the following:

- direct the enforcement of congressional statutes or Supreme Court rulings
- enforce specific provisions of the Constitution
- guide the administration of treaties with foreign governments
- create or change the regulatory guidelines or practices of an executive department or agency

Executive orders can be an important strategic tool, as they convey the president's priorities to the bureaucracy that implements the laws. For example, in 1948, President Harry Truman signed Executive Order 9981, which states, "It is hereby declared to be the policy of the President that there shall be equality of treatment and opportunity for all persons in the armed services without regard to race, color, religion, or national origin."[19] This executive order effectively banned segregation in the U.S. military. Why did Truman issue an executive order instead of working for congressional passage of a statute to desegregate the military? Many analysts think the reason is that Truman, who ardently believed that the military should be desegregated, not only doubted that Congress would pass such a measure but also faced pressure from early civil rights activists who had pledged an African American boycott of military service if the military was not desegregated. President George W. Bush drew criticism for his extensive use of executive orders, which served to create policy in various areas. For example, one Bush executive order froze the assets of any person who threatened the efforts at stabilization in Iraq; another created a uniform system for classifying national security information.[20]

Executive orders have very few limitations and stipulations. One limitation is that presidents cannot use them to create new taxes or appropriate funds, because the Constitution reserves these powers for Congress.

Emergency Powers   Broad powers that a president exercises during times of national crisis have been invoked by presidents since Abraham Lincoln's claim to **emergency powers** during the Civil War. Lincoln used emergency powers during the war to suspend the civil liberties of alleged agitators, to draft state militia units into national service, and to federalize the governance of southern states after the war.

In 1936, the U.S. Supreme Court acknowledged the existence of presidential emergency powers in *United States v. Curtiss-Wright Export Corp.*[21] In this case, the U.S. government charged the Curtiss-Wright Corporation with conspiring to sell fifteen machine guns to Bolivia, in violation of a joint resolution of Congress and a presidential proclamation. Without congressional approval, President Franklin D. Roosevelt had ordered an embargo on the machine gun shipment. The Court supported Roosevelt's order, ruling that the president's powers, particularly in foreign affairs, are not limited to those powers expressly stated in the Constitution. The justices also stated that the federal government is the primary actor in foreign affairs and that the president in particular has inherent powers related to his constitutional duties in foreign relations.

Executive Privilege Presidents also can exercise **executive privilege,** the authority of the president and other executive officials to refuse to disclose information concerning confidential conversations or national security to Congress or the courts. In invoking executive privilege, presidents draw on the idea that the Constitution's framework of separation of powers justifies the withholding of certain information from Congress or the judiciary,[22] a claim initially asserted when George Washington refused to grant Congress access to all documents pertaining to treaty negotiations. Typically, presidents claim executive privilege so they can get advice from aides without fear that such conversations might be made public or scrutinized by members of Congress or the judiciary. Presidents also have invoked executive privilege when negotiating with other heads of state, to shield these sensitive negotiations from being examined by the other branches of the federal government.

On occasion, the judicial branch of the federal government has successfully challenged executive privilege. For example, when President Richard Nixon refused to turn over tapes of Oval Office conversations to a special prosecutor investigating the Watergate scandal in 1974, the Supreme Court intervened. In *United States v. Richard M. Nixon,* the Court asserted that while executive privilege does exist, it was not applicable regarding the tapes because President Nixon's claim of executive privilege concerning the tapes was too broad.[23] (See pp. 463–465 for more on Watergate.)

More recent cases in which a president has invoked executive privilege are notable. President Bill Clinton attempted to do so to prevent White House aides from testifying before special prosecutor Kenneth Starr regarding the Monica Lewinsky scandal. (Clinton was accused of having extramarital relations with Lewinsky, a White House intern.) Clinton's maneuver failed, and his aides were compelled to testify. In 2007, President George W. Bush asserted executive authority in a showdown with Congress over the politically motivated firing of nine U.S. attorneys. Bush invoked executive privilege to prevent White House Counsel Harriet Miers and presidential adviser Karl Rove from testifying before Congress. The congressional inquiry continued without Miers's and Rove's testimony, however, and eventually Attorney General Alberto Gonzales stepped down as a result of the scandal.

In general, the courts have allowed executive privilege in cases where a clear issue of separation of powers exists—as with respect to international negotiations and conversations regarding matters of policy or national security. The courts have tended to limit the use of executive privilege when presidents have exercised it in an effort to prevent the revelation of misdeeds by members of the executive branch.

The People as a Source of Presidential Power

One of the most important sources of presidential power today comes from the people. Although one president generally will have the same formal powers as the next, presidents' ability to wield their power, to control the political agenda, and to get things done typically is a function of political skill, charisma, and what political scientist Richard Neustadt has called "the power to persuade."[24]

The President and the Bully Pulpit

Modern presidents work to persuade the public on a virtually continuous basis. They know that if they win popular support for their views and political agenda, they will have an easier time getting their policy priorities through Congress. In their efforts to persuade the people, they exploit the power of their office, using the presidency as a forum from which to speak out on any matter—and to have their views listened to. This ready access to the public ear and broad power of the president to communicate led President Theodore Roosevelt to exclaim, "I have got such a bully pulpit!"[25] In using their bully pulpit, presidents seek to communicate that their stances on important issues are the right choices and that their actions, particularly controversial decisions, should be supported.

The reason presidents work so tirelessly to win public support for their agenda is that they understand that getting Congress to act on policy priorities, to approve budgets, and to pass favored legislation depends heavily on the perception that the public supports presidential initiatives. Indeed, Richard Neustadt argues that the modern institution of the presidency is weak and that presidents in fact must rely on public and congressional support in order to enact their agendas.[26] Getting Congress to do what the president wants is more difficult when a president faces a divided government, the situation in which the president belongs to one political party and Congress is controlled by a majority of members of the other party. For example, when the Republicans lost control of both the House and Senate in the 2006 congressional elections, President Bush's chances of enacting his legislative priorities, such as privatizing Social Security, decreased significantly because the new Democratic majorities in Congress did not share these priorities.

But beyond partisan differences, presidents' ability to get things done in Congress also is a function of their popularity with the people. A popular president can use that clout to persuade members of Congress that his positions are the right ones; an unpopular president will face greater obstacles to having his legislative agenda enacted.

The President and Public Approval

When Barack Obama was sworn into office as president in January 2009, fully 67 percent of the American people approved of the way he was handling his job as president. As Obama's presidency matured during the spring and summer of 2009, his approval rating occasionally dipped below 60 percent. But by the fall of 2009, with declining approval ratings due in part to the controversy associated with his priority of reforming the nation's health care system, it was clear that Obama's **honeymoon period**—a time early in a new president's administration characterized by optimistic approval of the public—was over.

But the flow and ebb of presidential popularity during the administration of George W. Bush illustrates how essential the people's support is to the success of a chief executive's initiatives. After the September 11, 2001, terrorist attacks and President Bush's rapid and dignified response to them, he enjoyed record high approval ratings. **Approval ratings** are the percentage of survey respondents who say that they "approve" or "strongly approve" of the way the president is doing his job. Immediately after September 11, President Bush's approval ratings hovered in the high 80s, occasionally reaching 90 percent, meaning that 90 percent of those surveyed indicated that they approved of the way he was handling his job. (In contrast, the average presidential approval rating since the Franklin D. Roosevelt administration had been 56 percent.) During this time, Bush had enormous legislative successes. These included the passage of the USA PATRIOT Act of 2001, which gave law enforcement officers greater authority in handling suspected terrorist acts and the congressional declaration of a "war on terror." When Bush's popularity subsequently waned because of the people's dissatisfaction with the rate of progress in the war in Iraq, the high number of casualties in the war, and continued weakness in the American economy, so too did support decrease for the continuation of the war, the president's economic policies, and a proposed extension of the USA PATRIOT Act. By the end of his second term as president, Bush's approval ratings were dismal, with the failing economy dragging down his popularity. (For more on President Bush's and President Obama's approval ratings, see "Then, Now, Next.")

In general, presidential approval ratings reveal that some presidents are simply more popular than others. For example, presidents Reagan and Clinton tended to enjoy high approval ratings, with President Clinton's second-term ratings running particularly high, especially in light of the Monica Lewinsky scandal and the subsequent impeachment proceedings against him.

When the United States engages in a short-term military action or is the subject of an attack by terrorists, the president's approval ratings also tend to improve substantially; this is sometimes referred to as the **rally 'round the flag effect.**

A president rarely sustains high public approval continuously. Once achieved, however, high ratings help the chief executive to achieve his goals by demonstrating the people's support of the presidential agenda.[27]

The Media as a Tool of Presidential Influence

Modern presidents rely heavily on the mass media to convey their message to the people. The importance of the medium of television to presidents and would-be presidents was first realized in the televised presidential debates in 1960 between John F. Kennedy and Richard Nixon. After the debates, most of those who had listened to the two candidates on the radio judged Nixon to have won. But those who watched the contest of words on television came to a different conclusion. Years later, after having

Will President Obama Retain High Approval Ratings?

THEN: After the September 11, 2001, terrorist attacks, President George W. Bush had the highest public approval rating (90 percent) of any modern president. As two wars dragged on and the economy faltered, however, Bush's approval rating tumbled, bottoming out in October 2008 at 25 percent, the third-lowest approval rating ever (behind those of Richard Nixon during the Watergate scandal and Harry Truman at the end of his term).

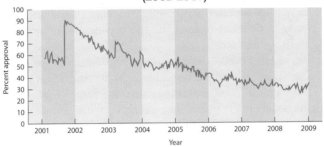

George W. Bush's Job Approval Ratings Trend (2001-2009)

Source: The Gallup Poll, http://www.gallup.com/poll/116500/Presidential-Approval-Ratings-George-Bush.aspx.

NOW: Since his election, President Obama has enjoyed comparatively strong approval ratings, ranging from a high of 69 percent (immediately following his inauguration) to a low of 49 percent in November 2009. The ratings started to decline as the president began trying to convince both Congress and the public of the need overhaul the nation's health care system.

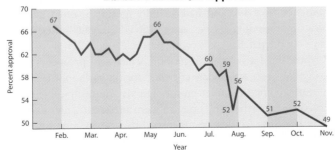

Barack Obama's Job Approval

Source: The Gallup Poll, http://www.gallup.com/poll/121934/Obama-Approval-Slips-Three-Points-Past-Week.aspx.

- What could cause Obama's approval ratings to reach their former levels? To decline further? How important will health care reform be in determining his approval ratings?

- How can the president be effective in convincing Congress to enact his policy agenda if his approval rating hovers below 60 percent in the future? How does the party composition of Congress mitigate the impact of low approval ratings?

- What other issues or circumstances might have an impact on presidential approval ratings in the future?

---

served as president, Nixon would comment on the influence of television in presidential campaigns, asserting that "in the television age, the key distinction is between the candidate who can speak poetry and the one who can only speak prose."[28]

Since the time of the Kennedy–Nixon debates, presidents' use of electronic media has increased significantly. Today's presidential candidates hire media consultants to assist them in preparing for televised debates. Teams of consultants create sophisticated media strategies that aim to integrate the presidential campaign's use of television, radio, and the Internet.

Once a president takes office, the expertise of the White House communications office kicks in to "spin" news in a favorable light for the administration. In particular, the White House communications director forges relationships with the most prominent media outlets by providing access, exclusive interviews, and scoops on breaking stories to reporters considered friendly to the administration.

Presidents use television to communicate directly with the American people. Important national speeches and the State of the Union address are televised, just as press conferences (usually) are. Interestingly, before the advent of television, presidential press conferences occurred more frequently than today, providing the best opportunity for the president to "talk to the people" and for reporters and their audiences to learn about presidential priorities.[29]

Table 12.3 summarizes the number of presidential press conferences President Kennedy and his successors have held. Not surprisingly, the presidents who communicated best through the medium of television tended to hold more press conferences than others. For example, compare the charismatic, persuasive John Kennedy with Richard Nixon, who was not telegenic and had an odd speaking voice. Yet sometimes the best communicators, including former actor Ronald Reagan—often called the Great Communicator—conducted few press conferences. Table 12.3 also shows that more recently, Bill Clinton held a below-average number of solo press conferences. Early in his tenure, George W. Bush was widely criticized for the rarity of his press conferences. In his first five years in office and after promising twice-monthly conferences, Bush held fewer solo press conferences than any other modern president. Later in his second term, Bush's number of solo press conferences increased to a nearly monthly rate, though the number tapered off toward the end of his term.

Although the nature of presidential press conferences and other media forums has evolved over time, the mass media have served as a key avenue by which modern

TABLE 12.3

Presidential Press Conferences

President	Months in Office	Number of Solo Press Conferences	Average Number of Solo Press Conferences per Month
Kennedy	34	65	1.91
Johnson	62	118	1.90
Nixon	66	39	0.59
Ford	30	39	1.30
Carter	48	59	1.23
Reagan	96	46	0.48
G. H. W. Bush	48	83	1.73
Clinton	96	62	0.65
G. W. Bush	96	37	0.41
Obama	8	8	1.00

Sources: Author's calculations based on data from www.whitehouse.gov and various news sources; Martha Joynt Kumar, "Presidential Press Conferences: The Importance and Evolution of an Enduring Forum," *Presidential Studies Quarterly* 35 (2005): 1.

presidents have communicated directly to the population at large. And because the nature of the president's relationship with his constituency is constantly evolving, so too is presidential power.

The Evolution of Presidential Power

Although the constitutional powers of the presidency have changed little over time, the power of the presidency has evolved a great deal.[30] In part, this development stems from some presidents' skillful use of powers not granted by the Constitution, such as the powers to persuade and to assert more authority. But the political environment within which presidents have governed has also contributed to the evolution of presidential power.[31]

The history of the early republic saw an incremental expansion of the power of the presidency, whereas the Great Depression of the 1930s and the election of Franklin D. Roosevelt in 1932 spawned an enormous growth of presidential authority.[32] As successor presidents inherited the large bureaucracy that Roosevelt built, presidential powers further expanded—gradually creating what historian Arthur Schlesinger Jr. has called the "imperial presidency."

Early Presidents and the Scope of Presidential Power

Thomas Jefferson's election to the presidency in 1801 marks one of the earliest expansions of presidential power. Jefferson broadened the powers of the office despite his Anti-Federalist reluctance to delegate too much power to the national government. Jefferson increased presidential power in two significant ways. First, as we have seen, Jefferson established the principle of inherent powers of the presidency by undertaking the Louisiana Purchase. Second, Jefferson's tenure of office witnessed the first time that a president had to act as party leader. Jefferson had no choice but to assume this role: if he had not, he would not have been elected president given the dominance of the Federalist Party during this era (see Chapter 8).

Twenty-five years later, Andrew Jackson would also adopt the role of president-as-party-leader, but he would add a new twist. Jackson's emphasis on *populism,* a political philosophy that emphasizes the needs of the common person, spawned a new source of presidential power, as Jackson was the first president to derive real and significant power from the people. Whereas earlier politics had mostly emphasized the needs of the elite, Jackson's populism mobilized the masses of common people who traditionally had not been civically engaged. This populism augmented the power of the presidency by increasing the popularity of the president and investing him with power that came from the people's goodwill.

In the twentieth century, the nature and scope of presidential power changed as a consequence of the prevailing political environment. One of the most extraordinary shifts in the nature of the presidency occurred during Franklin D. Roosevelt's administration, which lasted from 1932 until his death in 1945. (Roosevelt was elected to an unprecedented four terms; the Twenty-Second Amendment to the Constitution, which allows only two elected presidential terms, was ratified six years after his death.)

Having come to power during the Great Depression, Roosevelt engineered a significant change in the function of the federal government. He called for a New Deal for the American people, a series of social welfare programs that would provide employment for many of the nation's unemployed workers. Roosevelt's New Deal was based on the ideas of economist John Maynard Keynes, who argued for temporary deficit spending by the government (that is, going into debt) to spur the economy during economic downturns.

Roosevelt's primary weapon in his New Deal arsenal was the **Works Progress Administration (WPA),** a federal government program that employed 8.5 million people at a cost of more than $11 million between 1935 and 1943. The idea was that government-funded employment would create economic growth in the private sector because those employed by the government would have the money to buy goods and services, thus creating spiraling demand. The rising demand for goods and services would mean that the private sector could then employ more people, and the cycle of recovery and growth would continue. For example, if during the 1930s the government employed your great-grandfather to work on a road-building project in his town, he might have put his paycheck toward buying more bread and other baked goods than he previously could have afforded. If enough people in town could have similarly patronized the bakery, then the baker might have had to hire an assistant to keep up with demand, and consequently the assistant would have had money to spend on, say, new shoes for his children. In this way the increased demand for products and services would continue, creating additional economic growth.

Roosevelt's New Deal was important to the presidency for two reasons. First, it dramatically changed people's views of the role of the federal government. People now tend to think of the federal government as the provider of a "safety net" that protects the most vulnerable citizens—a safeguard that did not exist before the New Deal, when those needing assistance had to rely on the help of family, friends, churches, and private charities. Second, this popular perception and the programs that emerged—the Works Progress Administration, unemployment insurance, Social Security—meant that the federal government would have to grow larger in order to administer these programs. As a result, the president's role as chief executive would become much more important to modern presidents than it had been to those who served before Roosevelt.[33]

The Watershed 1970s: The Pentagon Papers, Watergate, and the "Imperial Presidency"

Americans' preference for strong presidents modeled after Roosevelt diminished drastically in the 1970s. In 1971, an employee of the Department of Defense named Daniel Ellsberg leaked a classified, top-secret 7,000-page history of the nation's involvement in and thinking on Vietnam dating from the Truman administration in 1945 to the Nixon administration then installed in the White House. Called the *Pentagon Papers,* the work first appeared as a series of articles in the *New York Times.* When the Nixon administration in 1971 successfully petitioned the Department of Justice to prevent the publication of the remainder of the articles, the *Washington Post* assumed publication of them. When the Department of Justice sued the *Post,* the *Boston Globe* resumed their publication. Two weeks later, in an expedited appeals process, the U.S. Supreme Court ruled in *The New York Times Co. v. The United States* that the government "carries a heavy burden of showing justification for the imposition of such a restraint" and that the government had failed to meet that burden, thus allowing the continued publication of the papers.[34]

The *Pentagon Papers* tainted the public's view of the presidency. The published work revealed miscalculations by policy makers in presidential administrations from Truman's to Nixon's, as well as arrogance and deception on the part of policy makers, cabinet members, and presidents. Specifically, the *Pentagon Papers* revealed that the federal government had repeatedly lied about or misrepresented the fact of increasing U.S. military involvement in Southeast Asia. In particular, the analysis in the *Pentagon Papers* indicated not only that U.S. marines had conducted offensive military maneuvers well before the public was informed but also that the U.S. military had engaged in other actions, including air strikes over Laos and military raids throughout the northern Vietnamese coastal regions. The Nixon administration's legal wrangling to prevent release of the *Pentagon Papers* cast a dark cloud over the public's perception of the presidency.

Cynicism about the presidency continued to grow in light of the **Watergate** scandal a year later. In 1972, men affiliated with President Nixon's reelection campaign broke into the headquarters of the Democratic National Committee (located

Evolution of the Modern Presidency

THEN (1970s)	NOW (2000s)
The presidency had become an increasingly powerful institution, shaped by the predecessors of Richard Nixon, who assumed office in 1969.	Presidential power is bolstered as the tragedy of September 11, 2001, necessitates strong leadership.
The presidency supplanted Congress as the epicenter of power in the federal government.	Presidential exercise of authority in the foreign policy realm serves to limit Congress's ability to rein in presidential power.
Backlash against abuses of executive power in the Nixon administration paved the way for the election of Jimmy Carter, a comparatively weak president.	Backlash against presidential policies leads to the election of Democratic President Barack Obama, and Democrats increase their majorities in both houses of Congress.

WHAT'S NEXT?

> How do you anticipate that the congressional election of 2010 will shape how President Obama exercises presidential authority?

> Will President Obama continue on the path of the imperial presidency created by his predecessors? Why or why not?

> What public policy issues will likely dominate in the months and years to come? How will these issues influence the ways presidential power is exercised?

in the Watergate Hotel in Washington, DC) to retrieve wiretaps that they had previously installed to monitor their opponents. *Washington Post* reporters Bob Woodward and Carl Bernstein, in a groundbreaking series of stories, traced the burglaries and the subsequent cover-up to high-level officials in the Nixon administration. This crime and the Nixon administration's attempts at cover-ups became known as the Watergate scandal. A Senate investigation revealed that President Nixon had secretly taped conversations in the Oval Office that would shed light on "what the president knew [about the break-in] and when he knew it."[35] Nixon claimed executive privilege and refused to turn the tapes over to a special prosecutor who had been appointed to investigate the scandal. When the U.S. Supreme Court ruled in *United States v. Richard Nixon* that Nixon must provide the tapes to the special prosecutor, one key tape was found to have a gap of almost twenty minutes where someone, reportedly his secretary, Rosemary Woods, had erased part of the recording.

Meanwhile, all of the Watergate burglars had pleaded guilty and been sentenced, and only one refused to name the superiors who had orchestrated the break-in. But the testimony of burglar James W. McCord Jr. linked the crime to the Committee to Re-Elect the President (CREEP), Nixon's campaign organization, and to high-ranking Nixon White House officials. The disclosure prompted John Dean, Nixon's White House counsel, to remark, "We have a cancer within, close to the presidency, that is growing."[36] With indictments handed down for many of Nixon's top aides, and with a Senate investigation and a special prosecutor's investigation in progress, the House Judiciary Committee took up the matter of impeachment. The committee handed down three articles of impeachment against Nixon—one for obstruction of justice, a second for abuse of power, and a third for contempt of Congress. When a newly released tape documented that Nixon had planned to block the investigations by having the Federal Bureau of Investigation and the Central Intelligence Agency falsely claim that matters of national security were involved, the tape was referred to as a "smoking gun."[37] Nixon lost the support of his few loyalists in Congress and on August 8, 1974, announced that he would resign from office the following day.

From a historical perspective, Watergate might seem like a relatively insignificant event in the history of the American presidency. But the impact of the Watergate scandal on the presidency has been enormous. Watergate badly wounded the natural trust that many Americans held for their president and for their government. Combined with the unpopularity of the Vietnam War and the release of the *Pentagon Papers,* it created a deep cynicism that pervades many Americans' perception of their government even today—a pessimistic attitude that has passed from generation to generation.

Watergate also dramatically demonstrated how enormously the presidency had changed. Modern presidents had supplanted Congress as the center of federal power and in so doing had become too powerful. Historian Arthur Schlesinger Jr. and other presidential scholars have decried the problem of the growth of the executive branch and, in particular, the imperial "courts"—the rising number of Executive Office of the President staff members, many of whom are not subject to Senate confirmation and share a deep loyalty to the person who is president rather than to the institution of the presidency. In juxtaposition with an attitude like that expressed by Richard Nixon in his comment that "when the president does it, that means it is not illegal,"[38] the imperial presidency left much room for abuse.

The Post-Watergate Presidency

With the election of Jimmy Carter to the White House in 1976, many observers believed that the era of the imperial presidency had passed. Carter, the mild-mannered governor of Georgia and thus a Washington outsider, seemed to be the antidote the nation needed after the display of power-run-amok during Nixon's tenure. But given the significant challenges Carter faced during his term, many people believed that he did not exercise *enough* authority—that he acted weakly when faced with various crises.

Ronald Reagan's election in 1980 in some ways represented a return to a more powerful, "imperial" presidency. Reagan, a former actor, was Hollywood swagger personified, speaking tough talk that many Americans found appealing. His administration was not unlike an imperial court, featuring a group of advisers with deep loyalties to Reagan. But the era of unchecked presidential power was gone for good. Reagan and his successors all attempted to set up administrations akin to imperial presidencies, each surrounding himself with a team of like-minded advisers and carving out strong policy agendas. But each also faced a much more aggressive media, dedicated to the kind of investigative reporting that had made Woodward and Bernstein famous.

Impeachment: A Check on Abuses of Presidential Power

Although presidential powers are flexible and can be shaped by the individuals holding the office, these powers do not go unchecked. One crucial check on presidential power is **impeachment,** the power of the House of Representatives to formally accuse the president (and other high-ranking officials, including the vice president and federal judges) of crimes. The Constitution specifically refers to charges of "Treason, Bribery, or other high Crimes and Misdemeanors," an appropriately vague description of the potential offenses a president could commit. An impeachment can be thought of as an indictment: if a majority of the members of the House of Representatives vote to impeach the president, the charges against the president, called the **articles of impeachment,** are forwarded to the Senate. The Senate then tries the president and, in the event of conviction for the offenses, determines the penalty. In convicting a president, the Senate has the authority to punish the president by removing him from office.

Although the Senate can force a president to step down, it has never done so in practice, and only two presidents have been impeached by the House of Representatives. The first was Andrew Johnson, who succeeded Abraham Lincoln as president in 1865 upon the latter's assassination. When he assumed the presidency, Johnson faced not only a divided nation but also a government in turmoil. The eleven articles of impeachment against him had to do primarily with his removal of the secretary of war, Edwin Stanton, who was working with Johnson's congressional opponents to undermine Johnson's reconstruction policies in the South. The so-called Radical Republicans in the House believed that Johnson's policies were too moderate; they sought to treat the Confederate states as conquered territories and to confiscate the land of slaveholders. These same House members wanted to protect their ally Stanton and prevent him from being removed from office. The Senate ultimately recognized the politically motivated nature of the articles of impeachment against Johnson and acquitted him on all counts.

The only other impeachment of a president occurred in 1998, when the House of Representatives approved two articles of impeachment against President Bill Clinton. On the basis of an investigation by a special prosecutor, the House impeached Clinton for lying to a grand jury about his relationship with White House intern Monica Lewinsky and for obstructing justice. The Senate acquitted Clinton on both counts.

During the Watergate scandal that rocked Richard Nixon's presidency, the House Judiciary Committee approved articles of impeachment against the president and sent them to the full House for a vote. Republican members of Congress convinced Nixon that the House would vote to impeach him and that the Senate would convict him and remove him from office. Faced with the inevitable, Nixon became the first president to resign from office before the House could vote to impeach him.

Evaluating Presidential Leadership

In 1998, while President Clinton was mired in impeachment hearings in Congress, his public approval ratings stood at 60 percent. Despite the Monica Lewinsky scandal and the risk that the president might be removed from office for lying about his relationship with the White House intern, a healthy majority of Americans separated Clinton's personal moral failings from his ability to govern successfully.

While a president is in office, people evaluate the president's performance on the basis of specific criteria. These include questions such as these: Does the president prioritize the same issues that I do? Is the president effectively managing the economy? Is the United States respected around the world? Is the president a strong leader, unafraid to exercise power? Does the president have a vision for the nation and for his administration? Is the president able to communicate that vision to the people? If presidents are successful in these areas, they tend to have generally high approval ratings. As we have seen, however, high approval ratings are difficult to sustain over the course of an administration.

In general, the average American's criteria for presidential greatness differ substantially from assessments by scholars of the presidency. The American public at large tends to emphasize recent presidents with strong communication skills, citing Ronald Reagan, John F. Kennedy, and Bill Clinton among the top four presidents in one survey (with Abraham Lincoln number three). Scholarly rankings tend to be more historically inclusive, with George Washington, Abraham Lincoln, Franklin D. Roosevelt, and Thomas Jefferson leading the list of the greatest presidents.

Women in the White House

Of the three branches of government, the executive branch has been the most challenging for women to gain entry into as formal participants. As we saw earlier in this chapter, no woman served as a cabinet member until the twentieth century, and to date, a woman has not been elected president. Yet cabinet positions are not the only place where women's influence in the executive branch has been felt. Historically, the women who have served as First Lady have influenced both presidents and policy.

> The office of the First Lady has been defined by the individuals who have occupied it. While taking an active ceremonial role, First Lady Michelle Obama has concentrated much of her energies on raising her daughters Natasha, known as Sasha (center), and Malia (right). Here, the Obamas read stories to children at the 2009 Easter Egg Roll on the south lawn of the White House.

Some recent First Ladies, among them Nancy Reagan and Hillary Clinton, have exercised undisguised public power. Upon President Obama's election, many Americans began to wonder whether First Lady Michelle Obama would take up the reigns as policy leader, but that has not been the case. And with women becoming an increasing proportion of the pool of candidates deemed eligible to be president, a woman's election to the presidency in the near future becomes nearly assured. Indeed, Senator John McCain's selection of Alaska governor Sarah Palin was seen by many analysts as an acknowledgment of the importance of women voters and the inevitability of a woman president. As President Richard Nixon remarked, "Certainly in the next 50 years we shall see a woman president, perhaps sooner than you think. A woman can and should be able to do any political job that a man can do."[39]

The First Lady

Much like the presidency itself, the office of the First Lady has been defined by the individuals who have occupied it. That women as different as Barbara Bush, the wife of President George H. W. Bush, and Hillary Clinton, the wife of President Bill Clinton, could consecutively and successfully serve as First Lady demonstrates the open-mindedness with which the American people view the role. Today, First Lady Michelle Obama eschews the policy-oriented role that Hillary Clinton forged, instead preferring to focus on raising the Obamas' young daughters, Malia and Sasha, and on the more ceremonial aspects of serving as First Lady.

Although the role of First Lady has historically been ceremonial in nature, many modern First Ladies have used the position as a platform for favorite causes, policies, and views. President Ronald Reagan noted, "If the president has a bully pulpit, then the First Lady has a white glove pulpit . . . more refined, restricted, ceremonial, but it's a pulpit all the same."[40] Recent initiatives of the white glove pulpit include Laura Bush's advocacy of literacy and Nancy Reagan's anti-drug-abuse ("Just Say No") campaign.

Other First Ladies have used their proximity to the chief executive to influence policy concerns more broadly and more forcefully. Some have acted "behind the scenes," as was the case with Edith Wilson, the wife of Woodrow Wilson. Others have taken a more public role. Eleanor Roosevelt, the wife of Franklin D. Roosevelt, fought for many causes during her husband's administration, including human rights and civil rights for African Americans. Hillary Clinton transformed the office of First Lady by serving, at her husband's appointment, as the chair of a presidential task force on health care reform. Her role in the task force, and indeed throughout the Clinton administration, proved to be a lightning rod for critics who thought that a First Lady should not be so prominent. Laura Bush, by contrast, was a more reserved and less public First Lady.

When a Woman Is Elected President

As First Lady, Barbara Bush speculated about the election of a woman president. She wryly commented, "Somewhere out in this audience may even be someone who will one day follow my footsteps, and preside over the White House as the president's spouse. I wish him well!"[41]

Over a period of time, pollsters have explored the possibility of whether Americans would vote for a qualified woman for president. Figure 12.3 shows that since 1937, when only 33 percent of Americans said they would cast their presidential

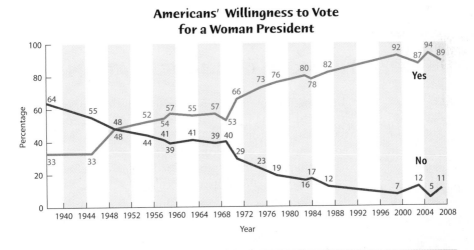

Americans' Willingness to Vote for a Woman President

POLITICAL INQUIRY

FIGURE 12.3 ■ What has been the trend since the late 1930s in the American electorate's willingness to vote for a women president? What factors do you think explain this shift?

Source: The Gallup Poll, www.galluppoll.com/content/?ci=8611&pg=1 and www.gallup.com/poll/18937, and www.gallup.com/poll/26875/Analysis=Impact=Personal=characteristics=Candidate=Support.aspx.

ballot for a qualified woman, that figure has steadily risen. By 1999, the number had risen to 92 percent of respondents who said they would vote for a female presidential candidate. Yet by 2005, that figured had declined to 89 percent. One explanation for this drop could be that Senator Hillary Clinton was frequently mentioned at the time of the poll as a likely 2008 presidential candidate and that respondents unwilling to support her candidacy responded that they were unwilling to vote for a woman for president.

Though Senator Clinton's bid for the White House was unsuccessful, inevitably, the United States will have to face the issue of the role of the First Gentleman. We can wonder about the dilemmas that might arise for the men who pioneer in this new role. Will the ceremonial functions of the first spouse remain the same? Will the First Gentleman choose the White House china; will he assist in the organization of state dinners and other social functions? Will he work in a private-sector job outside the White House? Will he have a voice in influencing administration policy?

We will learn the answers only when a married woman becomes president. In all likelihood, people's fascination with the role of First Gentleman will wane when the novelty of the office wears off. And similarly to the various interpretations of the role that First Ladies have created, it is likely that the role of First Gentleman will be flexible and adaptable, responding to the inclinations and the personalities of the men who occupy it, as well as to public preferences.

CONCLUSION: CONTINUING THE CONVERSATION

- The American presidency is a dynamic institution, one that is molded by the individuals who serve as president and by the American people—by their changing interests, viewpoints, struggles, and needs. The presidency has a symbiotic relationship with the larger culture in which it exists; it is at once shaped by, and shapes, the culture.

- The presidency is a product of both the design of the framers and the desires of the citizenry. As the country's need for stronger presidents has increased, the resources and authorities of presidents have grown to accommodate new powers. But at what point does the presidency become, in the minds of Americans, too powerful?

- The influence citizens of the future have on the presidency will depend on whom they elect to the highest office in the land, on how the people's opinions shape (or, in some cases, fail to shape) presidential actions, and on how the people's relationship with their presidents develops.

Summary

1. Presidential Elections

Presidential campaigns are key avenues by which individuals can become involved in the electoral process, such as through participating in nominating conventions, voting on Election Day, and voicing their opinions about the formal selection of the president through the Electoral College system.

2. Presidential Roles in the Domestic Sphere

As chief legislator, the president helps to define and influence Congress's agenda and can also veto legislation; as chief economist, the president shapes economic policy using the federal budget and key appointments; as party leader, the president acts as party chief and helps fellow party members at all levels get elected.

3. Presidential Roles in the Foreign Policy Sphere

As chief diplomat, the president and his administration shape the foreign policy of the United States. As commander in chief, the president is the leader of all branches of the armed forces.

4. Overlap in the President's Domestic and Foreign Policy Roles

As chief executive, the president is chief administrator of the entire executive branch of government, including the cabinet departments. As chief of state, the president is the ceremonial head of state, a function that is carried out by a separate officeholder in many other nations.

5. The President and the Executive Branch

Leading the executive branch of the federal government is among the president's top responsibilities. Key executive branch offices are the vice president, the cabinet, and the Executive Office of the President (EOP).

6. Presidential Succession

If a president dies in office, he or she is succeeded, in order, by the vice president, the Speaker of the House, the president pro tem of the Senate, and then by a specified order of cabinet officials, according to the Presidential Succession Act of 1947. When a president becomes incapacitated in office, the Twenty-Fifth Amendment to the Constitution prescribes the course of action.

7. Sources of Presidential Power

Article II, Sections 2 and 3, of the U.S. Constitution enumerate the expressed powers of the president: inherent powers emanate from the "take care" clause of the Constitution and have been asserted by presidents as constitutionally implied; statutory powers include powers that the Congress grants presidents; and special presidential powers include emergency powers, executive privilege, and the power to issue executive orders.

8. The People as a Source of Presidential Power

Because the people are a major source of presidential power, presidents continuously seek to nurture and secure public support. To this end, presidents exploit their easy access to the "bully pulpit" and the media.

9. The Evolution of Presidential Power
The presidential powers of George Washington contrast strikingly with the powers of contemporary presidents, with presidential powers expanding significantly during the administrations of Thomas Jefferson, Andrew Jackson, and Franklin Roosevelt.

10. Evaluating Presidential Leadership
Significant differences separate scholarly assessments of specific presidents from the views of the general population. In general, nonacademics tend to name modern presidents who have been effective communicators as among the greatest presidents, whereas scholars cite a number of earlier presidents as most effective.

11. Women in the White House
Some First Ladies, among them Eleanor Roosevelt and Hillary Clinton, have been much more powerful and visible public figures than others. As the pool of potential female presidential candidates increases, there is a growing likelihood that a woman will be elected president.

For Critical Thinking and Discussion

1. What is your opinion about the presidential election process? Would you favor a constitutional amendment eliminating the Electoral College in favor of a popularly elected president? Why or why not?

2. What do you think are the most important roles for presidents today? Why do these roles matter more than others?

3. Who do you think has been the greatest president in U.S. history? What characteristics do you admire about the president you chose?

4. What factors affect how frequently presidents veto legislation? Does vetoing legislation signify presidential strength or weakness? Explain.

5. What impact did Watergate have on people's perception of the presidency and of government? Have there been lasting effects from this scandal? Explain.

6. Would the people you know be willing to vote for a woman for president? Which demographic groups do you think would be more willing? Why? Which would be less willing, in your opinion—and why?

Key Terms

approval ratings 458
articles of
  impeachment 466
balanced ticket 445
cabinet 445
chief of staff 448
emergency powers 455
executive agreement 442

Executive Office of the
  President (EOP) 446
executive order 455
expressed powers 453
executive privilege 456
honeymoon period 458
impeachment 466
inherent powers 454

line-item veto 437
National Security Council
  (NSC) 449
Office of Management and
  Budget (OMB) 449
press secretary 449
rally 'round the flag
  effect 458

Internet Resources

A More Perfect Union **Web site**
www.mhhe.com/harrisonampule   Consult the book's Web site for study guides, interactive activities, simulations, and current hot-links that provide additional information on the American presidency.

270 to Win
www.270towin.com   This interactive Web site demonstrates how the Electoral College outcome is determined; users can experiment with altering the results of elections. It also contains past voting information for all states.

Center for the Study of the Presidency
www.thepresidency.org   This research center analyzes presidential leadership and offers seminars and symposia for presidential researchers, including the Center Fellows program for undergraduate students.

The White House
www.whitehouse.gov   The White House Web site contains information about current issues and news, the text of presidential speeches, links to cabinet departments and the EOP, and information about the First Lady and the vice president.

Recommended Readings

Borrelli, MaryAnne. *The President's Cabinet: Gender, Power, and Representation.* Boulder, CO: Lynne Rienner, 2002. An analysis of the evolution of presidential cabinets in terms of gender representation.

Neustadt, Richard E. *Presidential Power and the Modern President.* New York: Free Press, 1990. An update of the author's classic 1960 volumes, explaining the evolution of power in the modern presidency and probing, in particular, presidents' ability to persuade.

Schlesinger, Arthur M., Jr. *The Imperial Presidency.* Boston: Houghton Mifflin, 1973. A classic volume describing how the presidency has become a rarely checked, "imperial" institution.

Woodward, Bob, and Carl Bernstein. *All the President's Men,* 2nd ed. New York: Simon & Schuster, 1994. The classic work that launched investigative journalism, particularly concerning the presidency, in which the authors describe their investigation of the Watergate scandal that led to President Richard Nixon's resignation.

The federal bureaucracy under President George Washington had three departments and two offices serving a national population of 4 million.

Almost 3 million civilian federal bureaucrats—plus 35 to 40 million state, local, private for-profit, and nonprofit bureaucrats—serve a national population of over 300 million.

13

The Bureaucracy

Citizens turn to the government to solve their problems and provide services. Through policy-making processes, Congress and the president determine which problems the national government will address and what services it will provide. After Congress and the president approve policies, millions of public servants put them into action. The daily implementation of policy by public servants is the key to citizens' satisfaction with government.

President Barack Obama (2009–present) estimated the cost of providing national public services in his proposed 2010 budget to be about $3.6 trillion.[1] This staggering sum amounts to $9.8 billion per day, or $6.8 million per minute. Almost 3 million national civilian bureaucrats and 2 million military personnel provide public services. Beyond the legions of federal public servants, almost 20 million state and local bureaucrats assist in implementing national public policies. In addition, through grants and contracts with the national government, millions of employees in private for-profit businesses and in nonprofit organizations help to do the work of the national government.

Americans expect the millions of government and nongovernment employees to provide public services and benefits efficiently and effectively. In our democracy, citizens also want assurance that their tax dollars are spent properly and in furtherance of the public good. But such accountability is hindered by the complexities of public service delivery. Moreover,

NEXT

Will the volume of public service outsourced to private for-profit contractors continue to soar?

Will contracting-out boost the efficiency and effectiveness of public service delivery and save taxpayer dollars over time—or not?

Will the bureaucracy remain a target of criticism from citizens, candidates, and elected officials?

assessing performance is difficult when the services bureaucrats provide include ensuring justice and domestic tranquility, defending the nation, and promoting the general welfare.

Bureaucrats and Bureaucracy

Most people think of government agencies when they hear the word *bureaucracy,* and they think of government employees when they hear the word *bureaucrat*—and their thoughts are often negative. They typically focus on a large government organization with inefficient, dehumanizing procedures that require tedious paperwork. They visualize long lines at the Department of Motor Vehicles as lazy and uncaring workers (who they believe cannot be fired) slowly process mounds of forms.

Taxpayers are not the only people who think and speak negatively of the bureaucracy. Even our presidents—who rely on bureaucrats and bureaucracies to implement their policy promises—historically have not hesitated to criticize bureaucrats. In describing his initiative to improve the performance of the national bureaucracy, President Bill Clinton (1993–2001) stressed that his goal was "to make the entire federal government both less expensive and more efficient, and to change the culture of our national bureaucracy away from complacency and entitlement toward initiative and empowerment."[2]

Are the negative images and the criticisms of bureaucrats and bureaucracies fair? Before we can answer, we must understand who the bureaucrats are, what they are hired to do, and how they are expected to accomplish their work.

Who Are the Bureaucrats?

Who was the last government employee with whom you had a face-to-face interaction? Who was the last government worker to make a decision that directly affected you? Chances are, it was not an elected official, such as the president or a member of the Senate, nor was it an appointed federal judge. Rather, the government employees that you (and the people around you) interact with and are affected by on a daily basis are those individuals who are hired into executive branch agencies to implement public policy—that is, **bureaucrats.** Bureaucrats include government employees such as the administrator who reviews college students' Pell Grant applications, the Food and Drug Administration (FDA) inspector who monitors food and drug quality, and the Equal Employment Opportunity Commission (EEOC) lawyer who argues that an employer allowed sexual harassment of its workers. Bureaucrats provide the public services that elected officials authorize, and in doing so, they make decisions that affect people daily.

Because of perpetual criticism of bureaucracies and bureaucrats on the part of elected officials and ordinary citizens, individuals working in the national bureaucracy do not take being called a bureaucrat as a compliment. Bureaucrats prefer the term *public servant,* because that phrase captures how they see themselves and their essential job goal.[3]

Charles Goodsell, a respected scholar of public administration and public policy, notes that studies show government employees to be very hard workers who are motivated by the recognition of the importance of public service. This public service motivation is distinct from the motivation of private-sector employees, for whom salary levels and shorter work hours provide key incentives.[4] Compared to private-sector employees, public servants have higher levels of formal education, must comply with more stringent codes of behavior, and express a greater concern for serving the public.[5] In addition, government bureaucrats tend to report somewhat higher levels of job satisfaction than do their private-sector counterparts.[6]

Very few children say that they want to be a bureaucrat. Yet millions do aspire to careers as public servants, including teachers, police officers, lawyers, and health care professionals. National, state, and local governments hire professionals such as these to implement public policy—to do the business of government. Chances are, whatever your major in college, you can get a job as a public servant. Almost 23 million national, state, and local bureaucrats, engaged in every job and career imaginable, implement national public policy.

Joining the millions of government bureaucrats are the so-called **shadow bureaucrats**—employees on the payroll of private for-profit businesses and private nonprofit organizations with government contracts. Through a process of **contracting-out** (also called *outsourcing* or *privatizing*), the government signs work contracts with these organizations to assist in the implementation of national policy. In other words, shadow bureaucrats do the work of government, but they do not receive a government paycheck.

In summary, today, a mix of national, state, and local bureaucrats, as well as shadow bureaucrats, deliver national public services. In addition to having in common the delivery of public services, public and shadow bureaucrats also share a similar work environment. That is, they work in bureaucratic organizations.

Bureaucracy: An Organizational Structure

Max Weber (1864–1920), the "father of sociology," coined the word *bureaucracy* to describe large organizations, such as government, with the following features: a division of labor, specialization of job tasks, hiring systems based on worker competency, hierarchy with a vertical chain of command, and standard operating procedures. Weber argued that these features enhance the performance and accountability of large organizations. In our discussion, **bureaucracy** is any organization with a hierarchical structure, although this term is most commonly used to designate a government agency or the collection of all national executive branch organizations.

Organizations with these bureaucratic features are not unique to government. For example, colleges and universities are also bureaucratic organizations. They have a division of labor with specialization of tasks (consider the various academic departments, each specializing in a different discipline). They hire employees (such as professors, computer technicians, and student affairs staff) with the knowledge, skills, and abilities essential to doing their jobs well. Colleges and universities also have a hierarchy with a chain of command (faculty members report to department chairs, who report to a dean, who reports to the vice president for academic affairs, who reports to the president, who makes final decisions). University employees implement standardized procedures to register students for classes, determine financial aid eligibility, and punish violations of the conduct code.

So, although most people think of government when they hear the word *bureaucracy,* a bureaucracy is *any* organization with Weber's bureaucratic structure. Yet in this chapter, as is appropriate to our study of American government, we focus on the departments and agencies that compose the national government bureaucracy. And even though most people think of government employees when they hear the term *bureaucrat,* nongovernment employees, as we have seen, may also be paid with taxpayer money to serve the public, and so it is appropriate that we consider them, too.

Federal Bureaucrats

Political scientists distinguish among national bureaucrats according to several factors, including the process by which they are hired, the procedures by which they can be fired, and the grounds for which they can be fired. On the basis of these factors, we can differentiate among three categories of national civilian bureaucrats: political appointees, civil servants, and senior executive service employees.

Political Appointees

In 1863, President Abraham Lincoln, suffering from smallpox, told his secretary to "send all the office seekers in here. I finally have something I can give to them all." Indeed, before the creation of the civil service system in 1883, presidents had the authority to hire bureaucrats, selecting whomever they wanted and establishing whatever qualifications they desired, in a noncompetitive hiring system known as *patronage.* Under the patronage system, hordes of men seeking government jobs presented themselves to the president after each election.

Government has come a long way since 1863. Today federal agencies hire the majority of bureaucrats based on **merit**—a system of hiring and promotion based on an individual's competence—rather than patronage. Out of the 2.7 million bureaucrats in the national government today, only about 7,000 political appointees are hired through patronage.[7]

After the election of a new president, Congress publishes the **plum book,** which lists the top jobs in the bureaucracy to which the president will appoint people through the patronage system. There is no standard process for assessing the knowledge, skills, and abilities needed for appointive positions, nor is there open competition for these patronage jobs. Further, because citizens expect presidents to be responsive and accountable to them, and presidents rely on their political appointees to support their efforts to meet these expectations, presidents tend to appoint people who support their policy preferences to these top positions.

Patronage positions come with a downside for the appointees: no job security. The president not only hires but can also fire political appointees at his pleasure.

On December 1, 2008, fifty-one days before his inauguration, President-elect Barack Obama announced nominees for his national security team, Shown standing, left to right, are Eric Holder (attorney general), Arizona Governor Janet Napolitano (head of Homeland Security), Robert Gates (continuing as secretary of defense), Vice President–elect Joe Biden, Senator Hillary Clinton (secretary of state), retired Marine General James Jones (national security adviser), and Susan Rice (U.S. ambassador to the United Nations).

The merit-based civil service system, combined with Titles VI, VII, and IX of the Civil Rights Act, typically fosters a civil service with greater descriptive representation than any other category of government worker. What do you think accounts for the diversity of President Obama's national security team? Are concerns about the patronage system fostering the selection of unqualified political appointees valid? Why or why not?

More common than firing is the resignation or retirement of appointees who no longer enjoy presidential approval.

Civil Servants

During the first century of U.S. history, all national bureaucrats got their jobs through patronage. Then in 1883, mobilized by the assassination of President James Garfield (whose brief administration lasted from March to September 1881) by an unsuccessful seeker of a patronage position, Congress and President Chester Arthur (1881–1885) approved the Pendleton Civil Service Act. This law introduced a merit-based civil service system to the national government. The hiring principles of the **merit-based civil service** system are open competition, competence, and political neutrality. **Civil servants** are bureaucrats hired through the merit-based personnel system. The 1978 Civil Service Reform Act reinforced these merit principles and legislated the right to unionize for many federal civil servants.

Open Competition and Competence Today merit-based civil service jobs, which compose at least 85 percent of the national bureaucracy, are open and accessible to all who wish to compete for a position. The competition requires that candidates prove their competence to do the job (their merit). Jobs covered by the merit-based civil service system are analyzed and ranked on the basis of the knowledge, skills, and abilities needed to do the job competently. A job's rank determines its salary. The pay scales offer equal pay for jobs of equal worth, as determined by the job analysis. (See Table 13.1 for the pay scales and education requirements for

TABLE 13.1

Education Requirements and Salary Ranges for White-Collar Federal Service Positions* (2009)

Level	Salary Range	Qualifying Education
GS-1	$17,540–21,944	No high school diploma required
GS-2	$19,721–24,815	High school graduation or equivalent
GS-3	$21,517–27,970	One academic year above high school
GS-4	$24,156–31,401	Two academic years above high school, or associate's degree
GS-5	$27,026–35,135	Four academic years above high school leading to a bachelor's degree, or a bachelor's degree
GS-7	$33,477–43,521	Bachelor's degree with superior academic achievement or one academic year of graduate education or law school
GS-9	$40,949–53,234	Master's (or equivalent graduate degree) or two academic years of progressively higher-level graduate education
GS-11	$49,544–64,403	PhD or equivalent degree or three academic years of progressively higher-level graduate education
GS-12	$59,383–77,194	Completion of all requirements for a doctoral or equivalent degree (for research positions only)

*Table shows the amount and level of education typically required for each grade for which education alone can be qualifying. At GS-13 and above, appropriate specialized experience is required for all positions.

Sources: www.opm.gov/flsa/oca/09tables/html/gs.asp (salary data); www.govcentral.com/benefits/articles/1757-what-determines-where-you-stand-on-the-gs-scale (education level data).

white-collar government jobs for which education alone can be qualifying.) Today the national civil service comprises more than 900 occupational titles.

Several national laws have helped to make today's civil servants, as a group, look more like the U.S. population at large than they did in the past. Title VII of the 1964 Civil Rights Act, as amended, prohibits employers, including the government, from making personnel decisions based on factors irrelevant to job competence, such as sex, race, color, ethnicity, age, and disabilities that can be reasonably accommodated. The merit principles of the 1978 Civil Service Reform Act (CSRA) reiterate this prohibition against discrimination in personnel practices. The bans against discrimination in Title VII and the CSRA do not apply to the positions of elected officials or political appointees.

Title VI of the 1964 Civil Rights Act prohibits discrimination based on race, color, religion, and ethnicity in educational opportunities offered by institutions receiving federal funding. Title IX, which was added to the act in 1972, extended this prohibition to sex-based discrimination. Enforcement of these laws has increased the diversity of people who are able to gain the education and experience needed to do government jobs competently. The interaction of Titles VI, VII, and IX has fostered greater *descriptive representation* among civil servants than among any other category of government worker. This means that the people serving resemble the larger population whom they serve in terms of demographic characteristics such as race, age, ethnicity, sex, religion, and economic status. "Analyzing the Sources" on page 483 considers the influence these laws have had on the national civil service.

Political Neutrality   Merit-based civil servants cannot be fired merely because someone with different political beliefs is elected or appointed to supervise them. They can be fired due to poor quality of work (misfeasance) or nonperformance of their work (nonfeasance), or for violating the rules, regulations, or laws that guide their work (malfeasance). The system thus gives civil servants job protection and does not require them (unlike political appointees) to adhere to the president's policy preferences. Hence the civil service system supports political neutrality to ensure efficient and effective public service delivery.

In 1939, Congress approved the Hatch Act, limiting civil servants' rights to engage in political activity. The rationale behind this law's passage was that if civil servants stayed out of politics, they would be less inclined to allow party loyalty to influence their job performance. Over time, however, civil servants have contested the constitutionality of the legal limits on their political engagement. As a result, the Hatch Act has been modified in recent decades to loosen the restrictions on civil servants' political activities. This easing of limits on political engagement has allowed civil servants to exercise their First Amendment rights of expression, including political expression more freely and fully.

Civil Service Reform Act (1978)   "There is widespread criticism of federal government performance. The public suspects that there are too many government workers, that they are underworked, overpaid, and insulated from the consequences of incompetence."[8] With these words, President Jimmy Carter (1977–1981) announced proposed civil service reforms in 1978. The resulting Civil Service

The Federal Civilian Nonpostal Bureaucracy

THEN (1789)	NOW (2010)*
Public servants got jobs through a patronage system.	Civil servants get jobs through a merit-based system or by contract (the latter in the case of nonprofit and private for-profit employees).
Public servants were all white males.	The civil service workforce is 17% black, 7% Hispanic, 5% Asian, and 2% Native American, and 56% of civil servants are male.
Public service jobs were strictly clerical.	Civil service jobs are 34% administrative, 24% professional, 30% technical and clerical, and 11% blue collar.
Public servants worked exclusively in New York City.	About 15% of civil servants work in the Washington, DC–Maryland–Virginia–West Virginia metropolitan area; 82% work elsewhere in the United States; and about 3% work outside the country.

WHAT'S NEXT?

> Will the number of shadow bureaucrats continue to rise? Why or why not?

> Will the percentage of federal employees working outside the United States continue to grow as a result of globalization?

> How will minimum job qualifications for public service change with continuing technological advances and globalization?

* www.opm.gov/feddata/html/prof0906.asp.

Reform Act of 1978 (CSRA) reaffirmed and expanded the merit principles established by the Pendleton Act and reorganized the management of the national civil service. Carter's reforms also eliminated the Civil Service Commission (CSC), the central personnel office created by the Pendleton Act.

Three new independent administrative agencies—the Office of Personnel Management (OPM), the Merit System Protection Board (MSPB), and the Federal Labor Relations Authority (FLRA)—replaced the old Civil Service Commission.

Equal Educational and Employment Opportunity and Stratified Occupational Segregation

Laws prohibit race-based and sex-based discrimination in educational and employment opportunities. In addition, affirmative action requires most governments (as employers) and private businesses with government contracts to adopt and implement personnel plans detailing how they will actively recruit qualified women and minorities for open positions.

Evaluating the Evidence

① Review the accompanying chart and table. Do equal educational and equal employment laws work? Explain.

② Are there additional data you would want to review before answering question 1? If so, what kind of information would this supplementary data provide? Why?

③ Sex- and race-based occupational segregation occurs when women and minority men dominate low-paying, low-status jobs and white men dominate high-paying, high-status jobs. Based on the data presented here, does occupational segregation exist in the national civil service? Explain.

| Job category | GS 1–4 | GS 5–8 | GS 9–11 | GS 12–13 | GS 14–15 | Senior pay levels |

Percent women: 65%, 66%, 50%, 38%, 30%, 25%

Percent minority*: 43%, 40%, 30%, 24%, 18%, 14%

*Minority includes women and men with American Indian, Alaska Native, Asian, Pacific Islander, Black, or Hispanic origin.

Source: www.opm.gov/feddata/factbook/2007/2007FACTBOOK.pdf.

COLLEGE DEGREES CONFERRED BY SEX AND RACE/ETHNICITY			
DEMOGRAPHIC	BACHELOR'S	MASTER'S	DOCTOR'S*
Men	42.5%	41.2%	52.9%
Women	57.5%	58.2%	47.1%
White	70.0%	60.3%	56.2%
Black	8.7%	7.8%	5.1%
Hispanic	6.3%	4.4%	3.2%
Asian/Pacific Islander	6.2%	4.8%	4.9%
Native American	0.7%	0.5%	0.4%

*Doctor's degrees are the highest degree a student can earn for graduate study and include EdD, JD, and PhD.

Source: U.S. Department of Education, National Center for Education Statistics, http://nces.ed.gov/fastfacts/display.asp?id=72.

Today the OPM is the central personnel office, responsible for developing and implementing merit-based civil service personnel policies and procedures. The MSPB ensures proper implementation of the merit system. The CSRA also legislated for the collective bargaining rights (unionization rights) of national civil servants and created the FLRA to monitor the relations between unionized bureaucrats and the federal government.

Unionized Civil Servants   Three out of every five U.S. federal civil servants belong to labor unions.[9] The American Federation of Government Employees (AFGE) is the largest such union, representing 600,000 national bureaucrats. The level of union membership varies dramatically from agency to agency. Whereas about 90 percent of U.S. Postal Service employees are union members (not AFGE members but members of one of several unions for postal employees), the level of union membership among bureaucrats in the State Department is close to zero. Part of the explanation for the range of unionization levels across national agencies is the percentage of each agency's workers that is composed of blue-collar workers. In general, blue-collar workers are likelier to be union members than are white-collar workers.

Unionized civil servants have leverage to negotiate certain conditions of work. For example, they may bargain for improved training opportunities and enhanced due process protections in disciplinary matters. Unions representing national civil servants cannot negotiate salaries or work hours, however. And unlike private-sector unions, national civil servant unions do not have the legal right to strike. The prohibition of strikes by national civil servants is typically justified by the fact that these workers provide essential services that are vital to public safety. A strike by these workers would therefore threaten public safety and health.

The Senior Executive Service   One additional CSRA-mandated change to the national bureaucracy was the creation of a new category of civil servant, the **senior executive service (SES)** bureaucrat. SES positions are hybrids of political appointee and civil service positions. The SES includes most of the top managerial, supervisory, and policy positions that are not patronage positions.

At least 90 percent of SES bureaucrats are career civil servants (hired through an open competition based on competence) who have given up some job security for positions with higher pay. These employees can be moved from job to job and from agency to agency (less job security), but they are immune from firing except for proven misfeasance, nonfeasance, or malfeasance. The remaining SES bureaucrats are typically hired from outside the merit-based civil service system. Appointed with approval of the OPM and the White House Office of Presidential Personnel, these SES noncareer bureaucrats do not face open competition and do not have the job protection of merit-based civil servants.[10]

Supplementing the work of national political appointees, civil servants, and SES bureaucrats are armies of state, local, and shadow bureaucrats. The volume of national public policy executed by these non-national bureaucrats has been increasing dramatically since the 1960s due to devolution and a rise in contracting-out.

State, Local, and Shadow Bureaucrats

Today the overwhelming majority of the almost 20 million state and local bureaucrats, and possibly as many as 15 million shadow bureaucrats, provide various national public services. Through devolution and contracting-out, the national government relies on these non-national bureaucrats to serve the people's daily needs. National bureaucrats monitor these state, local, and shadow bureaucrats' compliance with the rules and regulations that come with devolution and outsourcing.

As you may recall from Chapter 3, devolution is the federal government's shifting of greater responsibility for financing and administering public policies to state and local governments, putting the implementation of national policy in the hands of state and local bureaucrats. Mandates in federal laws require state and local governments to implement national policies. In cases where national law preempts (takes precedence over) state and local law, state and local bureaucrats have to implement federal policy instead of state or local programs. Preemption is common, for example, in the area of environmental protection, where state and local officials must ensure private- and public-sector compliance with federal air, water, and landfill standards.

As we've seen, the national government also contracts with shadow bureaucracies—private for-profit and nonprofit organizations—to provide vital services as well as to produce certain resources needed to serve the public. Outsourcing, for example, includes the federal government's contracting-out with Lockheed Martin and Boeing for the production of defense resources such as helmets, fighter planes, and laser-guided missiles, and Blackwater, a private security firm, to provide security for U.S. diplomats in Iraq. Traditionally, too, the government undertakes large capital projects such as the construction of roads and government buildings through contracts with private businesses. Further, the federal government outsources medical as well as social research to cure disease and address the ills of society. And through government contracts, the Red Cross has dispensed disaster relief for decades.

The national government expects that contracting-out will reduce the expense of government by eliminating the overhead costs (including employee benefits and basic operating costs) of producing public goods and services. Outsourcing also provides a means by which the government can hire experts and specialists when they are needed and keep them off the payroll at other times. The government can eliminate these contracted personnel and their costs more easily than it can fire civil servants, who have job protection. The expectation is that the private- and nonprofit-sector employees and organizations will be more efficient and effective than government bureaucracies.

Even with the increased use of state, local, and shadow bureaucrats, the national bureaucracy itself is neither small nor streamlined. It is composed of thousands of bodies with a variety of names and organizational structures. The national bureaucracy, an evolving organism, continues to grow in complexity even as it privatizes and devolves more of its work.

The Evolution and Organization
of the Federal Bureaucracy

Four million people resided in the United States in 1789, the year George Washington was sworn in as the first president. Most of them lived off the land and were self-sufficient; they expected few services from the national government. The federal bureaucracy consisted of the Department of War, Department of Foreign Affairs, Treasury Department, Attorney General's Office, and Postal Services Office. These three departments and two offices handled the core functions demanded of the national government at that time: respectively, providing defense, managing foreign affairs, collecting revenues and paying bills, resolving lawsuits and legal questions, and delivering mail. Initially, other than for military personnel, the work of public servants was mostly clerical in nature.

Today, as the U.S. population tops 300 million, more than 2,000 executive branch units, employing 4 million bureaucrats (2.7 million civilian bureaucrats and about 1.3 million military personnel), implement volumes of national policies. The number of bureaucrats is equal to the nation's population in 1789.* Figures 13.1 and 13.2 show the growth in size and cost of the national bureaucracy since the 1940s.

Political scientists distinguish among five categories of executive branch organizations based on their structure and the type of work they perform: (1) departments, (2) independent administrative agencies, (3) independent regulatory commissions, (4) government corporations, and (5) agencies in the Executive Office of the President.

Within each category, there is much variation in size, structure, and function. When Congress and the president authorize a new policy, they must decide whether they will assign its implementation to an existing agency or create a new agency. If they choose the latter option, they must determine which type of agency to create.

Departments

The Department of Homeland Security, established in 2002, is the newest of fifteen federal **departments,** each responsible for one broadly defined policy area (see Figure 12.2 on page 447). The president holds the fifteen departments accountable through the appointment of a head official. *Secretary* is the title of this top political appointee in all departments except the Department of Justice, where the head is the attorney general. Although the Senate must confirm them, these top appointees serve at the president's pleasure. In addition to appointing the department secretaries, the president names bureaucrats to positions in several levels of the hierarchy

---

*The organization chart of the federal government, which provides a window on the breadth of the federal bureaucracy today, is included in the U.S. Government Manual at www.gpaccess.gov/gmanual/browse-gm-08.html.

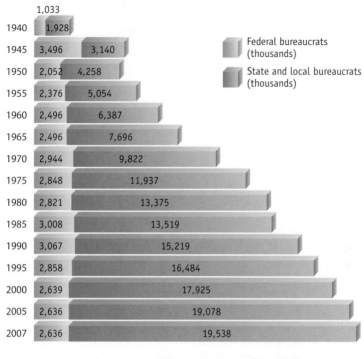

Growth in National Civilian Bureaucrats and State and Local Bureaucrats

Year	Federal bureaucrats (thousands)	State and local bureaucrats (thousands)
1940	1,033	1,928
1945	3,496	3,140
1950	2,052	4,258
1955	2,376	5,054
1960	2,496	6,387
1965	2,496	7,696
1970	2,944	9,822
1975	2,848	11,937
1980	2,821	13,375
1985	3,008	13,519
1990	3,067	15,219
1995	2,858	16,484
2000	2,639	17,925
2005	2,636	19,078
2007	2,636	19,538

POLITICAL INQUIRY

Figure 13.1 ▓ **What has been the trend in the growth of the national civilian bureaucracy since 1965? What has been the pattern for the growth of state and local bureaucracies over the same period? What explains these patterns?**

Sources: Table 17.5 in *Fiscal Year 2009 Historical Tables*, www.whitehouse.gov/omb/budget/fy2009/pdf/hist.pdf; Statistical Abstracts of the United States, 1941, 1946, 1961, 1981.

below the secretaries. These political appointees have titles such as *deputy secretary, assistant deputy secretary, agency director,* and *deputy director.* Table 13.2 on page 489 lists the fifteen departments and gives the number of employees and budget outlay for each in 2008.

Independent Administrative Agencies

Whereas each executive branch department has authority for a broadly defined policy area, a host of **independent administrative agencies** are each responsible for a more narrowly defined function of the national government. Congress and the president create these agencies to fulfill one of several purposes. Some of them, such as

Growth in Federal Expenditures, 1940–2009

Year	Budget
1940	$10
1945	$93
1950	$43
1955	$68
1960	$92
1965	$118
1970	$196
1975	$332
1980	$591
1985	$946
1990	$1,253
1995	$1,516
2000	$1,789
2005	$2,472
2010	$3,591 (estimate)

Budget in billions of current dollars
(rounded to nearest billion)

POLITICAL INQUIRY

Figure 13.2 ■ **What has been the overall trend in the growth of federal government spending since 1940? What would you say about the pattern since 2000? What political factors—domestic and international—explain the trend in federal spending over the past decade?**

Source: Table 3.1 in *Historical Tables Fiscal Year 2009*, www.whitehouse.gov/omb/budget/fy2009/pdf/hist.pdf.

the Smithsonian Institution, were established to handle new governmental functions that did not easily fall within the purview of existing departments. Other independent administrative agencies support the work of existing departments and agencies, including recruiting and training employees (Office of Personnel Management) and managing government properties and records (General Services Administration). Still others, such as the National Science Foundation and the National Aeronautics and Space Administration, focus on research and preservation of national resources.

Congresses and presidents create independent administrative agencies when they want to protect the agencies' decision making or functions from partisan politics. Thus

TABLE 13.2

Evolution of Federal Government Departments

Department and Year Created	Civilian Employees (FY 2008 average)	Budget Outlay in Billions of Dollars (2008)
State, 1789	35,724	$ 17.5
Treasury, 1789	112,366	548.8
Interior, 1849	68,414	9.9
Justice, 1870 (attorney general's office 1789; department status 1870)	107,790	26.6
Agriculture, 1889	97,584	90.8
Commerce, 1913 (separated from Department of Commerce and Labor, which had been created in 1903)	41,217	7.7
Labor, 1913 (separated from Department of Commerce and Labor, which had been created in 1903)	16,267	58.8
Defense, 1947 (previously, Department of War, created 1789; Army Department and Navy Department, created 1798)	680,025	640.5
Housing and Urban Development, 1965	9,559	49.1
Transportation, 1966	54,547	70.0
Energy, 1977	14,782	21.4
Health and Human Services, 1979 (created from Department of Health, Education and Welfare, established in 1953)	62,097	700.5
Education, 1979 (created from Department of Health, Education and Welfare, established in 1953)	4,281	66.0
Veterans Affairs, 1988	263,620	84.8
Homeland Security, 2003	164,592	40.7

Sources: Civil employee statistics from www.opm.gov/feddata/html/2008/july/table3.asp; budget information from www.whitehouse.gov/omb/budget/Historicals/, Table 3.1.

the structure of these agencies differs from the organization of the federal departments. A director, nominated by the president and usually needing Senate confirmation, heads each agency's board. The board is composed of members affiliated with both political parties, who are appointed by the president for a fixed term of a specified number of years. The expectation is that this structure will limit the president's influence over the independent agency because it relieves the director of the need to be loyal to the president's preferences to keep the job. Hence these agencies are supposed to be "independent" of partisan politics. Yet ultimately such agencies still need to earn the support of those who authorize the spending of money and who have the authority to restructure the agency or its mission—Congress and the president.

Independent Regulatory Commissions

Over time, Congress and presidents have recognized the need for expertise in regulating the country's diverse economic activities and their impact on the overall economy, workers, consumers, and the environment. Acknowledging their own lack of such expertise, they have created numerous **independent regulatory commissions,** bureaucracies with the authority to develop standards of behavior for specific industries and businesses, to monitor compliance with these standards, and to impose sanctions on those it finds guilty of violating the standards.

Initially, such government regulation centered on *economic regulation*—matters such as setting the prices of goods and services and ensuring competition in the marketplace. The first independent regulatory commission, the Interstate Commerce Commission (ICC, 1887), was set up to oversee the prices and services of the railroad industry. Beginning in the 1960s, Congress turned more in the direction of *social regulation,* establishing regulatory commissions that focused on how business practices affected the environment and the health and safety of consumers and workers. For example, legislation created the Environmental Protection Agency (EPA) in 1970 and the Consumer Product Safety Commission (CPSC) in 1972.

Independent regulatory agencies are under the direction of bipartisan boards whose members do not need to be loyal to the president's preferences. Typically, the president nominates and the Senate confirms an odd number of board members. Board members serve staggered fixed terms. This structure allows the agency to make decisions based on the expertise of its board members, not on the preferences of the president or Congress. Still, the agencies need both presidential and congressional support to survive.

Government Corporations

Like private businesses, **government corporations** sell a service or product; but unlike private businesses, they are government owned. Congress and the president create government corporations when they believe it is in the public interest for the national government to engage in a commercial activity, such as selling stamps to pay for the cost of delivering mail. (In fact, the best-known U.S. government corporation is the United States Postal Service.) Unlike the other categories of bureaucracies, government corporations are expected to make enough money to cover their costs.

A bipartisan board typically directs each government corporation. The president appoints the board members to serve for staggered fixed terms. Typically, the Senate is not required to confirm the board members. Like regulatory commissions and administrative agencies, government corporations are structured to be independent.

Executive Office of the President

By 1939, the national bureaucracy for which the president serves as chief executive officer had grown tremendously in size and diversity of structure and functions. Acknowledging that the president needed help to manage this constellation of departments, independent administrative agencies, independent regulatory commissions, and government corporations, President Franklin Roosevelt (1933–1945) and Congress created the Executive Office of the President (EOP).

The EOP is composed of dozens of offices and councils that assist the president in managing the complex and sprawling executive branch of the bureaucracy. The EOP has evolved into the locomotive of the national government—the engine driving the development and implementation of presidential policies and programs. The president appoints the top-level bureaucrats in EOP agencies, and the majority of these appointments are not subject to Senate confirmation. The president has the authority to fire these appointees at his pleasure. Therefore, the EOP serves the president; it is in fact the presidential bureaucracy. (See Chapter 12 for a detailed discussion of the EOP.)

In this section, we took stock of the executive branch organizations in which national bureaucrats implement policy. We next consider the nature of the essential roles bureaucrats play in all stages of public policy.

Federal Bureaucrats' Roles in Public Policy

Although the primary work of bureaucrats is implementation—putting public policy into action—bureaucrats play an active, vital role in all six stages of the public policy cycle. These stages are (1) agenda setting, (2) policy formulation, (3) policy approval, (4) resource allocation, (5) policy implementation, and (6) policy evaluation.

According to the **politics–administration dichotomy,** there is a clear line between *politics* (the formulation and approval of public policy and the allocation of resources to put the policy into effect) and the *administration* of public policy (the real-world implementation of the policy). The dichotomy says that elected officials (whom citizens hold accountable through the ballot box) have authority for politics and that competent bureaucrats (hired through merit-based civil service) have authority for policy administration. Theoretically, this arrangement fosters not only responsive government but also efficient and effective public services.

The politics–administration dichotomy may sound good, but the reality of public policy processes does not allow for such a clean separation between those who "do politics" and those who administer policy. Although bureaucrats are hired to implement policy made by elected officials, these officials tap the expertise of bureaucrats throughout the other five stages of the policy process, allowing bureaucrats to influence and even make policies themselves, as we now shall see.

Agenda Setting

In the first stage of the public policy cycle, elected officials place issues on their agendas to discuss, if not to address by formulating a *policy*—a plan of government action to deal with a particular public concern. Bureaucrats play an instrumental role in setting the policy agenda. Because their focus is to implement public policy at the street level, bureaucrats have a clear view of the societal problems that citizens are looking for the government to address and strong views on how best to address these problems. Political scientists use the term *iron triangle* to describe long-term collaborative efforts among bureaucrats in a government agency, the members of an interest group, and the members of a legislative committee to get their mutual concerns on the agenda and then to formulate the policies they deem necessary to address these concerns. *Issue networks,* which are temporary collaborations among bureaucrats, elected officials, and the members of several interest groups, also engage in lobbying to set the agenda, as well as to influence policy formulation. Bureaucrats, who want to get their concerns and proposed programs on the agenda, may work to create issue networks as well as iron triangles. For more about iron triangles and issue networks, see Chapter 7.

Policy Formulation

The second stage of the policy process, policy formulation, involves defining a problem that has made it to the agenda and setting a plan of action (a policy) to address the problem. (Note, however, that not all concerns that reach an elected official's agenda—or even the agendas of numerous elected officials—go further in the policy process.) Although anyone can formulate a public policy, only elected officials can officially introduce policy proposals into the lawmaking process. Thus individuals and groups outside government, as well as bureaucrats, must identify members of Congress who can introduce policy proposals for legislative action. The president can also make policy by issuing an executive order, an authority that lies outside the legislative process (see Chapter 12).

Because bureaucrats often have specialized knowledge of societal problems, elected officials rely on bureaucrats when formulating policies. House and Senate committees frequently call on bureaucrats to review and comment on bills that, if approved, they will implement and to testify in the hearings in which congressional members investigate and study problems. Thus bureaucrats regularly take part in policy formulation, whether at their own impetus or at the request of elected officials.

In recognition of bureaucrats' expertise, Congress often includes vague or ambiguous language in bills and relies on bureaucrats to fill in the program details after a bill is passed, during the policy implementation stage. Vague legislative language may also reflect the congressional sponsors' need to win majority votes in both the House and the Senate and to secure presidential approval of the policy. Fuzzy language means that if the bill becomes law, bureaucrats will need to discern what the policy is directing them to do before they can implement it.

Policy Approval

When Congress and the president vote to approve or reject the formulated policy, which is in the form of a proposed piece of legislation—a bill—they have reached the third stage, policy approval. Bills detailing the government's plan to address a problem are called authorization bills; when Congress and the president, or Congress alone over a president's veto, approve such bills, the laws thus created authorize government action. **Authorization laws** not only provide the plan of action to address a given societal concern but also identify the executive branch unit that will put the plan into effect. The law may authorize an existing executive unit to carry out the policy, or it may establish a new unit to do the job. Presidential executive orders, another form of public policy, direct bureaucrats in how to implement policy. Yet bureaucracies cannot implement a public policy until they have legal authority to spend money.

Resource Allocation

In the next phase of the policy process, resource allocation, Congress and the president specify how much money each bureaucracy will be authorized to spend during the budget year. Through the budget process (see Chapter 15), Congress and the president formulate appropriation bills, which are plans for the distribution of government revenue to government entities, including bureaucracies, legislative bodies, and judicial bodies. Approved appropriation bills—**appropriation laws**—give bureaucracies the legal authority to spend money.

Bureaucrats play three key roles in the budget process. First, at the request of the president, bureaucrats develop an annual budget request for their agencies. Second, before Congress approves the appropriation bills that distribute government revenues to the agencies, it calls upon bureaucrats to justify their budget requests. In turn, bureaucrats lobby members of Congress to allocate to their agencies the funds they requested. With limited money available, bureaucracies typically do not receive all the funding they request. Therefore, bureaucracies compete with one another for their piece of the limited budget pie. Once Congress and the president approve the appropriation bills, bureaucrats take on their third role in the budget process: they spend money to put the public policy into action.

Policy Implementation

Bureaucrats are at the center of the second-to-last stage of the policy cycle, policy implementation. In this phase, bureaucrats must first interpret the law and then carry it out. Congress and the president delegate to bureaucrats the authority to determine the best way to implement the policy; this authority is called **administrative discretion.** Applying administrative discretion, bureaucrats make the day-to-day decisions related to executing policy programs and enforcing the necessary rules and standards. Elected officials risk the loss of control over the content of public policy when they delegate administrative discretion to bureaucrats. However, they have numerous tools to limit this risk, which we discuss later in this chapter's section on federal bureaucratic accountability.

The process by which bureaucrats translate vague law into concrete plans of action is a quasi-legislative ("as-if legislative") process. It is "quasi-legislative" because bureaucrats in the executive branch, not legislators, make policy as they fill in the details needed to implement legislation. **Administrative rule making** is the name of this process by which upper-level bureaucrats use their administrative discretion and their expertise in the policy area to create rules, regulations, and standards that the bureaucracy will then enforce. For example, recognizing its lack of expertise in the specifics of how to prevent air and water pollution, Congress delegated to the Environmental Protection Agency (EPA) the authority to establish policy. The EPA sets specific pollution emissions standards in order to implement the Clean Water and Clean Air acts. Although Congress does not approve these EPA administrative standards, importantly, the standards have the force of law.

Agencies involved in administrative rule making also have a quasi-judicial ("as-if judicial") role. Through **administrative adjudication,** they determine when their rules are violated, and they impose penalties on the violators. Citizens who disagree with an agency's application of its administrative rules or those whom an agency finds guilty of violating its rules may challenge the agency's decisions through a lawsuit. Indeed, several states successfully sued the EPA in 2007 for its failure to set carbon dioxide emissions standards and hence its inadequate implementation of the Clean Air Act. Claiming that "the EPA's failure to act in the face of [the Supreme Court's 2007 ruling and] these incontestable dangers is a shameful dereliction of duty," Massachusetts attorney general Martha Coakley, along with the attorneys general of seventeen other states, as well as two cities and eleven environmental interest groups, sued the EPA in April 2008.[11]

Policy Evaluation

The last stage of the policy process is policy evaluation—the assessment of the intended and unintended effects of policy implementation. People do not assess government success by the number of laws passed or by the promises made in the language of the laws. Rather, the effectiveness and efficiency of public service delivery are what matter to the public. The implementation of policy by bureaucrats is thus the key to citizens' satisfaction with government—and the key to government success.

Since the 1970s, U.S. taxpayers have called for increased transparency in government, including evaluations of public policy implementation to determine how effectively government is using their tax dollars. The corruption of the administration of President Richard Nixon—which featured Nixon's misuse of the Internal Revenue Service to collect information on opponents, as well as the infamous White House cover-up of the break-in at the Democratic Party headquarters in the Watergate Building—partially explains the call for greater transparency in government. The publication in 1973 of political scientists Jeffrey L. Pressman and Aaron B. Wildavsky's study of a federally funded economic development program also fueled outcries for increased transparency and evaluation.[12] Their landmark research concluded that it is "amazing that federal programs work at all" given the hurdles that policy implementers encounter.

As a result, policy evaluation has become a larger component of the workload of legislators and bureaucrats in recent decades than it ever was before. Because elected officials and citizens want proof of the efficiency and effectiveness of implemented policies, agencies must document what they do and its impact. Because citizens do not elect bureaucrats, they do not have the opportunity to fire civil servants whose performance is unsatisfactory. Therefore, citizens defer the responsibility for bureaucratic accountability to members of Congress, the president, and the judges who preside over the courts because these elected and appointed government officials have legal means to monitor bureaucrats' work and to hold them accountable.

Federal Bureaucratic Accountability

When it comes to public service, everyone is watching. The courts, through the mechanism of lawsuits, review the actions of the executive and legislative branches to ensure that they are constitutional and legal. Congress and the president, as the creators and funders of bureaucracies, can threaten to revamp or eliminate any bureaucracy, or to decrease its funding, if its performance falls short of expectations. Congress and the president not only structure bureaucracies to foster efficient, effective, and accountable public service but also pass laws to increase self-policing by bureaucrats.

People outside government, including many ordinary citizens, also keep a close eye on bureaucracies. National **sunshine laws** open up government functions and documents to the public, ensuring transparency and the public's right to know about government business and decision making. But these laws are effective only if citizens know about and take advantage of them.

Accountability to the People

One of the first national sunshine laws for the enhancement of bureaucratic accountability to the people was the Administrative Procedure Act (APA) of 1946. The APA responded to citizens' and interest groups' concerns about the fast growth in the number of agencies involved in administrative rule making and about the lack of transparency and accountability of the bureaucratic rule makers. The APA, which applies to all federal agencies except those specifically excluded by legislation, standardized rule-making procedures and requires bureaucracies to publicize their proposed rules in the *Federal Register,* a daily national government publication. They also must publish an invitation for people to offer comments on the agency's proposals.

Once the agency collects and reviews the people's comments, it must publish its approved rules in the *Federal Register.* To facilitate this open process, the national government Web site www.regulations.gov posts proposed administrative rules and accepts electronically submitted comments on the rules. In this way, people can have a voice in administrative rule making. Such citizen input is essential to democracy because bureaucrats propose and approve more administrative rules each year than the pieces of legislation proposed and approved by Congress and the president.

The Freedom of Information Act (FOIA) is a 1966 amendment to the APA. The FOIA requires national agencies to give citizens access to government documents upon request and at a reasonable cost. After the terrorist attacks on September 11, 2001, however, the national government has denied an increasing percentage of such requests in the name of national security. The decreased access to government documents heightened tensions between people advocating government confidentiality, on the one hand, and individuals cherishing democratic openness and those dedicated to holding the national bureaucracy accountable, on the other. The American Society of Newspaper Editors was so concerned about the diminished access that it established Sunshine Week (first held March 13–20, 2005) to educate citizens about their right to know and to request information about what the bureaucracy is doing.

Another law that aims to make the federal bureaucracy open and responsive to the people is the Government in the Sunshine Act of 1976. This act of Congress requires all multiheaded national agencies, except those in the Executive Office of the President (EOP), to conduct open, public meetings where citizens can testify and present their concerns about these agencies' actions (past, current, and potential) and the procedures by which they make decisions.

National agencies are now also using the Internet to make government more transparent. In September 2000, the General Services Administration (GSA) of the national government launched its FirstGov Website, the national government's one-stop portal to national, state, local, and tribal government agency websites. It provides government information and services at your fingertips. In 2007, the GSA changed the name from FirstGov to USA.gov (www.usa.gov) in response to feedback from users who wanted a name that was easier to remember. (See "Then, Now, Next" for more on USA.gov as well as the new RECOVERY.gov site.)

Strongly supporting the use of the Internet as a means to enhance citizen access to government information and services, Congress approved and President Bush signed into law the E-Government Act of 2002. This law established a federal chief information officer within the Office of Management and Budget. Moreover, it requires national agencies to use Internet-based information technology. President Barack Obama has promised that under his administration the federal government will provide Americans with an "unprecedented level of openness, collaboration, and efficiency and effectiveness through the use of information technology."[13]

Private organizations that monitor and evaluate the activities of bureaucrats have certainly taken advantage of sunshine laws and e-government. For example, in 2007, Congress passed legislation to establish an independent, bipartisan commission to investigate U.S. wartime contracting in Iraq and Afghanistan. Senator Claire McCaskill (D-Missouri), the bill's cosponsor, praised "POGO's [the Project on Government Oversight] work in supporting these provisions, along with the support of other watchdog groups including Taxpayers for Common Sense, the Government Accountability Project, OMBWatch, Common Cause, U.S. PIRG and Iraq and Afghanistan Veterans of America."[14] In addition to taking advantage of their right to government documents under the FOIA, watchdog groups are also likelier than is the average citizen to use government Web sites to track bureaucratic activities.

In a democracy, bureaucrats, like elected officials, operate in a fishbowl. Working face to face, or computer screen to computer screen, with the people whom they serve, they are in full view of anyone interested in monitoring them. Sunshine laws

Will E-Government Improve the Obama Administration's Performance?

THEN: President Bill Clinton's administration initiated e-government in 2000 with the launching of Firstgov.gov, which later became USA.gov. The E-Government Act of 2002, signed into law by President George W. Bush, requires federal agencies to use the Internet as a means of providing services to citizens.

NOW: President Barack Obama and Congress turn to the Internet to ensure that implementation of the American Recovery and Reinvestment Act (2009), an unprecedented $787-billion economic stimulus package aimed at jumpstarting the national economy, will be transparent. The RECOVERY.gov website (1) explains the law, (2) shows how, when, and where the money is being spent, and (3) provides data so citizens can evaluate the law's progress and impact.

WHAT'S NEXT?

- Will the increased use of e-government lead to a decrease in the size and cost of the federal bureaucracy? Why or why not?

- Will e-government foster more efficient and effective government services, and therefore a decrease in citizens' criticism of the bureaucracy, or will the volume of criticism increase as citizens' expectations of more efficient service are not met?

- How might the digital divide—the fact that approximately 40 percent of U.S. homes are not connected to the Internet at all or have only limited access to technology—affect the level of government transparency and accountability in the era of e-government?

and e-government provide citizens with the means to find out what is going on in the bureaucracy. When citizens or watchdog groups identify a problem with bureaucratic operations, they frequently turn to the media to bring public attention to the issue, as the media are always ready to report on bureaucratic inefficiency and impropriety. A more expensive option for citizen and interest group action against bureaucratic waste and misconduct is the filing of a lawsuit.

Accountability to the Courts

As bureaucratic agencies implement policy, they must comply with constitutional guarantees of due process and equal protection of laws. A citizen who believes that bureaucrats have violated these rights can challenge bureaucratic actions through the agency's quasi-judicial processes. If the citizen is not satisfied with the result of this quasi-judicial recourse, he or she can sue the agency through the courts.

Through the litigation process, the U.S. judicial system seeks to ensure that administrative agencies conduct their quasi-legislative and quasi-judicial functions in compliance with the constitutional guarantees of due process (in the Fifth and Fourteenth amendments), as well as the Administrative Procedure Act of 1946. In 2006, for example, federal district judge Richard Leon ruled that the Federal Emergency Management Agency (FEMA) procedures and notices to Hurricane Katrina victims were so difficult to understand that evacuees were deprived of due process because they were unable to determine what the process was. According to the lawyer for ACORN, a housing advocacy group that brought the lawsuit, as many as 11,000 families may have been wrongfully denied long-term housing assistance by the lack of due process in FEMA procedures.[15]

Accountability to Congress

Bureaucrats must always keep in mind the preferences and agenda of Congress if they want to survive, for Congress approves the legislation that creates, regulates, and funds bureaucracies. The Senate has an additional mechanism for promoting bureaucratic accountability, in that more than one-quarter of the president's appointees are subject to Senate confirmation. The confirmation process for top bureaucrats gives senators a degree of influence over the leadership and direction of executive departments and agencies.

Another lever by which Congress encourages bureaucratic accountability is the monitoring of bureaucracies' policy implementation, a form of legislative oversight. When the media, citizens, or interest groups bring concerns about a bureaucracy's policy implementation to the attention of legislators, Congress might launch an investigation. If, consequently, Congress and the president are dissatisfied with that bureaucracy's performance or behavior, they can cut its budget, modify its legal authority, or even eliminate the agency.

In most cases, oversight does not occur unless citizens, interest groups, and the media push for congressional action, as occurred in the aftermath of September 11, 2001, when public pressure forced Congress to create the 9/11 Commission to investigate the terrorist attacks on the World Trade Center in New York City. An evaluation of bureaucratic performance can also be required in the authorization legislation by a

sunset clause, which forces the expiration of the program or policy after a specified number of years unless Congress reauthorizes it through new legislation.

Accountability to the President

The president also has several tools for holding bureaucracies accountable. Like Congress, the president can use the authorization and appropriation processes to ensure accountability. In addition, because most top political appointees serve at the president's pleasure, they are responsive to the president's policy preferences— and in this way they and their agencies are accountable to the president.

Today the Office of Management and Budget, an EOP agency, is the key lever in the president's efforts to hold the bureaucracy accountable. The OMB evaluates bureaucratic performance for the president. Based on OMB performance assessments, the president proposes budget increases or decreases, agency growth or elimination, or even a reorganization of the executive branch in which agencies are consolidated.

In addition to overseeing performance evaluations of bureaucratic agencies, the OMB spearheads the development of the president's budget, controls the implementation of appropriation laws, and regulates administrative rule making. Through its Office of Information and Regulatory Affairs (OIRA), the OMB ensures that regulations created by executive branch agencies are not "unnecessarily costly"[16] and support the president's policy preferences.

Internal Accountability

The president, Congress, the courts, and ordinary citizens have multiple means by which to hold bureaucrats accountable. But bureaucrats, who themselves are taxpayers, also worry about inefficiency and waste in public service. Legislated codes of behavior and whistle-blower protections help to foster accountability from within bureaucracies.

Codes of Behavior and the Ethics in Government Act

To ensure the best public service, bureaucracies have codes of behavior. These codes specify guidelines for ethical, efficient, and effective behavior on the part of bureaucrats. Each government agency has its own such code. In addition, in 1992, the Office of Government Ethics published a comprehensive set of ethical standards for national bureaucrats. Moreover, many of the professions in which bureaucrats are members (lawyers, doctors, nurses, accountants, engineers, and so on) have established codes of behavior. Importantly, however, codes of behavior are just guidelines. They do not stipulate what a bureaucrat should do in a given situation. Thus bureaucrats must use discretion when applying such codes to their daily work of providing public service.

The Ethics in Government Act of 1978 established the United States Office of Government Ethics (OGE), which is charged with preventing conflicts of interest by bureaucrats (political appointees, SES bureaucrats, and civil servants). A **conflict of interest** arises when a public servant is in a position to make a decision or take an action from which he or she can personally benefit. In such a situation, the public servant's private interest is in conflict with his or her responsibility to serve the public interest. A key to the prevention of conflicts of interest is the requirement that top government officials must disclose their finances.

Whistle-Blower Protections and Inspectors General Whistle-blower laws offer an additional means of internal accountability in the national bureaucracy. The 1978 Civil Service Reform Act provided some protections to civil servant **whistle-blowers**—employees who disclose government misconduct, waste, mismanagement, or abuse of authority, or a threat to public health or safety. The CSRA established the Office of Special Counsel to protect whistle-blowers' job security. Then in 1986, thanks to the lobbying efforts of many groups, including the Project on Government Oversight, Congress approved the False Claims Act. This law allows for a monetary reward for government whistle-blowers who expose fraud that harms the U.S. government.

In another attempt to improve internal accountability, Congress approved the Inspector General Act in 1978. This law aims to ensure the integrity of public service by creating government watchdogs, called **inspectors general,** appointed by the president and embedded in government agencies, to monitor policy implementation and investigate alleged misconduct. The law requires the appointment of the inspectors general without regard to their political affiliation and strictly on the basis of their abilities in accounting, auditing, or investigation. "We're supposed to check our politics at the door and call things as we see them. If we uncover things that reflect badly on the government, we're legally and morally obliged to report it. We're obliged to do that for the good of the country." So explained Clark Ervin, who held the position of inspector general at the State and Homeland Security departments.[17]

In summary, whistle-blower protection laws and inspectors general enhance the ability of the bureaucrats themselves to police the agencies in which they work, and sunshine laws give government outsiders various instruments for monitoring the bureaucracy. But many citizens and government officials believe that more needs to be done to improve bureaucrats' record of performance.

Can Bureaucratic Performance Be Improved?

In the United States, bureaucrats perform every job imaginable. They generally do their jobs so well that we rarely think about how their work positively affects us around the clock. We and our elected officials are nevertheless hair trigger–quick to bash the bureaucracy at the slightest hint of inefficiency. Similarly, the media seize upon any opportunity to report on problems with bureaucrats and bureaucracies. Our public discourse infrequently covers bureaucrats' *good* performance. When was the last time you heard a news report or were a party to a friendly conversation that praised a public servant?

Yet the U.S. Postal Service delivers hundreds of millions of pieces of mail six days a week, and rarely is a letter or package lost. Thousands of planes safely take off from and land at U.S. airports every hour, guided by federal bureaucrats in the person of air traffic controllers. Millions of senior citizens receive a monthly Social Security check on time every month. Even more people travel the interstate highway systems without incident each day.

> In August 2007, the I-135W bridge in Minneapolis collapsed, killing thirteen people. Barely one year after the collapse, the new replacement bridge opened to traffic. The private construction firm contracted by the state of Minnesota to design and build the new bridge completed the job three months earlier than the state's deadline and less than 2 percent over budget—unusual for a project of this magnitude. The success of this $234-million contract can be attributed to cooperation among local, state, and federal bureaucracies, all moving with record speed, as well as an innovative arrangement with the private contractor.

Public administration and policy scholar Charles Goodsell has found that two-thirds to three-fourths of Americans report their encounters with government bureaucrats and bureaucracy as "satisfactory."[18] However, research consistently shows that some national agencies perform better than do others.

The Best-Performing Bureaucracies

Political scientists William T. Gormley and Steven Balla reviewed national performance data and summarized the characteristics of national agencies that perform well.[19] They found that numerous factors correlate with better-performing bureaucracies—factors that individual bureaucrats have little control over. These include legislative language that clearly states the goal of the legislation and provides high levels of administrative discretion, allowing bureaucrats to determine the best way to achieve the goal. Better-performing bureaucracies tend to be those with easily measured goals, especially goals that include providing resources to citizens (such as Social Security checks) as opposed to taking resources (tax collection). Another factor correlated with good performance is high levels of support from elected officials, the media, and diverse groups of citizens for the legislated goal and the implementing agency. High levels of support typically result in an agency receiving ample resources. Effective leaders who develop and maintain high levels of support from government officials and interested parties outside of government are also important to well-performing bureaucracies.

Does Contracting-Out Improve Performance?

In addition to analyzing citizen satisfaction with public bureaucracies, Charles Goodsell has analyzed the body of research that assesses the efficiency of public policy implementation by government bureaucrats compared to the efficiency of private organizations. He found that "the assumption that business always does

> President Barack Obama attends a hurricane preparedness meeting at FEMA headquarters in Washington in May 2009. The president is joined by two of his confirmed appointees, Homeland Security Secretary Janet Napolitano (in the yellow jacket) and FEMA Director Craig Fugate (to the right of Napolitano).

better than government is not upheld."[20] In fact, Goodsell reports that "despite antigovernment rhetoric to the contrary, the federal government achieves essentially the same degree of satisfaction for its services as corporate America does for its products."[21] Nevertheless, many commentators and elected officials argue that private businesses are more efficient than are governments and therefore that more public service should be outsourced to private businesses.

Contracting-out to private businesses certainly decreases the number of bureaucrats on the national payroll. But does outsourcing foster more efficient and effective public service? Does it save taxpayer dollars? The evidence strongly suggests otherwise.

Outsourcing government work can lead to waste, fraud, overpricing, and corruption. In its evaluation of contract waste and fraud in Hurricane Katrina relief, the House of Representatives Government Reform Committee reported that "the main problems were no-bid contracts, layers of subcontracting that inflated costs, and a lack of oversight on the completion of work."[22] What causes these inefficiencies?

First, for-profit organizations must make a profit to survive. As contract law experts note, for many private government contractors, overestimating the costs of the work and then reaping illegally high profits are a common reality. Second, holding bureaucrats accountable for their performance is not easy in general, and determining whom to hold accountable for delays, cost overruns, and quality issues is complicated when policy implementation occurs through the shadow bureaucracy.[23] Unlike government bodies, private businesses can legally function behind closed doors—unless and until concerned citizens, watchdog groups, the media, and government officials force the doors open through congressional investigations or lawsuits.

Citizens' Role in Bureaucratic Performance

Citizens turn to the government to provide services and solve problems. As we have discussed, the government's success in serving the people well depends on many factors. Ultimately, even if all other factors correlated with a well-performing bureaucracy are in place, the bureaucracy will fail without the participation and compliance of the people it serves. The effectiveness of public policies depends on people's knowledge of and compliance with the law. It depends on their applying for the government programs for which they qualify and their conformity to the rules, regulations, standards, and directions of bureaucrats. This symbiotic relationship is essential to the success of government.

CONCLUSION

CONTINUING THE CONVERSATION

- In 1789, the federal bureaucracy was small in size and limited in scope. Today a sprawling, complex network of federal, state, local, and shadow bureaucrats distributes a huge number and diversity of public services that would have been unthinkable to earlier generations.
- Hiring based on merit, not patronage, the devolution of service to state and local bureaucrats, and outsourcing to shadow bureaucrats are now the norm in the federal bureaucracy.
- The hope and expectation have been that the work of the shadow bureaucrats would be more efficient and effective than that provided by federal bureaucrats. However, whistleblowers and scholars have regularly challenged the idea that the shadow bureaucracy does a superior job of delivering vital services.
- Criticism of the federal bureaucracy and bureaucrats has been a constant chorus, yet most citizens report satisfactory interactions with government bureaucrats and sufficient public services.

STUDY NOW

Summary

1. Bureaucrats and Bureaucracy
Traditionally, most people define bureaucrats as employees in the executive branches of the national, state, and local governments who deliver public service, and they think only of government agencies when they hear the word *bureaucracy*.

2. Federal Bureaucrats

The national government hires almost 3 million civilians into the federal executive branch, through patronage and merit-based personnel systems, to administer the policies established by elected officials.

3. State, Local, and Shadow Bureaucrats

The overall number of national bureaucrats has been stable over the past few decades. However, the number of state, local, and shadow bureaucrats has grown significantly due to the proliferation of federal grants-in-aid and mandates, and the practice of contracting out more and more public services.

4. The Evolution and Organization of the Federal Bureaucracy

Today federal government employees equal in number the nation's total population in the year 1789; work in agencies reporting to department secretaries and independent commissions, boards, and directors; and deliver a variety of services of which the founding fathers never could have dreamed.

5. Federal Bureaucrats' Roles in Public Policy

Federal bureaucrats lobby elected officials in all stages of the policy cycle, provide expertise to policy makers, and make policy regularly as they determine the detailed programs, rules, and standards that are needed to put policies in action. They also use administrative discretion daily to implement policies.

6. Federal Bureaucratic Accountability

Taxpayers, clients, the media, interest groups, and whistle-blowers, as well as the president, Congress, and the courts, hold bureaucrats accountable.

7. Can Bureaucratic Performance Be Improved?

Certainly citizens do not evaluate every agency as performing well, but for the most part, citizens report that their interactions with government bureaucrats are at least satisfactory.

For Critical Thinking and Discussion

1. Do citizens expect too much from government and hence from bureaucrats and bureaucracies? Explain your answer.

2. Does the profit motive of private businesses threaten the efficient use of taxpayer money when public services are contracted-out? Why or why not?

3. Identify at least one public service that you believe the national government should not contract-out to private-sector organizations, and defend your choice(s).

4. Compose a list of public services provided to you since you woke up this morning. Which of these were provided by national bureaucrats? State bureaucrats? Local bureaucrats?

Key Terms

administrative
    adjudication 494
administrative discretion 493

administrative rule
    making 494
appropriation law 493

authorization law 493
bureaucracy 477
bureaucrats 476

Internet Resources

***A More Perfect Union* Web site**
www.mhhe.com/harrisonampule Consult the book's Web site for study guides, interactive activities, simulations, and current hot-links that provide additional information on bureaucracy in government.

Office of Management and Budget
www.whitehouse.gov.omb This Web site provides access to the current and previous federal budget documents and historical budget tables.

Regulations.gov
www.regulations.gov You can review proposed and approved rules, regulations, and standards of federal executive agencies and submit your comments about them.

USA.gov
www.usa.gov Use this site as a one-stop portal to national, state, and local government officials, agencies, and documents.

Recommended Readings

Goodsell, Charles T. *The Case for Bureaucracy: A Public Administration Polemic,* 4th ed. Washington, DC: CQ Press, 2004. A review of the common myths and criticisms of bureaucracy, with evidence to show that they are indeed unsupported.

Gormley, William T., Jr., and Steven J. Balla. *Bureaucracy and Democracy: Accountability and Performance.* Washington, DC: CQ Press, 2004. Case studies and examples illustrating what the national bureaucracy does and why it is important, and drawing on social science theories to describe how bureaucracy works and the complex and conflicting demands put on it.

Wilson, James Q. 1989. *Bureaucracy: What Government Agencies Do and Why They Do It.* New York: Basic Books, 1989. A classic treatise on what government agencies do and why they function as they do, with analysis of how they might become more responsible and efficient.

A common-law tradition imported from England dominated in the U.S. legal system.

Through code law and further interpretation of common law, the courts respond to unprecedented developments, from a torrent of technology to a continuing terrorist threat.

NOW

14

The Judiciary

We think of the courts primarily as places where citizens turn when they have a dispute that they need to resolve. We venture into a courtroom when we encounter some difficult legal issue with either the government or a private individual or group. The resolution of disputes is indeed the primary function of the courts in the United States. But courts and judges are concerned with other, more significant and far-reaching endeavors. In this chapter, we consider how the judiciary, consisting of the federal and state court systems, provides one of the most important defenses that citizens have against abuses of power by the executive and legislative branches. The judiciary's role as protector of civil liberties and civil rights does not escape the recognition of the American people: courts typically receive higher approval ratings than the other institutions of government.[1]

In *Federalist* No. 78, Alexander Hamilton explains that the Constitution intentionally structures the judiciary to be the weakest branch of government. But the judiciary has evolved significantly, to the point that it shares an equal role with the other two branches. Today the courts play a central role in ensuring that power remains in balance among the three branches of government on the federal level, as well as between the federal government and the states.

NEXT

Will new laws successfully address the complexities of issues like technological advance and the terrorist menace?

Will shifting Supreme Court ideology influence government actions in response to the ever-present threat of terrorism?

Will courts with specific policy expertise supplant legislatures' policy making in areas such as technology?

Judges have powers that go well beyond the immediate case they are considering. This authority allows them to make law for future generations. In fact, on both the national and state level, lawmaking is a shared enterprise among the three branches—legislative, executive, and judicial. Although the Constitution created a government characterized by a separation of powers, lawmaking is far less compartmentalized.[2] It is simplistic to think that legislatures make law, executives enforce it, and courts interpret it; rather, lawmaking is a part of what all three branches are empowered to do.

The Origins of the U.S. Judiciary

The foundations of the U.S. **judiciary**—the branch of government comprising the state and federal courts and the judges who preside over them—reach back to colonial times and the early years of the republic that took shape after the colonies broke with England. The U.S. Constitution created the framework for the judiciary. The structure and authority of the federal judiciary have evolved further, and continuously, through compromises forged over the last 200-plus years.

The Constitution and the Judiciary Act of 1789: Establishing the Supreme Court and the Federal District Courts

During the debates over the ratification of the Constitution, the Anti-Federalists and Federalists sparred over what the powers of the national judiciary should be. The Anti-Federalists warned that a too powerful national judiciary would erode states' rights. For their part, the Federalists contended that a strong national court would be necessary to moderate conflicts between the states. Ultimately, the Constitution named the **U.S. Supreme Court** as the high court of the land, but the framers intentionally did not make the Court's powers specific. Only by saying little about the specific powers of the Supreme Court were they able to reach agreement on the judiciary.

One of the most important of the framers' compromises was to establish only one court, the Supreme Court, and to empower Congress to create all lower courts. Congress accordingly set up these inferior courts in the earliest days of its first session when it passed the Judiciary Act of 1789, creating the federal district courts.[3] The federal district courts' geographic jurisdictions matched state boundaries, with at least one federal court in every state. Congress intended that these courts would have strong ties to the states in which they were located and expected that in many cases federal judges would apply state, not federal, law. These federal district courts

> Prominent on the façade of the U.S. Supreme Court building, this quotation from the landmark decision in the case of *Marbury v. Madison* demonstrates the importance of John Marshall's tenure as chief justice and his role in shaping the judiciary.

drew strength from their ties to the states, but the federal judiciary was quite weak, with little authority.

Marbury v. Madison *and the Principle of Judicial Review*

Shortly after his election in 1800, President Thomas Jefferson barred the Supreme Court from meeting during the 1801–1802 term. Jefferson was concerned about the out-of-power Federalists' potential use of the federal judiciary to maintain control of the national government. Jefferson was perhaps right to worry, because in the following term, in the landmark case *Marbury v. Madison* (1803), the Federalist-led Supreme Court grasped for itself the power of judicial review.[4] As we saw in Chapter 2, judicial review is the Court's authority to review and to strike down laws passed by the other branches of the national government.

In the *Marbury* case, the Court argued something that it had never argued before: that it had the power not only to review acts of Congress and the president but also to decide whether these laws were consistent with the Constitution, and to strike down those laws that conflicted with constitutional principles. Legal scholar Joel B. Grossman observes that in *Marbury*, "[John] Marshall made it abundantly clear that the meaning of the Constitution was rarely self-contained and obvious and that those who interpreted it—a role he staked out for the federal courts but one that did not reach its full flowering until the mid-twentieth century—made a difference."[5] Judicial review is the most significant power the Supreme Court exercises. Over time, the Court has extended this power to apply not only to acts of Congress and the chief executive but also to laws passed by state legislatures and executives, as well as to state court rulings.[6]

The Judiciary Act of 1891: Expanding the Federal Courts

The middle level in the federal court structure, the courts of appeals, also known as **circuit courts** of appeals, were created some 100 years after the *Marbury* decision, through the Judiciary Act of 1891. This law sought to relieve the heavy caseload that the U.S. Supreme Court faced after Congress had gradually expanded the jurisdiction of the federal courts to include criminal cases during the nineteenth century.

Until the advent of separate circuit courts of appeals, federal district court judges and even Supreme Court justices had needed to ride by horseback around the circuits to hear intermediate-level appeals cases. They sometimes traveled thousands of miles in a year in the practice, which became known as **circuit riding.** Over time, they began to bitterly bemoan the hardships they faced in servicing the geographically expanding country and the increasing case docket. But it took a long time for the states and their representatives in Congress to become convinced of the necessity of **courts of appeals**—courts that review previous decisions made by courts in the federal or state judicial system. These courts were charged exclusively with reviewing the application of law in previous court decisions, rather than reviewing evidence or facts of the cases.

The Judiciary Act of 1891 divided the courts of appeals into nine geographic units, with each unit number corresponding to a circuit. The assumption in carving out these units was that each state should be grouped with states likely to have similar political cultures. Today there are twelve courts of appeals covering designated regions, and the thirteenth hears specific kinds of cases, among them cases involving international trade, governmental contracts, and patents. By creating these separate courts of appeals, Congress significantly reduced the Supreme Court's workload: in 1890, 623 cases were filed with the Court, but just two years later, after passage of the Judiciary Act, that number fell by more than half, to 275. The act also eliminated the requirement of circuit riding, thus easing the burden on Supreme Court justices. Significantly, in using statutes rooted in the common-law tradition, the Congress itself was creating a relatively new form of law: code law.

The Basis of U.S. Law

U.S. law combines two different kinds of law: common law, which is made principally by judges reaching decisions in cases, and code law, enacted primarily by legislators (and often referred to as *statutory law*) and by chief executives.[7] Although the U.S. legal system has roots in a common-law system, most legal disputes today center on disagreements involving the interpretation of code law.

The Language of U.S. Law

Understanding the language of the U.S. legal system is tricky. What do all the names mean in these cases? Who is opposing whom? What determines where a case is being heard? What is meant by that commonly heard word *litigation*? Let's begin with the last question. **Litigation** refers to the process by which cases are brought and decided in the American legal system. Every court case has a title, and the title is the shorthand way of naming the main parties in the case. For example, in 2000, the U.S. Supreme Court decided the case *Bush v. Gore.* In this case, George W. Bush (the first name in the case) is the **plaintiff,** that is, the person or organization bringing the case. Al Gore (the second name) is the **defendant,** the individual who is defending himself or herself against the plaintiff's accusation.

In the U.S. judicial system, there are two main types of cases. First, **civil law cases** involve a conflict between private individuals in which the plaintiff alleges that some action or inaction by the defendant has caused harm to him or her. Second, **criminal law cases** are brought by the government or a prosecutor against a defendant, alleging that he or she has engaged in conduct resulting in injury to another person and that this injury is so significant, it harms not only the individual but also the larger society.

Because criminal cases are concerned with the breach of an obligation owed by the individual to the larger society, criminal cases always involve either a state government or the national government (though sometimes civil cases can involve a government entity). For example, when the baseball legend and home run–record breaker Barry Bonds was indicted for allegedly having lied to federal authorities investigating the sale of steroids, the criminal case was filed as *The United States of America v. Barry Lamar Bonds.* In contrast, civil cases typically pit individual against individual, as in *Kevin Federline v. Britney Spears,* a lawsuit involving the custody of the celebrities' two sons. Civil cases typically center on the breach of some obligation owed by one individual to another. The most common civil cases are concerned with the family, a contractual matter, or an injury to a person or property (known as a **tort**).

The names in the case title may also reveal the stage of litigation. At the trial stage, the case names a plaintiff and a defendant. Subsequent changes in the order of names suggest that a case has moved to the appeals stage. To clarify: when one party believes that the trial court judge has misapplied or misinterpreted the law, that party has a right to appeal this decision to an appellate court. In the filing of this appeal, the names of the parties change. The party bringing the appeal becomes the **petitioner** (also called *appellant*) and is the first party named in a case name. The person arguing against the appeal becomes the **respondent** (also called *appellee*) and is the second name in the case title. For example, in 2005, when AT&T sued Microsoft in a patent dispute, the case was *AT&T Corp. v. Microsoft* and was heard in the U.S. District Court for the Southern District of New York. Microsoft later appealed the decision to the U.S. Court of Appeals for the Federal Circuit and finally to the U.S. Supreme Court. In 2007, the Supreme Court heard *Microsoft* (appellant) *v. AT&T* (appellee), as Microsoft was appealing the district court's decision in favor of AT&T, which the appeals court had affirmed (the Supreme Court ruled in favor of Microsoft).

Common Law

Law created by courts through the cases they decide is called **common law,** and it binds all courts considering similar cases in the future.

The Historical Basis of Common Law   England began using the common law as a means of unifying the country after the Norman invasion of 1066. In the 1100s, local courts began to write down this national, or "common," law to make it easy to use. Nobles soon realized that the law might be applied to limiting the power of the king and could protect the nobles against unfair and arbitrary actions by the monarchy. Most significant in the creation of common law was the Magna Carta ("Great Charter") of 1215, the first document to list the rights and protections granted to individuals in England. The Magna Carta is one of the core documents in the evolution of constitutional law.

In the common-law system, the jury provides a key check on the powers of the government. The English colonists of North America and later the framers of the Constitution embraced the right to a jury trial. This right rests on the belief that a jury of one's peers is best able to place itself in the shoes of the accused and to make a determination about whether a wrong has been committed. Serving on a jury, like voting in an election or volunteering for an interest group, is an important form of citizen engagement.

The Principle of *Stare Decisis*   In the evolution of the American judicial system, the colonists relied on the principle of *stare decisis,* a Latin phrase that means "let the decision stand." ***Stare decisis*** means that in deciding cases, judges must abide by the legal **precedent,** that is, the legal authority that earlier cases established, even in the instance of laws handed down hundreds of years before and in a society that was far different. The principle of *stare decisis* ensures that common law is not very quick to change. *Stare decisis* also ensures a consistency of legal expectations for individuals and the legal community. Common law was the predominant form of law in the United States in the nineteenth century.

Code Law

By the early twentieth century, rapid changes in society and the economy demanded much faster responses in the law than what common law could provide. Legislators in Congress and the states responded to these changes by creating laws to regulate the behavior of individuals and organizations and to deal with a vast array of new issues. The kind of law they developed is known as **code law.**

A similar, continuously changing social environment prevails today. Because of the steady flow of change and the fast pace of contemporary life, the prior body of law has become inadequate to deal with unprecedented developments in technology, commerce, communication, and even crime. In creating code law responsive to these new realities, legislators have had to become more knowledgeable and specialized about the topics of the laws they write. They have had to rely heavily on experts—police attempting to enforce laws, business and industry leaders, and other specialists—to help shape how laws are written.

Sources of U.S. Law

We have seen that code law and common law coexist in the United States and that judges, legislators, and presidents all contribute to lawmaking. What's more, these officials often cooperate in the lawmaking enterprise, interacting to clarify ambiguous provisions in the code law or to apply the common law to more specific situations. These lawmakers collectively create law that is distinct, but they do so in different ways, as we consider in this discussion.

In this section, we examine the five different sources of laws in the United States: the U.S. and state constitutions, statutes, judicial decisions, executive orders, and administrative and regulatory law. These sources differ not only in terms of who makes the law but also in their place in the hierarchy of the U.S. legal system. Moreover, lawmakers create law not only at the national level but in all fifty state governments as well.

The Federal and State Constitutions

Atop the hierarchy of the sources of U.S. law are constitutions—the U.S. Constitution and the constitutions of the fifty states. Constitutions are the highest form of law, taking precedence over all other laws, and they are the primary organizational blueprint for the federal and state governments. Constitutions delineate the powers of the government and the limitations on those powers. They also establish the structure and function of each of the branches—executive, legislative, and judicial—and define the relationship between the federal and state governments and between the government and the individual.

The body of law that comes out of the courts in cases involving constitutional interpretation is known as **constitutional law.** In cases concerning a provision of the federal Constitution, the high court is the U.S. Supreme Court, and its decisions bind all Americans, including Congress and the president.

Statutes

Laws written by legislatures are called **statutes.** Statutory lawmaking is the hallmark of any code law system. In such a system, legislative law reflects the core principles of the government system. For example, the **U.S. Code** is a compilation of all the laws ever passed by the U.S. Congress, and it reflects this body's priorities and concerns. The U.S. Code has fifty sections spanning a range of issues including agriculture, bankruptcy, highways, the postal service, and war and defense.

Judicial Decisions

When a judge or a panel of judges decide a case, they often write an opinion that justifies their decision and explains how they have applied principles of *stare decisis.* These judicial opinions then become part of the common law.

Under what circumstances do judges write an opinion? To answer that question, we must consider the resources for appealing cases on the federal and state levels. The federal court system comprises two levels of appeals, or appellate, court: the circuit courts of appeals, previously described, and the U.S. Supreme Court, which has the final say in cases. The state systems generally feature two appeals levels, and the final appellate court is the court of last resort, performing much the same function as the U.S. Supreme Court.[8] Judges serving in *courts of last resort*—that is, the U.S. Supreme Court and the state high courts—almost always write opinions in cases, and these opinions have the force of law. The Supreme Court's decisions govern all similar cases heard in all the federal courts and become the law of the land; a state high court's decisions become law in that state.

Executive Orders

Article II, Section 1, of the U.S. Constitution states that "the executive power shall be vested in [the] president of the United States." This power has been interpreted to allow the president to issue orders that create and guide the bureaucracy in implementing policy. Because executive orders have the force and effect of law, they represent a crucial tool in the president's lawmaking tool box. Historically, presidents have sometimes used executive orders to create policy that may not have garnered sufficient legislative support. For example, Chapter 12 describes President Harry Truman's use of executive orders to desegregate the military in 1948.

A president or governor can enact an executive order without input from the other branches of government, though executive orders are subject to judicial review and depend on Congress for funding. As described in Chapter 12, President Bush used executive orders extensively to address a wide range of issues. These included prohibiting new investment in Burma to punish that nation's repressive regime and improving the coordination and effectiveness of bureaucracies administering youth programs in the United States.[9]

Administrative Law

In addition to the executive order, presidents and governors have another source of lawmaking power: they head a vast bureaucracy of agencies that have their own lawmaking authority. As we saw in Chapter 13, bureaucrats get their power directly from Congress or the state legislatures. By delegating significant power to bureaucratic administrators with expertise in specific policy areas, Congress and the state legislatures help to ensure the effective implementation of the laws they pass.

Why, specifically, must legislators delegate such power? The reason is that lawmakers typically write vague or ambiguous bills. They do so to increase the chances that representatives and senators with differing ideologies will find a given bill acceptable for passage into law. But the result of vague or ambiguous wording might be that the law, once passed, is difficult to implement. Thus legislators must turn to bureaucrats with expertise and specialized knowledge to help them to administer the law.

This delegation of authority gives administrators substantial power. It allows them to act as quasi-legislators ("as-if legislators") in creating administrative rules, implementing them, and interpreting those rules as well. Administrative rule-making fleshes out the broad principles in the statutory law, much of which is interpreted by the federal courts.

The Federal Court System

Article III of the Constitution created only one court—the Supreme Court—and left it to Congress to create any additional federal courts that the country might need. As we saw earlier in this chapter, Congress responded with a series of laws that created inferior (or lower) courts in the form of federal district courts and federal appellate courts (or courts of appeals).

In addition to these constitutionally and legislatively created courts, each state has its own independent state court system structured by state constitutions. Because the U.S. judicial system has both federal and state courts, it is said to be a **dual court system.** Figure 14.1 shows that nearly every case, whether tried in a federal or state court, originates in a **trial court**—the court in which a case is first heard and which determines the facts of a case.[10]

Jurisdiction of Federal Courts

The ability of a court to hear a case depends on whether that court has **jurisdiction**—the authority of a court to hear and decide a case. Federal jurisdiction is strictly defined by Article III, Section 2, of the Constitution. In this passage, federal courts are empowered to hear only cases involving a federal question or a diversity of citizenship. A

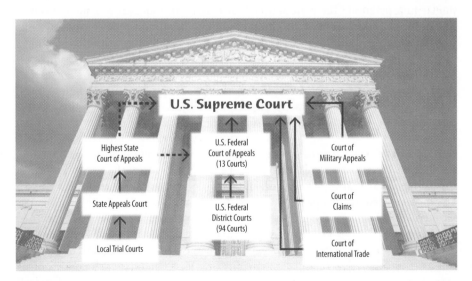

FIGURE 14.1

The U.S. Court System

federal question is a question of law based on interpretation of the U.S. Constitution, federal laws, or treaties. **Diversity of citizenship** means that the parties in the case are individuals from different states or that the case involves a U.S. citizen and a foreign government. It may also mean that the suit centers on the complaint of one or more states against another state or states.

When a court has **original jurisdiction** over a case, that court is the first one to hear the case—no other court has yet considered the legal issues in this case. In instances of original jurisdiction, the court must decide what happened in the case and must apply the existing law to resolve the dispute. In contrast, **appellate jurisdiction** empowers a court to review the decision of the court that has already heard a case. Usually, the appellate court is called upon to decide not what happened but rather whether the first court correctly applied or interpreted the law.

In the federal courts, the federal district courts have original jurisdiction in most cases. The U.S. courts of appeals handle first-level appeals of decisions made in those federal district courts. Most cases that reach the Supreme Court come to it under its appellate jurisdiction.

The Structure of the Federal Courts

The U.S. court system is a dual system in two ways. First, as noted above, parallel federal and state court systems operate largely independently of each other and make law in specific areas. Second, each of these systems has both trial courts and appellate courts. In the brief discussions that follow, we consider the different kinds of courts in the federal system.

Federal District Courts   The federal judiciary is structured hierarchically, similar to a pyramid. There are ninety-four federal district courts at the bottom of this pyramid. These are the trial courts in this system, and they do much of the work of the federal judiciary. The function of trial courts is straightforward: judges or juries decide what happened in a case and then apply the law. For example, in a terrorism case, the judge or the jury assesses whether the defendant is guilty of committing acts of terror as defined by federal law. If the defendant is found guilty, the court then looks to the law to impose a penalty. Federal district courts operate throughout the United States; every state must have at least one.

U.S. Courts of Appeals   At the middle level of the federal judicial pyramid are thirteen courts of appeals. As Figure 14.2 shows, twelve of these courts cover specific regions (circuits) plus the Federal Circuit located in the District of Columbia. The thirteenth court of appeals covers specific kinds of cases, involving such matters as international trade, government contracts, and patents. Congress has authorized 179 judgeships for these courts of appeals, though typically there are vacancies.

The size of each circuit varies depending on the size of the court's constituency and its caseload. Today, the smallest circuit is the First Circuit, which consists of six judgeships; the largest, the Ninth, has twenty-eight.[11] Each circuit court of appeals is supervised by a chief judge. The chief judge is the individual on the bench who has the most seniority but is under age 65. The judges who hear a case typically

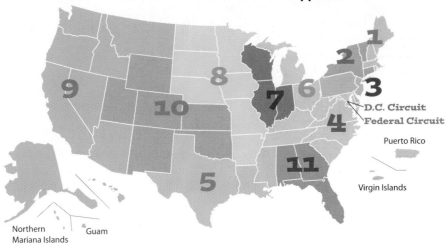

The Federal Circuit Courts of Appeals

D.C. Circuit
Federal Circuit

Puerto Rico

Virgin Islands

Northern Mariana Islands   Guam

POLITICAL INQUIRY

FIGURE 14.2 ■ **How many U.S. circuit courts of appeals are there today? What circuits (regions) do they cover, and what determines the size of each circuit? What kinds of cases does an additional, special court of appeals (not shown in the map) cover?**

include a three-judge panel made up of the courts of appeals judges. They are sometimes joined by visiting judges (usually from the corresponding federal district of the court of appeals) and retired judges. In deciding cases, the judges read briefs submitted by lawyers, which argue their clients' case, and then hear oral arguments. During this process, no new facts are admitted into evidence; instead, the court of appeals focuses on questions of procedure or the application of law that occurred in a decision of the lower court.

The Judiciary Act of 1891 carved out only nine geographic units for the courts of appeals. Congress has increased the number of circuit courts to the thirteen of the present day (see Figure 14.2) by splitting up existing circuits. Each new division has typically reflected Congress's desire to keep together states with similar legal and political cultures.

Courts of appeals are the courts of last resort for most federal cases because after a case has been decided by the appellate court, there is no automatic right to an appeal. Although some cases may be appealed to the U.S. Supreme Court, the Court ultimately chooses to hear only a small fraction of these.

Special Courts In addition to the federal district courts and the courts of appeals, Congress, acting under Article I of the Constitution, created several specialized courts. These include the Court of International Trade, the U.S. Court of Military Appeals, the U.S. Tax Court, and the U.S. Court of Veterans' Appeals.

Changing Caseloads: Fraud on the Internet

	THEN (2001)*	NOW (2008)**
Number of complaints processed by the federal government's Internet Fraud Complaint Center and referred to law enforcement agencies	33,940	275,284
Cumulative losses by victims of cybercrimes whose cases were processed by the federal government's Internet Fraud Complaint Center	$17.8 million	$265 million
Top three reported offenses	Internet auction fraud (63%)	Nondelivery of merchandise and/or payment (33%)
	General merchandise sales (11%)	Internet auction fraud (25%)
	Nigerian money offers (9%)	Credit/debit card fraud (9%)

WHAT'S NEXT?

> Have you been, or do you know anyone who has been, a victim of Internet fraud?

> Will cyberfraud continue to grow, in keeping with the present trend? What will be the impact of any growth on the court system?

> What new forms might Internet crime take in the future?

*www.ic3.gov/media/annualreport/2001_IFCCReport.pdf.
**www.ic3.gov/media/2009/090331.aspx.

Recent media coverage has highlighted the activities of another kind of specialized court, the Foreign Intelligence Surveillance Act (FISA) court. It was established by Congress in a 1978 act that spells out the procedures for the collection of human and electronic intelligence.[12] During the George W. Bush administration, FISA courts were charged with determining whether an individual could be subject to warrantless surveillance of his or her communications (see Chapter 4).

FISA courts are evidence of a notable trend in how the judicial branch is coping with the growing complexity of the types of cases that come before the courts. This trend involves increasing specialization, both by law, as in the creation of special courts such as FISA courts, and by practice, as when judges develop an "informal" expertise in a policy area—say, DNA testing or software patent law. Legal scholar Lawrence Baum assesses this trend as an effort by the courts to gain and apply the kind of expertise characteristic of the administrative agencies of the government:

> Whether judicial specialization is established by law or develops in practice, it reflects an effort to gain the perceived strengths of administrative agencies while retaining the form and name of the courts. The efficiency and expertise that are ascribed to specialization can help courts keep up with their caseloads and perhaps improve the quality of decision-making.[13]

Although this specialization may occur in both state and federal courts, it is not possible for the highest court in the land, the U.S. Supreme Court, to limit its expertise.

The U.S. Supreme Court within the Federal System   At the top of the federal judicial pyramid sits the U.S. Supreme Court. Although this court has a very limited original jurisdiction (which we examine later in this chapter), it hears appeals from both the federal and the state courts when cases decided there concern a federal constitutional question or when federal law is involved.

Nine judges, called **justices,** sit on the Supreme Court. One of these justices has been specially selected by the president to serve as the **chief justice,** the judge who provides both organizational and intellectual leadership on the Court. The chief justice has the same voting power as the other justices, called *associate justices.* But he or she has an important, distinctive role in the decision-making process. When the chief justice agrees with the majority, he or she chooses whether to write the majority opinion or assign it to another justice. The current chief justice is John Roberts, whom President George W. Bush appointed in 2005.

Selecting Judges for the Federal Bench

On July 19, 2005, President George W. Bush announced his nomination for the seat that had been occupied by Supreme Court Justice Sandra Day O'Connor, who retired at the end of the Court's 2004–2005 term. The president and many others had long anticipated a retirement on the Court, where no vacancies had opened up for more than a decade. Bush named circuit court of appeals judge John Roberts to fill the vacancy created by O'Connor's retirement. Then, shortly after the Roberts nomination, Chief Justice William Rehnquist died. Suddenly, Bush had to look for a successor to Rehnquist, who had served on the Court since 1972. The president decided to elevate Roberts's nomination to that of chief justice, and the Senate overwhelmingly confirmed him with a vote of 78–22.

Once federal court judges are confirmed by the Senate, they serve for life, as long as they do not commit any impeachable offenses. Both Chief Justice John Roberts, who was appointed to the Court at age 50, and Associate Justice Sonia Sotomayor, who was 55 when appointed by President Barack Obama, will each likely serve on the court for about 30 years. Both will also probably be among the longest-lasting legacies of the presidents who appointed them.

The Senate's Role in Appointment and Confirmation

The president and the Senate share power in the selection of federal court judges and Supreme Court justices. In this way, the nomination and confirmation process serves as a check on the respective powers of the presidency and the Senate.

In the case of the federal district court judges, a custom known as **senatorial courtesy** gives senators—though only those who are of the same political party as the president—a powerful voice in choosing the district court judges who will serve in their state. Under this tradition, a senator from the same political party as the president can veto the president's choice of a federal district court judge in the senator's state.

> Former Supreme Court Justice Sandra Day O'Connor was the first woman appointed to the high court. Chief Justice John Roberts was nominated to replace her upon her retirement, but then President George W. Bush appointed Roberts as chief justice upon the death of William Rehnquist. Roberts and O'Connor both attended Rehnquist's funeral in 2005.

Because circuit courts of appeals judges and Supreme Court justices serve more than one state, the individual senators from any one state play a far less powerful role in the appointment of these judges than they do in the selection of district court judges. Rather, in the selection procedure for circuit court judges and U.S. Supreme Court justices, the Senate Judiciary Committee, composed of eighteen senators, takes the lead. Committee members are charged with gathering information about each nominee and providing it to the full Senate. The Senate Judiciary Committee also typically votes on the nominee, and the full Senate uses this vote to signal whether the nominee is acceptable. Sometimes the judiciary committee does not make a recommendation about a candidate, as when members split their vote 7–7 on the nomination of Clarence Thomas to be a U.S. Supreme Court justice in 1991. (Thomas was confirmed by the full Senate.)

Judicial Competence

Appeals court judges and Supreme Court justices first and foremost must be qualified, and some nominees in recent decades have been rejected because of senatorial doubts about their qualifications. The Senate rejected two nominees of President Richard Nixon because of such concerns. And when President George W. Bush nominated his White House counsel Harriet Miers as an associate Supreme Court justice in 2005, he was forced to withdraw her nomination because of concerns about Miers's qualifications. These objections strongly indicated that Miers would face a steep uphill climb to achieve Senate confirmation. (Some in the media argued, however, that the questions about Miers's competence were in part a political smoke screen—a ploy by certain conservative Republican senators who would probably have voted to reject the Republican nominee because her ideological outlook may not have been conservative enough for them.[14])

Ideology and Selection to the Bench

Once the Senate establishes the competence of a circuit court or Supreme Court candidate, attention shifts to the nominee's ideology—his or her worldview. Mindful that federal judges typically serve far beyond their own tenure, presidents often regard these nominations as a way of cementing their own legacies. They give the nod to judges and, more significantly, to Supreme Court justices with whom they are ideologically compatible. When George W. Bush nominated John Roberts, he chose an individual who shared the president's own policy views, particularly with regard to issues such as abortion, church and state relations, and criminal due process protections.

Representation of Demographic Groups

When President Barack Obama faced the prospect of appointing a successor to replace the retiring Associate Justice David Souter, he encountered significant pressure from constituents and from interest groups (which created expectation in the

Will President Obama and Future Presidents Consider Demographic Characteristics When Making Court Appointments?

THEN: When Associate Justice Sandra Day O'Connor, the first woman appointed to the Supreme Court, announced her retirement in 2005, President Bush nominated John Roberts, a 50-year-old DC circuit court judge, to replace her. O'Connor characterized Roberts as "good in every way, except he's not a woman."* Before Roberts was confirmed by the Senate, however, Chief Justice William Rehnquist died, and Bush then

renominated Roberts to the chief justice post and nominated White House Counsel Harriet Miers. That nomination was withdrawn following questions about Miers's qualifications and level of experience. Bush then nominated Samuel Alito (shown

above left being sworn in by Roberts), a 54-year-old Caucasian male and another circuit court judge. Both Roberts and Alito were confirmed easily by Senate.

NOW: Early in President Obama's term, Associate Justice David Souter announced his retirement from the Court. From the outset, the media and analysts created the expectation that Obama would add to the diversity of the Court. He responded by selecting Sonia Sotomayor, the Supreme Court's first Hispanic member and third female. Sotomayor won confirmation handily.

- With three women having been appointed to the Supreme Court, will a judge's sex continue to be an issue when presidents make future appointments?

- The Court currently has one African American and one Latina Justice. What other demographic groups might seek to be represented on the Supreme Court?

- Will Republican presidents in the future face the same kind of pressure to select justices from diverse backgrounds that Obama had faced? Why or why not?

*Christina L. Boyd and Lee Epstein, "When Women Rule, It Makes a Difference," *The Washington Post,* http://www.washingtonpost.com/wp-dyn/content/article/2009/05/01/AR2009050103406.html

---

media) to appoint the first Hispanic justice to the Court (see "Analyzing the Sources"). Obama obliged, selecting Sonia Sotomayor, who sat on the second circuit of the U.S. Court of Appeals and is of the Puerto Rican descent. In selecting Sotomayor, Obama named the first Hispanic and third woman to the Court. Other presidents have faced similar expectations: when Thurgood Marshall, the Supreme Court's first African American jurist, retired in 1991, political analysts and the media expected President George H. W. Bush to appoint another African American to the seat. Bush obliged and appointed Clarence Thomas to the court. Even though the federal courts effectively underrepresent the population at large, because judges are overwhelmingly male, white, Protestant, and upper middle class, the current Supreme Court has a relatively diverse composition. In recent decades, an informal demographic composition of the Court has evolved with an African American seat (currently occupied by Associate Justice Clarence Thomas), a Jewish seat (both Associate Justices Stephen Breyer and Ruth Bader Ginsburg are Jewish), a Roman Catholic seat (now actually several such seats, with Chief Justice John Roberts and Associate Justices Anthony Kennedy, Antonin Scalia, Clarence Thomas, and Samuel Alito all being Catholic), and a woman's seat (occupied by Ginsburg as well as Sotomayor).

The impulse to recognize specific seats that reflect major groups in the population serves the goal of **symbolic representation,** which is the representation on the Court of the country's leading demographic groups. There is an implicit assumption that a justice occupying one of these seats will best serve the concerns of the racial, ethnic, gender, or other group to which he or she belongs. That is, the Latino justice will take the perspective of Latinos, the female justice will consider the policy preferences of women, and so on. In fact, however, the representation may be more symbolic than real because the issues of importance to Latinos, women, or any other group are hardly monolithic. These issues are so multidimensional that no one person could speak for all the members' concerns. Nevertheless, many public figures and citizens say that the Court should mirror as closely as possible the main contours of the national demographic profile. (See "Then, Now, Next for more on recent appointments as they relate to this goal.)

Clearly, the nomination and confirmation of federal judges does not take place in a vacuum. Beyond presidents' and senators' concerns about judicial qualifications, ideology, and demographic representation, these players are acutely aware of what

Does Demographic Representation Matter in Court Appointments?

In this cartoon by Ed Fischer, a Republican senator considers the nomination of U.S. Supreme Court Justice Sonia Sotomayor as two voters—representing 40 million Hispanic voters—look on.

Evaluating the Evidence

① Why would the cartoon specifically show a Republican legislator being especially conscious of Hispanic voters when considering the Sotomayor nomination?

② What does the size of the Hispanic man and woman suggest about the strength of the Hispanic vote in shaping the outcome of some elections?

③ Only nine Republican senators voted for Sotomayor's confirmation. Republican senators from both Texas and Arizona (where Hispanics constitute a sizable proportion of the electorate) voted against her nomination. Among those voting for Sotomayor was Senator Mel Martinez of Florida. Do you think Hispanic voters will consider their senators' position on the Sotomayor nomination when casting their ballot in future Senate elections? Why or why not?

© Ed Fischer. www.CartoonStock.com

their constituencies will think of any nominee and of what might happen at the confirmation hearings. For this reason, they continuously gauge public opinion throughout the nomination and confirmation process. In addition to being mindful of the voters, the president and the senators calculate how interest groups, particularly those that helped to put them in office, will view the nominee. In nominating John Roberts, George W. Bush sought to ensure that his nominee would be acceptable to one of his core constituencies, conservative voters.

Interest groups often have a significant voice in the confirmation hearings. Some groups almost always participate in the hearings, among them the American Bar Association, labor and civil rights organizations, law enforcement groups, and business interests. These groups do not hesitate to let the members of the Senate Judiciary Committee know clearly whether they support or oppose a given candidate.

The U.S. Supreme Court Today

The decisions of the U.S. Supreme Court's nine justices are binding on all other courts in the country, and no other court may overturn them. Decision making on the Court is a multistep process that provides many opportunities for conflict and compromise. As a **collegial court,** which means it is made up of a panel of justices, Supreme Court justices must work closely together as they navigate the process.

> The impulse to fill specific Supreme Court seats with nominees who represent major groups in the population serves the goal of symbolic representation. Such nominations are made with the implicit (though not necessarily accurate) assumption that a justice occupying one of these seats will best serve the demographic group to which he or she belongs. Associate Justice Ruth Bader Ginsburg is the Court's second female justice and was the sixth Jewish person ever to serve on the Supreme Court (Associate Justice Stephen Breyer, who is also Jewish, was nominated to the court a year after Ginsburg joined it). President Obama's appointment of Sonia Sotomayor, who is Hispanic, created the first "Hispanic seat." What other demographic groups will be vying for a symbolically representative appointment to the Supreme Court in the future?

The need for compromise on the Court is especially intense because of the sheer number of cases it hears and the fact that its decisions are final.

The Supreme Court's Jurisdiction

In the vast majority of cases, the Supreme Court is reviewing a decision made by a lower court rather than exercising original jurisdiction. The framers limited the Supreme Court's original jurisdiction to only those cases that concern ambassadors, public ministers, and consuls, and those involving two or more states. But over time, Congress, in cooperation with the Court, has decided that the Court should retain original jurisdiction only in cases involving suits between two or more states.

Choosing Cases for Review

Approximately 7,000 petitions are filed with the Court each year, each asking for the review of a case already decided. Each case is one that a party or parties are appealing from some other court because one or both sides dispute the decision in the case. Ultimately, the justices write decisions in only 80 to 90 cases, however. How do they decide which cases to hear? Like the other stages of the decision-making process, "deciding to decide," as Supreme Court scholar H. W. Perry puts it, is a joint activity.[15]

The decision to place a case on the Supreme Court's agenda is a collaborative one. Important in this process is the role of Supreme Court clerks. These young lawyers, who are recommended for the positions by certain "feeder professors" at select law schools, are charged with drafting a **pool memo,** a description of the facts of the case, the pertinent legal arguments, and a recommendation as to whether the case should be taken.

The chief justice distributes a list of selected cases, the **discuss list,** to the other justices before a regularly scheduled conference. A chief justice's decision as to whether to include a given case on the discuss list is primarily based on review of the Supreme Court clerks' pool memos. On Fridays throughout the Court's term, which lasts from October to June, the justices meet in conference to discuss the cases on the list.[16] At this point, they vote on whether to issue a writ of *certiorari*—a Latin term roughly translated as "a request to make certain"—for specific cases. The **writ of *certiorari*** is a higher court's order to a lower court to make available the records of a past case so that the higher court can determine whether mistakes were made during the lower court trial that would justify a review of the case.[17] The writ of *certiorari* falls within the Court's discretionary jurisdiction, meaning that the Court can choose whether to hear such cases (unlike those cases that have a mandatory appeal to the U.S. Supreme Court).

The justices determine whether they will consider a case according to a practice known as the **Rule of Four,** under which the justices will hear a case if four or more of nine justices decide they want to hear it. They do not need to give reasons for wanting or not wanting to hear a case—they simply must vote. The vast majority of the cases the Court hears reach the justices through a writ of *certiorari,* reflecting its role as primarily an appellate court.

On the Docket: Considering the Case

When a case makes its way onto the Court docket, the parties in the litigation shift into high gear (see Figure 14.3). The petitioner (the party that sought the Court's review in the first place) usually has forty-five days to file a written **brief**—a document detailing the legal argument for the desired outcome—with the Court. After the filing of this brief, the opposing party, the respondent, has thirty days to file its own brief with the Court.

Today, *amicus curiae* briefs are a common part of Supreme Court litigation. Filed within a specified time period by a person or group that is not party to the

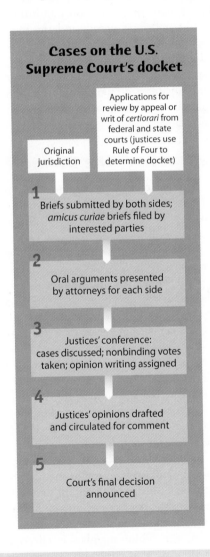

FIGURE 14.3

Decision Making on the Supreme Court

lawsuit, an *amicus curiae* **brief,** or **"friend of the court" brief,** is a document that aims to influence the Court's decision. Some cases trigger the filing of many *amicus* briefs; the largest number of such briefs (ninety) ever filed in a Supreme Court case came in two cases involving affirmative action at the University of Michigan.[18]

In docketing a case, the clerk of the court selects a date for **oral arguments**— attorneys' formal spoken arguments that lay out why the Court should rule in their client's favor. Heard in the Supreme Court's public gallery, oral arguments give the justices the opportunity to ask the parties and their lawyers specific questions about the arguments in their briefs. In typical cases, each side's lawyers have thirty minutes to make a statement to the Court and to answer the justices' questions. Although the public gallery is grand, and the mood is often somber and formal, the justices can sometimes be less than polite toward each other and the lawyers during the oral arguments. The justices frequently interrupt the attorneys during their opening statements and responses to questions and sometimes seem to ignore the lawyers entirely, instead talking with each other. This discourse takes place entirely within public view, and transcripts (and sometimes even tapes) are readily available to the public.

Meeting in Conference: The Deliberative Stage

After the justices have listened to the oral arguments in the case, they meet in conference to deliberate. At this point, each justice will signal his or her likely vote on the case and discuss the legal issues in play. We have few clues as to how the justices interact in conference, as these proceedings are entirely closed to the public. The late chief justice William Rehnquist once described conferences in which the most junior associate justice was seated closest to the door and was charged with answering any knocks on the door that might come about during deliberation.[19] But other than the anecdotal descriptions we have from justices, once a case enters this phase, it is in a kind of black box. We can only guess about how the justices deliberate and make their decisions because there is no public record of these proceedings.

We do know that the justices must work together at the deliberation stage if they hope to reach a decision that a majority of them will sign. Because cases are decided by majority rule, there is a strong incentive to cooperate. The chief justice plays a vital role in this process. After the likely votes of the other justices are tallied in the conference, the chief justice decides whether he is with the majority. If he is, he chooses whether he wants to write the majority opinion. If he declines, he can assign the task to one of the other justices in the likely majority. If the chief justice is not with the majority, the senior member of this majority decides whether to write the opinion or assign the opinion to another justice. By the time the justices have finished with the conference, they will have already read the briefs in the case, heard the oral arguments, and listened to each other's views. In assigning the majority opinion, the senior member is effectively giving a stamp of approval to the view of the case that either he or she or some other member of the Court has articulated.

The assignment of the opinion is a crucial stage. The justice who writes the opinion must consider the position of the other justices, especially those who are likely to vote with him or her in the majority. No justice who is assigned to write the majority opinion can afford to ignore the policy views of the other justices. At the opinion-writing stage, the justices must cooperate and try to hammer out a decision that at least five of them will agree to. Their discussion about the case often centers on the legal arguments that the parties have advanced or on the underlying factual issues.

Deciding How to Vote: Voting Blocs on the Court

How does each justice decide how to vote in a particular case? Frequently, the justices vote in blocs—those with similar views tend to vote together, especially in similar cases. By the late 1990s and early 2000s, Supreme Court watchers could predict with a great deal of certainty how specific justices would line up to vote in cases involving abortion restrictions, for example.

These voting blocs work as a kind of shorthand for the justices, who often look to other, like-minded justices to decide how they should vote in certain cases.[20] In cases involving broad areas of the law, such as civil rights and civil liberties, and in cases concerned with the separation of powers, the justices are remarkably predictable.[21] Their decision making follows patterns, with many justices voting together term after term. For example, in case after case brought before the Rehnquist Court (from 1986 to 2005, when William Rehnquist was chief justice), four of the nine justices lined up on each side and Justice Sandra Day O'Connor was the swing vote whose decision determined the outcome in these closely divided cases.[22]

In terms of political stance, we tend to talk about the justices as either conservative or liberal, with conservative justices tending to favor the state and state interests in cases involving civil liberties or civil rights, and liberal justices tending to favor the individual in these cases. The justices are arrayed in groups on a kind of spectrum, and Justice O'Connor occupied the central position for many years. Because the Court was so closely divided, she exercised significant power in the decision-making process.

Writing the Opinion

At the opinion-writing stage, give-and-take comes into play among the justices, especially if the case is particularly close, so that the justice writing the majority opinion must lock in all the available votes. This is an important consideration because at this point the justices are still free to change their minds about how they will vote or whose opinion they will join.[23] Although there are no records of the justices' deliberations, it is likely that the first draft of most majority opinions is modified to reflect the desires of at least some of the justices who agree to sign it.

There are significant incentives for the author of the draft opinion to take into account the perspectives not only of the justices who agree with his or her conclusions, but also of those who disagree. The reason is that the majority draft may not be the only draft circulating among the justices. When the justices disagree about a decision, it is likely that other drafts also circulate. Some of these drafts may become concurring opinions; others may become dissenting opinions. **Concurring opinions** agree with how the majority opinion decides the case but disagree with at least some of the legal arguments or conclusions reached in this majority opinion. **Dissenting opinions** not only disagree with these arguments and conclusions but also reject the underlying decision in the case.[24]

As drafts of the majority, concurring, and dissenting opinions circulate, the justices continue to gauge the level of support for each. It does not appear to be unusual for majority opinions to become concurring opinions, and vice versa. Again, the ability of the justices to persuade their colleagues on the Court is the primary indicator of which opinion will prevail as the majority decision.

After the opinions are written and signed off on, the Court announces the decision by publishing it. On rare occasions, the justices read their majority opinions, and sometimes their concurring and dissenting opinions, from the bench.

The Supreme Court Today: The Roberts Court

Although it is still early in the tenure of Chief Justice John Roberts, we can make some observations about his leadership and ideology on the basis of decisions to date by the Roberts Court. Many legal scholars say the Roberts Court, particularly in the absence of the moderate O'Connor and with the addition of the conservative Samuel Alito, is tilting more conservatively than the Rehnquist Court in which Justice Sandra Day O'Connor played the pivotal balancing role.[25] Figure 14.4 shows the shifts in

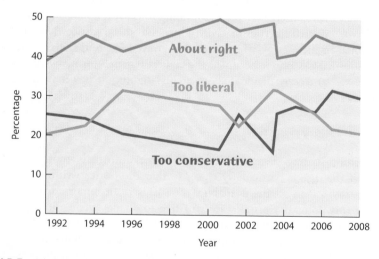

FIGURE 14.4

Citizens' Views on Supreme Court Ideology
Source: Gallup News Service, October 2, 2007.

public opinion that have accompanied these changes in the composition of the court. Today about one-third of Americans view the Supreme Court as "too conservative," and the percentage of people who say that the Court's ideology is "about right" dropped from nearly 50 percent in 2000 to about 42 percent in 2007.[26]

In 2009, several U.S. Supreme Court decisions shed some light on the path that the Roberts Court was taking. Many important cases dealt with the balance of power between individuals and government. One important case involved a 13-year-old suing her school district after she had been strip-searched when school officials suspected that she had provided over-the-counter ibuprofen to a classmate. In an 8–1 decision, the court ruled that while it was reasonable to search a student's backpack and outer garments, a strip search violated the student's right to privacy and was unreasonable.[27] Another case dealt with the issue of when federal courts may act to enforce federal mandates on states. By a 5–4 decision, the Court made it easier for state schools to shed federal supervision of their English language education programs, a decision that will affect other state institutions, including prisons.[28] In another 5–4 decision, the Court dealt a blow to the criminal justice systems in forty states by requiring that crime lab analysts testify in criminal proceedings, instead of allowing reports written by the analysts to substitute as evidence.[29] At the time of the ruling, laws in only ten states required testimony from analysts.

These decisions illuminate a distinct trend of the Court today: the justices' willingness to limit the exercise of authority by the states and the other branches of government. In another example, the Roberts Court weakened a key provision of a landmark campaign finance law, the Bipartisan Campaign Finance Reform Act of 2002, by loosening restrictions on campaign television ads. The Court's recent conservatism is also evident in a case in which the justices upheld a federal ban on partial birth abortion, a procedure in which labor is induced and suction is used to remove a fetus.[30]

Figure 14.5 shows the ideological distribution of the Supreme Court today and highlights its slight tilt toward the conservative side, with Justices Clarence Thomas, Antonin Scalia, Samuel Alito, and Chief Justice Roberts reflecting a conservative viewpoint and Justices John Paul Stevens and Ruth Bader Ginsburg taking a more liberal stance. While it is too early in Justice Sonia Sotomayor's tenure on the bench to determine her ideology precisely, her previous rulings indicate that she will probably fall on the liberal side of the court, slightly to the left of centrist Justices Stephen Breyer, a moderate liberal, and Anthony Kennedy, a moderate conservative.

Judges as Policy Makers

Courts make law—common law—by deciding cases and establishing legal principles that bind future litigants and judges. The lawmaking function of courts ensures that judges have a powerful role as public policy makers.[31] This is particularly true of judges who serve in appellate courts such as the state supreme courts, the federal circuit courts of appeals, and the U.S. Supreme Court.

FIGURE 14.5 ■ **THE IDEOLOGICAL DISTRIBUTION OF THE SUPREME COURT TODAY**
While it is too early in Sonia Sotomayor's tenure on the bench to determine her
ideology precisely, her previous rulings indicate that she will probably fall on the
liberal side of the Court. In what direction does today's Supreme Court tilt with
respect to ideology? How could that slant change? Given the current presidential
administration, what is the likelihood that it will?

Because of their policy-making role, judges participate in a larger political discourse that goes far beyond the concerns of individual litigants. As we consider in this section, judges are not free to act completely independently of the other branches of the government, but they *are* able to weigh in on some of the country's most important issues. Justice Antonin Scalia has colorfully described the crucial role that judges play in using the law to create policy. As Scalia sees it, the ideal judge is "one who has the intelligence to discern the best rule of law for the case at hand and then the skill to perform the broken-field running through earlier cases that leaves him free to impose that rule: distinguishing one prior case on the left, straight-arming another on the right, high-stepping away from another precedent about to tackle him from the rear, until (bravo!) he reaches the goal—good law."[32] Most recently, the courts have been called upon to resolve issues related to the war on terror, the death penalty, the powers of the chief executive, freedom of speech, abortion, euthanasia, and affirmative action.

What does it mean to be a policy maker? Recall from Chapter 13 that policy makers are individuals who have authority to influence, or to determine, solutions—public policies—that address the issues and problems a society faces. After choosing a policy, the policy maker must stand ready to adapt it to changed situations or new challenges.

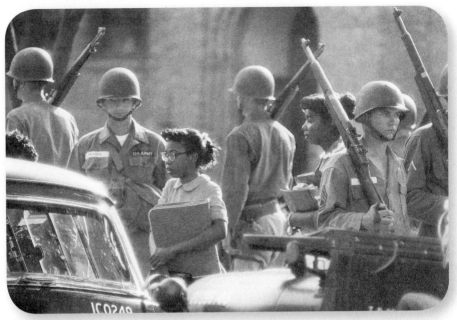

> The activist Warren Court rejected the constitutionality of racial segregation, including in schools. Here students integrating Little Rock (Arkansas) Central High are escorted to an Army station wagon waiting to drive them home after school in 1957.

Activism Versus Restraint

When considering the courts' role as policy makers, legal analysts often categorize judges and justices as exercising either judicial activism or judicial restraint. **Judicial activism** refers to the courts' practice of applying their authority to bring about particular social goals. It reflects the notion that the role of the courts is to check the power of the federal and state executive and legislative branches when those governmental entities exceed their authority.

During the Warren Court (the tenure of Chief Justice Earl Warren, from 1953 to 1969), the Supreme Court took an activist stance, most notably in rejecting the constitutionality of racial segregation. By barring southern states from segregation in a variety of contexts—including schools and other public facilities—the Warren Court powerfully bolstered the efforts of civil rights activists. The activism of the Warren Court was also instrumental in shaping the modern rights of the accused. During Warren's tenure, the Supreme Court established *Miranda* rights for individuals accused of a crime[33] and mandated that states provide counsel to such defendants when they cannot afford an attorney.[34] The Warren Court's activism also shaped modern definitions of the privacy rights of individuals,[35] which would later form the framework for the Court's thinking about abortion rights (see Chapter 4 for further discussion of these cases). Supported by presidents who enforced its rulings, the Warren Court took on a leadership role in changing the nature of U.S. society.

Some judges reject the idea that the courts' role is to actively check legislative and executive authority. Noting that officials in those branches are elected to carry out the people's will, these judges observe **judicial restraint**—the limiting of their own power as judges. Practitioners of judicial restraint believe that the judiciary, as the least democratic branch of government, should not check the power of the democratically elected executive and legislative branches unless their actions clearly violate the Constitution.[36]

By tradition, judicial activism and judicial restraint are linked, respectively, with the liberal and conservative ideologies. That neat categorization, however, breaks down when one tries to apply it to recent courts. The Rehnquist Court (1986–2005) was both conservative and activist.[37] That Court chose to hear a case, *Planned Parenthood of Southeastern Pennsylvania v. Casey* (1992), that checked the authority of the state of Pennsylvania to implement a state law that limits access to abortion. In its decision, the Court laid the framework for the tightening of abortion laws in many states by clarifying what measures the states could take in restricting abortions.

Competing Legal Interpretations

When judges and lawyers consider a case, the common-law tradition—specifically, the principle of *stare decisis*—means that they must consider past cases with similar facts and legal questions. They must be guided by how courts in these cases have interpreted the underlying legal issues. As we have seen, the legal principles that come out of these cases constitute case law.

But even though *stare decisis* binds jurists and attorneys to prior case law, this does not mean that judges, in ruling on new cases, simply apply previous decisions to new circumstances. Rather, in interpreting the legal precedent, they typically choose among several cases related to the legal issues at stake, and their choice often determines the outcome of the present case. For this reason, law school students become skilled at identifying the line of cases that might help them to succeed in making a particular argument. They must assume, however, that the lawyer on the other side of the courtroom will also select cases that best support that attorney's chances for success.

Checks on the Courts

The U.S. judiciary is a powerful institution. It operates as the equal of the legislative and executive branches of government yet is insulated from the influence of these other institutions. Despite the authority and power of the courts, judges and justices face checks and constraints that limit how they decide cases, make law, and act as policy makers. Among the most important checks on the judiciary's power are the other branches of government. But the law enforcement community, lawyers, interest groups, and individual citizens also check the courts and constrain their activism, as we next consider.

The Inner Ring: Legislatures and Chief Executives

Formidable checks on the judiciary come from what some analysts call the *inner ring*—the other core institutions of the government, namely, the legislative and executive branches. Article II of the Constitution explicitly gives the legislative and executive branches crucial checks on the structure of the courts. It grants Congress the power to create all federal courts other than the Supreme Court and gives both the president and the federal legislature important powers in determining who sits on all federal courts. Indeed, the procedures for choosing the judges who will serve on the federal bench afford both of these branches significant control over the judiciary. Executives check the judiciary through their appointment authority, and the legislature does so through the confirmation process.

Beyond giving the president a check on the judiciary by specifying the executive's power to appoint judges, the Constitution also empowers the chief executive to grant pardons to individuals for violations of the law. A further check on judges results from the courts' reliance on the executive branch for the enforcement of their decisions. Specifically, if presidents fail to direct the bureaucracy to carry out judicial decisions, those decisions carry little weight. Frequently, it is executive implementation that gives teeth to the judiciary's decisions.

The Constitution also creates a legislative check on the judiciary because the framers established only the Supreme Court and left it up to Congress to create the lower federal courts. In addition, Article I allows Congress to control the Supreme Court's appellate docket and even to remove whole categories of cases from the Court's consideration. Congress also can control the number of judges or justices who serve on the federal judiciary and can increase this number to get a majority of judges or justices to choose a preferred policy outcome. Moreover, the two houses of Congress have a central role in deciding whether to impeach federal judges. The House issues the articles of impeachment, and the Senate conducts the impeachment trial. Finally, Congress initiates the process of constitutional amendment. In fact, in several cases, Congress has embarked on such amendment procedures in direct response to a Court decision with which members of Congress or their constituencies have disagreed. For example, the Twenty-Sixth Amendment, which standardized the voting age to 18 years of age, came about after the Supreme Court ruled that states could set their own age limits for state elections.[38]

Additional constitutional checks limit the power of the judges. So, although the courts can check the lawmaking power of the legislative and executive branches by exercising judicial review (which, to recap, is the courts' power to decide whether the laws passed by the other branches are constitutional), the legislature and the executive can check the courts' power of judicial review through the creation of new laws. For example, Title VII of the 1964 Civil Rights Act bars sex discrimination in employment. In decisions reached in 1974 and 1976, the Supreme Court interpreted this prohibition narrowly, concluding that Congress did not mean to bar discrimination on the basis of pregnancy when it passed Title VII. Many legislators were angered by these decisions. Consequently, in 1976, Congress passed the Pregnancy Discrimination Act, which amended Title VII to state explicitly that sex discrimination encompassed pregnancy discrimination. The Court could do nothing to respond to this new law because Congress used the law specifically to clarify the Civil Rights Act. Only if the new act had been in conflict with the Constitution could the Court have taken action.

The Gatekeepers: Participants in the Judicial Process

Participants in the judicial process—especially law enforcement officers and interest groups concerned with issues of law—also provide checks on how judges and justices decide cases, make law, and act as policy makers.

Law Enforcers' Checks on the Judiciary   One way in which law enforcement officials check the judiciary is through the exercise of *discretion*. Every day, police officers face situations in which they must decide whether to investigate wrongdoing and whether to arrest suspects engaged in illegal acts. The use of discretion by the police and others who are in the front line of law enforcement means these citizens are effectively deciding how and whether to enforce the laws made by courts, legislatures, and chief executives.

For many years, local law enforcement agents closed their eyes to spousal abuse, for example. If they investigated domestic violence, they often treated the perpetrator much more leniently than they would have if the person had not been married to the victim. This decision to be less aggressive in enforcing the law against assault and battery in such cases made some sense, because police knew that entering a home where spousal abuse was occurring was dangerous and that the victim would be unlikely to cooperate in prosecuting his or her attacker. Police often acted on their own, disregarding what the lawmaking institutions, including the courts, required them to do. Only when victims or their families successfully sued police departments for their failure to act did agencies throughout the country begin to treat spousal abuse cases more seriously.

Interest Groups' Checks on the Judiciary   Legal scholar Andrew Jay Koshner argues that interest groups have transformed how the judiciary operates.[39] Lawyers and law firms assist interest groups in bringing their concerns to the judiciary. For example, when lawyers for the National Association for the Advancement of Colored People (NAACP) hit a roadblock in their attempts to persuade state legislatures to eliminate segregation in public schools, they pressed civil rights advocacy groups to go to court. The result was the landmark Supreme Court ruling in *Brown v. Board of Education* (1954), which established that segregation in public schools violated the equal protection guarantees in the Fourteenth Amendment.[40]

Experienced and trusted interest groups also constrain the courts by providing them with essential information. Courts need such information, especially in highly complex or technical cases involving issues far outside judges' expertise. Depending on what information and arguments they provide, these groups can constrain the courts' options in a case.

Intracourt Constraints

Confirmed judges and justices also face powerful internal constraints on their judicial actions. For lower-court judges, the higher courts, or those courts' decisions in previous cases, impose limitations. Federal district court and appeals court judges, for example, do not diverge far from Supreme Court precedent because if they did so, they would risk having their decisions overturned.

Even the Supreme Court faces substantial constraints, some of which arise from dynamics inside the Court itself. The relationships and interactions among the justices seem to place serious restrictions on their decisions. We have seen, for example, that compromise and negotiation are a central part of the Court's decision making, particularly at the opinion-writing stage. Justices who can persuade others to sign their opinions exercise significant power. This power takes a different form than it does in the other branches. Whereas in the executive and legislative branches the players exercise the power of the purse and engage in overt forms of vote trading, in the judiciary, this power is based on legal reasoning and persuasion.

The Outer Ring: The Users

In addition to these various other influences on the courts, an "outer ring" of *users*—the people whom a law directly affects—can considerably constrain the actions of judges. In the many cases where these users are the general public, the courts must consider how this public will receive their decisions and interpretations.

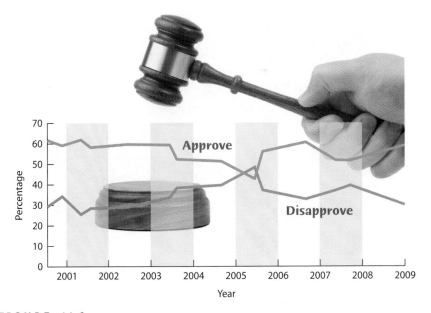

FIGURE 14.6

The Supreme Court's high approval ratings reflect the fact that it rarely breaks with public opinion in its decisions.

Source: Gallup News Service, June 19, 2009.

Indeed, public opinion seems to have a distinct impact on what the courts do, especially appellate courts such as the U.S. Supreme Court. The Court rarely issues a decision that is completely out of step with the thinking of the majority of the population. This trend is confirmed by the comparatively high levels of approval of the Court among Americans, illustrated in Figure 14.6. In fact, most cases seem to follow public opinion. When the Court does break with public opinion, as it has in prohibiting prayer in the public schools, it opens itself up to harsh criticism by the president, Congress, interest groups, and the general public.

Users can also constrain the courts by threatening to ignore their rulings. When members of the public disagree with judicial decisions, or with any law for that matter, they can engage in civil disobedience. In acts of civil disobedience, individuals or groups flout the law to make a larger point about its underlying unfairness. Keep in mind that the courts have little ability to enforce their decisions, and if people refuse to recognize those decisions and the other branches of the government fail to enforce them, the courts risk losing their authority and power. Fear of losing authority may partly explain why judicial decisions rarely fall out of step with the larger public stance on an issue. Like the inner ring and the gatekeepers, the outer ring imposes significant constraints on courts and probably limits how judges handle cases and interpret laws. These constraints may not be written into the U.S. Constitution, as the checks are, but they are nonetheless very powerful and probably have a significant impact on how judges decide cases.

> In the many capital punishment cases decided since *Gregg v. Georgia* (1976), the justices have upheld capital punishment in general but have barred states from imposing it on juveniles and people with mental retardation, using public opinion polls to justify their rulings. The lethal injection death chamber in the prison in Huntsville, Texas, shown here, is one of the most active in the nation.

CONTINUING THE CONVERSATION

CONCLUSION

- The American judiciary has evolved powerfully over the past two-plus centuries to accommodate a broad spectrum of societal changes in a continuously growing country. Rooted in a common-law tradition and framed by the Constitution, the judiciary in its early form strongly reflected its English heritage, with its emphasis on law made by judges.

- The judiciary has proved remarkably responsive to the sweeping societal changes that have occurred since those early beginnings. Specifically, the judicial branch has expanded to reflect both the rising population and citizens' increased use of courts to settle disputed matters.

- At the same time, the body of law that the courts interpret and apply has developed well beyond its common-law origins into a system based heavily on more explicit code law.

- Future courts will be challenged to interpret new laws addressing a host of thorny issues, including many currently unresolved dimensions of technology and terrorism.

- We can anticipate how the judicial branch will meet new demands by examining the strategies the courts have brought to bear in the past. We can see that the judiciary has responded to societal changes in incremental ways, through both revisions in code law and increased judicial specialization.

STUDY NOW

Summary

1. The Origins of the U.S. Judiciary

The Constitution and the Judiciary Act of 1789 created a weak judiciary, but in the landmark case *Marbury v. Madison* (1803), the Court asserted the principle of judicial review, which empowered the courts to check the democratically elected branches of government. The Judiciary Act of 1891 expanded the federal court system by creating federal appellate courts.

2. The Basis of U.S. Law

The American legal system has its basis in both common law and code law. Common law is created when judges reach decisions and write opinions in cases. Code law is made by the legislative and executive branches when they pass statutes or create regulations.

3. Sources of U.S. Law

There are five sources of law in the American system: the federal and state constitutions, statutes, judicial decisions, executive orders, and administrative law.

4. The Federal Court System

The Constitution expressly established the Supreme Court alone, and Congress created the appeals and district courts in a series of laws, beginning in 1789. The Supreme Court has almost total control over the cases it will hear, and compromise and negotiation mark deliberations among the justices.

5. Selecting Judges for the Federal Bench

Federal judges and justices are nominated by the president and confirmed by the Senate. In evaluating nominees, senators examine the nominee's competence and ideology and consider how the nominee's demographic characteristics might represent the population at large.

6. The U.S. Supreme Court Today

Although the Supreme Court has limited original jurisdiction, it is the highest court in the land. The cases the justices select tend to have broad repercussions in their application.

7. Judges as Policy Makers

Although U.S. legal culture encourages the view that there is only one way that a case can be decided, the reality is that judges often draw from multiple legal interpretations in deciding cases and weigh these options in determining which best promotes the goal or social good that they think should receive priority.

8. Checks on the Courts

Outside influences checking the courts include an inner ring consisting of legislatures and executives, a ring of gatekeepers comprising law enforcers and interest groups, and an outer ring of users, the people whom the laws directly affect. Within the judicial system, on the Supreme Court itself, legal precedent and the need to build coalitions restrict the justices' actions.

For Critical Thinking and Discussion

1. How did the American legal system come to be a blend of the common-law and code-law traditions? Which tradition better suits today's political, social, and economic realities? Why?

2. What is your view on the shared lawmaking by the three branches of American government? Are you satisfied that this shared system benefits the country? Can you think of some negatives to the U.S. system?

3. The Supreme Court has the power of judicial review, that is, the power to strike down federal and state laws that it views as in conflict with the U.S. Constitution. Can you think of any reasons why it would not be a good thing to allow the Court to overturn laws passed by the democratically elected branches?

4. When a president nominates a prospective federal judge, a number of factors are at play, and the nominee's qualifications are only one of these. What are these other factors? Should they be in play? Why or why not? In what ways do these factors reinforce or undermine democratic principles?

5. Which do you think impose greater limitations on policy making by federal courts: constitutional checks or intracourt and external constraints? Why?

Key Terms

amicus curiae brief ("friend of the court" brief) 528
appellate jurisdiction 516
brief 527
chief justice 519
circuit courts 510
circuit riding 510
civil law case 511
code law 512
collegial court 525
common law 511
concurring opinion 530
constitutional law 513
courts of appeals 510
criminal law case 511

defendant 511
discuss list 526
dissenting opinion 530
diversity of
   citizenship 516
dual court system 515
federal question 516
judicial activism 533
judicial restraint 534
judiciary 508
jurisdiction 515
justice 519
litigation 511
oral arguments 528
original jurisdiction 516

petitioner 511
plaintiff 511
pool memo 526
precedent 512
respondent 511
Rule of Four 526
senatorial courtesy 520
stare decisis 512
statute 513
symbolic representation 523
tort 511
trial court 515
U.S. Code 513
U.S. Supreme Court 508
writ of *certiorari* 526

Internet Resources

A More Perfect Union **Web site**
www.mhhe.com/harrisonampu1e   Consult the book's Web site for study guides, interactive activities, simulations, and current hot-links that provide additional information on the U.S. judiciary.

FindLaw
www.findlaw.com   This Web site provides a wealth of information about lawmaking in the federal and state judiciaries, as well as ongoing cases in the news. It allows users easy access to federal and state code law, case law, and regulatory law. It also helps prelaw and law students stay connected to helpful information about legal education and practice.

Oyez
www.oyez.org/oyez/frontpage   This interactive Web site allows you to access recordings of the oral arguments in a select group of cases. You can also take a virtual tour of the Supreme Court building and learn interesting trivia about the Court, including the most active lawyers before the Court.

U.S. Supreme Court
www.supremecourtus.gov   The official Web site of the U.S. Supreme Court is an excellent resource for doing research on the Court. You can access the briefs and oral argument transcripts for cases currently before the Court, as well as cases recently decided. The site also allows easy access to nearly all cases that the Court has decided, including historical decisions.

Recommended Readings

McGuire, Kevin T. *Understanding the Supreme Court: Cases and Controversies.* New York: McGraw-Hill, 2002. A book that uses real cases to examine the selection of justices, the Supreme Court's decision-making procedures, the influence of interest groups, and the impact of Court rulings.

Samuels, Suzanne U. *Law, Politics and Society: An Introduction to American Law.* Boston: Houghton Mifflin, 2006. A comprehensive survey of the foundations of the American legal system, lawmaking by institutions and groups, and law and public policy.

Tarr, G. Alan. *Judicial Process and Judicial Policymaking.* Belmont, CA: Thomson/Wadsworth, 2006. A broad outline of the institutions and main actors in the U.S. judicial system, explaining both judicial decision making and policy making.

van Geel, T. R. *Understanding Supreme Court Opinions.* New York: Pearson/Longman, 2005. An introduction to Supreme Court opinions and to the justices' use of different schools of legal argument and interpretation in these opinions.

PART V

PUBLIC

POLICY

National Journal

AFGHANISTAN: NEW LEASE ON A "LONG WAR"

The decision to surge thousands of troops to Afghanistan hinged on lessons learned from eight years of conflict.

President Obama's decision to dispatch more than 30,000 reinforcements to salvage the war in Afghanistan may well prove to be the most consequential decision of his presidency. Critics on the left accuse him of sinking the nation deeper into a Vietnam-like quagmire. Opponents on the right oppose his 18-month timeline, or reject a nation-building campaign that risks breaking the U.S. military on a hardscrabble land where, it is said, empires go to die.

As an important marker in the "long war" against violent Islamic terrorism and extremism, the Obama administration's Afghan deliberations illuminated a number of important issues. First and foremost, the Obama "surge" reveals how the hard lessons of counterinsurgency warfare now dominate U.S. military thinking and are fundamentally reshaping the Army in particular.

Indeed, if Obama had decided not to send reinforcements, he would have ignored the U.S. military's prevailing narrative of the past eight years of war.

The prolonged debate on Afghanistan also highlighted worrisome stress fractures in the overburdened all-volunteer force, and raised questions about whether the military's war-fighting skills and instincts are atrophying in the "soft power" realm of armed nation building. Moreover, the deliberations pointed to a growing fissure between a war-weary American public and military leaders who anticipate a conflict with Islamic terrorism that is likely to stretch well into the future.

"I'm afraid the analogy of a horse that has been ridden hard and put up wet is coming true," Lt. Gen. William Caldwell IV, who commanded the Army's Combined Arms Center at Fort Leavenworth, Kan., told *National Journal.* In terms of the physical well-being of our majors, recent classes have been the worst we've ever seen in 15 years of testing," said Caldwell, who has recently deployed to Afghanistan himself. "That's why we are starting to put in place systems that allow us to sustain this operations tempo for the next 20 years, because I think anyone who believes we'll have all of our forces out of Iraq and Afghanistan in the next five years is sadly mistaken. Even if we leave, we'll likely be deployed somewhere else. This really is the 'long war.'"

Bad Options

To grasp the power of the counterinsurgency narrative in shaping contemporary military thinking, consider the options that were presented to Obama. One was a "hybrid" strategy that involved sending fewer additional troops. It would have targeted Qaeda and Taliban leaders while leaving a lighter footprint on the ground. That is exactly the strategy that Gen. Stanley McChrystal, the top Afghan commander, pursued in Iraq when he headed the Special Forces hunter-killer teams there. That campaign led to the death or capture of numerous high-value targets, including the most-wanted terrorist in Iraq, Abu Musab al-Zarqawi, the leader of Al Qaeda in Iraq, who was killed in 2006. Yet that strategy did little to quell the insurgency that very nearly engulfed Iraq in an all-out civil war.

U.S. commanders also discussed the option of sending fewer additional troops and holding their current ground while accelerating the handoff of responsibilities to Afghan security forces. Army chief George Casey, the former Iraq commander, pursued such a strategy in Iraq between 2004 and 2007. It led to a persistent mismatch between an increasingly potent insurgency and an inexperienced and overwhelmed Iraqi security force that failed to halt the country's descent into chaos. In his West Point speech, Obama called this the "muddle through" option.

It's fair to ask whether **the military and the American body politic have reached different conclusions** based on the experience of the past eight years.

By contrast, Gen. David Petraeus, the head of Central Command who literally wrote the Army's counterinsurgency manual, took charge in Iraq in 2007 and implemented a population-centric strategy of "clear, hold, and build" with the help of 30,000 additional U.S. troops. Only then did the deteriorating security situation begin to stabilize.

By this telling, Petraeus's strategy encouraged Iraqis, who were finally provided a modicum of security and protection from retribution, to begin to identify the insurgents who had operated invisibly in their midst. Convinced that U.S. forces were staying, tribal sheiks and the "Sons of Iraq" in the Sunni insurgent stronghold of Anbar province sided with the United States

against Al Qaeda in Iraq. The "virtuous cycle" of counterinsurgency operations then began, with Iraqi security forces steadily gaining confidence in operations against the diminished insurgency, to the point that U.S. commanders now plan to withdraw 70,000 forces from Iraq by September 2010, and all U.S. forces by the end of 2011.

Classic Counterinsurgency

After two decades of deeply unsatisfying experiences in irregular warfare in places such as Somalia, Kosovo, Iraq, and Afghanistan, no one should underestimate the influence on current military thinking of the mythology surrounding Petraeus's counterinsurgency campaign in Iraq. When President Obama identified Afghanistan as the "central battlefield" in the conflict against terrorism, it was no surprise that McChrystal and Petraeus used the "Iraq surge" as the template for their strategy to turn that war around. The surprise would have been if they hadn't.

"Looking back, I think General Petraeus will prove a pivotal figure of this period, and he deserves a lot of credit for what he accomplished in Iraq," said Andrew Krepinevich, a counterinsurgency expert and the president of the Center for Strategic and Budgetary Assessments in Washington. "At a time when the stakes were extremely high and conventional wisdom held that the Iraq war was lost, he adopted this methodical strategy rooted in counterinsurgency doctrine that achieved a remarkable turnaround. And now in Afghanistan, he and McChrystal are again coming late to an insurgency that has gained all the momentum. That requires a surge of U.S. forces to buy time to train indigenous forces to assume most of the burden. That is essentially our way out of Afghanistan."

When Navy Adm. Michael Mullen, chairman of the Joint Chiefs of Staff and the president's top uniformed advisor, was asked how long the United States and its NATO allies would have to pursue such a comprehensive counterinsurgency campaign in Afghanistan, he referred once again to the Iraq template. "We have to be careful about the direct comparisons between Iraq and Afghanistan, because there are those [strategies] that work, and others that are different because [these] are two different countries. But I think [Afghanistan] does look a lot like Iraq in that regard. If I were to use the surge in Iraq in 2007, and look where we are right now [about three

years later, with an exit date scheduled two years hence], I think we can apply the same kind of timelines to Afghanistan. We think that's reasonable in terms of having the desired impact, and then being able to start thinning our forces out and bringing them back home."

Unending Deployments

Inevitably, the debate over reinforcing a counterinsurgency campaign in Afghanistan raised thorny near-term issues, beginning with the reliability of the Afghan government as a partner and options to pressure President Hamid Karzai to tackle the problem of endemic government corruption. The ability of the international aid community and civilian agencies such as the State Department and USAID to deliver economic help was another critical concern; establishing a blueprint for adequately training Afghan security forces in a realistic timeframe was another.

"Taken together, these additional American and international troops will allow us to accelerate handing over responsibility to Afghan forces, and allow us to begin the transfer of our forces out of Afghanistan in July of 2011," Obama said at West Point on December 1. "Just as we have done in Iraq, we will execute this transi-

tion responsibly, taking into account conditions on the ground."

The Obama administration plans to deploy all of the additional 30,000 U.S. troops by June of 2010, meaning that already busy U.S. ground forces are in for another period of frenetic activity.

Ghosts of Vietnam

For old soldiers of a certain age, the deliberations over Afghanistan, with their divisive political undertone and polls showing a majority of Americans opposed to sending more troops, echo an earlier troubling national debate. These veterans recall that after the 1968 Tet offensive, as American public opinion turned decisively against the Vietnam War, the military adopted a more population-centric counterinsurgency approach that included an accelerated transfer of responsibilities to South Vietnamese forces, or "Vietnamization." That strategy arguably worked until 1975, when Congress, reflecting the will of the people, pulled the plug on U.S. support and South Vietnam collapsed.

"After redirecting our attention to Iraq, having barely kicked the Taliban out of Afghanistan in 2002, we shouldn't be surprised that seven years later it's gone to hell; but I'm not sure [that] upping our investment now will recoup those lost years," said Richard Hart Sinnreich, a defense consultant who fought in Vietnam and taught at West Point and the Army's Command and General Staff College. "I certainly don't see us being successful in Afghanistan in less than five to 10 more years, and I don't think the American people are willing to support that kind of prolonged fight against a nationalist tribal movement in someone else's country. The public doesn't want to absorb the kind of U.S. casualties required to win in a gentle way, or inflict the kind of casualties required to win in a ruthless way. That raises the very good question of whether, strategically, we are designing a U.S. military force to fight wars which the American people will not support."

With the U.S. having already engaged in counterinsurgency operations for longer than it did in the Vietnam War, it's fair to ask whether the military and the American body politic have reached different conclusions based on the experience of the past eight years. The military has clearly concluded that it needs to develop the skills to improve its counterinsurgency operations, in hopes of buying public patience with some tactical successes in Afghanistan. But what if the American people have concluded that the nation had better end its involvement in such conflicts altogether?

Retired Army Gen. Barry McCaffrey is a former four-star head of the Southern Command and a highly decorated veteran of the 1991 Persian Gulf War and the Vietnam War. "Personally, I am 100 percent supportive of [Defense Secretary Robert] Gates's contention that we have to win the wars we're in right now, even if that means partially breaking our ground forces," he said in an interview. "And we're burning through upwards of $5 billion a month in Afghanistan during an unprecedented economic recession," McCaffrey said. "So my worry is that we are gradually creating a U.S. military focused on counterinsurgency operations but forgetful that its primary responsibility is to deter and, if necessary, prosecute high-intensity war against the armies of other nations, at a time when the American public has determined that it wants no more interventions in major Muslim countries. And I think the American people are right."

PUTTING AMERICA
TO WORK

PROJECT FUNDED BY THE
American Recovery
and
Reinvestment Act

RECOVERY.GOV

STATE OF OHIO
DEPARTMENT OF TRANSPORTATION

THEN

The federal government played a limited role in the economy, and there was consensus about the need for a balanced federal budget.

NOW

The federal government makes policy to achieve national economic health, and borrowing to balance the federal budget is the norm.

15

Economic Policy

From President George Washington's terms in office to the current administration, the involvement (some would say interference) of the national government in the nation's economy has evolved dramatically. Today, the national government enacts a variety of laws that seek to ensure economic prosperity, including tax laws, laws that regulate economic activity in the domestic and international marketplaces, laws that protect the health and safety of workers and consumers, and spending policies that encourage economic growth and provide for the public good. In addition, the Federal Reserve—the United States' central bank—makes policy decisions that affect the amount of money in circulation and hence consumer prices and employment rates.

Debates about the proper role for the national government in creating and maintaining a healthy economy have been ongoing since the birth of the American republic. The economic downturn experienced by the United States beginning in 2007 intensified the tone and volume of debates about U.S. economic policy among elected and appointed officials at the national and state levels, economists, corporate leaders, and taxpayers. As these debates raged, and the global economy faltered, the U.S. national debt grew to a staggering $11.5 trillion dollars.

Will continuing globalization impede the government's ability to maintain a healthy national economy?

Can the United States retain its dominance in the world economy?

Will your generation and future generations achieve the American dream?

Economic Health and the American Dream

The U.S. national government seeks a healthy economy so that it can raise the revenue it needs to serve the people in compliance with the mission laid out in the Preamble to the Constitution: to establish justice, ensure domestic tranquility, provide for the common defense, promote the general welfare, and secure the blessings of liberty. On a more personal level, many U.S. citizens desire a healthy economy so that they can achieve the **American dream**—a financially secure, happy, and healthy life, with upward social mobility, attained through an individual's hard work and persistence.

The desire for enough money to buy not only what we require to meet our basic needs (food, shelter, and clothing) but also what many people would consider luxuries seems natural to most Americans. In developed countries such as the United States, "luxuries" typically include owning a home instead of renting, owning a car or two, dining at a nice restaurant now and then, taking vacations, and sending children to good schools. The American dream includes sustaining this middle-class lifestyle through retirement and expecting our children's lives to be even better than our own.

Clearly, it takes money to live the American dream. For some, being born into a wealthy family or just dumb luck (winning the lottery!) may provide the means to live the American dream. For most individuals, however, the ability to earn enough money to attain the American dream is the product of several factors, including their education level and work ethic and the availability of well-paying jobs.

Why are you attending college? Are you taking classes to develop your intellectual capacities? To better understand yourself and the world around you? To get a better-paying job so you can live the American dream? If you read your college's mission statement, you will find that your institution hopes to facilitate all of these accomplishments. Probably the easiest accomplishment to measure is obtaining a well-paying job, and personal income is a logical indicator of whether that goal has been reached. Table 15.1 shows that personal income is positively correlated with educational attainment; generally, the more education you acquire, the higher your personal income will be. In addition, Table 15.1 shows that race and sex— two factors that you cannot control—are also correlated with personal income. So earning a college degree is the best step you can take in your quest to live the American dream. However, for women and nonwhite men, the income benefits of a college education are muted.

Although you may be able to increase your level of education, and you have some control over your work ethic, the availability of well-paying jobs commensurate with your level of education is not within your control. The health of the national economy determines the availability of jobs and their compensation (pay and benefits). So, although achieving the American dream depends on individual attributes and opportunities to develop those attributes, the health of the national economy also plays a major role.

Education, Race, Sex, and Mean Personal Income

TABLE 15.1

	High School	Associate's Degree	Bachelor's Degree	Master's Degree	Doctoral Degree
All groups	$31,071	$39,724	$56,788	$70,358	$103,944
Female	23,236	33,052	43,302	53,209	77,968
Male	37,356	47,575	69,818	87,981	116,473
Black	26,368	35,817	47,903	55,654	85,237
Female	22,643	35,328	44,326	50,916	*
Male	30,122	36,534	52,569	62,396	*
Hispanic	27,508	36,106	45,371	65,240	*
Female	20,608	31,675	38,825	51,344	*
Male	32,148	41,445	51,336	81,885	*
White	32,083	40,465	57,932	71,063	105,541
Female	23,334	32,889	43,142	53,062	78,389
Male	38,833	49,061	71,735	89,837	118,003

*Too few earning PhDs to meet statistical standards for reliability.

Source: U.S. Census Bureau, *Statistical Abstract of the United States: 2009*, 128th ed. (Washington, DC: 2008), Table 224.

A healthy national economy—with low unemployment, stable prices, and high productivity—supports a nation's ability to raise sufficient revenue to serve its people. The better the economy's performance, the greater the **tax base:** the overall wealth (income and assets, such as property) of citizens and corporations that governments tax in order to raise revenue.

The Nature of the American Economy

In the United States and other countries, national government policies influence the **economy,** the system of transactions by which goods and services are produced, distributed, and consumed. Economic policies are those aimed at creating and/or maintaining a healthy economy. Economists view a healthy economy as one in which unemployment is low, the price of consumer goods is relatively stable, and the productivity of individual workers, and of the economy as a whole, is increasing.

Although labeled as a capitalist economy, the U.S. economy is not an example of pure capitalism. In a **pure capitalist economy,** private individuals and companies own the modes of producing goods and services, and the government does *not* enact laws aimed at influencing the marketplace transactions that distribute these goods and services. In other words, a pure capitalist economy has a government-free marketplace. Although private ownership of the modes of production dominates the U.S. marketplace, it is not a government-free marketplace. National government policies in some cases encourage, and in other cases mandate, certain business practices that the government deems essential to sustain a healthy economy, as well as a clean environment and a safe and productive citizenry. Because of the many national policies enacted to influence the economy, the U.S. economy is an example of a **regulated capitalist economy (mixed economy),** not a pure capitalist economy.

People around the world want their governments to engage in actions that ensure a healthy economy. Yet the actions a government takes to ensure a healthy economy depend on the economic theories its lawmakers follow. In the United States, Democrats and Republicans traditionally disagree on economic policies, each justifying their policy preferences with different economic theories. Next, we survey several economic theories that have influenced U.S. national economic policy in various historical periods.

Economic Theories That Inform Economic Policy

Today's debates about the proper role of the government in the economy are nothing new. At the birth of the nation, the popular consensus was that the national government should play a very limited role in the economy. However, as the national economy evolved and experienced ups and downs, citizens and corporations sought greater government involvement in the economy, and economists developed new theories about the proper role for governments in creating and maintaining a healthy economy: laissez-faire economics, Keynesian economics, supply-side economics, and monetarism.

Laissez-Faire Economics: An Unrealized Policy

Until the late 1800s, a majority of the American people believed that the national government should take a relatively **laissez-faire,** or "hands-off," stance with regard to the marketplace. That is, they thought that the government should neither encourage nor discourage (through its laws) business practices that affected economic health. In his *Wealth of Nations* (1776), economist Adam Smith described the principles underlying the theory of laissez-faire. Smith's classical capitalist argument emphasized that the most effective means of supporting a strong and stable economy in the long term is to allow unregulated competition in the marketplace. According to Smith, people's pursuit of their self-interest in an unregulated marketplace would yield a healthy economy. While supporting a hands-off approach in general, the national government became involved in economic activity as early as 1789, when Congress approved and President George Washington (1789–1797) signed the first import tariff.

As a manufacturing economy replaced the predominantly agricultural economy during the nineteenth century, the general laissez-faire stance of the national government disappeared. Technological advances fueled industrialization and the movement of workers from farms to manufacturing jobs in the cities. As immigrants flocked to the United States in search of the American dream, the supply of cheap labor ballooned. Giant corporations formed, and individuals with money to invest accumulated great wealth. Monopolies and trusts also developed, limiting competition in a variety of industries. **Income inequality**—the gap in the proportion of national income held by the few at the top of the income ladder compared to the many on the lower rungs—grew. At the same time, the quality of life for the majority of working-class citizens deteriorated as additional family members, including children, needed to work to pay for life's basic necessities. As fewer and fewer people achieved the American dream, even with all family members working, many Americans began to look to the federal government to improve working and living conditions.

In the late nineteenth century, the federal government began to respond to workers' demands for better wages and working conditions and to business owners' calls for uniform (national) rules and regulations for business practices to replace the existing hodgepodge of state-imposed regulations. Moreover, by the early twentieth century, the national government took steps to protect public health by passing laws regulating the processing of foods and drugs and the cleanliness and safety of manufacturing plants. Though not directed at the health of the economy, such regulations increased the costs of doing business, hence affecting the economy. In addition to regulating working conditions, the national government began to use the tool of immigration policy to bolster the national economy and the wages of American-born workers. For example, the Chinese Exclusion Act of 1882 barred immigrants from China, who were willing to work to build the railroads for lower wages than American-born workers. The contemporary public debate about the impact of immigrants on the U.S. economy—in terms of wages, working conditions, and the cost of health, education, and welfare policies—is discussed in Chapter 16.

Clearly, the national government never fully implemented laissez-faire. Moreover, as the national economy grew with industrialization, Americans accepted and even called for a mixed economy featuring regulated capitalism. Today consensus continues on the need for some level of government involvement in the marketplace in order to ensure a healthy and sustainable economy, environment, and standard of living. But debate continues over how much government involvement is appropriate and what specific policies the government should enact.

Keynesian Economics

Before the Great Depression of the 1930s, government officials and economists believed that a **balanced budget**—a budget in which the government's expenditures (costs of doing business) are equal to or less than its revenues (money raised through taxes)—was important for a healthy economy. Yet officials and economists recognized that during wartime the government might need to engage in **deficit spending,** spending more than is raised through taxes, to pay for the military effort.

> Created in 1935 as one component of President Roosevelt's effort to end the Great Depression, the Works Projects Administration (WPA) put millions of unemployed people to work on public works projects such as highway and building construction. In his efforts to address the growing U.S. unemployment rate during the severe global recession of 2007–2009, President Obama signed into law the American Recovery and Reinvestment Act (ARRA), aimed at creating 3.5 million jobs, in February 2009. By June 2009, ARRA stimulus funds were being spent on hundreds of construction projects throughout the country.

During the Great Depression, when unemployment rates soared to 25 percent, President Franklin D. Roosevelt (1933–1945) and Congress supported deficit spending to address the nation's severe economic depression. The Roosevelt administration implemented numerous economic regulations and a number of innovative work and public assistance programs. These policies drove up government spending at a time of shrinking government revenues. A key objective of the government's increased spending was to trigger economic growth by lowering unemployment rates, thereby increasing demand for goods (because more employed people means more people with money to spend), thus boosting the national economy. Deficit spending, Roosevelt said, would provide the solution to the American people's economic woes.

The new economic theory of John Maynard Keynes supported Roosevelt's unprecedented peacetime deficit spending. **Keynesian economics** recommends that during a **recession**—an economic downturn during which unemployment is high and the production of goods and services is low—the national government should increase its spending (to create jobs) and decrease taxes (so that people have more money to spend) to stimulate the economy. Based on this theory, during a **depression,** which is a long-term and severe recession, deficit spending is justified. During times of rapid economic growth—an **economic boom,** which is the opposite of a recession/depression—Keynesian theory recommends cutting government spending and possibly increasing taxes. In the long term, deficit spending during recessions and collecting a surplus when the economy is booming should lead to a balanced budget. Hence, Keynesian economic theory advocates using **fiscal policy,** the combination of tax policy and spending policy, to ensure a healthy economy.

Following the tenets of Keynesian economics, in February 2008, Congress and President George W. Bush (2001–2009) approved tax rebates totaling $168 billion and tax cuts for select businesses. In September 2008, Congress and the president pledged to spend $300 billion to bring back to health two top mortgage companies (Fannie Mae and Freddie Mac) and the American International Group (AIG), a major international insurance and financial services organization. The Bush administration continued these fiscal policies in the fall of 2008 by winning approval from Congress for $700 billion to bail out faltering Wall Street financial institutions.

President Barack Obama (2009-present) and Congress continued to use fiscal policy to stimulate the sagging economy by enacting the American Recovery and Reinvestment Act (ARRA), which authorized a $787–billion economic stimulus package that combined tax cuts and increased federal spending. The goals of the ARRA were to create and save jobs, jump-start the nation's economy, and build the foundation for long-term economic growth. While Keynesian economics has informed the economic policies of Democratic and Republican administrations from Roosevelt to Obama, President Ronald Reagan (1981–1989) implemented a different economic theory in his efforts to deal with the economic downturn that began during the late 1970s.

Supply-Side Economics

President Reagan introduced the nation to a competing economic theory, **supply-side economics,** which advocates tax cuts and a decrease in government regulation to stimulate the economy in times of recession. Supply-siders argue that the government collects so much money in income taxes from workers that they are discouraged from working more than they absolutely need to (as any extra effort will just mean they pay more in taxes). In addition, high taxes drain the economy because they diminish people's ability to save and corporations' ability to invest to increase productivity. Therefore, the theory goes, if the government cuts taxes, workers will be more productive and people will have more money to save and invest, thus stimulating economic growth. Supply-siders also argue that because government regulation increases the cost of producing goods, **deregulation**—reducing or eliminating restrictions on business—will contribute to increased production at the same cost, thus increasing the supply of goods.

Republican President George H. W. Bush (1989–1993) initially continued the supply-side economic policies of Reagan, but before the end of his presidency, Bush broke his promise not to raise taxes in an attempt to begin to address the growing **national debt**—the total amount of money owed to others due to borrowing. In addition to increasing taxes, he signed into law new regulations. Democratic President Bill Clinton (1993–2001) battled a Republican-dominated Congress for most of his presidency. Clinton's proposed spending increases were muted by Congress, and Congress pushed for tax cuts. As a result of these policies and economic growth, by the end of the 1990s, the national government was no longer engaging in deficit spending. President George W. Bush, working with a Republican-dominated Congress for most of his presidency, pursued supply-side economics by cutting taxes and deregulating. (For more on policy makers' willingness—or unwillingness—to raise taxes, see "Then, Now, Next.")

When Will President Obama and Other Elected Officials Be Willing to Raise Taxes?

THEN: During his campaign in 1988, presidential candidate George H. W. Bush told voters to "Read my lips. No new taxes." As president, Bush broke that promise in an attempt to address the growing national debt. At a convention, a democratic supporter reminded delegates of Bush's broken promise.

NOW: Democratic presidential candidate Barack Obama promised not to tax employer-provided health care benefits, while Republican presidential candidate John McCain suggested that Obama *would* tax those benefits. Just six months after his inauguration, President Obama publicly stated that he might break this promise in order to get health care reform without increasing the national debt, yet quickly—at the urging of Democrats in Congress—Obama indicated that he would not break this promise after all.

WHAT'S NEXT?

- Should elected officials be confident that their reelection prospectus will not be harmed by voting for tax increases? Why or why not?
- Will the federal government be able to stop its pattern of deficit spending within the next few years merely by increasing taxes, or will it also have to cut spending? Explain your answer.
- What arguments can those concerned about the growing national debt use to persuade elected officials to stop the pattern of deficit spending?

Monetarism

Economist Milton Friedman, a onetime supporter of Keynesian economics, is today best known for yet another economic theory, **monetarism,** which advocates that the government's proper role in promoting a healthy economy is the regulation of the money supply to ensure that the rate of inflation remains low. **Inflation** refers to a rising price level for consumer goods, which decreases the purchasing power of money. The Bureau of Labor Statistics provides an inflation calculator (www .bls/gov) that allows you to determine what yesterday's dollar is worth today due to inflation. For example, according to the calculator, $1.24 in 2009 bought what $1.00 in 2000 could buy.

Monetarists believe that *too much* money in circulation leads to a high inflation rate, which slows economic growth as people spend less because of higher prices. In addition, as the rate of inflation increases, investors begin to worry about the health of the economy, and investments may decline as a result, ultimately limiting economic growth. On the flip side, the monetarists say, *too little* money in circulation means that there is not enough for new investments, and consequently, that new jobs are not created; this situation, too, retards economic growth. Today, monetarists target an inflation rate of 1–3 percent per year to ensure an adequate money supply for a healthy economy. They believe that the national government must use its monetary policy to maintain this level of inflation.

Should One Economic Theory Predominate?

Although economists, government officials, and citizens broadly agree that the government should act to ensure a healthy economy, there is perpetual debate over how involved the government should be in the economy and what specific policy actions it should take. Where people stand in this debate depends on which economic theory they advocate. Each theory supports the use of different government policies to promote a healthy economy. Before we discuss these various policies that theoretically promote economic health, we consider how governments measure economic health. Once we know what a healthy economy looks like, we can then consider the effects that various policies have on the health of the economy.

Measuring Economic Health

Economists and government officials describe a healthy economy as one that has the following characteristics: expanding gross domestic product (GDP), an increasing level of worker productivity, a low unemployment rate, and a low inflation rate.

These traditional measures of economic health together provide a useful snapshot of how the national economy is doing. Other measures of economic health focus on the general well-being of the people by accounting for factors such as rates of poverty and literacy and the financial situation of households. These less traditional measures include the United Nations Human Development Index, real median household income, income inequality, and the poverty rate.

GDP and Unemployment Rates: What Do They Measure?

Traditionally, no measure of economic health has the cachet of the gross domestic product (GDP). However, U.S. Senate hearings in March 2008 questioned the usefulness and accuracy of the GDP as currently formulated. Moreover, some economists argue that a more accurate economic assessment would combine an improved GDP with a measure of the quality of life. Employment status clearly correlates with a person's quality of life; however, some have questioned the current means by which the government measures this indicator.

The Gross Domestic Product

The U.S. Commerce Department calculates the *gross domestic product (GDP),* which it defines as the total value of all goods and services produced by labor within a country's borders for a specified period, usually one year. The GDP is calculated from the following formula:

$$GDP = CS + GS + BI + (Ex\text{-}Im)$$

where:

CS is the total amount of *consumer spending* to purchase goods and services

GS is the total amount of *government spending* to purchase goods and services

BI is the total amount of money *businesses invest* in new capital resources (such as equipment, computers and software, automobiles, and facilities)

Ex-Im is the nation's total net exports, which is the difference between the value of all its exports and the value of all its imports

The Unemployment Rate

Every month the Bureau of Labor Statistics of the Department of Labor reports

Traditional Measures of Economic Health

Most economists assume that growth in the gross domestic product translates into a prosperous nation with improving living standards—hence, progress toward living the American dream. **Gross domestic product (GDP)** is the total market value of all goods and services produced by labor within a country's borders. Another assumption made by most economists is that high productivity, or output per worker, also fosters improved living standards. Rising GDP and productivity are signs of an expanding economy, which means the production of more goods and services—and thus the availability of more goods and services for consumers.

Economists also expect a healthy economy to correlate with a low level of inflation. When inflation rises, consumers' purchasing power falls, and they cannot buy as much this year with the same amount of money they spent last year. The Bureau of Labor Statistics publishes the **consumer price index (CPI),** which measures the

the *unemployment rate,* which is the percentage of the labor force that does not currently have a job. To calculate the unemployment rate, each month over 2,000 trained Census Bureau employees interview people in 60,000 households that are representative of households across the United States. Collectively, these interviews are called the Current Population Survey (CPS).

The Census Bureau classifies individuals as employed if they did any work at all for pay or profit during the survey week, including part-time and temporary work. The Census Bureau also counts as employed people who have a job but did not work during the survey week because they were on vacation, ill, experiencing child care problems, taking care of some other family or personal obligation, on maternity or paternity leave, involved in an industrial dispute, or prevented from working by bad weather.

Persons are classified as *unemployed* if they meet the following criteria:

- They do not have a job, and
- They have actively looked for work in the prior four weeks, and
- They are currently available for work.

Evaluating the Evidence

1. The GDP does not include the value of unpaid work done in the home such as home-cooked meals, child care, adult care, house and clothes cleaning. Should it include these costs? Why or why not?

2. Does the fact that the "unemployment" rate does not account for people who have given up hope of finding a job and therefore stopped looking for work call into question the rate's accuracy? Justify your answer.

3. What measure, or combination of measures, would you argue provides citizens with the most accurate picture of the health of the economy? Explain your answer.

average change in prices over time of a "market basket" of goods and services, including food, clothing, shelter, fuel, transportation, and selected medical costs. The CPI is the most commonly used measure of inflation's impact on people. According to economists, when the economy is healthy, the inflation rate (measured by change in the CPI) ranges between 1 and 3 percent.

A low unemployment rate, 5 percent or less, is also characteristic of a healthy economy, according to economists. When more people are working, the financial situation of families overall should improve. In addition, in a growing economy with falling unemployment, government revenues should increase (as there is more corporate and personal income to tax), and government spending for social welfare programs should decrease (as fewer people should need public assistance). These trends create a healthier financial situation for government. (For a closer look at what the GDP and unemployment rates measure, see "Analyzing the Sources.")

In sum, a high or rising GDP, high or increasing rate of productivity, low inflation rate, and low unemployment rate suggest a healthy national economy. Yet, as the U.S. Department of Commerce's Bureau of Economic Analysis points out, "While the GDP is used as an indicator of economic progress, it is not a measure of well-being."[1] Therefore, we need to review other measures that attempt to assess the well-being of the people.

Other Measures of Economic Health

The United Nations (UN) created the **Human Development Index (HDI)** to measure the standard of living of the people of various nations. The HDI assesses three dimensions of human development that people in prosperous nations should be able to enjoy: a long and healthy life, educational opportunities, and a decent standard of daily living. These measures of economic health shed light on the ability of people to earn enough to *enjoy a decent quality of life.* Thus they are probing into something quite different from the traditional measures of national economic health that we have just discussed.

With an HDI score of .95 (1.0 is the highest score possible), the United States ranked fifteenth out of 179 nations in the *Human Development Report 2007/2008.*[2] How do we know what this rank means to American households and their ability to live the American dream? Additional measures—looking at household income, income inequality, and the level of poverty within the population—can help us answer this question.

Real median household income is an important measure of the financial wellbeing of American households. **Real income** is income adjusted for inflation so that it can be compared across years. **Household income** is the total pretax earnings of all residents over the age of 15 living in a home. **Median household income** is the income level in the middle of all household incomes; 50 percent of the households have incomes less than the median and 50 percent have incomes greater than the median. An increase in real median household income should characterize a healthy, expanding economy if we assume that increases in workers' productivity will translate into increases in workers' incomes.

To determine whether people at all income levels are benefiting from a healthy economy, the government calculates changes in the percentage of the total national income possessed by households in five income groups. Specifically, the government divides U.S. households into five *quintiles,* each composed of 20 percent of the households in the nation, based on total household income. The bottom group (bottom quintile) is composed of the 20 percent of households with the lowest incomes, and the top quintile comprises the 20 percent of households with the highest incomes. The government then determines the percentage of the total national income possessed by each quintile. Changes in the percentage of the total income held by each quintile over time indicate whether income inequality is growing or shrinking. The ideal is to see a shrinking of income inequality as the national economy expands.

The ideal healthy economy would also ensure that all workers earn enough to stay out of **poverty**—the condition of lacking sufficient income to purchase the necessities for an adequate living standard. The **poverty rate** is the percentage of the population with income below the nationally designated poverty level. The U.S. Census Bureau calculates the poverty rate by using its **poverty thresholds**—an annually updated set of income measures (adjusted for family size) that define who is living in poverty. According to the poverty thresholds for 2007, a family of four, with two children under the age of 18 years, earning less than $21,027 was living in poverty.[3] A family of the same size and makeup earning $21,028 was not living in poverty.

So we have seen that traditional economic measures, such as GDP, productivity, inflation, and employment, serve as indicators of national economic health, and other measures also shed light on the quality of life of people in the United States. With this context in mind, we next explore the way the national government uses fiscal policy to promote a healthy national economy that provides benefits to individuals and households.

Fiscal Policy and Economic Health

As noted earlier, fiscal policy comprises spending policy and tax policy. The national government, through its budget process, annually approves a twelve-month plan for raising and spending revenue. The twelve months in which the fiscal policy plan is implemented is a **fiscal year (FY),** running from October 1 through September 30 of the following calendar year. A government's fiscal year is named for the calendar year in which it ends. FY 2010 began on October 1, 2009, and ends on September 30, 2010.

National government expenditures accounted for 21 percent of the GDP of the United States in 2008—unquestionably, a substantial percentage of national economic output.[4] While government spending certainly can create jobs, its primary goal is to provide the services necessary to fulfill the Constitution's mission. The other side of the coin, tax policy, raises revenue needed by the national government to serve the people. While the main goal of tax policy is to collect revenue, taxation also decreases the amount of money taxpayers have to spend in the marketplace and corporations have to invest. Hence, taxation may reduce consumer demand for goods and services, with possible effects on the unemployment rate as well as company profits. It may also impact investment in economic growth. Thus tax policy, like spending policy, powerfully affects the economy.

To understand fiscal policy, we look next at the sources of the funds the federal government uses to run the nation, as well as the spending decisions that Congress and the president must make.

Tax Policy

The Constitution delegates the power of the purse to Congress. By the authority of the Constitution, Congress formulates and approves *tax laws* to raise money along with *appropriation laws*—legislation that authorizes the spending of government money for a fiscal year. The Constitution specifies that the House must introduce revenue-raising bills before the Senate can consider them. The House Ways and Means Committee and the Senate Finance Committee are the congressional standing committees from which tax bills emerge.

Figure 15.1 presents the tax mix proposed in the FY 2010 budget. Today the national tax on individual income is the largest revenue source for the national government. The federal individual income tax is imposed on each individual's *earned income* (salaries and wages) and *unearned income* (profits made from investments).

The second-largest revenue category, social insurance, includes taxes collected for Social Security, Medicare, and unemployment compensation. Because employers deduct from workers' paychecks the amount they owe for social insurance taxes, these taxes are referred to as *payroll taxes*. The federal government's third-largest revenue source is corporate income taxes. The national government also collects

FY 2010 Executive Budget

POLITICAL INQUIRY

FIGURE 15.1 ■ What is the government's top source of revenue in the FY 2010 executive budget? Do you project that the revenue from this source will remain high in future budgets? Why or why not? What are the other two main sources that provide national revenue?

Tax Brackets for Those Filing as Single Taxpayers*

THEN (2001)	NOW (2009)
15% for taxable income $0–27,050	10% for taxable income $0–8,350
27.5% for taxable income $27,050–65,550	15% for taxable income $8,350–33,950
30.5% for taxable income $65,550–136,750	25% for taxable income $33,950–82,250
35.5% for taxable income $136,750–297,350	28% for taxable income $82,250–171,550
39.1% for taxable income $297,350 and above	33% for taxable income $171,550–372,950
	35% for taxable income $372,950 and above

WHAT'S NEXT?

> Will calls for a more simplified tax structure result in legislation that replaces the six progressive tax brackets with a flat tax? Explain.

> Will the calls for a fairer tax structure encourage Congress to approve additional tax brackets? Why or why not?

> Will the growing national debt force an increase in the tax rates? Justify your answer.

*www.moneychimp.com/features/tax_brackets.htm.

excise taxes, which are taxes levied against a specific item such as gasoline or liquor; *estate and gift taxes,* and *customs duties* (import taxes).

Taxes levied by the federal government do not affect the income of all taxpayers in the same way. The national income tax is a **progressive tax** because it takes a larger percentage of the income of wealthier taxpayers and a smaller percentage of the income of less-well-off taxpayers. Most taxpayers view a progressive tax, theoretically based on a person's ability to pay, as fair and equitable. Some people believe that a **proportional tax (flat tax),** which takes the same percentage of each taxpayer's income, is fairer than a progressive tax. A flat tax of 10 percent would equal $3,500 for a person earning $35,000 and $13,500 for a person earning $135,000. Although these two taxpayers pay a different amount of money in taxes, the *proportion* of their income collected is the same—hence the name proportional tax. The third impact a tax can have is regressive. A **regressive tax** takes a greater percentage of the income of lower-income earners than of higher-income earners. States' sales taxes are the prime example of a regressive tax.

Another reason why taxes affect various taxpayers differently is the government's practice of granting **tax expenditures** (better known as *tax breaks* or *tax loopholes*). These are government financial supports to individuals and corporations to encourage behaviors that ostensibly enhance the public good. Tax breaks and loopholes allow these taxpayers to pay lower taxes on their income than they would otherwise pay. For example, to encourage home ownership, the government gives tax breaks to individuals paying interest on a home mortgage. The government also offers tax breaks to businesses for job creation and worker retraining.

State and local governments, as well as nonprofit organizations that provide a public service, pay no federal taxes. Thus we say that they are exempt from federal taxes. Included in this group of tax-exempt organizations are the overwhelming majority of colleges and universities, which are public or nonprofit institutions. They are tax exempt because they provide the public good of higher education without making a profit; they must invest any surplus money back into the institution.

Tax expenditures and tax cuts would not be such a big concern if the government raised enough money to balance its budget. Unfortunately, deficit spending is the norm for the national government. How is the government spending all this money?

Spending Policy

Decisions the federal government makes about spending significantly affect both the national economy and the ability of individuals to achieve their American dream. Although setting the budget is an annual process, with Congress and the president approving a spending plan one fiscal year at a time, not all national government spending is approved on an annual basis.

Mandatory spending pays for government programs, such as Social Security, that were created and authorized by legislation that also obligates the government to spend the money necessary to meet that program's commitments for as long as the program exists. For a mandatory spending program, the **budget authority**—the authority provided by law for agencies to obligate government spending—is established

Discretionary
nonsecurity
spending
19.6%

Discretionary
security spending
18.9%

Mandatory spending
61.5%

Social Security
18.6%

Medicare
12.7%

Interest
4.6%

Other
24.6%

FIGURE 15.2

Federal Expenditures by Budget Categories: FY 2010 Executive Budget

Source: The Budget for FY 2010, Historical Tables, Tables 3.1 and 8.3, http://www.whitehouse.gov/omb/budget/fy2010/assets/summary.pdf.

at the birth of the program and does not need to be reestablished each fiscal year; this is *open-ended budget authority*. Interest payments on the national debt are also included in the category of mandatory spending; the government is legally obligated to pay back the money it borrows. Mandatory spending is *uncontrollable spending*, which means that current law requires the government to spend money to meet these obligations no matter what the cost. As Figure 15.2 shows, the majority of the national budget pays for uncontrollable, mandatory spending.

Programs without open-ended budget authority in their authorizing legislation have their budget authority approved on an annual basis. Programs granted budget authority year by year in the annual budget process are **discretionary spending** programs with *controllable* spending. Each year, Congress and the president deliberate over how much budget authority to provide to these programs. Typically, Democrats and Republicans differ on their spending priorities, and when the percentage of the budget over which Congress has control (discretionary spending) shrinks, the partisan battles over spending become ever more intense. Although the number of programs covered by discretionary spending far exceeds the number of mandatory spending programs, a smaller percentage of the budget is spent on these programs.

The national government divides discretionary spending programs into two major categories: security spending and nonsecurity spending. As Figure 15.2 indicates, security spending is a smaller piece of the budget pie than is nonsecurity spending. Security spending includes expenditures for the Department of Defense—including military personnel, operations, maintenance, and procurement—for Homeland Security, and for international affairs. Nonsecurity spending covers an array of activities and programs, including the administration of justice, agriculture, education, energy, health, housing, income security for the poor and disabled, transportation, and veterans' benefits and services.

In the annual budget process, Congress and the president do not make decisions about most of the money spent by the national government because the majority of expenditures are mandatory. Other than interest payments on the debt, mandatory spending could be controlled by Congress and the president by rewriting the legislation that established these open-ended budget obligations. As recent attempts to rewrite the legislation that created the Social Security retirement program have shown, however, many mandatory programs are politically difficult to change. This is partly because elected officials fear the impact such changes would have on their reelection prospects, and partly because of partisanship. Not only do Democrats and Republicans disagree on the proper reforms, members of both parties disagree among themselves on specific reforms. Hence, mandatory spending continues to grow as a percentage of the federal budget.

Creating Fiscal Policy Through the National Budget Process

The federal government creates its programs through authorization legislation that specifies the program's goals and establishes whether its budget authority is obligated for the life of the program (mandatory spending) or must be set annually (discretionary spending). In an annual appropriation process, Congress and the president

> President Barack Obama's fiscal 2010 federal budget books, shown here at the White House in May 2009. President Obama conducted a line-by-line review of the budget, signing off on 121 cuts totaling $17 billion. Though this may sound like a large amount, it was only about one-half of 1 percent of the $3.4-trillion FY 2010 budget Congress approved.

establish yearly funding for discretionary spending programs and possibly change tax policy to increase revenue raised—to pay the bills—or to cut taxes in an effort to stimulate the economy. This process begins in the executive branch.

The President's Executive Budget   The budget process officially starts about a year and a half before the beginning of the fiscal year for which budget authority will be obligated. For example, work on the budget for FY 2010 began during the spring of 2008. The process begins when the Office of Management and Budget (OMB) sends the president's budget priorities (policy and financing preferences) to the executive branch agencies. Executive branch agencies use the president's guidelines to formulate their funding requests. Typically, these requests are incremental changes (small increases) to their current fiscal year's budget authority.

The budget requests work their way back up the executive branch hierarchy to the OMB. The OMB reviews the budget requests, conducts hearings in which the agencies justify their requests, and analyzes the requests in light of economic forecasts. The OMB then submits its budget recommendations to the president, who works with the OMB to create a proposed fiscal plan for the entire national government for the upcoming fiscal year. The OMB drafts a budget document and a budget message, collectively labeled the **executive budget,** which explains the president's fiscal plan. The president is required by law to submit the executive budget to Congress by the first Monday in February, eight months before the fiscal year begins.

Congressional Action   Once Congress receives the president's executive budget, the Congressional Budget Office (CBO), the legislative branch's counterpart to the OMB, swings into action. The CBO analyzes the executive budget in light of economic forecasts and predicted government revenues. The House Budget Committee and the Senate Budget Committee use the CBO's analysis, along with reports from other congressional committees, to develop the **concurrent budget resolution,** which establishes a binding expenditure ceiling (the maximum amount that can be spent) and a binding revenue floor (the minimum amount that must be raised), as well as proposed expenditure levels for major policy categories. The House and the Senate must both agree to the concurrent budget resolution. This agreement is to occur by April 15, less than six months before the fiscal year begins.

After approval of the concurrent budget resolution, the House and the Senate Appropriations Committees each draft appropriation bills to provide budget authority for discretionary programs. In order to comply with the concurrent budget resolution, Congress may also need to revise the legislation that authorized selected government programs. For example, the House and Senate may have to agree to change the open-ended budget authority in existing legislation in order to comply with the expenditure ceiling in the concurrent budget resolution. Or they may have to agree to changes in tax legislation to meet the revenue floor specified in the concurrent resolution. **Budget reconciliation** is the annual process of rewriting authorization legislation to comply with the concurrent budget resolution. The deadline for completion of the reconciliation process is June 15, less than four months before the fiscal year begins.

Congress has until the end of June to approve the twelve appropriation bills that fund the national government for the upcoming fiscal year. This timetable leaves two months for the president to approve the bills so that by October 1 the national government can begin the new fiscal year with budget authority for discretionary spending programs. If Congress and the president fail to approve one or more of the appropriation bills by October 1, Congress must approve a **continuing resolution** to authorize agencies not covered by approved appropriation laws to continue to spend money within their previous budget year's levels.

The nature of the annual budget process is such that, at any given time, some government body in the executive or legislative branch is preparing a future budget, even as the executive branch is implementing the current budget. At the same time, the Government Accountability Office (GAO) is evaluating the implementation of the previous fiscal year's budget. Thus, budgeting is a perpetual government activity, one that takes up a great deal of national officials' time.

Deficit Spending, Debt, and Economic Health

Most Americans highly value the ideal of a balanced budget, in which, as we have seen, the government spends no more than the revenues that it raises. Although the nation had a **budget surplus** (money left over when all expenses are paid) for several years at the end of the 1990s, **budget deficits** (more money spent than collected through revenues) recurred as the first decade of the twenty-first century unfolded. Indeed, deficit spending has become the norm, not the exception (see Figure 15.3). In March 2009, the CBO estimated the FY 2009 deficit at $1.8 trillion and the FY 2010 deficit at almost $1.4 trillion.[5] What impact does fiscal policy dominated by deficit spending have on the nation's economic health?

A government that engages in deficit spending borrows money and hence goes into debt. Even as politicians, some economists, and many concerned citizens call for a balanced budget—with some people even proposing a constitutional amendment mandating this objective—deficit spending continues, and so the national debt grows. The long-term impact of debt is the legal obligation to pay back not only the money initially borrowed (the *principal*) but also *interest,* an additional amount equal to a percentage of the amount initially borrowed. In the case of government borrowing, future generations must pay back the debt of their parents and grandparents. Today, to pay off the $12-trillion national debt, each citizen would have to chip in about $39,000.[6]

Public debate is ongoing about the economic impact of long-term deficit spending and the colossal national debt, which is almost three times the amount of money the national government spends in one year. Some economists argue that the more money the national government borrows, the less money businesses can borrow in order to invest and expand the economy. In addition, many citizens grow increasingly concerned that today's deficit spending will burden future generations with the bill for current policies. Complicating the picture, as the debt incurred from decades of deficit spending accumulates, the debt payment is becoming a larger proportion of the annual federal budget, increasing the percentage of the budget

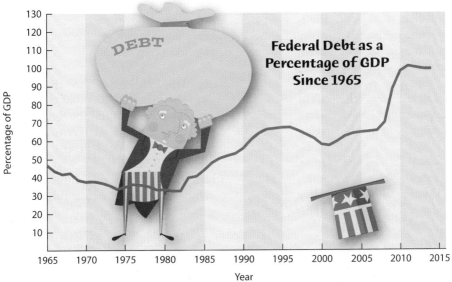

FIGURE 15.3 What do we mean by a budget deficit and a budget surplus? What trend in deficit spending does the graph indicate? In what recent years has there been a surplus rather than a deficit? What government expenditures do you think explain the rise in deficit spending since 2002? What is the federal debt? What trend does the graph show with respect to the federal debt since the late 1980s?

that pays for mandatory spending. Still, as the nation's economic recession continued in 2009, with the unemployment rate over 9.5 percent and housing foreclosures spiraling upward, President Obama and Congress engaged in deficit spending to jump-start the economy. By September 30, 2009, the end of FY 2009, the national debt had increased to almost $12 trillion.[7]

In order for the government to stop its deficit spending and ultimately reduce its debt, it must increase taxes, cut expenditures, or both. Elected officials do not like to reduce spending, however, because budget cuts often mean that some of their constituents will lose a service or their jobs. Nor do they like to raise taxes because higher taxes mean that some citizens must give even more of their income to the government. Elected officials fear that citizens harmed by spending cuts and tax increases will not vote for them on Election Day. While elected officials struggle with budget decisions and their impact on reelection hopes, appointed officials, who are not held accountable through the ballot box, make monetary policy.

Monetary Policy and the Federal Reserve System

The federal government seeks to influence the value of money by controlling its availability. When more money is in circulation, it is lower in value, and consequently consumers need to spend more to keep buying the same goods and services. Inflation is at work. The costs of running a business also increase with inflation. Because of these potential problems, the nation's central bank, the Federal Reserve, works to maximize employment, ensure stable prices (keep inflation low), and moderate long-term interest rates.

Congress and President Woodrow Wilson (1913–1921) established the Federal Reserve System (the Fed) in 1913. The Fed is composed of the Board of Governors (a government agency whose members the president nominates and the Senate must confirm), twelve Federal Reserve Banks, and the Federal Open Market Committee (FOMC). The Board of Governors, the president of the Federal Reserve Bank of New York, and the presidents of four other Federal Reserve Banks, who serve on a rotating basis, compose the FOMC. Today, the Fed's responsibilities include (1) setting **monetary policy,** the body of government policies aimed at maintaining price stability; (2) supervising and regulating banking institutions; (3) maintaining the stability of financial markets; and (4) providing financial services to depository institutions, the national government, and foreign official institutions—central banks of other nations and international organizations such as the International Monetary Fund.

The Fed has three primary tools for setting monetary policy. It can raise or lower the *reserve requirement*—the amount of money that financial institutions must keep out of circulation. In times of high inflation, the Fed may raise the reserve requirement to decrease the amount of money available through credit, hence decreasing the money supply. The Fed can also raise or lower the *discount rate*—the interest charged to financial institutions that borrow money from the Federal Reserve bank—and thereby make it more or less costly to borrow money. The Fed action that most influences the money supply, however, is its decision to buy or sell securities (stocks and bonds, which represent partial ownership in a company, and loans of money, respectively), primarily U.S. Treasury securities. The Fed sells securities when it wants to decrease the money supply and buys them to increase the supply.

Beyond its authority to set monetary policy, the Fed exerts supervisory and some regulatory authority over about 3,000 banks that are members of the Federal Reserve System (including all commercial banks chartered by the national government and those state-chartered banks that choose to join the Federal Reserve System), companies that control banks, and the U.S. activities of foreign banks. However, the Fed is not the only federal agency supervising and regulating the banking and financial industries. For example, the Office of the Comptroller of the Currency (OCC)—created in 1863 as a bureau within the Treasury Department—also charters, supervises, and regulates national banks. The Federal Deposit Insurance Corporation (FDIC)—an independent agency established in 1933—supervises state-chartered banks that are not members of the Federal Reserve System. Since the mid-1800s, the national government has created numerous regulatory agencies charged with ensuring the safety and soundness of the nation's banking and financial industries and systems, with the ultimate goal of promoting a healthy national economy.

Regulatory Policy to Prevent Market Failure

As stated by Adam Smith in 1776, in theory, the competition that characterizes a free, unregulated market serves the public good by producing the range of high-quality and affordable products and services that citizens need or demand. Free-market advocates assume that competition provides for the public good. Yet at times, the competition of a free, unregulated market may fail a nation and its people. **Market failure** occurs when marketplace competition harms consumers, workers, the environment, or the economy as a whole.

Indeed, competition among private entities, each trying to make a profit, may threaten public safety and health. Consider, for example, the unsafe products, including dangerous foods and drugs, that may be manufactured and sold to make a profit. Think about production and manufacturing processes that may pollute the air, water, and land, creating conditions that are injurious to public health. Competition may also lead firms to cut salaries and benefits to ensure their profits, or their very survival. Such cuts decrease workers' ability to earn wages and benefits that keep them in the middle class, or even out of poverty. Unsafe and unhealthful working conditions may be another "cost" that workers "pay" so that firms can hold down or reduce production expenses. Moreover, if marketplace competition leads to the elimination of all competitors, a monopoly develops, leaving consumers with goods that are overpriced and possibly of poor quality.

Most recently, the United States has experienced a market failure caused by risky decisions made by the financial and banking industries. Loans and credit lines extended to people without the means to repay the borrowed money sparked an increase in the number of people who could not pay their mortgages and therefore lost their homes. Hundreds of billions of dollars worth of mortgage-related investments had gone bad by the fall of 2008, and prominent financial and banking institutions collapsed. President Bush and Congress also began discussions about the need for new regulations for the banking and financial industries to prevent similar market failures in the future. President Obama's administration continued these discussions, focusing on protecting consumers of the banking and financial industries.

In the U.S. economy today, the government regulates marketplace practices to protect the public from market failure. This regulation occurs in two broad categories: business regulation and social regulation. **Business regulation** includes government policies that aim to preserve competition in the marketplace. **Social regulation** refers to government policies directed at protecting workers, consumers, and the environment from the harm caused by marketplace competition. In Chapter 13, we surveyed the administrative rule-making process by which executive branch agencies establish business and social regulations. In this discussion, we trace the evolution of these two types of regulatory policy.

Business Regulation

The federal government created the first agency for the purpose of regulating business, the Interstate Commerce Commission (ICC), in 1887. The ICC initially regulated the prices of and services provided by the railroad industry to protect the livelihood of farmers who relied on the nation's rail lines to transport their goods to distant markets. Next, in 1914, the federal government established regulations to prevent large corporations from engaging in business practices that harmed marketplace competition and established the Federal Trade Commission (FTC) to oversee these regulations.[8]

In 1934, during the Great Depression, the government created the Securities and Exchange Commission (SEC) to regulate and make transparent the nation's stock markets and financial markets. Another regulation of the Depression era, the National Labor Relations Act of 1935 (commonly known as the Wagner Act), authorized the national government to regulate interactions between management and labor unions. The Wagner Act empowered union members by creating the right of workers to unionize and elect representatives to bargain collectively with management for improved wages and working conditions. Moreover, the Wagner Act outlawed certain management practices that Congress considered unfair to labor—and hence a potential threat to the economy. Then in 1947, Congress overrode President Harry Truman's (1945–1953) veto and passed the Labor-Management Relations Act (Taft-Hartley Act), which identified and outlawed labor practices Congress deemed unfair and restricted the right to unionize to nonsupervisory employees only.

> Women carry their belongings from the headquarters of Lehman Brothers in New York in September 2008 after the 158-year-old investment bank filed for bankruptcy. Because of the credit crisis and devalued real estate market that devastated banking and financial institutions such as Lehman Brothers, the federal government proposed new regulations for these institutions.

Thus within fifty years of the creation of the first regulatory agency, the ICC, the national government had put in place a full range of business regulations. From regulating prices and standards in industries, to criminalizing business practices that impinge on marketplace competition, to making stock transactions transparent, to regulating labor-management relations—today the government regulates the marketplace in a wide variety of ways in the interest of creating and maintaining a healthy economy.

Social Regulation

The national government also uses social regulatory policy—which aims to protect the public's health and safety—to safeguard workers, consumers, and the environment from the potential harm created by the competitive quest for profits in the marketplace. Like business regulation, social regulation has an economic impact because it increases the costs of doing business.

Early Social Regulation   Scholars see precedents for social regulation in two 1906 laws that protected *public* health—the Pure Food and Drug Act and the Meat Inspection Act. Upton Sinclair's descriptions of the dangerous and unsanitary conditions in the Chicago meatpacking industry in his novel *The Jungle* motivated President Theodore Roosevelt (1901–1909) to sign these two laws. The Pure Food and Drug Act created the Food and Drug Administration (FDA) and charged it with testing all foods and drugs produced for human consumption. It also requires individuals to present prescriptions from licensed physicians in order to purchase certain drugs and mandates the use of warning labels on habit-forming drugs. The Meat Inspection Act requires government inspection of animals that are slaughtered and processed for human consumption and establishes standards of cleanliness for slaughterhouses and meat processing plants.

The federal government first addressed working conditions that jeopardized *workers'* health when it enacted the Fair Labor Standards Act (FLSA) in 1938. The FLSA established standards for a legal workweek, overtime pay for those working more than the standard workweek, minimum wages, record keeping of workers' hours, and limits on child labor. President Franklin D. Roosevelt characterized the law as the "most far-reaching, far-sighted program to the benefit of workers ever adopted."[9]

Consumer and Environmental Protection   In the 1960s, the government focused anew on growing concerns about product quality and safety. In his 1965 book *Unsafe at Any Speed,* attorney and consumer advocate Ralph Nader warned that "a great problem of contemporary life is how to control the power of economic interests which ignore the harmful effects of their applied science and technology."[10] Although Nader's book targeted the unsafe cars rolling off the assembly lines of the U.S. auto industry, his warning was equally relevant to the countless American industries that were discharging chemicals and toxins into the environment. Nader's book ignited a consumer safety movement, and a related environmental movement was born with the first Earth Day in 1970.

Lobbying by concerned citizens and interest groups led to passage of the Environmental Protection Act of 1970 and the Consumer Product Safety Act (CPSA) of 1973. These far-reaching federal laws aimed to regulate business practices that threatened consumers' health and safety, as well as the environment. The federal Consumer Product Safety Commission (CPSC), created through the CPSA, is charged by law with protecting the public from unreasonable risk of injury associated with more than 15,000 consumer products, including toys, products for children, products for inside and outside the home, and products made for sports and recreation. The CPSA can recall such products if it deems them unsafe, just as the FDA can recall food and prescription medicines it judges to be unsafe. The CPSC and the FDA post recall information on their Web sites (www.cpsc.gov/; www.fda.gov/opacom/Enforce.html).

The financial and economic free fall that began in 2007 sparked a national conversation about the need for additional regulation of the financial and banking industries. In 2009, President Barack Obama and Treasury Secretary Timothy Geithner proposed the creation of a new agency that would oversee financial products sold to consumers, such as credit cards and mortgages, in order to protect consumers and ultimately the economy. They also proposed restructuring the numerous existing federal agencies that regulate the financial and banking industries.

The Costs of Regulation

Marketplace regulation has unquestionably lowered the risk of harm to citizens and the environment caused by marketplace competition. It also has muted economic downfalls and market failures. But the burden of government regulations has driven up the cost of doing business, and in the end, consumers pay for these costs. In many industries, this increased cost poses greater problems for smaller firms than for larger ones. The higher costs caused by regulation may also put U.S. industries and firms at a competitive disadvantage in the global marketplace because many other countries do not impose regulations. Therefore, the production costs of firms in other countries are often lower than those in the United States.

The lack of regulations imposed by governments in other nations is a growing concern in the United States. The FDA and the CPSC are recalling numerous products manufactured in foreign countries and even some products manufactured in the United States that use ingredients or components from foreign sources. Because of these concerns, trade policy and the interdependence of the global economy are prominent contemporary issues.

Trade Policy in the Global Economy

The next time you are shopping, try to purchase only American-made products. Is it possible? Stores in the United States offer products that are domestic (that is, American-made) as well as imported (made overseas by American or foreign companies). Moreover, many American-made products have imported components and ingredients. For example, U.S. International Trade Commission data show that ingredients for food products are imported from more than 100 countries.[11] Today marketplaces in every country offer products grown and produced in countries from throughout the world. Hence national economies are integrated and interdependent—holistically forming the **global economy.**

To navigate in this global economy, each nation has its own **trade policy**—a collection of tax laws and regulations that support the country's international commerce. In addition, international organizations whose mission is to establish trade rules for all nations to follow have created a global trade policy. The goal of trade policy, like the other economic policies we have discussed, is ostensibly to promote prosperous economies.

Trade Policy: Protectionist or Free Trade?

A government's trade policy takes one of two basic forms: free trade or protectionism. **Protectionist trade policy** aims at protecting domestic producers and businesses from foreign competition through tariffs and nontariff trade barriers. A **tariff** is a special tax on imported goods. **Nontariff trade barriers** include government social and business regulations and government **subsidies**—tax breaks or another kind of financial support that encourages business expansion or decreases the cost of doing business so that businesses can be more competitive. Proponents of national government subsidies to U.S. farmers argue that decreasing these subsidies would place the farmers at a competitive disadvantage because European farmers receive even larger subsidies from their governments. Regulations include restrictions such as quotas on the number of imports allowed into the country and bans on the sale of imports that the government deems unsafe. For example, in 2007, the national government blocked imports of wheat gluten from a company in China after the FDA recalled a brand of pet food manufactured in Canada that contained this ingredient. The pet food caused cats and dogs throughout the United States to become ill and even to die.

From the 1790s until the 1930s, protectionism was the aim of U.S. trade policy. As the first secretary of the treasury, Alexander Hamilton argued successfully that taxes on imported goods could be set high enough to protect American-made products in the domestic marketplace. In 1930, even as the American economy was failing, Congress hiked tariffs 20 percent—so high that this action set off an international tariff war. This tariff hike fueled the Great Depression, whose economic toll was global in scope.

After World War II, the United States and its international partners gradually shifted toward a **free trade policy,** which aims at lowering or eliminating tariffs and nontariff barriers to trade. Free trade policies decrease the costs of bringing products to markets throughout the world and, in this way, open markets to a greater diversity of products and brisker competition. When other nations eliminate tariffs, American companies can participate in the global marketplace at a lower cost. These opportunities encourage an increase in the supply of U.S. goods and thus lead to an expansion of the U.S. economy. By the same token, when the United States eliminates its tariffs, more foreign products make their way into the American marketplace, increasing the diversity of consumer goods and producer competition and decreasing consumer prices in the United States.

International Trade Agreements

In 1947, the United States and twenty-three other nations signed the General Agreement on Tariffs and Trade (GATT). This multilateral agreement on guidelines for conducting international trade had three basic objectives. First, the signatory countries would not discriminate against each other in trade matters. Second, the signatory countries would work toward eliminating all tariff and regulatory barriers to trade among their countries. Third, the signatory countries would consult and negotiate with each other to resolve any trade conflicts or damages caused by the trading activities of another signatory country. Through multilateral negotiations, the GATT established the guidelines for international trade and resolved trade disputes from 1947 to 1995.

Then in 1995, the World Trade Organization (WTO) came into being. The WTO continues the GATT's advocacy of free trade and punishment of protectionism. Specifically, the WTO monitors adherence to international trade rules and resolves charges of rule violations raised by its member countries, of which there are over 130. The WTO Ministerial Conference meets every two years to discuss and deliberate on international trade rules. The meetings have become magnets for massive and sometimes violent demonstrations by protesters from around the world who believe that free trade is harming the environment, impeding human development in developing countries, and hurting the poor in all countries. Opponents of free trade argue that the deregulation of nontrade barriers has exacerbated deplorable working conditions, child labor problems, and poverty.

In the 1990s, bipartisan support for free trade in the U.S. Congress produced regional trade agreements such as the North American Free Trade Agreement (NAFTA), which the United States, Canada, and Mexico signed in 1993. NAFTA eliminated barriers to trade and financial investments across the economies of the three nations. Yet by the beginning of the twenty-first century, congressional legislators' concerns about possible damage to living standards and the health of the global environment, which many argue are caused by free trade, were growing, as was the nation's **trade deficit** (a negative balance of trade in which imports exceed exports).

Activists throughout the world are advocating policies to limit some of the harms they ascribe to free trade. Environmental groups fight for environmental protections to be included in international trade agreements. The International Labour Organization—a specialized agency of the United Nations that promotes internationally recognized human and worker rights—advocates for bans on forced labor and child labor, prohibitions against discrimination in personnel decisions and policies, and safeguards for workers' rights to organize and bargain collectively with employers (all forms of social regulation). Groups concerned about human development worry that free trade agreements ignore the economic status of small family farmers, craftspeople whose goods are sold in local markets, and poor people in general. In addition to these global concerns, American activists look closer to home, concerned about the impact of free trade on the ability to live the American dream.

The U.S. Economy, the Global Economy, and the American Dream Today

Between 2000 and 2006, according to traditional measures of economic health—the GDP, unemployment rates, and rates of inflation—the U.S. economy was expanding; however, it was the weakest economic expansion since World War II.[12] During the same period, in American households, the real median household income decreased[13] and the poverty rate crept up to 12.3 percent.[14] Moreover, income inequality grew. According to the U.S. Census Bureau, by 2007, the bottom quintile possessed just 3.4 percent of the total national income, while the top quintile held 50.5 percent, the largest share of the national income held by the top quintile since 1967.[15] Alan Greenspan, the renowned economist who chaired the Federal Reserve from 1987 to 2005, testified to Congress's Joint Economic Committee in 2005 about this paradox of a growing economy that disproportionately benefits those at the top: "This is not the type of thing which a democratic society—a capitalist democratic society—can really accept without addressing." He even suggested that this income gap seriously threatened the stability of the U.S. economy.[16]

Indeed, in 2007, the economy began to stagnate. The Fed used monetary policy in its efforts to try to stimulate the economy, cutting interest rates six times between September 2007 and March 2008. Senator Christopher Dodd (D-Connecticut), chair of the Senate Banking Committee, stated, "The current economic situation is more than merely a 'slowdown' or a 'downturn.' It is a crisis of confidence among consumers and investors."[17] This "crisis in confidence" sparked a call for the Fed to increase its regulation of the banking and financial investment industries in spring 2008.

President George W. Bush and Congress attempted to use fiscal policy to address this economic situation. In February 2008, they approved tax rebates totaling $168 billion and tax cuts for select businesses. Then in October 2008, President Bush signed the $700-billion Emergency Economic Stabilization Act, an economic bailout package allowing the federal government to buy assets from the biggest banks to shore them up and restore confidence in the financial system.

In his FY 2010 executive budget (published in February 2009), President Barack Obama summarized the economic status of the nation and the actions his administration planned to take in response to it: "We start 2009 in the midst of a crisis unlike any we have seen in our lifetime. Our economy is in a deep recession that threatens to be deeper and longer than any since the Great Depression. . . . The time has come to usher in a new era—a new era of responsibility in which we act not only to save and create new jobs, but also to lay a new foundation of growth upon which we can renew the promise of America." Obama then highlighted the planned investments in clean energy, education, health care, and infrastructure (such as roads, bridges, schools, and broadband lines) that are part of the American Recovery and Reinvestment Act of 2009. The hope was that these investments would maintain and create jobs. He also discussed the need for government to be more transparent and accountable to the people, beginning with the necessity of making tough decisions that will cut deficit spending.

The recession, which began in 2007 and deepened throughout 2008 and 2009, was a global phenomenon. Rising unemployment, shrinking confidence in financial institutions, decreasing availability of credit and hence decreasing investment, and slow economic growth were economic realities in countries throughout the world. In November 2008, leaders of twenty countries met in Washington, DC, for an emergency economic summit and agreed to work together to address the global recession. Central banks in European and Asian countries took actions to encourage investment and to shore up financial institutions. Many nations also put in place stimulus packages—taxing and spending plans—to combat the worst global economic crisis since the Great Depression.

It was during the Great Depression that historian James Truslow Adams coined the term "American dream." In his book *The Epic of America* (1931), Adams argued that what made America a unique nation was its inhabitants' "dream of a better, richer, and happier life" for all citizens based on equal "opportunity for each according to his [or her] ability or achievement."[18] For many, the American dream has come to mean owning a home, providing their children with good educational opportunities so they can advance in life, and saving for retirement. For others, it means being rich. Today, Americans tell pollsters that they are living better than their parents did. At the same time, Americans tell pollsters that today's children will *not* be able to live better than *their* parents did.[19] Indeed, *New York Times* columnist Bob Herbert summarizes several recent studies of the Millennial Generation (those born between 1980 and 2000) by stating that it "is in danger of being left out of the American dream—the first American generation to do less well economically than their parents."[20] Does the American dream mean doing better economically than your parents? Does it mean being rich? Or does the American dream mean living in a nation that has a stable, healthy economy and offers its citizens an equal opportunity to achieve (measured by homeownership, high levels of education, and a comfortable retirement) according to their ability and effort? If the American dream is the latter, can government policies—fiscal, monetary, regulatory, and trade—ensure a healthy national economy in today's interdependent global economy? In addition, can the government's domestic policies—which we discuss in Chapter 16—ensure an equal opportunity to achieve according to each citizen's ability and effort?

CONTINUING THE CONVERSATION

CONCLUSION

- The variety, complexity, and volume of economic policies have grown strikingly since 1789, when President George Washington took office.
- The president and Congress use fiscal policy, trade policy, and regulatory policy to achieve a prosperous economy, safe working conditions and consumer products, a healthy environment, and access to the American dream.
- The Fed aims to maintain price stability and high rates of employment through its control of monetary policy.
- The federal government's efforts to serve the people while creating and maintaining a healthy economy have frequently involved deficit spending, culminating in a national debt of almost $12 trillion by FY 2009.
- Adding to the complexity of achieving and maintaining a prosperous U.S. economy, safe working conditions and consumer products, a healthy environment, and good-paying jobs that provide opportunities to fulfill the American dream is the interdependence of today's global economy.

STUDY NOW

Summary

1. Economic Health and the American Dream

Though work ethic and education level influence personal income, a healthy national economy is essential to the ability of people to live a financially secure, happy, and healthy life—to realize the American dream.

2. The Nature of the American Economy

Because the government implements many policies that encourage, and sometimes mandate, certain business practices in the interest of creating and maintaining a healthy economy, the United States has what is known as a regulated capitalist economy.

3. Economic Theories That Inform Economic Policy

The national government's efforts to achieve and maintain a healthy economy have expanded as lawmakers have supported a variety of economic theories, among them Keynesian economics, supply-side economics, and monetarism.

4. Measuring Economic Health

Traditional measures of economic health include worker productivity, GDP, rate of inflation, and rate of unemployment; other measures include real median household income, income inequality, rate of poverty, and the Human Development Index.

5. Fiscal Policy and Economic Health

Taxing and spending decisions by the president and Congress influence how much money consumers have to spend, save, and invest; how much profit firms make and how much they have to invest in expanding business; and how much the government has to spend in order to serve the people.

6. Monetary Policy and the Federal Reserve System

The Fed, directed by a group of appointed officials, works to keep inflation and unemployment low by regulating the amount of money in circulation in the economy.

7. Regulatory Policy to Prevent Market Failure

Today, business regulation (to ensure competition) and social regulation (to protect workers, consumers, and the environment) are pervasive components of the U.S. economy, despite ongoing calls by business, some economists, and politicians to deregulate.

8. Trade Policy in the Global Economy

Protectionist trade policy dominated the United States until after World War II, when free trade policy became the goal of international agreements and U.S. trade policy.

9. The U.S. Economy, the Global Economy, and the American Dream Today

The recent global recession, the worst since the Great Depression of the 1930s, has sparked conversations about the nature of the American dream and if it is in fact achievable in the global economy.

For Critical Thinking and Discussion

1. If you were president of the United States and wanted to balance the annual budget, what cost cuts to programs do you think you could get American taxpayers to support? What tax increases or new taxes do you think you could get American taxpayers to support? Explain your choices.

2. Consider your family's financial situation. What economic policy would you propose the national government implement to improve your family's financial situation? Explain.

3. Which type of tax do you think is the most fair, progressive, proportional, or regressive? Explain your choice.

4. If the national government deregulates with regard to environmental protection, product safety, and/or working conditions, would there be negative consequences? Give some examples, or explain why there would not be any.

Key Terms

American dream 550
balanced budget 553
budget authority 564
budget deficit 568
budget reconciliation 567
budget surplus 568
business regulation 572
concurrent budget
  resolution 567
consumer price index
  (CPI) 558
continuing resolution 568
deficit spending 553
depression 554
deregulation 555
discretionary
  spending 565
economic boom 554
economy 551
executive budget 567
fiscal policy 554
fiscal year (FY) 561

free trade policy 576
global economy 575
gross domestic product
  (GDP) 558
household income 560
Human Development
  Index (HDI) 560
income inequality 553
inflation 557
Keynesian economics 554
laissez-faire 552
mandatory spending 564
market failure 571
median household
  income 560
monetarism 557
monetary policy 570
national debt 555
nontariff trade barrier 575
poverty 560
poverty rate 561
poverty thresholds 561

progressive tax 564
proportional tax
  (flat tax) 564
protectionist trade
  policy 575
pure capitalist
  economy 551
real income 560
recession 554
regressive tax 564
regulated capitalist
  economy (mixed
  economy) 552
social regulation 572
subsidy 576
supply-side
  economics 555
tariff 575
tax base 551
tax expenditures 564
trade deficit 577
trade policy 575

Internet Resources

A More Perfect Union **Web site**
www.mhhe.com/harrisonampule Consult the book's Web site for study guides, interactive activities, simulations, and current hot-links that provide additional information on economic policy in the United States.

American Enterprise Institute (AEI)
www.aei.org The AEI sponsors research on government policy and economic policy and advocates limited government involvement in the marketplace.

Economic Policy Institute
http://epinet.org This nonprofit organization aims to broaden public debate on strategies to achieve a prosperous and fair economy.

Office of Management and Budget (OMB)
www.whitehouse.gov/omb   The OMB's site has links to the most recent executive budget and historical budget documents.

Tax Foundation
www.taxfoundation.org   The Tax Foundation conducts policy research that monitors fiscal issues at the federal, state, and local levels. It collects and analyzes data related to taxes and tax burdens on U.S. citizens and corporations.

Recommended Readings

Derber, Charles. *People Before Profit.* New York: Picador, 2003. A disturbing analysis of globalization to date, with a blueprint for a new form of globalization that will lead to a more stable and just global community.

Schick, Allen. *The Federal Budget.* Washington, DC: Brookings Institute, 2000. A comprehensive, in-depth consideration of the national budget process.

Woodward, Bob. *Maestro: Greenspan's Fed and the American Boom.* New York: Simon & Schuster, 2000. A probing look into how the Fed operated under the leadership of Alan Greenspan from 1987 to 2000. The effect of the evolving global economy on the economic health of the United States is an intriguing part of Woodward's account.

In the 1930s, radical new federal government policies created a safety net that enabled economically distressed citizens to provide for their basic needs.

The federal government faces a host of domestic policy issues, from the high cost of maintaining the safety net to environmental degradation, scarce energy supplies, homeland security threats, and immigration.

NOW

16

Domestic Policy

According to the Declaration of Independence and the U.S. Constitution, the American government must ensure a just and safe society in which citizens can live their lives freely, in pursuit of their happiness. Essential to the achievement of these goals are the preservation and protection of the natural environment so that future generations can enjoy a quality of life comparable to today's. And implicit in these founding documents is the idea that government policy makers must recognize the long-term impact of their policies, as well as their lack of policies, on citizens, their communities, and the nation at large.

In our federal system, when citizens bring societal problems to the attention of government officials, the ensuing legislative and public debates typically revolve around several key questions. First, government officials must decide whether the problem is one that government should address. If the answer to this fundamental question is yes, then additional questions follow. What level of government has legal authority to address the problem? What level of government has the financial resources? What is the most cost-effective means to deal with the problem? Beyond the expected positive effects of a policy's implementation, what unexpected costs and negative consequences might occur?

NEXT

Will Social Security survive—and fund the retirement checks of *your* generation?

Will global warming and worldwide environmental degradation force U.S. policy makers to sign on to international treaties?

Will demographic change owing to immigration today bring new issues to tomorrow's policy agenda?

Citizen Engagement and Domestic Policy

The Constitution established a government that is by and for the people. Previous chapters have explored the many ways that individuals and groups engage with government officials and political processes in order to influence what government does and does not do. Yet a widespread national affliction is *NIMBY,* or "not-in-my-backyard" syndrome. People with *NIMBY* syndrome decline to participate in politics until a government action or inaction threatens them directly. When citizens experience a negative effect in their own backyard, they get involved. Lobbying government officials is a common first step in citizen engagement, and it may be as basic as making a phone call, sending an e-mail, or writing a letter, or as complex as mobilizing large groups for activism. Citizens may also use lawsuits to press government officials to focus on issues of concern and to address them through policy making.

Complicating the work of U.S. policy makers, the diversity of citizens' needs and expectations for government action means that almost every call for government action sparks a call for either a different action or no action. The plurality of citizens' needs, individuals' constantly changing priorities, and their range of political ideologies make for an ongoing public conversation and legislative debate over which policies warrant government spending and who will pay the taxes to cover the bills. Democrats and Republicans frequently disagree on these matters. Democrats typically are more liberal in inclination and tend to support **safety nets**—programs ensuring that every citizen's basic physiological needs (food, water, shelter, health care, and a clean environment) are met. Republicans more commonly have a conservative ideology and focus more on public safety and national security issues. Ultimately, elected officials—whose career goal, after all, is to get reelected—find it much easier to add new policies and programs, and consequently to drive up government expenses, than to eliminate programs or to decrease program costs.

As we have seen in preceding chapters, the government makes policy in several ways. For one, Congress and the president set policy by approving *authorization bills,* which establish a policy and identify who will implement it, and *appropriation bills,* which authorize the spending of national revenue. Federal, state, local, and shadow bureaucrats also make policy, through both the administrative rule-making process and their daily use of administrative discretion. In addition, the presidential power of the executive order amounts to making policy, as it gives the president the authority to tell bureaucrats how to carry out a national policy. Finally, the federal judiciary, through the various cases that come before the courts, has policy-making power by virtue of its authority to declare unconstitutional the laws made by the legislative and executive branches of national, state, and local government (the authority of *judicial review*). The courts also resolve conflicts over the meaning and proper implementation of laws. In summary, each of the three branches of the national government has policy-making authority that it uses to fulfill the government's constitutionally established mission to serve present and future generations.

Since 1788 (when the states ratified the U.S. Constitution), the national government's scope of responsibility for addressing domestic matters has gradually expanded as citizens and groups have lobbied to press for their interests. Federal authority now covers a diverse collection of public policies. Today's national budget lists seventeen superfunctions of the federal government (see Table 16.1).[1] The numbers in the table show that the majority of federal government functions and most government spending

TABLE 16.1

National Budget Superfunctions and Expenditures: Total Proposed National Budget Authority, 2010—$3,591,076 million ($3.6 trillion)

Defense and Foreign Policy
($762,954 million; 21.2% of budget outlays)*

National defense ($712,853 million; 19.9%)
International affairs ($50,101 million; 1.4%)

Domestic Policy
($2,740,462 million; 76.3%)

General science, space, and technology ($32,853 million; 0.9%)

Energy ($22,147 million; 0.6%)

Natural resources and environment ($43,592 million; 1.2%)

Agriculture ($26,047 million; 0.7%)

Commerce and housing credit ($85,998 million; 2.4%)

Transportation ($106,863 million; 3.0%)

Community and regional development ($27,977 million; 0.7%)

Education, training, employment, and social services ($134,585 million; 3.8%)

Health ($389,012 million; 10.8%)

Medicare ($457,815 million; 12.8%)

Income security ($547,451 million; 15.3%)

Social Security ($677,100 million; 18.9%)

Veterans benefits and services ($108,935 million; 3.0%)

Administration of justice ($55,663 million; 1.6%)

General government ($24,424 million; 0.7%)

Net Interest
($135,862 million; 3.9%)

*Numbers in parentheses represent (1) total outlay for each function and (2) percentage of total budget outlay, rounded to the nearest tenth of a percent.

Source: Budget of the United States Fiscal Year 2010, Historical Tables, Table 3.2, www.whitehouse.gov/omb/budget/Historicals/.

are directed at *domestic* policy matters: 76.3% for domestic policies and 21.2% for foreign and defense policies. The remaining percentage pays the interest on the national debt incurred by past borrowing to cover deficit spending.

Because it would be impossible for us to examine every domestic policy program, we limit our focus in this chapter to a subset of national domestic policies. Specifically, we concentrate on policies that address the most basic of human needs and are essential to sustaining life, liberty, and opportunities to pursue happiness: environmental, energy, income security, health care, and homeland security policies. We also look at the controversial policy area of immigration, defined by some as a national security concern, by others as an economic issue, and by still others as a humanitarian cause reflecting the United States' roots and highest ideals.

Tools of Domestic Policy

The national government attempts to address citizens' problems and to provide benefits and services to the people by using various policy tools. Domestic policy tools include laws and regulations, direct provision of public goods, cash transfer payments, loans, loan guarantees, and insurance, as well as contracting-out the provision of public goods to nongovernmental entities.

Laws and Regulations

At the federal, state, and local levels alike, government strives to accomplish its policy goals by creating laws with which individuals and organizations must comply. These include environmental laws, national narcotics laws, and laws addressing work

> National, state, and local governments hire public servants to monitor compliance with their laws and regulations. It is common for public servants from two or more levels of government, such as federal Drug Enforcement Administration (DEA) agents and state police officers, to work together in intergovernmental efforts to serve the public efficiently and effectively, as they do here in helping to transfer a Colombian drug lord to U.S. custody (several agents' faces are obscured for their safety).

standards and conditions. Many laws assign administrative agencies the authority to establish the specific rules, regulations, and standards that are essential to effective implementation of the laws.

Direct Provision of Public Goods

In addition to creating rules of behavior through law and regulations, governments provide services and benefits. Using the policy tool of **direct provision,** governments hire public servants—bureaucrats who receive a government paycheck—to dispense the service. For example, veterans hospitals hire doctors, nurses, and physical therapists to administer health care to veterans; the U.S. Postal Service hires mail carriers, postal clerks, and postal processing machine operators to deliver billions of pieces of mail each week. To provide for the country's common defense, the national government employs millions of military personnel. The workers hired by the national government to provide these services directly are on the payroll of the national government.

Cash Transfers

Another instrument of government policy is the **cash transfer**—the direct provision of cash (in various forms) to eligible individuals or to the providers of goods or services to eligible individuals. The main cash-transfer programs are of two kinds, depending upon their sources of revenue. For **noncontributory programs,** the general revenues collected by the government pay for the program. This means that a proportion of the money collected from all taxpayers funds the cash transfer. Temporary Assistance to Needy Families, the income security program for families with children who have no or very low income, is an example of a noncontributory cash-transfer program. In contrast, **contributory programs,** or **social insurance programs,** are funded by revenue collected specifically for these programs, and they benefit only those who have paid into the programs. Social insurance programs are **entitlement programs,** meaning the government guarantees the program's benefits to all who meet the eligibility criteria. Thus workers who pay the payroll tax for Social Security will receive Social Security checks when they retire.

With a **direct subsidy,** another type of cash transfer, the government provides financial support to specific persons or organizations that engage in activities that the government believes benefit the public good. Individual farmers and agricultural corporations, for example, receive money from the government to grow specified crops or to limit how much they grow. College students receiving Pell grants, which do not need to be paid back, are also recipients of direct subsidies funded through the federal government's general revenue.

Loans, Loan Guarantees, and Insurance

In addition to using tax breaks and grants to encourage behaviors that accomplish its goals, the national government lends money to individuals and organizations, and it guarantees loans made by private businesses. Some examples are government loan

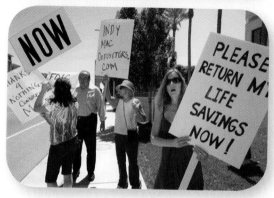

> Depositors, fearful that the money they had deposited had been lost, besieged banks such as this one in Passaic, New Jersey, after Wall Street crashed and the Great Depression began in 1929. To protect depositors' money, in 1933, the federal government created the Federal Deposit Insurance Corporation (FDIC), which today insures bank deposits of up to $250,000 per depositor, per insured bank. In July 2009, former IndyMac Bank depositors who had lost some of their savings when the bank failed (because they had deposited more than the insured amount), demonstrated on the one-year anniversary of the FDIC takeover of the bank.

programs to assist individuals in purchasing homes, and Perkins loans, which pay some of the college expenses of students from very low-income families. In addition, the government guarantees banks that it will repay the loans they provide to college students if the students cannot repay the loans themselves; these guaranteed loans are called Stafford loans. The national government is also in the insurance business. The Federal Deposit Insurance Corporation (FDIC) is one example of a national insurance program. The FDIC insures bank deposits of up to $250,000 in member banks to encourage people to save money for their own sake and for the good of the national economy.

Contracting-Out

The government also contracts with private and nonprofit organizations to produce essential resources or to deliver services historically provided by the government. One example of contracting-out, or outsourcing (see Chapter 13), is the government's contracts with corporations such as Lockheed Martin and Boeing to build the planes and missiles it needs to defend the country.

By means of contracting-out and the other various tools we have surveyed, the government delivers goods and services to its citizens now and in the future. In the rest of this chapter, we examine how government uses these tools to implement overall policy in several domestic policy areas, including the environment, energy, income security, health care, homeland security, and immigration.

Environmental Policy

At the most basic level, providing for the general welfare means ensuring that people have the basic necessities for sustaining life. These needs include clean and drinkable water, breathable air, and unpolluted land on which to grow food safe for consumption. No one argues against a clean environment. Yet there is no consensus on how to achieve and maintain one. In addition, appeals for environmental protection often conflict with demands for ample supplies of energy and for economic development. Government officials engage in a complex balancing act to protect the environment while ensuring an ample supply of energy and supporting economic development.

Environmental protection includes conserving natural resources and limiting the pollution emitted into the air and water and onto the land. By the late 1960s and 1970s, several environmental crises had brought the harm humans had caused to the natural environment, plants, animals, and people into stark view.

Environmental Degradation

Since the 1940s, farmers have used chemicals to destroy insects, weeds, fungi, and other living organisms that harm their crops. The threats such pesticides pose to air, water, and land became the focus of public concern and political debate after the publication of Rachel Carson's eye-opening best-seller *Silent Spring* in 1962. Carson's book documented how pesticides were contaminating the environment and getting into human food. The use of chemicals, she warned, threatened the existence not only of birds—whose extinction would mean a silent spring—but of humankind itself. Although the chemical industry tried to discredit Carson's findings, President John F. Kennedy (1961–1963) established a special panel to investigate them, and the panel found support for Carson's concerns.

Then, in 1969, these growing apprehensions became a spectacular reality when the heavily polluted Cuyahoga River in northeastern Ohio caught fire for the second time since 1952. Around the same time, arsenic was found in the Kansas River, and millions of fish went belly-up in major waterways such as Lake Superior, killed by the chemicals and untreated waste emitted by industrial plants and local sewage systems. In response, state and local governments banned fishing in many waterways, including Lake Erie, due to their excessive pollution.

The mounting environmental crises and additional governmental studies brought calls to action from both citizens' groups and elected officials during the 1960s and 1970s. U.S. Senator Gaylord Nelson (D-Wisconsin) responded by founding Earth Day. He later recollected that "all across the country, evidence of environmental degradation was appearing. . . . The people were concerned, but the politicians were not. . . . Suddenly, the idea occurred to me—why not organize a huge grassroots protest over what was happening to our environment?"[2]

Nelson's vision of a day of educational rallies in Washington, DC, became a reality on April 22, 1970, when more than 200,000 people gathered on the National Mall. Millions more congregated across the country to draw attention to environmental concerns. Earth Day 1970 was so successful at bringing attention to the environmental cause that many consider it the beginning of the environmental movement. Celebrated every year with rallies and teach-ins involving millions of people worldwide, Earth Day keeps concerns about environmental degradation on the public policy agenda.

Environmental Protection

A cascade of groundbreaking national legislation followed the first Earth Day. The Environmental Protection Act of 1970 established the Environmental Protection Agency (EPA) to oversee the implementation of laws protecting the quality of air, water, and land. The Environmental Protection Act mandates that all construction projects receiving federal funding must begin with an environmental impact study analyzing the project's effects on the environment and on endangered species. The act also has a sunshine component requiring the government to invite citizens' comments on proposed projects. Under these provisions of the law, environmental interest groups frequently bring lawsuits challenging the quality and accuracy of environmental impact studies and developers' lack of compliance with the sunshine provisions. Developers and parties probing into new energy sources view such lawsuits as a waste of time and money. But in fact, this litigation, combined with the broader work of various environmental groups, has become a driving force in environmental protection today.

Clean Air   The landmark Clean Air Act of 1970 delegates authority to the EPA to set air quality standards while giving state governments enforcement responsibility. Today states in turn typically delegate some of their enforcement responsibilities to local governments. If states and their local governments do not enforce compliance with the national standards, the EPA can take over. To bolster compliance with the Clean Air Act, the law gives citizens the right to sue those who are violating the standards. Citizens also have the right to sue the EPA if it does not enforce the Clean Air Act. In fact, in 2007, Massachusetts and eleven other states, three cities, and several environmental groups successfully challenged the EPA and President George W. Bush's (2001–2009) interpretation of the law, when the U.S. Supreme Court determined that carbon dioxide is a pollutant that the EPA has the authority to regulate.[3]

Clean Water   The Clean Water Act is actually the 1972 Federal Water Pollution Control Act as amended over the years. This law, which has the goal of making waterways clean enough to swim in and to eat fish from, authorizes the EPA to set water quality standards and to require permits for anyone discharging contaminants into any waterway. However, the direct discharge of pollutants into waterways is not the only source of water pollution. Runoff from farms, which carries animal waste and pesticides into waterways, contributes heavily to the problem. The Department of Agriculture joins forces with the EPA to prevent this indirect source of pollution.

Under the Clean Water Act, state and local governments must monitor water quality, issue permits to those discharging waste into waterways, and enforce the national standards. If states and localities fail to carry out these mandated responsibilities, the EPA can step in and do the job. The law also provides for federal loans to local governments, funneled through state governments, for building waste-water treatment plants.

The Safe Drinking Water Act of 1974 authorizes the EPA to establish purity standards for drinking water. Because states or localities typically operate water systems, this act effectively requires the EPA to regulate state and local governments. The act provides for national grants to state and local governments for research and for improving their water systems.

Clean Land   The United States produces more solid waste—from household garbage to toxic by-products of manufacturing—per person than any other country. If not properly disposed of or treated, all waste has the potential to harm the environment, as well as plants, animals, and people.

Some toxic by-products, such as the radioactive nuclear wastes produced in manufacturing nuclear weapons and generating nuclear power, cannot be treated or disposed of, but they dissipate over time—from 100 years for low-level radioactive waste to hundreds of thousands of years for high-level radioactive waste. In 2004, a federal appeals court ruled that the developers of the nuclear repository being built at Yucca Mountain, Nevada, to store nuclear waste for the long term had to ensure it would function successfully for hundreds of thousands of years.[4]

Citizens with resources, including money and the time to organize or to join an existing organization, are able to fight the location of such undesirable land uses in their communities. Lower-income communities are more likely than more affluent cities and towns to bear the burden of housing waste storage facilities. **Environmental racism** is the term used to describe the higher incidence of environmental threats and subsequent health problems in lower-income communities, which frequently are also communities dominated by people of color.[5]

The Resource Conservation and Recovery Act of 1976, administered by the EPA, regulates the disposal of solid and hazardous wastes and encourages recycling. Although this act authorized the cleanup of toxic waste sites, and the government identified thousands of such sites in the 1970s, no national funding was made available for the cleanup. Then in 1980, as Congress was debating how to address potential harm caused by toxic waste sites, an abandoned site for the storage, treatment, and disposal of hazardous waste in Elizabeth, New Jersey, exploded.[6] Shortly thereafter, Congress approved the Comprehensive Environmental Response, Compensation and Liability Act of 1980 (known as the Superfund law) to pay for cleanup of the nation's most toxic waste dumps.

Because U.S. air quality and water quality have improved tremendously since the 1970s, many citizens and government officials have shifted their attention to other societal concerns. At the same time, U.S. industries have become more resistant to legislative proposals to stiffen environmental standards and are increasingly challenging the implementation of environmental laws. In addition, a growing private property rights movement is challenging restrictions on land use that have been put in place in the name of environmental protection. Although no one is arguing against a clean environment, tensions persist between the need for environmental protection and other policy areas. The increasing demand for cheap energy is one such area.

Energy Policy

Energy creation—the production of electricity and heat, as well as fuels to power automobiles, trucks, planes, trains, and other transport vehicles—is essential to the prosperity of the U.S. economy and to the American way of life. The United States uses more energy than any other country in the world, and its demand for energy continues to rise. What underlies this increasing demand? Industrial and commercial expansion, the construction of larger houses, and soaring computer use all have contributed to the ballooning demand for electricity. Robust sales of trucks for personal use, as well as of gas-guzzling sport utility vehicles (SUVs), have driven up consumers' demand for gasoline. The ever-rising energy demands of the U.S. economy and the lifestyle of U.S. residents are problematic for several reasons, as we shall see.

Energy and Global Warming

The majority of energy consumed in the United States is produced by burning fossil fuels—oil, coal, and natural gas. Burning fossil fuels produces air pollution. The pollution produced by U.S. reliance on fossil fuels is not just a national problem; it is a global problem. Mounting evidence indicates that pollution from burning fossil fuels has increased temperatures worldwide, creating a **greenhouse effect**—so-called because in a greenhouse, the walls and roof trap solar heat, keeping the temperature inside warmer than it is outside. **Global warming,** the gradual average increase in the earth's temperature, is the result of pollution that traps solar heat in the earth's atmosphere.

International fears about the potential harm of global warming led to a treaty called the Kyoto Protocol of 1997. Countries that ratify the Kyoto Protocol agree to work toward eliminating the greenhouse effect by reducing their emissions of carbon dioxide and other gases believed to cause it. Although 184 parties have ratified the treaty, the United States has not.

Even though the federal government has not ratified the Kyoto Protocol, many state and local governments are collectively working to meet its provisions, with the goal of showing the national government the benefits of abiding by it. Currently, ten northeastern states have agreed to the Regional Greenhouse Gas Initiative (RGGI). The RGGI commits these states to capping emissions from power plants. Mayors in almost 200 cities have responded positively to the call of Seattle mayor

Greg Nickels to meet the Kyoto Protocol's goal of reducing greenhouse gas emissions to 7 percent less than 1990 levels by 2012.[7]

President Barack Obama (2009-present) came into office with global warming as one of his top priorities. With his support, the House of Representatives approved the American Clean Energy and Leadership Act in July 2009 and sent it to the Senate for consideration. With a goal of cutting greenhouse gas emissions by 17 percent from 2005 levels by 2020, the bill imposes the first-ever federal limits on carbon dioxide and other pollutants linked to global warming and calls for a change in direction for the nation's energy policy. Al Gore, who won a Nobel Peace Prize in 2007 for his work on global warming, posted a statement on his Web site declaring this bill "an essential first step towards solving the climate crisis."

National Energy Policy

Until the 1950s, the United States produced almost all the oil it consumed.[8] Today it imports almost half the oil it uses (see Figure 16.1). Moreover, about 38 percent of all energy consumed in the United States comes from burning oil, meaning that

Top Suppliers of U.S. Crude Oil Imports, 2007

54%
OPEC

46%
Non-OPEC

Other OPEC nations 9
Libya 31
Kuwait 64
Algeria 162
Iraq 177
Angola 181
Nigeria 395
Venezuela 420
Saudi Arabia 530

United Kingdom 37
Russia 41
Colombia 50
Brazil 61
Other non-OPEC nations 231
Ecuador 72
Mexico 514
Canada 681

Imports to U.S. in millions of barrels

POLITICAL INQUIRY

FIGURE 16.1 ■ What percentage of U.S. crude oil imports come, respectively, from OPEC and non-OPEC countries? Which OPEC country is the top source of this oil? What stands out about the OPEC countries that are shown, in terms of their location in the world? Which non-OPEC country provides the most crude oil to the United States?

Source: U.S. Census Bureau, *The Statistical Abstract 2009*, Table 895.

about 19 percent of U.S. energy comes from imported oil. This heavy reliance on foreign oil concerns citizens and the government because of the volatile political environments in some oil-producing countries in the Middle East and South America and because of conflicts between U.S. policies and the policies of some of these countries.

The Opec Embargo and Carter's Response   In 1973, for example, the Arab members of the Organization of Petroleum Exporting Countries (OPEC) implemented an embargo on oil supplies. This embargo was a reaction to U.S. support of Israel in that nation's Yom Kippur War of 1973 against Egypt and Syria over disputed lands. Outraged by what they saw as U.S. interference, OPEC member nations refused to sell oil to the United States and western European nations that supported Israel in the war. This five-month oil embargo, followed by OPEC production limits that kept oil prices high and produced hours-long waits in gas station lines, forced the United States to set national energy policies.

In 1975, the national government established the Strategic Petroleum Reserve, a growing supply of crude oil stored away in case of a future energy emergency or an interruption in the U.S. supply of imported oil. That same year Congress also set fuel-efficiency standards for passenger cars and light trucks, the Corporate Average Fuel Economy (CAFÉ) standards. In 2007, more than thirty-five years after establishing CAFÉ, Congress significantly increased the fuel efficiency standards for the first time. Automobile producers must meet the new 35-miles-per-gallon standard, up from 25 miles per gallon, by the year 2020.[9] However, it was not until May 2009, during President Barack Obama's administration, that the Department of Transportation finalized the rules needed to enforce the new CAFÉ standards. (For more on CAFÉ standards, see "Then, Now, Next.")

In 1976, the federal government established the Department of Energy to develop and oversee a comprehensive national energy plan. In 1977, President Jimmy Carter declared an "energy crisis" and announced policies stressing energy conservation through measures such as the regulation of temperature settings in public buildings and tax incentives to insulate homes. In addition, government regulation of oil and natural gas prices was curtailed during Carter's presidency.[10] Although the government had historically regulated the prices of these energy resources, the expectation was that if prices rose on the basis of supply and demand, people would conserve. Carter's energy policies also included increased financial support for research and development of alternative energy sources such as solar, wind, geothermal (produced by the earth's internal heat), and renewable biomass (fuels created from plant life, such as corn and switchgrass).

With deregulation, oil prices jumped by 1980 to more than ten times their 1972 level. But by 1986, oil prices had begun to fall. With lower prices through the 1990s came reduced federal government support for research and development of alternative energy sources. The public, too, lost interest in energy conservation, and the demand for energy grew, as did the production of gas-guzzling automobiles.

Will the Obama Administration Succeed in Enforcing the Fuel-Efficiency Standards Set by Congress?

THEN: In 2007, the national government legislated new fuel efficiency standards for cars and trucks (CAFÉ standards); however, President Bush's administration failed to write the regulations needed to enforce the standards. In addition, the Bush administration denied California's request to enact its own tougher standards.

NOW: Within the first week of his administration in January 2009, President Obama directed the Environmental Protection Agency to reconsider for approval California's application to set stricter limits on tailpipe emissions from cars and trucks. In May 2009, Obama announced the rules to enforce the new national CAFÉ standard of 35.5 miles per gallon by 2016.

WHAT'S NEXT?

- How do you think Americans will react to the prospect of driving smaller cars or cars that run on an energy source other than gasoline, which automakers will produce in order to meet the new emission standards?

- Do you think that Americans are concerned enough about climate change to buy smaller, more fuel-efficient cars even if gas prices go down significantly? Support your answer.

- President Obama's early record indicates a new direction in environmental and energy policy. Do you think national environmental and energy policy could revert to that of the Bush administration? What might cause such a reversion? What might prevent it?

An Energy Policy Focused on Fossil Fuels In 2001, Secretary of Energy Spencer Abraham sounded an alarm: "America faces a major energy-supply crisis over the next two decades. The failure to meet this challenge will threaten our nation's economic prosperity, compromise our national security, and literally alter the way we live our lives."[11] In response, President George W. Bush appointed Vice President Dick Cheney—a former oil company executive—to preside over a task force charged with formulating a new national energy policy. The result was an energy policy emphasizing the increased production of fossil fuels. This policy was in stark contrast to the conservation approach developed in the 1970s. Moreover, Bush's 2002 budget drastically cut funding for conservation initiatives and for research on alternative, renewable energy sources.

By the winter of 2005, government officials and citizens were increasingly concerned over the price and availability of oil. Hurricane Katrina had taken a toll on domestic oil production. The Iraq War and tensions with Iran jeopardized the stability of imports from the Middle East. President Hugo Chavez of Venezuela, the number-three U.S. oil supplier, was also threatening to limit the availability of his country's oil.

In response, President Bush emphasized in his 2006 State of the Union address how essential affordable energy is to the United States' success in the world economy. He stressed that Americans' "addiction" to oil must be reduced. Bush called for a 22 percent increase in funding for research in alternative renewable energy sources such as solar and wind, as well as in nuclear energy, and recommended increased use of coal. The president also called for expanded research in alternative means to power automobiles, including electricity, hydrogen, and ethanol (produced from corn, wood chips, and switchgrass).

Future Directions Supporters of the American Clean Energy and Leadership Act, which was approved by the House and sent to the Senate in the summer of 2009, called the bill a revolution in energy policy. Under this act, energy companies would pay a price for the greenhouse pollution they create through the purchase of pollution allowances, or they could shift to using cleaner energy sources, including solar, wind, geothermal, and nuclear. Automakers would be required to make more fuel-efficient cars. The bill's sponsors argued that another outcome of the bill would be the creation of new green jobs—such as making or installing solar panels and wind turbines, developing equipment to harness carbon emissions, and producing energy-efficient light bulbs, washing machines, and other home appliances. President Obama called on senators and all Americans to support the bill, which he argued would "open the door to a clean energy economy and a better future for America."[12]

Today limited supplies and high costs of traditional energy sources, along with the environmental impact of the continuing use of fossil fuels, threaten the quality of life of Americans and people around the globe. Americans are looking to national and state governments for public policy solutions to these energy-related and environmental problems. In a similar way, during the 1930s, Americans had turned to the national government to address the economic downturn that was impeding millions of Americans' ability to enjoy a decent quality of life, as we next consider.

Income Security Programs

Before the Great Depression of the 1930s, Americans who could not provide for their basic needs relied on relief from family, friends, charities, and, in some cases, local or state government. During the Depression, however, the excessively weak economy left one-quarter of the U.S. labor force unemployed. Families lost jobs, savings, and homes. Charities were overwhelmed. State and local governments lacked the resources to assist the millions of people without incomes. Citizens, as well as state and local governments, looked to the federal government for assistance.

Within his first hundred days in office, President Franklin D. Roosevelt (1933–1945) proposed a sequence of revolutionary bills to stimulate and regulate the depressed economy and to provide income to the needy. His administration's radical proposals placed the national government at the center of issues it had historically left to local and state governments. These and the subsequent New Deal policies approved in Roosevelt's first few years in office created jobs, established a government-regulated economy (see Chapter 15), and provided income security for retired citizens and a safety net for people in financial need. Many of the New Deal programs are still in place today, though in modified form.

Social Security

The Social Security Act of 1935, a centerpiece of the New Deal, established a range of landmark income security programs. To this day, these programs provide financial assistance to the elderly, disabled, dependent, and unemployed.

Old-Age and Survivors Insurance   The Social Security Act established the Old-Age and Survivors Insurance (OASI) Program, which initially provided income to individuals or families when a worker covered by the program retired. This contributory cash transfer program is the traditional retirement insurance component of Social Security; most people are aware of it and anticipate benefiting from it in retirement. OASI is a social insurance entitlement program, funded by contributions from employees and employers. Each year the federal government establishes the amount of earnings subject to the Social Security tax, which is called the *covered income*. Employees and employers each pay 6.2 percent (for a total of 12.4 percent) of the employee's covered income for Social Security. In 2009, income up to $106,800 was subject to the tax.

The 1937 Federal Insurance Contribution Act (FICA) established the pay-as-you-go funding mechanism for OASI. Through FICA contributions, current workers and employers deposit money in the Social Security Trust Fund, and the government uses the money contributed today to pay today's beneficiaries. The money left over after today's payments are made is invested so that the trust fund will grow; income from investments will be combined with future FICA revenues to pay for future Social Security checks.

Because Social Security is an entitlement, and because the government cannot predict how long a Social Security recipient will live—and therefore how many checks

The Future of Old Age and Survivors Insurance (OASI)

	THEN (1937)	NOW (2009)
Percentage of workers covered*	60%	97%
Payroll tax collected from employees to fund OASI*	1% on wages up to $3,000	6.2% on wages up to $106,800
Number of workers paying into OASI for per one retiree*	16	3
Normal retirement age*	65	67 (for those born after 1959)
Total receipts**	$747 million	$695,462 million (end of 2008)
Total benefit payments**	$1 million	$509,337 million (end of 2008)
Assets at end of year**	$766 million	$2,202,886 million (end of 2008)

WHAT'S NEXT?

> The Congressional Budget Office, the Social Security Trustees, and many economists forecast that, with only three workers paying into the system for every one retiree and with retirees living longer, the system is not sustainable over the long term. What can the government do to bring more money into the system to pay benefits to future retirees?

> Currently, every worker who pays into the system can apply for OASI benefits at their normal retirement age, even workers who continue to work and those earning money through investments, including millionaires and billionaires. What can the government do to cut the cost of benefit payments?

> The Social Security Trustees report indicates that within 30 to 75 years the OASI trust fund will be depleted. Is there a particular Social Security reform, or combination of reforms, that you believe the majority of U.S. citizens would support to fix this problem? Explain.

*http://www.newyorklife.com/cda/0,3254,5786,00.html (accessed July 28, 2009).
**http://www.ssa.gov/OACT/STATS/table4a1.html (accessed July 28, 2009).

the recipient will receive during his or her lifetime—the government cannot control or predict the annual cost of Social Security. With the increasing number of retirees and with those retirees living longer lives, the pay-as-you-go system will eventually reach the point of not covering the full costs of OASI. The surplus money in the Social Security Trust Fund is already shrinking. This situation has generated intense public debate over what the national government should do to ensure that Social Security funds are available for workers who are currently contributing to the program.

Amendments to the Social Security Act   Congress amended the Social Security Act in 1939 to provide benefits to the dependents and surviving spouse of a deceased worker. In 1956, the act was further amended to assist workers who, due to physical or mental disabilities, had to stop working after age 50 but before the OASI-designated retirement age. The new benefit program thus created, called Social Security Disability Insurance (SSDI), provides income to those covered by the Social Security program and to their families if they meet the guidelines for disability. Similarly to OASI, SSDI is a contributory (social insurance) program.

In 1972, Congress again amended the Social Security Act by establishing the Supplemental Security Income (SSI) program, a noncontributory program. Recipients of SSI include low-income elderly people whose Social Security benefits are so low they cannot provide for themselves, individuals with disabilities, and blind people. Unlike other Social Security programs, SSI is a **means-tested benefit,** meaning that the eligibility criteria to receive the benefit include a government-specified income level, which is very low.

The Social Security Act of 1935 created other income security programs, including unemployment compensation and Aid to Dependent Children. Three years after passage of the Social Security Act, the Roosevelt administration also enacted a minimum wage, and several decades later, in 1975, Congress established an additional income security program known as the Earned Income Tax Credit. We now turn to these other income security programs.

Unemployment Compensation

Together, employees, employers, the federal government, and state governments fund the unemployment compensation program created by the Social Security Act of 1935. Through this program, employees who lose their jobs through no fault of their own can collect unemployment compensation for up to twenty-six weeks. An employee fired for cause (not doing the job, doing it poorly, or violating work rules or the law) cannot receive unemployment compensation.

During economic recessions, the national government has sometimes extended the twenty-six-week benefit period if the unemployment rate remains high for a long time. For example, in February 2009, the federal government approved a new, temporary unemployment program that provides up to twenty additional weeks of unemployment benefits to certain workers. This extension was in addition to a 2008 extension that provided up to thirteen additional weeks of benefits to workers in states with unemployment rates of at least 6 percent. The federal government paid for these additional thirty-three weeks of extended benefits.[13]

Is the Minimum Wage a Living Wage?

The federal Fair Labor Standards Act (FLSA) covers more than 130 million American workers. The FLSA sets the federal minimum wage for covered employees, which is currently $7.25 per hour. As shown in the accompanying map, forty-five states also have minimum wage laws. When both state and federal minimum wage laws apply to an employee, the law guarantees the employee the higher of the two minimum wages. State minimum wage laws may, and in several cases do, cover employees that the federal minimum wage law does not cover. Four states have established a minimum wage lower than the federal minimum for some workers not covered by the federal law.

The minimum wage law applies to employees of enterprises that have an annual dollar volume of sales or business of at least $500,000. It also applies to smaller firms engaged in interstate commerce or in the production of goods for interstate commerce. Also covered are federal, state, and local government employees and most

domestic workers (such as housekeepers, full-time babysitters, and cooks).

The law allows various exceptions. For example, the law does not guarantee the federal minimum wage to full-time students, youths under age 20, employees earning tips and sales commissions, student learners, farm laborers, and seasonal and recreational workers.

Evaluating the Evidence

① An hourly employee working forty hours per week in 2009 and getting paid $7.25 per hour would earn $15,080 (before paying taxes). Is this a living wage? According to the poverty guidelines in Table 16.2 on page 607, would this individual be living in poverty? If this person were a single parent with one child, would he or she be living in poverty?

② Why might the governments of thirteen states and the District of Columbia have established a minimum wage higher than the federal minimum wage?

③ What explanations might justify excluding full-time students, youths under age 20, employees earning tips and sales commissions, student learners, farm laborers, and seasonal and recreational workers from minimum wage laws?

Minimum Wage

In addition to guaranteeing some income for workers who lose their jobs through no fault of their own, Congress in 1938 enacted the Fair Labor Standards Act, which established a minimum wage. The aim was to guarantee most employed workers a **living wage**—a wage high enough to keep them out of poverty. The federal government has amended this law several times to expand minimum wage coverage to additional job categories, yet there are still various exceptions to it. (See "Analyzing the Sources.") For workers guaranteed the minimum wage, employers

Consolidated State Minimum Wage Update Table (Effective Date: 07/24/2009)

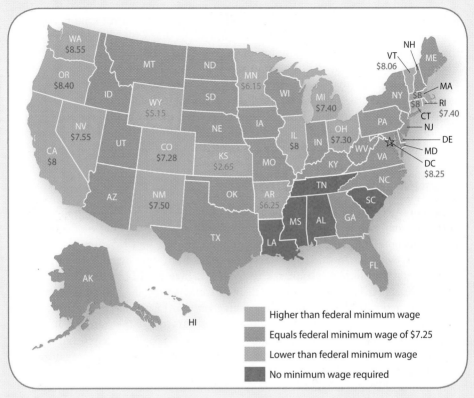

Source: U.S. Bureau of Labor Statistics.

must pay overtime (equal to one and a half times an employee's regular hourly rate) for all hours over forty worked during a workweek.

In 1938, the government set the federal minimum wage at twenty-five cents per hour. Over the decades, Congresses and presidents have had to pass new legislation in order to increase the minimum wage. Proposals to raise the minimum wage are always controversial, as revealed by the intense debate that preceded legislation in May 2007 that increased the national minimum wage from $5.15 (the wage set in 1997) to $7.25 per hour by July 2009. Senate Democrats, led by Senator Edward Kennedy (D-Massachusetts), included the provision for the minimum wage hike in a bill to continue funding for the Iraq War. In this way, they won needed votes from those who did not support the wage increase but did support the war funding. Speaker of the House Nancy Pelosi (D-California) said of the increase, "We are raising wages for the hardest-working Americans."[14]

State and local governments can establish a minimum wage higher than the federal minimum for covered workers, and they can extend a minimum wage to workers not covered by the federal minimum wage. In 2009, thirteen states and the District of Columbia had minimum wages higher than the new national minimum of $7.25 an hour.[15] But even in states that provide more generous benefits, the harsh reality is that many minimum wage workers, as well as many people earning several dollars over the national minimum wage—whom we collectively call the working poor—are still living in poverty. Hence, today's minimum wage is not a living wage. To reduce the financial hardship of minimum and low-wage workers, the national government established the Earned Income Tax Credit program.

Earned Income Tax Credit

In addition to providing cash transfers and regulating wages, the government supports income security through programs offering tax breaks. One of these is the Earned Income Tax Credit (EITC) program, established in 1975.

Citizens with low-to-moderate earned income from employment or from self-employment who file an income tax return are eligible for EITC benefits. Working parents are eligible for larger tax credits than are workers without children. The amount of the tax credit decreases (eventually reaching zero) as earned income increases. For example, in 2007, a parent with two children who earned $15,000 received an EITC of $4,716, and a parent with two children who earned $38,000 received no EITC.[16]

According to the Center on Budget and Policy Priorities, a research organization concerned with the status of poor people, the national EITC keeps more than 4 million people, the majority of whom are children, out of poverty each year and is the "nation's most effective antipoverty program for working families."[17] Yet the antipoverty program with which many Americans are most familiar began in 1935 as Aid to Dependent Children.

Temporary Assistance to Needy Families

The Social Security Act established Aid to Dependent Children (ADC), which evolved into Aid to Families with Dependent Children (AFDC) and was then replaced by Temporary Assistance to Needy Families (TANF). Initially supporting stay-at-home single widows with children, the ADC program evolved into TANF, with its emphasis on assisting needy single-parent and two-parent families with children. The focus moreover has changed from one of encouraging women to stay home with their children to one of requiring recipients to work (those in single- and dual-parent households) and requiring fathers (particularly those not living with their children) to take on greater financial responsibilities for their children.

Federal grants and state funds paid for the ADC and AFDC noncontributory cash transfer entitlement programs, and a formula in the national law determined what percentage of each state's annual program costs the federal government would cover. The federal law also gave each state discretion to determine the level of benefits and the eligibility criteria for program recipients in that state.

Beginning in the late 1950s the number of female-headed households with children living in poverty began to increase, a development referred to as the **feminization of poverty.** Although the overwhelming majority of AFDC beneficiaries were children, myths about a poor work ethic and irresponsible sexual practices on the part of their typically single mothers fueled many calls for reform.

With passage of the Family Support Act (FSA) of 1988, the federal government adopted as a goal cultivating self-sufficiency in AFDC recipients. The FSA provided funds for job training, childcare, and health benefits to help people get off AFDC, which cost more per recipient than issuing a monthly income security check. While in the longterm the FSA was expected to decrease in cost as welfare recipients became self-sufficient workers, the short-term spike in costs led to calls for further welfare reform. In response, the federal government offered states waivers from some of the AFDC grant conditions to encourage experimentation with new forms of income security for low-income families with children.

On the national level, in 1996 President Bill Clinton (1993–2001) signed the Personal Responsibility and Work Opportunity Reconciliation Act (PRWORA), which radically changed both the nature and the provision of income security for low-income families with children. PRWORA replaced the AFDC entitlement program and several other grant assistance programs for low-income families with one grant, Temporary Assistance to Needy Families (TANF). Unlike AFDC, TANF is not an entitlement program.

Although PRWORA gives state governments a great deal of flexibility in determining TANF eligibility, benefits, and programs, it comes with several very specific regulations. For example, a family can receive benefits only for two consecutive years and a lifetime maximum of five years. Moreover, program beneficiaries must work or be enrolled in an educational or a training program that prepares them for work. In addition, female TANF recipients must identify their children's fathers so that these men can be required to provide financial support for their children. Ultimately, the success of this radical approach to welfare reform depends on the availability of jobs that pay well and offer benefits; hence its success depends on the overall health of the U.S. economy.

Government Definitions of Poverty

Despite the various income security programs we have considered, tens of millions of Americans, including millions who work full-time, live in *poverty*—the condition of lacking sufficient income to purchase the necessities for an adequate living standard. Millions of others are one problem away from poverty, meaning that a health emergency, significant car repair, family relations issue, or job layoff could land them in poverty. The government defines poverty using two measures: poverty thresholds and poverty guidelines.

Since the 1960s, the U.S. Census Bureau has used the gauge of *poverty thresholds*—an annually updated set of income measures (adjusted for family size) that define who is living in poverty (see Chapter 15). The government uses these thresholds to collect data on how many families and individuals are living in poverty.

According to the Census Bureau, in 2007, 37.3 million individuals (12.5 percent of the U.S. population) were living in poverty.[18] Just under 12.3 million children below the age of 18 years (18 percent) were in poverty, and almost 3.6 million people over the age of 65 (9.4 percent) were as well. The poverty rate among blacks was 24.5 percent; Hispanics, 21.5 percent; Asians, 10.2 percent, and non-Hispanic whites, 8.2 percent.

Government agencies that offer additional safety-net programs beyond the ones we have considered so far do not use the Census Bureau's poverty thresholds to determine eligibility. Instead, many use the Department of Health and Human Services' (HHS) **poverty guidelines,** a version of the poverty thresholds simplified for administrative use. Table 16.2 presents the HHS Poverty Guidelines for 2009.

Most safety-net programs allow families with incomes of a certain percentage above the HHS poverty guidelines (say, 185 percent) to receive benefits. Administrators recognize that families with even those income levels experience difficulties in meeting their basic needs. Programs that use the HHS poverty guidelines as the basis for determining eligibility include the Food Stamp Program and the National School Lunch Program. These programs target the problem of **food insecurity,** the situation in which people have limited or uncertain ability to obtain, in socially acceptable ways, enough nutritious food to sustain a healthy and active life.

Health Care Policy

Lack of health insurance is an additional problem for low-income households. Further, it is a growing challenge for middle-income households because the number of employers providing medical insurance for their employees (at no cost or a shared cost) has decreased in recent years as the cost of medical care has skyrocketed.

According to the U.S. Census Bureau, in 2007, 45.7 million people in the United States (15.3 percent) were without health insurance.[19]Among these uninsured, 8.1 million (11.0 percent) were under 18 years of age. Approximately 70 percent of those with insurance had private insurance plans, and the rest had government-provided plans, including Medicaid and Medicare. These two programs were established in 1965 as part of President Lyndon Johnson's (1963–1969) "Great Society" plan, which included government programs to address the effects of poverty during a time of national economic prosperity. Medicare and Medicaid are part of today's safety net.

Medicaid

Title XIX, added to the Social Security Act in 1965, created Medicaid—a joint federal-state entitlement program providing health care to people meeting the means test. Because the national legislation delegates substantial discretion to state governments regarding eligibility and benefits, there are really fifty different Medicaid programs.

In this cash transfer program, state governments pay health care providers, and then the national government reimburses the states for a percentage of these bills.

TABLE 16.2

Poverty Guidelines, 2009 ($ per year)

Forty-Eight Contiguous States and the District of Columbia

Persons in Family	Poverty Guideline
1	$10,830
2	14,570
3	18,310
4	22,050
5	25,790
6	29,530
7	33,270
8	37,010

For families with more than 8 persons, add $3,740 for each additional person.

Alaska

Persons in Family	Poverty Guideline
1	$13,530
2	18,210
3	22,890
4	27,570
5	32,250
6	36,930
7	41,610
8	46,290

For families with more than 8 persons, add $4,680 for each additional person.

Hawaii

Persons in Family	Poverty Guideline
1	$12,460
2	16,760
3	21,060
4	25,360
5	29,660
6	33,960
7	38,260
8	42,560

For families with more than 8 persons, add $4,300 for each additional person.

Source: *Federal Register* 74, no. 14 (January 23, 2009): 4199–201.

The national government's share of each state's cost is based on a formula that takes into account the state's wealth. The national government pays as little as 50 percent of the Medicaid bill in the fourteen wealthiest states and as much as 77 percent in the poorest state, Mississippi.[20]

Medicaid beneficiaries fit in one of three broad categories: (1) low-income pregnant women, infants, and children up to age 6 in families with income less than 133 percent of the poverty guideline, and children up to 18 in families with income less than 100 percent of the poverty guideline; (2) low-income disabled citizens receiving SSI; and (3) low-income elderly people requiring nursing home or long-term care services or requiring assistance in meeting health care costs not covered by Medicare (a program of health insurance for the elderly; see below). States have the discretion to provide Medicaid to some additional groups, as defined by the national government. Although AFDC recipients were automatically eligible for Medicaid, today's TANF recipients are not.

The soaring cost of health care has drawn much attention to the Medicaid program. In the 1980s and 1990s, when the cost of Medicaid grew at an average annual rate of 20 percent, Congress tried to cut back its Medicaid costs by clarifying the health care fees for which the national government would reimburse state governments. At the same time, the rise in the percentage of *children* without health insurance generated bipartisan congressional support for the State Children's Health Insurance Program (SCHIP). Established in 1997, SCHIP covers medical costs for low-income uninsured children under the age of 19 who are not eligible for Medicaid. In this joint federal-state cash transfer program, eligibility is based on a family income that is generally less than 200 percent of the HHS poverty guideline. States participating in SCHIP can expand their current Medicaid program to cover these children, or they can create a new program that provides the standard coverage mandated by the national government.

Although the majority of persons benefiting from Medicaid are women and children, the bulk of Medicaid spending covers the health care costs of the elderly. The largest percentage of Medicaid spending pays for nursing home and long-term care services, which Medicare does not cover.

Medicare

In 1965, President Lyndon Johnson signed legislation enacting Medicare, a program that provides health insurance to persons over age 65 and those under 65 who have been receiving SSDI for at least two years. Today, Medicare has four components.

Part A, Medicare's Hospital Insurance Program, is a social insurance program funded by a 1.45 percent tax paid by employees and employers that helps to pay for hospital stays. (This tax and the Social Security tax make up the "FICA" deduction from your paychecks.) All who pay into Medicare are eligible for Part A benefits when they reach the age of 65. Also eligible for Part A are persons under age 65 who have been receiving SSDI for at least two years.

All persons eligible for Part A and any persons over age 65, even if they are not eligible for Part A, can opt into *Part B,* Medicare's Supplemental Medical Insurance. Part B covers a percentage of physician costs and other outpatient health care expenses, such as laboratory fees and ambulance services.

In 1997, Congress established a third Medicare component, *Part C,* Medicare + Choice. This component allows Medicare beneficiaries to choose private health plans that provide them with the same coverage found in Medicare Parts A and B.

Under pressure from the American Association of Retired Persons (AARP) and other senior citizen interest groups, Congress proposed and President George W. Bush signed the Medicare Prescription Drug, Improvement, and Modernization Act in 2003. This act established Medicare *Part D,* the core of which is a prescription drug plan that took effect in 2006. A complicated program, Part D requires Medicare beneficiaries to choose a prescription drug plan provided by a private insurer if they do not already have prescription coverage through another health plan.

The Future of Health Care

President Obama and Congress have been wrestling with health care reform legislation. Unlike the battle to reform health care during President Bill Clinton's administration, President Obama has doctors, insurance companies, and pharmaceutical manufacturers working with him to develop a plan that will guarantee health care to all who want it while at the same time containing health care costs. In this latest attempt at health care reform, there are five big questions: (1) Should the government mandate that employers provide health insurance to all their employees? (2) Should all people be required to have health insurance? (3) Should there be a government-sponsored health insurance option? (4) How will the government (think taxpayers) pay for government guaranteed health care? and (5) How can health care costs be reduced? In February 2009, at the beginning of the health reform battle, President Obama stated, "I suffer no illusions that this will be an easy process. It will be hard. But I also know that nearly a century after Teddy Roosevelt first called for reform, the cost of our health care has weighed down our economy and the conscience of our nation long enough. So let there be no doubt: health care reform cannot wait, it must not wait, and it will not wait another year."[21]

Homeland Security

The government's responsibility does not stop with ensuring basic necessities such as a clean environment, affordable energy, a secure income, and health care. Federal, state, and local governments also cooperate to prevent threats to personal safety, home, and health. Such threats may come from natural disasters such as hurricanes and earthquakes or from human-made calamities such as terrorist attacks.

President George W. Bush and Congress established the Department of Homeland Security in 2002 in response to the September 11, 2001, terrorist attacks on U.S. soil. The department's mission is to improve the coordination of efforts to prevent and respond to disasters, both human-made and natural, within the U.S. borders. Homeland security is a central theme in contemporary U.S. domestic policy and an ever-present concern in Americans' daily lives.

Four Dilemmas for Policy Makers

Four significant dilemmas present themselves in homeland security policy deliberations. The first deals with the question of how much intrusion into citizens' lives, in the name of prevention, is acceptable. The second dilemma concerns the appropriate level and distribution of national grants-in-aid to state and local governments for improved communication systems and response capabilities. A third dilemma has to do with the intergovernmental aspect of homeland security. How much discretion should devolve to state and local governments with the federal grants-in-aid? Although this is a common concern with respect to intergovernmental efforts for any policy area, the stakes can be very high, and the finger pointing and blaming especially vigorous, when disasters occur.

The fourth dilemma for policy makers is how to ensure that national, state, and local bureaucrats, as well as other first responders, are able to coordinate their efforts to prevent and respond to homeland disasters. Communication, leadership, authority, and cooperation have all proven to be problematic during disasters.

The Importance of Intergovernmental Coordination

Homeland security can succeed only as an intergovernmental effort. To prevent attacks, the government must rely on intelligence collected by both local and state law enforcement and federal agencies such as the Central Intelligence Agency (CIA), the National Security Agency (NSA), and the Federal Bureau of Investigation (FBI). Typically, the first-responders to attacks and natural disasters are police officers, fire fighters, emergency medical technicians, and other public servants hired by local governments. Federal and state agencies, when necessary, support first-responders. The Department of Homeland Security agencies that back up first-responders include the Federal Emergency Management Agency (FEMA), the Office of Domestic Preparedness, and the National Biological Warfare Defense Analysis Center.

Hurricane Katrina and its aftermath in September 2005 presented the first real test of the response capacity of the Department of Homeland Security. The department failed the test according to citizens living in the states damaged by the hurricane, and to local and state government officials, the media, and Bush administration investigators. According to the Bush administration's *Fact Sheet: The Federal Response to Hurricane Katrina: Lessons Learned,*[22] the hurricane and subsequent flooding of New Orleans "exposed significant flaws in our national preparedness for catastrophic events and our capacity to respond to them." The report highlights the crucial need for the integration of homeland security plans across national, state, and local governments, as well as across organizations in the private and nonprofit sectors.

Clearly, intergovernmental efforts are essential if we are to have secure homes, healthy lives, and opportunities to pursue happiness within the borders of the United States—the mission of domestic policy. The efforts of individual citizens are also vital.

Another facet of the Department of Homeland Security's work is the implementation of immigration policy and border security. Continuing concerns about potential acts of terrorism on U.S. soil, as well as debates over the economic effects of the increasing number of immigrants coming to the United States, have placed immigration policy reform high up on the national agenda.

Immigration Policy

The majority of immigrants to the United States are young people seeking two goals: reunification with family members residing here and work that will provide a better quality of life than they are able to achieve in their home countries. U.S. immigration policy, the collection of laws that specify which people the government will authorize to immigrate to the United States, allows approximately one million immigrants, in four categories, to immigrate legally each year. Figure 16.2 shows that these legal immigrants come from around the globe. In addition to the legal newcomers, about 500,000 unauthorized immigrants come into the United States annually. After September 11, 2001, citizens and their elected representatives, concerned about the impact of both authorized and unauthorized immigrants, began to analyze immigration policy anew. Debate on immigration policy reform has been ongoing ever since.

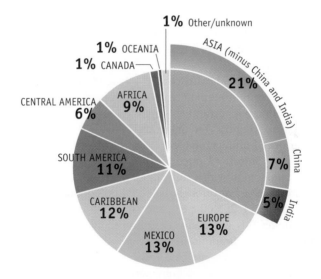

FIGURE 16.2 ■ GLOBAL SCOPE OF U.S. IMMIGRATION
What world region is the source of most legal immigrants to the United States today? With respect to the Americas, what country or larger geographical unit is the source of most legal immigrants to the United States?

Authorized and Unauthorized Immigration

Federal immigration policy determines who may immigrate to the United States as permanent residents and as temporary visitors (such as tourists, students, and guest workers). Since the Immigration and Nationality Act of 1965, the largest category of immigrants authorized to come to the United States permanently are those seeking to reunify with family members who are either U.S. citizens or authorized permanent residents. The second-largest category comprises individuals welcomed for their employment skills; this group includes highly skilled professionals and wealthy entrepreneurs expected to invest in job creation. Persons to whom the United States offers humanitarian protection from persecution (or likely persecution) because of race, religion, nationality, membership in a particular social group, or political views compose the third-largest category of authorized immigrants. The smallest category of permanent authorized immigrants gain entry through the country-quota system, which allows up to 25,000 people per country per year (selected by lottery) to enter the United States legally.[23] Figure 16.3 presents the breakdown of authorized and unauthorized immigrants for 2006.

Who is *not* eligible for permanent authorized immigration to the United States? In addition to foreigners who do not fall within one of the categories described above, foreign nationals perceived to be anarchists or political extremists have been excluded since 1901, when a Polish anarchist assassinated President William McKinley (1897–1901). More recently, in 2002, the USA PATRIOT Act established new criteria for denying entry to the United States. Today the national government can deny authorized immigration to foreigners who are perceived as a security or terrorist threat, have a criminal history, have previously been removed from the United States, or present a health risk.[24]

Why do half a million immigrants enter the United States without authorization each year? The answer to this question has several dimensions. One major dimension has to do with economic opportunities—the lure of jobs that are better than those available in the home country. Yet unless an individual fits into one of the four categories for authorized immigration, he or she has no basis on which to apply for permanent, legal entry into the United States. Another reason for the large volume of unauthorized immigration is that individuals applying for immigration under the family reunification category or through their country's quota system come up against the annual U.S. quota of 25,000 per country. There is a wide gap between the number allowed under this quota and the number of applications. The result is a backlog of millions of applications that may mean up to a twenty-year wait for authorized immigration.[25] These are just some of the obstacles that explain why approximately 500,000 unauthorized immigrants enter the United States each year.

Proposed Immigration Policy Reforms

The flood of unauthorized immigrants creates financial and other stresses and strains that have prompted calls for immigration reform. Although unauthorized immigrants are not eligible for safety-net benefits such as programs for income security and food security, all children born on U.S. soil—even those born to unauthorized

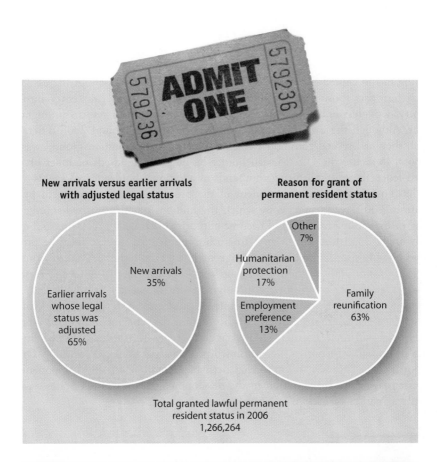

New arrivals versus earlier arrivals with adjusted legal status

- New arrivals 35%
- Earlier arrivals whose legal status was adjusted 65%

Reason for grant of permanent resident status

- Other 7%
- Humanitarian protection 17%
- Employment preference 13%
- Family reunification 63%

Total granted lawful permanent resident status in 2006
1,266,264

POLITICAL INQUIRY

FIGURE 16.3 ■ LEGAL IMMIGRATION TO THE UNITED STATES
For immigrants who were granted lawful permanent residence in 2006, what percentages, respectively, were (1) new arrivals and (2) earlier arrivals whose legal status was adjusted? What factor accounted for the most grants of permanent status?

immigrants—are citizens and hence are eligible for these benefits. Moreover, the government guarantees a public education to all children, citizens and unauthorized immigrants alike. State and local governments cover approximately 92 percent of the cost of public education, and the national government funds the remaining 8 percent. And with respect to legal rights, the Fourteenth Amendment to the Constitution guarantees all people, not just citizens, due process before the government can infringe on their life, liberty, or pursuit of happiness, as well as equal protection of the law. Typically, the costs of these constitutional guarantees fall to state and local governments. Most unauthorized immigrants *do* pay taxes and so are contributing to government revenues collected to pay these bills. Yet their tax contributions do not cover these costs, just as the taxes collected from low-income citizens and authorized immigrants do not cover the costs of their safety-net benefits.

Given the financial burden of supporting the 10 million unauthorized immigrants residing in the United States in 2005, and in light of concerns about the ease with which terrorists (posing as well-intended immigrants) might gain entry into the country, Congress and President Bush worked intensively to reform immigration policy. Although the various reforms proposed between 2005 and 2007 differed in detail, they had several common elements. One point of common ground was the proposal to secure the U.S.-Mexico border by building hundreds of miles of reinforced fence along it and hiring thousands of additional border patrol agents.

The most controversial component of the proposed reforms, put forth by the Senate in 2007, was a process by which the millions of unauthorized immigrants living in the United States could become authorized permanent residents and eventually apply for citizenship. Many Americans complained bitterly that the process would be unfair to the millions of foreign nationals who have been waiting out the application and authorization process so that they can legally enter the country. Others argued that unauthorized immigrants are inherently criminals and thus should not gain the benefit of legal permanent residence. On the other side of the debate were the countless employers who rely on the labor of immigrant workers (authorized and unauthorized), as well as some economists who stress the importance of immigrant labor to the continued prosperity of the U.S. economy. Others supporting the pathway to authorized permanent residency remind opponents of the essential role of immigration in the development of the United States—which is truly a "nation of nations"—since its founding.

CONCLUSION

CONTINUING THE CONVERSATION

- Prior to the Great Depression of the 1930s, the national government's domestic policy commitment was limited while state and local governments played the dominant role in addressing the day-to-day needs of the people.

- Today the objectives of the national government's domestic policy are twofold: the maintenance of a safety net that assists citizens in meeting their basic needs, and the protection of Americans' lives, homes, and natural environment from perils—human-made and natural.

- The increasing costs of safety-net programs from Social Security to health care have prompted questions about the sustainability of these programs.

- Environmental degradation is on the agenda of policy makers not only in the United States but throughout the world.

- Revising (some would say reestablishing) national energy policy and reforming immigration policy are frequent topics of conversation in public forums and in legislatures.
- After September 11, 2001, the increased concern for homeland security prompted President Bush and Congress to create the Department of Homeland Security.

STUDYNOW

Summary

1. Citizen Engagement and Domestic Policy

U.S. domestic policy addresses internal problems that threaten the people's well-being, domestic tranquility, civil liberties, and standard of living.

2. Tools of Domestic Policy

The national government accomplishes its domestic goals through a variety of policy tools, including laws, regulations, direct provision of public goods, cash transfers, loans, loan guarantees, insurance plans, and contracting-out.

3. Environmental Policy

Since the 1970s, the federal government has assumed the primary role in formulating environmental policy; however, through its regulatory policy, supplemented with grants-in-aid and loans, it has devolved the implementation of environmental protection to state and local governments.

4. Energy Policy

Most U.S. energy is produced by the burning of nonrenewable fossil fuels, which harms the environment, leading to calls for an energy policy that includes funding for research and the development of alternative, renewable energy sources, and imposing limits on the amount of greenhouse gases energy producers can emit.

5. Income Security Programs

Since the idea that the government should provide a "safety net" for citizens in financial need took shape during the Great Depression, the national government has been providing a range of income security programs for the elderly, persons with select disabilities, and citizens meeting government poverty guidelines.

6. Health Care Policy

Even with the protections of Medicare and Medicaid, and even with the recent expansion of these programs, millions of people, including many employed adults, do not have health insurance.

7. Homeland Security

The Department of Homeland Security's mission is to prevent terrorist attacks and to respond to domestic disasters (human-made and natural).

8. Immigration Policy

Concerns over taxpayer costs to provide for immigrants and over the ease with which terrorists might gain entrance into the United States have sparked new efforts for immigration policy reforms.

For Critical Thinking and Discussion

1. Many critics of current environmental policy argue that government regulation of pollution amounts to ineffective policy. Some claim that using cash transfer tools, including tax breaks, grants, and direct subsidies, would be more effective. Explain how the government could use at least one of the cash transfer tools to protect the environment.

2. Which cash transfer programs (including tax breaks) will the majority of Americans benefit from at some point in their lives? Explain.

3. Explain how at least two of the programs discussed in this chapter are important to a sustainable community.

4. What might explain why Social Security and Medicare are entitlements but TANF is not an entitlement? Keep in mind the nature of the programs (contributory or noncontributory) and the populations each program targets.

5. Frequently, a crisis or disaster is the catalyst for revolutionary new public policies. Discuss one or two crises or disasters that have occurred in your lifetime and that led to major changes in public policy.

Key Terms

cash transfer 589
contributory program (social insurance program) 589
direct provision 589
direct subsidy 589
entitlement program 589

environmental racism 593
feminization of poverty 605
food insecurity 606
global warming 594
greenhouse effect 594

living wage 602
means-tested benefit 601
noncontributory program 589
poverty guidelines 606
safety net 586

Internet Resources

A More Perfect Union **Web Site**

www.mhhe.com/harrisonampule Consult the book's Web Site for study guides, interactive activities, simulations, and current hot-links that provide additional information on domestic policy in the United States.

Center for Budget and Policy Priorities

www.cbpp.org The center focuses on the impact of public policies on low-income households. On the Web site, you will find links to numerous reports elaborating on the effects of public policies on such households.

Environmental Protection Agency

www.epa.gov/history/topics This section of the EPA's Web site provides historical overviews of toxic waste sites that the government has worked to clean up.

U.S. Census Bureau

www.census.gov/statab This link on the Census Bureau's Web site contains the *Statistical Abstract*, an annually published volume with summary statistics illuminating the social, political, and economic status of the United States.

USA Government Information

www.usa.gov This easy-to-use first stop for government information offers links to government agencies and their programs.

Recommended Readings

Carson, Rachel. *Silent Spring*. New York: Houghton Mifflin, 1990. A thorough and alarming description of how the pesticide DDT harmed the food chain, caused cancer and genetic damage, and threatened the world as we know it.

Ehrenreich, Barbara. *Nickel and Dimed: On (Not) Getting By in America*. New York: Henry Holt, 2001. Documentation of the author's experiences when she joined the millions of Americans working full-time, year-round, for wages higher than the minimum wage ($6 to $7 per hour) in jobs with no benefits.

Gore, Al. *Earth in the Balance: Ecology and the Human Spirit*. Boston: Houghton Mifflin, 1992. A comprehensive assessment of the major post–Cold War threat to the United States and the world: planetary destruction due to overpopulation, deforestation, soil erosion, air pollution, and water pollution. Written before his more popularly known *An Inconvenient Truth*, Gore recommends far-reaching and specific governmental and corporate actions.

Kettl, Donald. *System Under Stress: Homeland Security and American Politics*, 2nd ed. Washington, DC: CQ Press, 2007. A comprehensive presentation of the massive bureaucratic reorganization that created the Department of Homeland Security. The effectiveness of this reorganization is assessed in light of the disastrous governmental response to Hurricane Katrina.

Peters, B. Guy. *American Public Policy: Promise and Performance*. Washington, DC: CQ Press, 2004. A readable account of the policy-making process, with chapters on specific policy areas: economy, taxes, health care, income maintenance, education, energy, environmental protection, defense, law enforcement, and social regulation.

The emergence of the
United States as a
superpower and the
Cold War dominated
U.S. foreign policy in
the aftermath of
World War II.

The war on terror defines U.S.
foreign and national security
policy.

NOW

Foreign Policy and National Security

The conventional view is that foreign policy is all about wizened old statesmen negotiating treaties and about sophisticated ambassadors clinking wine glasses at chic
cocktail parties. It is true that top government officials in Washington, DC, formulate foreign
policy—the politics and programs by which the United States conducts its relations with
other countries and furthers American interests around the globe. But the broader, everyday
reality of U.S. foreign policy is that individual American citizens play an important part in
shaping and implementing the programs decided upon by foreign policy makers. Citizens also
play their part by staying informed about policy makers' decisions on war, peace, trade issues,
and policies that ensure national security in the post-9/11 world and by expressing their
personal views to their representatives in government and through the ballot box.

Of all the country's policy arenas, the foreign policy arena is the most volatile. Over
the past sixty years, the goals of U.S. foreign policy have shifted significantly, ranging
from preventing the spread of communism in the post–World War II era, to redefining the
national foreign policy agenda as the world's only superpower in the 1990s, to responding
to the terrorist attacks on U.S. soil of September 11, 2001. As the objectives and world-
views of policy makers have changed in concert with unprecedented world developments,
so too have their priorities and the instruments available to them in implementing U.S.
foreign policy.

NEXT

What long-term repercussions will the wars in Iraq and Afghanistan and
ongoing tensions with Iran and North Korea have on the future of U.S.
foreign policy and the United States' role as world leader?

How will the continuing threat of terrorism against the United States
influence foreign and national security policy in the future?

Will U.S. foreign policy in the coming years increasingly reflect a clash of
civilizations between Western democracies and fundamentalist Islamic states?

The Tools of U.S. Foreign Policy

Government officials use a variety of instruments to shape foreign policy. Among these are diplomacy, trade and economic policies, and military options.

Diplomacy

Covering a gamut of situations, diplomacy is often foreign policy makers' tool of choice. **Diplomacy** can be generally defined as the conduct of international relations, particularly involving the negotiation of treaties and other agreements between nations. It can include an occurrence as mundane as the communication between two embassies when a citizen of one country commits a crime in another. Or it can involve an event as significant as a major summit attended by world leaders. When diplomacy works, we typically do not hear about it.

Among the central figures in the diplomatic dance are **foreign service officers,** the diplomatic and consular staff at American embassies abroad. Foreign service officers, who are employees of the Department of State, conduct formal communications among nations. They are frequently responsible for negotiating many different types of international agreements, including economic and trade accords.

Trade and Economic Policies

U.S. foreign policy makers rely on trade policies, economic aid (foreign aid), and economic penalties to compel foreign governments to conform to the United States' will. Consider the example of most favored nation status. In international trade, conferring **normal trade relations (NTR) status** (formerly known as "most favored nation status") means that a country grants to a particular trading partner the same, least restrictive trade conditions (that is, the lowest tariff rates) that the country offers to its other favored trading partners—its "most favored nations." U.S. foreign policy makers can bestow NTR status on a country to influence it to enact policies the United States prefers. Conversely, they can withhold this status to punish a nation that does not institute policies supportive of the United States' goals. For example, the United States withheld most favored nation status from Vietnam for many years, in an attempt to get the Vietnamese to account for American prisoners of war and soldiers missing in action in the Vietnam War.

Governments also use trade agreements as a tool of foreign policy. Among the most important of these agreements in the United States is the North American Free Trade Agreement (NAFTA), whose members include the United States, Mexico, and Canada. NAFTA eliminated barriers to trade and financial investments across the economies of the three nations (see Chapter 15 for further discussion).

American foreign policy officials also use economic strategies to punish countries whose policies or behavior the U.S. government disapproves of. In May 2007, the United States imposed **sanctions**—penalties that halt economic exchanges (and that may include boycotts, trade embargoes, the suspension of financial flow from investments, and the cessation of cultural exchanges)—on Iran. The George W. Bush administration (2001–2009) and Congress objected to a laundry list of Iran's activities, including the pursuit of nuclear weapons, financial and intellectual support of terrorist organizations, the country's opposition to the Mideast peace process, and its role in destabilizing both Iraq and Lebanon.[1] However, as Senator Christopher Dodd (D-Connecticut), chair of the Banking, Housing, and Urban Affairs Committee, has noted, "Economic sanctions are a critical element of U.S. policy toward Iran. But sanctions alone are not sufficient. They must be used as effective leverage, undertaken as part of a coherent, coordinated, comprehensive diplomatic and political strategy which firmly seeks to deter Iran's nuclear ambitions and other actions which pose a threat to regional stability."[2]

Almost a century ago, President Woodrow Wilson made this observation:

> A nation that is boycotted is a nation that is in sight of surrender. Apply this economic, peaceful, silent, deadly remedy and there will be no need for force. It does not cost a life outside the nation boycotted, but it brings a pressure upon the nation which, in my judgment, no modern nation could resist.[3]

But others argue that sanctions actually may worsen conditions, particularly for the poorest people in a sanctioned nation.[4] And given the high levels of **globalism,** or interconnectedness, among the world's countries today, a nation on which boycotts or sanctions are imposed often has recourse—sometimes in the form of aid from allies—to withstand the pressure of the economic penalty. Thus, as Senator Dodd observed, sanctions are frequently only a part of a wider diplomatic and political strategy.

The Military Option

Since September 11, 2001, the United States has been involved in a multifront war that prominently features military actions in Iraq and Afghanistan. The September 11 terrorist strikes and subsequent U.S. government actions demonstrate how the creators of foreign policy use the military option as an instrument of foreign policy. Hungry for an enemy after the deadly attacks on American soil, the United States targeted Afghanistan's Taliban regime. The Taliban had supported and harbored members of **al-Qaeda,** the radical international Islamic fundamentalist terror organization that took credit for the 9/11 bloodshed. Foreign intelligence had pointed to Osama bin Laden, a Saudi millionaire living in Afghanistan, as the engineer of the attacks. U.S. military action in Afghanistan continues today, with President Obama prioritizing the need to stabalize Afghanistan by increasing the number of troops serving there in 2010.

Then–Secretary of State Colin Powell subsequently made a case to the United Nations and to the American people alleging that U.S. intelligence indicated that the Saddam Hussein regime in Iraq was harboring **weapons of mass destruction (WMDs)**—nuclear, chemical, and biological weapons.[5] In response to what at the time appeared to be a credible threat, on March 18, 2003, American troops invaded Iraq. The military strike toppled the Hussein regime, which the United States had supported for years through foreign aid.[6] Following the invasion, weapons inspectors conducted a thorough search of suspected weapons sites, but no WMDs were ever found, leaving many critics of the Bush administration to question the administration's motives and to ask whether the intelligence community had been pressured by administration officials to find intelligence rationalizing the war in Iraq.[7] Nonetheless, the military effort continues today.

When they use the military as an instrument of foreign policy, policy makers send a strong signal. When military conflict occurs on a grand scale—for the United States, that would include today's wars in Afghanistan and Iraq, as well as the Gulf War (1990–1991), the Vietnam War (1965–1975), the Korean War (1950–1953), and the two world wars (1914–1918 and 1939–1945)—the goal often is **regime change,** the replacement of a country's government with another government by facilitating the deposing of its leader or leading political party. That is, rather than attempting to change another nation's policies, the wars are fought to end the reign of the enemy nations' leaders. On the other hand, most military action by the United States in the past century has occurred on a smaller scale, as policy makers have sought to change the policy in another country or perhaps to protect U.S. interests or allies. For example, in 1999 during the Clinton administration (1993–2001), the United States took military action in Kosovo in the former Yugoslavia to halt ethnic cleansing in that region. Other military actions—in Somalia (1992–1994), Bosnia (beginning in 1993), and Panama (1989)—have also been on a limited scale with specific and smaller goals than those of the major conflicts.

Who Decides? The Creators and Shapers of Foreign Policy

In the United States, the executive and legislative branches are the primary foreign policy makers, with the president and the executive branch playing the dominant role. That said, a wide variety of interests—from the media to interest groups, other nations, and even private individuals—provide the context of the foreign policy process and contribute to shaping the policy outcomes of that process.

The President and the Executive Branch

The president of the United States is the foremost foreign policy actor in the world. This vast power partially derives from the constitutionally prescribed duties of the president, particularly the role of commander in chief of the U.S. armed forces. But presidents' foreign policy powers also have roots in the way the institution of the presidency has evolved and continues to evolve. Other government institutions, especially the U.S. Congress, have some ability to rein in the foreign policy authority of the president. But presidential resources such as cabinet departments and the national intelligence community, as well as the executive prestige that supplements presidents' legal and administrative powers, mean that U.S. presidents in the twenty-first century are the central figures in the foreign policy arena.

The Departments of State and Defense In the executive branch, the departments of State and Defense take the lead in advising the president about foreign and military policy issues. Specifically, the Department of State, headed by

the secretary of state, has more than 30,000 employees located both within the United States and abroad. (State Department employees work at more than 300 U.S. consular offices around the world.) These staff members are organized according to topical specialty (trade policy, environmental policy, and so on) and geographic area specialty (the Middle East or Southeast Asia, for example). Political appointees hold many of the top ambassadorial posts. These ambassadors and the career members of the foreign service who staff each **country desk**—the official operation of the U.S. government in each country with diplomatic ties to the United States—help to shape and administer U.S. foreign policy in that country.

The Department of Defense, often referred to as the Pentagon for its five-sided headquarters, is headed by the secretary of defense. The modern Department of Defense traces its history to the end of World War II, although it is the successor of the Department of War established at the nation's founding. The Defense Department is the cabinet department that oversees all branches of the U.S. military. Thus, although the Army, Navy, Marines, Air Force, and Coast Guard operate independently, administratively they are part of the Department of Defense. The commanding officers of each branch of the military, plus a chair and vice chair, make up the Joint Chiefs of Staff, important military advisers to the president. Increasingly, both the State and Defense departments rely on private contractors to perform some functions typically associated with these respective departments, particularly overseas.

The National Security Council and the Intelligence Community

As discussed in Chapter 12, the National Security Council (NSC), consisting of the vice president, the secretary of state, the secretary of the treasury, the secretary of defense, and the national security adviser, advises and assists the president on national security and foreign policy.

Through the input of the National Security Council, the president's administration considers the country's top security matters. The NSC also coordinates foreign policy approaches among the various government agencies that will implement them. A recent addition to the foreign policy apparatus, the national security adviser has traditionally competed with the secretary of state for influence over foreign policy—and for influence over the president as well. The tension between the two advisers also stems from the differing approaches each agency takes in shaping foreign policy. Frequently, the State Department has a long-term view of world affairs and advocates for foreign policies in keeping with long-term goals. In contrast, the National Security Council focuses more on short-term crises and objectives. These competing viewpoints have at times sparked media wars between the leaders of these foreign policy bureaucracies. Perhaps none of these battles was more contentious than the one between President Jimmy Carter's (1977–1981) secretary of state, Cyrus Vance, and Zbigniew Brzezinski, his national security adviser. Brzezinski publicly attacked Vance because he disagreed with Vance's push for increased diplomacy with the Soviet Union, advocating instead a tougher, more hawkish strategy.

A key resource in presidential foreign policy making is the intelligence community. Chief among the agencies in this community is the Central Intelligence Agency

(CIA). This independent agency of the federal government is responsible for collecting, analyzing, evaluating, and disseminating foreign intelligence to the president and senior national policy makers. The CIA's roots are the World War II–era Office of Special Services. Like the NSC, the modern CIA was created by the National Security Act of 1947 at the dawn of the Cold War to monitor the actions of the expansionist Soviet Union. Since that time, the CIA has expanded its mission, using agents to penetrate the governments of foreign countries, influence their politics, and foment insurrections when the president has deemed such tactics necessary to promote American interests.

The clandestine nature of the CIA's activities prompted some members of Congress to raise questions about the agency's operations abroad. In 1975, the Select Committee to Study Governmental Operations with Respect to Intelligence—called the Church Commitee after its chair, Senator Frank Church (D-Idaho)—began investigations into whether the CIA and the FBI had engaged in illegal activities while gathering intelligence. These probes led to a series of reforms aimed at increasing Congress's oversight of the CIA's activities. Primary among the reforms was creation of the Senate Select Committee on Intelligence. Today this committee and the House Intelligence Committee are the congressional watchdogs that oversee intelligence operations. Then, in the mid-1990s, following the collapse of communism, members of Congress again challenged the CIA's mission and operations.

> A key shaper of foreign policy, President Barack Obama meets with Ben Franklin and Clyde Combs (left), two veterans of World War II, on the sixty-fifth anniversary of D-Day, the Allied invasion at Normandy. French president Nicolas Sarkozy, British prime minister Gordon Brown, Canadian prime minister Stephen Harper, and Prince Charles of Britain look on. The D-Day invasion provided the foothold necessary for Allied forces to liberate France from the Nazis. The experience of fighting World War II and dealing with its aftermath forced U.S. policy makers to reassess the United States' role in the world.

These critics complained that the agency was behind the times in remaining focused on an enemy that no longer existed. Evidence that operatives working for foreign governments had infiltrated the CIA led to even louder congressional demands for reform of the agency's operations.

These calls for reform gained strength in the aftermath of the 9/11 attacks. Congress, the media, and the independent 9/11 Commission pointed fingers at both the domestic intelligence service—the Federal Bureau of Investigation (FBI)—and the CIA for failing to anticipate and to avert the terrorist strikes. Both agencies came under heavy scrutiny by Congress for lapses in intelligence and apprehension. Because the CIA and the FBI had been seriously understaffed in Arabic translators, neither agency had had the means to interpret intercepted messages that might have enabled them to prevent the tragedy.

In the agency's own investigation, the CIA inspector general also cited the CIA's failures to share intelligence with other governmental agencies and to view counterterrorism operations strategically.[8] A particular shortcoming identified by the inspector general was the agency's failure to develop its human intelligence (human spying networks) as fully as its electronic intelligence-gathering capabilities. And according to the 9/11 Commission, which in 2004 issued a report detailing the agency's failures, the CIA was also responsible for providing the information that Iraq possessed weapons of mass destruction.[9] The CIA director at the time, George Tenet, called it a "slam-dunk" case, which led President Bush to decide to invade that country and depose its president, Saddam Hussein, in March 2003. Later investigations determined, however, that no weapons of mass destruction existed and that the CIA had relied too heavily on information from Iraqi exiles eager to rid their country of Hussein. Some commentators even maintain that CIA analysts were under White House pressure to report that Iraq was developing weapons of mass destruction. But this allegation has never been proved.

Spurred by the 9/11 Commission's findings, in 2005 President Bush announced the appointment of a national intelligence czar, called the **director of national intelligence (DNI)**. This individual is responsible for coordinating and overseeing all the intelligence agencies within the executive branch.

But even since the appointment of the first DNI, other controversial policies used by the CIA have come under fire, specifically the use of **extraordinary rendition,** apprehending an individual believed to be a terrorist and transferring the person to another nation. Using this practice, the CIA transported alleged terrorists to countries where interrogation methods include methods of torture forbidden in the United States. At a press conference on March 16, 2005, President Bush was asked about U.S. involvement in "rendition," particularly the practice of taking suspects to countries where, according to the State Department, police routinely torture people held in custody. In "the post-9/11 world," President Bush responded, "the United States must make sure to protect our people and our friends from attack. That was the charge we have been given. And one way to do so is to arrest people and send them back to their country of origin with the promise that they won't be tortured. That's the promise we receive. This country does not believe in torture. We believe in protecting ourselves."[10]

Congress

Along with the president, Congress also enjoys significant constitutional authority in foreign policy making. The constitutional provisions that outline congressional authority with respect to foreign relations include, prominently, Congress's power to declare war. In modern times, however, presidential administrations have circumvented this congressional power by using U.S. troops without a formal congressional declaration of war. Such was the case in the Vietnam War, for example.

In response to this presidential tactic, Congress in 1973 passed the **War Powers Act.** This law limits presidential use of military forces to sixty days, with an automatic extension of thirty additional days if the president requests such an extension. But the nature of modern warfare has quickly made the War Powers Act less effective than in the days of traditional warfare, as most modern warfare (the Iraq War being an exception) is measured in weeks rather than months. Thus it has been possible for modern presidents to wage full-scale wars without congressional involvement. Because of this reality, some critics have argued that designating war powers to the president is a cowardly decision. Representative Ron Paul (R-Texas), a conservative Republican presidential candidate in 2008, observed that "Congress would rather give up its most important authorized power to the President and the [United Nations] than risk losing an election if the war goes badly."[11] Other critics contend that the war powers law itself violates the constitutional provision for the separation of powers by mitigating both the president's power as commander in chief and Congress's authority to declare war.

But Congress's ability to shape foreign policy does not rest merely with its authority to declare war. Congressional powers with respect to foreign relations also include the authority of the U.S. Senate to ratify treaties, as well as to confirm presidential appointees to ambassadorial posts and to cabinet positions (including those of the secretaries of defense and state). Furthermore, one of Congress's greatest powers is its control of the purse strings. This control means that although the president can order troops into action, the members of Congress must authorize spending for such an operation. This tension between Congress and the president is plainly evident in the numerous congressional votes to allocate funds for the war in Iraq, particularly after the Democratic Party won control of Congress in the midterm elections of 2006. Although the Democrats in Congress would have preferred not to allocate as much money to the war effort, their hands were tied because they did not want to relinquish their obligations to the troops already deployed in Iraq, nor did they want to alienate constituents in the military or defense communities who were benefiting from the increased expenditures.

The Military-Industrial Complex

In his farewell address, President Dwight D. Eisenhower (1953–1961), Supreme Allied Commander of Europe during World War II, warned the nation of the influence of the burgeoning military-industrial complex. Eisenhower stressed that the American people and their representatives in government must "guard against the acquisition of unwarranted influence" and noted that "only an alert and knowledgeable citizenry can compel the proper meshing of the industrial and military machinery of defense with our peaceful methods and goals so that security and liberty may prosper together."[12]

Eisenhower was describing the mutually advantageous—and potentially corrupting—collusion among the U.S. armed forces, the defense industry, and Congress. These three entities have the potential to develop "unwarranted influence" over foreign policy in general and defense spending in particular, for several reasons. First, the goals of the military and the goals of the defense industry often intersect. Consider, for example, the military's need to supply soldiers with the appropriate equipment to fight wars. Both the military complex and the defense industry benefit from doing so: the military wants to protect its troops and help ensure their success on the battleground, and the defense industry seeks to sell such goods to the military—and reap a healthy profit.

A second reason the military-industrial complex has the potential to be so highly influential is the close personal and professional relationships that flourish between the individuals in the military and their counterparts in the defense industry. These relationships are similar to the associations that develop in the case of iron triangles (see Chapter 13). Indeed, many retired military personnel often put their military expertise to work in "retirement jobs" with defense contractors or as congressional lobbyists.

For many congressional districts throughout the United States, spending by the federal government for military bases, personnel, and defense contracts represents an important infusion of money into the local economy. When this economic influence is combined with the clout members of the military, veterans, their interest groups, and their families can wield, we can see why many members of Congress support the military-industrial complex.

The Media

Because of the pervasiveness and reach of the media, foreign policy decisions provide prime fodder for news reporting. But the media go well beyond monitoring and reporting on foreign policy; they also frequently play a role in shaping the country's foreign policy and in influencing the conduct of that policy.

Since the beginning of the twentieth century, the U.S. government has used the news media in an organized way to promote its foreign policy priorities. During World War I, newspapers ran ads calling on Americans to take all kinds of actions to help the war effort, from cleaning their plates and planting "victory gardens" (to conserve food supplies for soldiers) to buying war bonds to help finance the war. By World War II, filmmakers spurred Americans to action, from enlisting in the armed services to conserving food fats and saving scrap metal for the war effort. In these various wartime initiatives, the media worked hand in hand with the government and took a generally highly patriotic and supportive stance. By the era of the Vietnam War, however, journalists, particularly television reporters stationed among U.S. troops in the faraway Asian country, painted a grimmer,

> Governments attempt to shape public opinion, especially in wartime. During the Vietnam War, however, journalists—especially television reporters—allowed Americans to see a harsher image of war. In an indelible 1972 image of that war, 9-year-old Kim Phuc, who had stripped off her burning clothes, flees an aerial napalm attack. Kim Phuc is now a Canadian citizen, and her spoken essay, "The Long Road to Forgiveness," was broadcast on National Public Radio in 2008.

more realistic canvas, focusing on the ravages of war that most Americans had never before seen.

As for the news media's influence over the conduct and substance of foreign policy, it can take a variety of forms including the following:

- **Agenda setting and public awareness.** By focusing public attention on policy makers in a certain area of the world or on a particular aspect of foreign policy, the media have an impact on setting the policy agenda. During the current conflict in Iraq, for example, the news media highlight the war's casualties on a daily basis. Newspapers report the names and sometimes print the photographs of soldiers killed in action; TV news specials scroll the names and hometowns of fallen U.S. troops and civilians. This coverage reminds policy makers and the American public alike about the human costs of war and can have an effect on subsequent policy-making decisions.
- **Investigations.** The media play a powerful role in determining that U.S. foreign policy is being implemented in a way that the policy makers intended. The news media also help to ensure that the men and women who carry out foreign policy "in the trenches" of real life cease to commit or rectify any abuses they

may be committing. Consider the media coverage surrounding U.S. soldiers' scandalous abuse of enemy prisoners at the Abu Ghraib prison in Iraq. Graphic photos published in print and online of American soldiers tormenting naked captives reached readers all over the world. These photos heightened public awareness of the culture that appeared to be prevalent at the prison and led to the court-martial of twelve soldiers.

Public Opinion

Public opinion shapes the context in which foreign policy decisions are made. In particular, public support of foreign policy is valuable if that policy requires a substantial commitment of resources—say, troops or large amounts of government aid—as in the beginning of the war in Iraq. But negative public opinion may constrain the actions of foreign policy makers. For example, President Obama in announcing a surge in the number of troops being sent to fight in Afghanistan felt compelled to provide a war-weary public with an exit strategy, saying that troops serving in Afghanistan would begin coming home in July 2011.

> The media play an important role in keeping tabs on those who carry out foreign policy on the ground and in shaping public opinion. In April 2004, the news magazine program *60 Minutes II* broadcast an investigation of prisoner abuses at the Abu Ghraib prison in Baghdad, Iraq. Among the images shown was this one from late 2003 showing Pfc. Lynndie England holding a leash attached to an Iraqi detainee. England and several other soldiers serving at the prison were convicted by the Army courts-martial. England served 521 days for inflicting sexual, physical, and psychological abuse on Iraqi prisoners of war. Though the soldiers claimed they were instructed by superiors to engage in the abuse, no commanding officers were convicted.

Hot-button foreign policy issues such as the abuse of prisoners and the fighting of costly wars generate high levels of media coverage. The public might voice strong opinions on these issues in the wake of the saturated media reporting. Yet when it comes to foreign policy matters, public opinion is rarely the strong force that it can be in setting the domestic policy agenda. In general, people tend to be less concerned, less informed, and less interested in foreign policy matters than in domestic issues. Thus the public at large is likely to accept the views and actions of the individuals who make their country's foreign policy.

Public opinion plays a comparatively small role in shaping foreign policy for a variety of reasons. First, foreign policy is made incrementally, over years and decades, and keeping up with international developments in different parts of the world is not something that many individuals or even news organizations do. Often, international issues must reach crisis proportions before media coverage becomes significant and exerts an impact on public opinion.

Many Americans also feel less connected to foreign policy decisions than they do to domestic policy issues. Individuals may feel empathetic toward Chinese citizens who endure human rights violations at the hands of their government or might express sympathy toward North Korean famine victims. Yet their compassion only goes so far because those incidents have less bearing on their own lives than, say, whether their mortgage payments will increase because of Federal Reserve policy or whether more student loans will be available to pay their tuition. Despite the disconnect between most people's everyday lives and pressing issues in foreign policy, individuals nonetheless can and do influence foreign policy decisions, as we now consider.

U.S. Foreign Policy in Historical Context: Isolationism and Intervention

As those who make and shape U.S. foreign policy continue to confront the challenges of a new century, they can look back on two broad historical traditions with respect to American foreign relations: isolationism and intervention. Historically, an initial policy of **isolationism,** a foreign policy characterized by a country's unwillingness to participate in international affairs, gave way to **interventionism,** the willingness of a country to take part and intervene in international situations, including another country's affairs.

The Constitutional Framework and Early Foreign Policy Making

In drafting the Constitution, the founders sought to remove the United States from international affairs. They reasoned that it was best for the new American republic to stay out of the deadly wars that had plagued Europe for centuries and that had

> Individuals can have an impact on the foreign policy process. Here, music director Lorin Maazel conducts the New York Philharmonic Orchestra near a North Korean flag during a rehearsal at the East Pyongyang Grand Theater in Pyongyang, North Korea, in 2008. The Philharmonic was the first major American cultural group to visit North Korea and the largest delegation from the United States ever to visit this isolated nation.

caused many Americans to flee their native lands. Because of this isolationist outlook, the founders structured the Constitution so that responsibility for conducting foreign affairs rests exclusively with the national government rather than with the states.

The Constitution and Foreign Policy Powers   The Constitution provides for shared responsibility for foreign policy making in the national government between the executive and legislative branches. The Constitution grants the president very specific powers. These include powers related to filling the role of commander in chief, to making treaties, and to appointing and receiving ambassadors. In comparison, Congress's powers in foreign policy making are broader. Moreover, the Constitution structures executive and legislative powers as complementary. Note that the Constitution provides for checks and balances: although the president is commander in chief, Congress declares war and raises and supports an army and navy. Political scientist Roger Davidson has termed the give-and-take between presidential and congressional power "an invitation to struggle," reflecting the founders' attempt to ensure that neither entity dominates the process.[13]

Early Isolationism   In keeping with the founders' emphasis on isolationism, President George Washington's Farewell Address in 1796 warned the young government against involving the United States in entangling alliances. Washington feared that membership in such international associations would draw a war-weary people and a war-weakened nation into further conflicts. He refused to accept the advice of either his secretary of state, Thomas Jefferson, who favored an alliance with France, or his treasury secretary, Alexander Hamilton, who wanted stronger ties to Great Britain. As a general who knew firsthand about the ravages of war and who also was the first American leader to connect foreign and defense policy, Washington set the tone for the United States' role in the world for the next 200 years.

Foreign Trade and the Erosion of U.S. Isolationism   During Washington's tenure as president and in successive administrations, the United States' primary activity in the international arena was trade. Rich in natural resources and blessed with an industrious labor force, the United States sought to increase its wealth by selling raw materials and supplies to all sides in the Napoleonic Wars (1792–1815), the latest in the never-ending series of European conflicts. The French empire took exception to the United States' provision of supplies to its enemies, and when France captured ships that it alleged were bound for enemy ports, the United States was forced into an undeclared naval war with that country in the 1790s.

Neutral international trade was a difficult feat to accomplish in the American republic's early years. American ships had to cross sea lanes where neutrality was not the governing principle; instead, pirates, warring nations, and the allies of warring nations controlled the seas, and nationality counted for little. When pirates off the Barbary Coast of Africa seized ships and their crews, which they held for ransom, the United States fought the Barbary Wars (1801–1805 and 1815) against the North African Barbary states (what are now Morocco, Algeria, Tunisia, and Libya).

Throughout the early nineteenth century, the seas proved a difficult place for American sailors. During that time, the British Navy began the practice of **impressment,** or forcing merchant sailors off U.S. ships—in effect, kidnapping them—on the spurious grounds that American sailors were "deserters" from the British Navy. In protest of this policy, Congress passed the Embargo Act of 1807, which forced U.S. ships to obtain approval from the American government before departing for foreign ports. But the British continued impressments, and the Embargo Act seriously curtailed the amount of U.S. goods being exported. Overall, the Embargo Act harmed the U.S. economy, as the decline in trade spurred more economic woes.

The tensions between the United States and Great Britain escalated as the practice of impressment continued. When the United States sought to increase its territory northward into Canada (then still part of the British Empire), the United States and Great Britain fought the War of 1812 over the United States' desire to annex portions of Canada and to put a halt to the practice of impressments. The war was relatively short-lived, ending with the signing of the Treaty of Ghent in 1814, when the British decided that their military resources could be better used against France in the Napoleonic Wars.

Hegemony and National Expansion: From the Monroe Doctrine to the Roosevelt Corollary

After the conclusion of the War of 1812 in 1814 and of the Napoleonic Wars in 1815, peace settled over the United States and Europe. Still, some American politicians feared that European nations—especially France, Spain, and Russia—would attempt to assert or reassert their influence in the Western Hemisphere. Thus the view arose in American foreign policy–making circles that the United States should establish hegemony over its own hemisphere. In 1823, President James Monroe declared that "the American continents by the free and independent condition which they have assumed and maintain, are henceforth not to be considered as subjects for future colonization by any European power." Known as the **Monroe Doctrine,** this declaration sounded more like bravado than policy, because the United States was still too weak militarily to chase a European power away from South America, Central America, or the Caribbean. But the United States' interest in preventing the colonization of the Americas was consistent with the interest of the British, who did not want to see European rivals dominating in the Americas. Thus Monroe's doctrine had the backing of the formidable British fleet.

With the Americas out of play, European countries were expanding their colonial empires in Africa and the Middle East during the first half of the nineteenth century. Meanwhile, the United States also extended its territories westward and solidified its borders. Supporters of the theory of **manifest destiny**—the idea that it was the United States' destiny to expand throughout the North American continent—used this concept to rationalize the spread of U.S. territory. As the philosophy of manifest destiny took hold in the popular imagination, the United States expanded west to the Pacific Ocean, as well as south and southwest.

During this era, too, the United States became increasingly active in profitable international trade, particularly with China and Japan. To facilitate this Pacific trade—which was a primary goal of American policy makers—the United States acquired the islands of Hawaii, Wake, and Midway and part of Samoa in the 1890s. In 1898, on the pretext of ending Spanish abuses in Cuba and instigated by a *jingoistic* (extremely nationalistic and aggressive) President William McKinley and press, the United States decided to fight Spain, which by then was the weakest of the colonial powers. The United States won the Spanish-American War handily, and the victory increased the country's international prestige.

Theodore Roosevelt, who later became president, achieved enormous national popularity during the Spanish-American War for his leadership of the Rough Riders, a cavalry regiment. Their charge up San Juan Hill in Cuba in 1898 was the war's bloodiest and most famous battle. As spoils, the United States obtained the Philippines, Guam, Puerto Rico, and—temporarily—Cuba from Spain. Roosevelt supported the United States' entry into the war and later, as president (1901–1909), added his own famous dictum to the Monroe Doctrine: the **Roosevelt Corollary.** He announced that to ensure stability in the region, the United States had the right to act as an "international police power" and intervene in Latin America—and indeed, the entire Western Hemisphere—if the situation in any country warranted the intervention of a "civilized society."

After Roosevelt became president, the United States intervened in Panama, where U.S.-backed revolutionaries there won independence from Colombia in 1903. The United States then immediately began construction on the Panama Canal in 1904. The canal improved the flow of trade by greatly reducing the length of time ships took to travel between the Atlantic and Pacific oceans. It also accomplished one of Roosevelt's more cherished dreams: to show off U.S. naval power. At one point, Roosevelt decided to send the navy around the world strictly for public relations reasons, as a "show of force." Congress protested the cost of this endeavor, however. In order to outsmart Congress, Roosevelt, who had enough funds in the treasury for half the trip, sent the troops as far as Tokyo Bay. To "bring the boys home," Congress had to ante up the rest of the money.

World War I and the End of U.S. Isolationism

Encouraged by its successful efforts at colonization and strong enough by this time to ignore George Washington's admonition about avoiding foreign entanglements, the nation became embroiled in two major European wars in the twentieth century: World War I and World War II. The United States' isolation from the world ended with these two wars, even though strong isolationist forces in Congress and the White House continued to play a role during the first half of the twentieth century.

World War I came about primarily because of the balance of power system that dominated the world's foreign policy decisions from the end of the Napoleonic Wars in 1815 until the conclusion of World War I in 1918. The **balance of power system** was a system of international alliances that, in theory, would balance the power of one group of nations against the power of another group and thus discourage war. For nearly a century, this attempt to bring order to international relations worked, and Europe enjoyed a long period of peace. But a flaw of the balance of power system was that a relatively small skirmish could escalate into a major international incident because of agreements for **collective defense**—the idea that allied nations agree to defend each other in the face of invasion—that were inherent in the system. Such was the case in 1914 in Sarajevo when a young Bosnian Serb student assassinated Archduke Ferdinand, heir to the Austro-Hungarian throne. The assassin was a member of a group seeking Bosnia's independence from the Austro-Hungarian empire. The empire demanded that Serbia respond to the assassination, and when it determined that Serbia had not so responded, it declared war. Austria-Hungary's declaration of war led to a sweeping domino effect that had the European continent in full-scale war within weeks of that initial declaration because of those alliances and collective defense obligations between nations.

The United States entered World War I in 1917, three years after the conflict began and largely at the behest of Britain. U.S. participation led President Woodrow Wilson to formulate the first conceptual framework for world governance that had ever been articulated. The most effective way to maintain peace, Wilson believed, was through **collective security**—the idea that peace could be achieved if nations agreed to collectively oppose any nation that attacked another country. By using this approach, nations at peace could prevent war by working together to restrain the lawlessness inherent in more unstable parts of the world.

Internationalism and the League of Nations

In negotiating the end of World War I at the Paris Peace Conference, Wilson sought to organize a **League of Nations,** a representative body that would ensure the collective security of nations. Wilson was successful in convincing representatives at the Paris meetings of the need for such an organization. But he was less successful in convincing Congress of the merits of the League of Nations. In 1918, the Republican-controlled Senate—Wilson was a Democrat—refused to ratify the Treaty of Versailles, which included among the terms for ending World War I the formation of the League of Nations. Without the United States, the League died a natural death before being replaced near the end of World War II by the United Nations.

In the dawning days of World War I, the United States was still heeding George Washington's call to avoid entangling alliances. At the war's conclusion, isolationism remained a key tenet of U.S. foreign policy. In the years immediately following the war, trade reasserted itself as the key component of U.S. foreign policy. The Industrial Revolution was in full swing, and the United States depended upon the import of raw materials and the export of manufactured goods to grease the wheels of its prosperous economy in the 1920s. During this time, however, Europe was healing from the ravages of World War I, and growth in its manufacturing sector meant serious competition for American industry.

The U.S. economy suffered another blow in 1929 when the stock market crashed, marking the beginning of the Great Depression. To protect American industry from international competition, in 1930, Congress passed the Smoot-Hawley Tariff, which imposed a significant tax on imported goods. Confronted with this measure, other nations responded in kind, placing tariffs on American goods imported into their countries. The result? International trade dropped dramatically, and the economies of various nations, burdened by lower demand for the goods they produced, faltered. Industrialists, as well as citizens who saw the economic impact of an isolated United States, began to question the isolationism that had characterized U.S. foreign policy to date—from the era of Washington to the era of Smoot-Hawley.

World War II: U.S. Foreign Policy at a Crossroads

World War I was supposed to be the "war to end all wars." In hindsight, however, many observers believed that the victors only sowed the seeds of World War II (1939–1945). By impoverishing the defeated Germany through the imposition of huge *reparations* (compensation paid by a defeated nation to the victors for war damages) and the loss of 13 percent of its territory, the Treaty of Versailles (1919) created the environment that gave Adolf Hitler, the fascist leader of Germany, the opportunity to succeed politically. With his aggressive foreign policy, Hitler aimed to expand the German homeland at the expense of non-Germanic populations.

Influenced by a strong isolationist group in Congress, the United States waited until two years after the official start of the war in 1939 to declare war. Following a deadly Japanese attack on the U.S. naval base at Pearl Harbor, Hawaii, in December 1941, the United States declared war first on Japan and then on the other Axis powers (Germany and Italy) after those countries declared war on the United States.

Following years of fighting on multiple fronts, in August 1945 the United States dropped two atomic bombs on the Japanese cities of Hiroshima and Nagasaki. These devastating attacks ended the war.

The question remains whether the United States would have joined the efforts of the Allies (the United States, England, France, China, and the Soviet Union) sooner had policy makers known about the **Holocaust**—the murder by Hitler and his subordinates of 6 million Jews, along with political dissidents, Catholics, homosexuals, the disabled, and gypsies. Newspapers did not report the genocide until 1943, well after the war was under way. The experience of fighting World War II and dealing with its aftermath forced U.S. policy makers to reassess the country's role in the world, as well as the policies that governed its entire approach to foreign affairs.

The Postwar Era: The United States as Superpower

The post–World War II era saw the emergence of two of the Allied victors, the United States and the Soviet Union, as **superpowers**—leader nations with dominating influence in international affairs. The United States' role as superpower in a new international system, and the relationship between these superpowers, would shape America's foreign policy for the remainder of the twentieth century. Increasingly important in this new era was the role that **multilateral** (many-sided, or supported by numerous nations) organizations and agreements would play.

International Agreements and Organizations

In the aftermath of World War II, the United States was intent on avoiding the mistakes of the Treaty of Versailles, which many policy makers felt had led directly to the conditions that produced the war. They proceeded to address these mistakes one by one, often forming international organizations equipped to respond to the public policy challenges confronting the postwar world.

A key component of the postwar recovery effort was the **Marshall Plan.** Named for Secretary of State George Marshall, the program provided the funds necessary for Western European countries—even the United States' enemies from World War II—to rebuild. War-ravaged nations, including defeated (West) Germany, soon became economic powerhouses, thanks to initial help from the Marshall Plan. Ironically, by forcing the Germans to demilitarize as a condition of their surrender, the Allies freed Germany from spending large amounts of its own tax money on defense, thus enabling the German people to devote more of their resources to economic development. Other countries impoverished by war also benefited from the Marshall Plan (see Figure 17.1), creating new markets for U.S. products. Eastern European nations, now securely under Soviet influence, were prevented from participating. Because of the plan's success in Western Europe, the United States recognized that economic development and peace were intertwined, that economic

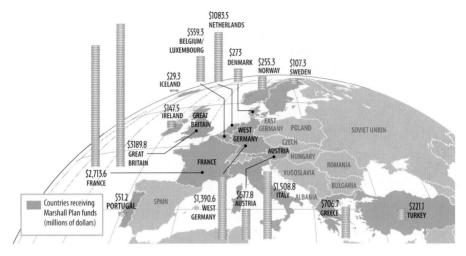

FIGURE 17.1

Recipients of Marshall Plan Aid, 1948–1951

Source: www.cnn.com/SPECIALS/cold.war/episodes/03/maps/.

stability was critical if future wars were to be prevented, and that an international approach was preferable to isolationism in foreign policy.

The United Nations   The Allied victors of World War II recognized the need for a structure to ensure collective security. In that spirit, U.S. officials organized a meeting in San Francisco in 1945 with fifty U.S. allies, all of whom agreed to create the **United Nations (UN).** Participants hoped that this international body, through collective security, would develop the capacity to prevent future wars. The charter of the United Nations created these components:

- A Security Council with eleven members, five of which—including the United States, the Soviet Union (now Russia), China, Great Britain, and France—are permanent members with the power to veto any action taken by the council. Today the Security Council consists of fifteen members, with the permanent members and their veto power remaining unchanged.
- A General Assembly consisting of all the member nations, each with a single vote (in 1945, there were 51 member nations; today there are 192).
- A Secretariat headed by a secretary-general with a staff at UN headquarters in New York. The secretary-general in 2010 is Ban Ki-moon of South Korea.
- Several specialized organizations to handle specific public policy challenges, including the Economic and Social Council, the Trusteeship Council, and the International Court at The Hague.

The United Nations' mission includes the promotion of economic and social development. Since its founding, it has added peacekeeping to its functions and has had some limited success in this endeavor in areas of the former Yugoslavia, the Middle East, and Africa. But in the immediate post–World War II era, the ability of the United Nations in general, and of the Security Council in particular, to provide for collective security was seriously undermined by the presence of the Soviet Union on the Security Council. Because the Soviet Union was a permanent member with veto power, any attempt by the Security Council to thwart Soviet aggression was blocked by the Soviets' veto.

NATO It did not take long for the United States and the Western democracies to be disappointed by the inability of the United Nations to provide for collective security. The UN's failure to halt the militaristic expansion of the Soviet sphere of influence particularly troubled them. Their frustrations led the United States and its Western allies to attempt to bring order to international relations through the creation of **regional security alliances,** which typically involve a superpower and nations that are ideologically similar in a particular area of the world.

The first regional security alliance was the **North Atlantic Treaty Organization (NATO).** Established in 1949, NATO created a structure for regional security for its fifteen member nations through a declaration that "an armed attack against one or more NATO nations . . . shall be considered an attack against them all."[14] Through the formation of NATO, the United States made a specific commitment to defend Western Europe in the event of a Soviet attack. In response to the creation of NATO, the Soviet Union and its seven satellite states in Eastern Europe formed a similar regional security alliance, the **Warsaw Pact,** in 1955.

The success of NATO at holding Soviet expansion into Western Europe at bay motivated the creation of the **Southeast Asia Treaty Organization (SEATO),** whose goal was to prevent communist encroachment in Southeast Asia. SEATO was a decidedly weaker organization than NATO; decisions had to be reached unanimously and rarely were. For example, SEATO was unable to agree to intervene in Cambodia, Laos, or Vietnam because member nations, including France, Pakistan, and the Philippines, objected to intervention.

Both NATO and the Warsaw Pact reflected the tensions and rivalry that existed between the United States and the Soviet Union. They also reflected the failure of the United Nations to provide for collective security, that is, the security of *all* nations. Instead, the regional security alliances more closely resembled the balance of power alliances established after the Napoleonic Wars.

International Financial Organizations In addition to establishing the United Nations and NATO for the purposes of conflict management and security, the United States recognized the need to relinquish a great deal of its own economic power in exchange for the economic stability that would come from international financial institutions. Doing so would benefit the global economy in general but also the U.S. economy in particular.

To this end, in 1944, an international agreement made in Bretton Woods, New Hampshire—the Bretton Woods Agreement—established the International Monetary Fund. The delegates to the meeting charged the **International Monetary Fund (IMF)** with regulating the monetary relationship among nations, including the establishment of exchange rates for major currencies around the world. To the present day, IMF member states provide the resources the IMF needs to operate through a formula by which nations pay amounts roughly proportional to the size of their economies. Based on these IMF contribution quotas, nations are then allocated votes proportional to their contributions. Thus the IMF perpetuates the dominance of the high-contributing economic powerhouses. Today the United States has nearly 20 percent of the IMF votes. The Bretton Woods agreement also established the institution that would become the **World Bank,** which initially focused on lending money to countries devastated in World War II. Today the World Bank lends money to developing nations in order to help them become self-sufficient.

Still reeling from the effects of high tariffs on international trade during the Depression, the United States also encouraged an international agreement that would heal the economies of nations by lowering tariffs and promoting international trade. In 1948, twenty-three nations signed the General Agreement on Tariffs and Trade (GATT). The GATT is based on the most favored nation principle.

In 1995, the **World Trade Organization (WTO)** replaced the GATT. Whereas the GATT was a series of agreements among nations, the WTO is an actual organization that negotiates, implements, and enforces international trade agreements. Today the WTO consists of 151 member nations (see Figure 17.2). Although it has a one-nation, one-vote policy, this policy is moot because the largest economies have the greatest say. The organization's goal—to remove all types of trade barriers, including obstacles to investment—is more ambitious than that of the GATT.

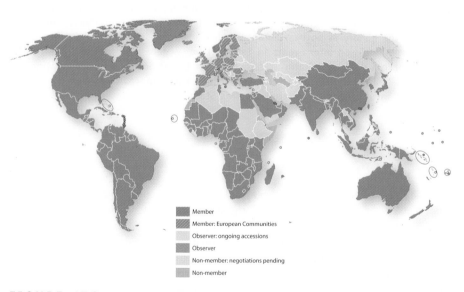

Member
Member: European Communities
Observer: ongoing accessions
Observer
Non-member: negotiations pending
Non-member

FIGURE 17.2

Membership in the World Trade Organization, 2008

The Big Three: British Prime Minister Winston Churchill, U.S. President Franklin Roosevelt, and Soviet Premier Joseph Stalin at the 1945 Yalta conference, which was crucial to the history of postwar Europe. Each leader came to the Yalta Conference with an agenda. Given later events in Eastern Europe, were Roosevelt and Churchill right to make a deal with Stalin at Yalta in order to get Soviet help in defeating Japan? What other choice could they have made? What choices do leaders of democracies have in dealing with dictators such as Stalin?

The Cold War: Superpowers in Collision

During World War II, the United States, Great Britain, and the Soviet Union were allies against the Nazis. But events at the wartime Yalta Conference in 1945—the second of three wartime conferences among British, U.S., and Soviet leaders—sowed the seeds of what would become known as the Cold War. The **Cold War** refers to the political, ideological, and military conflict that lasted from 1945 until 1990 between communist nations, led by the Soviet Union, and Western democracies, led by the United States. Each leader came to the Yalta Conference with an agenda. The United States' Franklin Roosevelt needed Soviet help in battling Japan in the naval wars of the Pacific. England's Winston Churchill sought democratic elections in Eastern Europe. And Soviet Premier Joseph Stalin wanted Eastern Europe as a Soviet sphere of influence, arguing that the Soviet Union's national security depended on its hegemony in the region.

At the conference, Stalin agreed to allow free elections in the region, but he later broke that promise. In response, former British prime minister Churchill warned Americans in a 1946 speech that the Soviets were dividing Europe with an "Iron Curtain." Churchill's characterization was accurate, because Stalin's brutal dictatorship, combined with the force of the Soviet Red Army, would install a communist government in every Eastern European nation. When Stalin also refused to cooperate in the planned allied occupation of Germany, the result was the division of Germany into separate zones, one administered by the Soviet Union and the other three by the United States, Great Britain, and France. In 1948, when the Soviets backed communist guerillas who were attempting to take over Greece and Turkey, U.S. president Harry Truman (1945–1953) committed the United States to "support free people who are resisting attempted subjugation by armed minorities or by outside pressures."[15] This policy—the United States' foreign policy commitment to assist efforts to resist communism—was called the **Truman Doctrine.**

U.S. Efforts to Contain Communism: Korea, Cuba, and Vietnam

The Truman Doctrine reflected the ideas of George F. Kennan, the State Department's Soviet expert at the time. Specifically, Kennan advocated the principle of **containment,** the policy of preventing the spread of communism, mainly by providing military and economic aid, as well as political advice, to beleaguered countries that were vulnerable to communist takeover. Kennan argued, "It is clear that the main element of any United States policy toward the Soviet Union must be that of a long-term vigilant containment of Russian expansive tendencies."[16] The idea of containment would spur the United States to fight in two protracted wars, the Korean War and the Vietnam War, in order to contain communism.

The Korean War, 1950–1953 The first military effort the United States engaged in to check the spread of communism occurred in 1950. In June of that year, North Korea, with the backing of Stalin and the Soviet Union, invaded South Korea in an attempt to reunify the Korean peninsula under communism. During that summer, the United States sent in troops as part of a United Nations force to help the South Koreans repel the attack. The defensive strategy quickly succeeded, but by October, the United States changed military strategy. Instead of merely containing the spread of communism, the United States sought to reunify North and South Korea—and, in doing so, to depose the communists from North Korea. But as U.S. and South Korean forces edged north, they also came closer and closer to the North Korea–China border.

That October, China, wary of a potential invasion, came to the aid of fellow communists in North Korea. The two countries' combined forces repelled the United Nations forces back to the 38th parallel, the original border between North and South Korea. Over the next two years, U.S. forces (as part of the UN contingent), North and South Koreans, and Chinese soldiers would continue to do battle, with very little territory changing hands. When an armistice was reached in July 1953, the border established was the 38th parallel—exactly what it had been before the war—although a demilitarized zone (DMZ) was created. Today U.S. and South Korean troops still patrol one side of the DMZ, while North Korean troops patrol the other.

The Korean War marked an escalation and expansion of the Cold War. Not only was the war the first occasion in which the two superpowers clashed militarily, but it also brought the Cold War outside the boundaries of Europe. Significantly, the outbreak of the Korean War also gave rise to the concept of **limited war**—a combatant country's self-imposed limitation on the tactics and strategy it uses, particularly its avoidance of the deployment of nuclear weapons. The idea of limited war would set the stage for subsequent conflicts.

The Cuban Missile Crisis, 1962   Another element of U.S. foreign policy during the Cold War involved the practice of brinkmanship, a phrase coined by John Foster Dulles, the secretary of state under President Dwight D. Eisenhower (1953–1961). In essence, **brinkmanship** meant fooling the enemy by going to the edge (the brink), even if the party using the brinkmanship strategy had no intention of following through to the incident's logical conclusion.

The Cuban Missile Crisis in October 1962 looks like an example of brinkmanship, even though that was not the intention of President John F. Kennedy (1961–1963). Reacting to Soviet premier Nikita Khrushchev's decision to put ballistic missiles in Cuba, Kennedy imposed a naval blockade around that island nation and warned the Soviet Union to withdraw its missiles, or else—never specifying what he meant by "or else." Although this confrontation seemed like brinkmanship, it was no bluff; rather, it was an act of bravado that could easily have led to nuclear war. Luckily for the United States and the rest of the world, the Soviets backed down, withdrew their missiles, and entered a period of improved relations with the United States.[17]

The Vietnam Conflict, 1965–1975   The United States' involvement in the war in Vietnam was motivated in large part by policy makers' acceptance of the **domino theory,** the principle that if one nation fell to communism, other nations in its geographic vicinity would also succumb. As described by President Dwight Eisenhower, "You have broader considerations that might follow what you would call the 'falling domino' principle. You have a row of dominoes set up, you knock over the first one, and what will happen to the last one is the certainty that it will go over very quickly. So you could have a beginning of a disintegration that would have the most profound influences."[18]

And so the United States again sought to contain the spread of communism in Southeast Asia. Although Vietnam was not of particular strategic importance to the United States, it represented the second "domino" in the faraway region. U.S. involvement in Vietnam started in the late 1950s, and by 1963, the United States became enmeshed in an all-out ground, naval, and air war there. The United States supported the South Vietnamese against the North Vietnamese in the decade-long civil war that would take the lives of almost 60,000 U.S. soldiers and at least 3 million Vietnamese soldiers and civilians. On April 29, 1975, when the South Vietnamese capital, Saigon, fell to the North Vietnamese Vietcong forces, the event marked the first military failure by the United States in its efforts to contain communism.

Détente: A Thaw in the Cold War Chill

Richard M. Nixon (1969–1974) was elected to the presidency in 1968 largely on his promise to conclude the war in Vietnam. Although several years would pass before the war ended, Nixon's approach to the top foreign policy issues of the day marked a departure from that of his predecessors. Specifically, the **Nixon Doctrine** emphasized the responsibility of U.S. allies to provide for their own national defense and security and sought to improve relations with the two communist world powers, the Soviet Union and China. As early as 1970, his administration sought **détente,** or the easing of tensions between the United States and its communist rivals. In keeping with this idea, the Nixon administration normalized diplomatic relations with China and began a series of nuclear arms control talks that would occur throughout the 1970s. Critics of the Nixon Doctrine argued that President Nixon's approach to foreign policy was accommodationist—that it sought the easy solution and ignored the moral and philosophical implications of improving relations between the Western democracies and their communist rivals.

Part of the motivation for détente was the recognition that any escalation of tensions between the superpowers would increase the probability of nuclear war. Since the early 1960s, the United States and the Soviet Union had engaged in a nuclear arms race in which each country attempted to surpass the other's nuclear capability. According to the doctrine of **mutual assured destruction (MAD),** if one nation attacked another with nuclear weapons, the other would be capable of retaliating, and *would* retaliate, with such force as to assure mutual annihilation. The advent of intercontinental ballistic missiles (ICBMs) meant that both the United States and the Soviet Union were capable of sending nuclear warheads through space to targets in their rivals' homelands. The goal of the arms race (which would continue through the 1980s) was first-strike capability, meaning that each nation sought the ability to use nuclear weapons against another nation and eliminate the possibility of that nation's retaliating in a second-strike attack.

Many foreign policy makers in both the United States and the Soviet Union believed in the power of **deterrence,** the idea that nations would be less likely to engage in nuclear war if the adversaries each had first-strike capability. But Nixon and his primary foreign policy adviser, Henry Kissinger (who served first as Nixon's national security adviser and then as his secretary of state), sought negotiations with the Soviets that would dampen the arms race.

Salt I and Salt II   In 1972, the United States and the Soviet Union concluded two and a half years of **strategic arms limitation talks (SALT talks)** that focused on cooling the superheated nuclear arms race between the two superpowers. The resulting treaty, **SALT I,** limited the two countries' antiballistic missiles (ABMs) and froze the number of offensive missiles that each nation could have at the number they already possessed, plus the number they had under construction.

The SALT II strategic arms limitation talks, begun during the Nixon administration and continuing through the Jimmy Carter presidency (1977–1981), resulted in the signing of the SALT II treaty in 1979. **SALT II** set an overall limit on all strategic nuclear launchers, including ICBMs, submarine-launched ballistic missiles (SLBMs), and cruise missiles. SALT II also limited the number of missiles that could carry multiple independently targeted reentry vehicles (MIRVs) with nuclear warheads and limited each nation to the development of only one new type of ICBM.

Later in 1979, however, the Soviet Union invaded Afghanistan, sparking a new round of U.S-Soviet tensions. In response, President Carter withdrew the SALT II treaty from consideration for ratification by the Senate. Nevertheless, Carter announced (as did his successor, Ronald Reagan) that the United States would abide by all of the terms of SALT II as long as the Soviet Union complied as well. During his one term in office, Carter also sought to engage the world in a campaign for human rights, while at the same time attempting to convert the vast U.S. military apparatus to peacetime functions—a policy known as **defense conversion.**

The Reagan Years and Soviet Collapse

Ronald Reagan's presidency (1981–1989) marked a pivotal time in U.S.-Soviet relations. On the one hand, the Reagan administration pushed for a *reduction* in missiles and nuclear warheads, not merely a limitation on increases. Because of this new direction, Reagan named these arms reduction talks the **strategic arms reduction talks (START talks).** Despite this overture, the Reagan administration was passionate in the pursuit of a ballistic missile defense system, called the **strategic defense initiative (SDI, or "Star Wars").** In protest of the development of this system, the Soviet Union walked out of the START meeting in 1983. The two superpowers would return to the table in 1985, after Reagan won reelection with a resounding victory.

In 1987, the United States and the Soviet Union signed the Intermediate-Range Nuclear Forces Treaty (INF), the first agreement that resulted in the destruction of nuclear weapons. It eliminated an entire class of weapons—those with an intermediate range of between 300 and 3,800 miles. A pathbreaking treaty, the INF shaped future arms control talks. It provided for reductions in the number of nuclear weapons, established the principle of equality because both nations ended up with the same number of weapons (in this case, zero), and, through the establishment of on-site inspections, provided a means of verifying compliance.

In retrospect, many analysts credit the Soviet Union's eventual collapse to President Reagan. During his tenure, Reagan ratcheted up the rhetoric with his many speeches referring to the Soviet Union as "the Evil Empire." Under his administration the U.S. defense budget also doubled, with much of the expenditure going toward the SDI. The Soviets reacted with fear and a surge in spending. These developments all came at a time when the Soviet Union was dealing with dissatisfied nationalities within its borders, as the fifteen republics that eventually would break away pressed for secession. The last straw, however, was the country's troubled economy because in order to compete with the United States, the Soviet Union had increased its military budget to the point where its economy collapsed—and with it, the government.

Post-Soviet Times: The United States as Solo Superpower in an Era of Wars

The START talks, which had resumed in 1985, resulted in a long-awaited agreement that reduced the number of long-range strategic nuclear weapons to 3,000 for each side. In 1991, the agreement was signed by U.S. president George H. W. Bush and Soviet president Mikhail Gorbachev, whose tenure had ushered in the ideas of *glasnost* (openness) and *perestroika* (economic restructuring) in the Soviet Union. That same year, after an attempted coup failed, the Soviet Union ended and Russia had its first democratically elected president, Boris Yeltsin.

Upon Yeltsin's election, in another series of talks called START II, Yeltsin agreed to even deeper cuts in nuclear weapons. Importantly, he also assented to the eventual elimination of all land-based missiles with multiple warheads (MIRVs). The START II agreement of 1992 between the superpowers was fully implemented in 2003 and significantly decreased the likelihood of a massive nuclear attack.

The 1990s proved to be a novel time in U.S. foreign relations. For the first time in over half a century, the United States was without an enemy, and it found itself the world's lone superpower. The tumult following the collapse of communism ushered in an era of wars—many of them fueled by long-standing ethnic rivalries or disputes—and the creation of new borders and new nations. And other events—such as fighting that erupted between UN and U.S. forces against Somali militia fighters loyal to warlord Mohamed Farrah Aidid in 1993; the 1998 attacks on U.S. embassies in Nairobi, Kenya, and Dar es Salaam, Tanzania; and the 2000 suicide bombing of the U.S. Navy guided missile destroyer USS *Cole* in the port of Aden, Yemen—were harbingers of clashes to come. It was as if a giant hand had lifted a rock at the end of the Cold War, freeing long-submerged problems to crawl out again and presenting new challenges for U.S. foreign policy makers as the United States assumed its role as the world's leader.

Defining U.S. Foreign Policy

THEN (1984)	NOW (2010)
The Cold War was the defining feature of U.S. foreign policy.	The war on terror is the defining feature of U.S. foreign policy.
The United States and the Soviet Union competed as the two world superpowers.	The United States is the world's only superpower.
The arms race resulted in unprecedented military spending.	A multifront war and national security needs result in unprecedented military and national defense spending.

WHAT'S NEXT?

> What new realities will shape U.S. foreign and national defense policy?

> Will the United States continue as the world's only superpower? How will a superpower be defined in the future? Will the term refer to military or economic might or a combination of these and/or other factors?

> What impact will continued military spending have on the U.S. and global economies?

U.S. Foreign Policy After 9/11

American foreign policy makers' challenges in the 1990s pale in comparison to those they have faced since the terrorist attacks of September 11, 2001. The incidents on that day have profoundly defined and determined recent American foreign policy.

One prism for viewing the 9/11 attacks is that posited by political scientist Samuel P. Huntington. He asserts that "the clash of civilizations will be the battle lines of the future."[19] Huntington's **clash of civilizations thesis** asserts that bitter cultural conflict will continue and escalate between modern Western democracies and fundamentalist Islamic states. Huntington, whose thesis remains controversial, argues that the ideological divisions that characterized the twentieth century—the clash between communism and democratic capitalism, for example—will be replaced by an older source of conflict: cultural and religious identity. Huntington initially posited his ideas in 1993, and his theories seemed particularly relevant during the 1990s when ethnic and religious warfare broke out in Bosnia and in parts of Africa. After 9/11, Huntington's neoconservative theory appeared to have significantly shaped the foreign policy of the George W. Bush administration.

Huntington's clash of civilizations thesis provides one explanation of *why* contemporary U.S. foreign policy has focused on the areas that it has. President George W. Bush himself articulated his views on the *how* of that policy's implementation. According to the **Bush Doctrine,** unilateral action (action by the United States alone) directly targeted at enemies is both justifiable and feasible. The Bush Doctrine also asserted that the United States should use its role as the world's only remaining superpower to spread democracy and to create conditions of security that will benefit itself and its allies.

A New Tenor in U.S. Foreign Policy

With the election of President Barack Obama (2009-present), the Bush Doctrine is less important in shaping U.S. foreign policy today. While ramping up the United States' involvement in Afghanistan, the Obama administration continues to scale back involvement in Iraq and has pledged to withdraw military forces from that country by 2011. In what was billed as an "address to the Muslim world," given in Egypt in 2009, Obama referred to the differences between his worldview and those of his predecessors:

> Violent extremists have exploited these tensions in a small but potent minority of Muslims. The attacks of September 11th, 2001, and the continued efforts of these extremists to engage in violence against civilians has led some in my country to view Islam as inevitably hostile not only to America and Western countries, but also to human rights. This has bred more fear and mistrust.
>
> So long as our relationship is defined by our differences, we will empower those who sow hatred rather than peace, and who promote conflict rather than the cooperation that can help all of our people achieve justice and prosperity. This cycle of suspicion and discord must end.
>
> I have come here to seek a new beginning between the United States and Muslims around the world; one based upon mutual interest and mutual respect; and one based upon the truth that America and Islam are not exclusive, and need not be in competition. Instead, they overlap, and share common principles—principles of justice and progress; tolerance and the dignity of all human beings.[20]

From his rhetoric, it appears that President Obama has rejected the notion of Huntington's "clash of civilizations," instead seeking to build bridges between the United States and the Muslim nations. In doing so, however, he faces not just the skepticism of many of his constituents but also that of many Muslim leaders and their constituents. (See "Then, Now, Next" for more on Bush's and Obama's policies.)

War in Afghanistan

One of President Obama's most important foreign policy initiatives has been to increase the number of troops in Afghanistan. In December 2009 he announced that an additional 30,000 troops would be sent to Afghanistan, nearly tripling the number serving there from when he assumed the presidency and bringing the total number of troops in Afghanistan to nearly 100,000. Obama's focus on Afghanistan came after increasing instability in that nation, which he said had not been given the strategic attention and resources that were necessary to bring stability and to ensure a peaceful transition to a stable Afghani government.

The United States' involvement in Afghanistan came about because of the role of Osama bin Laden and the al-Qaeda terror network in the September 11, 2001, terrorist attacks. For several years before 9/11, the fundamentalist Taliban regime in Afghanistan had allowed al-Qaeda training camps to operate in that country. In retaliation for the 9/11 strikes, in late 2001, the United States, a coalition of allies, and anti-Taliban rebels from within Afghanistan attacked the training camps and the Taliban government itself. Within weeks, the Taliban government fell. By toppling the Taliban as the leaders of Afghanistan, the United States fulfilled the policy goal of regime change.

The multilateral forces worked to create first an interim government in Afghanistan and then, in 2004, a democratically elected government. Nonetheless, U.S. forces and

> One impact of the war in Afghanistan in 2001 has been increased educational opportunities for women. Here Afghan girls listen to their teacher during language class in an open-air classroom after space ran out in their school. Shortages of supplies and overcrowded classrooms are commonplace as the nation's girls, who had been prohibited from attending school under the Taliban regime, now may receive an education, though they are often still at great risk.

Will President Obama's Approach to the Arab World Succeed?

THEN: Informed by the theory of a clash of civilizations between modern Western democracies and fundamentalist Islamic states, and compelled by the September 11, 2001, terrorist attacks, the Bush Doctrine relied on the principle of unilateral action. In engaging in essentially unilateral, multitheater wars in Iraq and Afghanistan, the United States evoked the ire of the Islamic world and disfavor among many traditional U.S. allies.

NOW: President Obama attempts to start a new chapter in U.S. relations with the Arab world, beginning with an address to Muslims throughout the world, delivered in Cairo in June 2009. Saying that he is proud to carry "the goodwill of the American people, and a greeting of peace from Muslim communities in my country: Assalaamu alaykum," Obama conveys his own experiences with the Islamic people, including his Muslim relatives, his time as a boy living in Indonesia, an Islamic society; and his experiences with Muslims in Chicago.

WHAT'S NEXT?

■ How might President Obama's conciliatory strategy work to build bridges to Islamic societies? In what ways might it fall short?

- Will a changed relationship with the Islamic world make it more or less likely that the United States will be the target of future terrorist attacks by Islamic extremists?

- What obstacles will this president and future administrations face in making foreign policy decisions as they confront differences between Western and Islamic cultures?

those of its allies must still deal with continued attacks from Taliban forces, and Osama bin Laden, believed to have escaped to the mountains of neighboring Pakistan, remains at large. Although the U.S. invasion of Afghanistan occurred largely in response to the Taliban's support of al-Qaeda, the invasion also demonstrated the potential consequences for nations that support terrorism against the United States.

War in Iraq

After the Taliban's fall, President Bush set his sights on changing another regime: that of Iraq's Saddam Hussein. During the presidency of Bush's father, George H. W. Bush (1989–1993), the United States had gone to war with Iraq when that country invaded Kuwait, an ally of the United States. During the younger Bush's 2003 State of the Union address, the president claimed that Iraq possessed weapons of mass destruction (WMDs) and said that the Iraqis were attempting to purchase the components of nuclear weapons. In the ensuing weeks, the Bush administration made a case for going to war with Hussein's regime to both the UN Security Council and the American people. In doing so, Bush introduced the concept of **preventive war,** the strategy of waging war on countries regarded as threatening to the United States in order to avoid future conflicts.

The concept of preventive war represents a shift in policy from responding to attacks to anticipating attacks. The idea of preventive war is in part an outgrowth of the drastically altered nature of warfare. The biological, chemical, and nuclear weapons of today can cross borders with far deadlier efficiency than troops, ships, or aircraft. In addition, U.S. enemies no longer declare themselves as openly as they did before. The national defense policy makers who advocate preventive war thus argue that the only way to defend the country against these various new threats is to invade *before* the fact, in hopes of deterring another attack.

Early Success, Followed by Stalemate   The invasion of Iraq in March 2003 was initially successful in toppling Saddam Hussein's regime. Despite insurgency violence that has prevented peace from taking root, elections were finally held in 2004 and 2005, and power officially passed to an elected government. In the face of continued violence, the Bush administration enacted a military surge policy, resulting in the addition of more than 20,000 troops in Baghdad and Al Anbar province. While not ending the conflict, the surge strategy was credited with quelling much of the violence in these areas.

The United States launched its invasion of Iraq without the support of two of its major allies, France and Germany. Indeed, the "coalition of the willing" turned out to be a group of small nations, some of which have already withdrawn their troops, while the commitment of others was minimal. Some countries, for example, gave their verbal support to the war but sent few troops. Great Britain alone was firmly committed to the U.S. initiative in Iraq, despite the unpopularity of the war among the British people, according to polls.

International support for the U.S. military action in Iraq, which was never very high, plummeted in light of evidence that U.S. soldiers had abused prisoners at the Abu Ghraib prison, discussed earlier in this chapter. Ironically, the United States, which had initially launched the campaign against human rights abuses, now found itself under attack from many parts of the world for not abiding by its own rules.

Problems with Nation Building   As the war in Iraq has stretched on for the better part of a decade, public support for the war has dwindled, and impatience for an end to the U.S. presence in Iraq has increased. What many Americans thought would be a quick and incisive victory turned into a protracted and deadly war, costing more than 4,300 U.S. soldiers their lives (as of December 2009), over 4,200 of whom were killed after President Bush declared "mission accomplished" in May 2003.

Nation building in Iraq proved troublesome—far more so than the rebuilding of Japan after World War II, for example. There, U.S. general Douglas MacArthur undertook the task of reconstructing the nation and creating a system of democratic self-governance. It took four years, but when MacArthur left for duty in Korea, Japan was as close to democracy as any Far Eastern country. Japan's feudal aristocracy had been abolished; the country had a new constitution that empowered the legislature to make laws; civil liberties and collective bargaining were guaranteed; the legal equality of the sexes had been established; and citizens had been given the right of habeas corpus. MacArthur also suspended banks that had financed the war, destroyed (at least temporarily) the giant monopolies, and refused to allow "war profiteers" to invade Japan at the expense of local businesses.

Fifty years later, as the United States sought to rebuild Iraq's war-torn infrastructure and feed its people after toppling Hussein's regime, a powerful insurgency thwarted American efforts. Unlike MacArthur, the U.S. military had allowed widespread looting in the early days of the occupation, including the looting of munitions warehouses. These munitions later helped to arm the insurgents. Also unlike MacArthur, who had some familiarity with Japanese culture, few U.S. commanders in Iraq knew either the Arabic language or Iraqi culture and rituals. Even fewer knew how to stem the war profiteering of the multinational corporations that had also "invaded" the country.

Iran and North Korea

In the twilight days of the Bush administration, the president continued to use antagonistic rhetoric toward two other nations that appeared to be on his list for regime change: Iran and North Korea. In his 2002 State of the Union speech, Bush had referred to Iraq, Iran, and North Korea as players in an "axis of evil," regimes that sponsored terrorism and were seeking weapons of mass destruction. Bush's characterization is in keeping with (or has shaped) the American public's perception of these nations (see "Analyzing the Sources").

U.S. Public Opinion of Various Countries

This figure provides a visual interpretation of data collected from Americans by the Gallup Organization in February 2007 in response to the question "Is your overall opinion of [the country whose name appears on the left] very favorable, mostly favorable, mostly unfavorable, or very unfavorable?"

Evaluating the Evidence

① In analyzing these data, what can you say about the United States' historical relationship with some of these countries and about the role that relationship might play in people's favorability ratings today?

② Is there evidence from these data that Cold War–era anticommunist sentiment among Americans still has a bearing on people's perceptions? Explain.

③ Do the data suggest that there is, in the phrasing of Samuel Huntington, a "clash of civilizations"? Is there evidence to dispute this suggestion? Explain.

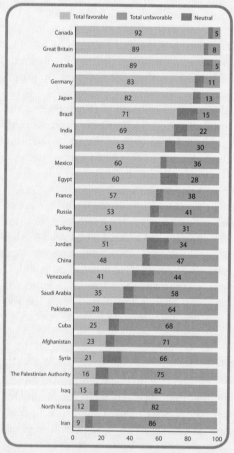

Source: http://brain.gallup.com/content/default.aspx?ci=1624.

Future Challenges in American Foreign Policy

The volatility and complexity of events in the global arena show no sign of abating. In the foreseeable future and beyond, U.S. foreign policy makers will undoubtedly continue to face a number of pressing issues. Certainly, among the most urgent of these problems is the ongoing, acute threat of further terrorism directed at domestic and foreign targets. Issues such as the environment, human rights, and technology promise to remain a fixture on the U.S. foreign policy agenda in the years to come.

The Ongoing Threat of Terrorism

As the terrorist attacks of 9/11 tragically demonstrated, foreign affairs can be unpredictable. There are nonetheless some clear challenges that U.S. foreign policy makers are certain to confront in the years to come. First among these is the continued threat of terrorism. As a tactic, terrorism has proven enormously effective in accomplishing the goals of the attackers. Specifically, terrorism breeds terror—it has disrupted economies, created instability, and acted as a polarizing force.

The advent of chemical and biological weapons also promises to be a tough challenge for U.S. and other foreign policy makers. The potential of these weapons of mass destruction to inflict enormous damage cannot be underestimated. Consider but one example: the death of five people and the panic that ensued after traces of the anthrax virus were found in letters mailed in the United States in the autumn of 2001.

Not all challenges to come are new ones, however. The continued proliferation of nuclear weapons presents a serious problem to foreign policy makers throughout the world. Figure 17.3 shows that eight nations have a declared nuclear weapons capability, including India and Pakistan; that another, Israel, has the undeclared potential; and that yet another, Iran, is seeking such potential. The fact that dangerous WMDs are in such wide distribution increases the likelihood of their use—either accidentally or intentionally.

Environmental Issues

When President Obama attended the United Nations Climate Change Conference in Copenhagen, Denmark, in December 2009, he broke with Bush administration policy, which had rejected the Kyoto Protocol—an international agreement whose objective is to reduce global warming by lowering the amount of greenhouse gas emissions. Obama announced that the United States planned to reduce U.S. greenhouse gas emissions by approximately 17 percent by 2020 compared to 2005 levels, and to work toward reducing U.S. carbon dioxide emissions by as much as 83 percent by 2050. Obama's attendance at the conference—and anticipated U.S. participation in a climate change agreement—marks a sea change in U.S. foreign policy that will

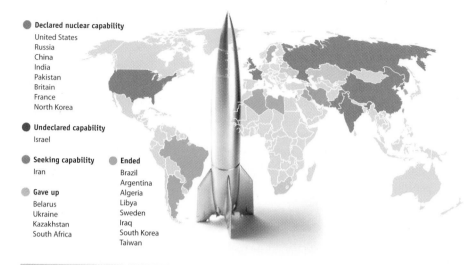

Declared nuclear capability
United States
Russia
China
India
Pakistan
Britain
France
North Korea

Undeclared capability
Israel

Seeking capability
Iran

Gave up
Belarus
Ukraine
Kazakhstan
South Africa

Ended
Brazil
Argentina
Algeria
Libya
Sweden
Iraq
South Korea
Taiwan

FIGURE 17.3 ■ THE NUCLEAR CLUB
What, if anything, do most or all of the countries that gave up or ended their nuclear programs have in common, either among themselves or with the countries that have nuclear capability? What do most or all of the countries that have nuclear capability—either declared or undeclared—have in common? What conclusions can you draw about these commonalities?

have significant implications for the future. Other environmental concerns that are sure to have a secure place in foreign policy makers' agendas for the future include the massive world consumption of fossil fuels, the deterioration of the oceans, worldwide deforestation, and ongoing air and water contamination.

Technology's Potential in Foreign Affairs

Although there are many uncertainties about what's next in the foreign policy arena, one certainty is that the impact of technology—as a tool in foreign policy and in citizens' efforts to influence the policies and institutions of government—will continue to increase. For example, in recent years, a number of countries have thrown off the shackles of one-person or one-party rule due to the revolution in communications technology, which has enabled citizens to see how governments in other countries work. Finding democracy preferable to their own form of government, in 2004, 28 million voters in the Ukraine overturned dubious election results and ousted the first victor, Prime Minister Viktor Yanukovych, installing in his stead another Viktor: Viktor Yushenko. The electronic media broadcast the "orange revolution" in the Ukraine—so called for the orange flags and orange garments of the protesters—for viewers around the world to see. The increasing inability of countries, including Iran, China, and North Korea, to limit access to technology and information from around the world will prove empowering to people everywhere.

CONTINUING THE CONVERSATION

- The nation's initial isolationism, spawned by a healthy suspicion of foreign powers and their motives, gave way to international relations in the limited sphere of trade.

- In both World War I and World War II, the importance of global alliances in helping to shape U.S. foreign policy became evident. With the end of World War II, the United States emerged as a superpower whose foreign policy came to be defined largely by its relations with its chief rival in the global arena, the Soviet Union.

- After the collapse of the Soviet empire in the 1990s, the foreign policy arena was murky, and U.S. and world policy makers searched for a new prism through which to view the nations of the world.

- On September 11, 2001, U.S. foreign policy instantly acquired a new focus. Ultimately, the administration's responses to the terrorist strikes showed that significant cultural and political differences separate the United States and the other Western democracies, on the one hand, and fundamentalist non-Western states that harbor terrorists, on the other. The attacks crystallized perceptions both among U.S. policy makers and in the general public that no longer could the terrorist states be viewed simply as potential threats or as insignificant to the United States' interests.

- Since assuming the presidency in January 2009, the Obama administration has signaled a departure from the tenor of the Bush administration. But it remains unclear whether President Obama's more conciliatory approach will prove effective in building relations with Arab and Muslim nations. It also remains to be seen whether national security measures put in place by both the Bush and Obama administrations will effectively deter future terrorist attacks on the United States.

- Given the distinctive nature of those who practice terrorism—their lack of geographic boundaries and their refusal to abide by the conventional rules of war—such a conflict surely would differ starkly from the last major clash of ideologies, the Cold War. In view of the unique qualities of terrorism, it is difficult to anticipate how the continued threat of terrorist acts will shape U.S. foreign policy. The randomness of terrorism confounds policy makers and other experts and prevents them from making accurate predictions and determining adequate modes of defense. Nonetheless, given the high stakes of another potential attack, the threat of terrorism—and the imperative to prevent it—clearly will remain a defining characteristic of U.S. foreign policy in the decades to come.

STUDY**NOW**

Summary

1. The Tools of U.S. Foreign Policy

The government officials who formulate U.S. foreign policy rely on diplomacy, by which nations conduct political negotiations with one another and settle disagreements; on economic policy to cajole other nations into enacting policies that the United States supports; and on military force, if needed, to force other countries to align with U.S. interests.

2. Who Decides? The Creators and Shapers of Foreign Policy

Because the Constitution grants important foreign policy–making powers to the president, the president along with the executive branch is the primary foreign policy maker in the United States. Congress also plays an important role in creating foreign policy, particularly through its decision making with respect to declaring war and appropriating funds.

3. U.S. Foreign Policy in Historical Context: Isolationism and Intervention

The conduct of foreign policy was at first influenced by a suspicion of foreign affairs. As the U.S. economy developed, government and business interests primarily concentrated on maximizing profits through international trade. In the twentieth century, the balance of power system drew the United States into global conflict in World War I. Although the United States retreated into an isolationist position during the Great Depression, an alliance with the British and Japan's attack on the U.S. naval base at Pearl Harbor, Hawaii, precipitated U.S. entry into World War II.

4. The Postwar Era: The United States as Superpower

After the Second World War, the United States and the Soviet Union emerged as competing superpowers locked in a Cold War of clashing ideologies. During this time, the United States also attempted to curb the spread of communism on the Korean peninsula, in Cuba, and in Vietnam. President Richard Nixon initiated a period of détente; President Ronald Reagan outspent the Soviets and forced the collapse of the Soviet economy. The end of communism in the Soviet Union and Eastern Europe meant drastic changes in the context of international relations.

5. U.S. Foreign Policy After 9/11

With the terrorist attacks of September 11, 2001, a new era in U.S. foreign policy commenced, seeming to reflect acceptance of the theory that a clash of civilizations—warfare over cultural and religious differences—was inevitable. But this paradigm was rejected by President Barack Obama, whose foreign policy has seemed to accentuate diplomatic solutions to foreign policy challenges thus far.

6. Future Challenges in American Foreign Policy

Among the greatest challenges for the United States in the foreign policy arena are the continued threat of terrorism and the accumulation of nuclear, chemical, and biological weapons. Environmental challenges and the impact of technology will also serve as focal points in the future.

For Critical Thinking and Discussion

1. How have the 9/11 terrorist attacks changed the structure of the foreign policy–making apparatus in the executive branch?

2. How did World War II change the way the United States was perceived by other nations around the world? How did the war alter U.S. policy makers' perceptions of what the international order should look like?

3. In retrospect, was the theory of containment an accurate description of how the United States should have attempted to stem the tide of communism during the Cold War? Why or why not?

4. Does Samuel Huntington's clash of civilizations theory accurately reflect the current state of world affairs? Explain. What present-day realities are in keeping with Huntington's theory? What other realities defy it?

5. What additional challenges, beyond those we examined in the text, are likely to face the makers of U.S. foreign policy in the next decade (2010–2020)?

Key Terms

al-Qaeda 621
balance of power
  system 634
brinkmanship 642
Bush Doctrine 647
clash of civilizations
  thesis 646
Cold War 640
collective defense 634
collective security 634
containment 641
country desk 623
defense conversion 644
détente 643
deterrence 643
diplomacy 620
director of national
  intelligence (DNI) 625
domino theory 642
extraordinary rendition 625
foreign service officers 620
globalism 621
Holocaust 636

impressment 632
International Monetary
  Fund (IMF) 638
interventionism 630
isolationism 630
League of Nations 635
limited war 642
manifest destiny 633
Marshall Plan 636
Monroe Doctrine 633
multilateral 636
mutual assured destruction
  (MAD) 643
Nixon Doctrine 643
normal trade relations (NTR)
  status 620
North Atlantic Treaty
  Organization (NATO) 638
preventive war 650
regime change 622
regional security
  alliance 638
Roosevelt Corollary 633

SALT I 644
SALT II 644
sanctions 620
Southeast Asia Treaty
  Organization
  (SEATO) 638
strategic arms limitation
  talks (SALT talks) 644
strategic arms reduction
  talks (START talks) 644
strategic defense initiative
  (SDI, or "Star Wars") 644
superpowers 636
Truman Doctrine 641
United Nations
  (UN) 637
War Powers Act 626
Warsaw Pact 638
weapons of mass
  destruction (WMDs) 621
World Bank 639
World Trade Organization
  (WTO) 639

Internet Resources

***A More Perfect Union* Web site**
www.mhhe.com/harrisonampule Consult the book's Web site for study guides, interactive activities, simulations, and current hot-links that provide additional information on American foreign policy.

Central Intelligence Agency
https://www.cia.gov This is the official Web site of the CIA. Its *World Factbook,* available online at this site, is an excellent resource for research on various nations. The site also hosts news and information, history, and career opportunities.

Cold War
www.coldwar.org This interactive Web site allows you to revisit the Cold War in a virtual museum. You can view relics of the Cold War, learn about the culture of the time, and play spy games.

North Atlantic Treaty Organization
www.nato.int This site hosts an informative eLibrary, as well as an impressive multimedia collection of documentation about NATO-related events and history.

State Department and **Defense Department**
www.state.gov and **www.defenselink.mil** These government sites offer a plethora of information from these two cabinet departments. Included are news and information, policy statements, career opportunities, virtual tours, and reports.

World Bank
www.worldbank.org This site explains the World Bank's policy priorities and offers data, research reports, and a wide variety of related international news.

Recommended Readings

Allison, Graham. *Nuclear Terrorism: The Ultimate Preventable Catastrophe.* New York: Times Books, 2004; and *The Essence of Decision: Explaining the Cuban Missile Crisis.* Boston: Little Brown, 1971. This key scholar of U.S. foreign policy making uses the Cuban Missile Crisis as a model to explain foreign policy making. In his more recent work, he analyzes the foreign policy dilemma of nuclear terrorism.

Jervis, Robert. *American Foreign Policy in a New Era.* New York: Routledge, 2005. An examination of the issues in and influences on American foreign policy in today's international circumstances.

Keohane, Robert. *Neo-Realism and Its Critics,* New York: Columbia University Press, 1986. A classic explanation of neorealism, a theory that emphasizes the power of state actors in international affairs.

APPENDIX A

THE DECLARATION OF INDEPENDENCE

In Congress, July 4, 1776

THE UNANIMOUS DECLARATION OF THE THIRTEEN UNITED STATES OF AMERICA

When in the Course of human Events, it becomes necessary for one People to dissolve the Political Bands which have connected them with another, and to assume, among the Powers of the Earth, the separate and equal Station to which the Laws of Nature and of Nature's God entitle them, a decent Respect to the Opinions of Mankind requires that they should declare the Causes which impel them to the Separation.

We hold these Truths to be self-evident, that all Men are created equal, that they are endowed, by their Creator, with certain unalienable Rights, that among these are Life, Liberty, and the Pursuit of Happiness.—That to secure these Rights, Governments are instituted among Men, deriving their just Powers from the Consent of the Governed, that whenever any Form of Government becomes destructive of these Ends, it is the Right of the People to alter or to abolish it, and to institute new Government, laying its Foundation on such Principles, and organizing its Powers in such Form, as to them shall seem most likely to effect their Safety and Happiness. Prudence, indeed, will dictate, that Governments long established, should not be changed for light and transient Causes; and accordingly all Experience hath shewn, that Mankind are more disposed to suffer, while Evils are sufferable, than to right themselves by abolishing the Forms to which they are accustomed. But when a long Train of Abuses and Usurpations, pursuing invariably the same Object, evinces a Design to reduce them under absolute Despotism, it is their Right, it is their Duty, to throw off such Government, and to provide new Guards for their future Security. Such has been the patient Sufferance of these Colonies; and such is now the Necessity which constrains them to alter their former Systems of Government. The History of the present King of Great-Britain is a History of repeated Injuries and Usurpations, all having in direct Object the Establishment of an absolute Tyranny over these States. To prove this, let Facts be submitted to a candid World.

He has refused his Assent to Laws, the most wholesome and necessary for the public Good.

He has forbidden his Governors to pass Laws of immediate and pressing Importance, unless suspended in their Operation till his Assent should be obtained; and when so suspended, he has utterly neglected to attend to them.

He has refused to pass other Laws for the Accommodation of large Districts of People, unless those People would relinquish the Right of Representation in the Legislature, a Right inestimable to them, and formidable to Tyranny only.

He has called together Legislative Bodies at Places unusual, uncomfortable, and distant from the Depository of their public Records, for the sole Purpose of fatiguing them into Compliance with his Measures.

He has dissolved Representative Houses repeatedly, for opposing with manly Firmness his Invasions on the Rights of the People.

He has refused for a long Time, after such Dissolutions, to cause others to be elected; whereby the Legislative Powers, incapable of Annihilation, have returned to the People at large for their exercise; the State remaining, in the mean Time, exposed to all the Dangers of Invasion from without, and Convulsions within.

He has endeavoured to prevent the Population of these States; for that Purpose obstructing the Laws for Naturalization of Foreigners; refusing to pass others to encourage their Migrations hither, and raising the Conditions of new Appropriations of Lands.

He has obstructed the Administration of Justice, by refusing his Assent to Laws for establishing Judiciary Powers.

He has made Judges dependent on his Will alone, for the Tenure of their Offices, and the Amount and Payment of their Salaries.

He has erected a Multitude of new Offices, and sent hither Swarms of Officers to harrass our People, and eat out their Substance.

He has kept among us, in Times of Peace, Standing Armies, without the Consent of our Legislatures.

He has affected to render the Military independent of and superior to the Civil Power.

He has combined with others to subject us to a Jurisdiction foreign to our Constitution, and unacknowledged by our Laws; giving his Assent to their Acts of pretended Legislation:

For quartering large Bodies of Armed Troops among us:

For protecting them, by a mock Trial, from Punishment for any Murders which they should commit on the Inhabitants of these States:

For cutting off our Trade with all Parts of the World:

For imposing Taxes on us without our Consent:

For depriving us, in many Cases, of the Benefits of Trial by Jury:

For transporting us beyond Seas to be tried for pretended Offences:

For abolishing the free System of English Laws in a neighbouring Province, establishing therein an arbitrary Government, and enlarging its Boundaries, so as to render it at once an Example and fit Instrument for introducing the same absolute Rule into these Colonies:

For taking away our Charters, abolishing our most valuable Laws, and altering fundamentally the Forms of our Governments:

For suspending our own Legislatures, and declaring themselves invested with Power to legislate for us in all Cases whatsoever.

He has abdicated Government here, by declaring us out of his Protection, and waging War against us.

He has plundered our Seas, ravaged our Coasts, burnt our Towns, and destroyed the Lives of our People.

He is, at this Time, transporting large Armies of foreign Mercenaries to complete the Works of Death, Desolation, and Tyranny, already begun with Circumstances of Cruelty and Perfidy, scarcely paralleled in the most barbarous Ages, and totally unworthy the Head of a civilized Nation.

He has constrained our fellow Citizens taken Captive on the high Seas to bear Arms against their Country, to become the Executioners of their Friends and Brethren, or to fall themselves by their Hands.

He has excited domestic Insurrections amongst us, and has endeavoured to bring on the Inhabitants of our Frontiers, the merciless Indian Savages, whose known Rule of Warfare, is an undistinguished Destruction, of all Ages, Sexes and Conditions.

In every Stage of these Oppressions we have Petitioned for Redress in the most humble Terms: Our repeated Petitions have been answered only by repeated Injury. A Prince, whose Character is thus marked by every Act which may define a Tyrant, is unfit to be the Ruler of a free People.

Nor have we been wanting in Attentions to our British Brethren. We have warned them, from Time to Time of Attempts by their Legislature to extend an unwarrantable Jurisdiction over us. We have reminded them of the Circumstances of our Emigration and Settlement here. We have appealed to their native Justice and Magnanimity, and we have conjured them by the Ties of our common Kindred to disavow these Usurpations, which would inevitably interrupt our Connections and Correspondence. They too have been deaf to the Voice of Justice and of Consanguinity. We must, therefore, acquiesce in the Necessity, which denounces our Separation, and hold them, as we hold the Rest of Mankind, Enemies in War, in Peace Friends.

We, therefore, the Representatives of the UNITED STATES OF AMERICA, in General Congress Assembled, appealing to the Supreme Judge of the World for the Rectitude of our Intentions, do, in the Name, and by Authority of the good People of these Colonies, solemnly Publish and Declare, That these United Colonies are, and of Right ought to be, Free and Independent States; that they are absolved from all Allegiance to the British Crown, and that all political Connection between them and the State of Great-Britain, is and ought to be totally dissolved; and that as Free and Independent States, they have full Power to levy War, conclude Peace, contract Alliances, establish Commerce, and to do all other Acts and Things which Independent States may of Right do. And for the Support of this Declaration, with a firm Reliance on the Protection of Divine Providence, we mutually pledge to each other our Lives, our Fortunes, and our sacred Honour.

John Hancock.

NEW-HAMPSHIRE	NEW YORK	PENNSYLVANIA	MARYLAND	NORTH CAROLINA
Josiah Bartlett	William Floyd	Robert Morris	Samuel Chase	William Hooper
William Whipple	Philip Livingston	Benjamin Rush	William Paca	Joseph Hewes
Matthew Thornton	Francis Lewis	Benjamin Franklin	Thomas Stone	John Penn
	Lewis Morris	John Morton	Charles Carroll	
		George Clymer		SOUTH CAROLINA
MASSACHUSETTS BAY		James Smith	VIRGINIA	Edward Rutledge
Samuel Adams	NEW JERSEY	George Taylor	George Wythe	Thomas Heyward, Jr.
John Adams	Richard Stockton	James Wilson	Richard Henry Lee	Thomas Lynch, Jr.
Robert Treat Paine	John Witherspoon	George Ross	Thomas Jefferson	Arthur Middleton
Elbridge Gerry	Francis Hopkinson		Benjamin Harrison	
	John Hart		Thomas Nelson, Jr.	
RHODE ISLAND	Abraham Clark	DELAWARE	Francis Lightfoot Lee	GEORGIA
Stephen Hopkins		Caesar Rodney	Carter Braxton	Button Gwinnett
William Ellery		George Read		Lyman Hall
		Thomas McKean		George Walton
CONNECTICUT				
Roger Sherman				
Samuel Huntington				
William Williams				
Oliver Wolcott				

November 22, 1787
JAMES MADISON

To the People of the State of New York:

Among the numerous advantages promised by a well constructed Union, none deserves to be more accurately developed than its tendency to break and control the violence of faction. The friend of popular governments never finds himself so much alarmed for their character and fate, as when he contemplates their propensity to this dangerous vice. He will not fail, therefore, to set a due value on any plan which, without violating the principles to which he is attached, provides a proper cure for it. The instability, injustice, and confusion introduced into the public councils, have, in truth, been the mortal diseases under which popular governments have everywhere perished; as they continue to be the favorite and fruitful topics from which the adversaries to liberty derive their most specious declamations. The valuable improvements made by the American constitutions on the popular models, both ancient and modern, cannot certainly be too much admired; but it would be an unwarrantable partiality, to contend that they have as effectually obviated the danger on this side, as was wished and expected. Complaints are everywhere heard from our most considerate and virtuous citizens, equally the friends of public and private faith, and of public and personal liberty, that our governments are too unstable, that the public good is disregarded in the conflicts of rival parties, and that measures are too often decided, not according to the rules of justice and the rights of the minor party, but by the superior force of an interested and overbearing majority. However anxiously we may wish that these complaints had no foundation, the evidence of known facts will not permit us to deny that they are in some degree true. It will be found, indeed, on a candid review of our situation, that some of the distresses under which we labor have been erroneously charged on the operation of our governments; but it will be found, at the same time, that other causes will not alone account for many of our heaviest misfortunes; and, particularly, for that prevailing and increasing distrust of public engagements, and alarm for private rights, which are echoed from one end of the continent to the other. These must be chiefly, if not wholly, effects of the unsteadiness and injustice with which a factious spirit has tainted our public administrations.

By a faction, I understand a number of citizens, whether amounting to a majority or a minority of the whole, who are united and actuated by some common impulse of passion, or of interest, adverse to the rights of other citizens, or to the permanent and aggregate interests of the community.

There are two methods of curing the mischiefs of faction: the one, by removing its causes; the other, by controlling its effects.

There are again two methods of removing the causes of faction: the one, by destroying the liberty which is essential to its existence; the other, by giving to every citizen the same opinions, the same passions, and the same interests.

It could never be more truly said than of the first remedy, that it was worse than the disease. Liberty is to faction what air is to fire, an aliment without which it instantly expires. But it could not be less folly to abolish liberty, which is essential to political life, because it nourishes faction, than it would be to wish the annihilation of air, which is essential to animal life, because it imparts to fire its destructive agency.

The second expedient is as impracticable as the first would be unwise. As long as the reason of man continues fallible, and he is at liberty to exercise it, different opinions will be formed. As long as the connection subsists between his reason and his self-love, his opinions and his passions will have a reciprocal influence on each other; and the former will be objects to which the latter will attach themselves. The diversity in the faculties of men, from which the rights of property originate, is not less an insuperable obstacle to a uniformity of interests. The protection of these faculties is the first object of government. From the protection of different and unequal faculties of acquiring property, the possession of different degrees and kinds of property immediately results; and from the influence of these on the sentiments and views of the respective proprietors, ensues a division of the society into different interests and parties.

The latent causes of faction are thus sown in the nature of man; and we see them everywhere brought into different degrees of activity, according to the different circumstances of civil society. A zeal for different opinions concerning religion, concerning government, and many other points, as well of speculation as of practice; an attachment to different leaders ambitiously contending for pre-eminence and power; or to persons of other descriptions whose fortunes have been interesting to the human passions, have, in turn, divided mankind into parties, inflamed them with mutual animosity, and rendered them much more disposed to vex and oppress each other than to co-operate for their common good. So strong is this propensity of mankind to fall into mutual animosities, that where no substantial occasion presents itself, the most frivolous and fanciful distinctions have been sufficient to kindle their unfriendly passions and excite their most violent conflicts. But the most common and durable source of factions has been the various and unequal distribution of property. Those who hold and those who are without property have ever formed distinct interests in society. Those who are creditors, and those who are debtors, fall under a like discrimination. A landed interest, a manufacturing interest, a mercantile interest, a moneyed interest, with many lesser interests, grow up of necessity in civilized nations, and divide them into different classes, actuated by different sentiments and views. The regulation of these various and interfering interests forms the principal task of modern legislation, and involves the spirit of party and faction in the necessary and ordinary operations of the government.

No man is allowed to be a judge in his own cause, because his interest would certainly bias his judgment, and, not improbably, corrupt his integrity. With equal, nay with greater reason, a body of men are unfit to be both judges and parties at the same time; yet what are many of the most important acts of legislation, but so many judicial determinations, not indeed concerning the rights of single persons, but concerning the rights of large bodies of citizens? And what are the different classes of legislators but advocates and parties to the causes which they determine? Is a law proposed concerning private debts? It is a question to which the creditors are parties on one side and the debtors on the other. Justice ought to hold the balance between them. Yet the parties are, and must be, themselves the judges; and the most numerous party, or, in other words, the most powerful faction must be expected to prevail. Shall domestic manufactures be encouraged, and in what degree, by restrictions on foreign manufactures? are questions which would be differently decided by the landed and the manufacturing classes, and probably by neither with a sole regard to justice and the public good. The apportionment of taxes on the various descriptions of property is an act which seems to require the most exact impartiality; yet there is, perhaps, no legislative act in which greater opportunity and temptation are given to a predominant party to trample on the rules of justice. Every shilling with which they overburden the inferior number, is a shilling saved to their own pockets.

It is in vain to say that enlightened statesmen will be able to adjust these clashing interests, and render them all subservient to the public good. Enlightened statesmen will not always be at the helm. Nor, in many cases, can such an adjustment be made at all without taking into view indirect and remote considerations, which will rarely prevail over the immediate interest which one party may find in disregarding the rights of another or the good of the whole.

The inference to which we are brought is, that the *causes* of faction cannot be removed, and that relief is only to be sought in the means of controlling its *effects*.

If a faction consists of less than a majority, relief is supplied by the republican principle, which enables the majority to defeat its sinister views by regular vote. It may clog the administration, it may convulse the society; but it will be unable to execute and mask its violence under the forms of the Constitution. When a majority is included in a faction, the form of popular government, on the other hand, enables it to sacrifice to its ruling passion or interest both the public good and the rights of other citizens. To secure the public good and private rights against the danger of such a faction, and at the same time to preserve the spirit and the form of popular government, is then the great object to which our inquiries are directed. Let me add that it is the great desideratum by which this form of government can be rescued from the opprobrium under which it has so long labored, and be recommended to the esteem and adoption of mankind.

By what means is this object attainable? Evidently by one of two only. Either the existence of the same passion or interest in a majority at the same time must be prevented, or the majority, having such coexistent passion or interest, must be rendered, by their number and local situation, unable to concert and carry into effect schemes of oppression. If the impulse and the opportunity be suffered to coincide, we well know that neither moral nor religious motives can be relied on as an adequate control. They are not found to be such on the injustice and violence of individuals, and lose their efficacy in proportion to the number combined together, that is, in proportion as their efficacy becomes needful.

From this view of the subject it may be concluded that a pure democracy, by which I mean a society consisting of a small number of citizens, who assemble and administer the government in person, can admit of no cure for the mischiefs of faction. A common passion or interest will, in almost every case, be felt by a majority of the whole; a communication and concert result from the form of government itself; and there is nothing to check the inducements to sacrifice the weaker party or an obnoxious individual. Hence it is that such democracies have ever been spectacles of turbulence and contention; have ever been found incompatible with personal security or the rights of property; and have in general been as short in their lives as they have been violent in their deaths. Theoretic politicians, who have patronized this species of government, have erroneously supposed that by reducing mankind to a perfect equality in their political rights, they would, at the same time, be perfectly equalized and assimilated in their possessions, their opinions, and their passions.

A republic, by which I mean a government in which the scheme of representation takes place, opens a different prospect, and promises the cure for which we are seeking. Let us examine the points in which it varies from pure democracy, and we shall comprehend both the nature of the cure and the efficacy which it must derive from the Union.

The two great points of difference between a democracy and a republic are: first, the delegation of the government, in the latter, to a small number of citizens elected by the rest; secondly, the greater number of citizens, and greater sphere of country, over which the latter may be extended.

The effect of the first difference is, on the one hand, to refine and enlarge the public views, by passing them through the medium of a chosen body of citizens, whose wisdom may best discern the true interest of their country, and whose patriotism and love of justice will be least likely to sacrifice it to temporary or partial considerations. Under such a regulation, it may well happen that the public voice, pronounced by the representatives of the people, will be more consonant to the public good than if pronounced by the people themselves, convened for the purpose. On the other hand, the effect may be inverted. Men of factious tempers, of local prejudices, or of sinister designs, may, by intrigue, by corruption, or by other means, first obtain the suffrages, and then betray the interests, of the people. The question resulting is, whether small or extensive republics are more favorable to the election of proper guardians of the public weal; and it is clearly decided in favor of the latter by two obvious considerations:

In the first place, it is to be remarked that, however small the republic may be, the representatives must be raised to a certain number, in order to guard against the cabals of a few; and that, however large it may be, they must be limited to a certain number, in order to guard against the confusion of a multitude. Hence, the number of representatives in the two cases not being in proportion to that of the two constituents, and being proportionally greater in the small republic, it follows that, if the proportion of fit characters be not less in the large than in the small republic, the former will present a greater option, and consequently a greater probability of a fit choice.

In the next place, as each representative will be chosen by a greater number of citizens in the large than in the small republic, it will be more difficult for unworthy candidates to practice with success the vicious arts by which elections are too often carried; and the suffrages of the people being more free, will be more likely to centre in men who possess the most attractive merit and the most diffusive and established characters.

It must be confessed that in this, as in most other cases, there is a mean, on both sides of which inconveniences will be found to lie. By enlarging too much the number of electors, you render the representatives too little acquainted with all their local circumstances and lesser interests; as by reducing it too much, you render him unduly attached to these, and too little fit to comprehend and pursue great and national objects. The federal Constitution forms a happy combination in this respect; the great and aggregate interests being referred to the national, the local and particular to the State legislatures.

The other point of difference is, the greater number of citizens and extent of territory which may be brought within the compass of republican than of democratic government; and it is this circumstance principally which renders factious combinations less to be dreaded in the former than in the latter. The smaller the society, the fewer probably will be the distinct parties and interests composing it; the fewer the distinct parties and interests, the more frequently will a majority be found of the same party; and the smaller the number of individuals composing a majority, and the smaller the compass within which they are placed, the more easily will they concert and execute their plans of oppression. Extend the sphere, and you take in a greater variety of parties and interests; you make it less probable that a majority of the whole will have a common motive to invade the rights of other citizens; or if such a common motive exists, it will be more difficult for all who feel it to discover their own strength, and to act in unison with each other. Besides other impediments, it may be remarked that, where there is a consciousness of unjust or dishonorable purposes, communication is always checked by distrust in proportion to the number whose concurrence is necessary.

Hence, it clearly appears, that the same advantage which a republic has over a democracy, in controlling the effects of faction, is enjoyed by a large over a small republic,—is enjoyed by the Union over the States composing it. Does the advantage consist in the substitution of representatives whose enlightened views and virtuous sentiments render them superior to local prejudices and schemes of injustice? It will not be denied that the representation of the Union will be most likely to possess these requisite endowments. Does it consist in the greater security afforded by a greater variety of parties, against the event of any one party being able to outnumber and oppress the rest? In an equal degree does the increased variety of parties comprised within the Union, increase this security? Does it, in fine, consist in the greater obstacles opposed to the concert and accomplishment of the secret wishes of an unjust and interested majority? Here, again, the extent of the Union gives it the most palpable advantage.

The influence of factious leaders may kindle a flame within their particular States, but will be unable to spread a general conflagration through the other States. A religious sect may degenerate into a political faction in a part of the Confederacy; but the variety of sects dispersed over the entire face of it must secure the national councils against any danger from that source. A rage for paper money, for an abolition of debts, for an equal division of property, or for any other improper or wicked project, will be less apt to pervade the whole body of the Union than a particular member of it; in the same proportion as such a malady is more likely to taint a particular county or district, than an entire State.

In the extent and proper structure of the Union, therefore, we behold a republican remedy for the diseases most incident to republican government. And according to the degree of pleasure and pride we feel in being republicans, ought to be our zeal in cherishing the spirit and supporting the character of Federalists.

Publius

APPENDIX C

THE FEDERALIST NO. 51

February 6, 1788

JAMES MADISON

TO THE PEOPLE OF THE STATE OF NEW YORK:

To what expedient, then, shall we finally resort, for maintaining in practice the necessary partition of power among the several departments, as laid down in the Constitution? The only answer that can be given is, that as all these exterior provisions are found to be inadequate, the defect must be supplied, by so contriving the interior structure of the government as that its several constituent parts may, by their mutual relations, be the means of keeping each other in their proper places. Without presuming to undertake a full development of this important idea, I will hazard a few general observations, which may perhaps place it in a clearer light, and enable us to form a more correct judgment of the principles and structure of the government planned by the convention.

In order to lay a due foundation for that separate and distinct exercise of the different powers of government, which to a certain extent is admitted on all hands to be essential to the preservation of liberty, it is evident that each department should have a will of its own; and consequently should be so constituted that the members of each should have as little agency as possible in the appointment of the members of the others. Were this principle rigorously adhered to, it would require that all the appointments for the supreme executive, legislative, and judiciary magistracies should be drawn from the same fountain of authority, the people, through channels having no communication whatever with one another. Perhaps such a plan of constructing the several departments would be less difficult in practice than it may in contemplation appear. Some difficulties, however, and some additional expense would attend the execution of it. Some deviations, therefore, from the principle must be admitted. In the constitution of the judiciary department in particular, it might be inexpedient to insist rigorously on the principle: first, because peculiar qualifications being essential in the members, the primary consideration ought to be to select that mode of choice which best secures these qualifications; secondly, because the permanent tenure by which the appointments are held in that department, must soon destroy all sense of dependence on the authority conferring them.

It is equally evident, that the members of each department should be as little dependent as possible on those of the others, for the emoluments annexed to their offices. Were the executive magistrate, or the judges, not independent of the legislature in this particular, their independence in every other would be merely nominal.

But the great security against a gradual concentration of the several powers in the same department, consists in giving to those who administer each department the necessary constitutional means and personal motives to resist encroachments of the others. The provision for defense must in this, as in all other cases, be made commensurate to the danger of attack. Ambition must be made to counteract ambition. The interest of the man must be connected with the constitutional rights of the place. It may be a reflection on human nature, that such devices should be necessary to control the abuses of government. But what is government itself, but the greatest of all reflections on human nature? If men were angels, no government would be necessary. If angels were to govern men, neither external nor internal controls on government would be necessary. In framing a government which is to be administered by men over men, the great difficulty lies in this: you must first enable the government to control the governed; and in the next place oblige it to control itself. A dependence on the people is, no doubt, the primary control on the government; but experience has taught mankind the necessity of auxiliary precautions.

This policy of supplying, by opposite and rival interests, the defect of better motives, might be traced through the whole system of human affairs, private as well as public. We see it particularly displayed in all the subordinate distributions of power, where the constant aim is to divide and arrange the several offices in such a manner as that each may be a check on the other—that the private interest of every individual may be a sentinel over the public rights. These inventions of prudence cannot be less requisite in the distribution of the supreme powers of the State.

But it is not possible to give to each department an equal power of self-defense. In republican government, the legislative authority necessarily predominates. The remedy for this inconveniency is to divide the legislature into different branches; and to render them, by different modes of election and different principles of action, as little connected with each other as the nature of their common functions and their common dependence on the society will admit. It may even be necessary to guard against dangerous encroachments by still further precautions. As the weight of the legislative authority requires that it should be thus divided, the weakness of the executive may require, on the other hand, that it should be fortified. An absolute negative on the legislature appears, at first view, to be the natural defense with which the executive magistrate should be armed. But perhaps it would be neither altogether safe nor alone sufficient. On ordinary occasions it might not be exerted with the requisite firmness, and on extraordinary occasions it might be perfidiously abused. May not this defect of an absolute negative be supplied by some qualified connection between this weaker department and the weaker branch of the stronger department, by which the latter may be led to support the constitutional rights of the former, without being too much detached from the rights of its own department?

If the principles on which these observations are founded be just, as I persuade myself they are, and they be applied as a criterion to the several State constitutions, and to the federal Constitution it will be found that if the latter does not perfectly correspond with them, the former are infinitely less able to bear such a test.

There are, moreover, two considerations particularly applicable to the federal system of America, which place that system in a very interesting point of view.

First. In a single republic, all the power surrendered by the people is submitted to the administration of a single government; and the usurpations are guarded against by a division of the government into distinct and separate departments. In the compound republic of America, the power surrendered by the people is first divided between two distinct governments, and then the portion allotted to each subdivided among distinct and separate departments. Hence a double security arises to the rights of the people. The different governments will control each other, at the same time that each will be controlled by itself.

Second. It is of great importance in a republic not only to guard the society against the oppression of its rulers, but to guard one part of the society against the injustice of the other part. Different interests necessarily exist in different classes of citizens. If a majority be united by a common interest, the rights of the minority will be insecure. There are but two methods of providing against this evil: the one by creating a will in the community independent of the majority—that is, of the society itself; the other, by comprehending in the society so many separate descriptions of citizens as will render an unjust combination of a majority of the whole very improbable, if not impracticable. The first method prevails in all governments possessing an hereditary or self-appointed authority. This, at best, is but a precarious security; because a power independent of the society may as well espouse the unjust views of the major, as the rightful interests of the minor party, and may possibly be turned against both parties. The second method will be exemplified in the federal republic of the United States. Whilst all authority in it will be derived from and dependent on the society, the society itself will be broken into so many parts, interests, and classes of citizens, that the rights of individuals, or of the minority, will be in little danger from interested combinations of the majority. In a free government the security for civil rights must be the same as that for religious rights. It consists in the one case in the multiplicity of interests, and in the other in the multiplicity of sects. The degree of security in both cases will depend on the number of interests and sects; and this may be presumed to depend on the extent of country and number of people comprehended under the same government. This view of the subject must particularly recommend a proper federal system to all the sincere and considerate friends of republican government, since it shows that in exact proportion as the territory of the Union may be formed into more circumscribed Confederacies, or States, oppressive combinations of a majority will be facilitated: the best security, under the republican forms, for the rights of every class of citizens, will be diminished: and consequently the stability and independence of some member of the government, the only other security, must be proportionately increased. Justice is the end of government. It is the end of civil society. It ever has been and ever will be pursued until it be obtained, or until liberty be lost in the pursuit. In a society under the forms of which the stronger faction can readily unite and oppress the weaker, anarchy may as truly be said to reign as in a state of nature, where the weaker individual is not secured against the violence of the stronger; and as, in the latter state, even the stronger individuals are prompted, by the uncertainty of their condition, to submit to a government which may protect the weak as well as themselves; so, in the former state, will the more powerful factions or parties be gradually induced, by a like motive, to wish for a government which will protect all parties, the weaker as well as the more powerful. It can be little doubted that if the State of Rhode Island was separated from the Confederacy and left to itself, the insecurity of rights under the popular form of government within such narrow limits would be displayed by such reiterated oppressions of factious majorities that some power altogether independent of the people would soon be called for by the voice of the very factions whose misrule had proved the necessity of it. In the extended republic of the United States, and among the great variety of interests, parties, and sects which it embraces, a coalition of a majority of the whole society could seldom take place on any other principles than those of justice and the general good; whilst there being thus less danger to a minor from the will of a major party, there must be less pretext, also, to provide for the security of the former, by introducing into the government a will not dependent on the latter, or, in other words, a will independent of the society itself. It is no less certain than it is important, notwithstanding the contrary opinions which have been entertained, that the larger the society, provided it lie within a practical sphere, the more duly capable it will be of self-government. And happily for the *republican cause,* the practicable sphere may be carried to a very great extent, by a judicious modification and mixture of the *federal principle.*

Publius

Seneca Falls Conference, 1848

When, in the course of human events, it becomes necessary for one portion of the family of man to assume among the people of the earth a position different from that which they have hitherto occupied, but one to which the laws of nature and of nature's God entitle them, a decent respect to the opinions of mankind requires that they should declare the causes that impel them to such a course.

We hold these truths to be self-evident: that all men and women are created equal; that they are endowed by their Creator with certain inalienable rights; that among these are life, liberty, and the pursuit of happiness; that to secure these rights governments are instituted, deriving their just powers from the consent of the governed. Whenever any form of government becomes destructive of these ends, it is the right of those who suffer from it to refuse allegiance to it, and to insist upon the institution of a new government, laying its foundation on such principles, and organizing its powers in such form, as to them shall seem most likely to effect their safety and happiness. Prudence, indeed, will dictate that governments long established should not be changed for light and transient causes; and accordingly all experience hath shown that mankind are more disposed to suffer, while evils are sufferable, than to right themselves by abolishing the forms to which they are accustomed. But when a long train of abuses and usurpations, pursuing invariably the same object, evinces a design to reduce them under absolute despotism, it is their duty to throw off such government, and to provide new guards for their future security. Such has been the patient sufferance of the women under this government, and such is now the necessity which constrains them to demand the equal station to which they are entitled.

The history of mankind is a history of repeated injuries and usurpations on the part of man toward woman, having in direct object the establishment of an absolute tyranny over her. To prove this, let facts be submitted to a candid world.

He has never permitted her to exercise her inalienable right to the elective franchise.

He has compelled her to submit to laws, in the formation of which she had no voice.

He has withheld from her rights which are given to the most ignorant and degraded men—both natives and foreigners.

Having deprived her of this first right of a citizen, the elective franchise, thereby leaving her without representation in the halls of legislation, he has oppressed her on all sides.

He has made her, if married, in the eye of the law, civilly dead.

He has taken from her all right in property, even to the wages she earns.

He has made her, morally, an irresponsible being, as she can commit many crimes with impunity, provided they be done in the presence of her husband. In the covenant of marriage, she is compelled to promise obedience to her husband, he becoming, to all intents and purposes, her master—the law giving him power to deprive her of her liberty, and to administer chastisement.

He has so framed the laws of divorce, as to what shall be the proper causes, and in case of separation, to whom the guardianship of the children shall be given, as to be wholly regardless of the happiness of women—the law, in all cases, going upon a false supposition of the supremacy of man, and giving all power into his hands.

After depriving her of all rights as a married woman, if single, and the owner of property, he has taxed her to support a government which recognizes her only when her property can be made profitable to it.

He has monopolized nearly all the profitable employments, and from those she is permitted to follow, she receives but a scanty remuneration. He closes against her all the avenues to wealth and distinction which he considers most honorable to himself. As a teacher of theology, medicine, or law, she is not known.

He has denied her the facilities for obtaining a thorough education, all colleges being closed against her.

He allows her in church, as well as state, but a subordinate position, claiming apostolic authority for her exclusion from the ministry, and, with some exceptions, from any public participation in the affairs of the church.

He has created a false public sentiment by giving to the world a different code of morals for men and women, by which moral delinquencies which exclude women from society, are not only tolerated, but deemed of little account in man.

He has usurped the prerogative of Jehovah himself, claiming it as his right to assign for her a sphere of action, when that belongs to her conscience and to her God.

He has endeavored, in every way that he could, to destroy her confidence in her own powers, to lessen her self-respect, and to make her willing to lead a dependent and abject life.

Now, in view of this entire disfranchisement of one-half the people of this country, their social and religious degradation—in view of the unjust laws above mentioned, and because women do feel themselves aggrieved, oppressed, and fraudulently deprived of their most sacred rights, we insist that they have immediate admission to all the rights and privileges which belong to them as citizens of the United States. In entering upon the great work before us, we anticipate no small amount of misconception, misrepresentation, and ridicule; but we shall use every instrumentality within our power to effect our object. We shall employ agents, circulate tracts, petition the State and national Legislatures, and endeavor to enlist the pulpit and the press in our behalf. We hope this Convention will be followed by a series of Conventions, embracing every part of the country.

Firmly relying upon the final triumph of the Right and the True, we do this day affix our signatures to this declaration.

Harriet Cady Eaton
Elizabeth M'Clintock
Mary M'Clintock
Margaret Pryor
Eunice Newton Foote
Margaret Schooley
Catherine F. Stebbins
Mary Ann Frink
Lydia Mount
Delia Matthews
Catharine C. Paine
Mary H. Hallowell
Sarah Hallowell
Catharine Shaw
Deborah Scott
Mary Gilbert
Sophrone Taylor
Cynthia Davis
Hannah Plant
Lucy Jones
Sarah Whitney
Elizabeth Conklin
Lucretia Coffin Mott
Mary Ann M'Clintock
Susan Quinn
Mary S. Mirror
Phebe King
Julia Ann Drake
Charlotte Woodard
Martha Underhill
Dorothy Matthews
Eunice Baker

Sarah R. Woods
Lydia Gild
Sarah Hoffman
Elizabeth Leslie
Martha Ridley
Rachel D. Bonnel
Betsey Tewksbury
Rhoda Palmer
Margaret Jenkins
Cynthia Fuller
Mary Martin
P. A. Culvert
Susan R. Doty
Rebecca Race
Martha Coffin Wright
Jane C. Hunt
Sarah A. Mosher
Mary E. Vail
Lucy Spaulding
Lavinia Latham
Sarah Smith
Eliza Martin
Maria E. Wilbur
Elizabeth D. Smith
Caroline Barker
Ann Porter
Experience Gibbs
Antoinette E. Segur
Hannah J. Latham
Sarah Sisson
Malvina Seymour
Phebe Mosher

Joel Bunker
Isaac Van Tassel
Thomas Dell
E. W. Capron
Stephen Shear
Henry Hatley
Amy Post
Frederick Douglass
Richard P. Hunt
Samuel D. Tillman
Justin Williams
Elisha Foote
Henry W. Seymour
David Salding
William G. Barker
Elias J. Doty
John Jones
William S. Dell
William Burroughs
Azaliah Schooley
Robert Smalldridge
Jacob Matthews
Charles L. Hoskins
Thomas M'Clintock
Saron Phillips
Jacob Chamberlain
Johnathan Metcalf
Nathan J. Milliken
S. E. Woodworth
Edward F. Underhill
George W. Pryor

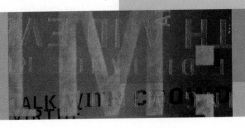

GLOSSARY

A

absentee voting The casting of a ballot in advance by mail in situations where illness, travel, or other circumstances prevent voters from voting in their precinct.

administrative adjudication The process by which agencies resolve disputes over the implementation of their administrative rules.

administrative discretion The authority delegated to bureaucrats to use their expertise and judgment when determining how to implement public policy.

administrative rule making The process by which an independent commission or agency fills in the details of a vague law by formulating, proposing, and approving rules, regulations, and standards that will be enforced to implement the policy.

advice and consent The Senate's authority to approve or reject the president's top appointments.

affirmative action In the employment arena, intentional efforts to recruit, hire, train, and promote underutilized categories of workers (women and minority men); in higher education, intentional efforts to diversify the student body.

agency review Part of the committee or subcommittee process of considering a bill, wherein committee members ask executive agencies that would administer the law for written comments on the measure.

agenda setting The determination by Congress of which public issues the government should consider for legislation.

agents of socialization The individuals, organizations, and institutions that facilitate the acquisition of political views.

al-Qaeda A radical international Islamic fundamentalist terror organization.

American dream The belief that in the United States hard work and persistence will reap a financially secure, happy and healthy life, with upward social mobility.

amicus curiae brief ("friend of the court" brief) A document submitted by parties interested in a certain case or issue in an attempt to provide the Court with information that may be used to decide the case.

Anti-Federalists Individuals who opposed ratification of the Constitution because they were deeply suspicious of the powers it gave to the national government and of the impact these powers would have on states' authority and individual freedoms.

appellate jurisdiction The authority of a court to review and overturn a lower court's decision in a case.

appropriation law A law that gives bureaucracies and other government entities the legal authority to spend money.

approval ratings The percentage of survey respondents who say that they "approve" or "strongly approve" of the way the president is doing his job.

articles of impeachment Charges against the president during an impeachment.

attentive public The segment of voters who pay careful attention to political issues.

Australian ballot A secret ballot prepared by the government, distributed to all eligible voters, and, when balloting is completed, counted by government officials in an unbiased fashion, without corruption or regard to individual preferences.

authoritarianism A system of government in which the government holds strong powers but is checked by some forces.

authorization law A law that provides the plan of action to address a given societal concern and identifies the executive branch unit that will put the plan into effect.

B

bad tendency test A standard established in the 1925 case *Gitlow v. New York,* whereby any speech that has the tendency to incite crime or disturb the public peace can be silenced.

balance of power system A system of international alliances that, in theory, would balance the power of one group of nations against the power of another group and thus discourage war.

balanced budget A budget in which the government's expenditures are equal to or less than its revenues.

balanced ticket The selection of a running mate who brings diversity of ideology, geographic region, age, gender, race, or ethnicity to the slate.

bandwidth The amount of data that can travel through a network in a given time period.

bicameral A legislative body composed of two chambers.

bill A proposed piece of legislation.

Bill of Rights The first ten amendments to the Constitution, which were ratified in 1791, constituting an enumeration of the individual liberties with which the government is forbidden to interfere.

Black Codes Laws passed immediately after the Civil War by the confederate states that limited the rights of "freemen" (former slaves).

blanket primary A type of primary that allows voters to vote in either party's primary, and voters can choose to vote in *both* parties' primaries for different offices.

block grant The intergovernmental transfer of money that has fewer conditions of aid than a categorical grant and is used for broadly defined policy areas; it is distributed based on complicated formulas.

blogosphere A community, or social network, of bloggers.

brief A document detailing the legal argument for the desired outcome in a court case.

brinkmanship The Cold War–era practice of fooling the enemy by going to the edge (the brink), even if the party using the brinkmanship strategy had no intention of following it through.

Brown v. Board of Education of Topeka The 1954 Supreme Court decision case ruling that segregated schools violated the equal protection clause of the Fourteenth Amendment.

budget authority The authority provided by law for agencies to obligate government spending.

budget deficit More money spent than collected through revenues.

budget reconciliation The annual process of rewriting authorization legislation to comply with the expenditure ceiling and revenue floor of the concurrent budget resolution for the upcoming fiscal year.

budget surplus Money left over after all expenses are paid.

bureaucracy Any organization with a hierarchical structure, although most commonly used to designate a government agency or the collection of all national executive branch organizations.

bureaucrats People employed in a government executive branch unit to implement public policy; a public administrator; a public servant.

Bush Doctrine The argument, articulated by President George W. Bush, that unilateral action directly targeted at an enemy is both justifiable and feasible.

business regulation Government rules, regulations, and standards, directed at protecting competition in the marketplace.

C

cabinet The group of experts chosen by the president to serve as advisers on running the country.

campaign consultant A paid professional who specializes in the overall management of political campaigns or an aspect of campaigns.

campaign manager A professional whose duties comprise a variety of strategic and managerial tasks, from fund-raising to staffing a campaign.

campaign strategy The blueprint for the campaign, including a budget and fund-raising plan, an advertising strategy, a staffing plan.

candidate committees Organizations that candidates form to support their individual election.

candidate-centered campaign A campaign in which the individual seeking election, rather than an entire party slate, is the focus.

capitalism An economic system in which the means of producing wealth are privately owned and operated to produce profits.

casework Personal work by a member of Congress on behalf of a constituent or group of constituents, typically aimed at getting the government to do something the constituent wants done.

cash transfer The direct provision of cash (in forms including checks, debit cards, and tax breaks) to eligible individuals or to providers of goods or services to eligible individuals.

categorical formula grant The intergovernmental transfer of money for a specified program area for which the amount of money a government is eligible to receive is based on a legislated formula.

categorical project grant The intergovernmental transfer of money for a specified program area for which recipients compete by proposing specific projects they want to implement.

caucus A meeting of all members of the political party in one chamber in which they elect leaders, approve committee assignments, and elect committee chairpersons.

centralized federalism The relationship between the national and state governments whereby the national government imposes its policy preferences on state governments.

chad A ready-made perforation on a punch card ballot.

checks and balances The mechanisms by which each branch of government can monitor and limit the functions of the other branches.

chief justice The leading justice on the Supreme Court, who provides both organizational and intellectual leadership.

chief of staff Among the most important staff members of the White House Office (WHO); serves as both an adviser to the president and the manager of the WHO.

circuit courts Also known as *courts of appeals;* the middle level in the federal court structure.

circuit riding The practice of traveling around the circuits by early Supreme Court justices and district court judges to hear appeals cases.

citizens Those members of the polity who, through birth or naturalization, enjoy the rights, privileges, and responsibilities attached to membership in a given nation.

civic engagement Individual and collective actions designed to identify and address issues of public concern.

civil disobedience Active, but nonviolent, refusal to comply with laws or governmental policies that are morally objectionable.

civil law case A conflict between private individuals in which the plaintiff alleges that some action or inaction by the defendant has resulted in harm to him or her.

civil liberties Constitutionally established guarantees that protect citizens, opinions, and property against arbitrary government interference.

civil rights The rights and privileges guaranteed to all citizens under the equal protection and due process clauses of the Fifth and Fourteenth amendments; the idea that individuals are protected from discrimination based on characteristics such as race, national origin, religion, and sex.

civil servants Bureaucrats hired through a merit-based personnel system who have job protection.

clash of civilizations thesis Samuel Huntington's idea that bitter cultural conflict will continue and escalate between modern Western democracies and fundamentalist Islamic states.

clear and present danger test A standard established in the 1919 Supreme Court case *Schenck v. U.S.*, whereby the government may silence speech or expression when there is a clear and present danger that this speech will bring about some harm that the government has the power to prevent.

clear and probable danger test A standard established in the 1951 case *Dennis v. U.S.* whereby the government could suppress speech to avoid grave danger, even if the probability of the dangerous result was relatively remote; replaced by the imminent lawless action (incitement) test in 1969.

climate control The practice of using public outreach to build favorable public opinion of an organization.

closed primary A type of primary in which voting in a party's primary is limited to members of that party.

cloture A procedural move in which a supermajority of sixty senators agrees to end a filibuster.

coattail effect The phenomenon by which candidates running for a lower-level office such as city council benefit in an election from the popularity of a top-of-ticket nominee.

code law Laws created by legislators to regulate the behavior of individuals and organizations.

Cold War The political, ideological, and military conflict that lasted from 1945 until 1990 between communist nations led by the Soviet Union and Western democracies led by the United States.

collective defense The concept that allied nations agree to defend one another in the face of an invasion.

collective goods Outcomes shared by the general public; also called *public goods.*

collective security The idea that peace could be achieved if nations agreed to collectively oppose any nation that attacked another country.

collegial court A court made up of a group of judges who must evaluate a case together and decide on the outcome; significant compromise and negotiation take place as members try to build a majority coalition.

commercial speech Advertising statements that describe products.

common law Law made by judges who decide cases and articulate legal principles in their opinions; based upon the British system.

concurrent budget resolution A document approved by the House and Senate at the beginning of their budget process that establishes binding expenditure ceilings and a binding revenue floor, as well as proposed expenditure levels for major policies.

concurrent powers The basic governing functions of all sovereign governments; in the United States they are held by the national, state, and local governments and include the authority to tax, to make policy, to implement policy, and the power of eminent domain.

concurring opinion A judicial opinion agreeing with how the majority decides the case but disagreeing with at least some of the legal interpretations or conclusions reached by the majority.

confederal system A structure of government in which several independent sovereign governments agree to cooperate on specified governmental matters while retaining sovereignty over all other governmental matters within their jurisdictions.

confederation A national government composed of a league of independent states and in which the central government has less power than the member states.

conference committee A bicameral, bipartisan committee composed of legislators whose job is to reconcile two versions of a bill.

conflict of interest In the case of public servants, the situation when they can personally benefit from a decision they make or an action they take in the process of doing their jobs.

conflicted federalism The current status of national-state relations that has elements of dual and cooperative federalism, with an overall centralizing tendency at the same time that elements of policy are devolved.

Connecticut Compromise (Great Compromise) At the constitutional convention, the compromise between the Virginia Plan and the New Jersey Plan that created a bicameral legislature with one chamber's representation based on population and the other having two members for each state.

consent of the governed The idea that, in a democracy, the government's power derives from the consent of the people.

conservatism An ideology that emphasizes preserving tradition and relying on community and family as mechanisms of continuity in society.

constitution A document that describes three basic components of an organization: its mission, foundational structures, and essential processes.

constitutional law The body of law that comes out of the courts in cases involving the interpretation of the Constitution.

constitutionalism Government that is structured by law, and in which the power of government is limited.

consumer price index (CPI) The most common measure of inflation, it measures the average change in prices over time of a "market basket" of goods and services.

containment The Cold War–era policy of preventing the spread of communism, mainly by providing military and economic aid, as well as political advice, to countries vulnerable to a communist takeover.

continuing resolution An agreement of the House and Senate that authorizes agencies not covered by approved appropriation laws to continue to spend money within their previous budget year's levels.

contracting-out Also called *outsourcing* or *privatizing;* a process by which the government contracts with a private for-profit or nonprofit organization to provide public services or resources needed by the government.

contributory program (social insurance program) A benefit provided only to those who paid the specific tax created to fund the benefit.

convergence The merging of various forms of media, including newspapers, television stations, radio networks, and blogs, under one corporate roof and one set of business editorial leaders.

cooperative federalism The relationship between the national and state governments whereby the two levels of government work together to address domestic matters reserved to the states, driven by the policy priorities of the states.

country desk The official operation of the U.S. government in each country that has diplomatic ties to the United States.

courts of appeals The intermediate appellate courts in the federal system that review previous decisions made by courts in the federal or state judicial system.

creationism A theory of the creation of the earth and humankind that is based on a literal interpretation of the biblical story of Genesis.

criminal due process rights Safeguards for those accused of crime; these rights constrain government conduct in investigating crimes, trying cases, and punishing offenders.

criminal law case A case brought by the government or a prosecutor against a defendant, alleging that he or she has engaged in conduct resulting in injury to another person, and that this injury is so significant that it harms not only the individual but also the larger society.

cross pressuring The presence of two conditions or traits that pull a voter toward different political parties.

D

de facto segregation Segregation caused by the fact that people tend to live in neighborhoods with others of their own race, religion, or ethnic group.

de jure segregation Segregation mandated by law.

dealignment The situation in which fewer voters support the two major political parties, instead identifying themselves as independent, or splitting their ticket between candidates from more than one party

defendant A person who is defending him or herself against a plaintiff's accusation.

defense conversion President Jimmy Carter's attempt to convert the nation's vast military apparatus to peacetime functions.

deficit spending Government expenditures costing more than is raised in taxes, leading to borrowing and debt.

democracy Government in which the supreme power of governance lies in the hands of its citizens.

department One of fifteen executive branch units responsible for a broadly defined policy area and whose top administrator (secretary) is appointed by the president, is confirmed by the Senate, and serves at the discretion of the president.

depression A long-term and severe recession.

deregulation The reduction or elimination of regulatory restrictions on firms and industries.

détente The easing of tensions between the United States and its communist rivals.

deterrence The idea that nations would be less likely to engage in nuclear war if adversaries each had first-strike capability.

devolution The process whereby the national government returns policy responsibilities to state and/or local governments.

digital divide The inequality of access to computers and Internet connections.

diplomacy The conduct of international relations, particularly involving the negotiation of treaties and other agreements between nations.

direct democracy A system of government that allows citizens to vote directly to approve or reject proposed

public policies or to force an elected official from office before the completion of his or her term.

direct provision A policy tool whereby the government that creates a policy hires public servants to provide the service.

direct subsidy A cash transfer from general revenues to particular persons or private companies engaged in activities that the national government believes support the public good.

director of national intelligence (DNI) The person responsible for coordinating and overseeing all the intelligence agencies within the executive branch.

discharge petition A special tactic used to extract a bill from a committee in order to have it considered by the entire House.

discretionary spending Payment on programs for which Congress and the president must approve budget authority each year in appropriation legislation.

discuss list Compiled by the chief justice, the list of cases on review that he thinks may be appropriate for the Court to hear.

dissenting opinion A judicial opinion disagreeing both with the majority's disposition of a case and with their legal interpretations and conclusions.

diversity of citizenship The circumstance in which the parties in a legal case are from different states or the case involves a U.S. citizen and a foreign government.

divided government The situation that exists when Congress is controlled by one party and the presidency by the other.

divine right of kings The assertion that monarchies, as a manifestation of God's will, could rule absolutely without regard to the will or well-being of their subjects.

domino theory The principle that if one nation fell to communism, other nations in its geographic vicinity also would succumb.

double jeopardy To be tried again for the same crime that one has been cleared of in court; barred by the Fifth Amendment.

dual court system A two-part judicial system such as that of the United States, which has both federal and state courts.

dual federalism The relationship between the national and state governments, dominant between 1789 and 1932, whereby the two levels of government functioned independently of each other to address their distinct constitutional responsibilities.

dual sovereignty The existence of two governments, each with sovereignty over different matters at the same time; neither level is sovereign over the other.

due process The legal safeguards that prevent the government from arbitrarily depriving citizens of life, liberty, or property; guaranteed by the Fifth and Fourteenth amendments.

E

earmark A designation within a spending bill that provides for a specific expenditure.

e-campaigning The practice of mobilizing voters using the Internet.

economic boom Rapid economic growth.

economic incentives Motivation to join an interest group because the group works for policies that will provide members with material benefits.

economy The system of transactions by which goods and services are distributed in the marketplace.

efficacy Citizens' belief that they have the ability to achieve something desirable and that the government listens to people like them.

electioneering Working to influence the election of candidates who support the organization's issues.

Electoral College A group of people elected by voters in each state to elect the president and the vice president.

elite theory A theory that holds that a group of wealthy, educated individuals wields most political power.

emergency powers Broad powers exercised by the president during times of national crisis.

entitlement program A government benefit guaranteed to all who meet the eligibility requirements.

enumerated powers The powers of the national government that are listed in the Constitution.

environmental racism The term for the higher incidence of environmental threats and subsequent health problems in lower-income communities, which frequently are also communities dominated by people of color.

equal protection clause The Fourteenth Amendment clause stating that no state shall "deny to any person within its jurisdiction the equal protection of the laws."

establishment clause The First Amendment clause that bars the government from passing any law "respecting an establishment of religion"; often interpreted as a separation of church and state but increasingly questioned.

exclusionary rule The criminal procedural rule stating that evidence obtained illegally cannot be used in a trial.

executive agreement An international agreement between the United States and other nations, not subject to Senate approval and only in effect during the administration of the president who negotiates the agreement.

executive budget The budget document and budget message that explains the president's fiscal plan.

Executive Office of the President (EOP) The offices, counsels, and boards that help the president to carry out his day-to-day responsibilities.

executive order The power of the president to issue orders that carry the force of law.

executive privilege The right of the chief executive and members of the administration to withhold information from Congress or the courts, or the right to refuse to appear before legislative or judicial bodies.

exit polls Polls conducted at polling places on election day to determine the winner of an election before voting officially ends.

expressed powers Presidential powers enumerated in the Constitution.

extradition The return of a person accused of a crime to the state in which the crime was committed upon the request of that state's governor.

extraordinary rendition Apprehending an individual believed to be a terrorist and transferring the person to another nation.

F

fairness doctrine The requirement that stations provide equal time to all parties regarding important

public issues and equal access to airtime to all candidates for public office.

federal question A question of law based on interpretation of the U.S. Constitution, federal laws, or treaties.

federal system A governmental structure with two levels of government and in which each level has sovereignty over different governmental functions and policy matters.

The Federalist Papers A series of essays, written by James Madison, Alexander Hamilton, and John Jay, that argued for the ratification of the Constitution.

Federalists Individuals who supported the new Constitution as presented by the Constitutional Convention in 1787.

feminization of poverty The phenomenon of increasing numbers of unmarried, divorced, and separated women with children living in poverty.

fighting words Speech that is likely to bring about public disorder or chaos; the Supreme Court has held that this speech may be banned in public places to ensure the preservation of public order.

filibuster A procedural move by a member of the Senate to attempt to halt passage of a bill, during which the senator can speak for an unlimited time on the Senate floor.

fireside chats President Franklin Roosevelt's radio addresses to the country.

fiscal policy Government spending and taxing and their effect on the economy.

fiscal year (FY) The twelve months during which the government implements its annual budget, beginning on October 1 and ending on September 30 of the following year.

527 A tax-exempt group that raises money for political activities, much like those allowed under the soft money loophole.

food insecurity The situation in which people have a limited or an uncertain ability to obtain, in socially acceptable ways, enough nutritious food to live a healthy and active life.

foreign service officers The diplomatic and consular staff at U.S. embassies abroad.

framing The process by which the media set a context that helps consumers understand important events and matters of shared interest.

free exercise clause The First Amendment clause prohibiting the government from enacting laws prohibiting an individual's practice of his or her religion; often in contention with the establishment clause.

free rider problem The phenomenon of someone deriving benefit from others' actions.

free trade policy The elimination of tariffs and nontariff trade barriers so that international trade is expanded.

freedom of assembly The right to form or join any type of organization, political party, or club without penalty.

full faith and credit clause The constitutional clause that requires states to comply with and uphold the public acts, records, and judicial decisions of other states.

fund-raising consultant A professional who works with candidates in identifying likely contributors to the campaign and arranging events and meetings with donors.

G

gender gap The measurable difference in the way women and men vote for candidates and in the way they view political issues.

general election An election that determines which candidates win the offices being sought.

generational effect The impact of an important external event in shaping the views of a generation.

gerrymandering The drawing of legislative district boundaries to benefit an incumbent, a political party, or another group.

global economy The worldwide economy created by the integration and interdependence of national economies.

global warming The rising temperature of the earth as a result of pollution that traps solar heat, keeping the air warmer than it would otherwise be.

globalism The interconnectedness between nations in contemporary times.

GOTV Get out the vote.

government The institution that creates and implements policy and laws that guide the conduct of the nation and its citizens.

government corporation An executive branch unit that sells a service and is expected to be financially self-sufficient.

grandfather clause A clause exempting individuals from voting conditions such as poll taxes or literacy tests if they or their ancestor had voted before 1870, thus sparing most white voters in the South.

grant-in-aid (intergovernmental transfer) The transfer of money from one government to another government (or from a government to a nonprofit organization, for-profit organization, or individual) that does not need to be paid back.

grassroots organizing Tasks that involve direct contact with voters or potential voters.

Great Depression Between 1929 and 1939, a time of devastating economic collapse and personal misery for people around the world.

greenhouse effect The heating of the earth's atmosphere as a result of humans' burning of fossil fuels and the resultant buildup of carbon dioxide and other gases.

gross domestic product (GDP) The total value of all goods and services produced by labor and properties within a country's borders.

H

habeas corpus An ancient right that protects an individual in custody from being held without the right to be heard in a court of law.

hard money Regulated campaign contributions that can specifically advocate the election of a candidate.

hate crime A crime committed against a person, property, or society, where the offender is motivated, in part or in whole, by bias against the victim's race, religion, disability, sexual orientation, or ethnicity.

hearings Sessions held by committees or subcommittees to gather information and views from experts.

heightened scrutiny test (intermediate scrutiny test) The guidelines most frequently used by the courts to determine the legality of sex-based discrimination; on the basis of this test, sex-based discrimination is legal if the government can prove that it is substantially related to the achievement of an important public interest.

Holocaust The genocide perpetrated by Adolf Hitler and the Nazis of 6 million Jews, along with political dissidents, Catholics, homosexuals, and gypsies.

honeymoon period A time early in a new president's administration characterized by optimistic approval by the public.

hopper A wooden box that sits on a desk at the front of the House of Representatives, into which House members place bills they want to introduce.

horizontal federalism The state-to-state relationships created by the U.S. Constitution.

House majority leader The leader of the majority party, who helps the Speaker develop and implement strategy and work with other members of the House of Representatives.

House minority leader The leader of the minority party, whose job mirrors that of the majority leader but without the power that comes from holding a majority in the House of Representatives.

household income The total pretax earnings of all residents over the age of 15 living in a home.

housing insecurity The situation in which people have limited or uncertain ability to obtain, in socially acceptable ways, affordable, safe, and decent-quality permanent housing.

Human Development Index (HDI) A UN-created measure to determine how well a country's economy is providing for a long and healthy life, educational opportunity, and a decent standard of living.

I

imminent lawless action test (incitement test) A legal standard established in the 1969 *Brandenburg v. Ohio* case whereby speech is restricted only if it goes beyond mere advocacy, or words, to create a high likelihood of imminent disorder or lawlessness.

impeach Formally charging a government official with not fulfilling constitutional duties or with committing a high crime or misdemeanor.

impeachment The power of the House of Representatives to formally accuse the president (and other high-ranking officials, including the vice president and federal judges) of crimes.

implied powers The powers of the national government that are not enumerated in the Constitution but that Congress claims are necessary and proper for the national government to fulfill its enumerated powers in accordance with the necessary and proper clause of the Constitution.

impressment The forcible removal of merchant sailors from U.S. ships on the spurious grounds that the sailors were deserters from the British Navy.

income inequality The gap in the proportion of national income held by the richest compared to that held by the poorest.

incorporation The process by which the Bill of Rights' protections were applied to state governments.

incumbency The situation of already holding the office that is up for reelection.

independent Often used as a synonym for unaffiliated voter.

independent administrative agency An executive branch unit created by Congress and the president that is responsible for a narrowly defined function and whose governing board is intended to be protected from partisan politics.

independent expenditures Outlays by PACs and others, typically for advertising for or against a candidate, but uncoordinated with a candidate's campaign.

independent regulatory commission An executive branch unit responsible for developing standards of behavior within specific industries and businesses, monitoring compliance with these standards, and imposing sanctions on violators.

indirect democracy Sometimes called a *representative democracy;* a system in which citizens elect representatives who decide policies on behalf of their constituents.

inflation The decreased value of money as evidenced by increased prices.

information equilibrium The dissemination of information outside traditional channels of control.

infotainment News shows that combine entertainment and news, a hybrid of the words *information* and *entertainment.*

inherent characteristics Individual attributes such as race, national origin, religion, and sex.

inherent powers Presidential powers that are implied in the Constitution.

initiative A direct democracy process in which citizens draft a desired policy and get a state-specified number of signatures on a petition in support of the proposal so that it is placed on the ballot for voters to approve or reject.

in-kind assistance A benefit program in which the recipient shops for a service provider who will accept payment from the government for the service or item purchased.

inspectors general Political appointees who work within a government agency to ensure the integrity of public service by investigating allegations of misconduct by bureaucrats.

instant runoff election A special runoff election in which the computerized voting machine simulates the elimination of last-place voter-getters.

instructed delegate model A model of representation in which legislators, as representatives of their constituents, should vote in keeping with the constituents' views, even if those views contradict the legislator's personal views.

intelligent design The theory that the apparent design in the universe and in living things is the product of an intelligent cause rather than of an undirected process such as natural selection: its primary proponents believe that the designer is God and seek to redefine science to accept supernatural explanations.

interest groups Organizations that seek to achieve some of their goals by influencing government decision making.

intergovernmental lobbying Efforts by groups representing state and local governments to influence national domestic policy.

intergovernmental relations (IGR) The collaborative efforts of two or more levels of government working to serve the public.

International Monetary Fund (IMF) The institution charged with regulating monetary relationships among nations, including establishment of exchange rates for major world currencies; established in 1944 by the Bretton Woods Agreement.

interstate compacts Agreements between states that Congress has the authority to review and reject.

interventionism A foreign policy characterized by a nation's willingness to participate and intervene in international situations, including another country's affairs.

iron triangle The interaction of mutual interests among members of Congress, executive agencies, and organized interests during policy making.

isolationism A foreign policy characterized by a nation's unwillingness to participate in international affairs.

issue network The web of connections among those concerned about a policy and those who create and administer the policy.

J

Jim Crow laws Laws requiring the strict separation of racial groups, with whites and "nonwhites" required to attend separate schools, work in different jobs, and use segregated public accommodations, such as transportation and restaurants.

joint committee A bicameral committee composed of members of both chambers of Congress.

joint referral The practice, abolished in the 104th Congress, by which a bill could be referred to two different committees for consideration.

judicial activism An approach to judicial decision making whereby judges apply their authority to bring about specific social goals.

judicial restraint An approach to judicial decision making whereby judges defer to the democratically elected legislative and executive branches of government.

judicial review Court authority to determine that an action taken by any government official or governing body violates the Constitution.

judiciary The branch of government comprising the state and federal courts and the judges who preside over them.

jurisdiction The power of a court to hear a case and to resolve it, given to a court by either a constitution or a statute.

justice Any of the nine judges who sit on the Supreme Court.

K

Keynesian economics The theory that recommends that during a recession the national government should increase its spending and decrease taxes, and during a boom, it should cut spending and increase taxes.

L

laissez-faire The hands-off stance of a government in regard to the marketplace.

lead committee The primary committee considering a bill.

League of Nations A representative body founded in the aftermath of World War I to establish the collective security of nations.

legitimacy A quality conferred on government by citizens who believe that its exercise of power is right and proper.

***Lemon* test** A three-part test established by the Supreme Court in the 1971 case *Lemon v. Kurtzman* to determine whether government aid to parochial schools is constitutional; the test is also applied to other cases involving the establishment clause.

letter to the editor A letter in which a reader responds to a story in a newspaper, knowing that the letter might be published in that paper.

libel False written statements about someone else that harms their reputation.

liberalism An ideology that advocates change in the social, political, and economic realms to better protect the well-being of individuals and to produce equality within society.

libertarianism An ideology whose advocates believe that government should take a "hands off" approach in most matters.

liberty The most essential quality of American democracy; it is both the freedom from governmental interference in citizens' lives and the freedom to pursue happiness.

limited government Government that is restricted in what it can do so that the rights of the people are protected.

limited war A combatant country's self-imposed limitation on the tactics and strategy it uses, particularly its avoidance of the use of nuclear weapons.

line-item veto The power of the president to strike out specific line items on an appropriations bill while allowing the rest of the bill to become law; declared unconstitutional by the Supreme Court in 1997.

literacy test A test to determine eligibility to vote; designed so that few African Americans would pass.

litigation The process by which cases are brought and decided in the American legal system.

living wage A wage high enough to keep workers and their families out of poverty and to allow them to enjoy a basic living standard.

lobby The practice of communicating directly with policy makers on an interest group's behalf.

logrolling The practice of members of Congress agreeing to vote for a bill in exchange for their colleague's vote on another bill.

loyal opposition A role that the party out of power plays, highlighting its objections to policies and priorities of the government in power.

M

majority rule The idea that in a democracy, only policies with 50 percent plus one vote are enacted, and only candidates that win 50 percent plus one vote are elected.

majority whip A go-between with the majority leadership and party members in the House of Representatives.

majority-minority district A legislative district composed of a majority of a given minority community—say, African Americans—the intent of which is to make it likely that a member of that minority will be elected to Congress.

mandates Clauses in legislation that direct state and local governments to comply with national legislation and national standards.

mandatory spending Payment for debt and government programs for which the legislation that creates the program also obligates the government to spend the money necessary to meet the program's commitments as long as the program is in existence.

manifest destiny The idea that it was the United States' destiny to spread throughout the North American continent; used to rationalize the expansion of U.S. territory.

Marbury v. Madison The 1803 Supreme Court case that established the power of judicial review, which allows the Court to strike down laws passed by the other branches that it views to be in conflict with the Constitution.

margin of error Also called *sampling error;* a statistical calculation of the difference in results between a poll of the sample and a poll of the entire population.

market failure A condition in which competition for profits in the marketplace causes harms to society, such as environmental degradation, unsafe working conditions, and low pay.

marketplace of ideas A concept at the core of the freedoms of expression and press, based on the belief that true and free political discourse depends upon a free and unrestrained discussion of ideas.

markup The process by which the members of legislative committees "mark up" a bill with suggested language for changes and amendments.

Marshall Plan The U.S. government program that provided funds necessary for Western European countries to rebuild after World War II.

McCullogh v. Maryland The 1819 case that established that the necessary and proper clause justifies broad understandings of enumerated powers.

means-tested benefit A benefit for which eligibility is based on having an income below a specified amount, typically based on a percentage of the poverty guideline.

media consultant A professional who brings the campaign message to voters by creating handouts and all forms of media ads.

media segmentation The breaking down of the media according to the specific audiences they target.

median household income The middle of all household incomes—50 percent of households have incomes less than the median and 50 percent have incomes greater than the median.

merit A system of hiring and promotion based on an individual's competence.

merit-based civil service A personnel system in which bureaucrats are hired on the basis of the principles of competence, equal opportunity (open competition), and political neutrality; once hired, these public servants have job protection.

minority whip The go-between with the minority leadership, whose job mirrors that of the majority whip but without the power that comes from holding a majority in the House of Representatives.

***Miranda* rights** A criminal procedural rule, established in the 1966 case *Miranda v. Arizona,* requiring police to inform criminal suspects, on their arrest, of their legal rights, such as the right to remain silent and the right to counsel; these warnings must be read to suspects before interrogation.

monarchy A government in which a member of a royal family, usually a king or queen, has absolute authority over a territory and its government.

monetarism The theory that says the government's proper economic role is to control the rate of inflation by controlling the amount of money in circulation.

monetary policy The body of government policies, controlled by the Federal Reserve System, aimed at influencing the supply of money in the marketplace to maintain price stability.

Monroe Doctrine President James Monroe's 1823 declaration that the Americas should not be considered subjects for future colonization by any European power.

muckraking Criticism and exposés of corruption in government and industry by journalists at the turn of the twentieth century.

multilateral Many-sided; having the support of numerous nations.

mutual assured destruction (MAD) The doctrine that if one nation attacked another with nuclear weapons, the other would be capable of retaliating and would retaliate with such force as to assure mutual annihilation.

N

narrowcasting The practice of aiming media content at specific segments of the public.

national debt The total amount of money the government owes to others due to borrowing.

National Security Council (NSC) The arm of the Executive Office of the President that the president consults on matters of foreign policy and national security, consisting of top foreign policy advisers and relevant cabinet officials.

natural law The assertion that standards that govern human behavior are derived from the nature of humans themselves and can be universally applied.

natural rights (unalienable rights) The rights possessed by all humans as a gift from nature, or God, including the rights to life, liberty and the pursuit of happiness.

naturalization Becoming a citizen by means other than birth, as in the case of immigrants.

necessary and proper clause (elastic clause) A clause in Article I, section 8, of the Constitution that gives Congress the power to do whatever it deems necessary and constitutional to meet its enumerated obligations; the basis for the implied powers.

neoconservatism An ideology that advocates military over diplomatic solutions in foreign policy and is less concerned with restraining government activity in domestic politics than traditional conservatives.

Net neutrality The idea that Internet traffic—e-mail, Web site content, videos, and phone calls—should flow without interference or discrimination by those who own or run the Internet pipeline.

netroots The Internet-centered political efforts on behalf of candidates and causes.

New Deal Franklin Roosevelt's broad social welfare program, in which the government would bear the responsibility of providing a "safety net" to protect the weakest members of society.

New Deal coalition The group composed of southern Democrats, northern city dwellers, immigrants, the poor, Catholics, labor union members, blue-collar workers, African Americans, and women that elected FDR to the presidency four times.

New Jersey Plan The proposal presented by states with smaller populations at the Constitutional Convention in response to James Madison's Virginia Plan.

new judicial federalism The practice whereby state judges base decisions regarding civil rights and liberties on their state's constitution, rather than the U.S. Constitution, when their state's constitution guarantees more than minimum rights.

new media Cable television, the Internet, blogs, and satellite technology.

Nixon Doctrine The policy emphasizing the responsibility of U.S. allies to provide for their own national defense and security, aimed at improving relations with the communist nations, including the Soviet Union and China.

noncontributory program A benefit provided to a targeted population, paid for by a proportion of the money collected from all taxpayers.

nontariff trade barrier Business and social regulations and subsidies aimed at creating a competitive advantage in trade.

normal trade relations (NTR) status The international trade principle holding that the least restrictive trade conditions (best tariff rates) offered to any one national trading partner will be offered to every other nation in a trading network (also known as *most favored nations*).

North Atlantic Treaty Organization (NATO) An international mutual defense alliance formed in 1949 that created a structure for regional security for its fifteen member nations.

O

obscenity Indecent or offensive speech or expression.

Office of Management and Budget (OMB) The office that creates the president's annual budget.

office-block ballot A type of ballot that arranges all of the candidates for a particular office under the name of that office.

oligarchy A government in which an elite few hold power.

ombudsperson A role in which an elected or appointed leader acts as an advocate for citizens by listening to and investigating complaints against a government agency.

open primary A type of primary in which both parties' ballots are available in the voting booth, and the voters simply select one on which to register their preferences.

oral arguments The stage when appeals court judges or Supreme Court justices meet with the petitioner and the respondent to ask questions about the legal interpretations or information contained in their briefs.

ordinary scrutiny test The guidelines the courts used between 1873 and 1976 to determine the legality of sex-based discrimination; on the basis of this test, sex-based discrimination is legal if it is a reasonable means by which the government can achieve a legitimate public interest.

original jurisdiction The power of a court to hear a case first, before other courts have decided it.

outsourcing The situation in which the government signs contracts with private-sector employers to do work previously provided by government workers.

oversight The process by which the legislative branch "checks" the executive branch to ensure that the laws Congress has passed are being administered in keeping with legislators' intent.

P

party identifiers Individuals who identify themselves as a member of one party or the other.

party in government The partisan identifications of elected leaders in local, county, state, and federal government.

party in the electorate Individuals who identify with or tend to support a party.

party organization The formal party apparatus, including committees, party leaders, conventions, and workers.

party system The categorization of the number and competitiveness of political parties in a polity.

party-column ballot A ballot that organizes the candidates by political party.

patronage The system in which a party leader rewarded political supporters with jobs or government contracts in exchange for their support of the party.

penny press Newspapers that sold for a penny in the 1830s.

petitioner Also called *appellant;* the party seeking to have a lower court's decision reviewed by the Supreme Court under the Court's discretionary jurisdiction.

plaintiff The party bringing the case to court.

platform The formal statement of a party's principles and policy objectives.

Plessy v. Ferguson The 1896 Supreme Court ruling creating the separate but equal doctrine.

plum book A publication that lists the top jobs in the bureaucracy to which the president will appoint people via the patronage system.

pluralist theory A theory that holds that policy making is a competition among diverse interest groups that ensure the representation of individual interests.

pocket veto A special presidential veto of a bill passed at the conclusion of a legislative session, whereby the president waits ten days without signing the bill, and the bill dies.

police powers The states' reserved powers to protect the health, safety, lives, and properties of residents in a state.

political action committee (PAC) A group that raises and spends money in order to influence the outcome of an election.

political culture The people's collective beliefs and attitudes about government and political processes.

political engagement Citizen actions that are intended to solve public problems through political means.

political ideology An integrated system of ideas or beliefs about political values in general and the role of government in particular.

political machines Big-city organizations that exerted control over many aspects of life and lavishly rewarded supporters.

political party An organization that recruits, nominates, and elects party members to office in order to control the government.

political socialization The process by which we develop our political values and opinions.

politics The process of deciding who gets benefits in society and who is excluded from benefiting.

politics–administration dichotomy The concept that elected government officials, who are accountable to the voters, create and approve public policy, and then competent, politically neutral bureaucrats implement the public policy.

poll tax A fee for voting; levied to prevent poor African Americans in the South from voting.

pool memo A description written by Supreme Court clerks of the facts of a case filed with the Court, the pertinent legal arguments, and a recommendation as to whether the case should be taken.

popular sovereignty The theory that government is created by the people and depends on the people for the authority to rule.

population In a poll, the group of people whose opinions are of interest and/or about whom information is desired.

populism A philosophy supporting the rights and empowerment of the masses as opposed to elites.

pork barrel Legislators' appropriations of funds for special projects located within their congressional districts.

poverty The condition of lacking the income sufficient to purchase the necessities for an adequate living standard.

poverty guidelines A simplified version of the poverty thresholds developed each year by the Department of Health and Human Services; used to set financial eligibility criteria for benefits.

poverty rate The proportion of the population living below the poverty line as established by the national government.

poverty thresholds A set of income measures adjusted for family size that the Census Bureau establishes each year to define poverty for data collection purposes.

precedent Legal authority established by earlier cases.

preemption The constitutionally based principle that allows a national law to supersede state or local laws.

president pro tempore Also called *president pro tem;* theoretically, the chair of the Senate in the vice president's absence; in reality, an honorary title, with the senator of the majority party having the longest record of continuous service being elected to the position.

press secretary The president's spokesperson to the media.

preventive war The strategy of waging war on countries that are regarded as threatening in order to avoid future conflicts.

primal scream format Loud, angry argument characteristic of many television and radio talk shows.

primary election An election in which voters choose the party's candidates who will run in the later general election.

priming Bringing certain policies on issues to the public agenda through media coverage.

prior restraint A form of censorship by the government whereby it blocks the publication of news stories viewed as libelous or harmful.

privileges and immunities The Constitution's requirement that a state extend to other states' citizens the privileges and immunities it provides for its citizens.

progressive tax A tax that takes a larger percentage of the income of wealthier taxpayers and a smaller percentage of the income of lower-income taxpayers.

property Anything that can be owned.

proportional representation system An electoral structure in which political parties win the number of parliamentary seats equal to the percentage of the vote the party receives.

proportional (flat) tax A tax that takes the same percentage of each taxpayer's income.

proposition A proposed measure placed on the ballot in an initiative election.

prospective voting A method of evaluating candidates in which voters focus on candidates' positions on issues important to them and vote for the candidates who best represent their views.

prosumers Individuals who simultaneously consume information and news and produce information in forms like videos, blogs, and Web sites.

protectionist trade policy The establishment of trade barriers to protect domestic goods from foreign competition.

public agenda The public issues that most demand the attention of government officials.

public goods Services governments provide that are available to everyone, like clean air, clean water, airport security, and highways.

public opinion The public's expressed views about an issue at a specific point in time.

public opinion poll A survey of a given population's opinion on an issue or a candidate at a particular point in time.

pure capitalist economy The system whereby private individuals and companies own the modes of producing goods and services, and the government does not enact laws aimed at influencing the marketplace transactions that distribute these goods and services.

purposive incentives Motivation to join an interest group based on the belief in the group's cause from an ideological or a moral standpoint.

push polls A special type of poll that both provides information to campaigns about candidate strengths and weaknesses and attempts to skew public opinion about a candidate.

Q

quota sample A method by which pollsters structure a sample so that it is representative of the characteristics of the target population.

R

rally 'round the flag effect The peaks in presidential approval ratings during short term military action.

random sampling A scientific method of selection for a poll in which each member of the population has an equal chance at being included in the sample.

rational abstention thesis A theory that some individuals decide the costs of voting are not worth the effort when compared to the benefits.

rational choice theory The idea that from an economic perspective it is not rational for people to participate in collective action when they can secure the collective good without participating.

real income Earned income adjusted for inflation.

realignment A shift in party allegiances or electoral support.

reapportionment Reallocation of seats in the House of Representatives to each state based on changes in the state's population since the last census.

recall A direct democracy measure by which citizens can remove an elected official from office before the end of his or her term.

recession An economic downturn during which unemployment is high and the production of goods and services is low.

Reconstruction era The time after the Civil War between 1866 and 1877 when the institutions and infrastructure of the South were rebuilt.

redistricting The redrawing of congressional district boundaries within each state, based on the reapportionment from the census.

referendum A direct democracy measure that places public policy drafted by government officials on the ballot for voters to approve or reject.

regime change The replacement of a country's government with another government by facilitating the deposing of its leader or leading political party.

regional security alliance An alliance typically between a superpower and nations that are ideologically similar in a particular region.

regressive tax A tax that takes a greater percentage of the income of lower-income earners than of higher-income earners.

regulated capitalist economy (mixed economy) An economy in which the government enacts policies to influence the health of the economy.

regulatory law (administrative law) A law made by executive and regulatory agencies, often pursuant to a delegation of lawmaking power from Congress.

regulatory policies Policies that mandate individual and group (corporate) behaviors that foster the general welfare.

report A legislative committee's explanation to the full chamber of a bill and its intent.

republic A government that derives its authority from the people and in which citizens elect government officials to represent them in the processes by which laws are made; a representative democracy.

reserved powers The matters referred to in the Tenth Amendment over which states retain sovereignty.

respondent Also called *appellee;* the party opposing the hearing of a case on the Supreme Court's discretionary docket.

responsible party model Political scientists' view that a function of a party is to offer a clear choice to voters by establishing priorities or policy stances different from those of rival parties.

retrospective voting A method of evaluating candidates in which voters evaluate incumbent candidates and decide whether to support them based on their past performance.

right to privacy The right of an individual to be left alone and to make decisions freely, without the interference of others.

Roosevelt Corollary The idea advanced by President Theodore Roosevelt that the United States had the right to act as an "international police power" in the Western Hemisphere in order to ensure stability in the region.

Rule of Four The Supreme Court practice by which the Court will agree to hear a case that comes to it under its discretionary jurisdiction if four or more justices vote to hear it.

Rules Committee One of the most important committees in the House, which decides the length of debate and the scope of amendments that will be allowed on a bill.

run-off election A follow-up election that is held when no candidate receives the majority of votes cast in the original election.

safety net A collection of public policies ensuring that the basic physiological needs of citizens are met.

salient Having resonance, in relation to a voting issue, reflecting intense interest.

SALT I The treaty signed in 1972 by the United States and the Soviet Union limiting the two countries' antiballistic missiles and freezing the number of offensive missiles that each nation could have at the number they already possessed, plus the number they had under construction.

SALT II The treaty signed in 1979 by the United States and the Soviet Union that set an overall limit on strategic nuclear launchers, limited the number of missiles that could carry multiple independently targeted reentry vehicles (MIRVs) with nuclear warheads, and limited each nation to the development of only one new type of intercontinental ballistic missile (ICBM).

sampling error Also called *margin of error;* a statistical calculation of the difference in results between a poll of a randomly drawn sample and a poll of the entire population.

sanctions Penalties that halt economic relations.

select committee A congressional committee created to consider a specific policy issue or address a specific concern.

selective incorporation The process by which, over time, the Supreme Court applied those freedoms that served some fundamental principle of liberty or justice to the states, thus rejecting total incorporation.

Senate majority leader The most powerful position in the Senate; the majority leader manages the legislative process and schedules debate on legislation.

Senate minority leader The leader of the minority party in the Senate, who works with the majority leader in negotiating legislation.

senatorial courtesy A custom that allows senators from the president's political party to veto the president's choice of federal district court judge in the senator's state.

senior executive service (SES) A unique personnel system for top managerial, supervisory, and policy positions offering less job security but higher pay than the merit-based civil service system.

seniority system The system in which the member with the longest continuous tenure on a standing committee is given preference when the committee chooses its chair.

separate but equal doctrine Established by the Supreme Court in *Plessy v. Ferguson;* it says that separate but equal facilities for whites and non-whites do not violate the Fourteenth Amendment's equal protection clause.

separation of powers The Constitution's delegation of authority for the primary governing functions among three branches of government so that no one group of government officials controls all the governing functions.

shadow bureaucrats People hired and paid by private for-profit and nonprofit organizations that implement public policy through a government contract.

signing statement A written message that the president issues upon signing a bill into law.

single-issue groups Groups that focus on one issue.

slander False verbal statements about others that harm their reputation.

social capital The ways in which our lives are improved in many ways by social connections.

social contract An agreement between the people and their leaders in which the people agree to give up some liberties so that their other liberties are protected.

social contract theory The idea that individuals possess free will, and every individual is equally endowed with the God-given right of self-determination and the ability to consent to be governed.

social movement The organized action of a broad segment of society to demand and effect improvement in the treatment of a specific group.

social regulation The government rules and regulations aimed at protecting workers, consumers, and the environment from market failure.

socialism An ideology that advocates economic equality, theoretically achieved by having the government or workers own the means of production (businesses and industry).

soft money loophole The Supreme Court's interpretation of campaign finance law that enabled political parties to raise unlimited funds for party-building activities such as voter registration drives and get-out-the-vote (GOTV) efforts.

soft news Events or topics that are not serious or broadly important.

solidary incentives The motivation to join an interest group based on the companionship and the satisfaction derived from socializing with others that it offers.

sound bites Short audio or video clips taken from a larger speech.

Southeast Asia Treaty Organization (SEATO) A regional security agreement whose goal was to prevent communist encroachment in the countries of Southeast Asia.

sovereignty Having ultimate authority to govern, with no legal superior.

Speaker of the House The leader of the House of Representatives, chosen by the majority party.

spoils system The practice of rewarding political supporters with jobs.

standing committee A permanent committee in Congress, with a defined legislative jurisdiction.

standing to sue The ability to bring lawsuits in court.

stare decisis From the Latin "let the decision stand," the principle that binds judges to rely upon the holdings of past judges in deciding cases.

statute A law enacted by Congress and the state legislatures to deal with particular issues or problems, sometimes more detailed and comprehensive than the common law.

statutory powers Powers explicitly granted to presidents by congressional action.

steering The practice by which realtors steered African American families to certain neighborhoods and white families to others.

strategic arms limitation talks (SALT talks) Discussions between the United States and the Soviet Union in the 1970s that focused on cooling down the nuclear arms race between the two superpowers.

strategic arms reduction talks (START talks) Talks between the United States and the Soviet Union in which reductions in missiles and nuclear warheads, not merely a limitation on increases, were negotiated.

strategic defense initiative (SDI, or "Star Wars") A ballistic missile defense system advocated by President Ronald Reagan.

stratified sampling A process of random sampling in which the national population is divided into fourths and representative counties and metropolitan statistical areas are selected as representative of the national population.

straw poll A poll conducted in an unscientific manner, used to predict election outcomes.

strict scrutiny test Guidelines the courts use to determine the legality of all but sex-based discrimination; on the basis of this test, discrimination is legal if it is a necessary means by which the government can achieve a compelling public interest.

subcommittee A subordinate committee in Congress that typically handles specific areas of a standing committee's jurisdiction.

subsidy A tax break or other kind of financial support that encourages business expansion or decreases the cost of doing business so that businesses can be more competitive.

sunset clause A clause in legislation that sets an expiration date for the authorized program/policy unless Congress reauthorizes it.

sunshine laws Legislation that opens up government functions and documents to the public.

Super Tuesday The Tuesday in early March on which the most primary elections are held, many of them in southern states; provided the basis for Super-Duper Tuesday in 2008.

superpowers Leader nations with dominating influence in international affairs.

supply-side economics The theory that advocates cutting taxes and deregulating business to stimulate the economy.

supremacy clause The paragraph in Article VI that makes the Constitution, and the treaties and laws created in compliance with it, the supreme law of the land.

supreme law of the land The U.S. Constitution's description of its own authority, meaning that all laws made by governments within the United States must be in compliance with the Constitution.

suspect classifications Distinctions based on race, religion, national origin, and sex, which are assumed to be illegitimate.

symbolic representation The attempt to ensure that the Supreme Court is representative of major demographic groups, such as women, African Americans, Jews, and Catholics.

symbolic speech Nonverbal "speech" in the form of an action such as picketing, flag burning, or wearing an armband to signify a protest.

T

take care clause The constitutional basis for inherent powers, which states that the president "shall take Care that the Laws be faithfully executed."

talk radio A format featuring conversations and interviews about topics of interest, along with call-ins from listeners.

tariff A special tax on imported goods.

tax base The overall wealth (income and assets of citizens and corporations) that the government can tax in order to raise revenue.

tax expenditures (Also, *tax breaks* or *loopholes*) Government financial supports that allow individuals and corporations to pay reduced taxes, to encourage behaviors that foster the public good.

telegenic Looks good on TV.

third party A party organized in opposition or as an alternative to the existing parties in a two-party system.

Three-Fifths Compromise The negotiated agreement by the delegates to the Constitutional Convention to count each slave as three-fifths a free man for the purpose of representation and taxes.

ticket splitting The situation in which voters vote for candidates from more than one party.

time, place, and manner restrictions Regulations regarding when, where, or how expression may occur; must be content neutral.

tort A wrongful act involving a personal injury or harm to one's property or reputation.

total incorporation The theory that the Fourteenth Amendment's due process clause requires the states to uphold all freedoms in the Bill of Rights; rejected by the Supreme Court in favor of selective incorporation.

totalitarianism A system of government in which the government essentially controls every aspect of people's lives.

tracking polls Polls that measure changes in public opinion over the course of days, weeks, or months by repeatedly asking respondents the same questions and measuring changes in their responses.

trade deficit Aa negative balance of trade in which imports exceed exports.

trade policy A collection of tax laws and regulations that supports the country's international commerce.

trial court The court in which a case is first heard and that determines the facts of a case.

Truman Doctrine Articulated by President Harry Truman, a foreign policy commitment by the United States to assist countries' efforts to resist communism in the Cold War era.

trustee model A model of representation in which a member of the House or Senate should articulate and vote for the position that best represents the views of constituents.

turnout rate The proportion of eligible voters who actually voted.

U

umbrella organizations Interest groups that represent collective groups of industries or corporations.

unanimous consent An agreement by every senator to the terms of debate on a given piece of legislation.

unicameral A legislative body with a single chamber.

unitary system A governmental structure in which one central government has sovereignty, although it may create regional governments to which it delegates responsibilities.

United Nations (UN) Established in 1945, an international body whose founders hoped would develop the capacity to prevent future wars by achieving collective security and peace.

U.S. Code A compilation of all the laws passed by the U.S. Congress.

U.S. Supreme Court High court with a limited original jurisdiction whose decisions may not be appealed; it serves as the court of last resort in the U.S. judiciary.

V

vblog A video blog.

V-chip Required by the Telecommunications Act of 1996, a computer chip in television sets that lets parents block programming they consider unsuitable for children.

veto An executive power held by the president, who can reject a bill and return it to Congress with reasons for the rejection.

Virginia Plan James Madison's proposal at the Constitutional Conversation for a new governmental stracture, which favored states with larger populations.

voter fatigue The condition in which voters grow tired of all candidates by the time election day arrives, and may thus be less likely to vote.

W

War Powers Act A law limiting presidential use of military forces to sixty days, with an automatic extension of thirty additional days if the president requests such an extension.

Warsaw Pact A regional security structure formed in 1955 by the Soviet Union and its seven satellite states in Eastern Europe in response to the creation of the North Atlantic Treaty Organization (NATO).

Watergate During the Nixon administration, a scandal involving burglaries and the subsequent cover-up by high-level administration officials.

weapons of mass destruction (WMDs) Nuclear, chemical, and biological weapons.

whistle-blower A civil servant who discloses mismanagement, fraud, waste, corruption, and/or threats to public health and safety to the government.

White House counsel The president's lawyer.

White House Office (WHO) The office that develops policies and protects the president's legal and political interests.

white primary A primary election in which a party's nominees for general election were chosen but in which only white people were allowed to vote.

winner-take-all An electoral system in which the candidate who receives the most votes wins that office, even if that total is not a majority.

Works Progress Administration (WPA) A New Deal program that would employ 8.5 million people at a cost of more than $11 million between 1935 and 1943.

World Bank The international financial institution created by the Bretton Woods Agreement of 1944 and charged with lending money to nations in need.

World Trade Organization (WTO) The organization created in 1995 to negotiate, implement, and enforce international trade agreements.

writ of *certiorari* Latin for "a request to make certain"; this is an order to a lower court to produce a certified record of a case so that the appellate court can determine whether any errors occurred during trial that warrant review of the case.

Y

yellow journalism An irresponsible, sensationalist approach to news reporting, so named after the yellow ink used in the "Yellow Kid" cartoons in the *New York World*.

REFERENCES

CHAPTER 1

1. Rogers Smith, *Civic Ideals: Conflicting Visions of Citizenship in U.S. History* (New Haven, CT: Yale University Press, 1997).
2. Robert A. Dahl, *Who Governs? Democracy and Power in an American City* (New Haven, CT: Yale University Press, 1961).
3. E. E. Schattschneider, *The Semi-Sovereign People* (New York: Holt, Rinehart & Winston, 1960).
4. E. J. Dionne Jr., *Why Americans Hate Politics: The Death of the Democratic Process,* 2nd ed. (New York: Touchstone, 1992).
5. Gallup Poll, "Trust in Government," www.gallup.com/poll/5392/Trust-Government.aspx.
6. Institute of Politics at Harvard University, "Attitudes Towards Politics and Public Service: A National Survey of College Undergraduates," April 11–20, 2000, www.iop.harvard.edu/pdfs/survey/2000.pdf.
7. Ibid.
8. Ibid.
9. Ibid.
10. Barbara Roswell, "From Service-Learning to Service Politics: A Conversation with Rick Battistoni," http://reflectionsjournal.org/Articles/V3.N1.Battistoni.Rick.Roswell.Barbara.pdf.
11. S. E. Finer, *The History of Government,* 3 vols. (London: Oxford University Press, 1997).
12. Martin A. Reddish, *The Constitution as Political Structure* (London: Oxford University Press, 1995).
13. Theodore Sky, *To Provide for the General Welfare: A History of the Federal Spending Power* (Newark: University of Delaware Press, 2003).
14. David Epstein, *The Political Theory of the Federalist* (Chicago: University of Chicago Press, 1984).
15. Thomas Hobbes, *Leviathan* (1651; New York: Oxford University Press, 1996), chap. 14.
16. *New York Times,* "America Enduring," September 11, 2002, http://query.nytimes.com/gst/fullpage.html?res=9A00E0DE1431F932A2575AC0A9649C8B63&scp=1&sq=america+enduring&st=nyt.
17. Oscar Handlin and Mary Handlin, *The Dimensions of Liberty* (Cambridge, MA: Harvard University Press, 1961).
18. Richard Labunski, *James Madison and the Struggle for the Bill of Rights* (London: Oxford University Press, 2006).
19. Jack N. Rakove, *Original Meanings: Politics and Ideas in the Making of the Constitution* (New York: Knopf, 1996).
20. Ira Katznelson and Martin Shefter, eds., *Shaped by War and Trade: International Influences on American Political Development* (Princeton, NJ: Princeton University Press, 2002).
21. *Wing Hing v. City of Eureka* (Calif.), 1886.
22. Clyde W. Barrow, *Critical Theories of the State: Marxist, Neo-Marxist, Post-Marxist* (Madison: University of Wisconsin Press, 1993).
23. Seymour Martin Lipset and Gary Marks, *It Didn't Happen Here: Why Socialism Failed in the United States* (New York: Norton, 2001).
24. Giovanni Sartori and Peter Mair, *Parties and Party Systems: A Framework for Analysis* (Oxford: European Consortium for Political Research).
25. Michael Delli Carpini, Director Pew Charitable Trusts, www.apa.org/ed/slce/civicengagement.html.

CHAPTER 2

1. Charles Hulse, "Filibuster Fight Nears Showdown," *New York Times,* May 8, 2005.
2. Charlie Savage, "Obama Issues Signing Statement with Public Lands Bill," *New York Times,* March 30, 2009.
3. Quoted in Katherine Seelye, "Clinton Backer Points to Electoral College Votes as New Measure," *New York Times,* March 25, 2008.
4. www.u-s-history.com/pages/h1211.html.
5. www.yale.edu/lawweb/avalon/amerrev/parliament/stamp_act_1765.htm.
6. www.historyplace.com/unitedstates/revolution/rev-prel.htm.
7. J. Alan Rogers, "Colonial Opposition to the Quartering of Troops During the French and Indian War," *Military Affairs* (1970): 7.
8. www.manhattanrarebooks-history.com/declaratory_act.htm.
9. http://ahp.gatech.edu/townshend_act_1767.html.
10. Russell Bourne, *Cradle of Violence: How Boston's Waterfront Mobs Ignited the American Revolution* (Hoboken, NJ: Wiley, 2006).
11. www.u-s-history.com/pages/h675.html.
12. C. Brian Kelly, *Best Little Stories from the American Revolution* (Nashville, TN: Cumberland House, 1999).
13. www.bostonteapartyship.com/.
14. www.ushistory.org/declaration/related/intolerable.htm.
15. www.yale.edu/lawweb/avalon/resolves.htm.
16. For further discussion of the impact of *Common Sense* on colonial attitudes and beliefs, see Edmund S. Morgan, *The Birth of the Republic: 1763–89* (Chicago: University of Chicago Press, 1992), 71–76.
17. www.geocities.com/presfacts/8/lee.html.

18. Council of State Governments, *The Book of the States* (Lexington, KY: Author, 2004), 10–11.
19. Charles Beard, *An Economic Interpretation of the Constitution of the United States* (New York: Macmillan, 1913).
20. www.usconstitution.net/consttop_ccon.html.
21. www.africanaonline.com/slavery_timeline.htm.
22. Alexander Hamilton, "Federalist No. 9," *The Federalist Papers* (Cutchogue, NY: Buccaneer Books, 1992), 37.
23. James Madison, "Federalist No. 51," *The Federalist Papers* (Cutchogue, NY: Buccaneer Books, 1992), 261–65.
24. James Madison, "Federalist No. 10," *The Federalist Papers* (Cutchogue, NY: Buccaneer Books, 1992), 42–49.
25. Alexander Hamilton, "Federalist No. 84," *The Federalist Papers* (Cutchogue, NY: Buccaneer Books, 1992), 436–37.
26. Thomas Jefferson, Letter to James Madison on the Bill of Rights debate, March 15, 1789. Courtesy of Eigen's Political & Historical Quotations.
27. John P. Roche, "The Founding Fathers: A Reform Caucus in Action," *American Political Science Review*, LV (1961).
28. Alexander Hamilton, "Federalist No. 78," *The Federalist Papers* (Cutchogue, NY: Buccaneer Books, 1992), 395–96.
29. Courtesy of Eigen's Political and Historical Quotations, www.politicalquotes.org/Quotedisplay .aspx?DocID=22447.
30. Larry Sabato, *A More Perfect Constitution: 23 Proposals to Revitalize Our Constitution and Make America a Fairer Country* (New York: Walker, 2007).
31. *Plessy v. Ferguson*, 163 U.S. 537 (1896).
32. *Brown v. Board of Education*, 347 U.S. 483 (1954).
33. Thomas Marshall, "Representing Public Opinion: American Courts and the Appeals Process," *Politics and Policy* 31, no. 4 (December 2003): 726–39.

CHAPTER 3

1. Kendra A. Hovey and Harold A. Hovey, *CQ's State Fact Finder: 2007* (Washington, DC: CQ Press, 2007), 220.
2. *Marbury v. Madison*, 5 U.S. 137 (1803).
3. Joe R. Feagin and Clairece Booher Feagin, *Racial and Ethnic Relations*, 7th ed. (Upper Saddle River, NJ: Prentice-Hall, 2003), 131.
4. Dennis L. Dresang and James J. Gosling, *Politics and Policy in American States and Communities*, 4th ed. (New York: Pearson Longman, 2004), 88.
5. *McCulloch v. Maryland*, 17 U.S. 316 (1819).
6. *Gibbons v. Ogden*, 22 U.S. 1 (1824).
7. *United States v. Lopez*, 514 U.S. 549 (1995).
8. www.oyez.org/cases/1990-1999/1994/1994_93_ 1260/.
9. *Helvering v. Davis*, 301 U.S. 619 (1937).
10. CNN, *CNN Reports: Katrina—State of Emergency* (Kansas City, KS: Andrews McMeel, 2005), 10.
11. Ibid., 11.
12. Ibid., 16.
13. Ibid., 176.
14. *Pruneyard Shopping Center & Fred Sahadi v. Michael Robins et al.*, 447 U.S. 74, 100 S. Ct. 2035 (1980).

15. David B. Walker, *The Rebirth of Federalism*, 2nd ed. (New York: Chatham House, 2000).
16. *National League of Cities v. Usery*, 426 U.S. 833 (1976).
17. *Garcia v. San Antonio Transportation Authority*, 469 U.S. 528 (1985).
18. *United States v. Oakland Cannabis Buyers' Cooperative*, 532 U.S. 483 (2001).
19. www.drugpolicy.org/marijuana/medical/challenges/ cases/conant/.
20. *Raich v. Gonzales*, 545 U.S. 1 (2005).
21. *Bush v. Gore*, 531 U.S. 98 (2000).
22. See, for example, David B. Walker, *The Rebirth of Federalism*.
23. *Massachusetts v. Mellon*, 262 U.S. 447 (1923).
24. *South Dakota v. Dole*, 483 U.S. 208 (1987).
25. U.S. Census Bureau, *Statistical Abstract of the United States 2006*, Table 421.

CHAPTER 4

1. Stephen L. Carter, *The Dissent of the Governed: Law, Religion, and Loyalty* (Cambridge, MA: Harvard University Press, 1998).
2. For an accessible and lively account of the central role of liberty in the American Revolution, see Thomas Fleming, *Liberty! The American Revolution* (New York: Viking, 1997).
3. For a history of civil liberties in wartime, see Geoffrey R. Stone, *Perilous Times: Free Speech in Wartime from the Sedition Act of 1798 to the War on Terrorism* (New York: Norton, 2004).
4. *Barron v. Baltimore*, 32 U.S. 243 (1833).
5. See *Hurtado v. California*, 110 U.S. 516 (1884), and *Turning v. New Jersey*, 211 U.S. 78 (1908), for a discussion of the standard the Court uses to determine whether a particular liberty should be incorporated into the Fourteenth Amendment.
6. *Gitlow v. New York*, 268 U.S. 652 (1925).
7. *Near v. Minnesota*, 283 U.S. 697 (1931).
8. *Palko v. Connecticut*, 302 U.S. 319 (1937).
9. Presidential Proclamation of September 24, 1862, by President Abraham Lincoln, suspending the writ of habeas corpus.
10. For two detailed accounts of the acts, see John C. Miller, *Crisis in Freedom: The Alien and Sedition Acts* (Boston: Little, Brown, 1951), and James Morton Smith, *Freedom's Fetters: The Alien and Sedition Laws and American Civil Liberties* (Ithaca, NY: Cornell University Press, 1956).
11. Ron Fournier, "Bush Orders Terrorist Trials by Military Tribunals," Associated Press, November 13, 2001. Executive order available at www.whitehouse.gov/ news/releases/releases/2001/11/20011113-27.html.
12. *Schenck v. United States*, 249 U.S. 47 (1919).
13. *Gitlow v. New York*.
14. *Dennis v. U.S.*, 341 U.S. 494 (1951).
15. *Brandenburg v. Ohio*, 395 U.S. 444 (1969).
16. *U.S. v. O'Brien*, 391 U.S. 367.
17. *Tinker et al. v. Des Moines Independent Community School District et al.*, 393 U.S. 503 (1969).
18. For a discussion of *Tinker* and similar cases, see Jamin B. Baskin, *We the Students: Supreme Court Cases for and About Students* (Washington, DC: CQ Press, 2000).

19. *Texas v. Johnson,* 491 U.S. 397 (1989).
20. *U.S. v. Eichman,* 496 U.S. 310 (1990).
21. *Miller v. California,* 413 U.S. 15 (1973).
22. *Chaplinsky v. New Hampshire,* 315 U.S. 568 (1942).
23. *New York Times v. U.S.,* 403 U.S. 713 (1971).
24. www.gallup.com/poll/1690/Religion.aspx.
25. The phrase "wall of separation" First appeared in Thomas Jefferson's 1802 letter to the Danbury Baptist Association. This letter is available at the Library of Congress Web site: www.loc.gov/loc/lcib/9806/danpre.html.
26. For a discussion of the doctrine of accommodationism, see Kenneth D. Wald, *Religion and Politics in the United States,* 3rd ed. (Washington, DC: CQ Press, 1997). For a discussion of neutrality, see Robert Booth Fowler, Allen D. Hertzke, and Laura R. Olson, *Religion and Politics in America: Faith, Culture, & Strategic Choices,* 2nd ed. (Boulder, CO: Westview Press, 1999).
27. *Everson v. Board of Education,* 330 U.S. 1 (1947).
28. *Lemon v. Kurtzman,* 403 U.S. 602 (1971).
29. *Zelman v. Simmons-Harris,* 539 U.S. 639 (2002).
30. *Engel v. Vitale,* 370 U.S. 421 (1962).
31. See, for example, the U.S. District Court ruling in *Tammy Kitzmiller et al. v. Dover Area School District et al.,* 400 F. Supp. 2d 707 (M.D. Pa. 2005).
32. *Prince v. Massachusetts,* 321 U.S. 158 (1944).
33. *Employment Division, Department of Human Resources of the State of Oregon et al. v. Smith,* 494 U.S. 872 (1990).
34. *Griswold v. Connecticut,* 381 U.S. 479 (1965).
35. *Roberts v. U.S. Jaycees,* 468 U.S. 609 (1984).
36. *Roe v. Wade,* 410 U.S. 113 (1973).
37. *Planned Parenthood v. Casey,* 505 U.S. 833 (1992).
38. *Bowers v. Hardwick,* 478 U.S. 186 (1986).
39. *Lawrence v. Texas,* 539 U.S. 558 (2003).
40. This is a point of agreement among the Court's opinion, the concurring opinion, and the dissenting opinion issued in *Lawrence v. Texas,* 539 U.S. 558 (2003).
41. *Weeks v. U.S.,* 232 U.S. 383 (1914).
42. *Mapp v. Ohio,* 367 U.S. 643 (1961).
43. See Chief Justice Warren E. Burger's dissent in *Coolidge v. New Hampshire,* 403 U.S. 443.
44. *Segura v. U.S.,* 468 U.S. 796 (1984).
45. *U.S. v. Leon,* 468 U.S. 897 (1984).
46. *California v. Greenwood,* 486 U.S. 35 (1988).
47. *Miranda v. Arizona,* 384 U.S. 436 (1966).
48. *Gideon v. Wainwright,* 312 U.S. 335 (1963).
49. *Furman v. Georgia,* 408 U.S. 238 (1972).
50. The de facto moratorium on the death penalty ended in 1976 in a series of cases starting with *Gregg v. Georgia,* 428 U.S. 153 (1976).
51. *Baze v. Rees,* 553 U.S. _____ (2008).
52. *Wilkerson v. Utah,* 99 U.S. 130 (1878).
53. For a strong argument against gun control, see John R. Lott Jr., *More Guns, Less Crime: Understanding Crime and Gun Control Laws* (Chicago: University of Chicago Press, 1998).
54. For a detailed look at different historical interpretations of the Second Amendment, see Carl T. Bogus, ed., *The Second Amendment in Law and History: Historians and Constitutional Scholars on the Right to Bear Arms* (New York: New Press, 2000).
55. For an articulation of this argument, see Carl T. Bogus, "What Does the Second Amendment Restrict? A Collective Rights Analysis," *Constitutional Commentary* 18, no. 3 (Winter 2001): 485–516.
56. *District of Columbia v. Heller,* 554 U.S. (2008).
57. www.millionmommarch.org.
58. http://2asisters.org.
59. For a recent report, see ACLU, "History Repeated: The Dangers of Domestic Spying by Federal Law Enforcement," May 29, 2007, www.aclu.org/images/asset_upload_file893_29902.pdf.
60. ACLU, "No Real Threat: The Pentagon's Secret Database on Peaceful Protest," January 17, 2007, available at www.aclu.org/safe-free/spyfiles/27988pub20070117.html.
61. Jo Mannies, "Ashcroft Defends Bush on Spying," St. Louis *Post-Dispatch,* February 10, 2008.
62. The full text of the law (H.R. 3162) is the Uniting and Strengthening America by Providing Appropriate Tools Required to Intercept and Obstruct Terrorism (USA PATRIOT) Act of 2001.
63. Protect America Act of 2007 (Pub.L. 110-55, S. 1927) signed into law by George W. Bush on August 5, 2007.
64. For an articulation of this argument, see Charles Krauthammer, "The Truth About Torture," *The Weekly Standard,* December 5, 2005.
65. For an articulation of this viewpoint, see Andrew Sullivan, "The Abolition of Torture," *New Republic,* December 19, 2005.
66. The full text of the Detainee Treatment Act of 2005 (H.R. 2863, Title X) is available at http://thomas.loc.gov/cgi-bin/query/R?r109:FLD001:S10909.
67. The full text of a statement delivered by Condoleezza Rice, the former U.S. secretary of state, at Andrews Air Force base in Maryland is available at www.timesonline.co.uk/tol/news/world/us_and_americas/article745995.ece.
68. European Parliament report, January 22, 2006, "Alleged Secret Detentions and Unlawful Inter-State Transfers Involving Council of Europe Member States."
69. David A. Harris, "'Flying While Arab,' Immigration Issues, and Lessons from the Racial Profiling Controversy," testimony before the U.S. Commission on Civil Rights (October 12, 2001).
70. OMB Watch, "Muslim Charities and the War on Terror: Top Ten Concerns and Status Update," revised March 2006, available at www.ombwatch.org//npadv/PDF/MuslimCharitiesTopTenUpdated.pdf.

CHAPTER 5

1. Rolan J. Pennock, "Rights, Natural Rights, and Human Rights—A General View," in *Human Rights,* eds. J. R. Pennock and J. W. Chapman (New York: New York University Press, 1981).
2. Raoul Berger, *Government by Judiciary: The Transformation of the Fourteenth Amendment* (Cambridge, MA: Harvard University Press, 1977).
3. Donald E. Lively, *The Constitution and Race* (New York: Praeger, 1992).
4. John Hope Franklin, *From Slavery to Freedom,* 7th ed. (New York: McGraw-Hill, 1994).
5. *Dred Scott v. Sandford,* 60 U.S. 393 (1857).

6. *Plessy v. Ferguson,* 163 U.S. 537 (1896).
7. George T. Blakey, *Hard Times and New Deal in Kentucky, 1929–1939* (Lexington: University of Kentucky Press, 1986).
8. Richard Kluger, *Simple Justice: The History of* Brown v. Board of Education *and Black America's Struggle for Equality* (New York: Knopf, 1976).
9. Raymond Wolters, *The Burden of Brown: Thirty Years of School Desegregation* (Knoxville: University of Tennessee Press, 1984).
10. Jo Ann Robinson, *The Montgomery Bus Boycott and the Women Who Started It* (Knoxville: University of Tennessee Press, 1987).
11. Taylor Branch, *Parting the Waters: America During the King Years, 1954–1963* (New York: Simon & Schuster, 1988).
12. *Browder v. Gale,* 142 F. Supp. 707 (1956).
13. John Lewis, *Walking with the Wind: A Memoir of the Movement* (New York: Simon & Schuster, 1998).
14. David J. Garrow, *Protest at Selma: Martin Luther King, Jr., and the Voting Rights Act of 1965* (New Haven, CT: Yale University Press, 1978).
15. Taylor Branch, *Pillar of Fire: America in the King Years 1963–65* (New York: Simon & Schuster, 1998).
16. Stokely Carmichael, "What We Want," *New York Review of Books,* September 22, 1966: 5–7.
17. Stokely Carmichael and Mike Thelwell, "Toward Black Liberation," *Massachusetts Review* 7 (1966): 639–51.
18. Steven Lawson, *Black Ballots: Voting Rights in the South, 1944–1969* (New York: Columbia University Press, 1976).
19. www.census.gov/prod/2001pubs/statab/sec08.pdf.
20. *Bradwell v. Illinois,* 83 U.S. 130 (1873).
21. *Minor v. Happersett,* 88 U.S. 162 (1875).
22. www.now.org/history/purpos66.html.
23. *Reed v. Reed,* 404 U.S. 71 (1971).
24. *Craig v. Boren,* 429 U.S. 190 (1976).
25. Joe R. Feagin and Clairece Booher Feagin, *Racial and Ethnic Relations* (Upper Saddle River, NJ: Prentice-Hall, 2003), 135.
26. Ibid., 149.
27. Ibid.
28. www.reuters.com/articlePrint?articleId=USN3061 859320080131.
29. Mark Hugo Lopez and Paul Taylor, "Dissecting the 2008 Electorate: Most Diverse in U.S. History," (Washington, DC: Pew Research Center, 2009), http://pewhispanic.org/reports/report.php?ReportID=108.
30. www.lulac.org/about/history.html.
31. Ibid.
32. *Mendez v. Westminister,* 64 F. Supp. 544 (1946).
33. Feagin and Feagin, *Racial and Ethnic Relations,* 218.
34. *Corpus Christi Independent School District v. Cisneros,* 404 U.S. 1211 (1971).
35. Texas State Historical Association, "The Handbook of Texas Online," www.tshaonline.org/handbook/online/articles/CC/jrc2.html.
36. U.S. Census Bureau, "Voting and Registration in the Election of November 2004," Table 8, www.census.gov/prod/2006pubs/p20-556.pdf.
37. Feagin and Feagin, *Racial and Ethnic Relations,* 278 and 310.

38. Ibid., 315.
39. *Sutton v. United Airlines,* 527 U.S. 471 (1999); *Murphy v. United Parcel Service, Inc.,* 527 U.S. 516 (1999).
40. *Bowers v. Hardwick,* 478 U.S. 186 (1986).
41. *Lawrence v. Texas,* 539 U.S. 558 (2003).
42. www.lambdalegal.org/our-work/publications/facts-backgrounds/recent-lgbt-advances. html.
43. *Romer v. Evans,* 517 U.S. 620 (1996).
44. *Regents of the University of California v. Bakke,* 438 U.S. 265 (1978).
45. Ward Connerly, "College Admissions, Let's Not Break the Law," 2007, www.acri.org/chairman.html.
46. www.acri.org/.
47. *Grutter v. Bollinger,* 539 U.S. 306 (2003).
48. *Parents Involved in Community Schools v. Seattle School District No. 1 et al.,* 551 U.S. _____ (2007), and *Meredith v. Jefferson County Board of Education,* 551 U.S. ____ (2007).

CHAPTER 6

1. Steven Pinker, *How the Mind Works* (New York: Norton, 1997), viii.
2. Aaron Nelson, "Update: Kids Tell Adults to 'Go Vote,'" *The Brownsville Herald,* November 7, 2006.
3. V. O. Key Jr., *Public Opinion and American Democracy* (New York: Knopf, 1961), 8.
4. Mark Hugo Lopez, Peter Levine, Deborah Both, Abby Kiesa, Emily Kirby, and Karlo Marcelo, *The 2006 Civic and Political Health of the Nation: A Detailed Look at How Youth Participate in Politics and Communities* (College Park, MD: Circle: The Center for Information and Research on Civic Learning and Engagement, 2006), 4.
5. Ibid.
6. Sidney Verba, Kay Lehman Schlozman, and Henry E. Brady, *Voice and Equality: Civic Voluntarism in American Politics* (Cambridge, MA: Harvard University Press, 1995), 439.
7. Frank Newport, "Clinton Has Edge Among Highly Religious White Democrats," The Gallup Organization, February 22, 2008, www.gallup.com/poll/104506/Clinton-Has-Edge-Among-Highly-Religious-White-Democrats.aspx.
8. Frank Newport, "Most in U.S. Want Healthcare Reform, but Vary on Urgency," July 24, 2009, http://www.gallup.com/poll/121883/Most-U.S.-Want-Healthcare-Reform-Vary-Urgency.aspx.
9. David L. Leal, Matt A. Barreto, Jongho Lee, and Rodolfo O. de la Garza, "The Latino Vote in the 2004 Election," *PS: Political Science and Politics* (2005): 46.
10. Joseph Carroll, "Only 11% of Blacks Satisfied with State of the Nation Right Now," www.galluppoll.com/content/?ci=28039&pg=1.
11. Lopez et al., *The 2006 Civic and Political Health of the Nation,* 20–21.
12. Karlo Barrios Marcelo, Mark Hugo Lopez, and Emily Hoban Kirby, *Civic Engagement Among Young Men and Women* (College Park, MD: Circle: The Center for Information and Research on Civic Learning and Engagement, 2007), 12.
13. David W. Moore, "Death Penalty Gets Less Support from Britons, Canadians Than Americans," Gallup News Service, February 20, 2006.

14. Elisabeth Noelle-Neumann, *The Spiral of Silence: Public Opinion—Our Social Skin,* 2nd ed. (Chicago: University of Chicago Press, 1993).
15. Susan Herbst, *Numbered Voices: How Opinion Polling Has Shaped American Politics* (Chicago: University of Chicago Press, 1993).
16. Robert S. Erikson, Gerald C. Wright, and John P. McIver, *Statehouse Democracy: Public Opinion and Policy in the American States* (New York: Cambridge University Press, 1994).
17. Walter Lippmann, *Public Opinion* (1929; repr. London: Free Press, 1997), 114.
18. "George Gallup, 1901–1984: Founder, The Gallup Organization," http://gallup.com/content/?ci=21364.
19. Herbert Asher, *Polling and the Public: What Every Citizen Should Know* (Washington, DC: CQ Press, 2001).
20. Ibid., 2.
21. Joseph Carroll, "Many Americans Use Multiple Labels to Describe Their Ideology," December 6, 2006, www.gallup.com/poll/25771/Many-Americans-Use-Multiple-Labels-Describe-Their-Ideology.aspx.
22. Randolph Grossman and Douglas Weiland, "The Use of Telephone Directories as a Sample Frame: Patterns of Bias Revisited, *Journal of Advertising* 7 (1978): 31–36.
23. Stephen J. Blumberg and Julian V. Luke, "Coverage Bias in Traditional Telephone Surveys of Low-Income and Young Adults," *Public Opinion Quarterly* 71 (2007): 734–49.
24. Clyde Tucker, J. Michael Brick, and Brian Meekins, "Household Telephone Service and Usage Patterns in the United States in 2004: Implications for Telephone Samples," *Public Opinion Quarterly* 71 (2007): 3–22.
25. Blumberg and Luke, "Coverage Bias in Traditional Telephone Surveys of Low-Income and Young Adults," 734–49.
26. Ibid.
27. George Terhanian and John Bremer, "Confronting the Selection-Bias and Learning Effects Problems Associated with Internet Research," Harris Interactive white paper, August 16, 2000.
28. G. Terhanian, R. Smith, J. Bremer, and R. K. Thomas, "Exploiting Analytical Advances: Minimizing the Biases Associated with Internet-Based Surveys of Non-Random Samples," *ARF/ESOMAR: Worldwide Online Measurement* 248 (2001): 247–72.
29. Quoted by Robert Niles, "Margin of Error," www.robertniles.com/stats/margin.shtml.
30. Irving Crespi, *Pre-Election Polling: Sources of Accuracy & Error* (New York: Russell Sage Foundation, 1988).
31. Benjamin I. Page and Robert Y. Shapiro, *The Rational Public: Fifty Years of Trends in Americans' Policy Preferences* (Chicago: University of Chicago Press, 1992).
32. Frank Newport, *Polling Matters: Why Leaders Must Listen to the Wisdom of the People* (New York: Warner Books, 2004).
33. James A. Stimson, *Tides of Consent: How Public Opinion Shapes American Politics* (Cambridge: Cambridge University Press, 2004).
34. Frank Newport, "U.S. Satisfaction at 15%, Lowest Since 1992," April 14, 2008, www.gallup.com/poll/106498/US-Satisfaction-15-Lowest-Since-1992.aspx.
35. Frank Newport and Joseph Carroll, "Iraq Versus Vietnam: A Comparison of Public Opinion," August 24, 2005, www.galluppoll.com/content/default.aspx?ci=18097&pg=2.
36. "Gallup Daily: State of the Nation," http://www.gallup.com/poll/111763/Gallup=Daily=State=Nation.aspx.
37. Jeffrey M. Jones and Joseph Carroll, "National Satisfaction Level Dips to 25%, One of Lowest Since 1979," May 16, 2007, www.galluppoll.com/content/?ci=27601&pg=1.
38. George C. Edwards III, with Alec M. Gallup, *Presidential Approval: A Sourcebook* (Baltimore: Johns Hopkins University Press, 1990).
39. David W. Moore, "Top Ten Gallup Presidential Approval Ratings," Gallup press release, September 24, 2001.

CHAPTER 7

1. Frank R. Baumgartner and Beth L. Leech, *Basic Interests: The Importance of Groups in Politics and in Political Science* (Princeton, NJ: Princeton University Press, 1998).
2. Peggy Daniels and Carol Schwartz, *Encyclopedia of Associations 1996* (Detroit, MI: Gale Research, 1995).
3. Alexis de Tocqueville, *Democracy in America: The Complete and Unabridged Volumes I and II* (1835–1840; New York: Bantam, 2000), 51.
4. Everett Carl Ladd, *The Ladd Report* (New York: Free Press, 1999).
5. Publius (James Madison), *Federalist #10,* 1787, www.ourdocuments.gov/doc.php?doc=10.
6. Robert D. Putnam, *Bowling Alone: The Collapse and Revival of American Community* (New York: Touchstone, 2000).
7. Claude S. Fischer, "Bowling Alone: What's the Score?" *Social Networks* 27 (May): 155–67.
8. Sylvia Hurtado and John H. Pryor, "The American Freshman: National Norms for Fall 2005," Cooperative Institutional Research Program (CIRP), Higher Education Research Institute (HERI) Graduate School of Education & Information Studies, University of California, Los Angeles, www.gseis.ucla.edu/heri/heri.html.
9. E. E. Schattschneider, *The Semi-Sovereign People* (New York: Holt, Rinehart & Winston, 1960), 132.
10. Earl Latham, *The Group Basis of Politics* (Ithaca, NY: Cornell University Press, 1952).
11. David B. Truman, *The Governmental Process* (New York: Knopf, 1951).
12. Hugh Davis Graham, *The Civil Rights Era: Origins and Development of National Policy, 1960–1972* (London: Oxford University Press, 1990).
13. Sidney Verba, Kay Schlozman, and Nancy Burns, *The Private Roots of Public Action: Gender, Equality, and Political Participation* (Cambridge, MA: Harvard University Press, 2001).
14. Quoted in Mark P. Petracca, *The Politics of Interests* (Boulder, CO: Westview Press, 1992), 347.

15. Julie Greene, *Pure and Simple Politics: The American Federation of Labor and Political Activism, 1881–1917* (New York: Cambridge University Press, 1998).

16. Elizabeth Sanders, *Roots of Reform: Farmers, Workers, and the American State, 1877–1917* (Chicago: University of Chicago Press, 1998).

17. Sharon E. Jarvis, Lisa Montoya, and Emily Mulvoy, "The Civic Participation of Working Youth and College Students: Working Paper 36" (Austin, TX: The Annette Strauss Institute for Civic Participation, and CIRCLE: The Center for Information and Research on Civic Learning and Engagement, 2005).

18. James Q. Wilson, *Political Organizations* (New York: Basic Books, 1973).

19. Dennis Hastert, *Speaker: Lessons from Forty Years in Coaching and Politics* (Washington, DC: Regnery, 2004), 256.

20. Jeffrey Berry, *The Interest Group Society,* 3rd ed. (New York: Longman, 1997).

21. Martin J. Smith, *Pressures, Power and Policy: Policy Networks and State Autonomy in Britain and the United States* (Pittsburgh, PA: University of Pittsburgh, 1994).

22. Herbert Alexander, *Money in Politics* (Washington, DC: Public Affairs Press, 1972).

23. Frank Sorauf, *Money in American Elections* (New York: Little, Brown, 1988).

24. Frank Sorauf, *Inside Campaign Finance: Myths and Realities* (New Haven, CT: Yale University Press, 1992).

25. Gary C. Jacobson, *Money in Congressional Elections* (New Haven, CT: Yale University Press, 1980).

26. Allan J. Cigler and Burdett A. Loomis, *Interest Group Politics* (Washington, DC: CQ Press, 1991).

27. http://thomas.loc.gov/cgi-bin/bdquery/z?d110: h.r.02419.

28. Lucy G. Barber, *Marching on Washington: The Forging of an American Political Tradition* (Los Angeles: University of California Press, 2002).

29. www.cc.org/mission.cfm.

30. American Music Conference Newsletter, "Sesame Street's Elmo Visits Congress on Behalf of Music Education," www.amcmusic.com/AMCNews/ newsletterSp02/elmo_dc.html.

31. Louise Overacker, *Money in Elections* (New York: Macmillan, 1932), 378.

CHAPTER 8

1. E. E. Schattschneider, *Party Government* (New York: Farrar & Rinehart, 1942), 1.

2. L. Sandy Maisel and Kara Z. Buckley, *Parties and Elections in America,* 4th ed. (Lanham, MD: Rowman & Littlefield, 2004).

3. Melanie Gustafson, Kristie Miller, and Elisabeth Israels Perry, *We Have Come to Stay: American Women and Political Parties, 1880–1960* (Albuquerque: University of New Mexico Press, 1999).

4. V. O. Key, *Politics, Parties, and Pressure Groups* (New York: Thomas Y. Crowell, 1964).

5. Seymour Martin Lipset and Stein Rokkan, *Party Systems and Voter Alignments* (New York: Free Press, 1967).

6. Geoffrey Layman, *The Great Divide: Religious and Cultural Conflict in American Party Politics* (New York: Columbia University Press, 2002).

7. Walter Dean Burnham, *Critical Elections and the Mainsprings of American Politics* (New York: Norton, 1997).

8. John Aldrich, *Why Parties? The Origin and Transformation of Party Politics in America* (Chicago: University of Chicago Press, 1995).

9. *Buckley v. Valeo,* 424 U.S. 1 (1976).

10. Regina Dougherty, "Divided Government Defines the Era," in *America at the Polls: 1996,* eds. Regina Dougherty, Everett C. Ladd, David Wilber, and Lynn Zayachkiwsky (Storrs, CT: Roper Center for Public Opinion Research, 1997).

11. Richard Hofstadter, "A Constitution Against Parties: Madisonian Pluralism and the Anti-Party Tradition," *Government and Opposition* 4, no. 3 (1969): 345–66.

12. Jefferson and Washington quoted in Richard Hofstadter, *The Idea of a Party System: The Rise of Legitimate Opposition in the United States, 1780–1840* (Berkeley: University of California Press, 1969), 2, 123.

13. Hofstadter, *The Idea of a Party System.*

14. James L. Sundquist, *Dynamics of the Party System: Alignment and Realignment of Political Parties in the United States* (Washington, DC: Brookings Institute, 1983).

15. Everett C. Ladd, *American Political Parties* (New York: Norton, 1970).

16. David R. Mayhew, *Electoral Realignments: A Critique of an American Genre* (New Haven, CT: Yale University Press, 2002).

17. William Nisbet Chambers, *Political Parties in a New Nation: The American Experience, 1776–1809* (New York: Oxford University Press, 1963).

18. Lance Banning, *The Jeffersonian Persuasion: Evolution of a Party Ideology* (Ithaca, NY: Cornell University Press, 1978).

19. Richard L. McCormick, *The Party Period and Public Policy: American Politics from the Age of Jackson to the Progressive Era* (New York: Oxford University Press, 1986).

20. Jules Witcover, *Party of the People: A History of the Democrats* (New York: Random House, 2003).

21. Lee Benson, *The Concept of Jacksonian Democracy* (Princeton, NJ: Princeton University Press, 1961).

22. Aileen Kraditor, *The Ideas of the Woman Suffrage Movement, 1890–1920* (New York: Norton, 1981).

23. Eric Foner, *Free Soil, Free Labor, Free Men: The Ideology of the Republican Party Before the Civil War* (New York: Oxford University Press, 1995).

24. William E. Gienapp, *The Origins of the Republican Party, 1852–1856* (New York: Oxford University Press, 1987).

25. Witcover, *Party of the People.*

26. McCormick, *The Party Period and Public Policy.*

27. Joel H. Silbey, *The Partisan Imperative: The Dynamics of American Politics Before the Civil War* (New York: Oxford University Press, 1985).

28. Lewis L. Gould, *Grand Old Party: A History of the Republicans* (New York: Random House, 2003).

29. Paul Kleppner, *The Third Electoral System, 1853–1892: Parties, Voters, and Political Cultures* (Chapel Hill: University of North Carolina Press, 1979).

30. Quoted in A. James Reichley, "Party Politics in a Federal Polity," in *Challenges to Party Government,* eds.

John Kenneth White and Jerome M. Mileur (Carbondale: Southern Illinois University, 1992), 48.

31. Kristi Anderson, *After Suffrage* (Chicago: University of Chicago Press, 1996), 30.

32. John Petrocik, *Party Coalitions: Realignment and the Decline of the New Deal Party System* (Chicago: University of Chicago Press, 1981).

33. David G. Lawrence, *The Collapse of the Democratic Majority: Realignment, Dealignment, and Electoral Change from Franklin Roosevelt to Bill Clinton* (New York: Westview Press, 1997).

34. Thomas F. Schaller, *Whistling Past Dixie: How Democrats Can Win Without the South* (New York: Simon & Schuster, 2006).

35. Edward G. Carmines, John P. McIver, and James A. Stimson, "Unrealized Partisanship: A Theory of Dealignment," *Journal of Politics* 49 (1987): 376–400.

36. www.galluppoll.com/content/default.aspx?ci=24655&pg=2.

37. David Karol, Hans Noel, John Zaller, and Marty Cohen, "Polls or Pols? The Real Driving Force Behind Presidential Nominations," www.brookings.edu/articles/2003/summer_politics_cohen.aspx.

38. Arend Lijphardt, *Electoral Systems and Party Systems: A Study of Twenty-Seven Democracies, 1945–1990* (New York: Oxford University Press, 1994).

39. Lipset and Rokkan, *Party Systems and Voter Alignments.*

40. Maurice Duverger, *Political Parties* (New York: Wiley, 1951).

41. Gary Orren, "The Changing Styles of American Party Politics," in *The Future of American Political Parties: The Challenge of Governance,* ed. Joel L. Fleishman (Englewood Cliffs, NJ: Prentice-Hall, 1982), 31.

42. This basis for this argument can be found in Larry J. Sabato and Bruce Larson, *The Party's Just Begun: Shaping Political Parties for America's Future,* 2nd ed. (New York: Longman, 2001).

43. Steven J. Rosenstone, Roy L. Behr, and Edward H. Lazarus, *Third Parties in America,* 2nd ed. (Princeton, NJ: Princeton University Press, 1996).

44. http://socialistparty-usa.org/platform/internationalpolicy.html.

CHAPTER 9

1. V. O. Key, *The Responsible Electorate* (Cambridge, MA: Harvard University Press, 1966).

2. Samuel C. Patterson and Gregory A. Caldeira, "Getting Out the Vote: Participation in Gubernatorial Elections," *American Political Science Review* 77 (1983): 675–89.

3. Barbara Norrander, *Super Tuesday: Regional Politics and Presidential Primaries* (Lexington: University of Kentucky Press, 1992).

4. Thomas E. Cronin, *Direct Democracy: The Politics of Initiative, Referendum, and Recall* (Cambridge, MA: Harvard University Press, 1999).

5. David Broder, *Democracy Derailed: Initiative Campaigns and the Power of Money* (New York: Harvest Books, 2001).

6. John F. Bibby, *Politics, Parties, and Elections in America* (Belmont, CA: Wadsworth, 2000), 253.

7. Pat Buchanan on NBC's *Today Show,* "The American Presidency Project," November 9, 2000, www.presidency.ucsb.edu/showflorida2000.php?fileid=buchanan11-09.

8. Ibid.

9. Mark Trahant, "Vote by Mail? OK, So I Was Wrong . . . ," *Seattle Post-Intelligencer,* September 25, 2005, http://seattlepi.nwsource.com/opinion/242020_trahant25.html.

10. Pippa Norris, ed., *Politics and the Press: The News Media and Their Influences* (Boulder, CO: Lynne Rienner, 1997).

11. See, for example, Matthew Dowd, "Campaign Organization and Strategy," in *Electing the President 2004: An Insider's View,* ed. Kathleen Hall Jamieson (Philadelphia: University of Pennsylvania Press, 2006).

12. Vivé Griffith, "The Influence of Media in Presidential Politics," Think Democracy Project, University of Texas at Austin, www.utexas.edu/features/archive/2004/election_media.html.

13. www.articles.latimes.com/2007/mar/11/nation/na-actblue11.

14. Gary Jacobson, *Money and Congressional Elections* (New Haven, CT: Yale University Press, 1980).

15. David Adamany, "Money, Politics and Democracy," *American Political Science Review* 71 (1977): 289–304.

16. *Buckley v. Valeo,* 424 U.S. (1976).

17. See Anthony Corrado, Thomas E. Mann, Dan Ortiz, Trevor Potter, and Frank Sorauf, *Campaign Finance Reform: A Sourcebook* (Washington, DC: Brookings Institute, 1997).

18. *Federal Election Commission v. National Conservative PAC,* 470 U.S. 480 (1985).

19. *McConnell v. Federal Election Commission,* 540 U.S. 93 (2003).

20. *Federal Election Commission v. Wisconsin Right to Life, Inc.,* 551 U.S. _____ (2007).

21. Norman H. Nie, Sidney Verba, and John R. Petrocik, *The Changing American Voter* (Cambridge, MA: Harvard University Press, 1976).

22. Angus Campbell, Philip Converse, Warren Miller, and Donald Stokes, *The American Voter* (New York: Wiley, 1960).

23. Jan Leighley and Jonathan Nagler, "Who Votes Now? And Does It Matter?" paper presented at the annual meeting of the MidWest Political Science Association, Chicago, 2007.

24. Norman H. Nie, Jane Junn, and Kenneth Stehlik-Barry, *Education and Democratic Citizenship in America* (Chicago: University of Chicago Press, 1996).

25. Jan E. Leighley and Jonathan Nagler, "Socioeconomic Class Bias in Turnout, 1964–1988: The Voters Remain the Same," *American Political Science Review* 86 (1992): 725–36.

26. The Annenberg National Election Study (ANES), "Voter Turnout 1948–2004," www.electionstudies.org/nesguide/2ndtable/t6a_2_2.htm.

27. Kim Nguyen and James Garand, "The Effects of Income Inequality on Political Attitudes and Behavior," paper presented at the annual meeting of the Midwest Political Science Association, Chicago, 2007.

28. Richard A. Brody, "The Puzzle of Political Participation in America," in *The New American*

Political System, ed. Anthony King (Washington, DC: American Enterprise Institute for Public Policy Research, 1978), 287–324.

29. Michael P. McDonald, "Up, Up and Away! Voter Participation in the 2004 Presidential Election," *The Forum* 2, no. 4 (2004), www. bepress.com/forum/vol2/iss4/art4.

30. Pippa Norris, "Retrospective Voting in the 1984 Presidential Election: Peace, Prosperity, and Patriotism," *Political Studies* 35 (1987): 289–300.

31. Daniel M. Shea, *Campaign Craft: The Strategies, Tactics, and Art of Political Campaign Management* (Westport, CT: Praeger, 1996).

32. Nie, Verba, and Petrocik, *The Changing American Voter.*

33. Samuel Kernell, "Presidential Popularity and Negative Voting," *American Political Science Review* 71 (1977): 44–66.

34. Shanto Iyengar and Jennifer A. McGrady, *Media Politics: A Citizen's Guide* (New York: Norton, 2006).

35. Warren E. Miller, "Disinterest, Disaffection, and Participation," *Political Behavior* 2 (1980): 7–32.

36. E. E. Schattschneider, *The Semi-Sovereign People* (New York: Holt, Rinehart & Winston, 1960).

37. Pew Research Center for People and the Press, "Beyond Red Versus Blue: Profiles of the Typology Groups," 2005, http://people-press. org/reports/display.php3?PageID=949.

38. Barbara Norrander and Bernard N. Grofman, "A Rational Choice Model of Citizen Participation in High and Low Commitment Electoral Activities," *Public Choice* 57 (1988): 187–92.

39. Sidney Verba and Norman H. Nie, *Participation in America: Political Democracy and Social Equality* (New York: Harper & Row, 1972).

40. Arend Lijphart, "Compulsory Voting Is the Best Way to Keep Democracy Strong," *The Chronicle of Higher Education,* October 18, 1996, B3–4.

41. Ruy A. Teixeira, "Just How Much Difference Does Turnout Really Make?" *The American Enterprise,* July/August, 1992, 52–59.

CHAPTER 10

1. James T. Hamilton, *All the News That's Fit to Sell: How the Market Transforms Information into News* (Princeton, NJ: Princeton University Press, 2003).

2. Matthew Robert Kerbel, *Remote and Controlled: Media Politics in a Cynical Age* (Boulder, CO: Westview Press, 1995).

3. William V. Kennedy, *The Military and the Media: Why the Media Cannot Be Trusted to Cover a War* (Westport, CT: Praeger, 1993).

4. Pippa Norris, *Women, Media and Politics* (New York: Oxford University Press, 1997).

5. David Weinberger, www.hillwatch.com/PPRC/Quotes/Internet_and_Politics.aspx.

6. New editions of all of these works are available: Tarbell (New York: Norton, 1969); Steffens (New York: Sangamore Press, 1957); and Sinclair (Cambridge, MA: Bentley, 1971).

7. Mark Wheeler, *Politics and the Mass Media* (Oxford: Blackwell, 1997), 228.

8. Robert Smith, "Running for Office via the Web," *NPR: Morning Edition,* January 23, 2007.

9. Howard Rheingold, "Using Participatory Media and Public Voice to Encourage Civic Engagement," in *Civic Life Online: Learning How Digital Media Can Engage Youth,* ed. Lance W. Bennett, The John D. and Catherine T. MacArthur Foundation Series on Digital Media and Learning (Cambridge, MA: MIT Press, 2008).

10. Norman H. Nie, Irena Stepanikova, Heili Pals, LuZheng, and XiaobinHe, *Ten Years After the Birth of the Internet: How Do Americans Use the Internet in Their Daily Lives?* www.stanford.edu/group/siqss/research/time_study_files/ProjectReport2005.pdf

11. See Howard Kurtz, *Spin Cycle—How the White House and the Media Manipulate the News* (New York: Simon & Schuster, 1998).

12. Patrick Healy, "To '08 Hopefuls, Media Technology Can Be Friend or Foe," *New York Times,* January 31, 2007, A15.

13. Howard Kurtz, "Throw Another Blog on the Fire," *Washington Post,* April 11, 2005, C1 and C8.

14. Christine Gibbs Springer, "Mastering Strategic Conversations," *PA Times,* September 2006.

15. Republican National Convention Speech, July 14, 1964, *Eisenhower's Post-Presidential Speeches,* www.eisenhower.archives.gov/speeches/Post-Presidential_speeches.pdf.

16. C. Richard Hofstetter, *Bias in the News: Network Television Coverage of the 1972 Election Campaign* (Columbus: Ohio State University Press, 1976); Michael J. Robinson and Margaret A. Sheehan, *Over the Wire and on TV: CBS and UPI in Campaign '80* (New York: Russell Sage Foundation, 1983).

17. William P. Eveland Jr. and Dhavan V. Shah, "The Impact of Individual and Interpersonal Factors on Perceived News Media Bias," *Political Psychology* 24, no. 1 (2003): 101–17.

18. Michael Parenti, *Inventing Reality: The Politics of the Mass Media* (New York: St. Martin's Press, 1986).

19. Tim Berners-Lee, "Neutrality of the Net," http://dig.csail.mit.edu/breadcrumbs/node/132.

CHAPTER 11

1. See, for example, David E. Price, *The Congressional Experience: A View from the Hill* (Boulder, CO: Westview Press, 1992).

2. Richard F. Fenno Jr., *Home Style: House Members in Their Districts* (New York: Longman, 2002).

3. *Davis v. Bandemer,* 478 U.S. 109 (1986).

4. Samuel Kernell, ed., *James Madison: The Theory and Practice of Republican Government* (Stanford, CA: Stanford University Press, 2003).

5. Richard F. Fenno Jr., *Congressional Travels* (New York: Pearson Longman, 2007).

6. Sue Thomas, *How Women Legislate* (New York: Oxford University Press, 1994).

7. Edmund Burke, *Speeches at His Arrival at Bristol,* November, 3, 1774, http://books.google.com/books?id=eNILAAAAYAAJ&pg=PA81&dq=Edmund+Burke,.+1774.+Speeches+at+His+Arrival+at+Bristol.+3+November,+3,+1774.&source=gbs_toc_r&cad=0_0.

8. Ibid.

9. Diana Evans, *Greasing the Wheels: Using Pork Barrel Projects to Build Majority Coalitions in Congress* (New York: Cambridge University Press, 2004).

10. Bret Schulte, "A Bridge (Way) Too Far," *U.S. News & World Report,* August 8, 2005, www.usnews.com/usnews/news/articles/050808/8highway.htm.

11. Ibid.
12. See, for example, Bruce Cain, John Ferejohn, and Morris Fiorina, *The Personal Vote: Constituency Service and Electoral Independence* (Cambridge, MA: Harvard University Press, 1987).
13. Walter F. Mondale, testimony in hearing before the Joint Committee on the Organization of Congress, July 1, 1993, www.rules.house.gov/Archives/jcoc2av.htm.
14. Walter J. Oleszek, *Congressional Procedures and the Policy Process,* 7th ed. (Washington, DC: CQ Press, 2007).
15. See Janet M. Martin, *Lessons from the Hill: The Legislative Journey of an Education Program* (New York: St. Martin's Press, 1994).
16. Gary Cox and Matthew D. McCubbins, *Setting the Agenda* (Cambridge: Cambridge University Press, 2004).
17. Woodrow Wilson, *Constitutional Government in the United States* (New York: Columbia University Press, 1911), 87.
18. David Butler and Bruce Cain, *Congressional Redistricting: Comparative and Theoretical Perspectives* (New York: Macmillan, 1992).
19. Christopher J. Deering and Steven S. Smith, *Committees in Congress,* 3rd ed. (Washington, DC: Congressional Quarterly, 1997).
20. Garrison Nelson, *Committees in the U.S. Congress, 1947–1992,* 2 vols. (Washington, DC: CQ Press, 1993).
21. Steven S. Smith, Jason M. Roberts, and Ryan J. VanderWielen, *The American Congress,* 5th ed. (New York: Cambridge University Press, 2007).
22. Lawrence C. Dodd and Bruce I. Oppenheimer, *Congress Reconsidered,* 8th ed. (Washington, DC: CQ Press, 2004).
23. Sarah H. Binder, *Minority Rights, Majority Rule: Partisanship and the Development of Congress* (New York: Cambridge University Press, 1997).
24. David W. Brady and Mathew D. McCubbins, *Party, Process, and Political Change in Congress: New Perspectives on the History of Congress* (Stanford, CA: Stanford University Press, 2002).
25. Joseph Martin Hernon, *Profiles in Character: Hubris and Heroism in the U.S. Senate, 1789–1990* (Armonk, NY: Sharpe, 1997).
26. Gary W. Cox, *Legislative Leviathan: Party Government in the House* (Berkeley: University of California Press, 1993).
27. Ronald M. Peters Jr., *The American Speakership: The Office in Historical Perspective,* 2nd ed. (Baltimore: Johns Hopkins University Press, 1997).
28. Susan Webb Hammond, *Congressional Caucuses in National Policy Making* (Baltimore: Johns Hopkins University Press, 2001).
29. Charles Babington and Jonathan Weisman, "Reid, Pelosi Expected to Keep Tight Rein in Both Chambers," *Washington Post,* November 10, 2006, A12.
30. Barbara Sinclair, *Majority Leadership in the US House and the Transformation of the US Senate* (Baltimore: Johns Hopkins University Press, 1990).
31. Barry C. Burden, *Personal Roots of Representation* (Princeton, NJ: Princeton University Press, 2007).
32. Sean Theriault, "Party Polarization in Congress," paper presented at the annual meeting of the American Political Science Association, Marriott Wardman Park, Omni Shoreham, Washington Hilton, Washington, DC, September 1, 2005, www.allacademic.com/meta/p40938_index.html.
33. Michael J. Malbin, *Unelected Representatives: Congressional Staff and the Future of Representative Government* (New York: Basic Books, 1980).
34. Burdett A. Loomis, *The Contemporary Congress,* 3rd ed. (Boston: Bedford/St. Martin's, 2000).
35. John R. Wright, *Interest Groups and Congress* (New York: Allyn & Bacon, 1996).
36. R. Douglas Arnold, *The Logic of Congressional Action* (New Haven, CT: Yale University Press, 1990).
37. For a discussion of the potential goals of demographic representation, see, for example, David T. Canon, "Representing Racial and Ethnic Minorities," in *The Legislative Branch,* eds. Paul J. Quirk and Sarah A. Binder (New York: Oxford University Press, 2005).

CHAPTER 12

1. George C. Edwards III, John H. Kessel, and Bert A. Rockman, eds., *Researching the Presidency: Vital Questions, New Approaches* (Pittsburgh, PA: University of Pittsburgh Press, 1993).
2. Theodore J. Lowi, *The Personal President* (Ithaca, NY: Cornell University Press, 1985).
3. Jean Reith Schroedel, *Congress, the President, and Policymaking: A Historical Analysis* (Armonk, NY: Sharpe, 1994).
4. William W. Lammers, *The Presidency and Domestic Policy: Comparing Leadership Styles, FDR to Clinton* (Washington, DC: CQ Press, 2000).
5. Andrew Rudalevige, *Managing the President's Program: Presidential Leadership and Legislative Policy Formulation* (Princeton, NJ: Princeton University Press, 2002).
6. Richard A. Watson, *Presidential Vetoes and Public Policy* (Lawrence: University of Kansas Press, 1993).
7. Robert J. Spitzer, *The Presidential Veto: Touchstone of the American Presidency* (Albany: SUNY Press, 1988).
8. Sidney M. Milkis and Mchael Nelson, *The American Presidency: Origins and Development, 1776–1998,* 4th ed. (Washington, DC: CQ Press, 2003).
9. www.abanet.org/media/releases/news072406.html.
10. George C. Edwards III and Steven J. Wayne, *Studying the Presidency* (Knoxville: University of Tennessee Press, 1983).
11. Louis Fisher, *Presidential War Power* (Lawrence: University of Kansas Press, 1995).
12. Cornell G. Hooton, *Executive Governance: Presidential Administrations and Policy Change in the Federal Bureaucracy* (Armonk, NY: Sharpe, 1997).
13. O. C. Fisher, *Cactus Jack: A Biography of John Nance Garner* (Waco, TX: Texian Press, 1978), chap. 11.
14. Bill Clinton, *My Life* (New York: Knopf, 2004), 414.
15. MaryAnne Borrelli, *The President's Cabinet: Gender, Power, and Representation* (Boulder, CO: Lynne Rienner, 2002).
16. Joel D. Aberbach and Mark A. Peterson, eds., *The Executive Branch* (New York: Oxford University Press, 2005).
17. William E. Leuchtenburg, *In the Shadow of FDR: From Harry Truman to Ronald Reagan* (Ithaca, NY: Cornell University Press, 1989).

18. Kenneth R. Mayer, *With the Stroke of a Pen: Executive Orders and Presidential Power* (Princeton, NJ: Princeton University Press, 2002).
19. www.trumanlibrary.org/9981.htm.
20. www.whitehouse.gov/news/releases/2007/07/20070717-3.html.
21. *U.S. v. Curtiss-Wright Export Corp.,* 229 U.S. 304 (1936).
22. Mark J. Rozell, *Executive Privilege: Presidential Power, Secrecy, and Accountability,* 2nd ed. rev. (Lawrence: University of Kansas Press, 2002).
23. *U.S. v. Richard M. Nixon,* 418 U.S. 683 (1974).
24. Richard Neustadt, *The Power to Persuade* (New York: Wiley, 1960).
25. *Outlook,* February 27, 1909.
26. Richard E. Neustadt, *Presidential Power and the Modern President* (New York: Free Press, 1990).
27. George C. Edwards III with Alec M. Gallup, *Presidential Approval: A Sourcebook* [Eisenhower to Reagan] (Baltimore: Johns Hopkins University Press, 1990).
28. After 1984 presidential campaign between Ronald Reagan and Walter F. Mondale, *New York,* November 19, 1984.
29. Jeffrey K. Tulis, *The Rhetorical Presidency* (Princeton, NJ: Princeton University Press, 1988).
30. Harry A. Bailey Jr. and Jay M. Shafritz, *The American Presidency: Historical and Contemporary Perspectives* (Pacific Grove, CA: Brooks/Cole, 1988).
31. Marc Landy and Sidney M. Milkis, *Presidential Greatness* (Lawrence: University of Kansas Press, 2000).
32. Harold J. Laski, *The American Presidency* (New York: Harper & Row, 1940).
33. William M. Goldsmith, *The Growth of Presidential Power: A Documented History,* 3 vols. (New York: Chelsea House, 1974).
34. *New York Times Co. v. U.S.,* 403 U.S. 713 (1971).
35. Statement of Sen. Howard Baker (R-TN) during the Senate Committee investigation.
36. John Dean, the Nixon presidential transcripts, March 21, 1973.
37. http://nixon.archives.gov/find/tapes/excerpts/watergate.html.
38. David Frost, *I Gave Them a Sword* (New York: William Morrow, 1978).
39. http://blog.washingtonpost.com/thetrail/2007/08/29/a_party_in_disarray.html/.
40. Barbara Gamarekian, "Washington Talk: The Presidency; First Ladies Step Further Out of Shadows," *New York Times,* March 10, 1988, B5.
41. Barbara Bush, commencement address at Wellesley College, June 1, 1990.

CHAPTER 13

1. http://www.whitehouse.gov/omb/budget/fy2010/assets/summary.pdf (accessed June 27, 2009).
2. http://govinfo.library.unt.edu/npr/library/speeches/030393.html.
3. For a review of the literature on public service motivation, see David J. Houston, "'Walking the Walk' of Public Service Motivation: Public Employees and Charitable Gifts of Time, Blood, and Money," *Journal of Public Administration Research and Theory* 16, no. 1 (2005): 67–86.

4. Charles T. Goodsell, *The Case for Bureaucracy: A Public Administration Polemic,* 4th ed. (Washington, DC: CQ Press, 2004), 104–106.
5. Norman J. Baldwin, "Public Versus Private Employees: Debunking Stereotypes," *Review of Public Personnel Administration* 12 (Winter 1991): 1–27.
6. Goodsell, *The Case for Bureaucracy,* 106.
7. www.gpoaccess.gov/plumbook/2004/index.html.
8. John T. Woolley and Gerhard Peters, "The American Presidency Project," www.presidency.ucsb.edu/ws/?pid=30436 (Santa Barbara: University of California, hosted, Gerhard Peters, database).
9. Robert B. Denhardt and Joseph W. Grubbs, *Public Administration: An Action Orientation* (Belmont, CA: Thomson Wadsworth, 2003), 231.
10. www.opm.gov/ses/features.asp.
11. www.msnbc.msn.com/id/23919234.
12. Jeffrey L. Pressman and Aaron Wildavsky, *Implementation: How Great Expectations in Washington Are Dashed in Oakland: Or, Why It's Amazing That Federal Programs Work at All* (Berkeley: University of California Press, 1973).
13. Office of Management and Budget, *FY 2008 Report to Congress on Implementation of the E-Government Act of 2002,* March 1, 2009: 3.
14. www.pogo.org/p/x/2007impact.html#contract.
15. Shaila Dewan, "FEMA Ordered to Restore Evacuees' Housing Aid," *New York Times,* November 30, 2006.
16. William T. Gormley Jr. and Steven J. Balla, *Bureaucracy and Democracy: Accountability and Performance* (Washington DC: CQ Press, 2004), 67.
17. Matt Kelley, "Probes at NASA Plummet Under Its Current IG," *USA Today,* January 11, 2008.
18. Goodsell, *The Case for Bureaucracy,* 139.
19. Gormley and Balla, *Bureaucracy and Democracy,* 164–78.
20. Goodsell, *The Case for Bureaucracy,* 54.
21. Ibid., 30.
22. www.house.gov/etheridge/Press-FEMAcontracts.htm.
23. Richard Stillman, *The American Bureaucracy: The Core of Modern Government* (Chicago: Nelson Hall, 1996), 308.

CHAPTER 14

1. "More Than Half of Americans Approve of the Job the Court Is Doing, Which Is Lower Than Approval Has Been at Some Recent Points but Still Much Higher Than Public Approval of President George W. Bush and Congress." Joseph Carroll, "1/3 of Americans Say U.S. Supreme Court Is 'Too Conservative,'" Gallup News Service, October 2, 2007.
2. Christopher N. May, *Constitutional Law—National Power and Federalism: Examples and Explanations* (New York: Aspen, 2004).
3. Morton J. Horowitz, *The Transformation of American Law, 1780–1860* (Cambridge, MA: Harvard University Press, 1977).
4. Charles D. Shipan, *Designing Judicial Review* (Ann Arbor: University of Michigan Press, 1997).
5. Joel B. Grossman, "Paths to the Bench: Selecting Supreme Court Justices in a 'Juristocratic' World," in *The Judicial Branch,* eds. Kermit L. Hall and Kevin T. McGuire (Oxford: Oxford University Press, 2005), 143.

6. Robert G. McCloskey, *The American Supreme Court*, 4th ed. (Chicago: University of Chicago Press, 2005).

7. Erwin Chemerinsky, *Constitutional Law: Principles and Policies* (New York: Aspen, 2006).

8. Robert A. Carp and Ronald Stidham, *The Federal Courts*, 4th ed. (Washington, DC: CQ Press, 2001).

9. www.whitehouse.gov/news/releases/2008/05/20080517-2.html.

10. The exception is those cases whose original jurisdiction is the U.S. Supreme Court, which is not typically considered a trial court.

11. www.uscourts.gov/faq.html.

12. 50 U.S.C. §§1801–1811, 1821–29, 1841–46, and 1861–62.

13. Lawrence Baum, "The Future of the Judicial Branch," in *The Judicial Branch*, eds. Kermit L. Hall and Kevin T. McGuire (Oxford: Oxford University Press, 2005), 523.

14. See, for example, Hugh Hewitt, "Why the Right Was Wrong," *New York Times*, October 28, 2005, www.nytimes.com/2005/10/28/opinion/28hewitt.html?ex=1288152000&en=53aee2bcf6872884&ei=5090&partner=rssuserland&emc=rss.

15. H. W. Perry Jr., *Deciding to Decide: Agenda Setting in the United States Supreme Court* (Cambridge, MA: Harvard University Press, 1994).

16. Bob Woodward, *The Brethren: Inside the Supreme Court* (New York: Simon & Schuster, 2005).

17. Henry J. Abraham, *The Judicial Process* (New York: Oxford University Press, 1998).

18. *Gratz v. Bollinger*, 539 U.S. 244 (2003), and *Grutter v. Bollinger*, 539 U.S. 306 (2003).

19. William H. Rehnquist, *The Supreme Court* (New York: Vintage Books, 2002).

20. Bernard Schwartz, *Decision: How the Supreme Court Decides Cases* (New York: Oxford University Press, 1996).

21. Jeffrey A. Segal and Harold J. Spaeth, *The Supreme Court and the Attitudinal Model* (New York: Cambridge University Press, 2003).

22. Jeffrey Toobin, *The Nine: Inside the Secret World of the Supreme Court* (New York: Doubleday, 2007).

23. Lawrence Baum, *The Supreme Court* (Washington, DC: CQ Press, 2004).

24. Paul J. Wahlbeck, James F. Spriggs II, and Forrest Maltzman, "The Politics of Dissents and Concurrences on the U.S. Supreme Court," *American Politics Quarterly* 27 (1999): 488–514.

25. *New York Times*, "The Roberts Court Returns," www.nytimes.com/2007/09/30/opinion/30sun1.html; Charles Lane, "Narrow Victories Move Court to the Right," *Washington Post*, June 29, 2007, A04; Linda Greenhouse, "Roberts Court Is a Conservative's Dream," *International Herald Tribune*, www.iht.com/articles/2007/07/01/news/scotus.php.

26. Carroll, "1/3 of Americans Say U.S. Supreme Court Is 'Too Conservative.'"

27. *Safford Unified School District v. Redding*, 557 U.S. _____ (2009).

28. *Horne v. Flores*, 557 U.S. _____ (2009).

29. *Melendez-Diaz v. Massachusetts*, 557 U.S. _____ (2009).

30. *Gonzales v. Carhart*, 550 U.S. _____ (2007).

31. Lee Epstein and Jack Knight, *The Choices Justices Make* (Washington, DC: CQ Press, 1998).

32. Lee Cokorinos, *The Assault on Diversity: An Organized Challenge to Racial and Gender Justice* (Lanham, MD: Rowman & Littlefield, 2003), 9.

33. *Miranda v. Arizona*, 384 U.S. 436.

34. *Gideon v. Wainwright*, 372 U.S. 335 (1963).

35. *Griswold v. Connecticut*, 381 U.S. 479 (1965).

36. Antonin Scalia, *A Matter of Interpretation: Federal Courts and the Law* (Princeton, NJ: Princeton University Press, 1998).

37. Thomas M. Keck, *The Most Activist Supreme Court in History: The Road to Modern Judicial Conservatism* (Chicago: University of Chicago Press, 2004).

38. *Oregon v. Mitchell*, 400 U.S. 112 (1970).

39. Andrew Jay Koshner, *Solving the Puzzle of Interest Group Litigation* (Westport, CT: Greenwood, 1998).

40. John E. Nowak and Ronald D. Rotunda, *Constitutional Law (Hornbook Series)* (St. Paul, MN: West, 2004).

CHAPTER 15

1. Bureau of Economic Analysis, "Measuring the Economy: A Primer on GDP and the National Income and Product Accounts," September 2007, www.bea.gov/national/pdf/nipa_primer.pdf.

2. http://hdr.undp.org/en/statistics/ (accessed July 5, 2009).

3. http://www.census.gov/hhes/www/poverty/thresh07.html.

4. http://www.whitehouse.gov/omb/budget/fy2010/assets/summary.pdf.

5. Lori Montgomery, "Deficit Projected to Swell Beyond Earlier Estimates: CBO Expects Trillions More in Borrowing," *Washington Post*, March 21, 2009.

6. www.brillig.com/debt_clock.

7. http://www.treasurydirect.gov/NP/BPDLogin?application=np.

8. Sherman Antitrust Act (1890); Clayton Antitrust Act (1914).

9. www.u-s-history.com/pages/h1603.html.

10. Ralph Nader, *Unsafe at Any Speed: The Designed-in Dangers of American Automobiles* (New York: Grossman, Publishing, 1965), ix.

11. Alexei Barrionuevo, "Globalization in Every Loaf," *New York Times*, June 16, 2007.

12. L. Josh Bivens and John Irons, "A Feeble Recovery: The Fundamental Economic Weaknesses of the 2001–2007 Expansion," Economic Policy Institute Briefing Paper #214, May 1, 2008, http://www.epi.org/publications/entry/4139 (accessed July 9, 2009).

13. Bernstein, Jared. 2008. "Real Wages Decline in 2007," Economic Policy Issue Brief #240, http://www.epi.org/content.cfm/ib240 (accessed May 12, 2008).

14. Jared Bernstein, Elise Gould, and Lawrence Mishel, "Income Picture: Poverty, Income and Health Insurance Trends in 2006," August 28, 2007, http://www.epi.org/content.cfm/webfeatures_econindicators_income20070828 (accessed May 12, 2008).

15. Ibid.

16. Peter Grier, "Rich-Poor Gap Gaining Attention," *Christian Science Monitor*, June 14, 2005, http://www.csmonitor.com/2005/0614/p01s03-usec.htm.

17. Edmund L. Andrews, "Top Officials See Bleaker Outlook for the Economy," *New York Times*, February 15, 2008.

18. Quoted in David Kamp, "Rethinking the American Dream," *Vanity Fair*, April 2009.

19. David Leonhardt, "Has the Jump in Wages Met Its End?" *New York Times,* September 12, 2007.
20. Bob Herbert, "Here Come the Millennials," *New York Times,* May 13, 2008.

CHAPTER 16

1. Visit the federal government's Web site (www .whitehouse.gov/omb/expectmore/index.html) for a more complete list of domestic programs.
2. http://earthday.wilderness.org/history/.
3. *Massachusetts v. EPA,* (2007) 549 U.S. _____.
4. "Roadblock at Yucca Mountain," *New York Times,* August 23, 2004.
5. David Hosansky, *The Environment: A to Z* (Washington, DC: CQ Press, 2001), 80–81.
6. Ibid., 243.
7. Josh Goodman, "Greenhouse Gumption: Whether You Call It Global Warming or Climate Change, It's an Issue That's Being Dealt with at the Grassroots," *Governing* 19, no. 8 (May 2006): 60–62.
8. Mary Cooper, "Energy Policy," in *Economic Issues: Selections from the CQ Researcher* (Washington, DC: CQ Press), 150.
9. Bill Vlasic, "Early Target for Fuel Economy Is Expected," *New York Times,* April 22, 2008.
10. Cooper, "Energy Policy," 146–49.
11. Ibid., 139.
12. Josef Herbert, "Climate Bill May Spur Energy Revolution: President Claims Measure Will Strengthen Economy," Associated Press, June 28, 2009.
13. http://opencrs.com/document/RS22915.
14. Stephen Labaton, "Congress Passes Increase in the Minimum Wage," *New York Times,* May 25, 2007.
15. Catherine Rampell, "Who Is Affected by a Higher Minimum Wage?" *New York Times,* July 24, 2009.
16. Erik Eckholm, "Tax Credit Seen as Helping More Parents," *New York Times,* April 1, 2007.
17. Amy Nagle and Nicholas Johnson, "A Hand Up: How State Earned Income Tax Credits Help Working Families Escape Poverty in 2006," Center on Budget and Policy Priorities, http://cbpp.org/.
18. Carmen DeNavas-Walt, Bernadette D. Proctor, and Jessica Smith, *Income, Poverty, and Health Insurance Coverage in the United States: 2007,* U.S. Census Bureau, Current Population Reports, P60-235 (Washington, DC: U.S. Government Printing Office, 2008).
19. Ibid.
20. Kendra Hovey and Harold A. Hovey, *CQ's State Fact Finder 2007* (Washington, DC: CQ Press, 2007), 143.
21. www.whitehouse.gov/issues/health_care/(accessed July 27, 2009).
22. www.whitehouse.gov/news/releases/2006/02/print/20060223.html.
23. Deborah Macmillan, "Overview: Federal Immigration Policy and Proposed Reforms," www.lwv.org/AM/Template.cfm?Section=LWVUSImmigration Study&TEMPLATE=/CM/ContentDisplay .cfm&CONTENTID=7426.
24. Ibid.
25. Patricia Hatch, "What Motivates Immigration to America," www.lwv.org/AM/Template.cfm?Section =LWVUSImmigrationStudy&CONTENTID =8179&TEMPLATE=/CM/ContentDisplay.cfm.

CHAPTER 17

1. "Dodd Assesses Efforts by U.S. to Increase Economic, Diplomatic, Political Pressure on Iran," March 21, 2007, http://dodd.senate.gov/index .php?q=node/3793.
2. Ibid.
3. Saul K. Padover, ed., *Wilson's Ideals* (Washington, DC: American Council on Public Affairs, 1942), 108.
4. www.unicef.org/sowc97/.
5. Secretary of State Colin L. Powell, remarks to the United Nations Security Council, February 5, 2003, www.state.gov/secretary/former/powell/remarks/2003/17300.htm.
6. www.npr.org/templates/story/story.php?storyId =4859238.
7. See, for example, James Risen, *State of War: The Secret History of the CIA and the Bush Administration* (New York: Free Press, 2006).
8. www.cia.gov/library/reports/Executive%20Summary _OIG%20Report.pdf.
9. Thomas H. Kean and Lee H. Hamilton, "The 9/11 Commission Report," ed. National Commission on Terrorist Attacks Upon the United States (Washington, DC: 2004).
10. www.nytimes.com/2005/03/16/politics/16text-bush.html?_r=1&pagewanted=4&oref=slogin.
11. "Congress Abdicates War Powers," *The New American,* November 4, 2002, 5.
12. www.ourdocuments.gov/doc.php?flash=true& doc=90.
13. Roger H. Davidson, "Invitation to Struggle: An Overview of Legislative-Executive Relations," *Annals of the American Academy of Political and Social Science* 499 (1988): 1, 9–21.
14. Article 5 of the North Atlantic Treaty, Washington D.C., April 4, 1949, www.nato.int/docu/basictxt/treaty.htm.
15. President Harry S. Truman's address before a joint session of Congress on March 12, 1947.
16. George F. Kennan, writing under the pseudonym "X," "Sources of Soviet Conduct," *Foreign Affairs* (July 1947): 25.
17. Graham T. Allison and Philip Zelikow, *Essence of Decision: Explaining the Cuban Missile Crisis,* 2nd ed. (New York: Longman, 1999).
18. www.nps.gov/archive/eise/quotes2.htm.
19. Samuel P. Huntington, "The Clash of Civilizations?" *Foreign Affairs* 72, no. 3 (Summer 1993): 22–49.
20. www.whitehouse.gov/the_press_office/Remarks-by-the-President-at-Cairo-University-6-04-09/

PHOTO CREDITS

CHAPTER 1 OPENER: © William Thomas Cain/ Getty; **p. 9 (top):** AP Photo/APTV; Fig 1.1: © Frederic J. Brown/AFP/Getty; **p. 19:** AP Photo/Leslie Close.

CHAPTER 2 OPENER: © Scott Olson/Getty; **p. 52:** AP Photo; **p. 60 (top left):** © American School/The Bridgeman Art Library/Getty; **p. 60 (top right):** © FPG/ Taxi/Getty; **p. 60 (bottom):** © Stock Montage/Hulton Archive/Getty; **p. 62:** The Granger Collection, New York; **p. 68 (top):** © Ron Sachs/CNP/Corbis; **p. 68 (bottom):** AP Photo/Brennan Linsley.

CHAPTER 3 OPENER: © Christopher Capozziello/ Getty; **p. 102 (top):** © Win McNamee/Reuters/Corbis; **p. 102 (bottom):** AP Photo/Pablo Martinez Monsivais; **p. 111:** © Win McNamee/Getty; **p. 117 (top):** © Corbis; **p. 117 (bottom):** AP Photo/Atlanta Journal-Constitution, Rich Addicks.

CHAPTER 4 OPENER: © David McNew/Getty; **p. 145:** © David Maxwell/AFP/Getty; **p. 164:** © Ron Sachs-Pool/Getty.

CHAPTER 5 OPENER: © P-59 Photos/Alamy; **p. 176 (left):** The Everett Collection; **p. 176 (right):** © New York Times Co./Hulton Archive/Getty; **p. 185:** © Bettmann/Corbis; **p. 187:** © Topham/The Image Works; **p. 193 (top):** © Bettmann/Corbis; **p. 193 (bottom):** © Shawn Thew/EPA/Corbis; **p. 200:** © Arthur Schatz/ Getty; **p. 204 (top):** © Porter Gifford/Liaison/Getty; **p. 204 (bottom):** © Chip Somodevilla/Getty.

CHAPTER 6 OPENER: © Jeff Greenberg/The Image Works; **p. 221 (left):** © Frances M. Roberts; **p. 221 (right):** © Scott Olson/Getty; **p. 243 (top):** © David White/Alamy.

CHAPTER 7 OPENER: © Eric Thayer/Reuters/ Corbis; **p. 254 (top):** AP Photo/Tupperware; **p. 254 (bottom):** © Duffy-Marie Arnoult/WireImage/Getty; **p. 274 (top):** © Kelly Wilkinson/The Indianapolis Star.

CHAPTER 8 OPENER: © Stan Honda/AFP/Getty; **p. 291 (top):** AP Photo/Morry Gash; **p. 291 (bottom):** © Brendan McDermid/Reuters/Corbis; **p. 305 (top):** © Bettmann/Corbis; **p. 305 (bottom):** © Richard Levine/ Alamy.

CHAPTER 9 OPENER: © Chris Fitzgerald/Candi-datePhotos/The Image Works; **p. 323 (left):** © Dennis Kitchen/Stone/Getty; **p. 323 (right):** © Sally Ryan/The New York Times/Redux; **p. 328 (left):** © Manic Photos/Alamy; **p. 328 (right):** © Manic Photos/Alamy; **p. 329:** AP Photo/ Gary I. Rothstein; p. 334: © Paul McMahon; **p. 341:**

© Photodisc/Getty; p. 344: © Reuters/HO/Swiftvets.com/ Landov; **p. 346:** AP Photo/Paul Vernon.

CHAPTER 10 OPENER: © Alex Wong/Getty; **p. 367:** © Bettmann/Corbis; **p. 371 (top):** © Bettmann/ Corbis; **p. 371 (bottom):** Official White House Photo by Pete Souza.

CHAPTER 11 OPENER: AP Photo/Evan Vucci; **p. 402:** © Bettmann/Corbis; **p. 405:** © Mark Wilson/ Getty; **p. 425 (top):** AP Photo/Gerald Herbert; **p. 425 (bottom):** © Martin H. Simon-Pool/Getty.

CHAPTER 12 OPENER: © Monika Graff/The Image works; **p. 439:** © Bill Pugliano/Getty; **p. 440:** © Mark Wilson/Getty; **p. 445:** AP Photo/The Scranton Times-Tribune, Butch Comegys; **p. 450:** © George Skad-ding//Time Life Pictures/Getty; **p. 452:** Official White House Photo by Pete Souza; **p. 468:** © Michael Reynolds/ EPA/Corbis.

CHAPTER 13 OPENER: AP Photo/John Amis; **p. 479:** AP Photo/Pablo Martinez Monsivais; **p. 501 (left):** AP Photo/Morry Gash; **p. 501 (right):** AP Photo/Jim Mone; **p. 502:** AP Photo/Gerald Herbert.

CHAPTER 14 OPENER: © Ron Sachs/CNP/Corbis; **p. 509:** © swatjester/Flickr; **p. 520:** AP Photo/Pablo Martinez Monsivais; **p. 522 (top):** AP Photo/Charles Dharapak; **p. 522 (bottom):** Official White House photo by Pete Souza; **p. 525:** © Peter Hvizdak/The Image Works; **p. 533:** © Bettmann/ Corbis; **p. 538:** © David J Sams/Stone/Getty.

CHAPTER 15 OPENER: AP Photo/The Plain Dealer, Scott Shaw; **p. 554 (left)** : © Bettmann/Corbis; **p. 554 (right):** © John Nordell/The Image Works; **p. 556 (top):** © Reuters/Corbis; **p. 556 (bottom):** AP Photo/ Charles Dharapak; **p. 566:** AP Photo/Ron Edmonds; **p. 573:** AP Photo/Louis Lanzano.

CHAPTER 16 OPENER: © Pool/Getty; **p. 588:** AP Photo/U.S. Drug Enforcement Administration; **p. 590 (top):** © Topham/The Image Works ; **p. 590 (bottom):** AP Photo/Nick Ut; **p. 597 (top):** AP Photo/Mark Avery; **p. 597 (bottom):** © culture-images GmbH/Alamy.

CHAPTER 17 OPENER: AP Photo/Jim MacMillan; **p. 624:** Official White House photo by Pete Souza; **p. 628:** AP Photo/Nick Ut; **p. 629:** AP Photo; **p. 631:** AP Photo/ Kyodo News; **p. 640:** © Public Record Office/HIP/The Image Works; **p. 648:** © Paula Bronstein/Getty; **p. 649 (top):** AP Photo/Adel Hana; **p. 649 (bottom):** Official White House photo by Pete Souza.

INDEX

A

AARP. *See* American Association of Retired Persons
absentee voting, 330–332, 331*f*
accommodationism, 151
Ackerman, Bruce, 170
ACLU. *See* American Civil Liberties Union
ACRI. *See* American Civil Rights Institute
Active Liberty: Interpreting Our Democratic Constitution (Breyer), 71
activism
  African American, 174–176, 175*f,* 176*f,* 182–187, 185*f*
  American colonists', 50
  anti-Vietnam War, 146, 149, 324
  Asian American, 174–176, 175*f*
  citizens with disabilities, 175*f,* 202–203, 212
  in civic life, 222
  family and community influences on, 222–223
  grassroots, 337*f*
  importance of, 7–8
  interest groups', 258
  judicial, 533
  Latino, 174–176, 175*f,* 198–201, 200*f*
  LGBT, 175*f,* 203–205, 204*f*
  media's role in strengthening engagement, 387
  Mexican American, 199–201, 200*f*
  Native American, 197–198
  Nelson's, 592
  netroots, 2, 337–338, 337*f,* 379–380
  restraint v., 533–534, 533*f*
  women, 191–196, 210
ACU. *See* American Conservative Union
ADA. *See* Americans for Democratic Action; Americans with Disabilities Act
ADA Restoration Act, 203
ADA Watch, 203
Adams, James T., 579
Adams, John, 300, 301
Adams, John Quincy, 301
Adams, Samuel, 50

ADC. *See* Aid to Dependent Children
administrative adjudication, 494
administrative discretion, 493
administrative law, 514–515
administrative powers, Congressional, 403*t*
administrative rule making, 494
advice and consent, 45
AFBF. *See* American Farm Bureau Federation
affirmative action, 206
  opposition to, 207–209, 208*f*
Afghanistan, funding of war, 425, 544–547
AFL-CIO. *See* American Federation of Labor-Congress of Industrial Organizations
African Americans, 25, 25*n,* 27, 27*f*
  Brown v. The Board of Education of Topeka, Kansas, 66, 183–184, 196
  Civil Rights Act (1964), 188, 195
  civil rights movement, 182–187, 185*f*
  in Congress, 428–429, 429*f*
  Democratic dominance: 1932–1968, 305–306, 305*f*
  electing Roosevelt, F. D., and Obama, B., 305–306, 305*f*
  Fifteenth Amendment: voting rights all male citizens, 91
  fighting for civil rights, 174–176, 175*f,* 176*f*
  government acceptance of discrimination, 181–182
  government response to civil rights movement, 187–191, 187*f*
  as loyal democrats, 291–292, 291*f*
  newly franchised, 302–303
  personal income, 551
  political party affiliation, 293*f*
  political socialization shaped by race/ethnicity, 227–229, 227*f*
  in presidential cabinet, 448*f*
  representation in Congress, 57*f*
  Supreme Court Justices, 521–524, 522*f,* 524*f*
  Thirteenth Amendment: abolishment of slavery, 90, 179
  voting rights, 187–188

age
  aging population, 25, 26*f*
  alcohol, 122
  child labor, 574
  -cohort effect, 232
  of Congress members, 427*t*
  as factor in voting, 348–349, 348*f*
  political party affiliation by, 293*f*
  voting, 65*t,* 95, 175–176
agency review, 413
agenda setting, 408
agents of socialization, 222
agricultural interests, 268–269, 269*t*
AH&LA. *See* American Hotel and Lodging Association
Aid to Dependent Children (ADC), 604–605
AIM. *See* American Indian Movement
AIPAC. *See* American Israel Public Affairs Committee
Albright, Madeleine, 81, 446
alcohol
  driving under the influence, 122
  MADD, 258
  Prohibition Amendment (Amendment XVIII), 65*t,* 92
  repeal of Prohibition Amendment, 65*t,* 93
Alien and Sedition Acts (1798), 142–143
Alien Enemies Act (1798), 143
Alito, Samuel, 423
AMA. *See* American Medical Association
amendment(s), 39, 46–48, 47*f.*
  See also Bill of Rights
  Article V on process of, 85
  Eleventh through Twenty-Seventh, 65*t,* 95
  postwar, 119–120
  that protect civil liberties, 65*t*
Amendments, Constitutional. *See also* Bill of Rights
  Eleventh Amendment, 65*t,* 89
  Twelfth Amendment, 65*t,* 89–90
  Thirteenth Amendment, 90, 179
  Fourteenth Amendment, 65*t,* 66, 90–91, 113, 119, 139–140, 174, 179, 192, 195, 206, 207–209, 208*f*

incorporation of Bill of Rights to apply to states, 139–140

intergovernmental authority interpreted by, 125

interpretation of enumerated/implied/reserved powers, 109–112, 111*f*

interpretation of Second Amendment, 67, 87, 110, 137*t*, 141*t*, 160–162, 161*f*, 171

intracourt constraints, 537

judges as policy makers, 531–534, 532*f*, 533*f*

judicial competence, 521

judicial process, 536

jurisdiction of, 526

Massachusetts v. Mellon, 122

new judicial federalism, 114

resolving conflicts among concurrent powers, 105

South Dakota v. Dole, 122

today, 525–531, 525*f*, 527*f*, 530*f*

www.findlaw.com, 71

The Supreme Court: Revised and Updated (Rehnquist), 127

supreme law of the land, 85–86, 107, 128

suspect classifications, 176

symbolic representation, 523

symbolic speech, 145

T

Taft, William Howard, 304, 315*f*

take care clause, 453–454

talk radio, 372

Tammany Hall, 304

TANF. *See* Temporary Aid to Needy Families

tariffs. *See also* taxes

GATT, 576–577

imposed on American colonists, 49–51

nontariff trade barriers, 575–576

Smoot-Hawley Tariff, 635

tax base, 551

tax breaks (loop holes), 564

tax expenditures, 564

tax laws, 561

tax policy, 561–564, 562*f*, 563*f*

taxes

Article I on, 72–73

campaign contribution, 314, 342–345, 343*t*, 344*f*, 494

earned income tax credit, 604

imposed on American colonists, 49–51

McCulloch v. Maryland, 109–110

national power to collect, 106*f*

services/taxes as functioning of government, 14, 21, 104

Sixteenth Amendment: personal and corporate income, 65*t*, 91

tax brackets, 563*f*

Taylor, Zachary, 301

Tea Act (1773), 50

Teamsters Union, 266

Teapot Dome scandal, 338

technology, new. *See also* Internet; media

Center for Democracy and Technology, 170

cost-benefit analysis altered by, 5

foreign affairs impacted by, 654

government employees in, 103*f*

politics changed by, 8–10, 17, 318, 356

Telecommunications Act, 386, 388

television, 370–374, 371*f*, 373*f*

GOTV, 323

public, 363

Temporary Aid to Needy Families (TANF), 33, 604–605, 608

Tenth Amendment. *See* Bill of Rights

terrorism, 653. *See also* Homeland Security

Before the Next Attack: Preserving Civil Liberties in an Age of Terrorism, 170

Obama, B., on terrorist surveillance program, 2–5

public opinion on, 242*f*

response preparedness, 609–610

September 11, 2001, 162–168, 163*f*, 164*f*, 166*f*, 169

USA PATRIOT Act v., 139, 165, 168, 170, 458, 612

Terrorism Risk Protection Act, 270

terrorist surveillance program, 2–5

Texas v. Johnson (1989), 146

The Social Contract (Rousseau), 53*t*

third-party candidates, 265, 307

impact of, 314–316, 315*f*

Nader, 271, 309, 313, 574

need for, 312–313, 312*f*

over slavery issue, 302–303

types of, 313–314

Thirteenth Amendment, 65*t*. *See also* Bill of Rights

Three-Fifths Compromise, 59

Thurber, James, 393

ticket splitting, 306–307

time, place, manner restrictions, 148

Tinker v. Des Moines, 146

Title IX, Equal Pay Act, 195

Title VII, Equal Pay Act, 195

Tocqueville, Alexis de, 254

tort, 511

torture/interrogation, 130–131

total incorporation, 129, 140

totalitarianism, 15

town meetings, American colonists', 18–19

Townshend Duties Act (1767), 49–50

toxic waste, disposal of, 593–594

tracking polls, 240

trade and professional interests, 269–270

trade deficit, 577

trade policy, 575

Traugott, Michael W., 251

treason, 84

Treasury Department, 489*t*

Treatise (Locke), 18, 53*t*

Treaty of Guadalupe Hidalgo, 199

Treaty of Versailles, 635

trial by jury, 138*t*. *See also* Bill of Rights

trial court, 515

Truman, Harry, 214, 306, 450, 641

cabinet of, 448*f*

trustee model, of congressional representation, 405

Twelfth Amendment, 65*t*. *See also* Bill of Rights

Twentieth Amendment, 65*t*, 92–93. *See also* Bill of Rights

Twenty-Fifth Amendment, 65*t*, 95, 450, 451, 452

Twenty-First Amendment, 65*t*, 93. *See also* Bill of Rights

Twenty-Fourth Amendment, 65*t*, 94, 181. *See also* Bill of Rights

Twenty-Second Amendment, 65*t*, 93. *See also* Bill of Rights

Twenty-Seventh Amendment, 65*t*, 95. *See also* Bill of Rights

Twenty-Sixth Amendment, 65*t*, 95, 175–176

Twenty-Third Amendment, 65*t*. *See also* Bill of Rights

Twitter, 243*f*, 316

two-party domination, 307–309

two-party system, 310–312, 312*f*, 318

continued socialization to, 309

third-party candidate v., 312–316, 312*f*, 315*f*

Tyler, John, 301

U

U. S. Code, 513

U. S. v. Eichman (1990), 146

U. S. v. O'Brien, 146

UFW. *See* United Farm Workers

ultra conservative ideology, survey of American's, 237*f*

ultra liberal ideology, survey of American's, 237*f*

Umbrella Organizations, 268

UN. *See* United Nations

unanimous consent, 415–416

Uncle Tom's Cabin (Stowe), 179

uncontrollable spending, 565

Underground Railroad, 177–179, 178*f*

unearned income, 562

unemployment, 117*f*

compensation, 601

rate, 558

unfunded mandate, 123

unicameral Congress, 54

unionized civil servants, 484

United Farm Workers (UFW), 200, 200*f*